Ukraine in the Seventies

Edited by
Peter J. Potichnyj

Papers and Proceedings of the McMaster Conference
on Contemporary Ukraine, October 1974

Mosaic Press
P.O. Box 1032
Oakville, Ontario

UKRAINE IN THE SEVENTIES

Copyright © 1975, Mosaic Press

Printed and bound in Canada

ISBN 0-88962-000-8

Table of Contents

CONFERENCE PROGRAMME

Friday, October 25, 1974

Opening Remarks
Dr. Arthur N. Bourns
President, McMaster University

Topic:	The Non-Renewable Resources of Ukraine
Speaker:	Mr. A. S. Romaniuk and Mrs. I. Slowikowski, Department of Mines and Energy Resources, Ottawa
Discussant:	Dr. V. N. Mackiw, Vice-President, Sherritt Gordon Mines, Ltd.

Topic:	Utilization of Renewable Resources in Ukraine
Speaker:	Mr. J. Holowacz, Policy Research Branch, Ontario Ministry of Natural Resources and Mr. W. Bien, Canada Centre for Inland Waters
Discussant:	Dr. B. M. Barr, University of Calgary
Chairman:	Dr. N. Field, University of Toronto

Topic:	The Present State of Cybernetics and the Republic-Level Economic Planning
Speaker:	Dr. V. Holubnychy, Hunter College, CUNY
Discussant:	Dr. A. J. Katsenelinboigen, University of California

Topic:	Ukrainian Agriculture: The Problems of Specialization and Intensification in Perspective
Speaker:	Dr. I. Stebelsky, University of Windsor
Discussant:	Dr. P. Woroby, University Of Saskatchewan
Chairman:	Dr. M. Boretsky, Department of Trade and Commerce, Washington, D.C.

Topic:	The Status of the Ukrainian Republic Within the Soviet Federation
Speaker:	Dr. J. N. Hazard, Columbia University
Discussant:	Dr. W. S. Tarnopolsky, York University
Chairman:	Professor J. E. L. Graham, McMaster University

Social Hour for Conference Participants
Courtesy of
Ukrainian Professional and Business Association of Hamilton

Performance by Trio "Kalyna"

Topic: Current Sociological Research in Ukraine
Speaker: Dr. A. Simirenko, Pennsylvania State University
Discussant: Dr. W. Isajiw, University of Toronto

Topic: The Growth and Redistribution of the Ukrainian Population
                    in Russia and the USSR: 1897-1970
Speaker: Dr. R. A. Lewis, Columbia University
Discussant: Dr. A. Romaniuc, Statistics Canada
Chairman: Dr. R. Blumstock, McMaster University

Topic: The Nature and Sources of Dissidence in Ukraine
Speaker: Dr. J. Birch, University of Sheffield, England
Discussant: Dr. B. R. Bociurkiw, Carleton University

Topic: The Communist Party of Ukraine After 1966
Speaker: Dr. Y. Bilinsky, University of Delaware
Discussant: Dr. B. Lewytzkyj, Munich, Germany
                    Dr. J. Pelenski, University of Iowa
Chairman: Dr. G. Hodnett, York University

Evening Programme

Chairman
Dr. R. C. McIvor, Acting Dean
Faculty of Social Sciences, McMaster University

CONFERENCE DINNER

Guest Speaker
Dr. S. Bialer, Columbia University
Detente and the Soviet Internal Developments

Panel Discussion: Ukrainian Studies in the West, Problems and Prospects
Participants: Dr. J. A. Armstrong, University of Wisconsin
                    Dr. C. Bida, University of Ottawa
                    Dr. G. S. N. Luckyj, University of Toronto
                    Dr. O. Pritsak, Harvard University
                    Dr. J. Reshetar, University of Washington, Seattle
Chairman: Dr. A. Bromke, McMaster University

Topic: The Social and Political Role of the Jews in Ukraine
Speaker: Dr. Z. Gitelman, University of Michigan
Discussant: Dr. I. L. Rudnytsky, University of Alberta

Topic: Russians in Ukraine and Problems of Ukrainian Identity
                    in the U.S.S.R.
Speaker: Dr. R. Szporluk, University of Michigan
Discussant: Dr. D. Pospielovsky, University of Western Ontario
Chairman: Dr. R. Johnston, McMaster University

CONFERENCE COMMITTEE:

P. J. Potichnyj, Political Science
Conference Chairman, Programme Chairman

L. J. Shein, Russian

R. E. Blumstock, Sociology

Members;

A. Bromke, Political Science

A. F. Burghardt, Geography

J. E. L. Graham, Economics

W. D. G. Hunter, Economics

R. H. Johnston, History

Jean Montgomery, Library

D. Novak, Political Science

K. H. Pringsheim, Political Science

A. Z. Szendrovits, Business

G. Thomas, Russian

PREFACE

The 1974 McMaster Conference on The Contemporary Ukraine, the eighth conference of an annual series held at McMaster University dealing with various aspects of Soviet and East European studies and the first conference ever held in North America focusing on Ukraine, has achieved a variety of degrees of success. The organizers hoped to draw together distinguished scholars for an exchange of views and to identify important problems which warrant further work: these objectives were certainly achieved at the Conference itself. It was also hoped that we could provide a source of published material on the contemporary Ukraine for students, established scholars and the interested public: the present volume will achieve this objective. Only one major objective remains unfulfilled, that is to stimulate further original research on the topic in the social sciences. It is hoped that the material published here will stimulate the achievement of this objective.

The Conference, held in October lasted for three days, comprising seven separate seminars at which twelve different problems were discussed by thirty-seven specialists. Such mathematics cannot do justice, however, to the interest generated both by the papers themselves and by the lively discussions that followed. The four hundred interested persons who participated, including many university students from Canada and the USA and some from Europe as well, assured the success of the Conference. It is unfortunate that the discussions, although recorded on tape, cannot be reproduced here.

This Conference can rightly be regarded as the first of its type in the Western world because of its scope, its content and its professionalism. It is to be regretted that no scholars from the Ukrainian SSR attended. Though formal invitations were extended by the Committee to several, none accepted. No responses whatsoever, in fact, were received. Moreover, Soviet reaction to the Conference was thoroughly negative, as the articles "Dobri baranchyky z MakMastera" (The Good Lambs from McMaster") in **Perets'** (November 22, 1974) and "Sydiachy na aisbergakh kholodnoi viiny" ("Sitting on the Icebergs of the Cold War") in **Radians' ka Ukraina** (No. 26 for January 31, 1975), clearly show. This reaction, based not on the materials of the Conference itself but on second-hand reports in the Ukrainian émigré press, betrays, besides a certain shallowness, the extreme sensitivity of the topic under discussion on the part of the Soviet establishment.

The Conference, through the papers and the discussions, developed an extremely interesting analysis of contemporary reality in Ukraine, beginning with the utilization of natural resources and moving to problems of demography, economic, social and political questions, and the state of Ukrainian studies in the West.

This Conference showed clearly that there exists a large group of specialists in the West who are systematically studying Ukrainian problems and who are thoroughly familiar with the field.

The materials from the Conference are presented here in six sections: resource development; economic problems; sociology and demography; non-Ukrainian nationalities; the relationships between Party, state and society; and Ukrainian studies in the West.

Most of the presentations have been left substantially unchanged in order to reflect, as much as possible, the attitudes and the atmosphere of the Conference. In some cases, however, the authors insisted on editing their papers and the authors of the appropriate commentaries have modified their statements accordingly. Also, several papers have been substantially revised either at the insistence of the editor or because they were too long in their original form to be published in a volume of this type. The original draft of Mr. Holowacz' paper, for example, was some 120 pages long and had to be revised downward to seventy pages. Mr. Bien, on the other hand, whose paper was more than one hundred pages long, decided not to condense his paper and, therefore, not to publish it here. Therefore, professor Barr's commentary, which was based on the original draft of these two papers had to be substantially reedited. Two commentators, Dr. Romaniuc of Statistics Canada and Dr. Pospielovsky, decided not to offer their commentaries for publication. Dr. Bialer's interesting discussion of "Détente" has been left out because it was indirectly relevant to the general theme of the Conference. Two other commentators, Dr. Lewytzkyj and Dr. Pelenski, have been persuaded to expand their commentaries into full-size papers for this publication.

In accordance with the policy of altering the original contributions as little as possible, no attempt has been made to bring uniformity into footnotes or spelling. The editor's preferences have been accommodated in only two cases: all Ukrainian place names or surnames are given here in transliteration from the Ukrainian and the name of the country under consideration is everywhere given without the definite article: "Ukraine", not the "the Ukraine". For those readers who find it difficult to make the transition from the more common versions of certain names a glossary is provided that lists both the Ukrainian names and the Russian equivalents.

Peter J. Potichnyj
Dundas, Ontario
March, 1975

Acknowledgements

I wish to express my thanks to the many people who helped to make this conference a great success. I should like to express my appreciation to Dr. Arthur N. Bourns, President of McMaster University and Dr. R.C. McIvor, the Acting Dean of the Faculty of Social Sciences for their cooperation and assistance, both material and moral. Professors L.J. Shein and R.E. Blumstock for their service on the Conference Committee. A special acknowledgement is due to Mr. N. Olchowy, President of Ukrainian Professional and Business Association of Hamilton. Thanks to his cooperation the social aspects of the meeting contributed to its overall success. To Messrs. I. Nalywayko J. Balaban, W. Klish, and Dr. N. Skaab, go my sincere thanks for their help in collecting funds for this publication. In addition, I wish to express the deep appreciation of the Committee to the Canada Council for the generous financial support, which made this conference possible, and to Mrs. Inger Moretensen-Gunby for her assistance in preparing the manuscript for publication. Finally, I wish in particular to express the Committee's thanks and my personal gratitude to Miss Jean Montgomery. Her generous service over a number of years to the Interdepartmental Committee has contributed to the success of our activities.

We, therefore, dedicate this volume to Miss Jean Montgomery.

OPENING REMARKS

It gives me the greatest pleasure to welcome you to the 8th Annual McMaster Conference on Soviet and East European Affairs. Those of you who have attended earlier conferences no doubt recognize by now that the President's introductory remarks are, unfortunately part and parcel of the proceedings. Nevertheless, I make it a point to open these conferences because of the important role which they have earned for themselves now in the scholarly life of our University. And I think it is fitting that the University acknowledge the significance of the papers and discussions at the Conference, also welcome the visiting scholars and other guests to McMaster.

I hardly need observe that we live in troubled times, nor that relations between East and West have constituted an enduring source of international tension, despite the hopeful signs of change in recent years. In the academic sphere we see such preferences in the joint participation of East European and Western scholars at the recent International Conference of Slavists in Banff, and of course on a lesser scale in the various academic exchanges and summer course programmes in Yugoslavia and Hungary sponsored by McMaster. In light of all this, it is distressing that the Soviet authorities did not see fit to respond to the invitation of the organizing committee to send seven participants. But we hope that Soviet scholars will attend future conferences in this series.

Some of our non-Canadian guests may not fully appreciate the extent to which cultures other than English or French have contributed to Canadian life. Canada is not the "melting pot" which some have claimed the United States to be. On the contrary it is an intricate ethnic as well as social mosaic, in which the Ukrainian community occupies a prominent position.

Ukrainians constitute a sizeable proportion of the population in a number of regions in Canada, and interest in Ukrainian culture has flourished across the country in recent years. There are few Universities from Montreal Westwards which do not offer courses in Ukrainian language or culture, and Ukrainian language is now being introduced as an elective in quite a few high schools in Canada.

Thus a conference devoted to the present day Ukraine is a natural concern of Canadian Ukrainians—as indeed of Canadians of other origins with their own cultural roots. At the same time one must note the intrinsic significance of Ukraine and some 40 million Ukrainians in the economics, politics and culture of the Soviet Union. The Conference organizers should feel particularly gratified in having succeeded in bringing together such an outstanding group of scholars to exchange ideas about this crucial aspect of Soviet affairs.

McMaster University and I myself, wish you the best in your deliberations and hope that you will have a pleasant three days at our University.

A. N. Bourns, Ph.D., D.Sc., F.R.S.C., F.C.I.C.
President and Vice-Chancellor, McMaster University.

Glossary of Place Names

In Ukrainian	In Russian
Kyiv	Kiev
Donets'	Donets
Donets'ke	Donetsk
Lviv	Lvov
Dnipro	Dnepr
Donbas	Donbass
Shebelynka	Shebelinka
Kharkiv	Kharkov
Kremenchuh	Kremenchug
Kryvyi Rih	Krivoi Rog
Zaporizhia	Zaporozhe
Dniprovs'kyi	Dneprovskii
Bilozers'ke	Belozersk
Kakhivka	Kakhovka
Kirovohrad	Kirovograd
Nykytivka	Nikitovka
Dniprodzerzhyns'ke	Dneprodzerzhinsk
Makiivka	Makeevka
Horlivka	Gorlovka
Luhans'ke	Lugansk
Voroshylovhrad	Voroshilovgrad
Sevastopil	Sevastopol
Simferopil	Simferopol
Ternopil	Ternopol
Chernivtsi	Chernovtsy
Ivano-Frankivs'ke	Ivano-Frankovsk
Odesa	Odessa
Podillia	Podolia
Chernyhiv	Chernigov
Cherkasy	Cherkassy
Vynnytsia	Vinnitsa
Zhytomyr	Zhitomir
Polisia	Polese

I
Resource Development

1

The Non-Renewable Resources of Ukraine

by
A.S.Romaniuk
and
I. Slowikowski
Department of Energy, Mines and Resources
Mines Branch
Ottawa, Ontario

1. INTRODUCTION

When we speak of non-renewable resources we are referring, of course, to mineral resources: those minerals which are sources for fuels, metals, certain chemicals and construction materials. Time and space unfortunately limit our discussion to the mineral fuels and metallics. We will not be able to discuss those minerals which form the raw material base for certain chemicals and construction materials.

In this paper we will look at the importance of Ukraine's mineral industry relative to other industries, look at current developments in individual commodity fields, and then briefly discuss trade.

I would like to mention some of the assumptions made by the authors. Ukraine we are discussing here is the existing Ukrainian Soviet Socialist Republic whose borders include the Crimea. As this is a conference on contemporary Ukraine, our concern has mostly been with current developments within her mineral industry, insofar as current information is available. For this reason data used to determine trends intentionally do not go back into historical times but rather begin with the 1950's.

The authors wish to acknowledge the assistance given by others in the search for data used in this report. In particular we thank Messrs. Holubnychy, Stebelsky and Holowacz.

3

FIGURE 1

TOTAL RESOURCES

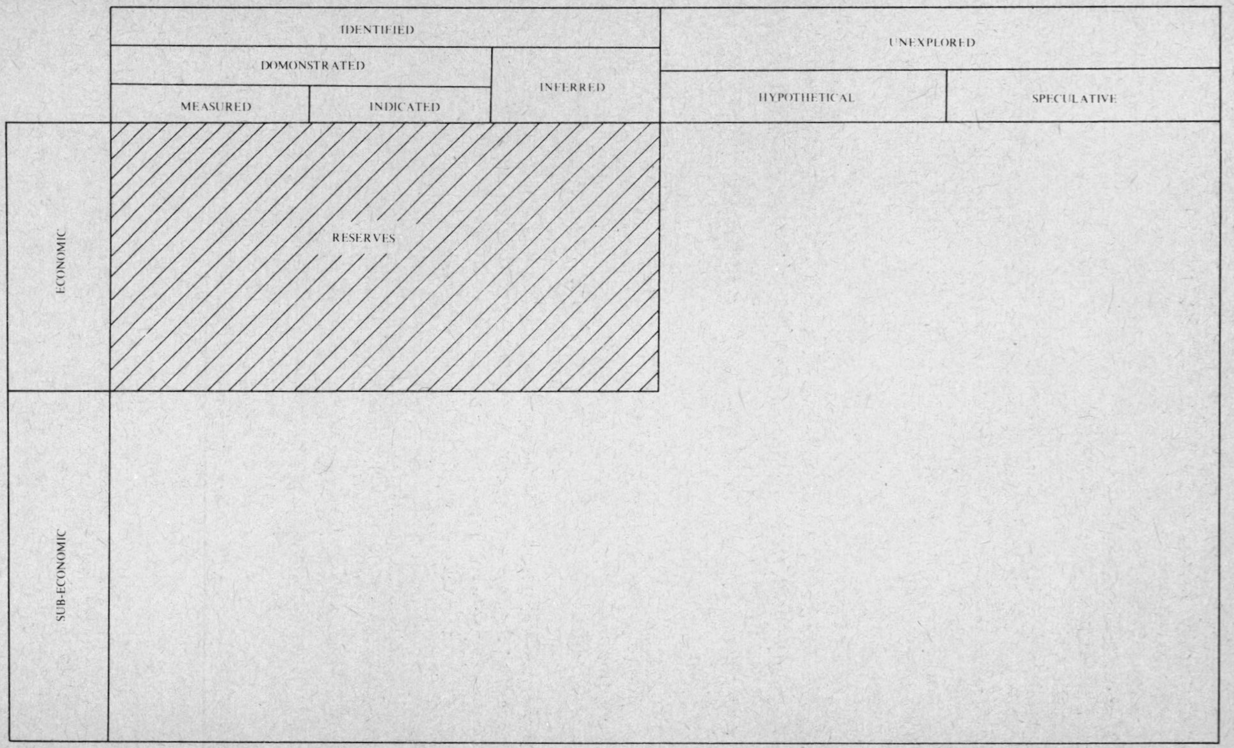

SOURCE: "CLASSIFICATION OF MINERAL AND ENERGY RESOURCES", Mining Magazine, March, 1974, p. 183.

4

2. RESOURCES vs RESERVES

In a paper on mineral resources it is wise to establish at the outset what the terms "reserves" and "resources" mean. "Mineral reserves" are limited to naturally occurring materials whose grades and quantities are measured or at least partly measured and which can be economically exploited at present prices with present technology. The term "mineral resources" includes reserves plus the total of additional material, explored and unexplored, which, if it is not presently of commercial value is likely to become so under certain assumed combinations of technology and economic conditions. Figure 1 illustrates the relationship.

In North American parlance reserves have traditionally been divided into three categories: measured reserves (proven); indicated reserves (probable); and inferred reserves (possible). The term "mineable reserves" is calculated by applying certain constraining factors to the measured category. For coal these factors would include depth of overburden, seam thickness and coal rank. Using a Canadian example, mineable reserves of Nova Scotia coal have been calculated using a maximum waste rock cover of 4,000 ft (1220m), and minimum seam thickness of 36 in. (0.9m). Finally there is the term "recoverable reserves" which applies to what you actually expect to be able to remove from a mineral deposit. Using underground mining methods recoverable reserves in Canada are usually given as 50 per cent of mineable reserves. For surface mining, recoverable reserves are usually given as 80 per cent of mineable reserves. North American reserve figures tend to be conservatively stated, because of these constrictions.

Turning now to terminology used in the Soviet Union we find their five classification categories are:

A_1: Prepared   (podgotovlennye)
A_2: Surveyed   (razvedannye)
B   Evident   (vidimye)
C_1: Supposed   (predpolagaemye)
C_2: Geological   (geologicheskiye) or future (perspektivnye)

Total resources are the aggregate of all known and projected resources and are categorized as "general" (obshchiye) resources. These have been tabulated by Shimkin as follows:

Figure II

Classification	Description
A_1	Reserves, assessed in detail, qualitatively and quantitatively, fully or partly ready for extraction in an existing mine.
A_2	Reserves, assessed in detail, qualitatively and quantitatively, not being exploited. (For priority industrial use).
B	Reserves, assessed in detail for quantity the quality and geological structure of which are not fully established, but only by tests in type sections of the body. (For industrial use. The prospecting data permits establishing processing schemes).
C_1	Reserves, qualitatively and quantitatively covered by reconnaissance prospecting. (For basing development plans and allocating reserves between users).
C_2	Reserves, established by surface surveys. (For long-range planning).

Source: D.B. Shimkin, "The Soviet Mineral-Fuels Industries, 1928-1958: A Statistical Survey," International Population Statistics Reports, Series P-90, *No.19, U.S. Department of Commerce, 1962, p.153.*

Shimkin has stated that for planning purposes each classification has its own significance. Development plans for existing mines, oil wells etc., are based on category A_1; the construction of new mines, wells and processing plants is based on category A_2 as well. For planning at the level of a regional trust, and in developing new fields, the aggregate of categories A_1, A2 and B (also called Industrial (promyshlennye) reserves) comes into consideration. Industry-wide preliminary plans, including the establishment of research projects on needed aspects of mining and processing technology, and also including estimates of the magnitude and distribution of national demand use Balance (balansovye) reserves, so-called for their relation to national economic balances. [2]

Soviet categories of reserves are only partly comparable to those used in North America. Very roughly, Industrial Reserves (A_1 plus A_2 plus B) correspond to our term measured reserves, Supposed Reserves (C_1) to our indicated reserves and Future Reserves (C_2) to our inferred reserves. Because the economic and technical conditions the Soviet Union places upon its reserves appear to be considerably less stringent than in the West, we would expect some overstatement of reserve figures.

3. RELATIVE IMPORTANCE OF THE MINERAL INDUSTRY

First let us look at the importance of "industry" relative to the other branches contributing to the economy of Ukraine. One gauge of this importance is the number of people employed which is shown in Figure III.

Figure III
Employees by Branch of Economy for the Ukraine (Annual Figures in thousands)
(% in brackets)

Branch of Economy	1950	1960	1970	1971	Remarks
Total	15,684	17,146	21,647	22,070	
	(100.0)	(100.0)	(100.0)	(100.0)	
Industry	2,509	4,028	6,036	6,143	refers to industrial
	(16.0)	(23.5)	(27.9)	(27.8)	production personnel
Construction	502	891	1,658	1,744	
	(3.2)	(5.2)	(7.7)	(7.9)	
Agriculture (Total)	9,352	7,456	6,630	6,585	
	(59.6)	(43.5)	(30.6)	(29.8)	
State Farms only	611	969	1,183	1,207	
	(3.9)	(5.7)	(5.5)	(5.5)	
Collective Farms only	8,741	6,487	5,447	5,378	figure for 1950 is for
	(55.7)	(37.8)	(25.2)	(24.4)	the month of July
Forestry	80	70	?	?	
	(0.5)	(0.4)			
Transport	710	1,062	1,502	1,551	
	(4.5)	(6.2)	(6.9)	(7.0)	
Communications	87	113	241	256	
	(0.6)	(0.7)	(1.1)	(1.2)	
Trade	613	854	1,465	1,526	
	(3.9)	(5.0)	(6.8)	(6.9)	
Housing	222	315	540	575	
	(1.4)	(1.8)	(2.5)	(2.6)	
Health Services	385	689	1,014	1,044	
	(2.5)	(4.0)	(4.7)	(4.7)	
Education and Culture	617	881	1,422	1,464	
	(3.9)	(5.1)	(6.6)	(6.6)	
Science	71	199	425	448	
	(0.5)	(1.2)	(2.0)	(2.0)	
Credit and Insurance	46	46	68	73	
	(0.3)	(0.3)	(0.3)	(0.3)	
Administration	333	216	337	344	
	(2.1)	(1.3)	(1.6)	(1.6)	
Others	157	326	309	317	may include some
	(1.0)	(1.9)	(1.4)	(1.4)	forestry

(Sums do not necessarily add up to 100.0 because of rounding off)

Source: *M. Feshback, S. Rapawy, "Labour Constraints in the Five Year Plan," Soviet Economic Prospects for the Seventies. Joint Economic Committee, Congress of the United States, June 1973, pp.534-535.*

The figures show that industry and agriculture are the dominant sectors employing people in Ukraine. (Figure III).

Only a quarter century ago, half the people employed in Ukraine were in agriculture. Since then the numbers in agriculture have dropped dramatically with the industry sector taking up much of the shift. This industrialization is one of the significant causes of social and economic changes in contemporary Ukraine. It is left to others at this conference to elaborate on this topic.

Using the employment indicator but breaking "industry" down into its components we have the results appearing in Fig. IV.

Figure IV
Average Yearly Number of Workers in Industry, Ukrainian S.S.R. (in thousands of workers)

	1960	1965	1970	1971	1972
All Industry	4,056	5,047	6,036	6,143	6,234
Fuel	598	600	572	558	538
Ferrous Metallurgy	388	452	508	503	496
Machine Building	1,169	1,725	2,188	2,272	2,343
Lumber & Related	261	298	307	310	311
Construction Material	338	356	428	437	442
Light Industry	514	607	805	821	823
Food	451	546	625	627	638

Source: Narodne hospodarstvo Ukrains'koi RSR v 1972 rotsi. Kyiv, 1974, p.112

4. MINERAL FUELS

Let us begin the overview of Ukraine's mineral fules with a brief look at developments and trends within the U.S.S.R. as a whole. Production of all major fuel commodities — coal, natural gas and oil — continues to increase but natural gas and oil are outpacing coal. In 1973 the U.S.S.R. produced 421 million metric tons of crude oil, 688 million tons of raw coal (including 173 million tons of coking coal) and 236,000 million cubic meters of natural gas. Increases were recorded of 5 percent for oil, 5 percent for natural gas and 2 percent for coal over 1972 production. Compared to 1970 production the projection for 1980 production of natural gas is to rise by 85 percent, oil by 70 percent and coal by 15 percent. It is a moot point if these production goals will be achieved, but they are a good indicator of the future importance being assigned to the various fuel commodities.

One reason for this trend is found in the relatively lower cost of producing and transporting oil and gas vs. coal. Melnikov makes the following comparison:

> If expenditures, worked out on the basis of recovery and processing costs, plus 10 percent from the capital expenditures (per metric ton of fuel equivalent, taking into consideration average distance of hauling) is taken as equal to 100 percent for fuel oil, then for natural gas they will be approximately 48 percent, for coal mined in open pits 79 percent and for coal mined underground 263 percent.

Let us now view the individual fuel commodities as they apply to Ukraine.

4.1 Coal

Within Ukraine, coal is mined in three basins: The Donets, the Lviv-Volyn' and Dnipro.

The Donets' Basin or Donbas is the most important coal producing basin in the U.S.S.R. and by far the most important in Ukraine. On a world scale it is second only to the Appalachian coal field in the United States. It extends eastward into Rostov Oblast of the Russian SRSR. In 1973, out of a total planned basin output of 212.2 million tons, 180.6 million tons (85 percent) were mined in the Ukrainian sector and 31.6 million tons (15 percent) in the Rostov section. This ratio has remained constant over the past decade. Most Donbas coal is high rank coal (anthracite and bituminous coal of which about half is coking coal), mined generally from thin seams using un-

7

derground longwall methods. Coal has been produced commercially from the Donbas since the 1820's. Its history could easily be the subject for a book. However our discussion in this paper must be limited to a brief examination of current problems and developments.

By comparison, development of the Lviv-Volyn' Basin began only in 1949 and the first bituminous coal was produced from underground operations in 1954. In 1973 some twenty mines produced 14.5 million tons of raw coal. The average cost of coal production here was said to be 9.5 roubles per ton, [3] at least for the first quarter of 1973. This is lower than the Donbas for reasons which will be detailed later. Average monthly productivity [4] per worker in 1973 in this basin was 65 tons of raw coal compared with Donbas productivity which ranges from a low of 34 to a high of 59 tons.

In the Dnipro Basin brown coal, which is a low calorific value coal, is mined by surface mining methods from pits which had to be reconstructed after World War II. Monthly productivity for this basin per worker is in the 135 to 177 ton range which is a direct reflection of the advantage of large-scale open pit mining as compared to underground methods. An obvious disadvantage is that arable land is rendered unproductive for agricultural purposes. For 1973 it was reported [5] that some 64 million cubic meters of material was stripped to produce 8.23 million tons of coal for a relatively high stripping ratio of 7.75 cubic meters per ton. Brown coal from this basin is used locally as fuel for thermal generating stations and in the form of briquettes as household fuel.

Current production of raw coal, by enterprise (kombinat), is shown in Figure V.

Figure V
1973 Coal Production in Ukraine (in thousands of metric tons)

Kombinat	Plan Total		Actual Total	
	All Coal	Coking Coal	All Coal	Coking Coal
Donets Basin	180,588	79,350	186,604	82,402
Donetskugol	19,868	14,776	20,727	15,322
Makeevugol	16,324	15,769	16,858	16,284
Krasnoarmeyskugol	22,934	10,219	23,798	10,456
Artemugol	13,340	12,411	13,728	12,703
Ordzhonikidzeugol	6,234	1,696	6,448	1,838
Shakhterskantratsit	12,595	160	13,095	193
Thorezantratsit	10,460	—	10,788	—
Voroshilovgradugol	10,450	2,975	10,746	3,211
Kadievugol	12,030	8,400	12,347	8,720
Pervomayskugol	10,943	3,360	11,039	3,428
Krasnodonugol	6,785	5,557	6,951	5,714
Donbassantratsit	23,463	—	24,396	—
Sverdlovantratsit	9,410	—	9,658	—
Trest Pavlogradugol	5,752	4,027	6,025	4,523
Lvov-Volyn Basin	13,642	—	14,455	—
Ukrzapadugol	13,642	—	14,455	—
Dneper Basin	11,270	—	11,524	—
Aleksandriyaugol	9,050	—	9,203	—
Trest Burugol	2,220	—	2,321	—
	205,500	**79,250**	**212,583**	**82,402**

Source: Ugol Ukrainy, *No.5, May 1974, p.51.*

A view of Ukrainian coal production relative to that of the U.S.S.R. as a whole is shown in Figure VI. Again, all figures are in terms of raw coal, i.e., coal which includes washing losses.

Although it is the Soviet Union's most important source of coal, especially for coking coals and anthracite, the Ukraine's share of the U.S.S.R. total is decreasing and this trend is expected to continue unless there is large-scale development of new reserves in the northern extension of the Donets Basin. The percentage factor in Figure VI shows the trend. Because of the dominant position of the Donbas, this decline is really the decline of the Donbas among the other major producing basins in

8

the U.S.S.R.

If we look at the profitability as a percentage of investment of the Ukrainian coal industry relative to other industry sectors we note that it is even lower than the electric utility sector. Incidentally the profit concept and significance of the monetary values given in Figure VII will not be discussed in this paper. The object of introducing the table is merely to show the trend and relative position of coal.

The problems facing the Donbas have their origin in the fact that most of the readily accessible coal has already been mined. On the positive side the Donbas has large reserves of coking coal, which has no better substitute in pyrometallurgy, especially steel-making. This factor combined with the favourable location of the Donbas near centres where its products are used assures it of an important, albeit diminishing, future.

Let us look at some of the basic operating parameters in the Donbas as they compare with the other major producing basins in the U.S.S.R. These basins together account for some 85 percent of the U.S.S.R.'s coal production. (Figure VIII).

The points that are brought out in Figure VIII would include the following:

(a) A high proportion of Donbas output is from thin seams (0.5 - 1.2m). Equipment for mining seams 0.5m thick is not yet available so waste rock is extracted with the coal. This in turn leads to an increasing ash content. In 1960 ash content averaged 18.9 percent and by 1970 this increased to 22.4 percent. [6] The trend is continuing as 1973 production reportedly has an ash content of 23.3 percent. [7] Soviet authorities have recognized the false economy of shipping and using inert material with coal rather than removing most of it at the mine site by simple mechanical means. It remains to be seen if quantity will be sacrificed for quality in this instance.

(b) The Donbas has a greater proportion of small mines than any other producing basin. As a rule small mines are less efficient than larger units. The trend, as in Great Britain, West Germany and France has been to consolidate units where possible and close down the smaller operations. Referring to Ukraine it has been reported [8] that from 1971 to mid-1973 some 143 mines and mine administrations were consolidated and 21 mines closed because of poor results. Practically all of these changes must have occurred in the Donbas.

(c) Donbas workings are the deepest in the U.S.S.R. with some now down to 1300 meters. Average depth in 1970 was 488 meters. Towards 1975 this should reach 570 meters and in 1980 about 650 meters. [9] In terms of production in 1970 some 60 million tons of coal were mined at a depth over 600 meters while for 1975 the projection is 68 million tons and for 1980 it is 79 million tons. [10]

There is a greater tendency at depth for the occurrence of roof and ground control problems in mine workings. Deep seams composed of hard coal and having thick overlying beds of strong rock give rise to rock bumps. In the Donbas deep seams tend also to be more gassy and outbursts (i.e., the violent outflow of coal gases) are a known problem. In response to these physical problems of mining at depth, practice in the Donbas is to extract seams which fall into the "safe" category before those which are known to be hazardous. This selective working rather than extracting in descending order is more costly, less productive and tends to decrease coal recovery. It has been reported[11]for example, that in a mine named after the XXII Party Congress, the cost of supporting 1 meter of mine development at the 800 meter level is 26.88 roubles compared with 17.76 roubles at the 600 meter level.

Two other problems associated with mining at depth in the Donbas are high rock temperatures and a greater tendency towards spontaneous combustion of coal. Rock temperatures at depths over 1000 meters are in the range 28-32 C (82 - 86 F).

9

Figure VI
COAL PRODUCTION IN UKRAINE (In Millions of Metric Tons)

	1950	1955	1960	1965	1970	1971	1972	1973	1974 Plan	1975 Plan
Ukraine	78.0	126.0	172.1	194.3	207.1	209.5	211.2	212.6	215.2	217.4
U.S.S.R.	261.1	389.9	509.6	577.7	624.1	640.9	655.2	661.4	670.0	694.9
% Ukr/USSR	29.9%	32.3%	33.8%	33.6%	33.2%	32.7%	32.2%	32.1%	32.1%	31.3%

Sources: Narodnoe Khoziaistvo SSSR v 1972 g., *Moscow, 1973, pp.170,209;* Entsyklopediya narodnoho hospodarstva Ukrains'koi RSR, *Kyiv, 1969, Vol.I, p.301;* Mining Annual Review, *1974, p.435.*

Figure VII
Profitability of Ukrainian Industrial Enterprises by Sector

	Profit in Millions of Roubles				Profit in Percent of Investment			
	1965	1970	1971	1972	1965	1970	1971	1972
Total Industry	3,972	10,171	10,276	10,699	12.9	21.8	20.4	19.6
Electric Power	218	502	548	511	8.5	10.8	10.6	8.8
Oil Extraction/Processing	88	198	197	209	27.3	29.4	25.4	24.5
Coal	812	395	352	300	18.2	7.2	6.2	5.0
Ferrous Metallurgy	454	1,598	1,657	1,714	7.4	17.5	17.0	16.7
Chemical	314	496	549	630	18.4	17.1	16.4	17.2
Oil-Chemical	25	85	97	104	16.2	27.2	27.3	25.5
Machine Construction/ Machinery	1,239	2,382	2,235	2,596	20.7	24.6	21.2	22.7
Lumber, etc.	125	243	254	263	18.6	34.6	34.0	33.3
Construction Materials	181	315	356	377	11.4	14.0	14.6	14.4
Light Industry	470	1,098	1,166	1,126	43.4	62.5	59.6	52.2
Food Industry	1,164	1,417	1,372	1,327	29.1	29.0	27.4	24.3

Source: Narodne hospodarstvo Ukrains'koi RSR v 1972 rotsi, *Kyiv, 1974, p.554.*

Figure VIII
Operational Parameters by Major Basins, 1970

	USSR Total (%)	Donbas	Kuzbass	Karaganda	Pechora	Moscow
Output in Relation to seam thickness						
Up to 1.2m (%)	36	68	5	2	10	—
1.2m to 3.5m (%)	52	32	64	58	82	89
3.5m to 6.5m (%)	7	—	14	29	8	11
›6.5m (%)	5	—	17	11	—	—
Output in Relation to Colliery Size						
Up to 500 t/day (%)	14	17	—	—	—	10
500 to 1,000 t/day (%)	21	25	2	—	8	31
1,000 to 2,000 t/day (%)	35	35	20	15	19	47
2,000 to 3,000 t/day (%)	16	15	25	32	42	8
3,000 to 5,000 t/day (%)	11	7	37	35	31	3
›5,000 t/day (%)	3	1	15	18	—	1
Output in Relation to depth of Working						
Up to 100m (%)	11	—	7	—	—	99
100 to 200m (%)	12	3	35	14	19	1
200 to 400m (%)	38	31	56	58	36	—
400 to 700m (%)	29	46	2	28	45	—
›700m (%)	10	20	—	—	—	—
Productivity						
Per Production Worker (t/shift)	2.1	1.7	2.6	3.3	2.9	3.2
Per Face Worker (t/shift)	6.2	5.1	7.6	9.1	9.8	10.2

Source: B.N. Whittaker, "The Coal Mining Industry of the U.S.S.R.," Mining Engineer, July 1974, p.465.

In the Krasnaya Zvyezda Mine rock temperatures at the 1200 meter level reach 36-40 C (97 - 104 F). Such temperatures obviously require increased ventilation and refrigeration of mine air. As for spontaneous combustion, out of 661 seams in the Ukrainian Donbas 132 are liable to spontaneous combustion. Most are in mines of the Kombinats Artemugol, Pervomaiskugol, Kadievugol and Ordzhonikidzeugol.[12]

(d) Donbas productivity is considerably lower than that of any other basin. This factor is a major contributor to the relatively high cost of Donbas coal.

Underground mining, which is the way Donbas coal is mined, is about three times more costly than strip mining.[13] On the matter of productivity another source[14] states that average monthly coal productivity of Soviet coal mines in 1971 was 310 tons in surface mines and 48 tons underground, i.e. over six times greater in surface mines as compared with underground mines.

The trend towards producing more coal from surface mines has been in progress in the U.S.S.R. as a whole for at least two decades and can be expected to continue. Figure IX shows the Ukraine moving against the trend. Its surface mining operations are comparatively minor in importance and there is little prospect this will change. To illustrate, of the total 1973 production, 204 millions tons were mined by underground methods and 8 million tons by open pits

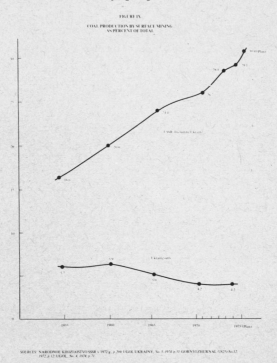

FIGURE IX
COAL PRODUCTION BY SURFACE MINING
AS PERCENT OF TOTAL

SOURCES: NARODNOE KHOZIAISTVO SSSR v 1972 g., p.209; UGOL UKRAINY, No. 5, 1974 p.37 GORNYI ZHURNAL (1825) No.12, 1972, p.12; UGOL, No. 4, 1974, p.71.

Nevertheless a comparison of the cost of high quality Donbas thermal coal and similar coal from the Kuznetsk Basin delivered to a central European Russian market such as Moscow does not show any marked advantage for Siberian coal. The reason is, of course, found in the much higher railway transport cost for Siberian coal. If we assume a railway transport cost for coal of 0.5 kopeck per ton-kilometer (a figure used by a recent Soviet source[15] and reasonably comparable to a North American rate of 1 cent per ton-mile) we get the following comparison.

	Donbas Coal	Kuzbas Coal
underground mining cost	19.0 rbls	-
open pit mining cost	-	6.0 rbls
rail transport cost: 1100 km	5.5 rbls	-
rail transport cost: 3700 km	-	18.5 rbls
Delivered cost per ton	24.5 rbls	24.5 rbls

On the subject of coal reserves in the Ukraine, we can refer to figures for the year 1956 which have been assembled by Hodgkins [16] and are reproduced in Figure X. More recent figures by Melnikov [17] are shown in brackets. It should be noted that total reserve figures assume a minimum thickness of 0.3 meters for hard coal and 0.6 meters for brown coal and a depth of 1800 meters. It remains to be seen if these are realistic assumptions, as the technology for mining coal seams 0.3 meters thick at depths approaching 1800 meters has yet to be developed. (Figure X)

Figure X
Geological Reserves of Coal as of January 1, 1956 in billions of metric tons

	Total	By degree of Reliability			By Depth Zones, in Meters			
		Proven	Probable	Possible	0-300	300-600	600-1200	1200-1800
U.S.S.R.	8,669.5	241.2	941.9	7,486.4	2,351.5	1,779.8	2,838.0	1,700.1
Ukraine	179.1	53.8	57.6	67.7	25.2	37.1	71.2	45.7
Donets'	173.1	49.0	56.6	67.6	20.9	35.5	71.1	45.7
Lviv-Volyn	1.8	1.7 (0.7)	0.1	—	0.1	1.6	0.1	—
Dnipro	4.2	3.1 (2.5)	1.0	0.1	4.2	—	—	—

Sources: *J.A. Hodgins,* Soviet Power. *Prentice Hall, N.J., 1961, pp. 158-159; N.A. Melnikov, "The Role of Coal in the Energy Fuel Resources in the U.S.S.R.;"* Canadian Mining and Metallurgical Bulletin, *June 1972, p. 79.*

In order to determine what kind of time-span is represented by these reserves let us first concern ourselves only with reserves in the "proven" category and round off the reserve figures to allow for production which has taken place since the figures were assembled. Finally, let us assume a 50 percent recovery for underground mining and 80 percent recovery for open pit mining.

For the Donbas the proven figure would be rounded off from 49,000 to 45,000 million tons. At the current rate of production of 180 million tons per year and a 50 percent recovery, the Donbas could operate for another 125 years. Assuming an 80 percent recovery this could be extended to 200 years.

Lviv-Volyn' reserves would be rounded off from 700 to 600 million tons. At the current rate of production of 14 million tons per year and a 50 percent recovery, this field could operate for another 21 years. If a recovery of 80 percent is assumed the figure would be 35 years.

The Dnipro reserve figures would be rounded off from 2,500 to 2,400 million tons. At the current annual rate of production of 11.5 million tons and a recovery of 80 percent it could operate for another 170 years.

4.2 Natural Gas

Natural gas, the main constituent of which is usually methane, is found either associated with crude oil or by itself. In Ukraine most gas (96 percent in 1971) is not associated with oil, and is produced from about forty deposits located in the following three geologically favourable areas:

— the Dashava area of the Subcarpathians, where the gas, about 97 percent methane, is associated with oil. Commercial production in this area began in 1924. The Subcarpathian along with the Dnipro-Donets' area, is being intensively explored for further deposits.

— the Crimean-Black Sea area, where some old but minor deposits are being exploited and considerable new exploration activity is taking place, especially within the Black Sea.

— The Dnipro-Donets' area which is the major producing area. It includes the Shebelinka field, centred about 35 miles south-east of Kharkiv, discovered in 1949— producing in 1956, and still likely the single largest source of natural gas in the

U.S.S.R. The original deposit was supplemented in 1965 with the discovery of another gas deposit at Yefremovka, 20 miles west of Shebelinka. Production here began in 1967. Mention has also been made [18] of the discovery in 1972 of the West-Yefremovski deposit along with further exploration of the Western-Krestishchenski deposit. Reserves in the latter deposit are said to be in the order of 180 billion cubic meters, which is close to the known reserves at Shebelinka. Intensive exploration continues in the Dnipro-Donets' area.

— Production of natural gas is shown in Figure XI.

Ukraine still appears to occupy first place in the production of natural gas in the U.S.S.R. Close to forty gas fields are in operation in the three major areas. Ukraine supplies gas to the Russian Republic, Belorussia, Moldavia, Lithuania, Poland, Czechoslovakia, and Austria to the extent of about one-fifth of her production.

Although there are gaps in the statistics, it appears production relative to the U.S.S.R. total peaked somewhere between 1955 and 1960. The republic's share has been more or less constant at just over 30 percent of the total up to 1972. The rapid development of deposits east of the Urals accounts for the correspondingly rapid decline of Ukraine's relative position since 1972. Unless very large reserves are discovered at depth it is unlikely this trend will be reversed.

Like coal, approximately three-quarters of U.S.S.R. natural gas reserves are located east of the Urals, while major consumers are located west of the Urals. This calls for the need to build major pipelines to move the gas some 1,500 to 2,200 miles (2,500 to 3,500 km).

Unquestionably natural gas and crude oil are the current star commodities in the Soviet energy picture. The stated objectives [19] of the current five-year plan reflect this, the objectives being:

(a) to raise natural gas production to 320 billion cubic meters (an increase during the five-year period of 122 billion cubic meters);

(b) to eliminate large losses of associated gas at oilfields and increase its use to 85-87 percent in 1975, as against 61.1 percent in 1970.

(c) to ensure the development of large gas deposits in the northern regions of Tyumenskaya Oblast, Turkmenia, Komi ASSR, Orenburgskaya Oblast, and the laying of 33,000 kilometers of main gas pipeline mostly with diameters of 1,020, 1,220 and 1,420 millimeters, which will constitute approximately 50 percent of the entire length of all previous gas pipelines built up through 1970;

(d) to ensure the complete refinement of gas so as to obtain from it gasoline, liquefied gases, sulphur, helium, and other valuable products.

Current plan objectives showing the regional shift in production are shown in Figure XII.

The U.S.S.R.'s gross reserves of natural gas (i.e. proven, probable and possible) are said to have increased from 3.6 trillion cubic meters at the beginning of 1966 to 15.7 trillion cubic meters at the beginning of 1971. [20] The largest deposits were discovered in Tyumenskaya Oblast, Turkmenia and near the city of Orenburg. The regional reserve picture is shown in Figure XIII.

Ukrainian reserves of natural gas (A plus B plus C$_1$) are given as 800 billion cubic meters in 1969 or about 5 percent of total U.S.S.R. reserves for 1971. [21] At the current annual production rate of 68 billion cubic meters the Ukraine's reserves would be depleted in about 12 years. This of course assumes no new discoveries. It is known that intensive exploration especially in the Dnipro-Donets area, the Subcarpathian area and the Black Sea, is adding to reserves at a rate at least equal to current production. It was reported that in 1973 six new deposits were found containing 90 billion cubic meters. [22]

On the subject of cost and productivity few recent figures are available. A somewhat dated tabulation by Woroniak and reproduced in Figure XIV is useful for comparative purposes. [23]

Figure XI
Production of Natural Gas (in billions of cubic meters)

	1950	1955	1960	1965	1970	1971	1972	1973	1974 (Plan)	1975 (Plan)
Ukraine	1.54	2.93	14.3	39.4	60.9	64.7	67.2	68.2	63.2	62.0
U.S.S.R. Total	5.76	8.98	45.3	127.7	197.9	212.4	221.4	236.0	256.8	320.0
% Ukr/USSR	26.7%	32.6%	31.6%	30.9%	30.8%	30.5%	30.4%	28.9%	24.6%	19.4%

Sources: Narodnoe khoziaistvo SSSR v 1972 g., *p.207;* Narodne hospodarstvo Ukrains'koi RSR v 1972 rotsi. *p.126;* SSSR i Soiuznye Respubliki v 1973 godu. *Moscow, Statistika, 1974.*

Figure XII
Natural Gas Production for Plan 1971-75 (production in billions of cubic meters)

	1970 Plan		1975 Plan	
	Planned Production	%	Planned Production	%
U.S.S.R. Total	198.0	100.0	320.0	100.0
European Part USSR + Urals	139.0	70.2	164.1	51.3
Orenburg Oblast	1.3	0.7	26.0	8.1
Komi ASSR	6.9	3.5	16.1	5.0
Regions east of Urals	59.0	29.3	155.9	48.7
Western Siberia	9.3	4.7	44.0	13.8
Turkmen SSR	13.1	6.6	65.1	20.3

Source: State Five Year Plan for the Development of the USSR, National Economy for the Period 1971-1975. *Moscow, English edition, p.107.*

Figure XIII
USSR, Natural Gas Reserves, by Regions as of January 1, 1971 (In billions of cubic meters) (Categories A,B, C₁)

	Reserves	% of Total
European Part of U.S.S.R.	3,358.1	21.3
Western Siberia	9,632.9	61.1
Central Asia and Kazakhstan	2,424.7	15.4
Eastern Siberia and Far East	346.3	2.2
Totals	15,762.0	100.0

Source: "The Mineral Industry of the USSR", United States Bufeau of Mines Minerals Yearbook. *Preprint from the 1971, p 41.*

Figure XIV
Gross Output and Cost of Gas Production in Seven Major Soviet Gas Fields

	1965			1968	
	Output[a]	Cost[b]	Output per Worker[c]	Output[a]	Cost[b]
Komi ASSR	0.6	2.94	3.1	0.6	3.47
Saratov Oblast	6.2	0.67	—	4.2	1.12
Krasnodarskii Krai	22.3	0.55	16.5	27.5	1.15
Stavropol'skii Krai	15.1	0.14	14.1	16.3	0.25
Kharkiv Oblast	27.1	0.27	35.0	33.7	0.33
Bukhara Oblast	16.0	0.19	27.5[d]	28.4	0.20

[a]*Billion cubic meters.*
[b]*Rouble per 1,000 cubic meters.*
[c]*Million cubic meters.*
[d]*Data represents Uzbek SSR.*

Sources: A. Woroniak, "Regional Aspects of Soviet Planning and Industrial Organization," The Soviet Economy in Regional Perspective. *New York, Praeger, 1973, p.288.*

As with the coal, a major factor favouring the Ukrainian natural gas industry is its location close to major consumers whereas distant sources need costly pipelines to bring their product to market.

Figure XV
Crude Oil Production, Including Gas Condensates (in Millions of Tons)

	1950	1955	1960	1965	1970	1971	1972	1973	1974 (Plan)	1975 (Plan)
Ukraine	0.29	0.53	2.16	7.58	13.9	14.3	14.5	14.1	15.0	16.4
U.S.S.R. Total	37.88	70.79	147.86	242.89	353.0	377.1	400.4	421.0	448.2	496.0
% Ukr/USSR	0.80%	0.70%	1.50%	3.10%	3.9%	3.8%	3.6%	3.3%	3.3%	3.3%

Sources: Narodnoe khoziaistvo SSSR v 1972 g., p.206; Narodne hospodarstvo Ukrains'koi RSR v 1972 rotsi, p.126; V.V. Strishkov, "Soviet Union", Mining Annual Review, 1974, p.435; Entsyklopedia narodnoho hospodarstva Ukrains'koi RSR, Vol. III, p.111.

4.3 Oil

The oil producing regions of Ukraine are of course the same as those already mentioned for natural gas: the Subcarpathian, the Dnipro-Donets and Crimean-Black Sea. In 1973 Ukraine's oil production decreased as compared with 1972, which likely means her output has levelled off and will remain at about 14 million tons per year. It may even be that Ukrainian production reached its peak in 1972.

Figure XV shows that Ukraine's portion of the U.S.S.R. total crude oil production is much less significant than for coal and natural gas. Ukraine cannot be considered as self-sufficient in this essential commodity — although it is a moot point what self-sufficiency in any commodity represents to a republic within the Soviet Union. If U.S.S.R. net production for 1972 (allowing for export and import of crude oil) is divided by her population we get a per capita consumption of 1.33 tons of crude. Using this indicator Ukraine would need to produce 63 million tons of crude oil to be self-sufficient. Actually it would need more than this because it is the most highly in-dustrialized and densely populated republic in the U.S.S.R.

Planned production for 1973 was 14.2 million tons so production was slightly below plan. The prospects of achieving the plan goal of 16.4 million tons in 1975 are not good. This under-achievement relative to plan applies especially to the old producing areas of Baku and Grozny. Transportation of West Siberian oil to major refineries and consuming centres in European U.S.S.R. appears to be a major bottleneck in overall plan achievement. Shortages of line pipe, compressors, and trained crews plus the supply and maintenance problems associated with developments in remote areas are some of the contributing factors.

As of January 1, 1971 reserves for U.S.S.R. crude oil in place were estimated at over 30 billion tons. No figures are known for Ukraine. [24]

In 1971 Ukraine's first offshore well was being drilled in the Black Sea, near Golitsino, where water depth reaches 35 meters. In the same year a 355 kilometer (220 miles) crude oil pipeline was completed between Kremenchuh and Kherson.

4.4 Peat

Peat is included among non-renewable resources of mineral fuels because one of its main uses is as a low-calorie fuel. Its other major use is in agriculture as a soil conditioner. Its occurrence in Ukraine is widespread but production is primarily in the Polissia area. Its use as a fuel is quite extensive especially in those rural areas where coal or natural gas are not readily available for home heating.

Figure XVI
Peat Production, for Fuel Purposes (in millions of tons)

	1950	1955	1960	1965	1970	1971	1972
Ukraine	2.9	4.1	4.7	4.3	4.1	4.4	4.6
U.S.S.R. Total	36.0	50.8	53.6	45.7	57.4	54.3	61.2
% Ukr/U.S.S.R.	8.1%	8.1%	8.8%	9.4%	7.1%	8.1%	7.5%

Sources: Narodne hospodarstvo Ukrains'koi RSR v 1972 rotsi, *p.126;* Narodnoe Khoziaistvo SSSR v 1972 g., *pp.170-171.*

The cost of producing peat varies considerably, depending on the form of the end product, and the degree to which this product is dried. Comparative cost figures have been given in roubles per ton as follows: [25]

Fuel Briquettes	10.6
Milled Fuel Peat	1.0
Lump Peat	3.9
Bulk (agricultural)	0.8

The cost of producing peat briquettes is within the range of the cost of coal delivered to the individual consumer so the use of peat as a fuel will likely gradually diminish. Its increasing use agriculturally will likely make up the difference so total production will not likely change very much.

Reserve figures have been given variously as ranging from 2.5 to 3.5 billion tons. Because peat is excavated within a few meters of the surface it can be assumed that virtually all reserves are recoverable.

5.METALLICS

5.1 Iron Ore

Ukraine's Kryvyi Rih iron ore mining complex in Dnipropetrovsk oblast is the largest in the world. Other producing basins are the Kerch in the Crimea, Kremenchug in Poltava oblast, and Bilozers'k in Zaporizhya oblast. The relative importance of these basins as producers is evident.

Figure XVII
Ukrainian Iron Ore Production by Basin (in millions of tons)

	Total	Kryvyi Rih	Kerch	Kremenchuh	Bilozerske
1950	21.0	21.0	—	—	—
1958	49.8	46.8	3.0	—	—
1965	83.8	79.2	4.6	—	—
1970	111.2	103.8	4.6	2.6	0.15
1971	117.0	104.8	4.7	6.5	1.00

Source: Gornyi Zhurnal (1825) No.12, December 1972, p.12.

The Kryvyi Rih Basin extends north and south some 38 miles and contains iron-bearing formations from one to four miles wide. It contains both high-grade (direct shipping) ores, with an iron content of 55 to 60 percent—mined mainly by underground methods, and low-grade iron quartzites with a metal content of 30 to 37 percent—mined mainly through open pits and requiring concentration in order to produce a marketable product. Geologically the host rocks of the Kryvyi Rih Basin are similar to those found in Knob Lake ores of Quebec-Labrador and the Mesabi Range in Minnesota, U.S.A.

By the mid-1950's much of Kryvyi Rih's rich, readily accessible iron ore had been mined out. This factor combined with the development of cheaper surface mining methods and concentrating and agglomerating technology resulted in a dramatic shift from underground to open pit production, as illustrated in Figure XVIII.

Within the period 1955-1970, six large concentrators with associated open-pit mines went into operation at Kryvyi Rih. These complexes (kombinats) account for more than half of Kryvyi Rih production. The trend is towards an ever increasing proportion of production to come from these complexes which mine lean ore. (See Figure XIX).

Kerch ore, by comparison to Kryvyi Rih's, is a low grade (approximately 45 percent iron in the concentrate) oolitic iron ore whose mineral content makes it difficult to concentrate. It is mined by open pit methods and mostly shipped in special ore carriers across the Sea of Azov to the Zhdanov steel mill. The ore is high in phosphorus and arsenic which are undsirable elements as well as manganese and vanadium which are useful.

Kremenchuh ore is similar to that of Kryvyi Rih as the Kremenchuh basin is considered a norther extension of the main basin. Underground mines here have serious water problems. The relatively new Dniprovski open pit mine is operated by the DneproGOK kombinat.

The Bilozers'k basin, on the left bank of the Dnipro River, is located east of the Kryvyi Rih Basin and is structurally similar. The basin is being developed by underground methods. Severe water problems made it necessary for vertical shafts to be sunk using a ground-freezing technique.

Ukraine produced 56 percent of the total Soviet iron ore in 1973, with half the Soviet total coming from the Kryvyi Rih Basin. Plans call for a 14 percent increase

FIGURE XVIII

Open Pit Mining of Iron Ore in Ukraine

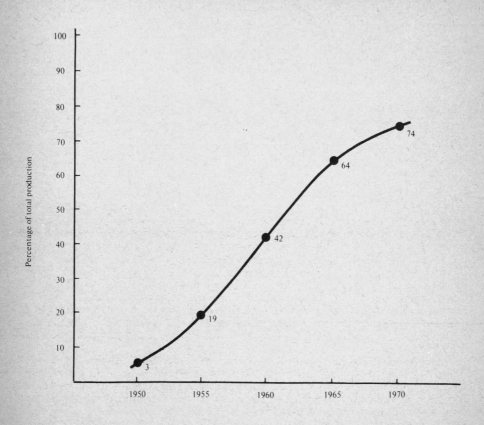

SOURCE: Gornyi Zhurnal (1825) No. 12, December 1972, p. 12

Figure XIX
Kryvyi Rih Mining — Concentrating Kombinats

Kombinat	Start-Up Year	1971 Production, in millions of tons	
		Crude Ore	Concentrate
YUCOK	1955	33.5	15.9
NKGOK	1959	16.1	6.2
Ts GOK	1961	20.0	7.2
Sev GOK	1964	33.1	14.3
In GOK	1965	27.7	12.2
Dnepro GOK	1970	13.5	6.5
Total		143.9	62.3

Source: Gornyi Zhurnal *(1825), No.12, December 1972, p.12.*

Figure XX
Production of Shippable Iron Ore (in millions of tons)

	1950	1955	1960	1965	1970	1971	1972	1973
Ukraine	21.0	39.9	59.0	83.9	111.2	117.0	119.5	121.0
U.S.S.R. Total	39.6	71.9	105.9	153.4	195.5	203.0	208.1	215.2
% Ukr/USSR	53.0%	55.5%	55.7%	54.7%	56.8%	57.6%	57.4%	56.0%

Sources: Gornyi Zhurnal *(1825), No.12, December 1972, p.12;* Narodnoe Khoziaistvo SSSR v 1972 *g., p.214;* Narodne Hospodarstvo Ukrains'koi RSR v 1972 rotsi, p.219.

during the 1971-75 plan. (**Fig. XX**).

Also in 1973 the mining capacity at both the New Kryvyi Rih and Inhulets complexes was expanded to provide ore for the giant No. 9 blast furnace under construction at the Kryvyi Rih iron and steel plant (working volume is 5,000 cubic meters for a rated capacity of 4 million tons).

Kryvyi Rih's future looks brighter than that of the Donbas for several reasons: its reserves of surface-mineable ore are great; the declining share of coke in the blast furnace charge tends to shift the location of steel works increasingly towards iron ore sources; and there is only one other major European source for iron ore in the U.S.S.R., namely the Kursk Magnetic Anomaly (KMA) which is about half way between Kryvyi Rih and Moscow. Like Kryvyi Rih, the Kursk basin has very large reserves of primarily low grade iron ore (30 to 40 percent iron) which is amenable to concentration along with localized deposits of direct shipping ore (55 to 60 percent iron). About 24.6 million tons of usable ore were produced from KMA in 1973 with plans to produce 30.7 million tons in 1974.[26] Presently it is the most rapidly expanding source of iron ore in the U.S.S.R. However there are two constraints which make the mining of KMA ore difficult; waste rock in the order of 1,000 ft. thick covers much of the reserves and serious water problems are common in both surface and underground mines.

By the same token Kryvyi Rih has an important operating problem which is that of ventilating its deep open pit mines during windless days or days during which there is a temperature inversion. The combustion products of blasting operations and engines of operating equipment must be removed artificially or mine operations under such conditions must stop.

Reserves figures for Ukraine which apply as of January, 1968 are compiled in Figure XXI.

Figure XXI
Iron Ore Reserves in the Ukraine (in millions to tons)

Basin or Deposit	Ore Type	A + B + C₁	C₁ (Speculative)
Kryvyi Rih	Total Ore	15,024	5,491
	rich ore	1,508	546
	lean ore	13,516	4,945
Kremenchuh	Total ore	1,149	1,004
	rich ore	168	52
	lean ore	981	952
Bilozerske	rich ore	452	228
Kerch	lean (brown) ore	1,747	386
Petrivsk	lean ore	228	50
Total		18,600	7,179

Source: Entsyklopedia narodnoho hospodarstva Ukrains'koi RSR. *Vol.II, p.82.*

The U.S.S.R. total of iron ore reserves for 1966 has been reported at 56,000 million tons for categories A+ B+ C₁, so Ukraine would have about one-third of the total. Most sources state the Kursk Magnetic Anomaly has greater reserves than those of Kryvyi Rih. Both unquestionably are very large. At present production rates Kryvyi Rih could continue operations for at least another half century. Its peak production years are still ahead of it.

Kerch ore reserves are sufficient for production at its current rate for over a century. However until improved ways of concentrating the ore and removing certain impurities are found, there will not likely be a dramatic rise in production from this basin.

5.2 Manganese

The Nikopol manganese basin south-east of Kryvyi Rih is the world's largest manganese producer. Its production in 1973 accounted for 79 percent of the U.S.S.R.'s total or over 27 percent of the world total. Mangnese is an essential element for the steel industry, used to counteract the harmful effects of sulphur in the production of steel and to impart toughness and hardness to certain specialty steels.

Two complexes or kombinats, the Ordzhonikidze in the west-end and Marganets in the east-end operate the basin. There were 18 underground mines, 10 open pit and 8 concentrators in operation in 1973 [27] with most of the ore being mined from open pits. The ore deposit is horizontal. At the west end of the basin the ore is from 2 to 3 meters thick and covered by 80 to 200 meters of overburden. In the eastern end the ore is 1.4 to 2.1 meters thick with overburden from 33 to 64 meters. High moisture, including groundwater, combined with weak rocks present some operational problems. A phosphorus content of about 0.3 percent in concentrates also presents problems to steel makers.

The first surface mines began operating in 1952 and produced 1.3 percent of the ore. The corresponding figures for surface mining in subsequent years are tabulated in Figure XXII.

Figure XXII
Raw Manganese Ore Production in the Ukraine (in millions of tons)

Year	Total	Underground	Open Pit	% by Open Pit
1950	1.94	1.94	—	—
1961	6.59	3.43	3.16	48.0%
1965	10.20	3.19	7.02	68.8%
1970	11.88	2.92	8.97	75.5%
1971	12.76	2.99	9.77	76.6%

Source: Gornyi Zhurnal *(1825) No.12, December 1972, p.14.*

Reasons for the shift are evident from some operational factors which apply to Ordzhonikidze operations in 1972. [28]

	Annual Output Per Man	Ore Losses	Ore Cost Per Ton
Open Pit	2720 tons	4.7 percent	4.86 roubles
Underground	583 tons	11.0 percent	6.75 roubles

Presumably the open pit costs include the cost of stripping which in 1970 totalled 94.8 million cubic meters for the whole of the Nikopol basin. The proportion of production coming from underground and open pit mines of unprocessed ore is shown in Figure XXII.

In 1970, 11.88 million tons of raw ore yielded 5.2 million tons of concentrates, or roughly 2.3 tons of run-of-the-mine ore to produce 1 ton of marketable ore. Figure XXIII shows production of concentrates.

Nikopol ore averages 26.4 percent manganese and is concentrated into two shippable products: concentrate containing 34 percent manganese and concentrate containing over 45 percent manganese.

The large reserves and proximity of mines to iron and steel centres favours expanded production in Ukraine rather than the other major source of manganese in the U.S.S.R. which is the Chiatura deposit of Georgia.

Reserves of 2.1 billion tons of raw ore [29] are sufficient for roughly 140 years of production at current mining rates. They are located in three deposits: Nikopol and Inhulets on the right bank and Velykyi Tokmak on the left bank of the Kakhivka Reservoir of the Dnipro River, and constitute 34, 19 and 47 percent respectively.[30] All three deposits are geologically related and constitute one Dneper manganese basin. Only the Nikopol is presently exploited.

Various nations are looking into ocean mining of manganese nodules. However there is little likelihood of this new source displacing Nikopol as the major producer. Metal content of nodules varies greatly but it is agreed that the most promising ocean mining belt is in the south-west and south central Pacific (5 N to 20 N and 110 W to 180 W) in water depths of 15,000—16,000 feet. In this area a dry assay of nodules would have the following approximate content:

Nickel	Copper	Cobalt	Manganese
1 per cent	0.8 per cent	0.2 per cent	20 per cent

The interest is in the nickel-copper values which represent some 80 percent of the total metal values in the ton of nodules represented by the above analysis. The amount of manganese to be derived from ocean mining will therefore depend upon demand for nickel and copper—assuming costs of ocean mining are comparable to mining at established mines on land.

5.3 Other Metallics

The Soviet Union's metals industry is organized into two divisions: one termed ferrous and the other non-ferrous. Statistics are not published on the latter which includes those metals we in North America refer to as base metals and precious metals. As a result the information that follows is somewhat fragmented.

It is generally agreed that Ukraine is deficient in most of the common base and precious metals. However, the republic is self-sufficient in mercury, titanium, zirconium and the rare earth metals. It is probably also self-sufficient in nickel and uranium, but not copper, lead or zinc.

Mercury

The Donets' Basin has the Soviet Union's oldest mercury mine and mill at Nikitovka, which was the U.S.S.R.'s main producer of mercury before World War II. Nikitovka is now second to producers in the central Asian region. The ore mineral is cinnabar which is easily reduced to mercury metal and occurs among beds of schist, sandstone, limestone and hard coal. Ore lenses averaging 0.2 to 0.3 percent mercury are mined by underground methods at depths to 270 and perhaps 330 meters. There are prospects for deeper mining which will probably be accompanied by difficult ground control problems. Production in 1970 was 1.73 times that of 1966. Reserves have been estimated [31] at 4.3 million tons. Other deposits of mercury are being mined near Shayan in the Tysa River valley of the Transcarpathians. Ore grades are said to be high but the deposits are small.

Nickel

During 1949-50 oxidized (lateritic) nickel ore deposits were discovered at

Figure XXIII
Manganese Concentrate Production (in millions of tons)

	1950	1955	1960	1965	1970	1971	1972	1973	1974 (Plan)	1975 (Plan)
Ukraine	0.90	1.62	2.72	4.65	5.20	5.62	5.89	6.5	?	6.8
U.S.S.R. Total	3.38	4.74	5.87	7.58	6.84	7.32	7.82	8.2	?	9.0
%Ukr/USSR	26.60%	34.20%	46.30%	61.40%	76.10%	76.80%	75.30%	79.2%	?	75.5%

Sources: Narodnoe khoziaistvo SSSR v 1972 g., *p.214;* Narodne hospodarstvo Ukrains'koi RSR v 1972 rotsi. *p.129.*

Pobuzhe, in Kirovohrad oblast. The ore has the following analysis: [32]

Ni	0.8	— 1.1 per cent
Co	0.05	— 0.07 per cent
Fe	17.5	— 26.5 per cent
Sio2	40	— 50 per cent
Mgo	3	— 7 per cent

The first stage of a ferronickel plant became operational in 1973. Ore is crushed, mixed with limestone and anthracite fines, heated to 800-870 C and the resulting hot billets are transported into electric furnaces. The furnace product is a crude ferronickel which is then upgraded into either a low-nickel or high-nickel ferronickel.

Uranium
    There are several reports of a major uranium mining operation at the northern end of the Kryvyi Rih basin at Zhovti Vody and Terny. The uranium is associated with the iron formation which was originally mined for its iron content. Grade is said to be good and reserves large. The largest uranium-plutonium plant in the USSR has apparently been constructed, along with associated research laboratories, near the deposit.

Titanium
    The Ukrainian titanium industry gained prominence as a major world producer about 1958. Heavy minerals dredged from river sands yield a titanium concentrate (the mineral constituents of which are ilmenite and rutile), a zirconium concentrate and a monazite concentrate (which is the principal ore mineral for the rare earth metals and thorium). The principal dredging centres are on the Irsha River, west of Kyiv, and at Volnohorsk, west of Dniprodzerzhinsk, on the Samotkan River. Three kombinats mine and refine the materials found in the sands of the middle Dnipro area.
— Zaporizhya titanium-magnesium kombinat
— Verkhnedniprovs'k mining-metallurgical kombinat, which as of 1961 is the largest supplier of raw material
— Irshans'k mining-beneficiation kombinat, constructed in 1960.
No data are available on titanium reserves. Titanium metal is produced by the magnesium reduction process.

6. TRADE IN MINERAL COMMODITIES

    Trade statistics by republic are not published so we must look at the export picture for the USSR in terms of commodities involved and their destinations and then make a calculated guess. Mineral commodities of special interest to Ukraine will be discussed individually.

Natural Gas
    Lee has recently summarized the Soviet trade picture for this commodity as follows:

> Until the last few years almost all of the natural gas produced in the U.S.S.R. was consumed domestically. In recent years small volumes of gas have been exported to Eastern Europe and to Austria but these exports have been more than offset by imports from Afghanistan and Iran. As a result of recent contracts signed with West Germany, Italy, France, and Finland and agreements with East European countries, the U.S.S.R. should become a net exporter of some 8 billion cubic meters of gas in 1975. [33]

Figure XXIV shows the trade picture for natural gas compiled primarily by Strishkov

Figure XXIV
Estimated Soviet Trade in Natural Gas (Billion Cubic Meters)

Country	1965	1970	1971	1972	1973	1975 plan
Exports	**0.4**	**3.3**	**4.5**	**5.1**	**7.0**	**22.5**
Eastern Europe	.4	2.3	3.1			11.5
Czechoslovakia	0	1.3	1.6			3.0
Poland	.4	1.0	1.5			1.5
Bulgaria	0	0	0			3.0
East Germany	0	0	0			3.0
Hungary	0	0	0			1.0
Western Europe	0	1.0	1.4			11.0
Austria	0	1.0	1.4			1.5
Finland	0	0	0			.5
Italy	0	0	0			6.0
West Germany	0	0	0			3.0
Imports	**0**	**3.6**	**8.1**	**11.0**	**12.0**	**14.0**
Afghanistan	0	2.6	2.5			4.0
Iran	0	1.0	5.6			10.0

Sources: V.V. Strishkov, "Soviet Union," Mining Annual Review, 1974, p.436; The Mineral Industry of the U.S.S.R., *Preprint 1971, p.43.*

of the United States Bureau of Mines.

Pipelines carry Shebelynka gas west to the Dashava field and then to Czechoslovakia and other nations outside the U.S.S.R. Very likely most of the 7 billion cubic meters of gas exported to Europe comes from Ukraine (at the same time the Donbas is provided with gas from Stavropol in the Russian S.F.S.R.).

Coal

The Soviet Union became a net exporter of coal and coke in 1956. Coal exports increased from 5.7 million tons in 1956 to 24.8 million tons in 1973 and coke exports rose from 2 million to 4.5 million tons. Coals exported to non-communist countries (some 35 percent of the total) are high quality coking coals and anthracite. Amongst the major markets for Soviet coal, Japan ranks first, followed by Italy, France and Austria. East Germany and Bulgaria are the major importers of Soviet coal and coke in the CMEA group of countries.

Soviet imports of coal and coke increased from 7 million tons in 1956 to about 10 million tons of coal and 0.7 million tons of coke in 1973. Poland is the only exporter of coal and coke to the U.S.S.R. Trade statistics, compiled mostly from United States Bureau of Mine sources, are shown in Figure XXV.

Of the 24.5 million tons of coal exported in 1970, about 2.9 million tons went to Japan. If we assume that no Donbas coal went to Japan, that all imported coal from Poland was consumed within Ukraine, and that all exported coal (except that to Japan) came from the Donbas, then in 1970 roughly 14 million tons of Donbas coal was exported outside the USSR. This, of course, is only a fraction of the Donbas coal which is moved out of Ukraine.

In 1955 the Ukrainian Donbas produced roughly 120 million tons of coal. Hodgkins[34] showed that 83 millions of Donbas coal was consumed within the "South", presumably Ukraine, 30 million within the Central Region, 5 million within the Volga Region, 4 million in the West, and 3 million in the Transcaucasus. This totals 136 million tons, or 16 million tons more than was produced in the Ukrainian Donbas. The difference is reasonably accounted for by production from the Russian part of the Donbas. Thus, in 1955 some 69 percent of Ukrainian Donbas coal was consumed within Ukraine. If one applies this factor to 1970 production of roughly 185 tons of Ukrainian Donbas coal, then we could reasonably assume 128 million tons is consumed within Ukraine, 14 million tons is exported outside the USSR and 57 millions to the Russian federated republic.

Figure XXV
USSR Trade in Coal and Coke (in millions of tons)

Output, consumption, and trade	1960	1965	1970	1971	1972	1973
Coal:						
Domestic output:						
Run-of-mine coal	509.6	577.7	624.1	641.0	655.2	661.4
Imports:						
From Communist countries	4.7	6.7	7.1	8.4	9.7	10.
Exports:						
Communist countries	8.2	15.2	14.8	16.4		
Non-Communist countries	4.1	7.2	9.7	8.5		
Total	12.3	22.4	24.5	24.9	24.4	24.8
Apparent consumption:						
Run-of-mine coal	502.0	562.0	606.7	623.1	640.5	646.6
Coke:						
Domestic output	56.2	67.5	76.0	78.0		
Imports:						
From Communist countries	0.7	0.7	0.7	0.8	0.6	0.7
Exports:						
Communist countries	2.2	2.8	3.2	3.4		
Non-Communist countries	0.4	1.0	0.9	0.9		
Total	2.6	3.8	4.2	4.4	4.5	4.5
Apparent consumption	54.3	64.4	72.6	74.4		

Sources: V.V. Strishkov, G. Markon, Z.E. Murphy, "Soviet Coal Productivity: Clarifying the Facts and Figures," Mining Engineering, *May, 1973, p.47; V.V. Strishkov, "Soviet Union,"* Mining Annual Review, *1974, p.436.*

Manganese Ore

The USSR trade picture for manganese ore is shown in Figure XXVI in terms of millions of tons of marketable ore.

Figure XXVI
Manganese Ore

	1970	1971	1972	1973
Total Soviet production	6.8	7.3	7.8	8.2
Ukraine production	5.2	5.6	6.0	6.5
Exported from USSR	1.2	1.4	1.3	1.3

Sources: Mining Annual Review, *1974, p.436;* Narodne hospodarstvo Ukrains'koi RSR v 1972, rotsi, p.129.

Of the 1.200 million tons of manganese ore exported in 1970, 0.365 million tons went to Poland, 0.175 million tons to East Germany, 0.153 million tons to Czechoslovakia, 0.109 million tons to France and 0.096 million tons to Japan. It is difficult to guess what proportion of exports came from Nikopol in Ukraine and what originated in Chiatura, Georgia. Nikopol is closer to most markets but Chiatura is more favourably located for shipment via the Black Sea port of Poti.

Iron Ore

Iron ore is one of the USSR's major export commodities and virtually all of this ore comes from Kryvyi Rih. Figure XXVII shows the trade picture in terms of millions of tons of marketable ore.

The 36.1 million tons exported in 1970 had the following destinations: Czechoslovakia 10.8; Poland 9.9; Romania 4.2; and East Germany 3.0.

Little information is available on how much Kryvyi Rih ore is consumed within the Russian SFSR, but the proportion is not great. The Kursk Magnetic Anomaly and Kola peninsula sources are much better situated geographically to supply central Russian pig iron producers.

Figure XXVII
Iron Ore

	1970	1971	1972	1973
Ukraine production	111.2	117.0	119.5	121.0
Exported from USSR	36.1	36.5	38.4	41.4

7. CONCLUSIONS

Ukraine for many decades has been the Soviet Union's most important source of the two commodities which are the pillars of heavy industry: coal and iron ore. The Donbas in 1973 accounted for over a quarter of the U.S.S.R.'s total coal production and Kryvyi Rih for half of the U.S.S.R.'s total iron ore production.

But the dominant position of the Donbas is declining although it will remain the Soviet Union's most important source of coking coal in the foreseeable future. As an energy source, coal in the whole of the U.S.S.R. is declining in importance relative to natural gas and oil because of the latter's lower cost to produce and transport. In absolute terms the U.S.S.R.'s, including Ukraine's, coal production will increase. The trend is towards developing Siberian coal resources which are more amenable to surface mining methods. These methods are less costly and more productive than underground mining which is used in the Donbas.

Similarly Ukraine's relative position as a natural gas producer is declining because of developments east of the Urals. The Shebelynka field is still the Soviet Union's largest producer.

Kryvyi Rih's dominant position will not likely diminish in the foreseeable future because of its extensive reserves if iron ore which can be mined by surface mining methods. Most of the ore mined is up-graded to produce a high grade product, a significant proportion of which is exported to various nations west of the U.S.S.R. The same situation applies to manganese ore mined in the Nikopol area which is the world's major producer of this metal.

Ukraine is also a major source of titanium and perhaps uranium.

The Republic's mineral industry is unquestionably vigorous, and ranks with agriculture in its contribution to the well-being of its people.

FOOTNOTES

1.   D. B. Shimkin, "The Soviet Mineral-Fuels Industries, 1928-1958: A Statistical Survey". **International Population Statistics Reports Series P—90**, No. 19, U.S. Department of Commerce 1962, p. 153.

2.   N. V. Melnikov, "The Role of Coal in the Energy Fuel Resources in the U.S.S.R." **Canadian Mining and Metallurgical Bulletin**, June 1972, p. 77.

3.   Ugol, No. 8 (August), 1973, p. 12.

4.   Ugol Ukrainy, No. 5 (May), 1974, pp. 53, 52.

5.   **Ibid.**

6.   Ugol Ukrainy, No. 11 (November), 1973, p. 43.

7.   Ugol Ukrainy, No. 5 (May), 1974, p. 53.

8.   Ugol Ukrainy, No. 11 (November), 1973, p.2.

9.   Ugol Ukrainy, No. 12 (December), 1971, p. 1, 4, 2.

10.   **Ibid.**

11.   **Ibid.**

12.   Ugol Ukrainy, No. 11 (November), 1973, p. 2.

13.   N. V. Melnikov, "The Role of Coal. .", **op. cit.**, p. 77.

14.   "The Mineral Industry of the U.S.S.R.", **United States Bureau of Mines Minerals Yearbook** 1971. Preprint p. 38.

15.   **Izvestiya Sibirskogo Otdeleniya Akademii Nauk SSSR,** 1974 No. 1 pp. 158-159.

16   J. A. Hodgkins, **Soviet Power.** Prentice-Hall, New Jersey, U.S.A., 1961, pp. 158-159.

17.   N.A. Melnikov, "The Role of Coal.., **op. cit.**, p. 79.

18.   **Neftyanaya i Gazovaya Promyshlennost',** No. 2, March-April, Kyiv, 1973, p. 2.

19.   **State Five-Year Plan for the Development of the U.S.S.R. National Economy for the Period** 1971-1975. Moscow, English edition, p. 106.

20.   **Ibid.**

21.   **Ukraine, A Concise Encyclopedia.** Toronto, University of Toronto Press, 1971, Vol. 2, p. 288.

22.   **Neftyanaya i Gazovaya Promyshlennost',** No. 2, March-April 1974, Kyiv, p. 2.

23.   A. Woroniak, **The Soviet Economy in Regional Perspective.** New York, 1973, p. 288.

24.   **The Mineral Industry of the U.S.S.R.,** United States Bureau of Mines Minerals Yearbook, 1971. Preprint p. 46.

25. Torfyanaya Promyshlennost', No. 4, 1974, pp. 5-7.

26. Soviet Geography, Review & Translation, Vol. XV, No. 6, June 1974, p. 377.

27. Mining Annual Review—1974, p. 439.

28. Gornyi Zhurnal (1825), No. 7 (July), 1973, p.22.

29. Kadastr Mineralnykh Resursiv Ukrainskoi RSR (Rudna i nerudna syrovyna dlya chornoi metalurhii), Kyiv 1971, pp. 22-23.

30. Ukraine: A Concise Encyclopedia. University of Toronto Press, 1971, Vol. II, p. 742.

31. Ukraine: Junior Encyclopedia, South Bound Brook, New Jersey, 1971.

32. Tsvetnye Metally, No. 4 (April), 1974, p. 16.

33. Soviet Economic Prospects for the Seventies. A Compendium of papers submitted to Joint Economic Committee, Congress of the United States, June, 1973. See paper The Soviet Petroleum Industry by J. R. Lee, pp. 289-90.

34. J. A. Hodgkins, Soviet Power, op. cit., pp. 62-63.

Comments on A.S. Romaniuk and I. Slowikowski
The Non-Renewable Resources of Ukraine

by
V.N. Mackiw
Sherritt Gordon Mines Limited

I would like to express to Mr. Romaniuk and Mrs. Slowikowski deep appreciation of all present today for such a comprehensive paper and excellent presentation. The value of this paper is an extensive research of Soviet literature resulting in a penetrating and up-to-date review of Ukraine's non-renewable resources.

It remains for me, perhaps for the purpose of initiating discussion, to make a number of secondary comments:

I agree with the authors that the methods used for the terminology and calculations of ore reserves in the Soviet Union do tend to overstate the potential ore reserves as compared to conservative methods used in North America; only future history can resolve which method is more correct. New technology tends to make marginal reserves more economical, or new economic conditions can justify higher price structures; I therefore believe that in the course of future generations larger natural resource reserves will be found than are presently estimated.

As regards economics of fuel production, there is no question that Melnikov is correct in stating that costs of production of natural gas and open-pit coal are lower than oil or underground coal. Naturally, costs of transportation to points of usage also have to be considered in making this comparison; therefore, depending on location, as the authors have shown, sometimes the costs of open-pit and underground coal are equalized if the cost of transportation by rail to the point of usage is different (page 13).

In view of the above, one has to come to the conclusion that relative economics of underground coal production in Ukraine will improve in view of the rapidly rising cost of transportation of open-pit coal from more distant areas. Also, the oil shortage in Ukraine will stimulate coal developments.

During 1974, the world came to realize that the value of fuel is not necessarily

31

related to its cost of production but to its commodity value. This especially applies to fuel oil and natural gas.

Natural gas is the lowest-cost fuel if produced and used in Ukraine. Unfortunately, Ukraine's reserves are relatively small — about twelve years. The main value of natural gas, in addition to its simple use for heating or power generation, lies in its use as feedstock for production of a number of chemicals, plastics, and chemical fertilizers. I am sure that Ukrainian and Soviet economists and planners are now considering methods for the conservation of natural gas from non-essential uses or exports, so that sufficient reserves are maintained in Ukraine for additional production of nitrogenous fertilizers, chemicals, etc. Otherwise Ukraine would, in future, have to rely on much more expensive gas brought by capital intensive pipelines from Siberia or Central Asia. It might perhaps be more advisable to direct capital to ammonia, urea, and similar plants, than to pipelines (at least for the immediate future).

I fully agree with the authors that iron ore and manganese ore production represent a very healthy segment of Ukrainian economy. For manganese, one can expect competition in about ten to twenty years from mining nodules from the bottom of the ocean.

It would be of interest to have a paper analyzing in detail how much the natural resources contribute to the development of the Ukrainian industry as a whole and to what extent the revenues obtained from exports of natural resources are used for further development of the Ukrainian industry.

Also as a suggestion, the review of Ukrainian non-renewable resources could be extended to non-metallic minerals, which play a significant role in the Ukrainian industry.

May I again express our thanks to the authors for this most interesting paper, which will contribute a solid basis to the understanding of industrial processes in Ukraine.

Forests of Ukraine
Their History and Present Status

by
Jaroslaw Holowacz

HISTORY OF FOREST COVER

General

As an industrially developed country, Ukraine is rather sparsely forested. On the average, the forests cover 12.9 per cent of the territory and in certain oblasts of the steppe they occupy less than 2 per cent. In the distant past forests occupied over one half of the present territory of Ukraine. What historical events contributed to their deforestation will be reviewed in the subsequent section of the paper.
section of the paper.

Between 1957 and 1961, the Ukrainian Scientific Research Institute of Field Husbandry conducted an extensive soil survey which, among other things, also attempted to determine whether any soils, currently in agricultural use, supported forest growth in the distant past (Vakuliuk, 1972). It was assumed that around the 1st century, the present territory of Ukraine had the maximum possible degree of forest cover. The soil survey's data were particularly useful in determining the degree of forest cover of the forest-steppe zone, while Polisia, the Carpathian and the Crimean Mountains were believed to have been, by and large, solidly forested during the 1st century.

Unfortunately, pedological information from the soil survey could not have been used to reveal the degree of forest cover of the steppe. Podzolized (or degraded) chernozems, which normally form under forest stands, turn into common chernozems soon after the removal of the forest and the evidence reflecting the existing forest vegetation in the past disappears permanently. In contrast, the evidence of podzolization in the forest-steppe zone persists apparently for centuries even in soils subjected to continual agricultural use on once forested land.

Judging from historical and contemporary information, forests grow readily on

33

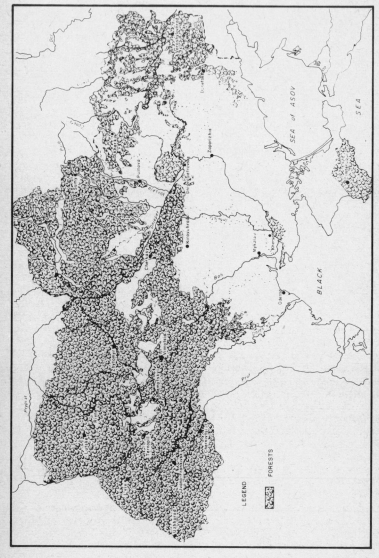

Fig 1 FORESTED AREA OF UKRAINE DURING THE FIRST CENTURY A.D. (RECONSTRUCTION)

AFTER HENSIRUK, S.A.,
AND BONDAR, V.S., 1973.

LEGEND

FORESTS

sandy and silty soils in the river valleys and outwash plains of the steppe zone. This observation could not have been substantiated in the presently denuded river valleys and on the outwash plains by pedological means because the evidence of podzolization is easily disturbed in the light soil structure of alluvial origin by flood activity. The non-applicability of the pedological evidence on what the forest cover may have been in the past in this zone, forced the researchers to rely on historical data and present-day information from areas in the steppe where forests regenerate themselves naturally. Forests in the steppe generally persisted on the north-eastern exposures of hillsides (balkas) forming the so-called bairak forests, and in sheltered areas, such as river valleys and eroded gullies. The forests which grew under these conditions frequently extended far into the open steppe. The river valleys, ravines, gullies and northern exposures of hills were relatively well-forested as is indicated by the description of Ukraine by the French cartographer, de Beauplan, who traveled through the Ukrainian steppe during the first half of the 17th century. Since, according to de Beauplan, forests still existed in the steppe at such a late date, it is, therefore, fair to assume that they were equally as widely distributed during the 1st century. According to the pedological data, historical information and the evidence as to the ease of a forest to regenerate itself naturally, it was possible to prepare a map depicting the probable degree of forest cover during the 1st century. (Fig. 1)

Five historical periods have been recognized by P. H. Vakuliuk and others during which the forested area of Ukraine had been substantially reduced. Those periods may be considered as a type of bench marks roughly coinciding with major political events which in their ultimate resolution exerted a noticeable influence on the biological environment of the people inhabiting the present territory of Ukraine. These periods, or stages, of deforestation of Ukraine start with the recorded beginnings of the Kyivan Rus' (9th cent.), followed by the periods centering around the Lublin Union of 1569 and the Peasant Reform of 1848-1861, and ending with the First and Second World Wars.

Kyivan Rus'

Around the time when Kyivan Rus' became an established state in Eastern Europe, the territory presently occupied by the Ukrainian SSR was relatively accessible to economic activity of the various tribes inhabiting it. The Sub-Carpathian and Carpathian regions were still densely forested. Here the forest occupied about 76 per cent of the area. Next followed Polisia with about 73 per cent of the area under forest. The forest-steppe and steppe zones show only a slight loss of forested area of approximately 2 per cent each in comparison to the approximations made for the first century. There is no information on the state of the forest cover of the Crimean Mountains during this period. It can be, however, argued that due to their structure, composition and above all, site, they have virtually remained intact in a broad sense since the 1st century. Thus only the Carpathian area and Polisia were significantly deforested apparently for agricultural use. The forest cover in the forest-steppe and steppe remained relatively stable suggesting that there was still plenty of good quality, non-forested agricultural land available for colonization. On the whole, during the early period of Kyivan Rus', forests covered nearly 26.7 million hectares, or 44 per cent, of the present territory of the Ukrainian SSR. Presently they cover 7.8 million hectares, or 12.9 per cent of the territory.

Until the end of the 14th century, deforestation of Ukraine had a rather isolated and sporadic character. Permanent and shifting forms of land cultivation were practiced particularly in the forest-steppe. What had been burned over for cultivation in one area was compensated by abandoned land elsewhere which ultimately reverted back to forest. On balance, the relationship of forested to non-forested land in the forest-steppe, an area of considerable activity during the period of Kyivan Rus', remained relatively stable. This is borne out by the evidence disccussed above.

A somewhat different pattern of deforestation emerged in the Carpathian and Polisia regions. Here the forested area had been reduced by about 25 per cent since the first century primarily due to the gradual expansion of agricultural activity.

35

The Lublin Union

When the Lublin Union was concluded (1569), smelting of iron ore, production of saltpeter (potasium nitrate), glass, potash, limestone, pitch, cooking salt, and wood tar had a wide distribution in Ukraine. All these activities required a considerable volume of high density wood either as a source of energy (iron ore, glass) or as raw material (potash, saltpeter, wood tar, charcoal and pitch), (Hensiruk and Bondar, 1973). In addition, high quality deals and staves as well as cooperage material were in demand in areas gravitating to the Vistula River basin. For example, to produce 100 kg of potash, it was necessary to burn 157 m^3 of high density wood, such as oak and beech, which grew primarily in the forest-steppe and the Sub-Carpathian regions.

In 1630, three noblemen, Ya.Vyshnevets'kyi, M. Potocki and M. Kalinowski signed an agreement to export 1,716 tons of potash from Halychyna via Gdaǹsk (Vakuliuk, 1972). Such a volume of potash required the burning of 2.7 million m^3 of high density hardwood timber. In order to supply this volume of wood, an area over 12,000 hectares had to be clear cut. The principal customer of potash from Ukraine was France. Until the time of the Lublin Union (1569), the arable land of Ukraine had been considered sufficient to sustain the existing population. This situation changed drastically on the newly acquired territories by Poland where Polish nobility exerted pressure on the peasantry in its domain to produce grain for export. The resulting increase in arable land brought about by the increased demand for grain occurred partly at the expense of forested land which was taken permanently out of forest production.

The deforestation wave following the Lublin Union extended over portions of the northern right bank territory and the areas to the west and south-west which came under Polish domination. The territory on the left bank of the Dnipro River and the entire steppe zone, including the Crimean Mountains, was relatively untouched.

Throughout the period extending from the 1st until the beginning of the 19th centuries, the deforestation process had been, by and large, gradual with the exception of the period following the Lublin Union when there was a sudden upsurge in the clearing of forests in response to the demand for arable land. The 19th century marks the beginning of an extensive clearing of forests even on soils too poor for uses other than forestry. This deforestation wave was, certainly, to a varying degree, taking place all over Europe during the 19th century. A number of factors contributed to this extensive and frequently indifferent removal of forest cover. In Ukraine, three factors are clearly indentifiable as the major ones, namely, railway building (1860), the expansion of arable land following the Peasant Reform (1848-1861) and the liquidation cuts of timber for export and local uses.

Peasant Reform (1848 & 1861)

The abolition of serfdom in Bukovyna and Halychyna in 1848, which were under Austrian domination, and in 1861 on the remaining territory, which was under Russian occupation, resulted in a new pattern of land use in Ukraine. The freed peasantry had a right to purchase land for farming but since the means of the peasantry to buy land were obviously limited, and since good agricultural land remained in the hands of the privileged foreign element, there was a strong tendency for the freed farmer to acquire forested instead of cleared land. In this manner, huge areas of forests were soon denuded and converted to agricultural use. The resulting high quality timber, such as oak and beech, was exported primarily to Austria and the remainder was either utilized as fuelwood or burned in situ.

The newly built railway lines running towards the western borders of Ukraine greatly facilitated timber trade. Internally, timber was still an almost exclusive source of fuel for both industrial and domestic uses. New, fuel-intensive industries, such as sugar manufacturing, further intensified the demand for fuelwood in addition to the making of potash, which began to decline towards the end of the 19th century. Over a period of 118 years on the territory of Ukraine occupied by the Russian Empire, the forested area decreased from 7,657,000 hectares in 1976 to 4,482,000 hectares in 1914, or by roughly 42 per cent (Hensiruk and Bondar, 1973). In the sparsely forested steppe of Ukraine, the rate of deforestation moved at an even faster pace. From the 15th century on until the end of the First World War the forest cover had been reduced from 15-20 to 2-7 per cent, or by an average of 74 per cent (Tarasenko, 1973).

Around the turn of the century, Ukraine was an already poorly forested country to such an extent that the sparse forest cover had a detrimental effect on the economic and cultural developments. The lack of a greater proportion of forest cover in the forest-steppe and steppe zones began to exert a negative influence on the local climate and, in turn, on the productivity of land in agricultural use.

The First World War

The fourth stage of deforestation of Ukraine took place during the First World War, including the post-war period lasting practically through to the beginning of the Second World War. According to Vakuliuk, between 1914 and 1920 about 667,000 hectares of forest were clear cut and not reforested and about 125,000 hectares of juvenile forests were destroyed by excessive grazing. In relative terms, the area of forests destroyed between 1914 and 1920 constitutes over 10 per cent of the currently forested area of Ukraine. The high demand for wood brought about by the industrialization scheme of the early five-year plan era was initially satisfied almost exclusively out of Ukraine's limited forest resources.

The extent of deforestation attributable to the Bolshevik period is not to be found in Soviet sources. However, the available reforestation data suggest that the damage inflicted on the forest during the war was not recouped during the subsequent inter-war period. About 792,000 hectares of forest were destroyed between 1914 and 1920 as contrasted to 686,000 hectares which had been planted and seeded between 1922 and 1941 (Soldatov et al. 1960). By adding the area of forest cut, but not regenerated during the forced industrialization period, it can be concluded that the deforestation of Ukraine under Soviet domination still continued during the inter-war period. On the territories under Polish and Romanian dominations, the existing forest cover was sustained, if not expanded, thanks partly to the care of the forest owners and the sluggish development of the respective economies lacking sufficient entrepreneurship to develop wood-using industries. The forests of the Carpatho-Ukraine were equally preserved in part due to their distant location with respect to the markets of Western Europe and partly due to the sound management practices carried out by foresters trained in the conservative traditions of the Austrian foresty school.

The Second World War

The fifth and most recent stage of deforestation is associated with the Second World War and the post-war reconstruction. About 165,000 hectares were destroyed by clear cutting and fire. Another 160,000 hectares of forest were degraded as a result of selective cutting. Due to the lack of appropriate management, such as tending and thinning, nearly 103,900 hectares of plantation forest were in need of drastic reconstruction after the war.

During the post-war reconstruction period the forests of Ukraine had been subjected to an excessive overcutting frequently exceeding four times the allowable cut during the late nineteen-forties (Hensiruk, 1971). The result of this excessive cutting was the virtual elimination of volume reserves in the mature and over-mature age classes. However, in contrast to the postwar period following the First World War, during that which followed the Second World War, the excessive overcutting was accompanied by a rather energetic reforestation program.

Today, the forested area of Ukraine constitutes 12.9 per cent of her territory which is the lowest in Europe in countries within roughly the same climatic zone. Were the forests of Ukraine at least moderately cared for since the second half of the 19th century, in accordance with the principles of forest management then applicable, one could reasonably expect the degree of forest cover of the territory to be in the neighbourhood of 30 to 35 per cent. Tripling the present extent of forest cover would

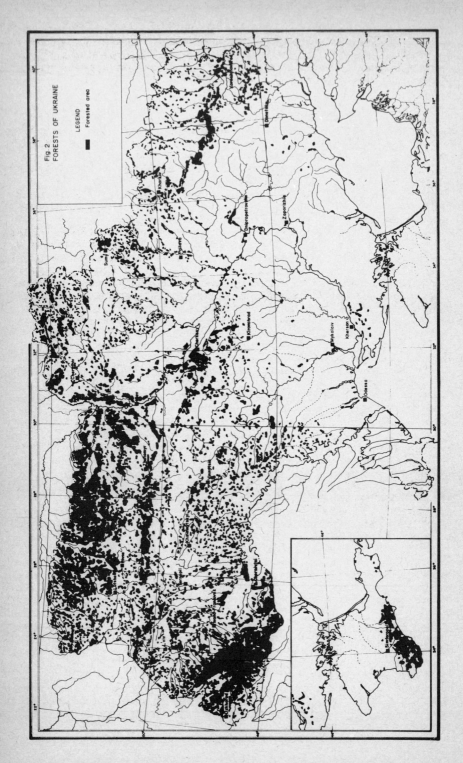

Fig 2
FORESTS OF UKRAINE

LEGEND

Forested area

38

have assured an all-sided development of forest-based industries, especially pulp and paper. A more extensive forest cover would have exerted a beneficial influence on the local climate, created conditions for the development of the tourist industry, sports, fisheries, hunting and the creation of a network of national parks, particularly in the Carpathian sub-zone and Polisia.

GENERAL PATTERN OF LAND USE

The territory of the Ukrainian SSR covers an area of 60,370 thousand hectares, or over 233 thousand British square miles. In Europe, Ukraine is the second largest country following Russia proper which occupies the first place by area. France, with which Ukraine is frequently compared, occupies an area of 55,100 thousand hectares versus Ukraine's 60,370 thousand hectares.

At the beginning of 1973, Ukraine had a population of 48,236.8 thousand with a population density of 79.9 persons per square kilometre. France's population reached 51,921 thousand with 94.2 persons per square kilometre.

Over 70 per cent of Ukraine's territory is in agricultural use (Table 1). Arable land covers an area of 56.5 per cent of the total territory. For a relatively industrialized country, the area occupied by land in agricultural use and that actually in cultivation, i.e. arable land, Ukraine ranks fairly high. In France, for example, comparable land categories constitute considerably lower proportions when compared to the entire territory. Land in agricultural use occupies 59 per cent, while that classified as arable accounts for slightly more than 39 per cent.

Table 1
Land classification of Ukraine by types

Types of land	Area in thous hectares	In per cent to total area
Arable land (1971)	34,114.4	56.5
Orchards, vineyards and other plantations (1971)	1,279.0	2.1
Meadowland (1971)	2,307.0	3.8
Pastureland (1971)	4,635.3	7.7
Total land in agricultural use	42,335.7	70.1
General forest land area* (1965 inventory)	9,787.0	16.2
Swamps (1971)	783.7	1.3
Reservoirs (1969)	2,168.2	3.6
Blow sands and gullies (1968)	557.0	0.9
Roads and road allowances	972.0	1.6
Other land	3,766.4	6.3
Total	60,370.0	100.0

*Includes forested land, non-forested forest land and land not suitable for forest production but surrounded by forest.

Sources: A.N. URSR, Entsyklopediia narodnoho hospodarstva Ukrains'koi RSR, Tom 2, Kyiv 1970 p.126.
S.A. Gensiruk, N.V. Turkevich, "Sovremennoe sostoianie lesnogo fonda Ukrainskoi SSR i vozmozhnyi ob'em rubok glavnogo pol'zovaniia" Lesnoi zhurnal 1969 No. 3 p. 27.
P.F. Vedenichev, Zemel'nye resusry Ukrainskoi SSR i ikh khoziaistevennoe ispol'zovanie Kyiv, [Naukova Dumka], 1972 p. 26
Narodne hospodarstvo Ukrains'koi RSR v 1971 rotsi Yuvileinyi statystychnyi shchorichnyk, Kyiv, Statystyka, 1972 p. 157.

From among the non-agricultural land classes, the largest area is occupied by the general forest land area, covering 9,787 thousand hectares, or 16.2 per cent of the territory. This land type comprises **forested land, non-forested forest land** and **non-forestry land**, or land not suitable for forest production. A rather small portion of the territory is occupied by land classes considered non-productive for principal uses, such as agriculture and forestry. These types of land include swamps, blow sands (Kherson obl.), eroded gullies (steppe), roads and other communication lines.

Forest Land Tenure and Grouping

According to the 1965 forest resources inventory, the overall, **general forest land area** for all tenure categories occupies 9,787 thousand hectares, or 16.2 per cent in relation to the entire territory of Ukraine (Table 2). This general land class comprises 7,770.1 thousand hectares of **forested land,**[1] or land currently under forest cover, while the remaining 2,017 thousand hectares consist of **non-forested forest land** and **non-forestry land.** The non-forested forest land can be defined as land which at the time of the inventory in 1965 was not supporting a forest stand but could support one were it reforested. Into this land class of non-forested forest land are also relegated recently established forest tree plantations in which the crowns have not closed. The non-forestry land is devoid of trees and not capable of supporting a forest stand without a major outlay of capital for purposes, such as drainage, terracing, irrigating or for other land amelioration work.

The non-forested forest land is continually being put into production, as a result of rather energetic reforestation operations. The land not suitable for forest production may even increase somewhat by the time the results of the 1973 forest resources become available due to water erosion of hillsides in the Carpathian Mountains brought about be excessive clear cutting operations in the past and frequent wind damage. In spite of the possibility that its area may ultimately increase, at present the non-forestry land class occupies about 1 million hectares, or 1.7 per cent, which is considered relatively small in relation to the entire territory of Ukraine.

The present tenure system and grouping of forest land in Ukraine, as well as in the entire USSR, evolved on the basis of a decision issued in April 1943 by the Council of Peoples' Commissars of the USSR governing the allocation of cut in the state forests. Over the years, three main tenure categories evolved, namely, **forests of national significance (Derzhlisfond), collective farm forests** and **assigned forests to**

Table 2
Distribution of forest land resources of Ukraine by tenure and land categories according to the 1965 forest resources inventory.

Tenure categories	Forested land		Non-forested land and non-forestry land*		General forest land area	
	Thous. hectares	Per cent	Thous. hectares	Per cent	Thous. hectares	Per cent
Forests of natl. significance (Derzhlisfond)						
Groups I and II	5,837.3	69.3	1,673.0	83.0	7,060.3	72.1
Collective farm forests	1,936.6	24.9	246.9	12.2	2,183.5	22.4
State farm forests and others	446.2	5.8	97.0	4.8	543.2	5.5
Total	7,770.1	100.0	2,016.9	100.0	9,787.0	100.0

*Within the "Derzhlisfond" category, land not suitable for forest production constitutes 882.9 thousand hectares. The remainder has been either recently reforested or may be suitable for reforestation purposes in the future.

Sources: S.A. Gensiruk, N.V. Turkevich, "Sovremennoe sostoianie lesnogo fonda Ukrainskoi SSR i vozmozhnyi ob'em rubok glavnogo pol'zovaniia, Lesnoi zhurnal, 1969 No.3, p.27

S.A. Hensiruk, V.S. Bondar, Lisovi resursy Ukrainy, ikh okhorona i vykorystannia, Kyiv, Naukova Dumka, 1973, pp.231,235, 238-240, 285.

state farms and other government enterprises. The first two categories have found a juridical expression in various decisions of the government, while the third tenure category has become a separate entity through convention rather than as a result of any legislative act. The assigned forest land is actually a part of the tenure category of forests of national significance allocated to various government institutions for use on a long-term basis.

The forests of national significance (Derzhlisfond) are managed by the Ministry of Forestry of Ukraine and the Ministry of Timber and Woodworking Industries of Ukraine. They represent the largest, economically most important block of forest land occupying over 72 per cent of the total general forest land area and are the main source of the annual timber harvest. Since 1943, forests in this category have been subdivided into three groups, each to perform a predetermined function subject to a rather strict regime of management.

Group I forests are essentially protection forests of a variety of profiles. Originally, that is after 1943, no commercial cuttings were permitted in Group I forests. In mature stands only sanitary removals of trees were tolerated. Since 1953, this rule has been relaxed and commercial cutting is being carried out in some of the environmentally less critical sub-classes of the Group I forests (Nikolaenko et al. 1973).

The relaxation of cutting regulations and the formal approval of allowable cut figures in 1967 by the State Committee of Forestry of USSR in Moscow, led to substantial differences of opinion between the central and the Ukrainian forestry authorities as to what the cut within this group of forests ought to be. The central authorities argued that the shipment of roundwood timber into Ukraine from the densely forested regions of the RSFSR unduly burdened the railway system. A larger cut of the growing stock volume, which accumulated in some of the Group I forests over the years of restriction, coupled with a greater utilization of Group II forests, would reduce substantially the necessity of annually shipping into Ukraine of timber and lumber over long distances amounting to some 28 million cubic metres in terms of roundwood equivalent. It was also argued that given the crisis in agriculture, specifically, the shortage of good quality arable land, it was unwise to maintain forests on potentially productive agricultural land. Such an approach would have helped to achieve two objectives simultaneously, at least in the short run. Increased cuttings in Ukraine would have reduced the demand for timber from the RSFSR, therefore lessening the burden on the railways, at the same time freeing land from under the removed forest for agricultural use. The Ukrainian forestry authorities maintained that increased cutting over a prolonged period of time would result in the virtual elimination of the woodlots (dibrovy) in the forest-steppe ultimately affecting regional water balance and agricultural productivity. It would appear that the republic view prevailed resulting in the reduction of allowable cut for Ukraine and increased timber shipments from the RSFSR.

Group II forests, subdivided into a number of sub-groups, are basically industrial forests of local nature. Cutting here in any year is not to exceed the mean annual increment (MAI) according to the rules governing forest management in the three groups. However, in Ukraine, the actual cut in Group II has, with the exception of just a few years, always exceeded the allowable cut. Group II forests provide the principal source of annual wood supply in Ukraine.

Group III forests are located beyond the borders of Ukraine principally in the RSFSR and the northern Kazakh SSR, and do not fall within the scope of the title of this paper.

The primary function of Group I forests is conservation in its broadest sense in areas where the stress on the natural environment is greatest. For this reason Group I forests have been set aside primarily in the steppe. Indeed, with the exception of a small area in the Kirovohrad oblast' (Onykiivskyi lishospzah), which belongs to Group II forests, all the remaining forests in the steppe are those of Group I.

Group II forests, constituting about 63 per cent of the general forest land area within the Derzhilsfond, predominate in Polisia and to a lesser extent in the Carpathian Mountains and the forest-steppe. In these three natural regions, the general forest land area making up Group II occupies the following proportions: Polisia 86.7 per cent; the Carpathian Mountains 68 per cent and the forest-steppe 56.7 per cent (Hensiruk and Bondar, 1973)

The collective farm forests account for almost 25 per cent of the forested land. As a tenure category, they have their origin since the collectivization of agriculture when tracts of forest land were set aside for the use of collective farms with a view to supplying them with building material and fuelwood. Like all the collective farm lands, they are administered by the agricultural authorities, but cut regulation and all the work relating to forest management and reforestation fall within the jurisdiction of the Ministry of Forestry of the Ukrainian SSR.

The third and smallest tenure category is made up of assigned forests. These are small areas in use on a long-term basis by state farms and other state organizations. As a group, the state farms hold about 52 per cent of the forested area in this category. Forest management operations in the assigned forests are under the control of the forestry authorities, that is, the Ministry of Forestry, while the day-to-day administration is the responsibility of the holding organizations.

The most reliable information on the condition of forests in Ukraine is available for those comprising the tenure category of forests of national significance (Derzhlisfond). Information on the remaining two tenure categories is either antiquated or incomplete and frequently non-comparable. For these reasons, here and in subsequent passages, references will be made primarily to the Derzhlisfond tenure category which, due to its size, is more representative of the forest conditions of Ukraine, while the remaining two categories will be only touched upon in passing.

Forested Land

Over the 15-year period between the forest resources inventories (1950-1965), the forested land area of Ukraine has been steadily increasing (Table 3).[2] This occurred in part as a result of afforestation of land formerly not under forest cover but already within the Derzhlisfond, and partly, due to the transfer of non-forested land from other uses, such as agriculture. On the whole, between 1950 and 1965, the forested land area has increased by 11 per cent, while that of the general forest land by 12.5 per cent. There has been a rather substantial increase in the recently planted area by about 2.4 times over a period of 10 years between 1955 and 1965. This trend is indeed welcome in light of experiences in other countries where forested areas have been

Table 3
Changes in forestry and non-forestry land within the forests of national significance (Derzhlisfond) over a period of 15 years.

Year	Forest Land			Non-forestry land*		General forest land area
	Forested land	Recently ** planted area	Non-forested forest land	Land assigned to special use	Swamps, blow sands, gullies, steep slopes	
	Thousand hectares					
1950	4,854.9	723.1		369.4	327.0	6,274.4
1955	4,960.3	251.9	287.2	259.6	329.3	6,088.3
1960	5,043.1	523.0	288.4	577.7	449.8	6,882.0
1965	5,387.3	599.9	190.2	503.4	379.5	7,060.3
	In per cent					
1950	100.0	—	—	100.0	100.0	100.0
1955	102.2	100.0	100.0	70.3	100.7	97.0
1960	103.9	187.6	100.4	156.4	137.6	109.7
1965	111.0	238.2	66.2	136.3	116.1	112.5

*Land not capable of supporting a forest stand.
**Plantations recently established in which the crowns have not closed.

42

steadily on the decrease. During the same period of time the non-forested forest land area has equally decreased by about 44 per cent apparently due to afforestation. The fluctuations in the two types of non-forestry land are probably due to changes in the interpretation of land use definitions and transfers of land from one non-forestry category to another.

GEOGRAPHICAL DISTRIBUTION OF FORESTS

The territory of Ukraine has been subdivided into three main natural zones and two sub-zones in accordance with the prevailing climatic, geomorphological and soil conditions. The three natural zones from north to south are **Polisia**, the **forest-steppe** and the **steppe**, while the two sub-zones, characterized by a vertical variability in vegetation cover, are the **Carpathian** and the **Crimean** Mountains.

Polisia
Table 4 shows the distribution of forest land and growing stock volume among the natural zones and sub-zones. The greatest proportion of forest land is concentrated in Polisia where the forest land occupies 36.6 per cent of the national total. The forests are distributed here over an extensive lowland area, cut up by wide meandering, sluggish and marshy rivers. Sodpodzolic and peat soils over a high water table predominate under the forest stands. The entire zone has a positive water balance and, over the years, has been the object of extensive drainage operations both for purposes of agriculture and forestry.

The area of Polsia is 29 per cent under forest cover as compared to 12.9 per cent for the entire country (Table 4). Coniferous species occupy 64.5 per cent, soft-leaved hardwoods 25.8 and hard-leaved hardwoods 9.7 per cent of the area of the zone (Hensiruk and Bondar 1973). Although Polisia occupies the number one position among the natural zones and sub-zones of Ukraine in terms of forest land area (36.6 per cent) it is however, in second place in accordance with the total growing stock reserves. The entire growing stock of the forests of Polisia accounts for 28.1 per cent of the total as opposed to that of the Carpathian Mountains which support 36.7 per cent. This makes it obviously clear that the forests of the Carpathian Mountains are both more productive and have a greater concentration of volume in older age classes than those of Polisia. Data in Table 4 demonstrate to that effect, indicating that the mature and overmature growing stock in Polisia constitutes 15.4 per cent of the national total while that of the Carpathian Mountains accounts for 57.2 per cent, or for almost four times as much.

The Forest-steppe
The forest-steppe zone is essentially a transition zone between the relatively moist and humid forests to the north and the dry steppe to the south. The climate here is moderately continental and the annual precipitation roughly equals the evapotranspiration, although in some areas of the forest-steppe the water balance may be negative. The relief of the zone is relatively level with extensive eroded gullies brought about by rapid deforestation in the past. Soils vary, ranging from chernozems and grey forest to peat, sedge, gley and even black alkali soils (solonets).

The area of the forest-steppe which is under forest cover is 11 per cent which is lower than the national average of 12.9 per cent. The pattern of the forest cover is spotty with small forested areas alternating with extensive areas of the non-forested steppe.

In accordance with the 1965 forest resources inventory (Table 4), forest land of the forest-steppe accounts for 28.7 per cent of the national total, being on the second place after Polisia. The zone's growing stock reserves constitute 28.6 per cent of the total, being higher than those of Polisia in spite of the latter's larger area under forest cover. The Left Bank of the forest-steppe is more densely forested than the Right Bank. Hard-leaved hardwoods predominate, accounting for 63.6 per cent of the zone's

43

Table 4
Forest land resources and growing stock of Ukraine by natural zones and sub-zones based on the 1965 forest resources inventory. (Area in thousand hectares; volume in million cubic metres).

Natural zones and sub-zones	Forest land categories						Growing stock						Per cent of territory covered by forests
	Forested land	Per cent	Non-forested land	Per cent	All forest land	Per cent	Juvenile growing stock	Per cent	Mature & over-mature growing stock	Per cent	All growing stock	Per cent	
Polisia	2,832.7	36.5	749.9	37.2	3,582.6	36.6	192.3	30.3	16.8	15.4	209.1	28.1	29
Forest-steppe	2,451.2	31.5	357.2	17.7	2,808.4	28.7	192.5	30.3	20.2	18.5	212.7	28.6	11
Steppe	674.8	8.7	440.8	21.9	1,115.6	11.4	23.2	3.7	5.8	5.3	29.0	3.9	3
Carpathian Mts.	1,555.7	20.0	392.3	19.4	1,948.0	19.9	216.2	34.0	57.2	52.5	273.4	36.7	34
Crimean Mts.	255.7	3.3	76.7	3.8	332.4	3.4	11.1	1.7	9.0	8.3	20.1	2.7	32
Total	7,770.1	100.0	2,016.9	100.0	9,787.0	100.0	635.3	100.0	109.0	100.0	744.3	100.0	12.9

forested area, and are followed by conifers — 24.6 and soft-leaved hardwoods — 11.8 per cent.

The Steppe
The steppe zone is characterized mainly by its dry, continental climate where the mean annual precipitation ranges between 450-300 mm (17.7 — 11.8 inches). Prolonged dry easterly winds, frequently coupled with dust storms, contribute to the zone's negative water balance which exceeds evapotranspiration from 2-3 times. Among the soils, the most widespread are various types of chernozems. In the southern steppe there appear dark chestnut soils with scattered saline outlers.

From among the natural zones and sub-zones, the steppe is the largest, occupying almost 40 per cent of the territory of Ukraine. Forest cover in the steppe is very sparse amounting to about 3 per cent, while the national average is 12.9 per cent. Equally small is the volume of the growing stock amounting to 3.9 per cent which is represented mainly by the juvenile age class which indirectly reflects accelerated reforestation effort taking place over the last 15 — 20 years. Hardwood forests predominate in the steppe, 74.6 per cent is occupied by hard-leaved hardwoods, 17.6 per cent by conifers and 7.8 per cent by soft-leaved hardwoods.

The Carpathian Mountains
Within Ukraine, the Carpathian sub-zone occupies a major portion of the eastern part of the Carpathian Mountains frequently referred to as the "Forested Carpathians". The complex vertical variations, the relative absence of exposed rocky cliffs and the lush vegetation covering the mountainsides, make the Carpathian Mountains a very picturesque region of Ukraine.

The combination of mild climatic conditions, high precipitation and deep and (as far as mountains go) relatively fertile soils, gave rise to a very healthy and productive forest. At present, the forests of the sub-zone cover 34 per cent of its territory, or almost three times the national average. The forested land area of the Carpathian sub-zone accounts for 20 per cent of the total for Ukraine but in terms of the growing stock reserves, it represents 36 per cent of the total and 57.2 per cent of the mature and overmature growing stock volume even after an uninterrupted over-exploitation of these forests since the Second World War.

The Crimean Mountains
The sub-zone of the Crimean Mountains is small in relation to the entire Crimean Peninsula where dry steppe predominates. Of the total area of the Crimean Peninsula, the mountainous sub-zone occupies some 23 per cent. The soils and vegetation of the sub-zone were formed under the influence of both the sub-tropical climate and the close proximity to the sea. Here the soils appear in a characteristic mountainous (vertical) zonality in accordance with the increase in elevation. Deciduous forests predominate on the northern and southern exposures on primarily brown alpine forest soils. Western exposures support the drought-tolerant, Crimean pine (**Pinus Pallasiana** Lamb), while on the eastern exposures are alpine meadows.

Along the main Yaila range, the mean annual precipitation reaches 1,000 mm (39.4 inches) decreasing sharply in the southerly direction and more gradually towards north-east to about 500 mm (19.7 inches). This precipitation in the mountains constitutes the major source of water of the rivers which flow through the steppe part of the Crimean Peninsula.

About 32 per cent of the mountainous part of Crimea is under forest cover. In the forests are found some 150 tree and shrub species. The hard-leaved hardwood group covers 89.2 per cent of the forested area, conifers 7.2 and soft-leaved hardwoods and shrubs 3.6 per cent. The most prevalent species are those of oak.

In terms of area covered by forests, the Crimean sub-zone accounts for 3.8 per cent of the total for the country. The growing stock too is limited amounting to about 2.7 per cent consisting mainly of trees of medium height (Table 4). Because of their small area and having primarily conservation function, the significance of the forests of Crimea from the point of view of the forest-based industry is small. Their greatest value lies in enhancing the tourist industry of the area.

THE GROWING STOCK

Volume Reserves

The total growing stock of forests of Ukraine amounts to over 744 million m³ (Table 5). The forest of national significance (Derzhlisfond) support the bulk of the growing stock, accounting for 86.7 per cent of the total. The remaining 13.3 per cent of growing stock is found on lands attached to collective farms, state farms and other state enterprises.

By examining the growing stock on a per unit area basis, shown in the last column of Table 5, one can get a general impression as to the present condition of the forests in each tenure category. Thus it becomes obvious that the forests within the Derzhlisfond are infinitely better stocked than those in the remaining two tenure categories. As far as volume per hectare is concerned, they occupy the fifth place in Europe.

Table 5
Growing stock distribution among tenure categories according to the 1965 forest resources inventory.

Tenure categories	Forested land thous hectares	Per cent	Growing stock in million m³	Per cent	In m³ per hectare
Forests of natl. significance (Derzhlisfond)	5,387.3	69.3	645.23	86.7	119.8
Collective farm forests	1,936.6	24.9	80.84	10.8	41.7
State farm forests and other	446.2	5.8	18.22	2.5	40.8
Total	7,770.1	100.0	744.29	100.0	96.1

Sources: S.A. Gensiruk, N.V. Turkevich, "Sovremennoe sostoianie lesnogo fonda Ukrainskoi SSR i vozmozhnyi ob'em rubok glavnogo pol'zovaniia," Lesnoi zhurnal, 1969. No.3 p.27

S.A. Hensiruk, V.S. Bondar, Lisovi resursy Ukrainy, ikh okhorona i vykorystannia Kyiv, Naukova Dumka, 1973. pp.231,235, 238-240, 285.

The low growing stock volume of 41.7 and 40.8 m³ per hectare in the collective farm and assigned forests reflects their prolonged abuse by excessive cutting and, probably, grazing as well. This can happen because the collective and state farms, as well as villagers in general, cannot obtain timber for their use in, what is officially called, "the planned order".

Species Composition

There are some 29 economically important tree and about 28 shrub species growing in Ukraine. In addition, there are also a few exotic tree species which have been introduced into Ukraine from other countries and which have become an integral part of the native landscape. The grouping of tree species is as follows, when the entire forested area is considered:

Conifers	42.3 per cent of forested area
Hard-leaved hardwoods	42.5 per cent of forested area
Soft-leaved hardwoods	15.2 per cent of forested area

Among the conifers, the most important species is the Scots or common pine, (**Pinus silvestris L.**) which is distributed all over the country. The genus spruce is represented by one species, namely Norway spruce, (**Picea abies (L.) Karst.**) distributed primarily throughout Polisia. The firs have only one representative in Ukraine in the species of silver fir (or Swiss pine), (**Abies alba Mill.**), distributed in the Carpathian Mountains. Larch, as a rule, does not appear in pure, natural stands in Ukraine. The native European larch, (**Larix decidua** Mill.), is found growing in association with other tree species in the Carpathian Mountains at an elevation of up to 1,800 m.

In contrast to the conifers, the hardwood group of species is more numerous. Individual species of this group usually appear in more complex plant associations than those of the conifers which as a rule form pure stands. The hardwood group of species is further sub-divided into two sub-groups, the **hard-leaved hardwoods** and the **soft-leaved hardwoods**. This sub-division appears to have been made partly on the basis of the hardness of wood and in part on the shade tolerance of the species involved. It seems to have very little to do with the actual hardness or softness of leaves. This subdivision is peculiar to the USSR and is not being applied elsewhere in Europe or North America.

Species belonging to the hard-leaved sub-group of hardwoods are relatively tolerant to shade and include those of oak, ash, maple, beech, elm, bluebeech and yellow birch.

The sub-group of soft-leaved hardwoods comprises white birch, linden, alder, poplar and willow. With a few minor exceptions, species belonging to this sub-group are generally of lesser economic importance as industrial raw material than those belonging to the hard-leaved sub-group. Birches and alders appear as the most important species in this sub-group as judged by the area occupied by each.

Table 6 shows species composition by area within the forests of national significance. The largest area of all is occupied by pine covering 34.7 per cent, followed by oak, distributed over 26.3 per cent of the forested area within this tenure category. A closer examination of the table shows that over 80 per cent of the forested area is covered by four genera: pine, oak, spruce and beech. Such a narrow range in species composition is characteristic of forests in the temperate zone. In Ukraine, this narrowness has been also enhanced by artificial regeneration which deliberately favoured the establishment of economically important species, such as pine, oak and spruce. This is well demonstrated by data in Table 7 where, over a period of fifteen years, the forested area under the three most important species increased by more than twice as compared to the average for the country. Only the area of spruce, from among the four most important species, decreased by almost 40 per cent. This

Table 6
Distribution of forested area among the predominating species within the category of forests of national significance (Derzhlisfond) according to the 1965 forest resources inventory.

Species	Area in thousand hectares	Per cent
Conifers:		
Pine	1,872.0	34.7
Spruce	531.3	9.9
Fir	73.0	1.4
Total for conifers	2,476.3	46.0
Hardwoods:		
Oak	1,419.0	26.3
Beech	502.8	9.3
Birch	290.2	5.4
Alder	226.7	4.2
Bluebeech	200.9	3.7
Ash	72.3	1.4
Poplar (P. tremula L.)	64.0	1.2
Total for hardwoods	2,775.9	51.5
Other species	135.1	2.5
Grand total	5,387.3	100.0

reduction in the area of spruce is attributable to primarily two factors:

1. Ruinous overcutting in the Carpathian Mountains which lasted well into the nineteen-sixties;

2. Widespread damage of spruce stands in the Carpathian Mountains by hurricane force winds, particularly during 1957-1964 when about 520 thousand hectares of forest were affected (Hensiruk, 1966). Spruce, being a shallow-rooted species, is most vulnerable to wind damage.

Information presented in Table 7 shows a definite trend in the increase of forested area supporting the economically more important species. Spruce is, of course, excepted for reasons given above. The same reasons can also be advanced in explaining the reduction in the area under fir betwen 1950 and 1965. Of particular importance is the reduction of the area supporting bluebeech which is a species of medium height, slow growing and the bole usually develops multiple ridges and crooks. Apart from its use as fuelwood, due to its relatively high density, the wood of bluebeech has little industrial application. Poplar, or rather aspen, is a pioneering species appearing usually in the early successional stages of stand development on sites not necessarily suited for healthy and uninterrupted growth. Under conditions of Ukraine, pioneering aspen stands originating after the cut of the main stand, are soon converted to a more durable species, such as oak, beech or pine. The much heralded expansion in 1956 aimed at the establishment of forests comprising certain fast-growing species, among which the cultivation of hybrid poplar was to occupy a prominent place, was of a magnitude not sufficient to have any substantial effect on the area under poplar. For these reasons, the area supporting this genus decreased by 23.5 per cent between 1950 and 1965 in favour of the first six species (Table 7) but not to the same extent as that under bluebeech.

Table 7

Shifts in the forested area by species within the forests of national significance (Derzhlisfond) between 1950 and 1965

	Forested land Thousand hectares		1965 in Per cent to 1950
	1950	1965	
Oak	1,112.7	1,419.0	127.5
Pine	1,507.1	1,872.0	124.2
Beech	426.1	502.8	118.0
Ash	63.7	72.3	113.5
Alder	200.5	226.7	113.1
Birch	261.2	290.2	111.1
Fir	564.5	531.3	94.1
Poplar (P.tremula L.)	83.7	64.0	76.5
Spruce	120.3	73.0	60.7
Bluebeech	370.0	200.9	54.3
Other species	145.1	135.1	93.1
Total	4,854.9	5,387.3	111.0

Age Structure

One of the cardinal objectives of forest management is to ensure a continual flow of primary forest products on an increasing basis in order to supply forest-based industries with raw material in perpetuity. In order to secure an increasing flow of goods and services from a given forest resource and to fully benefit from all its indirect influences, it is absolutely essential that the forest be so orgnaized in time and space as to make the realization of all those benefits attainable on an uninterrupted basis. It is, therefore, imperative that most, if not all, management units comprising the entire forest resource be reasonable regulated. This means that a forest of a management unit, district or country, managed over a prolonged period of time

Fig. 3

ACTUAL AND CALCULATED AGE STRUCTURE OF PRIMARILY INDUSTRIAL, GROUP II FORESTS
(DIAGRAM BASED ON DATA FROM HENSIRUK, S.A. AND BONDAR, V.S. 1973)

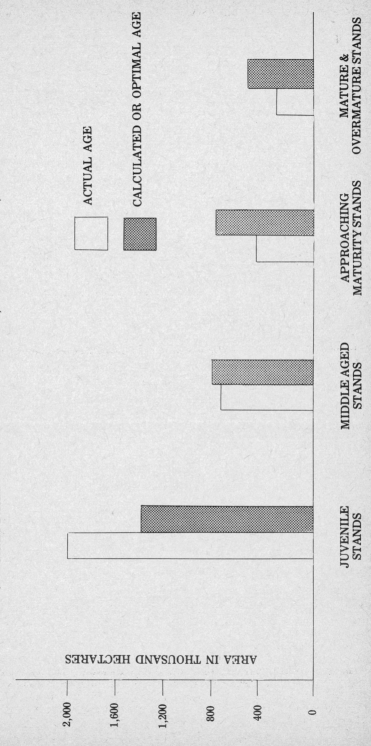

should have a uniform age class distribution. In other words, it should be fully regulated. If this is not the case, that is, if certain age classes (and hence sizes) are poorly represented, then the forest cannot supply on a continuous basis the principal part of its output which is usually timber.

The forests of Ukraine are relatively young. They are, on the average, 37 years old according to the last inventory. The oldest forests are found in the Carpathian Mountains with an average age of 63 years and the youngest in the steppe zone being 14 years old (Ulytskyi, 1970). The national, as well as the zonal, average ages are considerably below those that would be obtained were the forests fully regulated. Under the prevailing growing conditions of Ukraine, the average age should be between 50 and 60 years.

Table 8 shows the present age structure of forests belonging to the **Derzhlisfond** tenure category. An examination of the data in the table reveals an extremely unfavourable age class distribution over the forested area of Ukraine. The strong preponderance of juvenile stands, occupying over 55 per cent of the forested area, becomes clearly obvious. Under the conditions of a fully regulated forest, the proportion of the area under juvenile stands should be in the neighbourhood of 30-35 per cent.

Table 8
Age structure of forests of Ukraine by natural zones and sub-zones within the forests of national significance (Derzhlisfond).

Natural zones	Forested area in thousand hectares	Age Class distribution, in per cent			
		Juvenile stands	Middle aged stands	Stands approaching maturity	Mature & overmature stands
Polisia	1,989.0	64.1	20.9	10.6	4.4
Forest-steppe	1,636.0	57.3	26.5	10.4	5.8
Steppe	309.9	58.5	17.0	11.7	12.8
Carpathian Mts.	1,228.8	44.5	29.7	13.0	12.8
Crimean Mts.	223.6	16.4	38.5	16.5	28.6
Total	5,387.3	55.3	25.1	11.4	8.2

The most optimally represented age class is that of the middle-aged stands. Forests in that age class occupy slightly over 25 per cent of the forested area thus corresponding ideally with the requirements of a well-regulated forest.

The proportions of the area under the last two age classes is about one half of what it ought to be. Instead of 11.4 and 8.2 per cent of the area currently under these two age classes, they ought to support about 22 and 18 per cent respectively. Forests comprising the last two age classes are of harvestable size and, over the years, have been the objects of overcutting which contributed to their diminution dangerously below their optimal levels upsetting the entire temporal and spatial arrangement. The distortion in age class distribution brought about as a result of overcutting is illustrated in Fig. 3 which shows the existing age class distribution of forests in Group II in comparison to the calculated or optimal age class levels.

Equally lopsided age class distribution is observable in forests growing in the various natural zones and sub-zones. The Polisia zone, which accounts for 36.5 per cent of the forested area of the country, exhibits a very distorted age class distribution in its forests. The juvenile stands cover almost twice as large an area than that which would normally be contained in a reasonably regulated forest. The mature and overmature age classes occupy a mere 4.4 per cent of the area and that approaching maturity 10.6 per cent, or less than one half of what it ought to be.

From among the forests of the natural zones, only those growing in the Crimean Mountains exhibit a significantly different age structure. Here the proportion of the mature and overmature forested area far exceeds the level that might be considered optimal. The reason for this difference is in the fact that the forests of Crimea have been relegated to protection forests of Group I where exceptionally strict utilization regimes prevail. Furthermore, forests in this sub-zone grow very slowly on relatively poor sites (Site Class IV-V) located on hillsides producing timber of medium and small sizes in limited quantities not sufficient to supply the wood-using industry on a sustained basis.

Finally, Table 9 shows a historical overview of the age structure of forests of Ukraine. It is important to note that with the exception of the mature and overmature age class, which has been decimated, the remaining age classes have, over the years, maintained relatively similar distribution of the area covered. It will take at least one half of a century before some semblance of an approximate optimal age class distribution will evolve from the presently distorted age structure of the forests.

Table 9
Changes in age structure of forests within the national significance tenure category (Derzhlisfond) between 1945, 1950, 1955 and 1965.

Year	Juvenile stands	Middle aged stands	Stands approaching maturity	Mature and overmature stands	Total
	Area in thousand hectares				
1945*	2,603.7	1,055.9	564.1	597.9	4,821.6
1950	2,745.5	1,103.6	533.4	472.4	4,854.9
1955	2,605.7	1,225.0	581.8	569.3	4,981.7
1965	2,977.6	1,353.9	612.5	443.3	5,387.3
	In per cent				
1945*	54.0	21.9	11.7	12.4	100.0
1950	56.6	22.7	11.0	9.7	100.0
1955	52.3	24.6	11.7	11.4	100.0
1965	55.3	25.1	11.4	8.2	100.0

*Excluding forests of the Crimean Mountains.

Sources: S.A. Gensiruk, "O razmere glavnogo pol'zovanniia v lesakh Ukrainy," Lesnoe Khoziaistvo 1970, No.8, p.39
S.A. Hensiruk, and V.S. Bondar, Lisovi resursy Ukrainy, ikh okhorona i vykorystannia, Kyiv, Naukova dumka, 1973, p.247, 285.

In the column designated as mature and overmature stands, there occurred a sudden increase in forested area from 9.7 in 1950 to 11.4 per cent in 1955, followed by a drop to 8.2 per cent in 1965. These changes did not take place as a result of the recruitment of the forested area from the next lower age class, that is, stands approaching maturity, but were brought about by a deliberate decision during the fifties involving the reduction of rotation ages for commercially important species. The effect of this move resolved itself in the shifting of the age class distribution to the right, resulting in an artificial inflation of the older age classes with area supporting immature timber. Furthermore, the reduction of rotation ages for some species resulted in an increase of the volume of allowable cut bringing it closer in line with the actual cut. What impact this will have on the structure of the Ukrainian forest in the future remains to be seen. At this time, it is quite apparent that reducing the rotation ages of the commercially important species will result in smaller tree sizes being harvested, yielding products of lower quality for lumber and plywood.

In conclusion, it is necessary to point out that information on the age structure of the Ukrainian forest resource is available only for the **Derzhlisfond** tenure category. No information is available on the age structure of the remaining two categories, namely, assigned forests and forests in use by collective farms. Were these forests included in the analysis of the age structure, they would have further depressed the levels of the older age classes enhancing those of the younger ones thereby reinforcing the lopsided nature of age class distribution.

Productivity of Forests

The measuring yardstick of forest productivity in physical terms is the **Mean Annual Increment** (MAI). It is derived by dividing the total yield of timber by age of stand. Forest productivity as expressed by MAI may vary depending on management intensity, stand structure and origin, stand history, species characteristics, climatic and soil conditions. Productivity varies with age of stands; increasing rapidly during the juvenile period and gradually decreasing when the trees reach middle and mature ages.

Due to their young age and the relatively productive soil conditions, forests of Ukraine are highly productive. In terms of MAI, productivity of the forests of Ukraine exceeds that of the USSR by over 2 times (3.22 vs 1.35 m^3 per hectare per year). Nationally, the MAI of the forests within the **Derzhlisfond** tenure category stands at 3.22 m per hectare per year, being highest among conifers and lowest among hard-leaved hardwoods. (See Table 10). The higher level of MAI among soft-leaved hardwood species, as compared to those comprising hard-leaved, is due to the fact that the former are made up of younger stands and, therefore, grow faster, while the latter are older stands and, consequently, grow at a slower rate.

Table 10
Mean annual increment in forests of national significance (Derzhlisfond) by natural zones, sub-zones and species groups according to the 1965 forest resources inventory, in m^3 per hectare.

Natural zones and sub-zones	All forests within Derzhlisfond	Species groups		
		Conifers	Hardleaved hardwoods	Softleaved hardwoods
Polisia	2.99	3.10	2.64	2.83
Forest-steppe	3.24	3.71	2.98	3.75
Steppe	2.66	2.55	2.44	4.22
Carpathian Mts.	4.01	5.05	3.03	3.18
Crimean Mts.	1.51	1.82	1.51	1.12
Average for Ukraine	3.22	3.63	2.79	3.13

Regionally, the highest rate of growth is exhibited by the forests of the Carpathian Mountains with MAI of 4.01 m^3 per hectare per year, while those of the Crimean Mountains show the lowest rate of growth amounting to a MAI of 1.51 m per hectare per year. The difference is mainly due to the relative average ages of forests in both sub-zones, (older in Crimea), species composition (conifers more productive) and, of course, site productivity which is closely associated with the annual volume of precipitation which is by far higher in the Carpathian Mountains. In spite of the fact that over 64 per cent of the forested area of Polisia is covered by juvenile stands (Table 8) and, consequently, it would follow that the MAI would be higher, in actual

Table 11
Changes in mean annual increment by natural zones and sub-zones within the forests of national significance (Derzhlisfond) between the 1955 and 1965 forest resources inventories, in m^3 per hectare.

Zones and sub-zones	MAI in m^3/hectare		Per cent change 1955-1965
	1955	1965	
Polisia	2.54	2.99	117.7
Forest-steppe	2.91	3.24	111.3
Steppe	2.52	2.66	105.6
Carpathian Mts.	4.21	4.01	95.2
Crimean Mts.	1.45	1.51	104.1
Average for Ukraine	2.98	3.22	108.1

fact it is lower than that of the Carpathian Mountains and the forest-steppe. This difference in productivity may be attributed to the lower site productivity of forests in this zone, resulting from the excess moisture and predominance of waterlogged soil conditions as well as a shorter growing season. Well planned drainage operations could substantially improve forest site productivity in this zone.

Table 11 shows changes in forest productivity in terms of MAI between 1955 and 1965. While on the national basis the MAI increased by 8.1 per cent over the ten-year period, regionally there occurred an unexpected drop in the Carpathian Mountains from 4.21 to 4.01 m^3 per hectare. This drop in productivity is apparently due to the reduction in stand density brought about by extensive blow downs in recent years and excessive removal of trees through selective cuttings currently practiced in the Carpathian Mountains. The highest increase in MAI between 1955 and 1965 occurred in Polisia where young forests predominate.

INTENSITY OF FOREST USE

Removals

Removals are defined as quantities of wood products removed from a forested area over a period of one year. The volume of removals includes all the marketable timber which has been cut but for reasons of market availability, may or may not be taken out of the forest. Under the current timber supply conditions in Ukraine, nearly all the removed timber is utilized in one form or another with the exception of that cut in the remote areas of the Carpathian Mountains and perhaps Polisia where low quality wood and logging waste may be left on the ground.

Table 12 shows average annual volumes of wood removed from forests in the various zones and sub-zones. Since 1956 there has taken place a general decline in the volume of marketable timber removed. Of particular interest is the rather drastic reduction in volume cut between 1956-1960 and the 1966-1970 periods in the Carpathian Mountains from a high of 7,441 to a low of 3,620 thousand m^3, or by almost one half. During the first period (1956-1960) the forests of the Carpathian Mountains accounted for almost 46 per cent of the timber removed, dropping slightly to over 30 per cent during the last period. Over the three periods of time shown in Table 12, the levels of removal remained relatively stable in all the zones and sub-zones except, of course, in the Carpathian Mountains.

The disproportionate reliance on the Carpathian timber until about 1960 can be partly explained by the following factors: (a) the forests of this sub-zone occupy an area sufficiently capable of sustaining a modern logging industry over a prolonged period of time; (b) the growing stock volume of the mature age classes on a per unit area basis is highest among conifers which form highly productive, solid stands on higher elevations in the Carpathian Mountains. High volume per unit area results in higher labour productivity and more efficient use of available logging equipment thereby consistently assuring the fulfillment of planned production quotas. These factors, no doubt, influenced the decisions at the centre in favour of logging more timber in the Carpathian Mountains in total disregard of sound forestry principles.

Removals and Mean Annual Increment

Under conditions of a fully regulated forest, in which all ages are uniformly represented, the volume of annual removals should, on the average, equal the mean annual increment (MAI). In such an optimal situation whatever the forest grows is removed every year without impairing the productive capacity of the capital stock which is the living forest. Once a degree of regularity has been attained, the forest can provide an annual output of wood fibre equivalent in magnitude to MAI in perpetuity. In addition, the forest will also perform all the other social and biological functions that are commonly associated with its existence. A fully regulated, normal forest will produce an equal volume of fibre every year forever. By manipulating some of the inputs, modern forestry practice may change this constancy in the production pattern of the forest in an upward direction but only to a limited extent.

53

Table 12
Average annual harvest of marketable* timber within the forests of national significance (Derzhlisfond) between 1956 and 1970 by natural zones and sub-zones.

Natural zones and sub-zones	1956-1960		1961-1965		1966-1970	
	Thousand m³	Per cent	Thousand m³	Per cent	Thousand m³	Per cent
Polisia	4,441	27.4	4,535	34.0	4,151	34.9
Forest-steppe	3,852	23.8	3,997	29.9	3,672	30.9
Steppe	351	2.2	327	2.5	379	3.2
Carpathian Mts.	7,441	45.9	4,441	33.3	3,620	30.5
Crimean Mts.	118	0.7	45	0.3	63	0.5

*Including commercial timber, fuelwood, tree limbs and brushwood for wickerwork

As has already been demonstrated, the forests of Ukraine are still far from being fully regulated and substantial increases in wood fibre output could be obtained in the future by gradually balancing the forest's age class distribution. For this reason the rule "removals equal MAI" cannot be applied at the present time because of the irregular age class distribution (Tables 8 and 9). This fact has to be kept in mind while examining data in Table 13 which shows the relationship between removals and MAI by zones on a per unit area basis. Although the level of utilization of the MAI during the most recent period (1966-1970) was considerably below that of actual cut, it is still fairly high in light of the lopsided age class distribution which is so heavily represented by the juvenile age classes. The present MAI on the entire area of the Derzhlisfond (1966-1970) amounts to about 17,280 thousand m^3, while the average annual removals reached 11,885 thousand m^3 during the same period of time. The utilization of the MAI, therefore, is about 69 per cent. By including the low MAI and high removal figures of the collective farm and assigned forests in the above calculation, the resulting level of the utilization of the MAI would be considerably higher.

Table 13
Relationship between the mean annual increment (MAI) and annual actual cut for the forests of national significance (Derzhlisfond) between 1956 and 1970, in m^3 per hectare.

Natural zones and sub-zones	1956-1960			1961-1965			1966-1970		
	MAI	Actual cut	Per cent of utilization of MAI	MAI	Actual cut	Per cent of utilization of MAI	MAI	Actual cut	Per cent of utilization of MAI
Polisia	2.54	2.25	88.6	2.64	2.22	84.1	2.99	1.90	63.5
Forest-steppe	2.91	2.43	83.5	3.49	2.47	70.8	3.24	2.19	67.6
Steppe	2.52	1.47	58.3	2.55	1.45	56.9	2.66	1.30	48.9
Carpathian Mts.	4.21	7.57	179.8	3.97	4.55	114.6	4.01	3.60	89.8
Crimean Mts.	1.45	0.64	44.1	1.33	0.20	15.0	1.51	0.28	18.5
Average for the country	2.98	3.27	109.7	3.07	2.65	86.3	3.22	2.21	68.6

The Allowable Cut and its Utilization

A comparison of the MAI and the removal data under conditions of distorted age class distribution is only an approximate indication of the degree of forest use. Were the forests fully regulated then there would not be any problem determining their level of utilization because the annual removal, or cut, would equal the MAI which, in turn, would automatically be accepted as the allowable cut. Forests have a rather long production cycle which, within the temperate climate, may extend from about 20 years in the case of fast-growing, hybrid poplars, to 200 years required to produce fully grown oak trees. Over such a long period of time, the area committed to forest production may be subjected to a number of upheavals, such as fire, flood, drought, insect and disease damage. Major social, economic and political events and their aftermaths may, in many ways, influence the age structure, geographic distribution and density of forests. For example, a prolonged major famine may lead to an elimination of certain forested areas for use in agriculture. War activites may result in both extensive damage and overcut of the existing forests. Unfavourable balance of payments may lead to an overcutting of domestic forests in countries depending partly on wood supplies from foreign sources. Throughout history, all these events had taken place in Ukraine and left their mark on the general structure of the forests. For these reasons, it is very difficult to attain a level of what might be considered a fully regulated forest in which the annual cut would equal the MAI. A fully regulated forest is something to be aimed at but seldom, if ever, achieved. To attain such an ultimate level, at least approximately, it is necessary to order the forests in time and space by means of various silvicultural methods, chief among these being the magnitude of the annual cut.

Many factors enter into the consideration of the magnitude of what the annual cut ought to be and there are a number of methods according to which the allowable cut can be calculated. The ultimate purpose of a properly calculated allowable cut is to prevent the depletion of wood capital, to assure a steady flow of primary forest products, to attain and maintain a uniform age class distribution with a veiw to creating a fully regulated forest and to arrange the forest cover in time and space in such a manner as to enable it to exert all the beneficial influences on other activities within a lnadscape.

Table 14 shows the relationship betwen the allowable and actual cuts since the end of the Second World War. The actual cut figure reflects that of the principal cut (clear cut) and is comparable to that of the allowable cut. By examining the column showing the utilization of the allowable cut, it becomes obvious that the forests of Ukraine have been subjected to an extremely heavy regime of overcutting which persists to this day. Were this excessive utilization of the allowable cut not attended by a comparable reforestation effort it would be reasonable to expect a reduction in the forest cover of the Ukrainian territory. Since 1966, the per cent utilization of the allowable cut began to decline gradually and it is hoped that over the next five years, the actual cut will be brought in line with that of the allowable.

Table 14
Utilization of the principal allowable cut in the forests of national significance (Derzhlisfond) since the end of WW II

Period	Average annual volume in thousand m³		Per cent utilization of allowable cut
	Allowable cut	Actual cut	
1945-1950	4,998	11,584	232
1951-1955	5,981	11,111	186
1956-1960	6,403	11,775	184
1961-1965	5,936	7,844	132
1966-1970	5,301	5,663	107

An examination of the overll nationall figures on allowable cut frequently obscures the reality in the regions. An overcutting in one area may be compensated by undercutting, or no cutting at all, in another. For example, the forest resources in an inaccessible, remote area may remain entirely untouched, while those in closer proximity to the centres of demand may be overcut many years ahead of time, yet the national average may indicate a balance between the actual and the allowable cuts. Under such conditions the national figure may not entirely reflect the true situation. It is, therefore, necessary to examine allowable and actual cuts on a regional basis to determine the real distribution of forest use.

Such a comparison is partially demonstrated in Table 15 which reflects the allowable cut utilization within the Derzhlisfond, Group II forests of the South-Western Economic Region of Ukraine. Nearly 75 per cent of the forested area of Ukraine is distributed throughout this region where the Group II industrial forests predominate. As can be seen from Table 15, the excessive utilization of the forests in this region has persisted during the nineteen-sixties. Only during 1965 and 1967, were the actual cuts below those of the allowable, while during the remaining years the reverse was true.

It would not be an exaggeration to state that the intensity of forest use in the Carpathian Mountains since the end of the Second World War, until about the middle nineteen-sixties, had been nothing else but ruinous. For example, in 1949, the volume

Table 15
Comparison of allowable and actual cuts within group II forests of national significance (Derzhlisfond) of the South-Western Economic Region* of Ukraine (Principal cut only).

	1961	1962	1963	1964	1965	1966	1967	1968	1969	1970
Allowable cut, thous. m³	5,525	5,470	5,705	5,704	5,708	5,707	5,707	4,549	4,549	4,547
Actual cut, thous. m³	8,695	8,060	7,239	7,596	5,683	6,474	5,480	5,186	5,004	4,676
Per cent utilization	157.4	147.5	126.9	133.2	99.6	113.4	96.0	114.0	110.0	102.8

*Comprises: Vinnytsia, Volyns'ka, Zhytomyr, Zakarpats'ka, Ivano-Frankivsk, Kyiv, L'viv, Rivne, Ternopil, Khmel'nyts'kyi, Cherkasy, Chernyhiv and Chernivtsi oblast's. The South-Western Economic Region supports 74.6 per cent of the forested area of Ukraine.

Source: Prepared on the basis of a chart in: V.I. Pyla, Rozvytok lisopererobnoii promyslovosti na osnovi kompleksnoho vykorystannia derevyny, Kyiv Tekhnika, 1973, p.40.

of timber actually cut in the Chernivtsi oblast' amounted to over 4 times that of the allowable. There is also a certain amount of inconsistency between the allowable cut figures for the individual years and the corresponding volume of timber removed per unit area. As a case in point, in 1949, the allowable cut in the Ivano-Frankivs'k oblast' was utilized by 260 per cent and the volume of timber removed per one hectare amounted to 4.96 m^3. For the same obalst' seven years later (1956), the allowable cut was utilized by only 162 per cent, but the volume of timber removed per hectare suddenly shot to 8.55 m^3. What really happened was that the allowable cut for the Ivano-Frankivs'k oblast' was increased from 876.8 thousand in 1949 to 1,740.5 thousand m^3 in 1956, or by 98.5 per cent. There is no plausible explanation for this anomaly. As has been demonstrated before, there was no great preponderance of mature and overmature age classes in the Carpathian forest to justify this sudden increase in the allowable cut which resulted in the removal of 8.55 m^3 of timber per hectare, amounting to twice the volume of the MAI. This was not an error during a single year, since it persisted into the early nineteen-sixties, but a deliberate effort at camouflaging the consistent overutilization of the allowable cut by those in the logging industry aiming for high production targets. Removing 8.55 m^3 on a per acre basis by means of the principal (harvest) cut in a forest with a MAI of 4.21 m^3, having the mature and overmature age class poorly represented, can be considered only as an act devoid of professional responsibility. Even the timber barons in North America at times demonstrated a greater responsibility and compassion towards the future of the forest resource than the managers of the socialist forestry enterprises in the Carpathian Mountains.

FOREST REGENERATION

Artificial regeneration of forest in Ukraine had its beginnings during the 17th century when the Cossacks planted oak in the vicinity of **Zaporozhian Sich** for use in ship-building. The Cossacks also planted trees along fortification belts (zasiky) which were to be cut in the event of an attack with tree crowns facing in the direction of the approach of the enemy, thereby slowing down its initial assault. Trees cut in this manner were especially effective against attackers on horseback.

During the latter part of the 17th century and early part of the 18th, attempts at establishing oak were made under the instigation of Peter I in the pre-Azov steppe. These oak plantations were established with a view to providing timber for building ships to be used in the Azov-Black Sea basins. Extremely severe penalties were meted out to those who, in any way, cut or interfered with the naval plantations.

Attempts at establishing forests were also made during the settlement of the steppe. The new settlers planted trees on their own in the hope of obtaining building material and fuelwood in this sparsely forested region. The Mennonite settlers were particularly diligent in trying to afforest the steppe.

A more regular work on artifical regeneration had been conducted since the establishment of the Ministry of State Properties in 1838. Under the auspices of this Ministry, the first trained forester of the Empire, V.E. Graff, established a 157-hectare plantation in the steppe of eastern Ukraine. Presently, this forest is known as **Velykyi Anadol'** located near the city of Zhdanov in the Donets'ke oblast'. Following extensive site preparations, the work of V.E. Graff proved that it was possible to establish and maintain forest growth in the dry steppe (ppt. 300 mm, or 11.8 inches) on areas which had never been under forest cover before. Graff's proof was in contradiction to the opinions held in Europe at that time which maintained that forests established in the steppe could not be sustained over a longer period of time on account of persistent low humidity of the air. Experience gained at Velykyi Anadol' served later as a basis for the establishment of the shelterbelt network in the steppe which attained widespread prominence when the "**great nature transformation plan**" was unveiled in 1948.

Prior to the nineteen-twenties, reforestation efforts in Ukraine had a rather isolated and sporadic character. Forestry continually competed for land with agriculture; the latter use receiving consistently a greater priority. Although nationalization and collectivization, which followed the Bol'shevik Revolution brought about widespread destruction in agriculture and great suffering among rural population, in forestry it made possible an agglomeration of suitable land for reforestation purposes. About 686,000 hectares of land had been planted and seeded between 1922 and 1941 on the territory then within the Ukrainian SSR (Soldatov et al. 1960). The area thus reforested was still considerably below that from which forests were removed during the First World War and the Revolution.

Energetic reforestation operations began to expand following the Second World War. Not only was the backlog of cut-over areas put back into production, but also certain marginal agricultural lands were afforested. By 1950, the reforested area under all the tenure categories already exceeded the area classified as having been clear cut (Table 16).

The forest regeneration effort of Ukraine peaked during 1951-1955. From then on, it began to decline partly as a result of discontinuation of the shelterbelt establishment program and, in part, due to a shortage of appropriate non-forested land that could be afforested. The principal, or clear cut method of logging had been progressively replaced by various other forms of partial cutting, resulting in a further reduction of area that could be used in reforestation.

Table 16
Forest regeneration operations in Ukraine since the end of the Second World War, in thousand hectares.

Type of operation	1944-1950	1951-1955	1956-1960	1961-1965	1966-1969
Planting and seeding within the Derzhlisfond	440.0	535.0	550.4	593.3	284.4
Average annual effort	62.8	107.0	110.0	118.6	70.8
Assistance to natural regeneration	42.1	96.2	85.8	49.4	27.7
Afforestation of gullies and sands	70.8	285.1	156.7	168.6	145.4
Shelterbelt establishment	140.7	220.1	44.4	22.4	29.2
Area of principal cuts (clearcuts) within the Derzhlisfond	454.0	260.4	302.3	228.8	125.2
Planting and seeding on areas under the tenure of collective farms	14.0	37.0	82.3	47.9	32.4

Source: P.H. Vakuliuk, "Lisorozvedennia i lisovidnovlennia nä Ukraini," Lisove hospodarstvo, lisova, paperova i derevoobrobna promyslovist', 1970, No.2, p.18.

Future forest regeneration effort in Ukraine will ultimately even out and will restrict itself mainly to areas clear cut and lands transferred from other uses. Such a declining trend is becoming apparent in the forest regeneration effort projected for the current Five-Year-Plan (1971-1975). Once all the exposed hills, eroded ravines and blow sands become afforested, then subsequent to this, the entire reforestation effort will be sustained within the limit of about 200 thousand hectares annually.

The reforestation and afforestation effort carried out in the past resulted in a marked transformation in the structure of the forest resource of Ukraine. As has been indicated before, the active reforestation effort brought about significant changes in age class distribution making it lopsided in favour of the juvenile age classes (Table 10). The degree of forest cover of the territory has also increased somewhat since the end of the Second World War as a result of the accelerated reforestation effort. There also occurred a qualitative shift in species cover. Economically less significant species (bluebeech) have been replaced by those of greater value, such as pine, oak and beech.

All these factors and influences resulted in marked changes in the makeup of forests by origin. At present, one third of the forests classified under the tenure category of "Derzhlisfond" are of artificial origin. In the steppe zone, forests established by man cover almost 58 per cent of the zone's forested area; in the forest-steppe 46 per cent and in Polisia almost 30 per cent. In Europe, only Germany (East & West) has a higher proportion of artificially established forests.

Zones which support less than 20 per cent of forests of artificial origin are the mountainous regions of Ukraine. High precipitation in the Carpathian Mountains greatly favours natural regeneration even on areas cut clear. This makes it practically unnecessary to engage in artificial reforestation to attain desirable stocking. In the Crimean Mountains, the forests have never been subjected to extensive industrial exploitation. Whatever cutting had taken place was of a magnitude that did not adversely affect the natural regeneration processes.

In terms of roundwood equivalent, Ukraine consumes some 47 million m^3 of commercial timber annually (Lahutov et al. 1973). In this total, supplies from domestic sources account for only 17 per cent, while the remainder (83 per cent) is imported from the densely forested regions of the RSFSR in various stages of manufacture. The current annual lumber output alone requires almost 19 million m^3 of commercial timber in roundwood form, while the total domestic cut of the same type of timber amounts to about 7.3 million m^3.

The relatively high proportion of stands of artificial origin comprising the forest resource base of Ukraine will bring about substantial increases in the domestic supply of wood once these stands reach maturity. Barring any major natural disasters, and assuming that the presently distorted age class distribution will be faithfully balanced, the forests of Ukraine will be capable of supplying about 25 million m^3 of marketable timber within the next 20 years. This increased yield will be possible to realize in the fully stocked, artificially established stands once they reach the age at which they can be profitably thinned. Based on the present consumption pattern of timber in Ukraine, this increased supply may satisfy about 50 per cent of expected domestic needs.

FOOTNOTES

1.   According to the preliminary data for the 1973 forest resources inventory, the forested land of Ukraine has increased by about 700,000 hectares, or by about 9 per cent, since 1965.

2.   Since 1965, the forested area within the category of forests of national significance (Derzhlisfond) has increased by about 1.1 million acres, or by about 20 per cent, according to the preliminary data for the 1973 forest resources inventory. The increase in forested area in Ukraine occurred as a result of afforestation of lands hitherto non-forested.

LITERATURE CONSULTED

Biallovich, Iu. P., "Normativy optimal'noi lesistosti ravninnoi chasti Ukr. SSR." In Piatnitskii, S.S. (ed.) Lesovodstvo i agrolesomelioratsiia. Kyiv, Urozhai, Vypusk 28, 1972, pp. 54-65.

Bradis, Ye. M. (Ed.) Roslynnist' URSR, Lisy URSR. Kyiv, Naukova Dumka, 1971, p. 434.

Dobrovol's'kyi, V., Obraztsova, N., "Zemel'ni resursy Ukrains'koi RSR ta ikh vykorystannia", Ekonomika Radians'koi Ukrainy, No. 12, 1969, pp. 57-62.

Entsyklopediia narodnoho hospodarstva Ukrains'koi RSR (Iampol's'kyi, S.M., ed.), Kyiv, 1970, Vol. 2, pp. 384-386, Vol. 3, pp. 479-489.

Gensiruk, S.A., Turkevich, N.V., "Sovremennoe sostoianie lesnogo fonda Ukrainskoi SSR i vozmozhnyi ob'em rubok glavnogo pol'zovaniia," Lesnoi zhurnal, Izvestiia vysshikh uchebnykh zavedenii, No. 3, 1969, pp. 26-30.

Gensiruk, S.A., "O razmere glavnogo pol'zovaniia v lesakh Ukrainy", Lesnoe khoziaistvo, No. 8, 1970, pp. 38-40.

Gensiruk, S.A., Kompleksnoe lesnoe khoziaistvo v gornykh usloviiakh. Moscow, Lesnaia promyshlennost', 1971, pp. 93-113.

Hensiruk, S., "Osnovni zavdannia dokorinnoho polipshennia lisovoho hospodarstva radians'kykh Karpat", Ekonomika Radians'koi Ukrainy, No. 11, 1965, pp. 56-63.

Hensiruk, S.A., "Lisove hospodarstvo Karpat i shliakhy yoho dal'shoho rozvytku." In Rozmishchennia produktyvnykh syl Ukrains'koi RSR, Vydavnytstvo Kyivs'koho Universytetu, Kyiv, Vypusk 3, 1966, pp. 129-133.

Hensiruk, S.A., Bondar, V.S., "Lisovi resursy Ukrainy, ikh rozmishchennia, vykorystannia ta vidnovlennia. In Pohrebniak, P.S. (Ed.) Problemy heohrafichnoi nauky v Ukrains'kii RSR. Kyiv, Naukova Dumka, 1972, pp. 100-116.

Hensiruk, S.A., Bondar, V.S., Lisovi resursy Ukrainy, ikh okhorona i vykorystannia. Kyiv, Naukova Dumka, 1973, pp. 230-249, 283-286.

Iarmola, I.S., Voprosy lesosnabzhennia v SSSR. Moscow, Lesnaia promyshlennost, 1972, p. 238.

Ivanytsky, Borys, "Ukrainian Forestry," The Annals of the Ukrainian Academy of Arts and Sciences in the U.S. Vol. III, No. 1 (7), Spring-Summer, 1953, pp. 553-595.

Iwanitskyj, Borys, "Die Entwaldung der Ukraine," Zeitschrift fuer Forst-und Jagdwesen, Jahrgang 60, Juni 1928, pp. 272-379.

Lahutov, D.P., Patsera, A.D., "Udoskonaliuvannia prognozuvannia i planuvannia rozvytku okremykh vyrobnytstv lisovoi paperovoi i derevoobrobnoi promyslovosti," Lisove hospodarstvo, lisova, paperova i derevoobrobna promyslovist', No. 2, 1973, pp. 28-32.

Luk'ianov, B., "Pidvyshchuvaty produktyvnist' lisiv, ratsional'no vykorystovuvaty lisovi bahatstva," Ekonomika Radians'koi Ukrainy, No. 7, 1973, pp. 11-17.

Luk'ianov, B.M., "Za dal'shu intensifikatsiiu lisohospodars'koho vyrobnytstva," Lisove hospodarstvo, lisova, paperova i derevoobrobna promyslovist', No. 5, 1971, pp. 1-4.

Luk'ianov, B.M., "Zbil'shuvaty viddachu kozhnoho hektara lisu," Lisove hospodarstvo, lisova, paperova i derevoobrobna promyslovist', No. 4, 1972, pp. 1-3.

Luk'ianov, B.N., "Lesnoe khoziaistvo Ukrainy — na puti progressa," Lesnoe khoziaistvo, No. 12, 1972, pp. 22-27.

Narodne hospodarstvo Ukrains'koi RSR u 1972 rotsi, Statystychnyi shchorichnyk. Kyiv, 1974, pp. 143-144, 206-207, 466.

Narodnoe khoziaistvo SSSR v 1972 g., Statisticheskii ezhegodnik. Moscow, Statistika, 1973, pp. 238-239, 240-243.

Nikolaenko, V.T., Plotnikov, L.A., Voronina, A.P., Lesa 1 gruppy. Moscow, Lesnaia promyshlennost', 1973, pp. 164-165.

Sereda, N., "Vozrast rubki i potreblenie drevesiny v Ukr. SSR," Lesnaia promyshlennost', No. 12, 1957, pp. 27-28.

Soldatov, A., "Eshche o lesopol'zovanii v Ukr. SSR." Lesnaia promyshlennost', No. 1, 1965, pp. 23-24.

Soldatov, A.H., Tiukov, S.Iu., Turkęvych, M.V., **Lisy Ukrainy**. Kyiv, Vydavnytstvo Ukrains'koi Akademii Sil's'kohospodars'kykh Nauk, 1960, pp. 182-183.

Tarasenko, V.P., "Formirovanie optimal'nogo porodnogo sostava lesa i ustanovlenie optimal'noi lesistosti mestnosti — vazhneishii put'intensifikatsii lesnogo khoziaistva," In Zima, I.M. (Ed.), **Vsesoiuznaia nauchno-proizvodstvennaia konferentsiia po roprosam sovershenstvovaniia lesnogo khoziaistva; Tezisy dokladov.** Kyiv, 1973, pp. 22-24.

Ulyts'kyi, P.M., "Dynamika zmin u lisovomu fondi Ukrainy," **Lisove hospodarstvo, lisova, paperova i derevoobrobna promyslovist'**, No. 2, pp. 21-23.

Vakuliuk, P.G., "Povysit' protsent lesistosti Poles'ia, Karpat i lesostepi Ukrainy," **Lesnoe khoziaistvo**, 1972, No. 10, pp. 77-80.

Vakuliuk, P.H., "Lisorozvedennia i lisovidnovlennia na Ukraini," **Lisove hospodarstvo, lisova, paperova i derevoobrobna promyslovist'**, No. 2, 1970, pp. 15-18.

Vakuliuk, P.H., "Zmina lisystosti Ukrainy z davnykh chasiv do nashykh dniv," **Lisove hospodarstvo, lisova, paperova i derevoobrobna promyslovist'**, No. 2, 1972, pp. 15-19.

Vedenichev, P.F., **Zemel'nye resursy Ukrainskoi SSR i ikh khoziaistvennoe ispol'zovanie.** Kyiv, 1972, p. 96.

Comments on J. Holowacz,
Forests of Ukraine
Their History and Present Status

by
Brenton M. Barr
University of Calgary

The purpose of this discussion is to evaluate critically a presentation by J. Holowacz to the McMaster Conference on the Contemporary Ukraine, October 25-27, 1974. The criteria used to evaluate this report are taken from Science, 1960, volume 131, pp. 1182-1186, and are employed here to ensure objectivity in evaluation. This review considers the substantive nature of the report, the author's purposes, the extent to which the purposes were fulfilled, and the quality of presentation.

The author has attempted to evaluate a particular aspect of the natural resources of the Soviet Ukraine. Although he has accepted as his definition of the region the present territorial boundaries of the Ukrainian SSR, Holowacz generally views Ukraine as a country, rather than as a constituent region of the Soviet Union. He has devoted himself almost entirely to an analysis of problems within Ukraine and has not considered the extent to which many of the problems and processes he evaluates may in fact be part of a wider spatial or geographical continuum within the territory of the USSR, eastern Europe, or the Eurasian land mass. He has sought to present large amounts of information about a particular area of the world, but to rely on the absolute nature of the facts, not on their comparative or relative significance, to develop his case. Holowacz, in fact, leads the reader carefully through his meticulous calculation of many aspects of the Ukrainian forest and enables the reader to appreciate the great technical skill required to evaluate forest resources whether in Ukraine or elsewhere. Most of the Holowacz report is concerned with evaluation of the quantitative and qualitive aspects of the resource.

He does not, however, inform his reader of the purpose of the research or of the presentation. Consequently, discussion or review of the report is very difficult because the reader is never quite sure why the materials were presented. Consequently, in this evaluation, the assumption is made that the Holowacz presentation basically attempts to show how a technical analyst compiles the necessary data in order to make statements concerning the age and species structure of the Ukrainian forest, and the relationship of the resource to the demands made upon it by forest based industries. All further comments are made on the basis of this assumption and this reviewer must be forgiven if he has misunderstood other implicit objectives of the report.

The report is extremely long and attempts to cover more material than one would normally expect to be presented at a conference in the social sciences. It is really a symposium report and in its present form deserves to be presented at a meeting of specialists rather than at one comprising those generally interested in the diverse contemporary problems of Ukraine. The presentation is far too long and detailed in its present form if its is to make an impact on the general public who attended the conference. The report should be abstracted and the issues in it more clearly and more succinctly defined and presented. The presentation, however, is a logical and well-organized report. The basic value of the material to this conference should be in what it reveals about the resource problems of Ukraine — the issues and problems — and not in a ream of statistics which strike this reviewer as basically meaningless to a general audience. A brief consideration of the tables of contents of the report will suffice to show its ambitious scope.

The Holowacz report — in present draft form 120 typewritten pages — was initially meant also to include description of administration, education of labour, research organization, forest-based industries, multiple use of forests, national parks system, fisheries, wildlife, and a bibliography — the last item not being included in the present report. The present report, even without the above items, is still very comprehensive and contains sections devoted to the history of forest cover — land area population, geographical distribution of forests, the growing stock, species, species composition by area and their shifts, the degree of forest cover, age structure of forests, productivity of forests, removals, forest regeneration, and the timber supply balance of Ukraine.

Holowacz's report is, in this writer's opinion, thus suitable for publication as the only authoritative handbook on forest resources of Ukraine — it is not a conference paper but a document of great technical significance both to scientists in Ukraine, the USSR, and in Canada, not to mention in numerous other countries. The contents of the report have value to foresters, economists, geographers, planners, environmentalists and many other professionals concerned with resource development. The report is a definitive statement on the quality and quantity of Ukrainian forest resources but in its present form is far too detailed to comprise a conference report in which it would probably be advisable to present a summary overview of the chief issues, and to speculate on broader areas of concern to the forest industry such as possible tradeoffs between forest land and agricultural land, the geographical hiatus between location of wood supplies and location of converting industries, the problem of excessive hauls of wood on Soviet railways and waterways, and the possible economic benefit both to Ukraine and the USSR by developing more efficient forest industrial firms and improving the general system of their geographical relations.

The Holowacz paper is thorough and analytical in relation to specific aspects of Ukrainian forests. It proceeds upon a fine data base built up over nearly two decades of painstaking research, and takes cognizance of related functional aspects of Ukrainian forestry which extend into other Soviet regions; although, for the most part, this report could legitimately focus on Ukraine without detracting from its scientific value. However, to be entirely effective, any analysis of a constituent region of the Soviet Union must take great cognizance of the fact that so many processes are influenced by decisions made in Moscow, and that many problems are the consequence of the internal distribution of economic forces throughout the national spatial economy of the USSR. Therefore, this reviewer suggests that the major topic dealt with should at least be explicitly formulated within the context of the centralized federal milieu which comprises the USSR.

While the author has avoided the pitfall of being doctrinaire, this reader wishes that he had been less cautious and perhaps even speculated or followed up some of the leads which his material suggested. One wishes that J. Holowacz had been able to assess in greater depth why Ukrainian forest practices have resulted in excessive overcutting, and why central policies emanating from Moscow have taken their present form. In this day of behavioral approaches to social science, this reader would certainly have welcomed some analysis of the perception of Ukrainian forests by those both in Ukraine and in Moscow who are responsible for their administration and utilization. Inference and speculation are at best very risky by analysts but it is still tempting to think that the Soviet economic administration is not devoid of human foibles and human behavior which are perhaps a direct result of the excessive centralization of that state. This reader would love to know the extent to which Ukrainian foresters either in Ukraine or in Moscow are able to effect measures which in the long run at least would be of benefit to their "homeland". Perhaps matters such as these might eventually constitute a further phase of Holowacz's work once the back-breaking task of assembling the relevant statistical information has been completed.

In view of the assumed purposes of the report, we much conclude that the author has generally fulfilled his objectives. Certainly Holowacz has presented his readers with a masterful account of key problems in the forests of Ukraine. There is no substitute in English or apparently in other languages for the work presented here. The work is thorough, comprehensive, and a major addition to knowledge.

And finally we must consider the extent to which the report has been well written. The Holowacz report is precise, succinct within its sections, and developed on the basis of pertinent tables and maps. He could, however, improve his presentation by a reduction in reliance on words and an increase in visual materials such as photographs. Descriptions of regional differences in forest species composition, or in the general nature of the landscape, for example, could be adequately served by photographs usually obtained by western analysts such as geographers from Soviet news agencies for inclusion in books, monographs and articels about the USSR. Holowacz' sharp, precise prose, however, is worthy of emulation.

Lest the reader of this evaluation think that we have been excessively critical of some aspects of the material reviewed, attention should be drawn to the fact that the report is very long and very demanding of time and effort taken to evaluate it. The suject is of too great importance to be passed over lightly or glibly; the author is to be commended for undertaking such a major task but he is encouraged to consider the likely reaction of his audience when confronted by such a comprehensive, but excessively technical, evaluation of a resource problem which is not easily understood even by those in Ukraine who deal with it on a first-hand basis.

II
Economics

The Present State of Cybernetics and Republic-Level Economic Planning

by
Vsevolod Holubnychy
Hunter College of the
City University of New York

I. THE STATE OF THEORETICAL CYBERNETICS

1. The beginnings

Cybernetics began to develop in Ukraine a bit earlier than in the rest of the Soviet Union. The year 1947 is given as its birth date, which is 10 to 12 years behind its beginnings in the West. The main stimulus came from practical needs of the military defense [1] and the confluence of theoretical automatics and mathematics, [2] both of which had long and successful development in Ukraine in the past. Theoretical cybernetics began as an attempt at designing, during 1947-1950 of an analog machine for combinatorial modelling and automatic solution of linear equations up to the eighth degree. Such a machine was built at a laboratory of the Electrotechnical Institute of the Ukrainian Academy of Sciences under academician S.O. Lebedev. This lab became then specialized in discrete computer technology, and later, in 1957, was upgraded into the Computer Center, and finally, in 1961, into the Institute of Cybernetics of the Academy. [3]

In 1949-1951, in the Lebedev lab, they built the first electronic-tube-mini-computer "MESM," which is claimed to be not only the first computer in the USSR, but also in the Continental Europe. [4] It was an experimental machine, designed for testing the theories of computation and of building such machines. It served as such for the construction, in 1952, of the first Soviet large-scale "BESM" computer (with 4,000 tubes) at the Moscow Institute of Precision Mechanics of the Academy of Sciences of the USSR. [5] All six series of the "BESM" that were built so far were used mostly for military defense and space research purposes. They were practically hand-made,

71

cumbersome and relatively slow, but served their purpose well. "BESM-6" was considered in the West as comparable with all but the most powerful American machines for a while.[6]

Until the end of 1957 relatively little was conspicuous about cybernetics in Ukraine, perhaps because all its efforts were in the service of the military. More conspicuous were the Computer Centers in Moscow (established in 1955) and Tbilisi, Georgia (1955). Then, in December 1957, a Computer Center of the Ukrainian Academy of Sciences was created with V.M. Hlushkov at the head, and various branches of cybernetics began to bloom in the open. The Computer Center served not only the various institutes of the Academy, but also directed the designing of new computers and trained personnel in its "aspirantura." New machines were developed: an universal computer, "Kiev", in 1959 (its second version was installed at the nuclear research center at Dubna);[7] the specialized medium scale "SESM"; the quasi-analog computer "EMSS-7" which was later produced serially, etc.[8]

The emphasis in designing was put, however, not on data processing computers and peripheral equipment, as was the case in the West, but on computers suitable only for scientific and engineering research and for control of technological processes. "Kiev" was used, for example, for control of steel casting via telegraph. At the time this was a common policy for the whole USSR and also the main reason why the USSR had been lagging so far behind the West in the uses of computers in economic planning and business management.[9]

The first broad decision on development and production of "experimental models" of computers and systems "for automation of production processes" in the USSR was the decree of the USSR Council of Ministers of 5 April 1962.[10] It obligated the Councils of Ministers of the RSFSR, Ukraine, Belorussia, Georgia, and Azerbaidzhan, as well as ten USSR state committees and ministries, to carry out appropriate research, development, and production work during 1962-1965. The USSR State Committee for radio-electronics was made responsible for the quality of electronic computers. A large number of ministries and state committees were instructed to organize laboratories for mathematical description of their production and technological processes. Scientific research institutes for this purpose were established in Perm and Tbilisi, while in Ukraine construction of an electronic computer plant was decreed to be carried out during 1962-1964 in Kyiv. Ukraine was also to produce the magnetic tapes and ferroink for the computers.[11]

However, all these measures still had nothing to do with the application of computers for planning and economic management. Mathematical economics as a science was still struggling for recognition, which came only — and that only partially — as late as 1964, when the Lenin Prize was bestowed upon the three musketeers of mathematical economics, V.S. Nemchinov, L.V. Kantorovich, and V.V. Novozhilov.

In Ukraine theoretical economic cybernetics dates from 1960,[12] when it began to develop at the Academy of Sciences under V.S. Mykhalevych. Its scope had the following three subdivisions: (1) theory of economic systems and models, including econometrics, mathematical programming, and the theory of games: (2) theory of economic information and semiotics, including analysis of decision processes; and (3) theory of economic controls and management.[13] However, publications in the field of economic cybernetics did not come to full bloom until 1965 when the bimonthly journal Kibernetika (in Russian) appeared under the editorship of V.M. Hlushkov. This journal is translated into English in the United States.[14] Since then Kyiv has become the center of the Soviet Union's theoretical cybernetics.

The Institute of Cybernetics of the Academy of Sciences of the Ukrainian SSR was created in 1961. By the end of 1966 it had already 32 departments, grouped into four sectors: (1) theoretical cybernetics and computational methods, headed by V.M Hlushkov, who is also the Institute's director; (2) specialized computer technology and technical cybernetics, headed by G. Ye. Pukhov; (3) economic cybernetics and systems techniques, headed by V.S. Mykhalevych; and (4) biological cybernetics, headed by M.M. Amosov.[15]

72

2. The Scope and Structure of Theoretical Economic Cybernetics

On the basis of research papers that have been published in **Kibernetika** and in other publications of the Ukrainian Academy of Sciences, [16] the scope and structure of economic cybernetics is described in Fig. 1. It compares well with similar data about Western cybernetics, and is certainly at the world level. [17]

Some titles selected from **Kibernetika** more or less at random may also illustrate what really exciting topics have been under discussion. For example: I.I. Yeremin, "On Convex Programming Problems with Inconsistent Constraints"; U.I. Rizhikov, "On a Store Control Problem with Demand Distribution Parameter Unknown"; V.L. Makarov, "One Model of the Concurrent Economic Balance" — with reference to the Arrow-Debreu model; I.A. Krass, I.A. Poletaev, "Cooperation in Leontief's Models"; Pshenichny B.N., "A Dual Method in Extremal Problems"; L.D. Dryuchenko, V.V. Ivanov, V.E. Truten, "Reducing the Long-Term Prediction Problem to the Problems of Linear Integer Programming"; M.S. Nikolsky, "One Non-Linear Pursuit Problem"; N.N. Moiseev, "Hierarchical Structures and Game Theory"; G.Ts. Dzyubenko, "Linear Differential Games with Information Delay"; A.M. Andronov, "Single-Server Bulk-Servicing System with Finite Number of Demands"; Y.A. Zak, "Models and Methods of Constructing Compromised Plans in Problems of Mathematical Programming with Several Objective Functions"; A.I. Yastremsky, "Some Properties of Stochastic Analogue of Leontief's Model"; A.B. Pevnyi, "Speed of Convergence of Some Methods of Finding Minimax and Saddle Points"; V.M. Hlushkov, "On Prognostication Based on Expert Estimates"; F.L. Chernousko, "On Weighting Factors in Expert Estimates"; X.B. Tupchienko, "Optimal Control of the Poisson Process"; V.I. Zhukovsky, "On the Differential Game Theory with Integral Payoff"; V.A. Yemelichev, "Discrete Optimization: Sequential Schemes of Solution"; S.G. Antimonov, "Problems of Optimal Management for Economic Cooperation"; A.A. Chikriy, "On One Class of Linear Discrete Games of Quality"; M.I. Vaitsman, A.G. Shmidt, "The Principle of Maximum for Discrete Economic Processes Over the Infinite Time Interval"; B.G. Mirkin, "On One Axiom of the Mathematical Utility Theory"; Yu. M. Yermolyev, V.P. Gulenko, "The Finite Difference Method in Optimal Control Problems"; D.I. Golenko, N.A. Levin, "Some Questions of Optimization of Many-Topic Investigations in Network PERT and Control PERT with Reference to Several Resources"; V.S. Mykhalevych, "The Method of Sequential Analysis of Variants for Determination of Optimal Solutions"; V.V. Shkurba, "Computational Schemes for Solving Scheduling Theory Problems"; etc., etc.

In fact it is difficult to find a topic which has been discussed in the world mathematical economics which has not been at least touched upon by the Ukrainian economic cyberneticists. [18] However, one detrimental thing is clearly noticeable: the work of economic cybernetics has not been practice-oriented. It has been highly abstract, quite remote from practical application in the everyday business of a computerized economy. The probable reason is, of course, that that economy has not been computerized yet. Moreover, as yet they seem not to have found a system of evaluation of the usefullness of their own research work. [19]

II. THE STATE OF COMPUTER TECHNOLOGY

1. Designing of the machines

Computers are classified into "generations" as follows: the first generation used vacuum tubes; the second used transistors; third relies on miniature integrated circuitry; and the fourth uses pipe-line processing.

The second generation of computers was introduced in the USSR when in 1961 the Institute of Cybernetics of the Ukrainian Academy built the first fully transistorized machine called "Dnipro." [20] In the United States the second generation came into being in 1958. Since 1962 the "Dnipro" has been produced serially and in quantities which presumably permitted the USSR to outproduce "some capitalist countries" [21] at least for a while. The "Dnipro" has been used mainly to control technological and production processes in metallurgy, shipbuilding and chemical industries. [22] The "Dnipro" is a medium-size computer.

Next in the second generation came two Institute of Cybernetics' mini-computers called "Promin" (1962) and "Mir" (1964). [23] They are serially produced at the second Ukrainian computer plant at Severodonetsk, and are used in engineering designing work. [24] These two computers were the only ones in the whole USSR awarded the sign of state standard (GOST) as of January 1, 1972. [25] The GOST is awarded only to such products which are adjudged to be on the world technological level. This means that all other Soviet computers, by recognition of Soviet authorities, were not up to the world standards by that date.

Ivan Berenyi has estimated that by 1970, in the USSR and Eastern Europe fewer than 5 percent were computers of the third generation, whereas some 35 to 38 percent were still the first-generation machines, the rest being of the second generation. In the U.S. and Western Europe at the same time, 60 to 80 percent of the computers belonged to the third generation, with the remainder being of the second generation. [26] Berenyi's Soviet data may have been somewhat overstated, especially in view of the above-mentioned GOST qualifications. The 5 percent third-generation computers were probably imported into the USSR, rather than produced there, because one of the first calls for the development of the third-generation computers stems from August 1971, [27] and the first Soviet-produced third-generation computers were exhibited in Moscow only in May 1973. [28]

An American estimate of 1966 stated that "the USSR lags about five years behind the United States in the use of computers for data processing." [29] This was said at the time of the second-generation computers. Our data quoted above indicate that (not in data processing, but in the technological process control) the gap was actually only three years. Later, however, that gap substantially increased, as the switch was made (in the West) to the third generation. Today's estimate by R.C. Seamans, Jr., President of the U.S. National Academy of Engineering, is that the USSR has computers "still not as advanced as the equipment that we were using 10 years ago." [30] Fourth-generation computerization is now in full swing in the United States and Western Europe, whereas in the USSR it is still in the design stage. [31]

The main reason the USSR has bogged down at the switch to the third generation seems not to have been the lack of knowledge of integrated circuitry. According to Berenyi, between 1969 and 1972 the USSR placed order for importation of 15 third-generation computers from the United Kingdom, France, Italy, and West Germany. [32] Presumably, the orders were filled. Also, the I.B.M. Trade Corporation, after first refusing the Soviet order for the 360 / 40 model, agreed to sell it the 360 / 50 model. [33] Lately also, the Monsanto Company of the U.S., [34] the Control Data Corporation, [35] and the Sperry-Rand Corporation [36] entered into agreements with the USSR to supply it with advanced computer technology. It may be that the Western export controls only slowed down somewhat the acquisition of third-generation technology by the Soviet Union.

The main reason for Soviet slowness seems to have been the different directions that the development and application of the second and third-generation computers took from the beginning in the USSR and in the West. In the West, particularly the United States, huge demand for the data processing computers has arisen in the economy. Computers came to be applied in almost every phase of business activity from market research to accounting and record-keeping. There was no such demand in the USSR, where computers were mainly used in scientific and engineering research and for control of production processes. This is particularly evident from the fact that Soviet computers usually lacked high operation speeds, large internal and external memory systems, input-output peripheral equipment, and similar things which characterize data processing computers and not computers of other purposes. [37] The USSR has also had little experience in the linking of computer systems and in telecommunications. [38]

74

Fig. 1.   The Types of Research Done by Economic Cybernetics

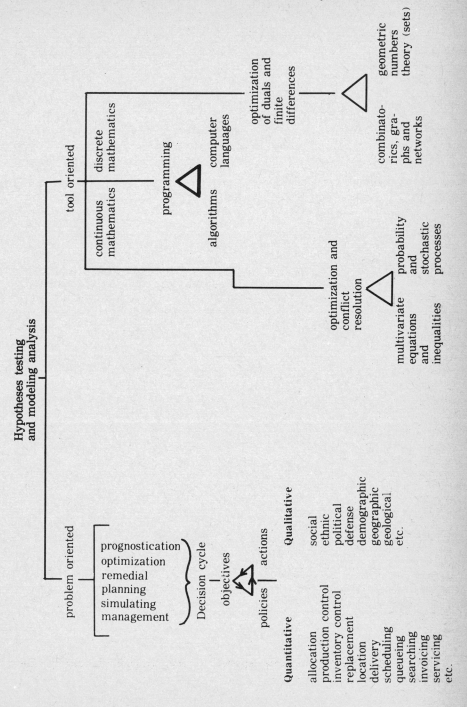

75

2. Production and installation

Soviet statistics on production and installation of computers undoubtedly belong to the category of "state secrets." They have been officially divulged in a very confusing aggregate form, first as the total ruble production figures of "automation instruments, computing technology and spare parts" ('**pribory, sredstva avtomatizatsii i vychislitel'noy tekhniki**'), and recently as those of the "means of computing technology and spare parts" ('**sredstva vychislitel'noy tekhniki**'). But what is "computing technology" ('**vychislitel'naya tekhnika**')? According to one authoritative source, it includes not only computers, but also the calculators, adding machines, logarithmic rules, and abacuses! [39] Whether the statistical definition of "computing technology" is the same is not known, but it is not excludable, because according to one official statistical handbook "computing technology" was being produced in the USSR in 1940. [40]

The latest figures on production of "computing technology and spare parts" in the USSR and the RSFSR (in million rubles of 1967 prices) has been divulged as follows: [41]

	USSR	RSFSR
1967	260.8	n.d.
1970	709.7	372.0
1971	879.4	459.0
1972	1213.5	633.0

This means that between 1967 and 1972 production of "computing technology" grew in the USSR at an annual rate of 36 percent! This is quite an impressive showing, especially if one takes into account the American estimate that between 1958 and 1965 that rate of growth was only 29.3 percent, as compared to 21.3 percent at the same time for the United States. [42]

For the Ukrainian SSR official production figures for the "computing technology and spare parts" (apart from "instruments of automation") have been divulged only for 1972 and 1973. The report on the fulfillment of the 1973 plan stated that the output in 1973 was 232 million rubles and that this was 122 percent of 1972. [43] This is, however, probably not in the 1967, but in the 1972 prices, which makes the figures not comparable with those of the USSR and the RSFSR. [44]

Together with the "instruments of automation," production of "computing technology and spare parts" was distributed in 1971 as follows: [45]

	Million rubles	Percent of the USSR
USSR	3,487	100.0
RSFSR	2,089	59.9
Ukraine	717	20.6
Belorussia	318	9.1
Armenia	66	1.9

This territorial distribution probably reflects production of computers in the republics today, except that the share of the RSFSR, as the figures quoted above show, may be smaller — only about 52 percent of the USSR (in 1967 prices).

Can the ruble production figures of "computing technology and spare parts" be somehow translated into absolute numbers of computers produced? An experiment in this can be made with the help of the official figures on the exports of "electronic computers and parts". It has been reported that in 1968 the USSR exported 16 complete computers at an average price of 462,375 rubles apiece; 46 and in 1969 — 28 computers at 499,965 rubles apiece. [47] Assuming that these export prices were not too different from the constant 1967 prices, by dividing the ruble production figures by these average prices, we obtain the following approximate figures on production of some "average" computers in the USSR:

1967	542
1970	1,475
1971	1,828
1972	2,522

It is also known that the USSR imported during 1970, 1971, and 1972, 26, 32, and 22 complete computers respectively.[48] Assuming an autarkic foreign trade policy with regards to computers especially, and that foreign trade amounted to from 1 to 5 percent of production at home, the above foreign trade data suggest that the USSR's production level between 1968 and 1972 was about 550 — 2,750 computers a year. This finding seems to square with the above. (Ukraine's part in the USSR's production should be about twenty percent).

These calculations may be compared with other Western estimates of Soviet production of computers. Without showing how the figures were arrived at, they assumed production level for the end of the 1960's to be around 1,000 computers a year, [49] and for the year 1970 — 2,000. [50]

The installed park of computers in the USSR was estimated to be 5,500 as of January 1970 [51] and 6,000 as of 1970, [52] of which 3,500 were operating in the economy. [53] It is also not known how these figures were arrived at. Computers "in the economy" presumably exclude not only those used by the military, but also those used in scientific establishments. The number of military computers is probably not known at all, and is excluded altogether.

On the latter assumption, these figures can be cross-checked against the following data. Ye. Sokolsky, the chief of administration of computer projects at the Central Statistical Administration of the Ukrainian SSR reported that "close to 800 various computers were used in the national economy" of the Ukrainian Republic in January 1972. [54] Assuming that this is 19 to 20 percent of the whole USSR (for example, the number of employees in planning and record-keeping in Ukraine in the 1970 census was 19.3 percent of the USSR [55]), the total computer population in the whole Soviet Union should have been 4,000 — 4,210 on the same date. Thus Western estimate of the number of Soviet computers "in the economy" seems to be verified.

It may also be worth noting that at the time of the national debate, in 1966, over the installation of the proposed network of computer centers in the Central Statistical Administration of the USSR (of which more below), Academician A. Dorodnitsyn had estimated that more than 4,000 medium to large-size computers would be required to put such a network to work.[56] The goal was 1970 and skepticism was expressed whether this would be possible to achieve. [57] It seems now that by 1972 they might have achieved this goal, but by small-size computers. The number of large-size computers still seems to be small because, according to Soviet Ukrainian press, their number in the economy of the Republic at the beginning of 1969 was only 84. [58]

To estimate the relative level of development of computerization of the Soviet economy, it is necessary to compare Soviet park of computers with those of other countries. Computer statistics in the United States and in the United Kingdom are imprecise because there are too many computers; the markets for mini-computers, especially, are presently flooded. In 1970 it was estimated that there were 70,000 computers in operation in the United States, with 18,000 additionally installed per year. [59] In the United Kingdom in 1972 there were estimated 8,000 computers in operation, specifically excluding small computers. [60] But other countries keep more exact statistics, including mini-computers. Assuming that, in 1972, the USSR had 4,000 of them in its economy, the Ukraine 800, the following table illustrates their relative standing.[61] On the per capita basis the table makes it obvious that the Soviet Union still ranks among the underdeveloped economies with regards to computerization — on the level with Brazil and Mexico. Even Spain and Yugoslavia are ahead of it, and by much.

	Total number of computers in the economy	Number of computers per one million of the population
West Germany	46,078	743
France	16,348	327
Japan	12,809	121
Netherlands	5,219	389
Italy	4,620	85
USSR	4,000	16
Spain	3,700	107
Switzerland	2,500	397
Sweden	2,020	245
Australia	1,594	123
Brazil	1,219	13
Yugoslavia	1,054	51
UKRAINE	800	17
Mexico	694	14
Israel	293	93

These relate explicitly to the uses of computers in the economy. If, however, one objected that some of the computers in the USSR for scientific research cannot be clearly distinguished from their uses in the economy, still nothing would change significantly in these conclusions, even if the number of Soviet computers were doubled.

3. The Uses of Computers

The same Ye. Sokolsky who revealed that there were 800 computers installed in the Ukrainian economy in 1972, said about their utilization the following: "Theoretically, the computer can and should run 20 hours per day, excluding preventive maintenance. Yet the loading of all computers which were used in the republic was on the average 11.6 hours per day,"[62] that is, only 58 percent of capacity! He attributed this fact to the sloppy work of unskilled programmers, insufficient demand for computer time, and lack of general knowledge of what computers can do on the part of their users. In 1971, according to his survey, in the computer centers of various ministries and departments of the Republic alone, "15,800 hours of computer time were lost owing to the lack of work."[63]

In another piece of official criticism it has been pointed out that computers are used presently only as bookkeeping and accounting machines, and not for an analysis of operations, prognostication, or choice among alternative decisions. As a result of lack of know-how, the printouts are used excessively and customers get 10-20 times more paper back from the machine than if the machine were not used at all.[64]

Of course, these deficiences in the use of computers are not unknown in the West: they also plague Western computer centers and Western users of computers, though, undoubtedly, the idleness of the computers is not as large as 42 percent here. Western computer centers would go bankrupt with such idleness.

However, such a widespread lack of know-how in the uses of computers as is indicated in the USSR confirms that conclusion reached earlier in this paper, viz., that the theoretical cybernetics, despite its high quality, has not been practice-oriented. Training of Soviet computer programmers is also extremely deficient.

Sokolsky says that out of nearly 10,000 people in Ukraine who service computer centers, only a little more than 4,000 have a higher education. [65] Moreover, many Soviet computers have been designed in such a manner that they cannot accept instructions in automatic programming languages, and computers have not been provided with the input-output equipment needed for the use of automatic languages. Hence, programmers have to prepare instructions in numerical form, and this is redundant and time-consuming process.

For the first time in October 1969 **Pravda** reported that courses to train specialists in applied cybernetics and computational techniques were being set up at Soviet higher and technical schools. [66] In 1971 it reported that engineering schools in Ukraine included such courses into their programs. [67]

III THE STRUGGLE FOR COMPUTERIZATION OF THE ECONOMY

1. The Economic Reform and the Unified System of Statistical Computer Centers

As every other major decision in the Soviet economy, the decision to begin computerization had to pass through a process of protracted political struggle, in which its proponents had to overcome stiff resistance from the opponents. The struggle for computerization began with the end of, and failure of, Khrushchev's decentralization reforms. Already in 1962, for example, an author reported a successful experiment at the Computer Center of the State Economic Council of the USSR (Gosekonomsovet) to simulate on computers the complete planning and management of a large machinebuilding factory; he declared unequivocally that "that action proves the possibility of **centralized** determination of productive capacities in industry." [68]

Early in the debate over the preparation of the 1966 economic reform, V. M. Hlushkov of the Ukrainian Institute of Cybernetics was reported to have come to the conclusion that "the preservation of the existing system of economic planning and management until 1980 will require the employment of the entire adult population . . . in the sphere of planning and management. And since that is impossible, it is necessary to limit the surging information about the national economy." [69] Hlushkov proposed the speedy establishment of a system of statistical computer centers all over the economy. His proposal did not emphasize the need for centralization in the computerized planning and management of the whole economy of the Soviet Union, even though he imagined the system to be based on the present lines of economic administration, viz., union, ministries, republics, etc. But Hlushkov clearly advocated the reduction in information flows, and thus his proposed system was designed to fit into the proposed economic reform, advocated by Kosygin, which would reduce the number of centrally determined targets in the plans and would raise the role of profit and of bonuses in the fulfillment of the plans. [70]

On the eve of the adoption of the 1966 economic reform the ranks of the economic cyberneticists and mathematicians were divided. V. Hlushkov and N. Fedorenko led those who advocated the establishment of the network of computer centers along the lines of the present economic administration, which combined both elements, centralization and decentralization. V. F. Pugachev led those who proposed increased centralization, with planned targets assigned for all goods to every enterprise. At the same time, the cyberneticists and mathematical economists were strongly opposed by a powerful group of conservative economists with some knowledge of mathematics (A. Boyarskiy, A. Kats et al.), who opposed introduction of mathematical techniques into planning and management altogether and advocated the preservation of the existing system. The theoretical lines in this debate have been aptly discussed in the West,[71] except that political consequences of this debate were not noted.

There is, however, strong evidence that some sort of political struggle took place around these issues just before and at the XXIII CPSU Congress. On 20 February 1966 **Pravda** published the draft of the CC CPSU directives on the 1966-1970 Five-Year

Plan, and there was nothing in it about the introduction of computers into the economy. On 6 March 1966, however, the CC CPSU and the USSR Council of Ministers adopted the decree concerning the establishment of the unified system of computer centers, (it is discussed below). Then on 8 April 1966, the XXIII CPSU Congress adopted its final directives on the five-year plan. In them nothing was said about the unified system of computer centers, but a paragraph was inserted (as compared to the Pravda's text of the draft), which called for "broad utilization of electronic computers in planning of the national economy and in management of production, transportation, commerce and scientific research."[72]

Since this Congress adopted the 1966 economic reform and since it did not mention the unified system, nor put out any targets for its establishment, it seems plausible to conclude that there was opposition to the unified system at the Congress, coming, perhaps, from the side of economic reformers who might have feared that the unified system would result in overcentralization of planning and management. From the stenographic report of the Congress, if it is complete, it also comes out that the proponents of computerization were not allowed to address the Congress.

Yet the time of the Congress V. N. Starovskiy, chief of the Central Statistical Administration, published a report in the press explaining the decree on the establishment of the unified system of statistical computing centers.[73] In it he announced that by 1970, within the existing network of the state statistical administration, computer centers and maching calculating stations would be established in all Union Republics, krais and oblasts as well as more than 650 machine calculating stations in administrative rayons and cities. Even though this network had as its purpose mechanization of statistical reporting, rather than of planning and management, its structure implied a step towards victory for the Hlushkov-Fedorenko concept, since the system was to be territorial, and not along the ministerial lines as proposed by Pugachev and others. Of course, this was not yet supposed to be a fully computerized system as foreseen by Hlushkov — obviously because there were not enough computers. But the skeleton of the possible future system was already laid down.

But the fact that the Party Congress did not support the new network explicitly might have been ominous. The decree establishing the system, as it was published later,[74] omitted mentioning the 650 target figure for the year 1970, though it placed heavy emphasis on the fact that the system was to include computerized centers. There is some evidence, however, that the system — although fully established by now — was not completed exactly on target.

2. The Inter-Congress Period of Flux

The period between the XXIII and XXIV CPSU Congresses, 1966-1971, was characterized by the piecemeal progress of economic reform, when one industry after another was decreed to be transferred to the reform basis. At the same time, computerization of the economy also proceeded in piecemeal fashion. There were special decrees directing computerization of individual ministries, such as that of the metallurgical plants of the Ministries of Ferrous and Non-Ferrous Metallurgy.[75] But not all such decrees were made public. The Ministry of Instruments, Means of Automation and Management Systems was made responsible for coordination of production and installation of computers, and in 1970 it acquired for this purpose its first five-year plan.[76] In 1971 there was also an interesting decree providing for contractual agreements among ministries and their enterprises about the transfer of new technology among them,[77] computers presumably included. This decree provided for agreements in prices, delivery dates, etc. It appears from it that various customers could now order new technology from producers in accordance with their own decisions. If so, this explains the piecemeal character of the computerization that was going on.

On 29 August 1969, the Council of Ministers of the USSR selected the city of Leningrad and the Leningrad oblast for the establishment of the first experimental "automatic management system" (Russian abbreviation: ASU) of industry, agriculture, and municipal economy.[78] All major industrial enterprises were to establish "interconnected computing centers" (**kustovye vychislitel'nye tsentry**) by the end of 1972. Ten state farms were to have a computer center in the city of Pushkin. The municipal economy of Leningrad was to be computerized as a unit. Scientific supervision over the establishment of the ASU was vested in the Leningrad branch of the USSR Academy of Sciences. Similar experimental ASUs were established also in other parts of the country, though without publicity.

In Ukraine, by 1972, more than 100 such automatic management systems and subsystems were in operation.[79] In 1969, B. Paton, president of the Ukrainian Academy of Sciences, announced plans for the creation of an Institute of Economic Cybernetics within the Economics Division of the Academy.[80] Its functions would have been to create, in industries and individual enterprises, complex automatic system for management of production, work, and administration, and to work out methods of optimum development of enterprises. This announcement, however, was premature: for some reason the Institute was not established. Perhaps it was in connection with this failure that P. Shelest, the CP of Ukraine's first secretary at the time, while discussing scientific management in **Pravda**, called for "taking better care of local peculiarities" in the development of automatic systems of management.[81]

This reference to local peculiarities was quite unusual, and clearly implied some sort of struggle between Ukraine and Moscow even in this area. Further light on the political nature of this struggle was recently thrown by a demand for the establishment, within the system of "ASU-science," of a separate Ukrainian Geological Information and Computer Center. The author of this demand, V. Sidorov,[82] explained that there were two wings in the approach to the "ASUscience": those who advocated a "regional" approach and those whom he called "fundamentalists." Whoever they are, they are not "regionalists" and are therefore, probably, centralizers. The geological computer center has not yet been established.

3. Decisions of the XXIV Party Congress

By the time the 24th CPSU Congress convened on 30 March — 9 April, 1971, it became clear that the devotees of computerization of the economy had won a decisive victory over their opponents. The Congress came out fully in favor of computerization. The only problem remaining now was how and when.

In his report to the Congress, in connection with the discussion of planning, Brezhnev spoke out in favor of the methods of "economico-mathematical model-building" and "systemic analysis." These methods should be used "to speed up creation of the ('otraslevye') systems of automatic management ('ASU') while keeping in mind that, eventually, we must create a state-wide ('ob-shchegosudarstvennuyu') automatic system for collection and analysis of information." For this, said Brezhnev, we need not only "appropriate technology" but also "skilled personnel."[83]

By the "eventually" he probably meant the year 1980. Of greatest significance, however, was his reference to "branch" ASUs' the territorial remained unmentioned. Also his reference to a "state-wide" system left the republics unmentioned. All this probably means that, at the moment, centralized concepts of computerization, like that of Pugachev, have won the upper hand over the concept of Hlushkov-Fedorenko. But this may only reflect Brezhnev's personal preferences for the time being — however significant they are, no doubt.

In his report to the Congress on the 1971-1975 five-year plan, Kosygin added the following: "Automatic management systems ('ASU') are now successfully used in a number of ministries and in many enterprises. Computer centers have been established at the Gosplan, Gossnab, Central Statistical Administration and a number of other administrations ('vedomstv'). During the next five years it has been proposed to make operational not less than 1,600 automatic systems of management of enterprises and organizations in industry, agriculture, communications, trade, and transportation.''[84]

From the nuances of Kosygin's speech and from his emphasis on computerization of the enterprises, he appeared to be more pragmatic than Brezhnev; or at least he spoke of the short run, rather than the "eventual future". In his speech to the Congress M. V. Keldysh, the president of the USSR Academy of Sciences, was more empirical than anyone else. He reminded his audience that "we must multiply our efforts to develop more advanced equipment" than was presently available; that "we must bring about" that the "machines are produced in centralized complexes, including the electronic processors, advanced auxiliary equipment, and with mathematical supplies" ' he also called for "radical acceleration of the growth of the means of communication." [85] In other words, he made all this a pre-condition for the success of the development of computerized management.

The 24th Congress resolved in its directives for the 1971-1975 five-year plan the following: [86] (1) to continue developing theoretical and applied cybernetics for the use in the economy; (2) to achieve production of all computers, including mini-computers and means of communication, and that in complete systems, including all the in-put and out-put equipment and standard programs; (3) increase production of the "means of computing technology" 2.4 times, including that of computers 2.6 times; (4) achieve serial production of "a new complex of electronic computers based on integrated schemes" 9 i.e., third generation); (5) create a complex of technical means of automatization of registration, collection, storage, and transmission of information; and (6) new technical means for a unified automatic communications network on a nation-wide basis.

The above-mentioned means of "computing technology" obviously include not only computers but also calculators, adding machines, accounting and bookkeeping machines, etc. In the actual text of the five-year plan that was published later, [87] the planned growth of production of the "means of computing technology" was increased from 2.4 to 2.8 times, while the production figure for computers remained the same — 2.6 times.

The plan also foresees "increased application of economico-mathematical methods and contemporary computer technology" in planning, [88] although in the introduction to the plan's text it is admitted that, for this plan, computers were used in two cases only: in the calculation of capital investment material balances (in money terms) and in the fuel-energy balance calculations. [89]

IV.   THE AUTOMATIZATION OF PLANNING AND MANAGEMENT

1.   The Existing System of Economic Controls

Figure 2 represent a schematic rendering of the present system of controls over Soviet industrial enterprises. It incorporates the results of the latest extension of the economic reform to the ministerial level: abolition of main administration (glavki) of the ministries and the consolidation and merger of small and medium enterprises into new organizations — combines (kombinaty) and amalgamations (ob'yedineniya). Vertically in Figure 2 are represented the so-called branch controls. The maze is as amazing as always. There are five to six lines of vertical subordination alone, which necessitates tremendous paper work and makes very slow flow of information inevitable.

It is against this kind of cumbersome system that the cybernetic revolution is potentially directed. The computerization of the economic controls has been finally recognized by Soviet leaders for two main reasons. Firstly, because of the increasing difficulty of coping with the flood of information that accompanies economic growth; secondly, because of the growing conviction that mathematical methods and tools can be highly useful in economic controls.

2. ASU - Automatic Systems of Management

An ASU consists of (a) systematic use of mathematical methods and standardized procedures, (b) automatic machines and computing technology, and (c) decision-making with their aid at different levels of controls over the economy.[90] As Kosygin mentioned at the 24th Party Congress, ASUs are used now in a number of ministries and many enterprises, but individually in a disjointed manner. He also mentioned that computer centers exist in all upper echelons of the Gosplan, Bossnab, and the CSA, presumably, down to the Republic level. Curiously, he failed to mention the existence of ASUS in the financial sector — at the banks and the Ministry of Finance — and it seems that, indeed, in contrast to the situation in the West, this sector is least computerized of all in the Soviet Union, except, perhaps, agriculture.

The 1,600 ASUs that are planned to be operational in the USSR by 1975 will still be largely disjointed. It is only by 1980, according to Brezhnev, that a GASU — State Automatic System of Management — will unify all the ASUs into something like one single system. This unification will presumably be achieved through the use of large third and fourth-generation computers through a system of time-sharing, which makes it possible for many individual ASUs in remote locations to use the same huge machine simultaneously via terminals and telephone or telegraph lines. Various dispersed computers and data banks will also be linked together, so that widely separated installations could share data. Information will thus become widely accessible, and with it controls over knowledge and decision-making.

The term "automatic" or "automatized" may appear somewhat confusing. It does **not** mean that the systems will run as one single machine with operations reduced to pushing buttons. Not at all! All decisions at all levels will still be made by men, no doubt. It is only the **procedures** for decision-making that will be, it is hoped, "automatized," that is, systematized and standardized, and controlled by computers. "controlled" implies checking and rechecking for correctness of decisions for their accord with standard procedures. As a result, human decisions will, it is hoped, become more accurate, more precise, more rational, and quicker.

At least in the initial stages of implementation, ASUs do not make relations within the existing systems of decision-making easier. On the contrary, such relations become more complicated.[91] Nevertheless, studies show that the use of ASUs pays. At a typical industrial enterprise in Ukraine a study has found that the use of ASU resulted in the following: 7-10 percent increase in production due to optimal planning; 15-20 percent reduction of inventories; 5-8 percent reduction in the time of the circulation of variable capital; and 10-15 percent reduction in defective output and the cost of fines therefrom. In general, it is asserted that investment into the ASU is 2-3 times more effective than into any otherpart of the enterprise.[92]

3. ASPR — Automatic System of Calculations of the Plan

The ASU for the purposes of planning has been dubbed ASPR, or "Avtomatizirovannaya Sistema Planovykh Raschetov" (Automatized system of planning calculations). In the system of management of the economy it will cap the ASUs. The work on the ASPR began in 1966, and by May, 1972, the first stage of the work was finished. But to finish the whole system, still "several years" and the third generation of computers were still required.[93]

The work on the ASPR has been directed by the Computer Center of the Gosplan of the USSR, with more than one hundred scientific institutions participating.[94] What has been accomplished so far is described as a standardized system of operations consisting of three stages: (1) manual calculation of plan's target with the help of desk calculators, which is checked for errors twice; (2) feeding these calculations into automatic printing calculators, which permit variation of different versions of the plan; and (3) calculation and documentation on printing calculators of several alternative versions of the final plan, ready for choice and decision-making.[95] This is then the standard procedure in the Gosplan of the USSR and the republics. As is evident, at this first stage of the ASPR computers are not used — obviously because they are not available yet for such a general use.

In its ultimate form "the ASPR will function on the basis of the mutually interconnected **models of optimal planning** of the socialist national economy," a complex of which "must be coordinated for all classes of tasks of national economic planning and secured by the appropriate mechanism of the realization of plans.." "..The basic, skeletal economico-mathematical model of the ASPR in all kinds of plans and at all levels and stages of national-economic planning must be the **intersectoral balance**, in its various modifications and cross-sections, including territorial and financial." [96]

The underlined points speak for themselves. The "appropriate mechanism for the realization of plans" is still a big question mark in the ASPR: should the "optimal plans" be enforced as before, or should a system of economic incentives be developed to guide the economy towards their realization? The inclusion of the territorial and financial plans is an admission of weaknesses that still plague the ASPR. The quoted editorial of the **Planovoe Khoziaystvo** admits, among other things, that "lately, the circle of the theoretical as well as applied studies for the creation of models of territorial planning has narrowed, which is due, obviously, to the underestimation of its significance." [97] Obviously, viz., "**ochevidno**," indeed.

4. Operational Planning Models Today

Soviet planners have already acquired considerable experience with relatively large but **ex post** inter-sectoral and inter-branch input-output models both on the USSR level [98] and specifically in Ukraine.[99] **Ex ante** operational planning projections are more difficult to develop, and they are still in the nascent state. But it is on this **ex ante** intersectoral input-output models that the whole ASPR system will rest.

According to the project, [100] the ASPR system will consist of more than 800 subsystems and "hundreds of millions" of indices.* There will be more than 300 branch subsystems of the USSR Gosplan and of the Gosplans of the union republics. At the core there will be 40 sectoral subsystems of the Gosplan of the USSR. The implementation of the ASPR is to begin in 1977..[101]

By 1972, however, only a dynamic 18-branch inter-sectoral model was operational, which was used in drawing up the Ninth (1971-1975) Five-Year Plan of the USSR.[102] For the Ukrainian Five-Year Plan an 11-variable model was used, based on the 1959-1968 statistical returns and extrapolated to 1975.[103] No such **ex ante** models were reported for other republics so far. However, in the ASPR project, the Ukrainian and Lithuanian Republics were designated as responsible for developing the ASPR systems for the union republics: Ukraine with the **oblast** sub-divisions and Lithuania without them.[104] The Lithuanian mathematical economists have already published their model. [105] At the core of the model they have used simulation of a plan.

V. PROBLEMS IN REPUBLIC-LEVEL PLANNING

1. The Legacy of the 1966 Economic Reform

After Khrushchev's 1957-1964 territorial management system was abandoned and the centralized ministerial rule was restored, republican economies were not completely subordinated to Moscow's direct rule comparable to Stalin's days. Because of the growth of these economies, such a complete subordination was no longer possible.

After the 1966 reform industries located in the territory of the Ukrainian republic,

---

*Just for laughs the opposition of a "Lysenko" of Soviet mathematical economics, A. Boyarskiy, may be noted. He wrote that "remaining within rational framework, one cannot speak of **millions** of indices" ..because such computers still don't exist. **Planovoe Khoziaystvo**, No. 11, November 1973, p. 30. But if they don't exist, they will! There is no limit to the size of the computers, in principle.

for example, were subordinated to more than 100 separate ministries and departments, but Union subordination accounted for only slightly more than one quarter of all the industries. The share of Union enterprises in the gross industrial output of the republic in 1967 was 30.5 percent, the share in capital investments — about 21 percent. [106] Hence, the rest of the Ukrainian economy was to be directly planned by the Gosplan in Kyiv. The same was also the case in other republics.

However, very numerous complaints indicate that the republic-level planning was grossly inhibited by the dearth of information coming from the Union organizations. A member of the Ukrainian Gosplan stated bluntly, for example, that because Union organizations do not furnish data to the Ukrainian Gosplan on time, nor in full scope, efficient and rational planning at the republic level is made thus practially impossible. [107] Practically the same was stated by a member of the RSFSR Gosplan, too. [108] Recently a member of the Uzbek Gosplan suggested that the relations between republic Gosplans and the Union organizations be placed on legal footing: they should be mutually obliged by law to furnish each other all the necessary data. [109]

The issues are clearly political, however. The bias against republican planning is embedded even in the official instructions from the Union Gosplan on how to prepare the plans. In principal, the structure of the republican plans is identical with the All-Union plans (except for the defense sector), but the said instructions suggest that all territorial plans should be first of all five-year plans, rather than annual, which really matter most. [110] As a result it seems certain that the republican annual plans today are second-hand documents, patched up from bits and pieces of information, and are definitely not so balanced as they should be.

2. The New Vertical Integration of Industries

New complications in republic-level planning have arisen recently from the decision of the Party and Government to eliminate, during 1973-1975, the multi-tier structure of the management of branches of industry, and to establish, instead of the ministerial departments ('glavki'), industrial amalgamations ('ob'yedineniya') and combines ('kombinaty'). [111] Instead of the multi-tier structure, two and three-tier structure has been introduced (see Fig. 2) through merger of small and medium-scale enterprises into large amalgamations and combines.

The elimination of the ministerial departments, on one hand, and of the small, backward enterprises, on the other, is undoubtedly economically justified. However, there is also a strong element of centralization embedded in this reform. It is evident from the fact that, as an editorial in the KOMMUNIST points out, amalgamations and combines should not be limited in their organization by the presently existing boundaries of the territorial administrative units. [112] In other words, All-Union amalgamations can cross the boundaries of the republics and be supra-republican; combines can cross the boundaries of the **oblasts**, etc. The impression is that the editorial actively advocates such centralization, which would diminish the prerogatives of the local organs of government. And this is certainly not the only example of the centralizational bias in the Brezhnev administration.

3. Computerization and Centralization of Economic Administration

The question that arises at this juncture is whether or not computerization leads to more centralization in economic controls, rather than to less.

In its nature, cybernetics is the science of **optimal controls**. Control necessarily means some sort of a hierarchical structure, triangular with a peak point. But optimal means minimax, or maximin — a sort of average among the extremes, any movement from which will distort the equilibrium. Hence, ideally, cybernetics should not be conducive to over centralization; neither should it be conducive to excessive decentralization of controls. It should produce an optimal relationship between the centralized and decentralized controls through an appropriate disaggregation of aggregate decisions.

In practice, however, at the start of the introduction of computers, the trend is towards centralization. This conclusion derives not from the Soviet Union, but from the West. In the local governments of the United Kingdom the use of computers began spontaneously, but then had to be nationally centralized for better efficiency.[113] The same trend towards centralization in local governments' use of computers was noted in the the United States.[114] In the non-governmental structures, such as the corporation and other business enterprises, and in scientific organizations, the trend is the same.

That this trend has been induced by computer technology, there is no doubt. The third-generation computers — not to speak of the fourth — made time-sharing and pipe-lining economically more efficient than the use of disjointed, "independent" computers. Whether there was also an admixture of supra-local-government and corporate politics is also a plausable question. Wider and more precise information that comes with the linked computers means better knowledge, and an appetite for better knowledge, at the center.

Such was the experience with the initial stage of computerization in the West, and this experience is probably even more valid for the Soviet Union. But this is, probably, a temporary experience. With more computers available, the optimal satiation point for information hunger may be reached at the center, and decentralization may follow as with the law of diminishing returns. After all, not all information can fit into given computers. When information will be generated by computers there may be too much of it, and the computer channels will be glutted. Selection will become necessary, and, therefore, disaggregation and decentralization.

As an American study of modern trends in the corporate management concludes:[115]

It is easy to think of examples where authority now dispersed might be efficiently reconcentrated at the top with the aid of computers. But such reconcentration is not the main trend in organization today. Since the new information technology began coming into use in the Fifties, the trend toward decentralization has probably been accelerated, indicating that there were better reasons for decentralization than the lack of instant information at headquarters. Computers can be used to reinforce either a centralizing policy or its opposite; the probability increases that decentralization will in the coming decades be carried to lengths unheard of ten years ago.

VI. SOME CONCLUSIONS FOR THE THEORY OF ECONOMIC SYSTEMS

1. Computers and the Evolution of Capitalism

Writing in 1858, Kark Marx foresaw that the ultimate stage of Capitalism will be its automation. Capital, he said.[116]

passes through different metamorphoses, whose culmination is the machine, or rather, an automatic system of machinery (system of machinery: the automatic one is merely its most complete, most adequate form, and alone transforms machinery into a system), set in motion by an automation, a moving power that moves itself; this automation consisting of numerous mechanical and intellectual organs, so that the workers themselves are cast merely as its conscious linkages.

At this stage, science and knowledge "become a direct force of production."[117] The present computer revolution seems to fall well within this prediction. But, as Marx foresaw, Capitalism does not change its essential nature because of automation. Neither does it in reality. However, for lack of imagination or whatever, some Soviet writers assume that Capitalism cannot fully digest the computer:[118]

Lately, in a number of capitalist countries the signs have appeared that computers do not justify themselves any longer, in connection with which it is possible that their rate of production will slow down. The reason is that the organization of the flows of information with the help of computers inside corporations has achieved the maximum point, while to optimize the flows of information among corporations, at the level of industry and of the whole national economy, is impossible because of private property and competition.

The authors evidently do not know, and cannot imagine, that a computer center can be established as a company on an industry-wide or inter-industry level, and that its machine time could be shared among and leased to different customers simultaneously. Yet this is precisely what is happening now with the third and fourth-generation computers!

Moreover, big banks offer increasing amounts of computerized services to their nation-wide customers, and even on an international level. [119] Under these systems point-of-sales transfers of funds are made directly between bank computers from one customer's account to another without the use of cash or cheques. The EFTSs also make possible automated payroll deposits and withdrawals, preauthorized bill payments, and descriptive billing on the clearing-house operations principle. This is almost the "cashless society" that Marx also foresaw as possible. Yet it remains Capitalism as long as it is based on private property.

2. Computers, Markets, and Socialism

When Oskar Lange developed his theory of Market Socialism in the running polemics against Hayek and Robbins thirty-five years ago, computers did not exist. Yet Lange lived long enough to see the advent of computers and to write a piece of reconciliation with them. [120] According to him, computers beat the market on many counts, such as speed of operations, predictable convergence of simulated iterations, and absence of income effects of oscillations upon the consumers. Yet because to Lange the "market" was simply the freedom of consumers to choose without rationing, he concluded that computers still must be used in combination with, rather than in place of, the market in a socialist economy. Thus he saved his model of "market Socialism."

This is, however, largely a play of words. The market is of course something much larger than merely the freedom of consumers' choice, and no opponent of the market economy has ever seriously advocated putting consumers on rationing. Market economy exists when producers are free and independent of each other in their economic behaviour, and so are the consumers, consumers being not only the buyers of final consumer goods, but also producers who buy their inputs. Market economy is possible only when independence of the enterprises is guaranteed by law, that is, when enterprises are in private or group property ownership. The market system has been criticized mainly for producing business cycles, depressions, unemployment, bankruptcies, financial crisis, and various other instabilities and disequilibria. Central planning has been advocated as a substitute for these deficiencies of the market mechanism.

Computers fit equally well into both the market system and the central planning system. They come not as their replacement, but as an improvement on both of them.

This is why it is difficult to agree with the following judgement: [121]

. . . Cybernetics, which has become a new faith in the Soviet Union, may turn out to be the ideological prop the Soviets need to permit them to accept the use of market mechanisms.

3. Decentralization of the Governments and the Market

It is not only ideology that does not permit the Soviet Union to return to the N.E.P., or to "State Capitalism," as Lenin called it, or to the "Market Socialism,"

87

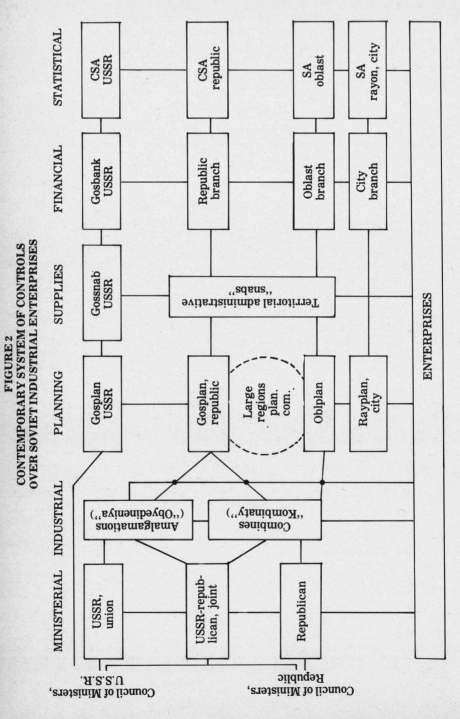

FIGURE 2
CONTEMPORARY SYSTEM OF CONTROLS
OVER SOVIET INDUSTRIAL ENTERPRISES

MINISTERIAL   INDUSTRIAL   PLANNING   SUPPLIES   FINANCIAL   STATISTICAL

Council of Ministers, U.S.S.R.

Council of Ministers, Republic

USSR, union

USSR-republican, joint

Republican

Amalgamations ("Obyedineniya")

Combines ("Kombinaty")

Gosplan USSR

Gosplan, republic

Large regions plan. com.

Oblplan

Rayplan, city

Gossnab USSR

Territorial administrative "snabs"

Gosbank USSR

Republic branch

Oblast branch

City branch

CSA USSR

CSA republic

SA oblast

SA rayon, city

ENTERPRISES

from which the N.E.P. did not differ much. It is also the Constitution of the USSR, as long as it is not changed. And it is also the political system of international relations, including nations of the USSR and of the Soviet bloc. Ultimately it is national economic self-interest. The Soviets had already their experience with the N.E.P., and they watch closely the experience of Yugoslavia with her "Market Socialism." They are convinced that their present system is capable of generating more capital formation than the N.E.P. or "Market Socialism" can, and this is all that matters for them now. They are ever in need of the maximum capital formation. Otherwise they would lose their status of a super-power in the world and at home.

The Soviet economy is nationalized. This is not a meaningless matter of the Constitution. There is neither private ownership of the means of production nor group control as in Yugoslavia's workers' management system. Everything in the Soviet economy is administered by governments of various levels. Hence, if reforms are to come, they will come by way of the decentralization of the governments, and not via outright restoration of the market mechanisms. The latter would be equivalent not to reform but to an outright revolution, and this is unconstitutional.

And the reform of the government administration of the economy is already well under way. The abolition of 'glavki' in the ministries and the establishment of the amalgamations and combines witness to this. With the computerization of the planning system being immanent, "it will become possible in the near future to pass over the centralized calculations of demand (**'potrebnosti'**) for all major resources, and to give up drawing on the ministerial planned demands (**'plany-zayavki'**)." [122] Thus the powers of the ministries will be circumscribed even more, and the industries will deal directly with the planning system.

Where do these reforms lead to? It appears that the ultimate goal of the computerization of the planning system is to integrate everything with it directly and to make the vertical structure of the Gosplan (see Figure 2) supreme over all other vertical control structures in the economy. One thing is obvious, though. There is no evidence that the present reforms are aimed at the restoration of the market system.

FOOTNOTES

1.   V.M. Hlushkov, "Kibernetyka v teoriyi i na praktytsi" (Cybernetics in theory and practice), **Nauka I Kul'tura: Ukrayina 1966** (Science and Culture: Ukraine 1966), Kyiv, T-vo Znannia, 1966, p. 41.

2.   V.M. Hlushkov, "Kibernetyka na Ukrayini" (Cybernetics in Ukraine), **Narysy z istoriyi tekhniky i pryrodoznavstva: Respublikans'ky Mizhvidomchy Zbirnyk** (Outlines of history of technology and natural sciences: Ann interdepartmental republican symposium), Kyiv, Naukova Dumka, Vypusk X, 1968, p. 24.

3.   **Istoriya Akademiyi Nauk Ukrayins'koyi RSR** (History of the Academy of Sciences of the Ukrainian SSR), Vol. 2, Kyiv, URE, 1967, p. 34.

4.   **Entsyklopediya Kibernetyky** (Encyclopedia of cybernetics), Vol. 2, Kyiv, URE, 1973, p. 36.

5.   **Ibid.**, Vol. 1, p. 154.

6.   I. Berenyi,"Computers in Eastern Europe," **Scientific American**, New York, Vol. 22, No. 4, October 1970, p. 104.

7.   Hlushkov, "Kibernetyka na Ukrayini," **op. cit.**, p. 25.

8.   **Ukrayins'ka Radians'ka Entsyklopediya** (Ukrainian Soviet encyclopedia), Vol. 10, Kyiv, URE, 1962, p. 245.

9.   K. Miller, "Computers in the Soviet Economy," **New Directions in the Soviet Economy** (Studies prepared for the Subcommittee on Foreign Economic Policy of the Joint Economic Committee, Congress of the United States) 89th Cong., 2nd sess., Part II-A, Washington, CPO, 1966, pp. 329-330.

10.   **Resheniya Partii i Pravitel'stva po khoziaystvennym voprosam** (Party's and Government's decisions on economic questions), Vol. 5, Moscow, Izd-vo Polit. Literatury, 1968, p. 51.

11.   **Ibid.**, pp. 52-53.

12.   **Istoriya Akademiyi Nauk...**, **op. cit.**, Vol. 2, p. 35.

13.   **Ekonomichny Slovnyk** (Economics dictionary), eds. P. I. Bahriy and S. I. Dorohuntsov, Kyiv, URE, 1973, pp. 149-150.

14.   **Entsyklopediya Kibernetyky, op. cit.**, Vol. 1, p. 488.

15.   **Istoriya Akademiyi Nauk..**, **op. cit.**, pp. 33-34.

16.   **Kibernetika i Vychislitel'naya Tekhnika** (Cybernetics and computer technology) — republican interdepartmental symposium, Kyiv, appearing two — three times a year; **Zbirnyk prats z obchysliuval'noyi matematyky i tekhniky** (Collection of papers on computational mathematics and technology), 3 vols., 1961; **Primenenie matematicheskikh metodov i vychislitel'noy tekhniki v ekonomike** (Application of mathematical methods and computers in economics), Donetsk, about once a year; **Avtomatika** (Automatics), Kyiv, bi-monthly, etc.

17.   Compare, for example, T. L. Saaty, "Operations Research: Some Contributions

to Mathematics," Science, Washington, Vol. 178, No. 4065, 8 December 1972, p. 1062.

18. Cf.P.I. Bahriy,"Razvitie ekonomiko-matematicheskoy nauki v Ukrainskoy SSR" (Development of economic-mathematical science in the Ukrainian SSR), Ekonomika i matematicheskie metody (Economics and Mathematical Methods), Moscow, Vol. 8, No. 6, 1972, pp. 813ff.

19. Cf. W.E. Sounder, "Analytical Effectiveness of Mathematical Models for R&D Project Selection," Management Science, Vol. 19, No. —, 1973, pp. 907ff.

20. Entsyklopediya Kibernetyky, op. cit., Vol. 1, p. 273.

21. V. M. Hlushkov, "Kibernetyka na Ukrayini," loc. cit., p. 27.

22. Ibid.

23. Entsyklopediya Kibernetyky, op. cit., Vol. 2, pp. 55 and 329.

24. Hlushkov, op. cit., pp. 28-29.

25. Ukazatel Gosudarstvennykh Standartov SSSR 1972 (Index of State Standards óf the USSR 1972), Moscow, Izd-vo standartov, 1972, p. 88.

26. Berenyi, loc. cit., p. 104.

27. B.E. Paton, "Nauka — proizvodstvu" (Science to industry), Ekonomicheskaya Gazeta (Economic Gazette), No. 34, August 1971, p. 17.

28. T. Shabad, "Moscow Unveils Computer System," The New York Times, 7 May 1973, p. 9.

29. Miller, loc. cit., p. 329.

30. " 'We Have To Be Concerned' When U.S. Skills Go to Russia," Interview with Robert C. Seamans, Jr., U.S. News & World Report, 23 September 1974, p. 73.

31. V. M. Hlushkov, Yu. V. Kapitonova, A. A. Letichevskiy, "Metodika proyektirovaniya vychislitel'nykh mashin chetvertogo i sleduyushchikh pokoleniy" (Methods of designing the computers of the fourth and subsequent generations), Kibernetika, Kyiv, No. 1, January-February 1973, pp. lff.

32. Berenyi, op. cit., p. 106.

33. "Watson Doubtful of Soviet Computer Deal," The New York Times, 8 October 1970, p. 71; "Moscow Places Order for I.B.M. Computer," The New York Times, 6 November 1971, p. 13.

34. The New York Times, 12 October 1973, p. 65.

35. U.S. News & World Report, 5 November 1973, p. 52.

36. Der Spiegel (Hamburg), No. 23, 3 June 1974, p. 71.

37. This is clearly recognized, e.g., by Entsyklopediya Kibernetyky, loc. cit., Vol. 1, pp. 470-471.

38. Berenyi, loc. cit., p. 108.

39. **Bol'shaya Sovetskaya Entsiklopediya** (Great Soviet Encyclopedia), 3rd ed., Moscow, 1971, Vol. 5, p. 570.

40. TsSU SSSR, **Narodnoe Khoziaystvo SSSR v 1972 g. Statisticheskiy Yezhegodnik** (National economy of the USSR In 1972: Statistical annual), Moscow, Statistika, 1973, p. 227.

41. Ibidem and TsSU RSFSR, **Narodnoe khoziaystvo RSFSR v 1972 godu: Statisticheskiy yezhegodnik** (National economy of the RSFSR in 1972: Statistical annual), Moscow, Statistika, 1973, p. 108.

42. Miller, loc. cit., p. 333.

43. **Radians'ka Ukrayina** (Soviet Ukraine), 1 February 1974. As translated in the **Digest of the Soviet Ukrainian Press** (New York), March 1974, p. 4.

44. **Resheniya Partii i Pravitel'stva..**, loc. cit., Vol. 8, p. 123; on the change of wholesale prices to the 1972 base.

45. **SSSR i soyuznye respubliki** (The USSR and union republics), Moscow, Statistika, 1972, pp. 8, 32, 54, 77, 255.

46. **Vneshniya torgovlia SSSR za 1969 god: Statisticheskiy obzor** (Foreign trade of the USSR in 1969: Statistical survey), Moscow, Izd-vo Mezhdunarodnye Otnosheniya, 1970, p. 24.

47. **Ibidem.**

48. **Ibidem..** za 1971 (1972, 1973) god, pp. 40, 40 and 40 respectively.

49. **Entsyklopediya Ukrayinoznavstva** (Encyclopedia of Ukraine), Paris, Molode Zhyttia, 1970, Vol. 6, p. 2362.

47. **Ibidem.**

48. **Ibidem..** za 1971 (1972, 1973) god, pp. 40, 40 and 40 respectively.

49. **Entsyklopediya Ukrayinoznavstva** (Encyclopedia of Ukraine), Paris, Molode Zhyttia, 1970, Vol. 6, p. 2362.

50. **Neue Zurcher Zeitung**, No. 148, 2 June 1971, p. 5.

51. Berenyi, loc. cit., p. 104.

52. **Neue Zurcher Zeitung**, op. cit.

53. H. Owen (ed.), **The Next Phase in Foreign Policy**, Washington, Brookings Institution, 1973, p. 116.

54. **Robitnycha Hazeta** (Workers' Gazette), Kiev, 26 September 1972, p. 3; as translated in the **Digest of the Soviet Ukrainian Press**, New York, December 1972, p. 15.

55. TsSU SSSR, **Itogi Vsesoyuznoy perepisi naseleniya 1970 goda** (Summary of the All-Union census of the population of 1970), Moscow, Statistika, Vol. VI, pp. 23 and 43.

56. **Pravda**, Moscow, 23 February 1966, as quoted by Miller, loc. cit., p. 331.

57. Skepticism was expressed by Miller, op. cit., who also estimated that there were probably not more than 3,000 computers installed in the whole country in 1966.

58. Entsyklopedia Ukrainoznavsta, loc. cit., p. 2362.

59. H. Owen, loc. cit., p. 116.

60. U.S. Department of Commerce. Bureau of International Commerce, Global Market Survey: Computers and Related Equipment, Washington, GPO, October 1973, p. 117.

61. Ibidem, pp. 10, 24, 39, 47, etc.

62. Robitnycha Hazeta, op. cit.

63. Ibid.

64. V. Skurykhin, A. Stohniy, "Avtomatychni systemy keruvannia" (Automatic control systems), Nauka i Kul'tura: Ukrayina 1971 (Science and culture: Ukraine 1971), Kiev, Znannia, 1971, p. 109.

65. Robitnycha Hazeta, op. cit.

66. F.D. Kohler, D.L. Harvey, "Administering and Managing the U.S. and Soviet Space Programs," Science, Washington, Vol. 169, No. 3950, 11 September 1970, p. 1054.

67. A. Titarenko, "Na puti sozidaniya" (On the road of creativity), Pravda, Moscow, 23 March 1971, p. 1.

68. N. Fetisov, "Obosnovanie planov s ispol'zovaniem vychislitel'noy tekhniki" (Determination of plans with the use of computers), Planovoe Khoziaystvo (Planned economy), Vo. 39, No. 10, October 1962, p. 39. Emphasis added.

69. A.G. Aganbegian, "K sozdaniyu optimal'noy sistemy planirovaniya i upravleniya narodnym khoziaystvom" (Towards creation of an optimal system of planning and management of the national economy), Vestnik Akademii Nauk SSSR (Herald of the USSR Academy of Science), No. 6, 1964, p. 66.

70. V. Hlushkov, N. Fedorenko, "Problemy shirokogo vnedreniya vychislitel'noy tekhniki v narodnoe khoziaysťvo" (Problems of broad application of computers in the national economy), Voprosy Ekonomiki (Problems of economics), No. 7, July 1964, pp. 87ff.

71. J.P. Hardt, M. Hoffenberg, N. Kaplan, H.S. Levine, Mathematics and Computers in Soviet Economic Planning, New Haven, Yale University Press, 1967, 298 pp.

72. XXIII s'yezd Kommunisticheskoy Partii Sovetskogo Soyuza: Stenograficheskiy otchet (23rd CPSU Congress: Stenographic report), Moscow, Izd-vo Polit. Literatury, 1966, Vol. 2, p. 327.

73. Ekonomicheskaya Gazetta, No. 13, April 1966, p. 25.

74. Resheniya Partii i Pravitel'stva . . . , loc. cit., Vol. 6, pp. 21ff.

75. Ibid., Vol. 8, p. 104.

76. **Ibid.**, pp. 61ff

77. **Ibid.**, p. 556.

78. **Ibid.**, Vol. 7, pp. 530-533.

79. B. Paton in the **Komunist Ukrayiny** (Communist of Ukraine), No. 12, 1972; as translated in the **Digest of the Soviet Ukrainian Press**, New York, September 1973, p. 17.

80. B. Paton in **Radians'ka Ukrayina** (Soviet Ukraine), 6 April 1969; as translated in **ibidem**, May 1969, p. 10.

81. P. Shelest, "Ovladevat naukoy upravleniya" (To master the science of management), **Pravda**, Moscow, 20 August 1971, p. 2.

82. V.M. Sidorov, "Zastosuvannia informatsiynykh system u heolohiyi" (On the use of information systems in geology), **Vistnyk Akademiyi Nauk Ukrayin-s'koyi RSR** (Herald of the Academy of Science of the Ukrainian SSR), No. 2, 1974, pp. 103-104.

83. **XXIV s'yezd Kommunisticheskoy Partii Sovetskogo Soyuza: Stenograficheskiy otchet** (24th CPSU Congress: Stenographic report), Moscow, Izd-vo Polit. Literatury, 1971, Vol. 1, p. 92. Emphasis added.

84. **Ibidem**, Vol. II, p. 53.

85. **Ibid.**, Vol. I, p. 269.

86. **Ibid.**, Vol. II, pp. 253, 254, 267.

87. **Gosudarstvenny piatiletniy plan razvitiya narodnogo khoziaystva SSSR na 1971-1975 gody** (State five-year plan of development of the national economy of the USSR in 1971-1975), Moscow, Izd-vo Polit. Literatury, 1972, pp. 126, 130, 347.

88. **Ibid.**, p. 341.

89. **Ibid.**, p. 14.

90. V.M. Hlushkov, "Osnovnye printsipy postroyeniya avtomatizirovannykh sistem upravleniya" (Main principles of the construction of automatized systems of management), **Kibernetika i vychislitel'naya Tekhnika** (Cybernetics and computing technology), Kyiv, Vypusk 12, 1971, pp.5ff.

91. A.N. Pirmukhamedov, "Pravo i avtomatizirovannaya sistema planirovaniya khoziaystva soyuznoy respubliki" (The law and the automatized system of planning of the economy of a union republic), **Sovetskoe Gosudarstvo i Pravo** (Soviet state and law), No. 3, March 1971, p. 22.

92. V. Skurykhin, A. Stohniy, **loc. cit.**, p. 114.

93. "Zozdanie ASPR - zadacha obshchegosudarstvennaya" (Creation of the ASPR is a state task), **Planovoe Khoziaystvo** (Planned economy), No. 8, August 1972, pp. 3-4, 6. pp. 3-4, 6.

94. "Vazhny etap rabot po sozdaniyu ASPR" (Important stage in the work on the

creation of the ASPR), **Planovoe Khoziaystvo** (Planned economy), No. 9, September 1973, p. 3.

95. D. Yurin, "Operativnaya obrabotka dannykh v Gosplan SSSR" (Operational work on the data in the USSR Gosplan), **Planovoe Khoziaystvo** (Planned economy), No. 7, July 1973, pp. 100-101.

96. "Sozdanie ASPR . . . ," **op. cit.**, pp. 4-5. Added emphasis.

97. **Ibid.**, p. 5.

98. Cf. V.G. Treml, "Input-Output Analysis and Soviet Planning," in J.P. Hardt, et al., **loc. cit.**, pp. 70ff.

99. TsSU URSR, **Narodne hospodarstvo Ukrayins'koyi RSR v 1970 rotsi: Statystychnyi Shchorichnyk** (National economy of the Ukrainian SSR in 1970: Statistical annual), Kyiv, Statystyka, 1971, pp. 61-77. And also P. Nahirniak, V. Krasheninnikov, "Pro rozrobku pershoho mizhhaluzevoho balansu suspil'noho produktu Ukrayiny" (About the work on the first inter-branch balance of the social product of Ukraine), **Ekonomika Radians'koyi Ukrayiny** (Economy of the Soviet Ukraine), Kyiv, June 1968.

100. N. Lebedinskiy, "Organizatsiya proektirovaniya i vnedreniya av-tomatizirovannoy sistemy planovykh rashetov"(Organization of designing and implementation of the ASPR), **Planovoe Khoziaystvo** (Planned economy), No. 8, August 1972, p. 10.

101. **Ibid.**, p. 14

102. **Ibid.**, p. 15.

103. Cf.A. Yemel'yanov, F. Kushnirskiy, "Dinamicheskaya model razvitiya narodnogo khoziaystva respubliki" (A dynamic model of development of the nationl economy of the republic), **Planovoe Khoziaystvo**, No. 11, November 1970; and the same, "Raschet osnovnykh pokazateley narodno-khoziaystvennogo plana s primeneniem ekonomiko-statisticheskikh modeley" (Calculation of basic indices of a national economic plan with economico-statistical models), **Planovoe Khoziaystvo** (Planned economy), No. 3, March 1972.

104. "Sozdanie ASPR . . . ," **op. cit.**, p. 8.

105. R. Raiackas, S. Zemaitaitite, **Informatsiya - prognoz - plan** (Information prognosis, plan), Moscow, Ekonomika, 1972, 190 pp.

106. F. Khyliuk, "Voprosy sovershenstovovaniya planirovaniya v respublike" (Problems in improving planning in the republic), **Planovoe Khoziaystvo** (Planned Economy), Moscow, No. 5, 1967, pp. 23-24.

107. **Ibid.**, p. 27.

108. A. Shulman, "Problemy tsentralizovannogo i territorial'nogo planirovaniya" (Problems in centralized and territorial planning), **Planovoe Khoziaystvo.** (Planned Economy), No. 5, 1967, p. 18.

109. A.N. Pirmukhamedov, **loc. cit.**, p. 22.

110. Gosplan SSSR, **Metodicheskie ukazaniya k sostavleniyu gosudarstvennogo plana**

razvitiya narodnogo khoziaystva SSSR (Methodical instructions on the preparation of the State Plan of development of the national economy of the USSR), Moscow, Ekonomika, 1969, p. 673.

111. Cf. "Polozhenie o proizvodstvennom ob'yedinenii (kombinate)" (Statute of industrial amalgamations and combines), **Sobranie Postanovleniy Pravitel'stva S.S.S.R.** (Collection of decrees of the USSR Government), No. 8, 1974, art. 38.

112. "Sovershenstvovat upravlenie, povyshat' effektivnost' promyshlennogo proizvodstva" (Improve management, raise efficiency of industrial enterprise), **Kommunist** (Communist), Moscow, No. 11, July 1973, p. 32.

113. P. Bartram, "Data Processing for the People," **Data Systems**, Vol. 12, No. 4, 1971, pp. 51, 53.

114. R. Keston, "Information Systems in Urban Government," **Computers And Automation**, Vol. 20, No. 9, 1971, pp. 21ff.

115. M. Ways, "Tomorrow's Management: A More Adventurous Life in a Free-Form Corportion," **Fortune**, 1 July 1966, reprint.

116. K. Marx, **Grundrisse: Foundations of the Critique of Political Economy** (Rough Draft). Tr. by M. Nicolaus. Harmondswoth, Penguin Books Ltd., 1973, p. 692. See also pp. 704-705.

117. **Ibid.**, p. 706.

118. M.Y. Loziuk, V.P. Stepanenko, **Naukovo-tekhnichna revolyutsiya i zahostrennia superechnostey suchsnoho kapitalizmu** (Scientific-technical revolution and sharpening of contradictions in contemporary capitalism), Kýiv, Naukova Dumka, 1974, pp. 54-55.

119. " 'Electronic Money' — What It Is and the Changes It Will Bring," **U.S. News & World Report**, Vol. LXXVII, No. 6, August 5, 1974, pp. 50-51.

120. O. Lange, "The Computer and the Market," in C.H. Feinstein (ed.), **Socialism, Capitalism and Economic Growth: Essays Presented to Maurice Dobb**, Cambridge, Cambridge University Press, 1967, pp. 158-161.

121. H.S. Levine, "Introduction," in J.P. Hardt, et al., **Mathematics and Computers in Soviet Economic Planning**, loc. cit., p. xxi.

122. N. Lebedinskiy, **loc. cit., Planovoe Khoziaystvo** (Planned Economy), No. 8, August 1972, p. 15.

Comments on Professor Vsevolod Holubnychy

The Present State of Cybernetics and Republic-Level Economic Planning

by
A. Katsenelinboigen
University of Pennsylvania

In Professor Holubnychy's report various questions concerning the utilization of computer technology in the USSR, especially in Ukraine, are examined in a very competent fashion.

I will begin with two personal observations, the first of which has no direct bearing on the basic ideas of the report.

Professor Holubnychy correctly notes the prominent role of academician Lebedev in the development of computer technology in the USSR. Lebedev's pioneering works in this sphere were accomplished while he was living in Kyiv, before he moved to Moscow in the 1950's. If one remembers how, during the Stalinist era, any initiatives in the field of cybernetics led to persecution, one can appreciate that it would have taken a truly brave individual, who put a high value indeed on all that is new, even to contemplate working in this direction. Academician Lebedev, as far as I can tell, was precisely that sort of man, as one may infer from other facts of his life.

While in Moscow, academician Lebedev and his wife supported new trends in painting and made it possible for young artists to realize their own talents for finding new and, for the Soviet people, unusual forms for the expression of artistic images. For this, courage and great respect for the "New" were required.

My second observation concerns the following assertion, which Professor Holubnychy makes in connection with his analysis of the creation of the data-processing network:

"Even though this network had as its purpose the mechanization of statistical reporting, rather than of planning and management, its structure implied a step towards victory for the Hlushkov-Fedorenko concept, since the system was to be territorial, and not along ministerial lines as proposed by Pugachev and others."[1]

This assertion by Professor Holubnychy is erroneous — or, more precisely, a mistake of a sort has been made here.

The point is that the article for academicians Hlushkov and Fedorenko was prepared by Pugachev, who was employed in TsEMI in the Academy of Sciences of the USSR, of which Fedorenko is the director.

In my comments I should like to expand on, and to express in a more systematic fashion than is done in this paper, those problems of planning technology which are basic to the computerization of an economy.

In the USSR, in my opinion, we see the following approaches to the technology of planning: first, the preservation in toto of the existing technology; second, is the adoption of a system of optimal functioning for the economy; third, the utilization of administrative methods which are based on decision theory; and, fourth, the creation of a western style economy in the USSR (a French or a Japanese type, for example) in which the technique of indicative planning is used.

The leader of the first trend is academician Hlushkov, who for many years now has been an antagonist of academician Fedorenko and of the other proponents of meaningful changes in planning technology.

Even though Hlushkov works in Kyiv, he has in fact influenced the development of planning systems in the USSR as a whole, as Professor Holubnychy's paper correctly reports. He is chairman of a number of All-Union scientific councils in this field and is chairman of the department in a Moscow business school where the Soviet economic and party manager elite is educated.

It should be noted that at the beginning of his activity in setting up systems of economic administration, Hlushkov actively supported new trends in planning of technology. Thus, in Kyiv in 1960 Hlushkov organized an All-Union seminar on the problems of managing the economy. The leading figure at this seminar was academician L. V. Kantorovich, who is the originator of the methods of optimal planning in the USSR. In Kyiv, at that time, under the guidance of V. Mykhalevych, work was successfully completed on the application of the methods of dynamic programming for deriving optimal variants of highways.

In recent years, apparently after realizing the impossibility of rapid change in the planning technology, Hlushkov has chosen, as a basic strategy, to automate the existing technology. This type of automation has a well-known indirect effect: the point is, that when computers are introduced it becomes necessary to rationalize the organization of production, and in fact this rationalization, as a rule, promotes higher production efficiency. Computers introduced into an existing planning system can also be used as a new technology. It would appear that the negative side of Hlushkov's approach is an excessive hope for achieving great efficiency of production within a very short time after the introduction of computers. It should be added here that Hlushkov and those closest to him do not have specialized education in the socio-economic field: they just use common sense. Quite often they act more sensibly than economists armed with a traditional education. However, they do act less sensibly than economists armed with contemporary socio-economic knowledge. One does find economists of this latter type in the USSR but Hlushkov does not actively seek to involve them in his activities. As a result, Hlushkov sometimes comes out with suggestions which are primitive—from the social point of view. For example, he proposed using computers to control consumer spending and thus to put an end to theft in the nation.

The second ideological scheme of management technology emanates from the Central-Economic-Mathematical Institute of the Academy of Sciences of the USSR. Academician Fedorenko is the head of this institute. He was born in Ukraine, although he became strongly Russianized, and he still feels the attraction of his native region: he dreams of using his accumulated savings to build a good school in the village where he was born.

The ideology of optimal planning would require a substantial rejection of the current planning techniques and the overcoming of the exisiting gap between the physical and the cost aspects of implementation. Also, elements of decentralization would increase, particularly on account of the broadening role of horizontal component mechanisms. To do this, of course, would not be to introduce market relations. I agree with Professor Holubnychy in his understanding of a market as a mechanism in which the participants are responsible for the activities that they undertake on the basis of the property that they own.

In addition, these notions of optimal planning have well-known ideological significance from the viewpoint of the interrelationships between the republics and the All-Union government. The point here is that an optimal planning model for the national economy can be given in at least two forms: one with global criteria for optimality and one as a model with vectoral optimization. [2]

As far as the results are concerned, as long as they are obtained under relatively normal conditions, these two methods can be interchanged. However, with respect to their primary perception of the images which they bear, these two methods are not equivalent. In the first method, at least in the first instance, the interrelations between the republics and the centre are concealed in the descriptions that use global criteria for optimality. In the second method these are at once revealed as obvious forms, because the objective of optimal development of every republic is immediately presented. The system of limiting conditions defines what portion of the income from the available resources of a given republic that the given republic's population will receive and what portion will be given out to other republics, and how much will be allocated to production of collective goods.

In this respect, it is interesting to compare "The Complex Program for Furthering and Improvement of the Cooperation and Development of Socialist Economic Integration of the Member Countries of the Council of Mutual Economic Assistance" (COMECON), which was adopted in 1971, and, on the other hand, the interrelations between the All-Union government and the republics within the USSR. For the interrelations between COMECON countries conditions obtain which provide that each individual nation has the right to receive all the revenue from its own resources. There is no such provision in the relations between the All-Union government and the republics: practically all revenues are taken over by the All-Union government and are distributed according to its own interests.

The third approach to perfecting the technology of planning in the USSR involves use of "decision theory".

First, in decision theory, attention is directed toward the way the system functions under conditions of uncertainty. Under such conditions there is no way to discover a regular procedure for predicting optimal activities in the future. Under these conditions the planning process, as is clearly shown in the works of H. Simon, R. Ackoff and others, is reduced in the first instance to discovering a satisfactory realm in which decisions may be made. This theory does not reject the principles of optimal planning, but rather limits their field of implementation to conditions under which a clear-cut objective in terms of attaining a specific maximum or minimum goal can be formulated.

Second, in "decision theory", notice is taken of the fact that planners must operate on the basis of what they call informalized information, in which cases the mechanism of decision—making must be based on expertise.

Computers can be useful for locating the field of satisfactory solutions. Writing the computer program in such cases presents considerable difficulties, however, in which chess—playing programs can be useful. This is because in chess the game situation is also one of indeterminacy—although of course on a very simple level.

In the USSR several years ago a corresponding member of the Academy of Sciences of the USSR, Moiseev, tried to propose to Soviet leaders the adoption of the principles of "decision-making" theory for perfecting the mechanisms of planning and management. He thought it necessary to include, directly in the mechanisms of decision-making, on the highest level, scholars bearing a wealth of non-formalized information. But, naturally, this idea did not appeal to the Soviet leaders, because they could not imagine working with scholars on a day-to-day basis. We know from history that only the most intellectually gifted leaders would risk trying to involve scholars in administration. As a matter of fact, scholars have not always proven to be good practical workers. One might surmise that scholars prefer to work at a profound level toward overcoming specific limitations over a considerable period of time, rather than making day-to-day decisions within the framework of such conditions as may be existing at the time.

The fourth type of planning technology is connected with the economic reform which was introduced in 1965 and which was rather quickly phased out. Under this reform, in fact, attention was focused on the social aspects of decentralization of the economy: freeing the economy from party control, the possibility of introducing unemployment, competition, etc. Inasmuch as the utilization of computers was associated in people's minds with a strengthening of the centralized system, supporters of the reform sometimes were, in fact, biased against computers. Professor Holubnychy quite correctly draws attention to the possibility of such a conflict. The following fact, however, is worth noting: A. Kosygin, in his article "Sotsial' no-ekonomicheskoe razvitie sovetskogo mnogonatsional'nogo gossudarstva",[3] while analyzing various ways of improving the state planning system, ignores the role, in this case, of mathematical methods and computers. He does mention the role of computers in connection with scientific-technological progress, but only at a level no higher than that of a branch in the administrative system.

"Solving the problems of automating production and those of perfecting communications and management require a broad application of contemporary computing techniques and electronic means. The utilization of systems of managing the technological processes of separate enterprises and, shortly, of whole branches, on the basis of computer techniques, appears to be one of the most important components of the scientific-technological revolution."[4]

It is even possible that the transferral of the planning and operation of the All-Union network of computer centres to the TsSU in the mid 1960's reflects a compromise between the supporters of centralization and the "reformers".

I should also like to express the following observations concerning Professor Holubnuchy's remarks about the liquidation of the Glavki and the introduction of "obedinieniia" (agglomerations) as a continuation of the reform. I see this matter somewhat differently.

Obedineniia undermine the whole ministerial apparatus, since approximately two-thirds of the ministerial apparatus is composed of workers from the Glavki. It was suggested that the obedineniia be set up in such a way that they would incorporate the overlapping functions of various branches of industry. This would lead to a sharp reduction of the ministerial apparatus and to the amalgamation of ministries. Because of the variety of enterprises which they unit within themselves the obedineniia will, in many cases, have to be subordinated to the oblast party committees. Such a reorganization would be advantageous to the party organs. Here the situation is analogous to that of the Sovnarhozy. When Khrushchev took over the party apparatus and depended on the obkom, it was to his advantage to put the administration of the economy to a large extent under the leadership of the obkoms. The fact that the creation of the obedineniia has run into difficulty shows that the leaders of the party apparatus do not yet have sufficient power to overcome the opposition of the Politburo members who represent the economic managers.

Of course, the creation of obedineniia can lead to a certain decentralization of management, to the extent that the obedineniia may even obtain the right to carry on independent external trade. It is obvious, nevertheless, that the monopoly on external trade will be preserved — although the monopoly function of the Ministry of Foreign Trade will be weakened. But this decentralization will mean a strengthening of the party organs. The consequences of such developments are difficult to predict.

FOOTNOTES

1.   See V. Holubnychy's paper in this volume.
2.   A. Katsenelinboigen, "On the Various Methods of Describing the Socialist Economy." **Matekon**, Vol. X, No. 2, 1973.
3.   A. Kosygin, "Sotsial'no-ekonomicheskoe razvitie sovetskogo mnogo-natsional'nogo gosudarstva", **Kommunist**, No. 7, 1972, pp. 15-41.
4. **Ibid.**, p. 20.

Ukrainian Agriculture: The Problems of Specialization and Intensification in Perspective*

by
Ihor Stebelsky
University of Windsor

INTRODUCTION

The trend towards agricultural specialization and intensification in modern farming are widely recognized.[1] In a free market economy, as farming becomes more closely integrated with transportation, processing, and marketing, and as market prices for certain commodities become attractive, the farmer frees himself from producing a wide selection of domestic necessities, increases his operation, specializes, and gains greater economies of scale. When land becomes a serious contraint, the farmer, under favourable market conditions, substitutes other inputs and thus achieves an increased output from the same land area or, in other words, intensifies his operations. When many farms in the same area specialize in the same commodities and encourage special services and processors to locate in their vicinity further economies are gained, and a regional specialization emerges. Favourable international market conditions encourage further specialization in commodities that are destined for export.

In the Soviet Union, whilst the economies of specialization and the need for intensification are widely recognized, these processes cannot be left to the spontaneous decisions of individual farmers.[2] For ideological reasons, specialization and intensification must be centrally planned within the framework of collective and state farms. Thus, when full-scale collectivization was undertaken, the party called for a

*Appreciation is expressed to T. Thorpe, V. Holubnychy, W. Isajiw, and P. Potichnyj for their aid in the preparation of this paper. The author is happy to express his appreciation to the Russian and East European Center at the University of Illinois for granting him a Summer Research Laboratory Associateship to support research for this paper.

TABLE I

FOOD PRODUCTION AND CONSUMPTION IN 1970
(Per capita in kg. per year)

Commodity	Production (A)		Recommended Soviet Norm[c]	Consumption (B)		Difference (A-B)	
	U.S.S.R. Average[a]	Ukrainian S.S.R.[b]		U.S.S.R. Averaged	Ukrainian S.S.R.[e]	U.S.S.R. Average	Ukrainian S.S.R.
Meat and fat	51	61	81.8	48	49	3	12
Milk	343	397	433.6	306	311	37	86
Eggs	168	195	292.0	157	156	11	39
Sugar	42	127	36.5	39	41	3	86
Oil (vegetable)	11.5	22.7	10.0	6.8	7.4	4.7	15.3
Vegetables	88	123	146.0	82	103	6	20
Potatoes	400	419	96.7	130	156	270	263
Grain	773	773	120.4	149	155	624	618

[a]Narodnoe Khoziaistvo SSR v 1972g. Moscow, 1973), pp. 7, 265, 267, 270, 340, 342, 370.
[b]Narodne hospodarstvo Ukrainskoi RSR u 1972 rotsi (Kyiv, 1974), pp. 7, 173, 236, 244, 245, 276, 279, 280.

[c]K.P. Obolenskii, Teoriia i praktika spetsializatsii sel'skogo khoziaistva (Moscow, 1970). p. 26.
[d]R.A. Groundwater, "Soviet Union", Agriculture Abroad (August, 1974), p. 17.
[e]P.G. Dubinov, "Sil'ske hospodarstvo Ukrainskoi RSR — do 50-richnoho iuvileiu Radians'koho Soiuzu," Visnyk sil'skohospodars'koi nauky, No. 11 (1972), p. 8.

fundamental change in the distribution of all crops across the territory of the Soviet Union, including the achievement of a higher level of specialization. A "rational" distribution of agricultural production, from the standpoint of the central planners in Moscow, was (1) to assure self-sufficiency in basic agricultural commodities and (2) to achieve a maximum utilization of agricultural resources throughout the U.S.S.R. at a minimum cost.[3] Large collective and state farms, specializing in the production of planned commodities, were to introduce significant economies of scale.

The zealous implementation of this programme, however, combined with ambitious procurements on the one hand and inadequate investment on the other, strained the existing storage, transportation, and processing facilities and resulted in much waste. Moreover, the heavy demands placed on the agricultural sector coupled with a "class war" against the "kulak" deprived many villagers of their subsistence. In order to avoid disaster, the leadership allowed the peasants to toil on their "private plots" to meet the basic needs of the household, the village, and even the nearby town. This freed the planners from the burden of small detail and allowed them to mould their grand designs on the socialized sector of the collective and state farms.

Within the framework of the goals set by the Communist Party of the Soviet Union, the contribution of Ukrainian agriculture is impressive. Its importance becomes even more striking when a number of its key specialties are considered. The purpose of this paper is to evaluate the importance of Ukrainian agriculture to the Soviet Union, to trace the evolution of agricultural specialization in the Ukrainian S.S.R., to adduce reasons for them, and to assess the trends in Ukrainian agriculture during the current Soviet drive for agricultural intensification and specialization.

PRESENT CHARACTERISTICS OF UKRAINIAN AGRICULTURE

The Ukrainian S.S.R. is a major world agricultural producer in its own right. It produces as much grain as Canada, and its production of wheat is surpassed only by the two world giants, the United States and the R.S.F.S.R. As the largest producer of corn in the Soviet Union, Ukraine has harvests equal to those of India or France. After the Russian Republic, Ukraine is the second largest producer of potatoes, having surpassed the declining potato production of West Germany nearly a decade ago. Indeed, in the production of sugar beets the Ukrainian S.S.R. has no equal in the world.[4]

The livestock sector of Ukraine is somewhat less impressive. Its meat production is surpassed by France, West Germany, Argentina, R.S.F.S.R. and the United States. More milk is produced by France, West Germany, R.S.F.S.R., the United States and India. Finally, the U.S., R.S.F.S.R., France, West Germany, the United Kingdom, Italy and Japan produce more eggs than the Ukrainian S.S.R.

With such a large production capacity and a population smaller than that of Italy, France, West Germany, or United Kingdom, the Ukrainian S.S.R. produces more than is needed to feed its population. On a per capita basis, it produces more food than the U.S.S.R. average, a country that, except for several recent huge grain imports, has remained relatively self-sufficient in basic food supplies. In all seven commodities except grain, the Ukrainian S.S.R. exceeds the Soviet average per capita production, in some cases by a very wide margin (Table I). By contrast, the per capita food consumption in Ukrainian S.S.R. is not better than that of the Soviet average. Both trail behind the recommended Soviet norms for meat, milk, eggs, and vegetables, and exceed the norms in sugar, potatoes and grain. A greater than average intake of potatoes and vegetables suggest the added benefits the Ukrainian population derives from its more productive private plots. Clearly, the "surplus" food production of the Ukrainian S.S.R. in all commodities except potatoes and grain serves to improve the food intake in other parts of the Soviet Union.

The contribution of Ukrainian agricultural production to the Soviet total is impressive. With a population of slightly over 19 percent, the Ukrainian S.S.R. accounts for more than 23 percent of the gross value of Soviet agricultural production (Table II). Of the two sectors in agriculture, crop production contributes more than animal husbandry. Even so, both crop and livestock sectors contribute a greater share of the Soviet total (25 and 22 percent respectively) than that consumed by the Ukrainian population (20 percent). Indeed, this has been the case, with minor fluctuations, throughout the Soviet period and, with a smaller share of the livestock sector, before the First World War (Table II).

The outstanding feature of Ukrainian agriculture is its high land productivity. It produces nearly one-quarter (23.3 percent) of the total Soviet agricultural production on a mere 2.7 percent of the Soviet land area, which contains 7.7 percent of the Soviet land used for agriculture and 15.2 percent of all the Soviet cultivated land. It is well known that Ukraine possesses a large portion of the best agricultural lands in the Soviet Union. Endowed with a predominantly flat to rolling topography with slopes seldom too steep for plowing and drainage seldom impeded, the Ukraine has more than 80 percent of its agricultural land in cultivation, more than any other republic in the Soviet Union. Such an emphasis on field crops, however, has led to a reduction of hayfields and pastures to the point where today they occupy only 6 and 11 percent of the farmland respectively. As a result, the livestock sector must rely predominantly on field grown crops.

Extensive areas of rich black soils, adequate moisture and abundant heat and sunshine are the chief comparative advantages of growing field crops in Ukraine. The latter constitute a broad variety where each competes for the best natural conditions. In comparing the crop composition of Ukraine with the Soviet Union as a whole a number of crops exceed the average for all field crops, and some stand out as true specialties of the republic (Table III). Clearly, corn for grain holds the commanding position (67.5 percent of the Soviet area sown to corn), followed by sugar beets (48.8 percent), root and melon fodder crops (39.6 percent), sunflowers (35.8 percent), and winter wheat (32.2 percent). In addition, the republic's share of fruit tree and berry plantings (32.3 percent) and vegetables (31.1 percent) is impressive. Even silage corn (24.8 percent) and pulses (25.3 percent) represent large shares, and are essential components of Ukraine's feed structure for the livestock industry.

TABLE II

UKRAINIAN S.S.R.'s SHARE OF SOVIET AGRICULTURAL PRODUCTION
(In percent of U.S.S.R., contemporary boundaries)

Value of Gross Agricultural Production
(Computed in average, 1965 Soviet prices)

Year	Population	Total	Crop	Livestock
1913	22.1	23.5	26.2	19.0
1940	21.3	26.3	28.4	23.5
1950	20.5	23.9	24.4	24.4
1960	20.0	23.3	23.9	23.2
1970	19.5	22.5	22.9	22.1
1960-64 av.	19.8	23.7	25.0	22.3
1965-69 av.	19.6	23.3	25.1	21.7
1970-72 av.	19.5	23.3	24.7	21.9

Sources:
Narodnoe Khoziaistvo SSSR v 1967g. (Moscow, 1968), p. 329; . . . v 1968g. (Moscow,1969), p. 317; . . . v 1969g. (Moscow, 1970), p. 291; . . . v 1970g. (Moscow, 1971), p. 277; . . . 1922-1972, p. 222; . . . v 1972g. (Moscow, 1973), pp. 289-90; **Sil's'ke hospodarstvo Ukrains'koi RSR** (Kyiv, 1969), pp. 24-25; **Ukraina za piatdesiat' rokiv** (1917-1967), (Kyiv, 1967), p. 133.

The livestock sector of Ukraine tends to be intensive. Only in Georgia and Armenia do livestock densities compare to those encountered in Ukraine.[5] Among the branches of the livestock industry, pig breeding displays a definite specialty, taking advantage of the local availability of corn (Table IV). Fowl of all kinds appear to be well represented, reflecting not only the availability of feed grains but also possibly a strong cultural attachment to these small domestic animals. Horses, sheep and goats remain well below the Soviet proportion. The shortage of natural pastures explains the low proportion of sheep and goats, but the low proportion of horses, considering the fact that the supply of motive power per agricultural worker in Ukraine lags behind the U.S.S.R. average by about one-third,[6] cannot be explained from an economic standpoint.

TABLE III

FIELD CROPS AND PLANTINGS, 1970

	U.S.S.R. (1,000 ha.)	UKRAINIAN S.S.R. (1,000 ha.)	(Percent of U.S.S.R.)
All field crops	206,655	32,782	15.9
All grain	119,261	15,518	13.0
Winter wheat	18,505	5,960	32.2
Spring wheat	46,725	70	0.2
Rye	10,020	833	8.3
Corn for grain	3,353	2,262	67.5
Barley	21,297	3,370	15.8
Oats	9,250	881	9.5
Millet	2,691	521	19.4
Buckwheat	1,879	364	19.4
Pulses	5,070	1,280	25.3
Technical crops	14,486	3,939	27.2
Sugar beets	3,368	1,659	48.8
Sunflowers	4,777	1,710	35.8
Flax (fibre)	1,284	230	17.9
Potatoes	8,064	1,988	24.7
Vegetables	1,499	466	31.1
Fodder crops	62,846	10,733	17.1
Silage corn	18,010	4,465	24.8
Root and melon	1,800	713	39.6
Annual grasses	17,959	3,421	19.0
Perennial grasses	21,725	1,947	9.0
Fruit tree and berry plantings	3,848	1,243	32.3

Sources:
Sel'skoe khoziaistvo SSSR (Moscow, 1971), pp. 109, 114-28, 130-33, 135; **Narodne hospodarstvo Ukrains'koi RSR u 1972 rotsi (Kyiv, 1974), p. 210.**

TABLE IV

LIVESTOCK, 1970

TYPE OF ANIMAL	U.S.S.R.	UKRAINIAN S.S.R.	
	(million head)	(million head)	(Percent of USSR)
Cattle (all kinds)	95.2	20.3	21.3
Cows	40.5	8.7	21.4
Pigs	56.1	17.2	30.7
Sheep	130.7	8.3	6.3
Goats	5.2	0.4	7.3
Horses	7.5	1.3	17.5
Fowl (all kinds)	590.3	142.5	24.1
Laying hens	137.5	30.3	21.9

Source:
Sel'skoe khoziaistvo SSSR (Moscow, 1971), pp. 251, 256, 263, 267, 270, 272, 274.

One should bear in mind, of course, that the figures presented here are for the Ukrainian S.S.R. as a whole. Within that territory there are considerable environmental and economic variations, with the land use, crop compositions, and livestock husbandry reflecting these differences. The northwestern fringe, known as Polissia or the forest zone, consists of a lowland with a high water table, frequent marshy conditions, much woodland, a high proportion of meadows and hayfield, and crops that tolerate the sandy acidic soil, such as oats, rye and barley. South of this, the so-called wooded-steppe zone extends from the western borders of Ukraine and the Carpathian mountains eastward towards Kharkiv and beyond. Possessing the most favourable conditions for farming, it boasts sufficient precipitation and enough heat for the two rivals, sugar beets and corn. The southern third of Ukraine consists mainly of the steppe zone, which occupies the coastal lowland, the Donets upland, and beyond. Here precipitation becomes marginal and droughts, especially the dreaded hot dry winds (sukhovii) become more common. Consequently grain farming can best survive under such conditions, and the driest areas, near the isthmus of Crimea, still retain dry pastures for sheep. This zone, however, receives most heat during the summer and, with the help of irrigation, can produce valuable mid-latitudinal heat loving plants. Finally there are two small mountain regions: the Crimean Mountains protect a narrow sloping coast of marginal Mediterranean climate, whereas the Carpathians shelter the warm, well watered, but tiny Tysa lowland suitable for corn and grapes.

Around urban centers and industrial districts the farms tend to specialize more in the production of vegetables, potatoes and milk for fresh consumption. Perhaps the most specialized of these are the state farms that raise chicken for eggs and meat. But most of the eggs and vegetables and a good portion of meat, milk and potatoes still come from the private plots of the peasants working on collective farms within acceptable travel distance of the cities. In the meantime, the socialized sector caters to the larger designs of the state.

Finally, agronomic and economic considerations limit the extent to which farms or regions specialize in a few selected crops. If a certain crop is planted repeatedly in the same field year after year, the yields will tend to decline, whilst diseases specific to that crop will build up and attack it in epidemic proportions. On the other hand, if crops are rotated in succession, a broader spectrum of nutrients and trace elements is withdrawn from the soil, other valuable materials may in fact be added by preceding crops and a build-up of specific diseases is avoided. At the same time, the need to apply heavy doses of fertilizers, pesticides and fungicides is alleviated. Other purely economic considerations also discourage monoculture. If one crop is destroyed by adverse weather conditions, a different one may survie and pose as "insurance". If one crop has a peak labour demand in one month, another may require work in another, and a good choice of crops can spread the work load over a longer season, providing a more efficient use of labour and a more stable income.

These patterns, of course, are not static, and undergo continual change. Such a change may reflect changes in the population pressure, demand for specific crops, land tenure condition, advances in agronomy, political policies of the elite in power and so forth. A brief review of the evolution of Ukrainian agriculture will identify some factors that moulded the present pattern.

EVOLUTION OF THE AGRICULTURAL PATTERN IN UKRAINE AND THE SOVIET GOVERNMENT POLICIES

Farming in the most favourable environment of the wooded-steppe zone can be traced back five thousand years, when the neolithic occupants of Ukraine cultivated wheat, barley and millet and cared for domestic animals. A millenium or two later other traditional crops were added, and the farming activity diffused into the heavily wooded areas, whilst livestock keeping predominated in the steppe zone. Exotics from the New World made their appearance in the seventeenth and eighteenth centuries, but the geographical patterns persisted until the second half of the nineteenth century.

The Beginnings of Modern Agriculture

Modern commercial agriculture began in Ukraine on gentry estates that acquired new technology and spurred production of marketable good, processed them on the spot, if necessary, and channelled them off to the market. The sparsely peopled steppe zone was colonized and assimilated with new iron plows to become the granary of Europe. Railways enabled the movement of bulky grains and perishable products. By 1913 Ukraine contained nearly one-quarter of the grain area of the Russian Empire (Table V) but generated about three-quarters of the imperial grain exports (mainly barley and wheat) and ranked as the largest grain exporter in the world. [7]

In the densely settled wooded-steppe zone near Kyiv a new labour-intensive specialty — the cultivation of sugar beets — was introduced. By the turn of the century it represented the major sources of domestic sugar of the Russian Empire (Table V). The crop demanded deep plowing, had heavy manuring, practices that transformed the ancient three-field system into modern crop rotation. Beet tops and by-products from the sugar beet mills, used as fodder, allowed for higher livestock densities to develop.

In addition, a number of commercial oil-bearing plants were grown, among which the sunflowers gained prominence during the 1880's near Poltava and Kharkiv. [8] Attempts by the Russian "Free Economic Society" to convert corn into a commercial feed crop in Ukraine met a limited success. [9] Suburban vegetable specialization was observed near Kyiv, Kharkiv, Katerynoslav and Odesa and several other locations of specialized vegetable growing emerged on the basis of favourable environmental conditions and accessibility to the main railway lines. The large commercial gentry orchards of Podillia and Eastern Ukraine were supplemented with young southern orchards of Kherson and Crimea. [10] Even livestock production continued to supply not only the distant cities of Moscow and St. Petersburg, but also the export of animals and their products beyond the confines of the Russian Empire. [11]

Most agronomic progress, it should be noted, was made on private estates. The peasantry, who by 1909 managed to purchase more than half of all the agricultural land, still farmed mainly with traditional tools and pursued the production of grain. Indeed, over 88 percent of the sown area in Ukraine was devoted to grain, a level that was to decline in succeeding decades (Table VI).

TABLE V

CHANGING WEIGHT OF CROPS GROWN IN UKRAINIAN S.S.R.
(In percent of U.S.S.R. total, contemporary boundaries)

	1913	1940	1950	1960	1965	1970
Total sown area						
million ha.	28.0	31.3	30.7	33.6	33.8	32.8
percent	23.7	20.7	21.0	16.5	16.2	15.9
All grain						
million ha.	24.7	21.4	20.1	13.7	16.5	15.5
percent	23.6	19.3	19.5	11.9	12.9	13.0
Winter wheat						
million ha.	3.1	6.3	5.4	3.7	7.4	6.0
percent	37.3	44.1	43.1	30.6	37.1	32.2
Corn for grain						
million ha.	0.9	1.6	2.8	3.0	1.8	2.3
percent	39.2	52.3	57.1	59.7	57.1	67.5
Sugar beets						
million ha.	0.6	0.8	0.8	1.5	1.9	1.7
percent	82.5	66.9	63.3	47.9	48.0	49.3
Sunflower						
million ha.	0.1	0.7	0.9	1.5	1.8	1.8
percent	7.7	20.3	24.9	35.9	36.5	35.8
Potatoes						
million ha.	1.1	2.0	1.9	2.2	2.1	2.0
percent	25.7	26.2	22.3	23.9	24.5	24.7
Vegetables						
1,000 ha.	267	485	374	474	465	466
percent	41.2	32.2	28.7	32.1	33.1	31.1
Vineyards						
1,000 ha.	46	74	50	115	262	237
percent	24.5	22.4	19.5	26.9	34.3	29.2
Fruit and berry plantings						
1,000 ha.	233	346	361	467	586	888
percent	35.6	33.2	42.4	39.4	39.2	36.5
Fodder crops						
million ha.	0.9	4.4	5.2	13.4	10.3	10.7
percent	26.8	24.6	25.3	21.2	18.7	17.1

Sources:
Narodnoe khoziaistvo SSSR v 1960g. / Moscow, 1961), pp. 392-99, 402, 404-06, 444, 407;
. . . v 1964g. (Moscow, 1965), pp. 278-80, 283, 287-89, 291, 334-35; Sel'skoe khoziaistvo
SSSR (Moscow, 1971), pp. 114-16, 119, 125-28, 130, 235-36.

TABLE VI

CHANGES IN THE STRUCTURE OF SOWN AREA
(In percent of total sown area)

	1913	1940	1950	1960	1965	1970
Total sown area						
million ha.	28.0	31.3	30.7	33.6	33.8	32.8
percent	100.0	100.0	100.0	100.0	100.0	100.0
All grain	88.4	68.2	75.4	40.9	48.8	47.3
Winter wheat	11.0	20.2	17.6	11.0	21.7	18.2
Spring wheat	20.6	2.9	3.8	0.8	1.5	0.2
Winter rye	16.2	11.8	12.7	4.0	4.2	2.5
Corn for grain	3.1	5.0	9.0	9.1	5.4	6.9
Spring barley	20.8	12.7	9.0	7.2	7.7	9.9
Oats	10.5	7.3	5.9	2.6	1.7	2.5
Millet	1.9	3.0	1.8	2.3	1.3	1.6
Buckwheat	2.5	2.3	2.1	1.2	1.2	1.1
Pulses	1.6	2.7	2.5	2.3	3.5	3.9
Technical crops	3.2	8.6	9.4	10.7	12.6	12.0
Sugar beets	2.0	2.6	2.7	4.3	5.5	5.1
Sunflower	0.3	2.3	2.9	4.5	5.3	5.2
Potatoes and vegetables	5.0	9.0	8.1	8.4	8.1	7.9
Potatoes	3.9	6.6	6.2	6.5	6.2	6.0
Fodder crops	3.4	14.2	17.1	40.0	30.5	32.8
Root and melon	—	1.1	1.3	1.7	1.9	2.3
Silage corn	—	—	—	22.3	12.9	13.6
Annual grass	1.4	5.7	9.1	11.4	11.0	10.4
Perennial grass	1.8	6.5	5.7	3.7	4.1	6.0

Sources:

Sil'ske hospodarstvo Ukrainskoi RSR (Kyiv, 1969), p. 51; Narodne hospodarstvo Ukrainskoi RSR u 1972 rotsi (Kyiv, 1974), pp. 208, 210-11.

Peasant Diversification and Intensification

Following the Bolshevik revolution and their invasion of Ukraine the gentry estates were toppled and, for a brief period, peasant farming prevailed. The wartime destruction, followed by a change in land tenure and the collapse of the Western European grain market, prevented sown acreage from recovering to the 1913 level, reduced the sown areas of wheat and barley by about one-third, but permitted an increase in other food grains such as rye, buckwheat and millet, and fodder crops, most notably corn. The household production of potatoes and vegetables registered considerable increase, whilst sugar beets and flax, their processing plants in disarray, were displaced by the cottage technical crops such as sunflowers and hemp. Livestock numbers recovered from the war and increased rapidly. In general, until 1928 the peasantry were not only diversifying their farms to better satisfy their needs but also intensifying agricultural production. Only the threat of Bolshevik harassment restricted their commercial growth. [12]

Collectivization and Regional Specialization

Mass collectivization, thrust upon the Ukrainian peasantry in January, 1930, was an imposition of a new coercive structure that would carry out the policies of the Soviet Union. At the same time, the First Five-Year Plan envisaged that collectivization would be accompanied by an orderly development of regional specialization. [13] The large and highly specialized state farms and, to a lesser extent, collective farms, would form zones of regional specialization that would assure the needs of Soviet industry and make the most efficient use of the natural conditions of the country

However, this ambitious programme of specialization was short-lived and doomed to failure. The Soviet economic priorities rested with the heavy industry, and the government was not willing to divert resources to produce fertilizers or build storage and transportation facilities to enhance the required regional exchange. Moreover, collectivization brought with it a complete disruption of the farming economy, a catastrophic decline of livestock, and hunger. By 1933 a new policy of regional self-sufficiency and farm diversification emerged.

Regional Self-Sufficiency and Farm Diversification

The policy of regional self-sufficiency that endured until after Stalin's death tended to de-emphasize Ukraine's specialty crops (Table V). The sugar beets were dispersed farther afield, including Central Asia, the Altai Krai of Western Siberia, and the Soviet Far East. The production of wheat was favoured over rye, and was expanded into the cool northern European zone and the dry eastern margins. Even cotton, traditionally grown in Central Asia, was cropped, with miserable results, in the southern steppe of Ukraine until 1956. [14]

The key agronomic element during this period was the grass-field crop rotation, which required the use of fodder crops, especially grasses, in rotation with other crops. From an agronomic standpoint it was an escape from the dead end imposed by a shortage of fertilizer and a lack of animal manure resulting from the decline in livestock. From an economic standpoint it was to have provided an adequate amount of feed to improve the livestock herds, but poor harvesting practices resulted in declining yields and a shortage in the feed supply.

Specialization Re-Examined

After Stalin's death his successors began to search for ways of improving the poor diet of the population. [16] In order to speed up agricultural production beyond the rate of population growth the party once more called for a correct geographical distribution of agricultural activities. In 1956 it acknowledged the merits of agricultural specialization and commissioned geographers to study the problem and draw up agricultural regions. [17]

Nevertheless, the regime was in no position to plan agricultural specialization on a scientific basis. The maps of agricultural regions designed by geographers and economists were too schematic and lacked statistical definition to be of use for planning purposes. [18] The complex system of agricultural prices made it impossible to calculate a collective farm's cost of production, let alone profit. When a new uniform price structure was introduced in 1958 and zoned to reflect production costs, the zones were drawn arbitrarily to follow administrative borders. [19] It became clear that a comprehensive land inventory was essential; methodological research began, but the survey of the Soviet Union still has to be completed. [20]

Lacking an effective mechanism for planning agricultural specialization, the leadership implemented broad changes of crop distribution on a trial and error basis. Khrushchev personally launched the spectacular Virgin Lands campaign and forced the equally well known corn programme. [21] As the dry steppe east of the Volga was plowed up to grow vast stands of wheat, the climatically moister areas, especially Ukraine, replaced their former wheat fields with corn (Table VI). Grain and fodder increases were to come from increased sown area, for investment in agriculture and the resultant intensification would take a long time in coming.

Although the programmes increased agricultural production, they generated much waste and failed to enjoy unqualified success. Wheat harvests in the "Virgin Lands" proved to be erratic, whereas the corn programme failed to improve the quality of fodder. Indeed, the widespread cultivation of corn for silage in Ukraine competed directly with the production of corn for grain and displayed the even more valuable winter wheat and barley. [22] Grain supplies declined to a point where unprecedented imports of food and feed grain had to be made in 1963 to avert disaster. In the eleventh hour Khrushchev committed the party to massive investment in agriculture, but could not preside over its implementation as he was removed from office.

Specialization and Intensification Adopted

The new leadership immediately put an end to Khrushchev's excesses, introduced five-year crop contracts, and allowed for a finer readjustment of the distribution of crops according to their performance in different environments. Unprecedented investments were channelled into agriculture in the form of mechanization, chemicalization, land improvement, price support, material incentives and industrialization. [23] Such investments launched agricultural intensification and started creating the necessary conditions for agricultural specialization. Indeed, the directives of the 23rd Congress of the C.P.S.U. (1965) urged a more efficient use of land, capital, technical, and labour resources by means of increasing the specialization of the collective and state farms. [24] The October, 1968 Plenum of the Central Committee reaffirmed that the planting and agricultural organs as well as collective and state farms must intensify their effort of bringing about agricultural specialization. It also warned the planners not to indulge in a carbon copy approach, but to consider local conditions and experience. [25]

Directives of this nature have again sent scientists scurrying to their desks (and computers) to work out methods and even schemes for agricultural specialization both at the farm and at the regional level. The Russian agricultural geographer Rakitnikov, together with his professional colleagues from other republics, updated his scheme of agricultural regions for the Soviet Union. [26] Kuznetsov, a geographer of the Land Management Institute in Moscow, published a definitive monograph on the geography and planning of agricultural regions. [27] That same year the agroclimatologist, Kolaskov, worked out a regionalization scheme for each crop depending on its physiological characteristics. [28] Two agricultural economists considered the established agricultural distribution in the Soviet Union so antiquated that they argued for its complete overhaul on the basis of agricultural specialization. [29] Perhaps the most ambitious project of all came from the think-tank of the Lenin All-Union Academy of Agricultural Sciences which proposed a methodology for planning optimal distribution of crops and livestock and presented a set of maps, based on their computer-calculations, for each type of crop or animal. [30] It remains to be seen to what extent their recommended methodology and distributions will be utilized by the

113

Irrigation assumed new, large-scale dimensions after the Kakhovka reservoir on the Dnipro was completed. Lime became available in larger quantities to neutralize the acidic soils of Polissia and gypsum was introduced to make the solonchak soils of the steppe productive. Fertilizer delivery was also speeded up after the crop failures of 1963. Previous delays in these investments can only be explained by the fact that the regime gave high priority to industry, leaving agriculture at the wayside.

Current performance and plans for expanding drainage and irrigation in the future indicate a determination, on the part of the regime, to redress the neglect. In 1970 there were nearly one million hectares of land prepared for irrigation and over one and one half-million drained. By 1975 an additional 400,000 hectares should be prepared for irrigation, another 600,000 hectares should be drained, and one-half of this tiled.[35] By 1985 the party envisages more than 3.7 million ha. prepared for irrigation and 3.3 million ha. drained, of which 2.1 million ha. would be tiled.[36] Eventually the irrigated land of Ukraine should reach 10 million ha., and all the drainable land — a total of 4 million ha. — will be drained.[37] By then the limits of drainage and irrigation will have been reached, and the efficiency with which such land can be utilized will assume paramount importance.

From the practical standpoint, however, the limits to which drainage or irrigation can be pushed are much smaller. A recent Soviet Geographical publication warned that the widespread drainage of Polissia would lead to wide seasonal fluctuations of the local rivers, a drop in the ground water level and, with the onset of the summer dry weather, the possible reactivation of drifting sands and dust storms.[38] It recommends that a large portion of this land be left in its natural state to regulate the water balance of the upper Dnipro basin.

More expensive technical modifications can extend the limits. Under conditions of seasonal drought the best results can be achieved if drainage is accompanied by irrigation. In Ukraine, however, such practice is exceptional and is now being slowly introduced on an experimental basis. Most drainage systems consist of simple, open trenches, and even the more efficient underground tile drainage systems are scarce. Presumably, if sufficient funds are made available, the technological problems can be solved. In the 15 year period (1971-1985) the regime will spend, it is reported, 10 billion rubles for irrigation and drainage projects in Ukraine and reconstruct 1.7 million hectares of the old drainage systems [39] — equal to the entire drainage system in Ukraine in 1972. Presumably the new techniques of two-way water control with sprinkler irrigation and tile drainage would then be installed.

It is more difficult, however, to cut through the red tape of bureaucracy that leads to systems prepared for drainage going unused for several years. In the Trubizh drainage district, for example, the farms were not ready to use the drained lands made available to them because they lacked the special equipment, additional fertilizers and lime, seeds and other inputs for farming on peat lands. Funds were not advanced to the farms to acquire such inputs in time. If a regional planning agency were allowed to encompass all the facets of the operation in the drainage district, Volik suggests, such shortcomings could be avoided.[40]

Irrigation faces even greater restrictions because of the impending shortages of water. According to calculations made a decade ago, the surface waters of Ukraine could provide for the irrigation of not more than 6.9 million hectares.[41] However, the availability of surface water in Ukraine is gradually being reduced. As a result of higher moisture retention in the soil from deep, fall plowing, increasing water consumption by industries and cities, increased evaporation of water from the huge reservoirs built on the Dnipro in the last two decades, plus the expected withdrawal for irrigation, the geographer L'vovich estimates that the flow of the Dnipro near its mouth will be reduced by 35 percent by 1980. The other rivers of southern Ukraine are expected to experience similar reductions of flow.[42] As a result it is now estimated that by 1980 there will be sufficient surface flow to irrigate only 5.7 million hectares.[43] To reach the ultimate goal of 10 million ha., as envisioned by the party, additional water would have to be diverted from the northern rivers into the Dnipro system, and ground water for irrigation would have to be withdrawn. Regardless of whether the

TABLE VII

PLANNED PRODUCTION OF MAJOR FOOD COMMODITIES NINTH FIVE YEAR PLAN

COMMODITY	U.S.S.R.		UKRAINIAN S.S.R.	
	Annual Average Production 1971-1975	Percent Increase Over 1966-1970	Annual Average Production 1971-75	Percent Increase Over 1966-1970
Grain (million tons)	195	116.3	40	120
Meat (million tons)	14.3	123.5	3.2	119
Milk (million tons)	92.3	114.6	20.3	113
Eggs (billions)	46.7	130.2	10.4	126
Wool (thousand tons)	464	116.6	27	112

Source:
Gosudarstvennyi piatiletnii plan razvitiia narodnogo khoziaistva SSR na 1971-1975 gody (Moscow, 1972), pp. 167, 262.

government planning agencies to make radical changes in the future, and how these changes would affect the patterns of Ukrainian agriculture.

The Current Five-Year Plan

According to the current plan Ukraine is developing its agriculture along its traditional lines of specialization, with a notable focus on grains (Table VII). In the Soviet Union as a whole the production of meat, eggs and wool is to proceed at a faster rate than that of grain. In Ukraine, however, the rates of growth for the animal products, including milk, are expected to be lower than in the Soviet Union as a whole. Apparently Ukraine may be geared to assume the role of supplying feed grains at a low cost to the more northerly livestock regions while at the same time increasing its own output of meat, milk and eggs to meet the yet unfulfilled demand for a properly balanced protein diet of its population.

Corn, the chief feed grain, leads all the grains in the projected rate of increase of production by 1975. In addition, sizeable production increases are expected in the labour-intensive preparation of flax fibre (exported for processing to Czechoslovakia), fresh vegetables, fruits and berries and grapes.[31] The last three groups are expected to cater to the rising republican demand for them, although the development of early potatoes and vegetables along the Donets River and elsewhere suggests an interest, on the part of planners, to cater to the large Moscow urban market. Similarly the higher purchase prices offered to potato and vegetable growers of Crimea is specifically designed to improve the food supply of these perishables to the resort cities on the Black Sea coast.[32]

In order to attain the planned increases, Ukrainian agriculture will have to intensify its farming even more. Various means of raising the productivity of land, plants, animals, capital investment and people have been suggested.[33] However, the current Five-Year plan specifically mentions only three ways in which agricultural intensification would be pursued in Ukraine: increased specialization, the use of improved seeds, and especially drainage and irrigation.[34] A brief review of the two most publicized modes of agricultural intensification — drainage and irrigation — is in order. This will be followed by an examination of the most recent trends in agricultural specialization.

Drainage and Irrigation

The programme of drainage and irrigation constitutes only one, albeit the most spectacular, of a number of measures designed to increase the productivity of agricultural land. The other measures include various agronomic techniques designed to reduce soil erosion and improve soil structure, the chemical treatment of poor soil to make it usable for growing crops, and the application of fertilizers to increase crop yields and improve soil cover. The effectiveness of improving land to attain consistently higher yields depends not so much on a rapid advancement in any one of the inputs, such as drainage and irrigation, but on the entire complex of inputs, including a well-balanced fertilization programme that would satisfy all the requirements of the plants grown. Therefore, as we shall see, the problems of drainage and irrigation cannot be considered in isolation from the other inputs essential in farming.

For a long time Ukrainian agriculture relied on the natural productivity of its farmland. Marshy conditions precluded extensive agriculture in Polissia. Recurring droughts in the southern steppe brought untold losses to grain production. Even in the favourable parts of Ukraine where moisture was adequate the constant cultivation of the land combined with a limited use of manure and a lack of fertilizers contributed to very low yields by European standards.

In the last two decades a belated effort was started to improve land productivity in Ukraine. The drainage of marshy lands, begun long before the revolution, increased at a faster rate after World War II and especially after 1965 (Table VIII).

116

TABLE VIII

LAND MELIORATION AND FERTILIZER SUPPLY

Year	Land Prepared for Drainage on Collective and State Farms Total drainage network (1,000 ha.)	Tile drainage (1,000 ha.)	Land Prepared for Irrigation on Collective and State Farms (1,000 ha.)	Supply of Fertilizer to Collective and State Farms in terms of nutrient content (1,000 tons)
1917	454	n.d.	17.4	n.d.
1953	870	n.d.	156	n.d.
1956	961	n.d.	n.d.	n.d.
1957	n.d.	n.d.	218	n.d.
1958	n.d.	n.d.	n.d.	459
1960	1,056	38.3	268	482
1965	1,278	128	503	1,286
1970	1,467	259	923	2,165
1971	1,536	304	1,012	2,436
1972	1,617	363	1,096	2,677

Sources:

Narodnoe khoziaistvo SSSR v 1965g. (Moscow, 1966), pp. 357, 362, 365; . . v 1970g. (Moscow, 1971), p. 349; . .1922-1972g. (Moscow, 1973), pp. 353, 361, 363; Sel'skoe khoziaistvo SSSR ((Moscow, 1960), pp. 258-59; Ukraina za 50 rokiv (Kyiv, 1967), p. 144.

water transfer schemes are ultimately implemented or not, it is clear that water for irrigation is in short supply, and that it should be used for irrigation as efficiently as possible. In present-day Ukraine this is not the case.

The older irrigation schemes, and especially the large ones built until 1966, were designed for surface channel and flood irrigation. To save money on construction, canals were not lined. This resulted in considerable seepage, water logging and salinization, destroying good agricultural land and wasting water. Such massive wastages, of course, cannot be tolerated, and recently it was disclosed that 20 million rubles were spent to re-build some portions of the Inhulets irrigation system that was put into operation in 1963.[44]

The new installations reportedly use concrete troughs, steel pipes and, in most cases, sprinkler irrigation. Such facilities reduce the wastage of land and water, save on labour, improve the management of crops, and avoid soil erosion.[45] Moreover, along the North Crimean canal, the new large irrigated areas will perform a dual function. The scientists hope that, in addition to providing water for crops on the spot, the plots of irrigated land will have a moderating micro-climatic effect that the farms could put to good use. They plan to alternate narrow strips of non-irrigated land with wider strips of irrigated plots. The increased atmospheric humidity over irrigated plots, they hope, will protect the grains grown on the non-irrigated strips from the hot dry winds (sukhovii) that occasionally blow through the region.[46]

In addition to the large projects, utilizing water diverted from the Dnipro, the party initiated, in 1963, a drive to expand small-scale irrigation.[47] Each farm was, and is still being urged, to tap groundwater and irrigate a plot of land 50 to 100 hectares in size in order that targets for increased yields of wheat and the output of wheat for the republic be met.[48] This approach cannot be considered economical from the standpoint of farms that must purchase scarce specialized equipment (if they are fortunate enough to get it) and other inputs for a very limited fund at their disposal. A greater concentration of irrigation on larger areas and fewer farms would, no doubt, yield higher returns on the investment, but the state prefers to save its own funds by laying the burden of investment on the farms themselves.

What the large irrigation projects may save on economies of scale they lose because of the vested interests of the ministry that builds the projects. The Ministry of Land Reclamation and Water Resources not only acts as the designer and builder, but also as its own client and inspector. As a result the work performed does not serve the best interests of agriculture, but simply provides for the fastest and cheapest way of expanding the area prepared for irrigation. To alleviate this problem, the economist V. Tregobchuk suggests that the functions of the client and inspector be transferred to the Ministries of Agriculture and of State Farms.[49]

The expansion of irrigation opens up wide possibilities of selecting those crops that would be most responsive to additional water and benefit most from the warmer climate of the southern steppe. It is widely known that corn responds much better to irrigation than wheat, and will benefit much more from supplemental irrigation in the southern steppe. It is also known that vegetables, potatoes and especially grasses increase their yield much more as a result of irrigation than wheat or barley.[50] Irrigated orchards and vineyards give the highest returns per unit land area.[51] Yet according to the latest statistics wheat or barley occupies a larger area on irrigated land than corn, and the area under vegetables is exceeded by that of grains by almost two times. Orchards and vineyards occupy a very small fraction of the irrigated land.[52] A much higher output could be derived from further re-structuring and specializing of sown areas under the irrigation but this hinges, at the same time, on a greater input of fertilizers, herbicides and pesticides,[53] availability of labour, and less pressure on Ukraine to meet its grain commitments.

Specialization

The Marxist-Leninist ideology assumes, as a basic truth, that large-scale specialized operations, whether in industry or agriculture, are progressive and more efficient as they benefit from the economies of scale. It was this ideological foundation that had to justify, from an economic standpoint, collectivization throughout the Soviet Union. It was again an ideological crutch for justifying the amalgation and enlargement of collectives during the 1950's. Now it is invoked again as a new approach is being taken to gain economies of scale by means of specialization.[54]

The new approach differs considerably from the abortive gigantomania that swept the state farms in the trying years of the First Five Year Plan. The new approach recognizes that a large specialized operation depends on the smooth functioning of its links with suppliers and purchasers and a sophisticated network of services. After a cautious beginning, the past party congress (1971) has generated considerable enthusiasm for organizing agro-industrial complexes and inter-farms cooperation.[55]

In its broadest sense, the agro-industrial complex integrates different branches of the national economy and brings about better interaction among them in order to promote rapid advancement in agriculture. According to the Soviet economist Lemeshev, this programme would assure a smooth and balanced allocation of resources and transmission of goods and services among the interrelated branches that, at the present time, suffer from administrative isolation and high levels of inefficiency.[56] Another aspect of the programme would involve the "industrialization" of agricultural production in order to increase labour efficiency in agriculture. This would require not only the mechanization of all the processes of farm production, but also farm specialization, with related increase of inter-farm cooperation and vertical integration.[57]

In a narrow sense, the agro-industrial complex relates to the vertical integration between a processing plant and the adjacent, specialized farms.[58] This integration, it is claimed, secures a new level of concentration of production and a high level of specialization with the fullest and broadest use of the raw materials, by-products and wastes at the processing plant. Moreover, it creates pre-conditions for the most efficient flow patterns to emerge, and allows for a "rational" use of the labour force, reducing the high seasonal fluctuations.[59] In the Ukrainian S.S.R. certain kinds of agro-industrial complexes have been functioning already for some time. For example, the Ministry of Food Industry has 455 plants in wine-making, vegetable and fruit canning sugar beet processing, and sunflower-oil extracting operations, of which 217 are organized on the basis of an agro-industrial complex. The latter, together with 222 specialized state farms, make up 200 separate agro-industrial complexes.[60] However, basic questions of accountability among the enterprises within each agro-industrial complex still remain to be worked out.[61] For this reason, at least, the enthusiastic claims of high efficiency do not appear entirely convincing at this time.

The inter-farm cooperation involves the establishment of a center that would perform a service from which the participating, share-holding collective farms would benefit. Perhaps one of the oldest and certainly the most widespread type is the inter-farm building organization. In 1961 there were 562 such organizations in Ukrainian S.S.R. that encompassed, among their share-holding members, 92.6 percent of the republic's collective farms. By 1965 their membership had increased to 96.7 percent.[62]

More recently, new kinds on inter-farm associations began to appear that related specifically to the production process. Among these the earliest involved the establishment of inter-farm feedlots, but their development was slow and by 1965 numbered only 36.[63] Far more widespread were the livestock feeding inter-farm associations that allowed for each of the participating farms to specialize in any one stage of animal raising, from breeding the young to fattening and finishing. Both efforts were crowned with a measure of success in that meat output expanded considerably. However, the meat processing plants and storage facilities in Western Ukraine were neglected to the point where the fattened cattle cannot be handled and must be shipped, live, as far as Armenia, suffering serious weight losses.[64]

The broiler industry, relying heavily on incubators, gained considerably from specialization and inter-farm cooperation. Even the state farms specializing in the production of bird meat have formed regional associations. For example, the two main centers near Kyiv incubate the young, then deliver the birds to their associated satellite farms for feeding, and finally receive the grown and fattened birds from the satellite farms for slaughter. The satellite farms obviously benefitted from sharing the incubating and slaughter facilities at the main centers, and as a result the volume of the combined operations increased by 1.5 times. [65]

The supply of feed rich in protein and vitamins was and remains a criticial bottleneck in expanding meat production. [66] To solve this problem the collective farms pooled together their funds to establish inter-collective farm mixed feed plants. Presently there are more than 200 such plants capable of an output greater than that of the state-funded enterprises, but their expansion of production is restricted by the fact that they can get from the state only one-fourth of the premixes and protein-vitamin supplements they need. [67]

On the whole, inter-farm cooperation in the production functions has demonstrated its potential usefulness. Unfortunately, its effectiveness is greatly hampered by the lack of local road networks that the farms themselves must finance, [68] and a declining availability of transportation resources in comparison to the rising farm needs.[69] The efforts are also thwarted by a lack of adequate vertical managerial links with the industry because of administrative isolation.

Even more difficulties are encountered when the republican planning body tries to exert administrative pressure to have collective farms assume higher levels of specializations. Whenever problems arise, the local (oblast and raion) planning organs are blamed: either they ignore or oppose the wishes of the republican planners, or they employ a heavy-handed administrative approach of simply reducing the mix of the required deliveries without providing the farms with adequate funds to reorganize their operations. Indeed, they are blamed for stifling the incentive of collective farms to reorganize by presenting them not only with a specific annual target for sales of different commodities, but also with livestock numbers, livestock productivity, sown acreage, and yields of crops. They are even blamed for frequently changing their plans, which not only upsets good farm management but violates the decision of the March (1965) Plenum of the Central Committee of the C.P.S.U. All these sins reflect the lingering habits of the local administrators, who disrupt rather than help in the planning of farming operations. [70]

The local administrators, however, may have a valid reason for perpetuating the practice of procuring a broad mix of commodities and for resisting imposed specialization. The removal of a small, though essential, branch of production on collective farms has resulted in local shortages of the product, for collective farmers encountered difficulties purchasing these commodities from state stores or from neighbouring farms. [71] Even Brezhnev noted, at the 3rd All-Union Congress of Collective Farmers, that the elimination of peasant self-sufficiency in food, especially under condition of poor transport, is not normal. Although our path obviously leads to the specialization of farms, he observed, it is not permissible to endulge in extremes and leap across stages of development. [72]

Even if extremes are not reached, a mere increase of the most productive branch and a reduction or elimination of the less productive one does not in itself provide for more efficient farming. When an optimal combination of various key branches of the farm is not maintained, the main, expanded branch will enjoy an increased income from use of diverted resources, but the entire farm will experience a decreased income. [73]

Obviously, the path of converting farms to more highly specialized operations is no easy matter. It is not surprising, therefore, that in February, 1974 the party officialdom in Kyiv called a special conference to discuss the matter. After some deliberation it urged every oblast, raion and farm to make use of the expertise of scientists, and with their help to devise a well defined programme of agricultural specialization and concentration of production for the future.[74]

CONCLUSION

Agricultural specialization is directed to meet the goals of the Soviet Union: self sufficiency in the main agricultural produce and adequate provision of food for major industrial districts. By virtue of its natural endowments, the Ukrainian S.S.R. performs a leading role in this task. It produces more than enough to feed its population and contributes more sugar beets and corn for grain than the rest of the Soviet Union. As the demand for agricultural products continues to grow, Ukraine is expected to intensify agricultural production in all the specialties it had developed since the turn of the century. In order to achieve this goal, the party envisions increasing the potential by means of various inputs, including irrigation and drainage, and farm specialization. The land improvement objectives are grandiose, but for ecological reasons greater efficiency will have to substitute for their contemplated scale. Farm specialization may contribute to more efficient production, but this is difficult to reach because of the abysmal neglect of rural services in the past and, despite the fanfare surrounding the agro-industrial complex, the present administrative isolation between agriculture and industry.

In the past Ukrainian agriculture benefitted the Russian Empire with enormous grain exports and production of numerous commodities for home consumption, including sugar. After the revolution, the grains were diverted to Russian northern industrial cities and the profits from selling this cheaply procured grain went a long way to industrialize the entire Soviet Union. Presently the price zonation on grains is such that Ukrainian agriculture supplies the small though strategic shipments of food and grain to Cuba and earns hard currency with occasional sales of sugar, oil and grain to European countries outside the Soviet bloc and to Japan.

FOOTNOTES

1.   See, for example, H. H. McCarty and J. B. Lindberg, **A Preface to Economic Geography** (Englewood Cliffs: Prentice-Hall, 1966), pp 216, 222-24; W. B. Morgan and R. J. C. Munton, **Agricultural Geography** (London: Methuen & Co., 1971), pp. 66-69; W. W. Wilcox, W. W. Cochrane and R. W. Herdt, **Economics of American Agriculture** (3rd ed; Englewood Cliffs: Prentice-Hall, 1974), pp. 21-27; H. F. Breimyer, **Individual Freedom and the Economic Organization of Agriculture** (Urban: University of Illinois Press, 1965), p. 63.

2.   K.P. Obolenskii, **Teoriia i praktika spetsializatsii sel'skogo khoziaistva** (Moscow, 1970), pp. 5-11.

3.   **KPSS v rezoliutsiiakh i resheniiakh sezdov, konferentsii i plenumov TsK** (Moscow, 1954), 3:56.

4.   Figures for this and the following paragraph are based on the F.A.O. statistics as reported in their production yearbooks. The figures for Ukraine are taken from official Soviet publications.

5.   The densities are in the order of 50 head of cattle equivalent per 100 hectares of farmland or more. **Atlas sel'skogo khoziaistva SSSR** (Moscow, 1960), p. 179.

6.   **Sel'skoe khoziaistvo SSSR** (Moscow, 1971), p. 377.

7.   The figures relate to Ukraine within the boundaries of contemporary Ukrainian S.S.R. According to Kubiiovych, who used the ethnographic limits of Ukraine, the figures are somewhat higher. I.O. Hurzhii, **Ukraina v systemi vserosiiskoho rynku 60-90kh rokiv XIXst.** (Kyiv, 1968), pp. 52-53, 60; V. Kubiiovych, **Heohrafiia Ukrainy i sumezhnykh kraiv** (Krakow, 1943), pp. 398-400.

8.   Hurzhii, **op. cit.**, pp. 60-61.
9.   J. Anderson, "A Historical-Geographical Perspective on Khrushchev's Corn Program", in J. Karcz, ed., **Proceedings of Conference on Soviet and East European Agriculture** (Berkeley: University of California Press, 1967), p. 105.

10.   Hurzhii, **op. cit.**, pp. 60, 68-72.

11.   **Ibid.**, pp. 73-76.

12.   A general discussion of these trends with occasional references to Ukraine may be found in V.P. Timoshenko, **Agricultural Russia and the Wheat Problem** (Palo Alto, California: Standford University Press, 1932), pp. 172-95.

13.   A more detailed discussion of this intention and its fate may be found in W.A.D. Jackson, "The Problem of Soviet Agricultural Regionalization," **Slavic Review**, Vol. 20, No. 4 (December, 1961), 656-78.

14.   A. Archimovich, "Botanical-Geographical Changes in the Distribution of the Field Crops of the Ukraine During the Last Fifty Years," **The Annals of the Ukrainian Academy of Arts and Sciences in the United States**, Vol. 11, No. 1-2 (31-32) (1964-1968), 60-61.

15.   For further details see N. Jasny, **Khrushchev's Crop Policy** (Glasgow, 1965), pp. 46-51.

16.   Jackson, **op. cit.**, pp. 668-70.

17. N.A. Gvozdetskii, "Raboty geografov po raionirovaniiu SSSR v interesakh sel'skogo khoziaistva," **Izvestiia Akademii Nauk SSSR. Seriia geograficheskaia** (1962) 5:89.

18. Jackson, **op. cit.**, pp. 674-78.

19. This is discussed in greater detail in R.G. Jensen, "Regionalization and Price Zonation in Soviet Agricultural Planning," **Annals of the Association of American Geographers**, Vol. 59, No 2 (June, 1969), 324-47.

20. **Ibid.**, p. 343. The basic physical land survey, by 1970, had covered 97.7 percent of the agricultural land of the Ukrainian S.S.R. (N.R. Obraztsova, "Oblik i vykorystannia zemel'noho fondu Ukrains'koi RSR," **Ekonomika i orhanizatsiia sil'skoho hospodarstva** (1970), 24:84. However, a uniform methodology for the qualitative and economic evaluations of agricultural land still has to be determined and implemented to complete the land inventory. V.A. Semenov, **Kachestvennaia otsenka sel'skokhoziaistvennykh zemel'** (Leningrad, 1970), p. 4; I.R. Mikhasiuk, **Ekonomicheskaia otsenka zemli i regulirovanie rentnykh dokhodov kolkhozov** (Moskva, 1970), p. 21.

21. These have been described by J. Anderson, **op. cit.**, pp. 104-28, and W.A.D. Jackson, "The Virgin and Idle Lands Program Reappraised," **Annals of the Association of American Geographers**, Vol. 52, No. 1 (March, 1962) 69-79.

22. R.L. Turner, "Growing Crops by Decree: Khrushchev's Corn Campaign in the Ukraine" (unpublished M.A. thesis, Wayne State University, Detroit, 1970), p. 65.

23. See, for example, V.A. Golikov, ed., **Itogi i perspektivy: sel'skoe khoziastvo posle martovskogo Plenuma TsK KPSS** (Moscow, 1967); **Sel'skoe khoziaistvo SSSR na sovremennom etape: dostizheniia i perspektivy** (Moscow, 1972). The impressive results of these high rates of investment have been recognized by western observers, such as Keith Bush. See his "Soviet Agriculture: Ten Years Under New Management," unpublished Radio Liberty Research Paper, Munich, August, 1974, p. 1.

24. **Materialy XXIII s'ezda KPSS** (Moscow, 1966), p. 251.

25. **Pravda**, October 31, 1968 quoted by Obolenskii, **op. cit.**, pp. 3-4.

26. A.N. Rakitnikov, **Geografiia sel'skogo khoziaistva** (Moscow, 1970), chapters 4, 5 and map 8.

27. G.A. Kuznetsov, **Geografiia i planirovka sel'sko-khoziaistvennykh raionov** (Moscow, 1971).

28. P.I. Koloskov, **Klimaticheskii faktor sel'skogo khoziaistva i agroklimaticheskoe raionirovanie** (Leningrad, 1971).

29. I.I. Zametin and P.P. Pertsev, **K voprosu o spetslalizatsii sel'skogo khoziaistva** (Moscow, 1970), p. 33.

30. **Razmeshchenie i spetsializatsiia sel'skogo khoziaistva SSSR** (Moskva, 1969).

31. P.H. Dubinov, "Sil'ske hospodarstvo Ukrains'koi RSR — do 50-richnoho iuvileiu Radians'koho Soiuzu," **Visnyk sil'skohospodars'koi nauky** (1972), 11:6; V. Makarenko and D. Putov, "Harantuvaty mil'iard pudiv," **Ekonomika Radians'koi Ukrainy** (1974), 2:5, 12; editorial interview with P.L. Pohrebniak, the Minister of

Agriculture of Ukrainian S.S.R. entitled "Milliard pudov Ukrainskogo khleba," **Zernovoe khoziaistvo** (1973), 9:2-4.

32. Z.I. Kuropiatnyk, "Spetsializatsiia ovochivnytstva — osnova pidvyshchennia ioho efektyvnosti," **Ovochivnytstvo i bashtannytstvo** (1974) 17:121; T. Mykhailenko, "Pro zbil'shennia vyrobnytstva rannikh ovochiv u raionakh pivdennostepovoi zony Ukrainy," **Ekonomika Radians'koi Ukrainy** (1973), 2: 16-23.

33. I.A. Chepurnov and V.Z. Makarenko, "Tempy i proportsii razvitiia sel'skogo khoziaistva Ukrainy v deviatoi piatiletke," **Organizatsiia i planirovanie otraslei narodnogo khoziaistva** (1972), 26-27: 157-66.

34. **Gosudarstvennyi piatiletnil plan razvitiia narodnogo khoziaistva SSSR na 1971-1975 gody** (Moscow, 1972), p. 264.

35. **Oroshaemoe zemledelie na Ukraine** (Kyiv, 1971), p.8.

36. S.M. Alpat'ev, "Dosiahnennia nauky v haluzi hidrotekhniky i melioratsii na Ukraini," **Visnyk sil'skohospodars'koi nauky** (1970) 4:91; M.A. Harkusha, "Stan i perspektyvy rozvytku melioratsii na Ukraini," **Visnyk sil'skohospodars'koi nauky** (1970), 4:82.

37. V.F. Volik, K.V. Primak and S.P. Khvorostian, "Ekonomicheskie problemy razvitiia melioratsii na Ukraine," **Organizatsiia i planirovanie otraslei narodnogo khoziaistva** (Kyiv, 1972), 26-27:192.

38. A.M. Marinich, ed., **Ukraina: obshchii obzor** (Moscow, 1969), p. 233.

39. Alpat'ev, **op. cit.**, 4:91.

40. V.F. Volik, "Puti povysheniia urovnia intensivnosti ispol'zovaniia osushennykh zemel'," **Organizatsiia i planirovanie otraslei narodnogo khoziaistva** (Kyiv, 1970), 14:176-80.

41. M.I. L'vovich, **Reki SSSR** (Moscow, 1971), p. 269.

42. **Ibid.**, pp. 309-12.

43. A.M. Marinich and M.M. Palamarchuk, eds., **Ukraina i Moldaviia** (Moscow, 1972), p. 409.

44. **Pravda**, Jan. 23, 1974, p. 2.

45. Harkusha, **op. cit.**, p. 79; L.I. Haidarova, "Do pytannia zroshennia zemel' na Ukraini," **Problemy heohrafichnoi nauky v Ukrains'kii RSR** (Kyiv, 1972), pp. 285-86.

46. Marinich and Palamarchuk, **op. cit.**, p. 412.

47. P. Golovko, "Maloe oroshenie na Ukraine," **Zemledelie** (1970), 5:55.

48. Editorial, **Radians'ka Ukraina**, Oct. 20, 1972, p.1

49. **Pravda**, Jan. 23, 1974, p. 2

50. V. Tregobchuk, "Razvitie irrigatsii na Ukraine i rezervy povysheniia ee effektivnosti," **Voprosy razvitiia narodnogo khoziaistva Ukrainskoi SSR** (Kyiv, 1967), pp. 163-64.

51. B. Kruhliak, "Efektyvnist' kapital'nykh vkladen' u zroshuvanomu zemlerobstvi," **Ekonomika Radianskoi Ukrainy** (1972), 6:26.

52. Narodne hospodarstvo Ukrainskoi RSR u 1972 rotsi (Kyiv, 1974), pp. 255, 257-61.

53. Tregobchuk, op. cit., p. 166.

54. V.D. Iaroshenko and N.V. Pisachenko, "Nauchnye osnovy spetsializatsii sotsialisticheskikh sel'skokhoziaistvennykh predpriiatii," **Trudy Kharkovskogo Ordena Trudovogo Krasnogo Znameni Sel'skokhoziaistvennogo Instituta imeni V.V. Dokuchaeva** (1969), 84:11; Obolenskii, op. cit., pp. 509.

55. V.A. Karlov, "XXIVs" ezd KPSS o dal'neishem razvitii sel'skogo khoziaistva," **Sel'skoe khoziaistvo SSR na sovremennom etape** (Moscow, 1972), p. 18.

56. M.Ia. Lemeshev, "On the elaboration of a program for the development of the agro-industrial complex in the USSR," **Problems of Economics**, Vol. 14, No. 4 (August 1971), 40-41.

57. V. Venzher, "Social and economic problems in the industrialization of agricultural production," **Problems of Economics**, Vol. 14, No. 9, (January, 1972), 68-9.

58. I.V. Nikol'skii, "Industrial'no-agrarnye energoproizvodstvennye tsikly i agrarno-agrarno-promyshlennye kompleksy," **Vestnik Moskovskogo Universiteta, Seriia V, Georgrafiia** (1973), 6:36-9

59. M. Makeenko and R. Khalitov, "Agroindustrial associations and their effectiveness," **Problems of Economics**, Vol. 15, No. 9, (January, 1973), 71-89.

60. Iu. P. Lebedinskii, ed., **Problemy formirovaniia i razvitiia agrarnopromyshlennykh kompleksov** (Kyiv, 1971), p. 41.

61. B. Umetskii, "Agrarno-promyshlennaia integratsiia i interesy predpriiatii," **Voprosy ekonomiki** (1973), 8:107-16.

62. M.S. Suhoniako and V.B. Alekseev, "Rozvytok mizhkolhospnykh ob'ednan' — kharakterna rysa suchasnoho etapu kolhospnoho budivnytstva," **Pytannia politychnoi ekonomiky** (1968), 45:17.

63. Ibid., p. 19.

64. Izvestiia (January 23, 1974), p. 3.

65. A.A. Sennikov, "Naukovo obhruntovane rozmishchennia i spetsializatsiia radhospiv Ukrainskoi RSR," **Visnyk sil's'kohospodars'koi nauky** (1970), 4:31.

66. V.P. Shamrinskaia, "K voprosu o strukture kormov v kolkhozakh Ukrainskoi SSR," **Organizatsiia i planirovaniia otraslei narodnogo khoziaistva** (1969), 13:111-17; V. Shamryns'ka and A. Tipko, "Pidvyshchennia efektyvnosti vykorystannia kormiv — vazhlyva umova rozvytku tvarynnytstva," **Ekonomika Radians'koi Ukrainy** (1974), 2:57-62.

67. Izvestiia (January 23, 1974), p. 3.

68. I.A. Chapurnov, "Ratsional'na struktura — naivazhlyvisha umova pidvyshchennia ekonomichnoi efektyvnosti sil'skohospodars'koho vyrobnytstva,"

Pytannia politychnoi ekonomii (1969) 54:121-22; also see a brief popular article in Radians'ka Ukraina (January 26, 1972), p. 2.

69. V.I. Koteliants, "Voprosy sovershenstvovaniia sel'skokhoziastvennogo transporta," Organizatsiia i planirovanie otraslei narodnogo khoziaistva (1971), 24:140-44. 44.

70. B. Kuzniak, "Sovershenstvovanie planirovaniia zagotovok v sviazi so spetsializatsiei kolkhoznogo proizvodstva," Ekonomika Sovetskoi Ukrainy (1970), 10:20-24.

71. I. Kuznetsov, "Zemledelie i trebovanie spetsializatsii," Ekonomika sel'skogo khoziaistva (1971), 4:36.

72. P.G. Dubinov, "Problemy rozmishchennia i spetsializatsii sil'skohospodars'koho vyrobnytstva," Visnyk sil'skohospodars'koi nauky (1970), 4:18-19.

73. O.O. Shchypanovskii, "Deiaki pytannia spetsializatsii sil'skohospodarskoho vyrobnytstva," Visnyk sil'skohospodars'koi nauky (1969), 10:14, 17.

74. Radians'ka Ukraina (February 20, 1974), p. 1. The presence of scientific expertise and theoretical research in the area is not absent, as evidenced by the writings of K.G. Teleshek and others in Trudy Kharkovskogo Ordena Trudovogo Krasnogo Znameni sel'skokhoziastvennogo instituta imeni V.V. Dokuchaeva, Vol. 28 (1969).

75. Vovko, op. cit., pp. 60, 88. It should be noted, however, that most of the "Soviet grain delivered to Cuba originates from Canada or the United States.

Comments on Professor Ihor Stebelsky

Ukrainian Agriculture: The Problems of Specialization and Intensification in Perspective

by
Peter Woroby [1]
University of Saskatchewan

A. In the opinion of the discussant, **the scope of the paper** is much too wide.
   Historically, it reaches into the period before 1914 and then describes the successive stages of intensification and specialization under the Soviet regime — the Stalin, Khrushchev and Kosygin-Brezhnev periods — which were diametrically opposed to each other and had differing effects on Ukraine. It appears that no significant loss would have occurred if the paper had concentrated on the present conditions and omitted the historical content. The contemporary measures of intensification and specialization are very real, still in existence, and among others they represent the most serious approach to the solution of the problem. Technically, the omission of historical references would have given more opportunity to discuss and evaluate individual agricultural policies which have not received sufficient attention in the paper. The latter statement particularly applies to the exploits of intensification such as an improved use of seeds, fertilizer, machinery, etc.

   The aim of Dr. Stebelsky's paper is "to evaluate the importance of Ukrainian agriculture to the Soviet Union, to trace the evolution of agricultural specialization in the Ukrainian S.S.R., to adduce reasons for them, and to assess the trends in Ukrainian agriculture during the current Soviet drive for agricultural intensification and specialization." Applying these objectives, the author has presented a comprehensive survey of the relevant factors and meaningful conclusions. At the same time, one may argue that the questions of specialization and intensification of the Ukrainian agriculture could have been tackled somewhat differently by emphasizing the analytical results more and the historical facts less. Thus, one could disagree with the scope of the problem, exert some criticism regarding the methodology of inquiry,

B. In the field of **methodology**, one should be concerned with the yardsticks of assessing various steps of intensification and specialization. In following this pursuit two different approaches can be used. Firstly, one can compare the contemporary stage of development with past achievements (**historical or vertical evaluation**) by emphasizing the growth of returns and improvements. Secondly, one can rate the present economic status of Ukrainian agriculture in terms of the optimal development. Although the latter standard is very difficult to define, it can be approximated by referring to various benchmarks such as the average profile of agricultural conditions in the U.S.S.R. and the standing of other economically advanced countries. Sometimes this criterion can be defined through the process of rational deduction, rather than through comparisons, yielding scientific norms for the required supply, technical performance, input-output relationships, etc. The above analysis (**horizontal evaluation**) is very important and one should make extensive use of it while being very cautious of the underlying limitations. For example, international comparisons should be confined to countries or regions which are homogenous in regard to the climatalogical and soil conditions.

The discussed paper does not make full use of the above possibilities. It has no important international evaluations and the domestic comparisons (Ukraine vs. U.S.S.R.) are exclusively confined to global economic indicators with two significant exceptions (irrigation and agro-industrial complexes). The author does not attempt to appraise the level and effectiveness of individual measures of intensification and specialization. There is only one recorded use of the optimal criterion, when evaluating the performance of Ukrainian agriculture vs. the dietary standards of the required consumption.

In answering the above questions, one should make extensive use of various statistical measures such as: global totals, relative shares and per unit outputs (e.g., per capita and per hectare values). The author appears to be aware of the available techniques, but he does not use them with the appropriate skill in the required situations. For instance, he misuses the **global outputs** of Ukraine in international comparisons. His enumeration of the world standings of Ukraine for various products (including those where the country is relatively deficient) as significant landmarks is a bit redundant and misleading. Everybody knows that the magnitude of the population and territorial dimensions of Ukraine, coupled with the favourable natural endowments, should place her high in external relations. It appears that the author fell under the spell of Soviet propaganda which favours such evaluations.

Comparisons of the above kind do not reveal anything about the development status of the potential capability of Ukrainian agriculture, which does not match the Western European or North American standards. It would have been more rewarding if he had used the varying rates of specialization and intensification in various countries. He could have exemplified this by referring to the percent areas occupied by various crops, yields per hectare and agricultural worker, intensity of livestock investment in the total investment, or per hectare of farmland, degree of mechanization (value of machinery per worker and / or per hectare of applicable farmland) etc.

There is also an exaggerated use of **relative numbers** (percent shares) illustrating the participatory role of Ukraine in the Soviet economy. Some of them, such as percent of the total population (table 2) are quite justified. They could and should have been amplified. For instance, the gap between a 22.1 percent share in 1913 and 19.5 percent share in 1970-72 can be simply translated into an absolute deficit of 6,500,000 persons, which measures the excess toll (above the average effect) of famine, wars, and deportations. However, the application of percent figures, say, to the use of fertilizers is practically useless. While retaining approximately the same share of supply, Ukraine did not fare worse or better than the entire Soviet Union. Instead a reference to the absolute volumes reveals a significant step up in the intensification measures recently. Thus, the usage between 1964 and 1972 increased 2½ times and by extending this comparison two years back (1962) this ratio amounts to five times. It appears that calculation of the fertilizer supply per hectare of farmland would have supplied the author with stronger arguments of analysis. [3]

One can also object to the unqualified use of the **per capita values** of agricultural production. Fortunately, the author has confined this approach exclusively to the internal Soviet data (Ukraine vs. U.S.S.R.). Although errors which are hidden behind such figures are of lesser magnitude than they would be in international evaluations, they are nevertheless there. Since Ukraine has a higher percent of farm population than the U.S.S.R., which is more industrialized [4], the per capita outputs appear to be unduly favourable, even for livestock and livestock products (see table 2). It is much better to illustrate this point by relating the outputs of crops and livestock to the resource base as was done in the original draft. [5] The illustrated figures revealed that Ukraine has a 55 percent higher productivity in crop yields but no margin of efficiency in livestock production. (The latter effect is the result of the newly assigned specialization in grains — it was different in 1950 when it exceeded the U.S.S.R. average by 36 percent.)

C. Before one undertakes the **evaluation of the individual measures** of specialization and intensification judging them by their effectiveness and efficiency one should first define the major criteria to be used in the overall assessment. Ultimately these can be identified as the raised standard of living of the people (individual benefits) and / or improvement in the economic conditions of the region (collective benefits).

With regard to the material returns to the local residents there is a very interesting documentation in the paper (table 1) which shows the ratios of actual consumption in Ukraine vs. recommended Soviet standards. The results show that the Ukrainian population is short 50 percent in egg consumption, 40 percent in meat and fat consumption, 30 percent in milk and vegetables consumption and 25 percent in the use of vegetable oils. The only recorded surpluses apply to potatoes (60 percent), grain products (30 percent) and sugar (15 percent). It would be of great interest to compare these findings with some international figures, particularly of the economically advanced countries.

While one would certainly expect the outcome to be quite unfavourable, one cannot deny that a considerable improvement in the **standard of living** of the rural population in the U.S.S.R. and Ukraine has taken place in recent years. Working hours have declined and earnings have gone up. The "trudoden" system has been replaced by guaranteed wages and pay is not longer a residual charge on kolkhoz income after all other operating expenditures are met. There appears to be a genuine attempt on the side of the authorities to close the gap between urban and rural incomes. Improvements can also be noted in the provision of social and educational services, reconstruction of buildings etc. [6] No equality, however, has been achieved between village and town yet and probably will not be for some time, since one recognizes the fact that the latter conditions are far removed from the ideal mark.

While one can answer the first question in more or less a positive manner, asserting that the standard of living in Ukraine is not worse than in the rest of the Soviet Union, one should not forget its latent maximum potential. Taking into account the rich endowments of Ukrainian agriculture, one must logically expect that the accrued benefits here would exceed significantly the returns in other regions. Thus, we attempt to answer the second question; namely, to what extent the measures of specialization and intensification assigned to Ukraine are truly compatible with her own interests? Would Ukraine maintain the same pattern of agricultural production if it applied the principle of autarchy which is valid for the U.S.S.R. to its own territory, or, paraphrasing the issue politically — could or would the present specialization and intensification be followed by an independent Ukraine? Does not the optimization of the economic operations in large areas automatically contribute to the one-sided and often non-optimal developments in their parts? Thus the **rationality of labour division** (specialization) which might be very useful for the U.S.S.R. as a whole is not necessarily advantageous to Ukraine.

This point is amply illustrated under various headings in the paper. It lacks, however, a concluding summary evaluation. For instance, the reduction of hay fields in Ukraine, the decline of livestock operations, the export of feed grain, potatoes and vegetables to Central Russia, unfavourable zone prices, etc., clearly illustrate the colonial status of Ukraine depriving her of an autonomous self-sufficiency. It is not only quantitative exploitation of Ukraine in traditional staple products such as grain (emphasized by the author) but also qualitative discrimination with a deliberate attempt to make her more economically dependent.

Referring to the individual measures of specialization and intensification, the author pays sufficient attention to the former subject, but not enough coverage is devoted to the latter effects. It is worthwhile to review them briefly since only two topics, land drainage and irrigation, and agro-industrial complexes have been adequately discussed in the paper.

One has to agree with the detailed and accurate assessment of **drainage and irrigation** problems. The possible erosion of soil in the dried out marshes ("reactivation of drifting sands and dust storms") and shortage of water for irrigation purposes due to the excessive evaporation of water reservoirs, sloppy construction techniques of water canals and uneconomic use of water for grain production are sufficient examples of cumulative shortcomings. They prove how difficult it is for man to balance the ecology of environment and learn suitable lessons from past mistakes. In the case of the three water reservoirs on the Dnipro-River (Kakhovka, Kremenchuk and Kyiv) one should also consider the tremendous economic losses attributed to the flooding of the most fertile lands and the improvised and incompetent resettlement of villages and towns from the river bank areas.[7]

The timely completion of farm operations in the U.S.S.R. with the relatively short sowing, growing and harvesting periods require a considerable amount of **farm-machinery**. Various attempts have been made to estimate their "optimal park" out of which the most known are Khrushchev and Ponomarev's standards.[8] By evaluating 1973 machinery inventories by more modest criterion (Khrushchev's), one finds a general shortage of 20 percent for tractors, trucks and combines. Ponomarev's requirements, instead, yield a 35 percent deficit for tractors and trucks and 25 percent for combines. The unsatisfactory degree of mechanization is often supplemented by "volunteered" or "borrowed" help from the non-agricultural sector. The above conditions appear to be even less satisfactory in Ukraine which has a lower degree of "motive power at the disposal of workers" (approximately 23 of the U.S.S.R. average).[9] The reasons for it could be manifold: milder climate (longer working periods) than in other parts of the U.S.S.R., a higher share of less mechanized crops such as potatoes and sugar beets, and surplus of labour and, last but not least, economic discrimination.

The use of **mineral fertilizer** adds considerably to the increase in the yields of grain, fodder and technical crops. This has been recognized by Soviet authorities in the recently adopted measures of intensification which I mentioned when discussing the methodology of the paper. What is interesting to note is that in spite of consistent and accelerated efforts, the level of fertilizer application is still very low. In 1968, the Soviets used only 38 kgs of mineral fertilizer per ha. of plowed land vs 82 kgs in the U.S., 206 Kgs in West Germany and 224 kgs in the U.K. "By 1973, the Soviet rates of application had reached about one-half of the U.S. levels." [10] (This must be equivalent to some 60 kgs per ha. now.

Short of machinery and chemical ingredients, the agricultural economy of the U.S.S.R. is relatively **labour intensive**. This is even more pronounced in Ukraine which lags some 10 percent in overall labour productivity.[11] This must be the effect of various factors including the already mentioned effect of undermechanization. Additional features to be considered here are the unbalanced pattern of the population pyramid (excess of females and older people) and the seasonal effect of farmwork (peaking tendencies during the summer) leading to a partial underemployment. This is somewhat compensated by work on private plots, which unfortunately is progressively diminishing in importance (apparent lack of interest on the side of the very young, and a graduate relinquishing of such activity by the aged and infirm).

Another measure of intensification can be found in the rural **reconstruction** programme. It aims to consolidate many small localities into the optimal size communities. It is directly connected with Khrushchev's agricultural reform which abolished the institution of MTS and allowed the distribution of farm machinery among collective farms. Regarded as a progressive step initially, the authorities soon found out that some farm units were too small to be able to cope with the assigned tasks. Consequently, a drive has been started for an increase in the scale of collective farms by encouraging economic unions and amalgamations among neighbouring localities. This policy has brought about a smaller number of collective farms which, although farming one economic unit, are separated in space and are not fully efficient in their communal efforts. Therefore, the proposed resettlement of households from smaller localities is not unexpected; it represents the necessary step of streamlining management operations by reducing the cost of worker transportation and increasing the scale of central farm premises. (This is not necessarily a bad measure as viewed by the author.)

To offset seasonal unemployment, to increase labour efficiency in agriculture and to enhance the scale of operations, the Soviet authorities initiated the establishment of **agro-industrial complexes** and interfarm cooperation. In conventional terms, this is a return to the local processing of agricultural products and auxiliary non-farm occupations which were known in the Ukrainian village for a long time. Although minimal in scale, they were thriving economically during the NEP period and in the prewar times. They were entirely wiped out and absorbed into governmental enterprises during the time of collectivization. The new agro-industrial complexes represent vertical integration between the processing plant (owned by the collective farm or an association of farms) and the output of the farms. They attempt to use the raw materials to the fullest extent by eliminating wastes, utilizing by-products, reducing transportation costs, etc. In Ukraine, such processing operations are comprised of "wine making, vegetable and fruit canning, sugar beet processing and sunflower-oil extracting operations".

The economic results so far have been not very convincing. In my opinion these undertakings will survive when the economics of scale are such that they can compete with the large scale state enterprises. In other cases, their gains are only temporary, at most to be considered as stop-gap measures. A classical example is the construction by many collective farms of hydro and thermal electric stations. They cease to operate as soon as the grid power system reaches the vicinity of the farm. The dimunitive scale and high cost of operation make them instantly obsolete. On the other hand, no machine can simulate or reproduce the work of folk art and craft which do deserve full governmental and community support.

The **interfarm cooperation** in the fields of construction, feed lots, livestock exchange, and broiler industry seem to be reasonable attempts to rationalize and maximize the individual farm's operation. Presently, they face certain bureaucratic obstacles of red tape and interference. Given more freedom and initiative, these establishments can add significantly to the economy of Ukrainian agriculture.

Apply urban-rural standards to Ukraine, one has to stress the aspect of **agricultural overpopulation** which is idential with the **lack of urbanization**. This statement, particularly regarding the development status of cities, might be shocking to some of the readers. Nevertheless it is a fact, which becomes apparent when one eliminates the urban agglomeration of Donbas, Kyiv, Kharkiv, Odesa and two or three addtional centers. The great expanses of Ukrainian territory lack focal points of major industrial activity. This is not the case, however, in West-Central Russia, characterized by the concentration of manufacturing and urban centers which are highly supported by the U.S.S.R. government.

A significant decline in rural population has taken place in Ukraine in the past two or three decades. Some rural out-migrants, no doubt, have settled in the Ukrainian urban communities, while others (probably a majority) were coaxed or forced to move outside the borders of the Republic (very likely into similar farm occupations).

At the same time it was the Russian element, personified by the skilled labourer and bureaucrat, which moved into Ukrainian cities. Thus, the goals of industrialization and rural depopulation were cleverly combined with the intended effects of **ethnic exchange** and **assimilation**. [12]

D. The conclusions of this review are as follows:

1. There have been significant improvements in the agricultural techniques in recent years.

2. The conditions of work and the standard of living have also gained considerably.

3. In spite of this Ukrainian agriculture subsidizes the remaining regions of the U.S.S.R.: it does it not only quantitatively, but also qualitatively by performing the inferior role of specialization.

4. Agro-industrial complexes are a favourable innovation. They will survive in competition with governmental enterprises provided they reach an adequate scale of operation and the authorities do not interfere with local initiatives and decisions. Similar qualifications apply to interfarm associations.

5. The Ukrainian republic is agriculturally overpopulated and under-industrialized. This evaluation is valid from both internal Soviet standards of comparisons and the optimal point of view of development.

6. The rural out-migration, which is ethnically Ukrainian, is deliberately directed into areas outside of the Republic, while at the same time urban growth in Ukraine continuously attracts the inflow of Russian immigrants.

7. Reversal of the above negative effects may come only in the case of some liberalization and decentralization of political power in the U.S.S.R.

FOOTNOTES

1. This discussion is based on the original draft of the paper which has been significantly changed in the final version. The main points of criticism raised at that time, however, are still valid at the present.

2. This has partially been achieved by reducing the historical content in the present version of the paper.

3. See findings in table 8. The original evaluation of the relative share of Ukraine has been omitted in the final version of the paper. The same treatment has also been unnecessarily applied to the drained land, with the apparent detrimental effect. The percent shares were quite appropriate for this type of data.

4. In 1959 the rural-urban ratios were 54.3 percent and 52.1 percent respectively. The apparent gap assumed much wider proportions for employment on collective farms (41.4 percent vs. 31.4 percent).

5. Unfortunately this valuable information has been removed from the current presentation.

6. Refer to descriptive and illustrative examples in the recently published **History of Towns and Villages of Ukraine.**

7. Refer to the critical observations in the essay "Kakhovske More" by O. Dorzhenko.

8. K. Bush, "Soviet Agriculture: Ten Years Under New Management," Radio Liberty Research Paper, 1974, p. 10.

9. This presently missing statistical information was listed previously in the original draft.

10. K. Bush, "Soviet Agriculture: Ten Years Under New Management," Radio Liberty Research Paper, 1974, pp. 12 and 13.

11. Recorded previously in the original submission.

12. The Russian element which is predominantly urban increased from some three million in 1926 to nine million in 1970.

III
Sociology and Demography

Current Sociological Research in Ukraine

by
Alex Simirenko
The Pennsylvania State University

It is generally known that Ukrainians in and out of Ukraine made a major contribution to the development of sociology in the Russian Empire. It was Mykhailo Drahomaniv (1841-1895) who was the first to call himself a sociologist and earn himself the wrath of the Tsarist government, which took the term to be synonymous with socialist. Drahomaniv went on to edit the first sociological periodical in Ukrainian, called **Hromada** (Society), which he began publishing in Geneva in 1878. Drahomaniv had famous predecessors and contemporaries among whom towers the figure of Volodymyr Antonovych (1834-1908). Around the turn of the century the talents of such famous scholars N.I. Ziber, M.M. Kovalevsky, M.I. Tuhan-Baranovsky, M. Hrushevskyi and M. Shapoval emerged. These names, however, give only an inkling of the sociological work which was being carried out throughout the second half of the 19th century by the local societies throughout Ukraine which were dedicated to the gathering of information on history and folklore as well as on the current state of society.

It was natural, then, to expect that the revival of sociology in the post-Stalin era[1] in the Soviet Union as a whole would also contribute to the flowering of sociology in the Ukrainian Republic. Such development, however, has not taken place and sociology in Ukraine is relatively primitive in comparison to its Russian counterpart. Sociological research produced in Ukraine is quantitatively insubstantial and qualitatively inferior. This research, with exception perhaps in the field of demography, reflects little originality, it generates no excitement, and it reveals little awareness of its past, not only of the pre-Revoluntionary period but also of the 1920's when much research was still carried on. An American scholar visiting the Soviet Union in recent months was shown a map at the Institute of Sociological Research in Moscow which depicted the distribution of all the laboratories for sociological

137

research throughout the country. He estimates that the total number of these laboratories was in the neighbourhood of 90 to 120. The Ukrainian Republic had no more than 5 to 6 laboratories on the map. This ratio pretty well approximates the amount of sociological research coming out of Ukraine. From a publication of sociologists in Ukraine we know that there are laboratories at the University of Kyiv, the University of Kharkiv, and the University of Lviv. Research is also being conducted in the cities of Zaporizhia, Dnipropetrovs'k, Kryvy Rih, Zhdanov, and some others, but evidently without the support of established research centers. [2]

Explanations for Underdevelopment of Sociology in Ukraine

A variety of explanations can be advanced to account for the underdevelopment of sociology in Ukraine. In the opinion of this writer, several interrelated factors may be responsible for this state of affairs and the most obvious ones are not necessarily the most significant. Without the aid of first-hand information from sociologists working in Ukraine, the best that can be essayed is a fuzzy and incomplete sketch of the predicaments faced by Ukrainian sociologists.

Since one can assume that no significant developments in the USSR occur without guidelines from the Central Committee Apparatus, it is only fair to ask the question whether the underdevelopment of sociology in Ukraine, and in some other Soviet Republics such as Lithuania, is a deliberately planned phenomenon. There are certainly indications that sociologists in Ukraine, of whatever nationality, are not particularly trusted as representatives to the various international conferences held in the West or as exchange scholars for the purpose of acquainting them with Western sociology. As best as it could be ascertained one of the first, if not the first, Ukrainian sociologist from Ukraine to have been sent to the West participated in the VIII World Congress of Sociology, in Toronto, in August, 1974. N.V. Honcharenko from the Institue of Philosophy in Kyiv was one of a group of some 80 Soviet delegates, and his paper entitled "Humanistic Impact of Culture on Scientific and Technological Progress" made no mention of Ukraine and provided no empirical data.

Some may suggest that the very undevelopment of sociology in Ukraine may keep its sociologists at home. The fact is, however, that the majority of Soviet sociologists who are permitted to travel abroad are some of the least imaginative scholars that the country has to display, something which was well demonstrated at the World Congress in Toronto. For some inexplicable reason, even the best of Soviet scholars who came to Toronto felt obliged to exhibit their safest and least exciting work.

Even assuming that there has been no deliberate policy on the part of the Party to keep sociology in Ukraine in an underdeveloped state, it is quite likely that the traditional distribution of resources and rewards leads to a continuous migration of talent from Ukraine. There are certainly plenty of sociologists with Ukrainian names working outside of Ukraine, even if they are not the most prominent figures, to argue for the existence of a "brain-drain." We would need, however, considerably more data to say anything conclusive on this subject.

Another rather obvious factor is the political risk that is involved in being an innovative sociologist in general and one working in Ukraine in particular. No matter how dull Soviet sociology may look to many of us in the West, it is regarded as an extremely exciting and popular discipline within the Soviet Union. This is mainly due to the efforts of Soviet sociologists in their examination of formerly taboo subjects. This has made them vulnerable to periodic attacks by the Party in which they are accused of "gross theoretical and methodological mistakes" and are reminded that "sociology is a Party science." [3]

It can be imagined what such attacks could do to the sociologists in Ukraine if joined with the issue of nationalism. This is the period when such a thoroughly Ukrainian journal as **Folk Art and Ethnography**, established in 1925 and published by the Academy of Sciences and the Ministry of Culture of the Ukrainian Republic, is seemingly devoting all its efforts to the denunciation of Ukrainian nationalism and praising the superior experience of the Russian working class. The situation is even worse for such Ukrainian journals as **Filosofska dumka** (Philosophic Thought) or

Ukrainskyi istorychnyi zhurnal (Ukrainian Historical Journal), which also publish sociological material. It is not surprising, therefore, that the most imaginative research conducted in Ukraine is done by non-Ukrainians residing outside of Ukraine.

There is sufficient evidence available in the so-called underground publications coming out of Ukraine to suspect that there may be at least some resistance to sociological research either on ideological or patriotic grounds. In the pre-Revolutionary period the work of sociologists aided in the raising of national consciousness and it must be realized, at least by some, that sociology can also be used to destroy it. Here again, however, the evidence is fragmentary and inconclusive.

Perhaps the most subtle factor in holding down the development of sociology in Ukraine is the current state of Soviet sociology which is mainly concerned with survey research, when traditionally Ukrainians have favoured historical and developmental approaches to the study of society.[4]

Arutiunian's Study of a Ukrainian Village

Having examined over twenty pieces of sociological research conducted in Ukraine, it can safely be asserted that the best of them by far is that by I. V. Arutiunian, an Armenian sociologist who was on the faculty of the Moscow State University at the time of the study. His study[5] of the village of Terpinnia in the region of Zaporizhia is a politically daring work which ranks with the best of current Soviet studies.

Arutiunian's study contrasts markedly with the work of sociologists in Ukraine. For one thing, he shows no fear of demonstrating his familiarity with sociological research of the 1920's and 1930's, citing over thirty studies of villages in this period, several of which were published in Ukraine. Examining carefully the studies conducted by sociologists in Ukraine, we find no more than two references to past studies, one published in 1925 and one in 1930. While Arutiunian is not afraid to refer to the decline of sociological research in the Stalin era, no sociologist in Ukraine ever mentions this subject. Most refreshing of all is Arutiunian's humour in reference to politically sensitive subjects, while the prose of sociologists in Ukraine is deadly serious, even when they are discussing a potentially humourous subject such as a wedding.

The major flaw in Arutiunian's report of the study, common to most Soviet sociological research, is his failure to provide sufficient methodological details. To simply state, for example, that the subjects were randomly selected and therefore are representative of the population is not sufficient information for forming a judgment of the study. Arutiunians's report, however, is a model of perfection in comparison with reports of empirical research conducted by sociologists in Ukraine. There are also other, more subtle aspects of the study which seem to have been made possible by the fact that Arutiunian is not a Ukrainian national. For example, the name of the village — Terpinnia — suggests "endurance in the face of suffering" and, therefore, could easily be connected with dissident nationals if studied by Ukrainian sociologists.

Arutiunian claims that he was attracted to a study of Terpinnia by virtue of the fact that the village was studied by economists in 1935. Two thousand questionnaires were collected at that time but never processed, having been stored in the archives ever since. According to Arutiunian, no comparable study of a village population was undertaken in the Soviet Union during the 1930's. Thus, Terpinnia presented the possibility for a unique study of a village in its transformation over a thirty year period. Having said this, Arutiunian unfortunately presents only a couple of comparisons for the two periods, so that we remain ignorant of what the village was like in the middle of the 1930's.

On a theoretical level, Arutiunian addresses himself to the nature and dynamics of social classes within the Soviet Union and thus comes to question the most precious concepts of Soviet Marxism. The fixed division of the Soviet Union into two classes, industrial, office and professional workers on the one hand and peasants on collective farms on the other, is too "crude" a distinction to be of any serious sociological use. In

Arutiunian's view, this "anachronism" should be abandoned in favour of detailed studies of the relationships within specific classes. Furthermore, the concept of property ownership is also outmoded in a society where everything belongs to the people and nothing, therefore, to anyone in particular. According to Arutiunian, it is not ownership but use and control of property that is important in a socialist society. From this standpoint, collective-farm peasants emerge as truly disadvantaged members of Soviet society since they have the use and control of only one-tenth of all the resources of society. With this formulation, Arutiunian emerges as the main defender of collective-farm peasnts.[6]

Although six years have elapsed since the publication of Arutiunian's book, his ideas are still being largely ignored. This is particularly true of sociologists in Ukraine, who are likely to wait for the official Party pronouncement on the subject. In the meantime, they are determined to stick to the repetitious and propagandistic but nevertheless safe slogans. Iu. I. Shiriaev, in his articles on the Soviet intelligentsia, suggest that if the intelligentsia is to be thought of as a distinct class because it performs mental labour, we would then have to designate workers and peasants as members of one and the same class because they perform physical labour. [7] He insists that this, of course, cannot be the case. Arutiunian, however, following his initial assumptions, felt that what naturally followed was the need to divide labour into physical and mental types. In at least two instances, sociologists continue to insult the collective-farm peasantry by insisting that "the working class represents the decisive force for the building of a communist society." [8]

In Kharkiv a study of social mobility, intended to show how all strata of the population have access to mobility, continues to use the "crude" distinctions. The children of collective-farm peasants constituted 7.3 percent of the student body at Kharkiv University in 1965 and 1966, but increased to 15 percent in 1967 and 15.4 percent in 1968. At the Kharkiv Pedagogical Institute, however, there was hardly any change in the same period, from 9.8 percent to 10.9 percent. [9]

In still another work, Ia. S. Mostovy contends, without presenting evidence to that effect, that the introduction of technical and industrial progress into a village leads to the elimination of differences between physical and mental labour. [10] Arutiunian's research, on the other hand, demonstrates that such technical progress leads to the introduction of differentiation between physical and mental labour.

Selected Results of Arutiunian's Study

In 1963, the village of Terpinnia consisted of 1,722 households with a population of 5,158. Fifty-one percent of these belong to a collective farm and the rest were divided between workers in a local lime factory and other government institutions in the spheres of culture, education and trade. In 1964-65, questionnaires were filled out for 520 families covering 1,782 people or 34 percent of the village population. For purposes of comparison, data was also gathered on state farm workers located in two nearby settlements. Sampling was done in such a way as to distribute each of the four occupational categories (collective farmers, state farmers, factory workers, and government establishment workers) into four additional groupings: trained and untrained mental labour and skilled and unskilled physical labour. Such a differentiation permitted Arutiunian to claim, on the basis of concrete evidence, that each occupational category is in itself a complex structure which is not easily generalizable and certainly should not be used as a label.

The complex nature of each economic category is demonstrated by Arutiunian through the income of the various groups. This also gives him the opportunity to compare incomes of the 1935 period, which clearly indicate some of the reasons for the burial of this earlier study in the archives of the Ministry of Agriculture. Not only does it indicate the cruel exploitation of collective-farm peasants in 1935, but also the even more shocking decimation of the peasant population, through famine and destruction, to just about two persons per family. Arutiunian keeps silent about this feature of his data and only suggests that he wants to show the lack of serious functional differentiation among the peasant population in 1935. He prefers to point out the continued economic sacrifices of the collective-farm peasants at the present time. Arutiunian's data is presented below. [11] (Tables I and II.)

It has always been part of Soviet Marxist dogma to ascribe the cultivation of private plots to the collective-farm peasants who supposedly have not reached the proper level of class consciousness as have the workers. Arutiunian's study puts such ideas to rest, demonstrating that indeed some members of all strata of the population, including the state-farm peasantry, are involved in the raising of personal fruits and vegetables and maintaining a cow. To be sure, the collective-farm peasants are preoccupired to a greater degree with private agriculture, but this, according to Arutiunian, is necessary to supplement their inadequate incomes. The study reveals that the more stable and adequate the income, the lesser the involvement in private agricultural pursuits.

State-farm peasants, being more adequately remunerated, are not compelled to supplement their income to the same degree as those on a collective farm. Results of a budget study conducted in 1961, cited by Arutiunian, revealed that state-farm peasants supplemented their income from private plots by 23 percent, while collective-farm peasants supplemented their income by 42 percent. Arutiunian also concludes that the cultivation of private plots simply reveals the rural location of those who cultivate them, rather than being a major index of the class position of collective farmers. In his words: "It is, of course, not the class consciousness of workers in the city which prevents them from raising cabbage on the sidewalk." [12]

The maintenance of private plots by collective-farm peasants has always been a favourite whipping boy of Soviet agitators to whom the enormous productivity of such plots suggests a corresponding lack of devotion to the maintenance of collective production. After all, of the total yield, 60 percent of potatoes, 35 percent of vegetables, 42 percent of meat, and 73 percent of eggs come from private plots. [13] Arutiunian conclusively demonstrates, on the basis of his study as well as those of others, that private plots are maintained not by the able-bodied peasants but by their young children, the old, the sick, nursing mothers, and women taking care of many children. Quite clearly, it is the collective-farm peasant who is in the exploited position and not the other way around.

There is more to Arutiunian's study than it is possible to review at this time. It presents a wealth of data on a Ukrainian village which has not been available since the 1920's. The major focus is on the material culture of the villagers: the nature of their living quarters, the contents of their living quarters, inventories of beds, linens, dishes, furniture, incons, newspapers, magazines, etc. The work is in marked contrast to the recently published "study" of a Kuban' village by P. Simush, whose conclusion is "that we are witnessing the emergence of a completely new type of peasant." [14] While it can be easily recognized that Simush's study is a piece of propaganda dressed as a sociological study, there is nothing in Arutiunian's study to suggest that the village of Terpinnia has produced a "new type of peasant."

The Investigation of the "New Man" and Other Problems

No matter how inadequate the efforts of sociologists in Ukraine, some are nonetheless exposing the major myth of the Stalin and post-Stalin years, that of the formation of the "new Soviet man." Arutiunian's study has demonstrated that what we have is the "old man" who is forced to fashion his survival under new circumstances. The results of other studies, even if less adequate, point to the same conclusions.

V.O. Tykhonovych, in a book-length study of motivation towards productivity, reaches the following conclusion: "But at the current stage of development of our society and well into the future, material interest will remain one of the major incentives for the raising of work productivity. This necessitates a complete and thorough investigation of the material interests of the people . . . " [15]

The work of sociologists justifying material incentives simply follows the economic indicators showing that collective-farm peasants refuse to part with their products unless adequately remunerated. The more obscure, specialized literature on

141

the subject of various aspects of Soviet production is rather open on this point. A discussion of the sunflower production of Ukrainian collective-farm peasants, for example, reports that the government is forced to put out more money or face the withdrawal of this commodity from the market, as a result of either the reduction of the area sown or by "conversion of the seeds into oil on the spot" and its sale on the collective farm market. [16]

The survival of the "old man" is also indirectly documented in other studies by sociologists in Ukraine. In a letter to the editor of **Molod' Ukrainy**, a ninth-grade student asked an embarrassing question as to the reasons why certain occupations are disdained while others are worshipped. To her it seemed that all occupations are valuable to society. [17] A sociologist who responded to her avoided the crux of the matter by telling her which occupations are more prestigious. The studies conducted by sociologists in Ukraine also avoid facing up to the basic failure to instill pride and respect for all work. [18]

Mention should also be made of three studies on subjects which are rarely investigated. Samborsky conducted research on collective-farm peasants' participation at the meetings of their collectives. The peasants from two villages in the Kharkiv region responded that 69 percent of them remain silent during the deliberations. He concludes that some of them are simply not used to speaking up at public meetings, but that many also do not say anything because the collective is being run so well that no questions are necessary. [19]

Mialovytsky's study of the causes of divorce is prefaced by the inevitable reference to the growth and development of the new Soviet family, which is built on some new qualitative changes in the relationship between spouses. The causes of divorce which he lists do not seem to be very different, however. The number one cause of divorce in 25 percent of cases is said to be the couple's inadequate knowledge of one another and lack of preparation for married life. This followed by drunkenness and sexual meandering in 19 percent and 17 percent of cases, respectively. [20]

Nor has the new society been able to eliminate crime and delinquency, a subject which has been studied by two Ukrainian sociologists. We learn that in the city of Dniprodzerzhinsk teenagers, mainly between the ages of 16 and 18, have been committing theft of personal and governmental property, assault and rape. [21]

National Consciousness of Children in Nationally Mixed Families

In the decade from 1959 to 1970, the ratio of families in which man and wife are of different nationalities has increased from 11 percent to 13.5 percent. Ukraine has some of the highest figures in this respect, reaching 20 percent for the Republic as a whole and 35 percent for the cities. The Party has seized upon this condition as a sign of the internationalization of life for all Soviet nationalities. Sociologists in Moscow have begun studying the nationally mixed families, the best of which thus far was conducted by L. N. Terentieva. [22]

The passport declarations of sixteen year olds were studied in seven capitals of Union Republics and three capitals of autonomous republics: Kyiv, Minsk, Kishinev, Vilnius, Riga, Tallin, Ashkhabad, Kazan, Cheboksary, and Saransk. Two districts were studied in each city, one of which was always in the central part of the city and one in the suburbs. For some reason Terentieva did not find it necessary to study any Russian cities.

In Kyiv, 72.2 percent of families with mixed nationalities were composed of a Ukrainian and a Russian, 15 percent of a Ukrainian and some other nationality, 9.8 percent of a Russian and some other nationality, and only 1.5 percent of other nationalities. Ukrainians and Russians were also heavily intermarried in the other cities studied: Minsk, 10.9 percent; Kishinev, 35.1 percent; Vilnius, 17.0 percent; Riga, 22.8 percent; Tallin, 23.2 percent; Ashkhabad, 29.2 percent; Kazan, 25.8 percent; Cheboksary, 14.0 percent; and Saransk, 24.4 percent.

The figures for cities outside of Ukraine are rather important, because the chance is quite high that the children of these mixed families will declare themselves as Russian. If the father is Russian and the mother Ukrainian, almost 90 percent of teenagers declare their nationality as Russian, except for Tallin, where for some reason only 75 percent do so. The situation is somewhat better when the father is Ukrainian and the mother Russian. In this instance, from 17 percent to a high of 48 percent (in Vilnius) declare themselves as Ukrainian.

These findings made Terentieva so happy that she was unable to disguise her basic Russian chauvinism. She concluded that this reflects a trend-setting pattern, or in her words "the intensity and the general direction of the internationalization of the life of Soviet families." [23] The choice of Russian nationality is described as based on the "ethnic kinship of the three Slav peoples" and the "predominant role of the Russian language as the basic language of communication." [24]

In the pre-revolutionary period Ukrainian mothers always played an extremely significant role in the formation of the national consciousness of their children in families of mixed nationality. Therefore, one suspects that these official figures reflect, at least in part, a strategy of national survival. We can well expect that a large number of "dormant" Ukrainians are criss-crossing the country with Russian passports.

Conclusion

Sociology as a science of society is by its very nature a potential tool which can be used for the benefit of people as well as against them, depending upon those who control it. In the Soviet Union, sociology is under the complete control of the Party which insists on using it for its own purposes. In the words of Academician Rutkevich, who is presently in charge of Soviet sociology: "The Marxist sociologist, be he a scientific, Party, or economic worker, cannot adopt the pose of a 'disinterested researcher'." [25] Under these circumstances, the most rational response of patriotic Ukrainians whould probably be to resist the invasion of privacy and, therefore, to prevent the successful development of sociology as a discipline. The underdevelopment of sociology in Ukraine may be a reflection of a national strategy for survival.

TABLE I
VILLAGE INCOME DISTRIBUTION — 1935

1935 Yearly Average Wage

	Gov't. Inst.		Factory		Collective Farm	
	Family	1 Person	Family	1 Person	Family	1 Person
Trained Mental Labour	4,103	1,521	3,300	900	273	136
Untrained Mental Labour	2,066	683	3,300	900	235	114
Skilled Physical Labour	1,718	545	1,668	586	245	104
Unskilled Physical Labour	976	343	1,263	445	226	101

TABLE II.
VILLAGE INCOME DISTRIBUTION — 1964-65

1964-65 Monthly Average Wage Per Person

	Gov't. Inst.	Factory	Collective Farm	State Farm
Trained Mental Labour	36.8	33.6	24.2	39.4
Untrained Mental Labour	27.0	—	21.2	27.0
Skilled Physical Labour	28.2	28.2	20.0	30.6
Unskilled Physical Labour	19.6	21.6	16.1	28.6

FOOTNOTES

1. The revival of sociology in the post-Stalin era has received considerable attention in the writing of Western sociologists: Robert K. Merton and Henry W. Riecken, "Notes on Sociology in the USSR." **Current Problems on Social-Behavioral Research, Symposia Studies** No. 10. Washington, D.C. National Institute of Social and Behavioral Science (March, 1962), pp. 7-14; Leopold Labedz, "The Soviet Attitude to Sociology " **Soviet Survey**, 10 (1956), and in A. Simirenko, ed., **Soviet Sociology: Historical Antecedents and Current Appraisals**, Chicago: Quadrangle Books, 1966, pp. 210-223; Leopold Labedz, "Sociology as a Vocation," **Survey**, 48 (July, 1963), pp. 57-64 and in A. Simirenko, **ibid.**, pp. 224-232. Lewis S. Feuer, "Meeting the Soviet Philosophers," **Survey** (April, 1964), pp. 60-74. George Fischer, **Science and Politics: The New Sociology in the Soviet Union**. Ithaca: Cornell University, 1964. George Fisher, ed., **Science and Ideology in Soviet Society**. New York: Atherton, 1967. Elizabeth A. Weinberg, **Soviet Sociology, 1960-1963**. Boston: Massachusetts Institute of Technology, Center for International Studies, 1964; Talcott Parsons, "An American Impression of Sociology in the Soviet Union," **American Sociological Review, XXX**, No. 1 (February, 1965), pp. 121-125; Allen Kassof, "American Sociology Through the Soviet Eyes," **American Sociological Review, XXX**, No. 1 (February, 1965), pp. 114-121; Paul Hollander, "The Dilemmas of Soviet Sociology," **Problems of Communism** (November-December, 1965), pp. 34-46; and in A. Simirenko, ed., **op. cit.**, pp. 306-326; Alexander Vucinich, "Science and Morality: A Soviet Dilemma," **Science**, 159 (March, 1968), pp. 1208-1212; Alvin W. Gouldner, **The Coming Crisis of Western Sociology**. New York: Basic Books, 1970; Zev Katz, "Soviet Sociology: A Half-Way House," **Problems of Communism** (May-June, 1971), pp. 22-40; Alex Simirenko, ed., **Soviet Sociology: Historical Antecedents and Current Appraisals**. Chicago: Quadrangle Books, 1966; Alex Simirenko, **Social Thought in the Soviet Union.-** Chicago: Quadrangle Books, 1969.

2. L.V. Sokhan, ed., **Sotsiolohiia na Ukraini.** Kyiv: Naukova Dumka, 1968, pp. 5-6.

3. See M. Rutkevich, "Sociology and the Management of Society," **Pravda**, September 14, 1973, p. 3.

4. In the words of Howard Becker and Harry Elmer Barnes, "It may be mere coincidence, or there may be a determining cultural situation, but for whatever reason the Ukrainians seem to have displayed an especial fondness for historical sociology." Cf. **Social Thought from Lore to Science**. Second Edition. New York: D.C. Heath and Co., 1953, p. 1068.

5. Iu. V. Arutiunian, **Opyt sotsiologicheskogo izucheniia sela.** Moscow: Moscow University Publishing, 1968. For translation see **Soviet Sociology**, Vol. X, No. 1-4 (1971-72).

6. **Ibid.**, pp. 36-39

7. Iu. I. Shiriaev, "pro strukturu radianskoii intelihentsii," in L. V. Sokhan, ed., **Sotsiolohiia na Ukraini**, op. cit., p. 59.

8. V. Ia. Zavadiaka, "Vplyv zahal'noii osvity na zminu struktury robitnychoho klasu," in L. V. Sokhan, **ibid.**, p. 71. See also V. O. Romantsov, "Pro zminy struktury robitnychoho klasu URSR za stattiu ta vikom v pisliavoennyi period," **Ukrainskyi istorychnyi zhurnal**, Vol. 14, No. 4 (April, 1971), pp. 27-34.

9. V. I. Astakhova, "V. I. Lenin pro mistse intelihentsii v sotsialnii strukturi sotsialistychnoho suspilstva," **Filosofska dumka**, No. 2 (1970), p. 99.

10.   La.S. Mostovy, „Vplyv naukovo-tekhnichnoho prohresu na zmist silskohospodarskoi pratsi,” **Filosofska dumka, No. 2** (1971), **p. 57.**

11.   Arutiunian, **op. cit.**, p. 49-50.

12.   **Ibid.**, p. 55.

13.   **Ibid.**, p. 56.

14.   P. Simush, **The Soviet Collective Farm: A Sociological Study.** Moscow: Progress Publishers, 1971, p. 143.

15.   V.O. Tykhonovych, **Motyvy trudovoi aktyvnosty osoby.** Kyiv: Naukova dumka, 1972, p. 139.

16.   M. Kruchinin, "Material Incentives for Sunflower Production," **Zernovye i maslichnye kultury,** No. 8 (1970), p. 10.

17.   See **Molod' Ukrainy,** August 8, 1969.

18.   See I. M. Nazymov, "Deiaki sotsialno-psykholohichni faktory vyboru profesii shkoliaramy," in L. V. Sokhan, ed., **op. cit.,** pp. 102-14, and V. O. Pravotorov, "Osoblyvosti formuvannia profesiinoho interesu studentiv," **Filosofska dumka,** No. 4 (1971), pp. 64-71.

19.   E.K. Samborsky, "Aktyvnist'kolhospnoho selianstva," in L.V. Sokhan, ed., **op. cit.,** p. 133.

20.   A. V. Mialovytsky, "Deiaki resultaty doslidzhennia prychyn rozirvannia shliubiv," in **ibid.,** p. 145.

21.   M. M. Mykheenko and V. V. Leonenko, "Z dosvidu konkretno-sotsiolohichnoho doslidzhennia zlochynnosti nepovnolitnikh ta orhanizatsii borot'by z neiu," in **ibid.,** pp. 153-65.

22.   L. N. Terentieva, "Forming of Ethnic Self-consciousness in Nationally Mixed Families in the USSR." Paper delivered at the VIII World Congress of Sociology, Toronto, Canada, August 17-24, 1974.

23.   **Ibid.,** p. 9.

24.   **Ibid.**

25.   M. Rutkevich, **op. cit.,** p. 3.

Comments on Professor
Alex Simirenko
<u>Current Sociological Research</u>
<u>in Ukraine</u>

by
Wsevolod W. Isajiw
University of Toronto

Professor Simirenko has singled out six reasons for under-development of sociology in Ukraine. We may add that many of these reasons are connected with the nature of sociological empirical research itself. Sociological research requires group organization or team work. Hence, like all group activities in the Soviet Union, unless sanctioned or sponsored by the Communist Party any systematic sociological research is liable to be politically suspect. The party, however, as Professor Simirenko has pointed out, sees sociological research as an instrument of efficiency in carrying out its policies, especially as useful means of improving production — since probably the best sociological research in the Soviet Union deals with the industrial workers. One can presume that in regard to research in industrial workers. One can presume that in regard to research in industrial sociology, the party feels that results of research under-taken by Russians and in the Russian republic are good enough for application in all republics of the Soviet Union, and hence there is no need for much independent sociological research in Ukraine.

However, if sociology is to develop in Ukraine at all, it must have the possibility to develop in a cumulative manner. A sociological journal would be a natural requirement for this. It is, however, highly unlikely that such journal would be allowed in the near future. For this reason the publication in 1968 of the collection of sociological essays under the title **Sotsiolohia na Ukraini** (Sociology in Ukraine) from which Professor Simirenko has quoted several studies, is of special importance. The studies are methodologically primitive and conceptually weak; the ideological baggage is heavy. Nevertheless, to my knowledge the collection is the very first attempt in Ukraine to bring empirical sociological research together. As I understand, the group of sociologists behind this undertaking had to bear stormy consequences after the publication of this collection and nothing similar has been published for some time after.

Professor Simirenko has given an excellent analysis of the highlights of empirical sociological research which is being done in contemporary Ukraine. However, because of all the difficulties surrounding the current development of sociology in Ukraine and the fact that this development is still in its early stages, to evaluate it more completely one should also look at other areas of work which at least potentially can have relevance to sociological empirical research. Hence, in addition to the material reviewed by Professor Simirenko, at least the following areas should be examined: (1) related areas of empirical research, in particular social psychology; (2) writings which although themselves are not pieces of primary sociological research, nevertheless bring together and discuss statistical data collected in an **ad hoc** manner; (3) writings which are neither systematically sociological, nor written by persons who would claim to be sociologists, but in which genuine sociological questions are raised; (4) writings which use Marxism to interpret history.

All I can do at the moment is simply point to isolated examples of each of these types of writings. An example of the first type is the work of Mykhaylo Horyn' referred to by V. Chornovil in his **Lykho z rozumu.** Horyn's studies have dealt with psychology of work and include such topics as "Psychological requirements in the organization of the bench-worker's work area," "Questionnaire for the study of conditions and psychological atmosphere of work in a frame-press workshop," "Psychological characteristics of universal screw-cutting lathe operators," "Psychological-methodical instructions for the organization of the training process in workshops for apprentices," "The peculiarity of control and its distinction from the concentration among workers of the machine-building industry," and others.

An example of the second type of works, i.e., writings which give a review and interpretation of social statistical data, can be such article as in the No. 6, 1973 issue of **Filosofs'ka Dumka,** by V. Kovalevsky, L. Matvienko and L. Sandiuk, entitled "Some social aspects of migration in the U.S.S.R." In this article the authors use very general statistical data to demonstrate migration between villages and cities in the Soviet Union and try to explain why migration to cities is twice as large as that from the cities to the villages. They suggest dissatisfaction with the character of work in the villages as the main motive for the move to the cities. In Ukraine today probably the majority of works on sociological topics are of this kind. They are very much like sophisticated journalistic articles, and although they deal with significant topics one is never certain about the basis for the data used, or how the data are linked together. Usually, their conclusions follow the ideological mold and tend to end with normative statements. Nevertheless, it is possible to find in them some worthwhile formulations of sociological problems. For example, in the article mentioned above the authors raise the question as to how the rural migration into cities influences the cities' social-psychological character.

The third type of writings offers, indirectly, a good illustration of Professor Simirenko's conclusion that the underdevelopment of sociology in Ukraine may be a survival technique resorted to by those genuinely interested in sociological questions about Ukrainian socity. It is this type of writing which raises the most interesting questions about Ukrainian society. Indeed, to raise good sociological questions one probably must at least in some way disturb the official interpretations of society. Sociological research is potentitally dangerous to any monolithic ideology. The case in point are some parts of the writings of Ivan Dzyuba and Valentyn Moroz.

Dzyuba in his **Internationalism or Russification?** is also interested in the problem of the village and the city. But he sees the problem between the two not simply as a socio-economic problem, but also and especially as a linguistic-national problem. The decline of the vitality of the village, demoralization, indifference, drunkedness in the villages, should be understood as relating to the fact that the village is Ukrainian, and the city in Ukraine, Russian. He suggests that the answer may be found in the social-cultural inferiority complex of the village and the contempt for the village and the village people by the city. But it is not just anybody in the city whom Dzyuba holds to be contemptuous of the village. Very significantly, from the sociological point of view, he singles out the intelligentsia, who happen to be mostly Russian, and who, as he says, "like to talk about the universally human principle but actually themselves contribute to the creation of an atmosphere in which a person's dignity and his whole being can be trampled down." [1]

V. Moroz in his "A Chronicle of Resistance" talks symbolically about the Hutsul from Kosmach whose identity has been threatened many times but who has nevertheless remained a Hutsul. It is the ability to persevere which makes resistance to the identity and uniqueness levelling forces possible. But Moroz goes further: ability to persevere also makes high cultural attainment possible. As he says, "high cultural attainment is possible only through uninterrupted tradition. Lose nothing, and keep adding layer upon layer. Only in this way can spirituality grow." [2] Then, referring to Masaryk's statement that the misfortune of Soviet Russia is that it is still semi-educated, Moroz points to a set of deep-going sociological issues in the following statement

Semi-education results when a person is first deprived of his traditions and then educated. Semi-education results when culture does not develop naturally, but is stuffed into a person according to a Five-Year-Plan, or some other accelerated program. Semi-education is manifest when people recognize the value of Kosmach icons, but see no wrong in stealing them. [3]

In the beginning of his paper Professor Simirenko states that traditionally Ukrainians have favored historical rather than survey research approach to the study of society. I don't know specifically which or whose works he has in mind. Perhaps what he means is that among Ukrainian thinkers one can discern an interest in seeing history as social process, an interest in genetic explanations. However, Marxist thought itself has encouraged social interpretations of history and one can easily find works along these lines in contemporary Ukraine. Possibly we can consider these as the fourth type of writings which have some relation to sociology in Ukraine. An example can be such work as D. I. Myshko's **Sotsialno-ekonomichni umovy formuvannya ukrainskoi narodnosti** (Social and economic conditions in the formation of Ukrainian peoplehood), published in Kyiv in 1963.

In many ways the book appears as both bad history and bad sociology. Since I am not a historian, I cannot adequately evaluate the historical data and sources used in the work. From the sociological aspect, however, there is no doubt that Marxism as used here serves like the Procrustean bed into which historical facts have been selected and fit.

Yet, it could be said that this is true of any model when used to interpret history. Note, for example, Neil Smelser's study of the social change in the Industrial Revolution. The model used is Parsonian, but the use of historical data appears to be also selective. This raises the question as to what extent the use of models in interpreting historical records is logically legitimate. However, the problem with Myshko's work, as with many other similar works in the Soviet Union, is that to interpret history Marxism is used as an ideology rather than as a genuinely analytical model. Hence its intellectual yield is dubious. But since as an ideology Marxism is used in Ukraine to interpret social phenomena, a relevant question here is to what extent Marxist thought itself is consonant with the traditional Ukrainian social and political thought. This, however, would require a spearate discussion which would go beyond the scope of the present task.

FOOTNOTES

1. Ivan Dzyuba, **Internationalism or Russification?**, M. Davies, ed. (London: Weidenfeld and Nicolson, 1968), p. 195.

2. Yaroslav Bihun, ed., **Boomerang: The Works of Valentyn Moroz** (Baltimore, Md.: Smoloskyp Publishers, 1974), p. 107.

3. **Ibid.**, p. 111.

The Growth and Redistribution of the Ukrainian Population of Russia and the USSR: 1897-1970*

by
Robert A. Lewis
Columbia University

Richard H. Rowland
Columbia University

Ralph S. Clem
Florida International University

INTRODUCTION

Within the past century, and particularly over the last fifty years, dramatic social, economic, and political changes have occurred across the territory now known as the Union of Soviet Socialist Republics. These changes have had a profound influence upon the population of the Russian Empire and the USSR and in turn, demographic forces have shaped broader social trends.

The essential fact about the Soviet Union is, of course, that it is a multinational state, or, more precisely, a federation of ethnically-based units. Most multinational states are characterized by some form of ethnic stratification, and the USSR does not appear to be an exception to this generalization. Ethnic stratification implies a hierarchical ranking of nationalities according to relative political-military power and cultural traits.[1] In any multinational country, because of ethnic-stratification, the effects of social and economic change (such as those which accompany moder-

* This research was supported by Grant Number HD 05585-03 of the Center for Population Research of the National Institute of Child Health and Human Development, and the International Institute for the Study of Human Reproduction, Columbia University.

151

nization) can be expected to have a differential impact upon the various ethnic groups. Thus, the interplay between social and economic change and the vital dimension of ethnicity is an especially important topic for consideration.

It is within this framework, the mutually influencing forces of population change and the role and status of ethnicity, that we propose to describe and explain the major demographic characteristics and trends of the Ukrainian population of the Russian Empire and the Soviet Union. The long-term effects of modernization, the most profound mode of social and economic change, has wrought considerable alterations in the Ukrainian population and in the Ukrainian national homeland. By modernization we mean the complex of economic, social, demographic, and psychological changes which began in Western Europe in the late eighteenth century and spread to Central and Eastern Europe, the Soviet Union, Anglo-America, Japan, and a few other areas. The effects of modernization are reflected in tangible changes such as economic development, industrialization, a decline in fertility and mortality, urbanization, higher levels of education, a redefinition of the status of women, and also in a number of more subtle and difficult to define changes involving personal aspirations, values, and attitudes.[2]

Although modernization has had a significant influence upon Ukrainians and Ukraine, demographic changes associated with political and military events and with non-modernizing developments such as agricultural colonization have likewise strongly altered Ukrainian population characteristics. Few, if any, of the many nationalities of the former Tsarist Empire or present-day USSR have felt the impact of the violent upheavals of war, civil unrest, or famine to such an extent as the Ukrainians. Accordingly, the effects of these isolated events and trends not related to modernization must be included in any analysis of Ukrainian demographic history.

The chief sources of data for this study are the Russian census of 1897, the Soviet censuses of 1926, 1939, 1959 and 1970, and various East European censuses for areas formerly outside but now within the USSR.[3] Although censuses provide perhaps the best data base for the analysis of any society, the use of Russian and Soviet materials have been very limited in the past, due mainly to problems of territorial comparability and definitional consistency. Over the years there have occurred radical changes in internal political-administrative units, the definition of crucial census categories such as "urban" and "nationality," and even the territorial limits of the country, changes which have rendered any comparisons or analysis over time extremely difficult if not impossible.

During the last decade, we have fundamentally reordered data from the censuses into a comparable set of regions (we have utilized the nineteen economic regions proposed by the Soviets in 1961, and based upon a consistent set of definitions.[4] Thus, for the first time we have available a wide range of demographic variables (such as age, sex, work force, literacy, and nationality) for regions constituting the contemporary USSR, with the census years serving as benchmarks for the later Tsarist era (1897), the early years of Communist power (1926), and the post-World War II (1959) and present-day (1970) Soviet periods.

In any such extensive data analysis a number of operational problems arise. Foremost among the problems having a direct bearing on the present study, that is, reflecting directly upon an analysis of the Ukrainian population, is the fact that the definition of "nationality" differed between the Russian and Soviet censuses. Whereas the Soviet censuses have included data for individual nationalities, the 1897 census provided data for only those people speaking a given native language. Although, "native language" is a fairly reliable surrogate for nationality (especially in 1897), and was accordingly used as such, certain problems did result, particularly in the case of Ukrainians. Because a substantial number of Ukrainians consider Russian to be their native language, they were thus recorded as Russians in the 1897 census. In addition, the strong Russification policies of the Tsarist government in the late nineteenth century undoubtedly induced an unknown number of Ukrainians to declare Russian as their native language to avoid any stigma attached to being non-Russian. The end result is that the Ukrainian population as enumerated in the 1897 census was almost certainly smaller than the actual Ukrainian population. This bias is not significant in terms of overall trends, but it will be mentioned in subsequent sections whenever it has some bearing on the demographic trends of the Ukrainians.

Our analysis of the Ukrainian population includes three broad aspects of demographic change: (1) the growth of the population; (2) the regional distribution and redistribution of the population; and (3) the urbanization of the population. Trends among Ukrainians with respect to these three aspects will be related to the trends of the total population of the country and of the Russians to provide meaningful comparisons.

Growth of the Ukrainian Population

Between 1897 and 1970, the Ukrainian population of the presentday USSR grew relatively slowly (Table 1). It increased from 24.3 million to 40.8 million, or by only 0.7 percent per annum. This rate was lower than rates for both the total and Russian populations (0.9 and 1.2 percent annually). The Ukrainian growth rate would be even lower if the problem of nationality definition in the 1897 census were not present, because this bias resulted in an underestimation of the 1897 Ukrainian population. As a result of its relatively slow growth, the Ukrainian share of the total population of the country declined from 19 percent in 1897 to 17 percent in 1970, although the Ukrainians still remain by far the second largest nationality in the USSR.

In order to understand the comparatively slow rate of increase of the Ukrainian population, the components of population growth must be analyzed. These components are births, deaths, and in a multinational state, ethnic assimilation. Inasmuch as we are concerned with the total Ukrainian population of the USSR, and since foreign emigration was not a major consideration, we will not include an analysis of the migration component. It should be understood, however, that whatever foreign emigration did take place further compounded the slow Ukrainian growth rate. The relatively slow increase in the numbers of Ukrainians, then, can be explained by trends in the birth component (fertility), by the number of deaths (due to natural causes and to war, civil unrest, and famine), and by ethnic assimilation (in this case, Russification).

Between 1897 and 1926, the Ukrainian population grew by 1.3 percent per year. However, in the 1896-1900 period, the natural increase rate of the political units which comprise present-day Ukraine averaged about 20 per thousand, with crude birth rates in the 40's or 50's per thousand and crude death rates generally in the 20's. In 1926 the crude birth rate for the Ukrainian SSR was reported at 42 per thousand, the crude death rate at 18, and crude natural increase at 24 per thousand.[5] Thus, under normal conditions it might be expected that the Ukrainian population would have grown by roughly 2 percent per year during the 1897-1926 period. That it did not grow this rapidly can be largely explained by the wars during this period. Although Ukraine was not a major battle area during World War I, the Ukrainians probably sustained their proportionate share of direct military deaths and a decline in fertility as a result of mobilization. Ukraine, however, was a major area of military conflict during the Civil War, as competing armies, including the Germans, attempted to control this vital grain-producing area; the result was hunger, economic disruption, and considerable population losses. The famine of 1922-23, although centered in the Volga and Urals, also affected southern Ukraine and the Crimea.[6] In short, the Civil War period was very chaotic in Ukraine and the loss of life was great.

Between 1926 and 1959, the Ukrainian population increased at by far its lowest rate during any of the intercensal periods being investigated: 4.1 percent or by only 0.1 percent annually. In fact, within the 1926 boundaries of the USSR, the Ukrainian population actually declined between 1926 and 1939 by 10 percent or some three million people. Lack of substantial population growth can be partly accounted for by the considerable chaos during the 1926-1959 period. Collectiviation occurred in the 1930's and a major famine plagued Ukraine from 1932 to 1934. Losses from the famine must have been in the millions, although they are difficult to estimate with any precision. [7] The 1939-1959 period included World War II, and because Ukraine was occupied by the Germans and was a major area of battle, the number of Ukrainian lives lost must have been very high.

Russification was another major factor in the virtual lack of growth of the Ukrainian population between 1926 and 1959. Because this factor particularly involved certain regions of the RSFSR (especially the North Caucasus and Central Chernozem), it is more appropriate to discuss Russification in greater detail in the following section concerned with regional patterns of the Ukrainian population. We have estimated Ukrainian losses due to assimilation during this period at between three and four and-a-half million; this estimate must of necessity remain imprecise because of the complicating influences of World War II. Suffice it to say at this point that millions of Ukrainians apparently declared themselves as Russians in the 1959 census, further impeding the growth of the enumerated Ukrainian population.

A decline in fertility and natural increase also contributed to the extremely slow growth of the Ukrainian population during the 1926-1959 period. Between 1926 and 1960 the crude birth rate of the Ukrainian SSR declined by about 50 percent to 21 per thousand. In addition, the child-woman ratio (another measure of fertility, defined here as the total population aged 0-9 per woman aged 20-49) of the Ukrainian population also declined by about 50 percent between 1926 and 1959. Crude death rates of the Ukrainian Republic declined from a reported 18 per thousand in 1926 to 7 in 1960; thus natural increase declined from 24 to 14 per thousand. [8]

Between 1959 and 1970, the Ukrainian population continued to grow slowly (0.8 percent per year). This relatively slow increase was mainly the result of a continued declined to six per thousand in 1970 and the crude birth rate to 15 per thousand. The Ukrainian child-woman ratio also declined further during this period and is now one of the lowest in the USSR. In addition, in 1970 the average family size of the Ukrainians was only 3.4. In short, the Ukrainian population has apparently nearly completed the demographic transition from high to low birth and death rates.

Losses from Russification were probably in the hundreds of thousands. These losses can be estimated by assuming that the natural increase rate for the Ukrainian population between 1959 and 1970 equalled the median natural increase rate for the Ukrainian SSR during this period (i.e., for 1964), projecting the 1959 population forward to 1970, and comparing it with the enumerated population in 1970. The 1970 Ukrainian population as enumerated in the census is about 800,000 less than what it would be by projecting the 1959 population to 1970 on the basis of that rate.

We have no adequate explanation at this time for the sharp decline in natural increase, particularly the fertility component, among the Ukrainian population. We plan, however, to investigate fertility decline in the USSR in much greater detail at a later date, so deeper insights into the processes of fertility must await this future study. Suffice it to say at this juncture, among the indicators of modernization, fertility is the one variable that is probably the most difficult to effect and that nationalities vary considerably in terms of fertility decline and their resistance to the forces of modernization, probably largely because of cultural reasons. A central problem in this respect in the study of Soviet fertility is why has there been a significant decline in such rural Slavic areas as Ukraine, whereas most Turkic-Muslim rural areas have maintained high levels of fertility. In short, the processes of modernization result in a general desire for smaller families, although different groups within the society are affected to a greater or lesser degree. The legalization of abortion and the increasing availability of contraceptives have provided the means to limit family size once the motivation for smaller families developed. The decline in fertility in Ukraine and in the USSR is a complex phenomenon and has been studied relatively little. Among the many factors, however, which may account for this decline are: (1) rapid urbanization; (2) rising educational levels; (3) a very high rate of female participation in the work force, which is particularly influential in the modernized sectors of the economy; (4) an adverse sex ratio because of male losses during the war, although currently this factor is of little importance; (5) changes in the proportion of women in the reproductive ages; (6) a sharp decline in infant mortality; (7) shortages of services and housing; and (8) a general rise in material aspirations. Mortality is easier to explain, generally being primarily related to economic development and the availability of modern medicine.

Regional Distribution and Redistribution of the Ukrainian Population

The regional distribution of Ukrainians has been modified by three components of population redistribution: differential regional natural increase, migration, and ethnic assimilation. Not only did the Ukrainian population increase quite slowly between 1897 and 1970, but it also did not experience any significant geographical shift. In particular, it experienced relatively little dispersal from its homeland. Indeed, between 1897 and 1970, the enumerated Ukrainian population outside of the Ukrainian SSR for all practical purposes did not increase at all, totalling slightly more than five million people each year. At the same time, the Ukrainian population of the Ukrainian SSR has increased by more than 16 million people. Thus, the Ukrainian population has actually become relatively more concentrated in the Ukrainian SSR, with roughly four-fifths of its population residing in Ukraine in all four census years (Table 2). Within Ukraine itself, this stability combined with slightly increased concentration has also been noticeable. In all four census years, the Southwest Region accounted for slightly less than one-half of the total Ukrainian population, the Donetsk-Dnipro Region for roughly one-fourth to one-third, and the South Region for less than one-tenth, and between 1897 and 1970 the share of the Ukrainian population residing in each of these three regions also increased (Table 2).

The virtual absence of dispersal on the part of the Ukrainian population is somewhat surprising for a number of reasons. First, during the same period, the total and Russian populations were experiencing considerable dispersal, particularly in an easterly direction. In addition, the share of the Ukrainians residing outside of Ukraine might have been expected to increase greatly, because of the great loss of life within Ukraine associated with collectivization and war. In fact, paradoxically, the increased concentration of the Ukrainians in Ukraine between 1897 and 1970 occurred primarily between 1926 and 1959, the period which included collectivization, famine, and World War II. During this period, the Ukrainian population of Ukraine increased by only 0.5 percent per year, but the total Ukrainian population of the USSR nevertheless became increasingly concentrated in Ukraine. Because the Ukrainian population of Ukraine was growing very slowly during this period, it is apparent that this increased concentration was not due to a massive influx of Ukrainians back to Ukraine.

The prime explanation for this unexpected increased concentration in Ukraine has been the substantial decline in the Ukrainian population outside Ukraine. Outstanding in this regard are two regions of the RSFSR which are adjacent to the Ukrainian Republic: the North Caucasus and the Central Chernozem. These were the two main regions of Ukrainian settlement outside the Ukrainian SSR in 1897 and 1926. In 1926, for example, they accounted for 8.7 and 4.7 percent of the total Ukrainian population, respectively. The North Caucasus even had more Ukrainians than did the South Region, one of the three regions of the Ukrainian SSR. By 1959, however, the North Caucasus and the Central Chernozem contained only 1.0 and 0.8 percent of the Ukrainian populations, percentages roughly duplicated in 1970. Between 1926 and 1959, the predominantly rural Ukrainian population in the North Caucasus declined by 88.2 percent, or from more than 3,100,000 to less than 400,000; in the Central Chernozem the decline was by 82.9 percent from more than 1,600,000 to less than 300,000. In short, between 1926 and 1959 the large Ukrainian population of the North Caucasus and Central Chernozem Regions declined by roughly four million people, not taking into consideration natural increase.

Russification was probably the prime reason for this sharp reduction. It has been noted, for example, that the growth of the Russian population of the USSR has, perhaps, been partly due to the assimilation of other peoples, in particular, the Ukrainians of the Kuban' and other portions of the North Caucasus Region.[9] Ivan Dziuba notes that during the 1930's the Ukrainian cultural and educational centers in the North Caucasus were "dispersed by the terror," and defenders of the "Ukrainian character" were wiped out. According to Dziuba, many Ukrainians in this area have been afraid to admit to being Ukrainians ever since.[10] The propensity towards the Russification of Ukrainians in the North Caucasus was also apparent in the 1926 census. In the "North Caucasus Krai" in the 1926 census, a region roughly similar to the North Caucasus Region of this study, nearly one-half (42.9 percent) of the Ukrainians considered Russian to be their native language. In comparison, corresponding figures for the USSR as a whole (1926 boundaries) and the USSR outside the Ukrainian Republic (1926 boundaries) were only 12.6 and 33.1 percent, respectively. It is generally acknowledged that the adoption of another language as the native tongue is highly related to ethnic assimilation. Therefore, the high degree of linguistic Russification in the North Caucasus may be viewed as a prelude to complete Russification.[11]

A similar pattern was not apparent at this time in the Central Chernozem Region, however. In the analogous "Central Chernozem Region" of the 1926 census, only 10.3 percent of the Ukrainians regarded Russian as their native language. By 1959, however, a very high degree of Russification in the Central Chernozem Region was apparent. In this year, 75.3 percent of the Ukrainians in the Central Chernozem regarded Russian as their native language, a truly incredible figure given the fact that the vast majority of the Ukrainians in this region still resided in rural areas. Not unexpectedly, this figure was well above the Union-wide average of 12.1 percent, and the average for the USSR outside the Ukrainian Republic of 48.4 percent. The North Caucasus continued to have a relatively high percentage (57.5) in 1959.

These linguistic patterns suggest that the great decline in the Ukrainian population of the North Caucasus and the Central Chernozem Regions was probably due to the fact that the bulk of the Ukrainians in these areas simply declared themselves to be Russians in the 1959 and 1970 censuses. This high degree of Russification apparently resulted from the fact that the Ukrainian rural population resided for quite a long time among a more numerous Russian population and had little access to Ukrainian cultural and educational institutions.

A similar situation has probably been responsible for the lack of a substantial increase in the enumerated Ukrainian population of many other regions. Between 1926 and 1959, the Ukrainian population also declined considerably in West Siberia, the Volga, and Kazakhstan. Like the North Caucasus and Central Chernozem, these regions were areas where large Ukrainian populations resided for quite a long time within major areas of Russian settlement. It is worthwhile to emphasize that the Russification of Ukrainians has occurred primarily in **rural** areas. This is quite unusual in that the Russification of non-Russian nationalities has tended to be much greater in urban areas than in rural areas.

Accordingly, it must be acknowledged that one of the reasons for the lack of dispersal of the enumerated Ukrainian population has been the high degree of Russification of the Ukrainians residing beyond the Ukrainian Republic. It appears that more substantial numbers of Ukrainians did move eastward, but such movements were not apparent in the census data, because by the time a later census was taken, many Ukrainians decided to declare themselves as Russians.

However, although a greater migratory dispersal of the Ukrainians actually occurred than census data would at first indicate, this migration was not associated to any significant degree with modernization, because it involved mainly a rural-to-rural movement. In addition, even if the Ukrainians who dispersed still declared themselves to be Ukrainians, it is unlikely that the Ukrainian population would have dispersed as much as the more modernized Russians.

That the Ukrainians have not migrated from their homeland to a more significant extent appears to be the result of the following factors: (1) their comparatively low educational level, which impedes their migration towards major areas of modern economic development outside the Ukrainian Republic (Table 3); (2) the presence of substantial opportunities within the Ukrainian Republic itself, including those resulting from the relatively good, in the Soviet context, local agricultural resource base, and significant local industrialization; indeed, in 1970, this republic was the leading republic with respect to the percent of total land area comprised by arable land, and it contained a greater number of industrial workers than any other republic save the RSFSR; [12] (3) the lack of chronic rural population pressure, due not only to the fairly good agricultural resource base, but also to low rural fertility, to the extensive loss of life associated with collectivization, famine, and war, and to its being colonized rather late; it is interesting to note that although such an indicator is not a completely valid measure of rural population pressure, the ratio between the rural population and hectares of arable land in Ukraine is lower than that of most other Soviet republics. [13]

Urbanization of the Ukrainian Population

Urbanization is perhaps the most important single aspect of population change associated with modernization. As such, the level of urbanization of a particular group is a good indicator of the degree to which the group has been integrated into modernized society. Operationally, urbanization measures the number of persons living in cities (however defined) against the total population. Increases in the level of urbanization normally occur when people migrate from rural to urban areas, a movement associated with modernization, but increases in the level of urbanization also takes place if the rural natural increase is lower than urban. It should be noted that our consistent definition of "urban" includes all centers of 15,000 or more, regardless of legal status.

Between 1897 and 1970, the Ukrainians experienced a substantial increase in their level of urbanization, as have most nationalities in this most rapidly urbanizing country. During this period, the Ukrainian level increased by 35.4 percentage points, an increase enhanced by rapid urban growth (1338.9 percent) coupled with almost no rural growth (only 5.5 percent for the 73-year period) (Table 4). In the post-1926 period, the Ukrainian rural population actually declined. Not unexpectedly, the biggest loss in the number of rural Ukrainians occurred between 1926 and 1959, the period of collectivization, famine, and World War II. Over four-fifths (86.5 percent) of the decline in the Ukrainian rural population between 1926 and 1970 occurred between 1926 and 1959, when this rural population declined by more than 7 million, or by more than one-fifth (-22.8 percent).

But, the Ukrainian urbanization process has not been as substantial as has that of the total USSR and Russian population. Whereas the Ukrainian level increased by 35.4 percentage points, the Union-wide and Russian levels increased by 36.7 and 43.3 percentage points, respectively; during the Soviet era (1926-1970) similar patterns existed (Table 4).

In addition to a relatively low increase in the level of urbanization (in the Soviet context), the Ukrainian level was also below the Unionwide and Russian levels in all four census years (Table 4). By 1970, the Ukrainian rural population still outnumbered its urban population by some 8 million people and the Ukrainian level of 40.1 percent was about 6 percentage points below the Union-wide level and 16 points below the Russian level. Whereas the Russian level of urbanization is now roughly comparable to that of such highly developed areas as Western Europe and Japan, the Ukrainian level is more on a par with those of such lesser industrial areas as Southern Europe, Eastern Europe, Southern Africa, and Mainland Middle America. [14]

Like most nationalities the Ukrainians are more urbanized outside their homeland than within it. In 1970, for example, the Ukrainian level of urbanization outside the Ukrainian SSR was nearly 20 percentage points higher than that within the republic (54.3 percent vis-a-vis 35.5 percent). Generally speaking, those who migrate from their homeland tend to be relatively highly educated and, accordingly, more urbanized. This is reflected by the fact that urban Ukrainians of the RSFSR have higher educational levels than do urban Russians of the RSFSR and urban Ukrainians of the Ukrainian SSR. In 1970, for example, 9.2 percent of all urban Ukrainians aged 10 and over in the RSFSR had a completed higher education, whereas the corresponding percentages for the urban Russians of the RSFSR and the urban Ukrainians of the Ukrainian SSR were only 5.7 and 5.2 percent, respectively.

However, most urban Ukrainians (80.9 percent in 1970) still reside within the Ukrainian Republic. Of the three economic regions comprising this republic, the Donets'k-Dnipro Region is the main region of Ukrainian urban settlement. In 1970, this region had more than 6,000,000 urban Ukrainians, by far the highest total for any of the 19 economic regions, and accounted for 42.9 percent of all urban Ukrainians in the USSR and 53.0 percent of all urban Ukrainians in the Ukrainian SSR. The Ukrainian level of urbanization has been much higher in the Donets'k-Dnipro than it has in the South and Southwest Regions; in 1970, respective levels of urbanization were 53.2, 38.2, and 23.6 percent, although the Southwest Region does contain Kyiv, which has more Ukrainians (over one million in 1970) than any other single city in the USSR. Yet, even in the Donets'k-Dnipro Region the Ukrainian level is below the level of urbanization for the total population of the region (59.7 percent).

That the Ukrainian urbanization process has not been more appreciable is perhaps somewhat surprising in light of the fact that the Ukrainian SSR has been an outstanding region of mining and manufacturing. The Donets'k-Dnipro, in fact, now ranks as one of the top two or three industrial regions in the USSR, and is the leading region of ferrous metallurgy in the USSR. The lack of a more considerable Ukrainian rural-to-urban movement has been partly due to many factors which were discussed in the preceding section: (1) the absence of chronic rural population pressure in Ukraine; and (2) the relatively low educational level of the Ukrainian populace, which impedes their participation in modern economic activities.

As in many other non-Russian areas of the USSR, the deficiencies of the indigenous work force have led to a considerable influx of the relatively highly-educated Russians towards nodes of modern economic activity in the homeland of these non-Russian peoples. In fact, although the migration of Russians to cities in Central Asia and Kazakhstan has received much notice lately, it should be pointed out that Ukraine has been the prime area of Russian urban settlement outside the RSFSR. Between 1897 and 1970, over two-fifths (42.5 percent) of the growth of the Russian urban population outside the RSFSR occurred in the Ukrainian Republic. This percentage has been remarkably stable: 34.4 percent during 1897-1926; 43.9 percent, 1926-1959; and 41.1 percent, 1959-1970. The relatively low percentage for 1897-1926 undoubtedly would have been somewhat higher had not there been the problems associated with defining "Russian" and "Ukrainian" in the 1897 census; these problems led to an over-enumeration of the Russian population in 1897, thus resulting in a smaller growth of the Russian population than might have been expected. This over-enumeration is reflected in the fact that the "Russian" share of the population of Kyiv declined from 54.4 percent in 1897 to 24.5 percent in 1926.

Not unexpectedly, the highly industrialized Donets'k-Dnipro Region has been the major region of Russian urban settlement in Ukraine. In 1970, the Donets'k-Dnipro / still had a larger Russian urban population than any other region outside the RSFSR. It contained nearly one-third (29.1 percent) of the total Russian urban population out-side the RSFSR and almost two-thirds (64.5 percent) of the Russian urban population in the Ukrainian Republic. In addition, in 1970, of all the 19 economic regions, the Russian level of urbanization reached its greatest extent in the Donets'k-Dnipro (72.7 percent). Furthermore, even though the Donets'k-Dnipro is the leading region of Ukrainian urban settlement, the Russians still managed to comprise roughly one-third of its urban population in all four census years (for example, 35.5 percent in 1970). A map in a study by the Soviet Ukrainian demographer V.I. Naulko revealed that Russians accounted for roughly one-half of the population of many large Donets'k-Dnipro cities in 1959, particularly in the Donbas: Makiyivka (52 percent), Donets'k (51), Horlivka (47), and Lugansk, now Voroshylovhrad (47). [15]

The Russian share of the urban population of the Ukrainian SSR has been most outstanding in the South Region in general and the Crimean Oblast in particular. In all four census years Russians comprised roughly two-fifths of the urban population of the South (43.6 percent in 1970). In the Crimea the Russian share has been even greater: 67.3 percent of the total population and 72.9 percent of the urban population in 1970, and in 1959, Russians accounted for more than 70 percent of such major cities as Kerch' (81 percent), Feodosiya (80), Sevastopil' (77), Yalta (73), Simferopil' (71), and Yevpatoriya (71).[16] The Crimea is truly a Russian exclave, although officially part of the Ukrainian Republic.

The presence of outsiders in the cities of Ukraine is fraught with implications. First, it has to be regarded as an additional factor impeding the local rural-to-urban movement of Ukrainians, since many cities of Ukraine are considerably non-Ukrainian in culture. This has been true not only in the southern and eastern Ukraine, where the Russian urban presence is especially noticeable, but also in Western Ukraine, where Jews and Poles have comprised a sizable share of the urban population. Thus, a circular chain of events is put into operation: the deficiencies of the Ukrainian work force impede local rural-to-urban migration and enhance an influx of Russians, which in turn acts to impede local rural-to-urban migration.

The extent to which the large number of outsiders in Ukraine has impeded the integration of Ukrainian and modernized society is reflected in data recently presented in a study by the Soviet sociologist Arutyunyan.[17] His figures indicate that in the census years of 1926, 1939, and 1959, the percentage of employed Ukrainians in the non-agricultural work force of the Ukrainian SSR was slightly lower than the comparable figure for the total population (indicating that the outsiders held a disproportionately large share of such jobs.) While Arutyunyan's data indicate a relative improvement in this respect between 1926 and 1959 in the industrial sector, the Ukrainians actually lost ground in the "mental work" category.[18]

The Russian presence in cities also has been a force towards Russification of the Ukrainians. Although a great number of Ukrainians in rural areas of predominately Russian settlement have been highly Russified, the more common situation of greater Russification in cities than in rural areas has also been in evidence in Ukraine. In 1970, for example, 17.1 percent of the Ukrainian urban population of the Ukrainian SSR considered Russian to be its native language, whereas in rural areas of Ukraine the corresponding percentage was only 1.3.

Summary and Conclusions

In summary of the demographic trends experienced by the Ukrainian population of the USSR since 1897, several key points stand out:

1. The growth of the Ukrainians was very slow in any context, Soviet or otherwise.
2. The slow growth was mainly due to heavy war losses, both civilian and military, to deaths from famine and collectivization, and a sharp decline in natural increase.
3. Assimilation or Russification also had a strong impact on growth, accounting for the "loss" of over three million Ukrainians.
4. The Ukrainian population has remained relatively concentrated in its own republic, due to the assimilation of Ukrainians beyond Ukraine and to a low incidence of migration.
5. Although the Ukrainians have experienced substantial urbanization, the percentage of Ukrainians in cities and the change in that percentage was below the Union-wide averages and considerably below the Russians.

The effects of war and famine upon the Ukrainian population requires little explanation beyond the fact that the Ukrainian national homeland has been an arena contested by major powers for centuries, resulting in the periodic visitations of havoc upon its inhabitants.

The effects of modernization, however, can be at least partly understood by reference to the aforementioned concept of ethnic stratification. The relative non-integration of Ukrainians into modernized society, particularly as reflected in their relatively low level of urbanization, is due principally to the fact that the system of ethnic stratification in the Russian Empire and the Soviet Union has partially excluded them from advanced sectors. This phenomenon has been true to some degree of almost all non-Russian nationalities of the USSR.

The Russians, as the dominant group in Imperial and Soviet society, modernized relatively early and pre-empted advanced sectors in most non-Russian areas (such as the Donbas). Certain other nationalities, because of cultural traits and a history of enterprise and education, also succeeded in entering modernized society at an early stage. In the Ukrainian context this is particularly true of the Jews. The presence of large numbers of non-Ukrainians in Ukrainian cities almost certainly impeded the urbanization of the indigenous Ukrainians and their entry into non-agricultural sectors of the economy.

The USSR was conceived as a federation of ethnic republics and, although this arrangement has been viewed by Soviet theorists as a transitional stage, it can be argued that the nationality units have assumed some permanence and legitimacy. If this is the case, then the benefits which have accrued to Ukrainians in their own republic vis-a-vis outsiders is of some importance. At the present, the Ukrainians remain relatively disadvantaged within their nationality republic, a fact which has been prominently and cogently argued by Soviet Ukrainian dissidents such as Ivan Dziuba.

In over half-a-century, Soviet rule has resulted in many material gains for the Ukrainians. Yet, the equalization of levels of socio-economic development among Soviet nationalities, a basic principle of Leninist nationality policy, remains an unattained goal. The extent to which the Soviet leadership succeeds in the modernization of the Ukrainians and other non-Russians will no doubt be an important factor in the future of the USSR.

TABLE 1

AVERAGE ANNUAL GROWTH RATES OF UKRAINIAN, RUSSIAN, AND TOTAL USSR POPULATIONS: 1897-1970
(in percent)

	Ukrainians	Russians	Total USSR
1897-1926	1.3	1.2	1.0
1926-1959	0.1	1.1	0.7
1959-1970	0.8	1.1	1.4
1897-1970	0.7	1.2	0.9

TABLE 2

PERCENTAGE OF UKRAINIANS RESIDING IN THE THREE REGIONS OF THE UKRAINIAN SSR: 1897-1970

Region	1897	1926	1959	1970
Southwest	46.6	44.3	47.8	47.3
Donets'k-Dnipro	23.9	26.4	30.8	30.7
South	7.4	5.8	7.7	8.6
Total Ukrainian SSR	77.9	76.5	86.3	86.6

TABLE 3

EDUCATIONAL LEVELS OF UKRAINIAN, RUSSIAN, AND TOTAL USSR POPULATIONS: 1970

Percentage of population aged 10 and over with:

	higher education (complete & incomplete)	higher and middle education (complete & incomplete)
Ukrainians	4.5	47.6
Russians	5.9	50.8
Total USSR	5.5	48.3

TABLE 4

LEVELS OF URBANIZATION OF UKRAINIAN, RUSSIAN, AND TOTAL USSR POPULATIONS: 1897-1970

	Ukrainians	Russians	Total USSR
1897	4.7	13.0	9.9
1926	7.3	16.1	13.3
1959	31.3	46.0	38.2
1970	40.1	56.3	46.6
Percentage point change, 1897-1970	35.4	43.3	36.7

FOOTNOTES

1. Tamotsu Shibutani and Kian M. Kwan, **Ethnic Stratification: A Comparative Approach** (New York: Macmillan, 1965).

2. C.E. Black, **The Dynamics of Modernization** (New York: Harper and Row, 1966), pp. 1-34; Calvin Goldscheider, **Population, Modernization, and Social Structure** (Boston, Little, Brown, and Company, 1971), Chapters 4-7.

3. Tsentral'nyy Statisticheskiy Komitet Ministerstva Vnutrennikh Del, **Pervaya Vseobshchaya Perepis' Naseleniya Rossiyskoy Imperii**, 1897 G., 89 vols.; Tsentral'noye Statisticheskoye Upravleniye SSR, **Vsesoyuznaya Perepis' Naseleniya 1926 Goda**, 66 vols.; Tsentral'noye Statisticheskoye Upravleniye pri Sovete Ministrov SSR, **Itogi Vsesoyuznoy Perepisi Naseleniya 1959 Goda**, 16 vols.; and Tsentral'noye Statisticheskoye Upravleniye pri Sovete Ministrov SSR, **Itogi Vsesoyuznoy Perepisi Naseleniya 1970 Goda**. For a listing of the East European censuses, see footnote 3 of: Robert A. Lewis and Richard H. Rowland, "Urbanization in Russia and the USSR: 1897-1966," **Annals of the Association of American Geographers**, LIX (December, 1969), p. 777.

4. J. William Leasure and Robert A. Lewis, **Population Changes in Russia and the USSR: A Set of Comparable Territorial Units** (San Diego: San Diego State College Press, 1966).

5. A.G. Rashin, **Naseleniye Rossii za 100 let** (Moscow: Gosudarstvennoye Statisticheskoye Upravleniye, 1956), pp. 217-18.

6. Eugene Kulischer, **Europe on the Move** (New York: Columbia University Press, 1948), p. 69.

7. Dana G. Dalrymple, "The Soviet Famine of 1932-1934," **Soviet Studies**, XV (January, 1964), p. 259.

8. Tsentral'noye Statisticheskoye Upravleniye pri Sovete Ministrov SSR, **Narodnoye Khozyaystvo SSR v 1970 G.** (Moscow: "Statistika," 1971), p. 50.

9. **Narody yevropeyskoy chasti SSR**, Vol. 1 (Moscow: Izdatel'stvo "Nauka," 1964), p. 22.

10. Ivan Dzyuba, **Internationalism or Russification?** (2nd ed., London: Weidenfeld and Nicolson, 1968), p. 188.

11. Brian D. Silver, "Ethnic Identity Change Among Soviet Nationalities," Unpublished Ph.D. Dissertation, University of Wisconsin, 1972, pp. 28-40.

12. Tsentral'noye Statisticheskoye Upravleniye pri Sovete Ministrov SSR, **Narodnoye Khozyaystvo SSR v 1970 G.**, pp. 159 and 291.

13. **Ibid.**, p. 300.

14. United Nations, **Growth of the World's Urban and Rural Population**, 1920-2000 (ST / SOA / Series A / 44), pp. 121-22.

15. V.I. Naulko, **Heohrafichne rozmishchennya narodiv v URSR** (Kyiv: Naukova Dumka, 1966).

16. **Ibid.**

17. Yu. V. Arutyunyan, "Izmeneniye sotsial'noy struktury sovetskikh natsiy," *Istoriya SSR*, No. 4 (1972), pp. 3-20.

18. **Ibid**.

IV
Non-Ukrainian Nationalities

The Social and Political Role of the Jews in Ukraine

by
Zvi Gitelman
University of Michigan

For several centuries the Jews have played the role of "the third nationality" in Ukraine. At least since the sixteenth century, they have been involved in triangular relationships with other nationalities. In the sixteenth and seventeenth centuries Jews played an intermediary economic role between Ukrainian peasants and Polish landowners; more recently, they have been part of a Russian-Jewish-Ukrainian relationship. Of course, other nationalities have always inhabited Ukraine, making ethnic relations there extremely complex. According to a Soviet scholar, at the end of the 1950's 120 nationalities lived in Soviet Ukraine.[1] Though in areas such as the Crimea and Bukovina, now included in Soviet Ukraine, there were important contacts with other nationalities, in the main the Jews of Ukraine have had their ethnic situation defined primarily by their relationships with Russians, Ukrainians, and in an earlier period, Poles.

Even the casual student of East European history is aware that these relationships generally have not been the most tranquil. A fundamental problem for the Jews in Ukraine which has dogged them for at least three hundred years has been their intermediary position between two larger, more powerful, and mutually hostile nationalities. In the seventeenth century, when Jews served — as much by necessity as by choice — as stewards and lessees for Polish nobles owning land worked by Ukrainian peasants, Jews became an object of Ukrainian hostility. They presented a visible, immediate, and accessible target for resentments brought about by economic exploitation, and so when Bohdan Khmelnytskyi led a Ukrainian uprising against the Poles in 1648 the Jews were caught between the warring sides. Thousands of Jews fell victim to both Poles and Ukrainians in what was probably the largest massacre of Jews between the Crusades and the twentieth century. The enormity of the tragedy,

167

preserved in Jewish literature and liturgy and in the historical memory of the people, has conditioned Ukrainian-Jewish relations ever since. Especially because Khmelnytskyi's uprising has been celebrated by Ukrainians as a glorious moment in their history — and the Soviets have continued this tradition, albeit giving a Marxist interpretation to the events — the Jews have not been able to forget these events and are obliged to reflect on their meaning for their own people. Thus, a historical event has been transformed into a living reminder and symbol of conflicting interests ending in violence and mutual hatred.

There have been long-range constant factors in the Ukrainian-Jewish relationship which have been sources of friction, mutual distrust and outright hostility. The fact that Ukrainians were overwhelmingly rural and Jews mostly urban meant that ethnic differences coincided with and overlay rural-urban tensions. The further association of Jews with specific economic roles and of Ukrainians with others contributed to mutual stereotyping, and since these roles were adversary and competitive, economic differences reinforced and exacerbated ethnic differences, and vice versa. In their survey of the literature on ethnicity, LeVine and Campbell conclude that "the greater the degree to which any single activity dominates the interaction between two groups, the more intergroup imagery will be dominated by the attributes of that activity."[2] Yiddish and Hebrew literature of the nineteenth century, accurately reflecting popular images among Jews, portray the Ukrainian almost always as a peasant, sometimes comical, usually ignorant, given to drunkeness and antisemitic outbursts, economically unsophisticated but with a certain "peasant slyness," and generally leading a kind of primitive and benighted existence. Undoubtedly, Ukrainian lore and literature portrayed Jews in stereotypical terms as well, though in both cultures there are undoubtedly more differentiated and sophisticated portrayals of Jews and Ukrainians.

In this century (and earlier) Russians have replaced Poles as the third actor in the triangular relationship. Again, Ukrainians have been able to perceive Jews as the allies of the "other" nationality which threatens Ukrainian culture, welfare, and independence. Once again perceiving themselves as subject to a neighboring, but foreign, people, many Ukrainians could regard Jews as being the "objective" and perhaps "subjective" allies of the Russians who were attempting to restrict Ukrainian cultural, political, and economic development. This perception is made credible by the fact that when Jews assimilated linguistically and otherwise, it was (and is) Russian, not Ukrainian, culture which attracted them. Russian culture has been conceived of by Jews in Ukraine as a more sophisticated, urban, widespread, and hence useful, culture than the Ukrainian. Thus, Jews have added to the total numbers of Russian speakers, students in Russian schools, and consumers and creators of Russian culture in Ukraine.

Since the 1930's there have been a great many theories advanced in the West which attempt to explain prejudice through psychological factors operating in a social context. A common theme is that frustration leads to aggression against outgroups which are perceived as the cause of the frustration.[3] Applied to our case, this line of reasoning would hold that Ukrainians, frustrated by Russian predominance and an inability to independently determine their own fate, displace their frustration not only on the Russians but also on the Jews who could be construed as weaker, but no less pernicious, allies of the national enemy.

In the absence of survey and other attitudinal data, we cannot determine what the attitudes of Ukrainians and Jews are toward each other today. Even statements about the past are of necessity broad generalizations which must be taken as such and not as absolute truths by any means. But both historical events as well as situational factors, obtaining today as well as in the past, enable us to at least determine why there would be grounds for ethnic tensions in Ukraine, particularly between Jews and Ukrainians, but also between Jews and other groups (not to speak of Russians and Ukrainians).

One situational factor which has varied little over time in its broad outlines is that the Jews have constituted what John Armstrong has called a "mobilized diaspora," and perhaps nowhere more so than in Eastern Europe.

While internal proletariats appear to be a feature of late stages of modern industrialized societies, "mobilized diasporas" clearly accompany early stages of modernization. By definition a diaspora is a geographic dispersion of a small minority of the total population. But few diasporas exhibit a degree of social mobilization sufficient to enable them to occupy a special functional position in a modernizing society. Those that do qualify as mobilized diasporas are highly urban, have high relative educational levels, have access to mass media, and are geographically mobile. While mobilized diasporas are distinct in culture (frequently because of religious distinctiveness), their attachment to their own language is usually not too deep. They readily employ the dominant language in their homes as well as at their work. Partly as a consequence of this linguistic ability, members of this group are especially skilled in trade, communication, human relations, and other white-collar occupations. Members of mobilized diasporas have a very high achievement orientation, and women as well as men are mobilized. Therefore mobilized diasporas may be extra-ordinarily useful in a modernizing society where these characteristics are rare. On the whole, members of mobilized diasporas fill attractive jobs. As the society becomes more fully modernized, members of other ethnic groups seek to obtain these positions, frequently before their skills make them competitively equal to mobilized diaspora members. The result is resentment and, frequently, discrimination against the mobilized diasporas. The calssic example of the mobilized diaspora in Western civilization is the Jews, but the Parsees in India, the Chinese in Southeast Asia, and the Lebanese in West Africa also fit the model.[4]

Thus, it is not only the economic role that Jews have played that has brought them into conflict with other nationalities, but also a distinctive social role which, at time, has become also a distinctive political role.

The political dimension in Ukrainian-Jewish relations assumed great prominence during the Russian Revolution and the Civil War that followed. During 1917-21 most Jews in Ukraine, and the political parties which represented them, were reluctant to support Ukrainian political independence for fear that Jews would not fare well in an independent Ukrainian state. Jews were represented in the Ukrainian Central Rada which had granted them broad national, political and cultural autonomy in 1917. But even those Jewish representatives who voted to proclaim Ukrainian independence in November, 1917 did so reluctantly, and by January, 1918 they were even less willing to support Ukrainian independence. [5] In turn, Ukrainian nationalists were dismayed at the failure of the Jews to support their cause. The Central Rada took no effective action against elements of the Ukrainian population who pogromized the Jews, and by 1919, when the Directory in Kyiv, headed by Symon Petliura, controlled at least part of Ukraine, mass pogroms broke out. These were the worst anti-Jewish riots in Eastern Europe since 1648. Though the White armies of Denikin, anarchist bands, bandits, and even the Red Army perpetrated many pogroms, the Jews came to fear the Ukrainian nationalist forces most of all. It has been estimated that of the 1,236 recorded pogroms in Ukraine in 1918-19, 493 were committed by elements of the Ukrainian nationalist forces. [6] Between 1917 and 1921 more than two thousand pogroms occurred, with the result that half a million Jews were left homeless and twenty-eight percent of Jewish homes were destroyed. The direct loss of Jewish life exceeded thirty thousand and approximately one hundred and fifty thousand Jews, or ten percent of the Jewish population, died as a direct or indirect consequence of the pogroms. [7] One of the immediate effects of the pogroms was to drive the Jews, hitherto largely indifferent or hostile to Bolshevism, into the hands of the Red Army as a means both of self-defence as well as of taking revenge. [8] Naturally, this further widened the already enormous gulf between Ukrainian nationalists and Jews, while drawing Jews closer to the Bolsheviks, the one major political element in the entire spectrum of Russian-Ukrainian politics which had renounced antisemitism and took vigorous steps to combat it within and without its ranks.

A longer range consequence of the pogroms was the decline of the Jewish population of Ukraine. The economic life of the Jewish population was severely crippled, and social problems, such as homeless children, were both created and exacerbated.

With the consolidation of Bolshevik power, ethnic tensions in Ukraine assumed less violent forms and perhaps even diminished absolutely. While in the 1920's within the Ukrainian Communist Party there were well known debates and struggles over national questions, resulting in purges of "nationalists" and, to a lesser extent, of "great power chauvinists," in Ukraine as a whole the Party's policy of "nativization" (korenizatsiia) provided greater latitude for national-cultural expression and activity not only for the Ukrainian nationality but also for the national minorities. Schools, trade unions, courts, and even Party cells began to operate in non-Russian languages, and the regime gave a great deal of support to national cultural activities, as long as they remained within the boundaries of ideological and political orthodoxy. Ukrainian and Jewish intellectuals, supported materially and psychologically by a regime for the first time, increased their interest in each other's work and, at least on the level of the intelligentsia, there seemed to be increased understanding among the various nationalities. Of course, there may have been a variety of motives at work here. As one Jewish writer noted, "The Ukrainians and the Belorussians drive us very hard to publish in Yiddish — of course, not as much from 'love of Mordecai' as from 'hatred of Haman,' hatred of the Russians." [9]

Jews had achieved political equality as a result of the Revolution, but their economic problems were exacerbated by it, by the ravages of the Civil War, the policies of War Communism and the general crisis of the Soviet economy. One way of ameliorating the economic situation was to settle Jews on land. Whereas under the tsars Jews had been forbidden to own land, except in special circumstances, the Soviet regime was eager to encourage economic rehabilitation through agricultural colonization, and some Jewish activists saw this also as a means of national consolidation and preservation of Jewish consciousness and culture. In Ukraine in 1925 fifteen thousand Jewish families registered for agricultural settlement and Jewish farm colonies were formed. In some instances this aroused the hostility of peasants who felt that the Jews were taking away their lands and were getting more financial and other aid than they. At the Tenth All-Ukrainian Congress of Soviets, Vlas Chubar, chairman of the Ukrainian Council of People's Commissars, found it necessary to reassure the population that the Jews were not being granted special privileges. A Ukrainian journalist reported that "'the yids will take over all power on the steppes,' hooligans whispered. And in some places priests even prayed to God to 'save us from the Jewish nemesis.'" [10] But settlement on the land and integration into industry proceeded apace, and the Jewish social structure was being transformed. In 1926, 15.22 percent of Ukrainian Jews were classified as workers, 20.67 as employees (white collar), 0.60 percent as professionals, and 3.85 percent as agricultural workers. Another 22.95 percent were in artels and over 16 percent were either unemployed or had no visible means of support. [11]

Beginning in 1928, with collectivization and the first Five-Year Plan, the Jewish socioeconomic structure was transformed along with that of the country as a whole. The categories of unemployed and self-employed, as well as those who employed others, disappeared. Jewish agricultural colonies were thoroughly collectivized and they were also "internationalized," that is, they were merged with non-Jewish collectives in order to change their specifically national character. Industry proved a greater attraction than agriculture to the Jews of Ukraine, as well as of other parts of the USSR, and large numbers of Soviet Jews entered diverse branches of the developing Soviet industry. A concomitant of industrialization was large population movements. For Ukraine as a whole this involved rural-to-urban movement, and for the Jews it meant moving from the shtetl to the larger towns, from the towns and cities of the Pale of Settlement to those which had previously been closed to the Jewish population, and from the former Pale provinces in Ukraine, Belorussia (and Poland and Lithuania) either to areas in these territories which had been previously forbidden to the Jews or out of these Western territories altogether and into the RSFSR. Whereas in 1926 73.9 percent of Soviet Jews lived in Belorussia and Ukraine, in 1939 only 63.2 percent did. In the early 1930's Jewish cultural activity seemed to be still on the upswing, with the emergence of the Institute of Jewish Proletarian Culture attached to the All-Ukrainian Academy of Arts and Sciences, the continued growth of the Yiddish school network, the publication of ten Yiddish newspapers in Ukraine (1935), and the activity of at least ten Yiddish theaters in various Ukrainian cities. By the mid-1930's, however, it was clear that a strong reverse trend was in the making. Along with a myriad of other sins catalogued by the Great Purge, "bourgeouis nationalism" became a cardinal error whose presence was discovered among all the nationalities of the Soviet Union. The leaderships of the national sub-units of the Party were severely affected by the anti-nationalist purges, as were prominent political and and cultural figures among the national minorities. In the late 1920's and early 1930's about fifty pamphlets and books propagandizing the population against antisemitism were published by the Soviet state, but after 1934 nothing on the subject was published (except for a small pamphlet by Academician Struve published in 1941 after the Nazi-Soviet alliance had broken down).[12] By the late 1930's the number of Yiddish books published in Ukraine (and elsewhere in the USSR) had declined drastically; only four Yiddish theaters remained in Ukraine; only five Yiddish newspapers were published, and beginning in 1934, the number of Yiddish schools and of students in such schools declined.[13] The Jewish political and cultural elites were seriously weakened by the purges, and together with the secular trends which had uprooted Jews from their traditional areas of habitation and had seriously weakened or destroyed the traditional way of life, these had the effect of reducing national consciousness among Jews and acculturating them rapidly into non-Jewish cultures.

This trend was partially deflected by the absorption into the USSR of the Western territories from Poland, the Baltic States, and Romania during the 1939-41 period. Over one million Jews from these areas were now under Soviet administration. Secularization and de-nationalization had not made nearly as much headway among them as it had among Soviet Jews, and the entry of this unassimilated Jewish population re-introduced traditional mores and folkways to the Soviet Jews.

Just as Soviet Ukrainians were affected by contact with Ukrainians from Poland (Halychyna), so too were Ukrainian Jews affected by their contacts with the less assimilated, more Jewishly active West Ukrainian Jewish population. But it was the Nazi occupation of Ukraine and the policy of annihilating the Jews which forced even those Jews who were reluctant to do so to realize that however they might regard themselves the non-Jewish world regarded them as Jews and did not differentiate very much between those who spoke good Russian or Ukrainian and those who clung to the Yiddish or Hebrew languages and cultures. The infamy of Babyn Yar is but one instance in the tragic history of slaughter and destruction which Ukrainian Jewry underwent during the war. It is impossible to generalize about "the Ukrainian attitude" toward the Jews at this time, for we are dealing with attitudes and actions of individuals and not of a nation acting as a collectivity, but there were sufficiently numerous incidents of collaboration with the Nazis by individual Ukrainians, whether as members of special police detachments, as concentration camp guards or simply as participants in anti-Jewish actions, to have created the impression among large numbers of Jews that the majority of the Ukrainian people were still infected with antisemitic attitudes and some were prepared to translate them into actions. Jewish partisan groups in all parts of the occupied territories had difficulties with other Soviet partisans and citizens, but in Ukraine such groups also faced the problem of dealing not only with the Nazis but with the Ukrainian Nationalist Organization (OUN) which hailed "a great independent Ukraine without Jews, Poles, and Germans. Poles — beyond the San; Germans — to Berlin; Jews to the gallows!"[14] The question of Ukrainian-Jewish relations in this period is complex, and undoubtedly controversial, and we cannot discuss it fully here.[15] For our purposes what is important is that the subjective perception by Ukrainian Jews was that all too many of their neighbors were willing either to observe passively or, in a smaller number of cases, to participate actively in a wholesale slaughter of the Jewish population. At the same time, Nazi propaganda, which was very intensive in Ukraine, attempted to

171

convince the Ukrainian people that their sufferings during the war were due to the "Jewish-Bolshevik" conspiracy which had exploited then and that the Jews were somehow avoiding the horrors of war while Ukrainians and others bore the brunt of the fighting. In sum, as a result of the war, mutual suspicion and tension among all the nationalities in Ukraine probably increased and was further exacerbated in the immediate post-war period when the Soviet state reasserted control in Ukraine and had to confront Ukrainian nationalism head on. Though one can debate the effects of the war on attitudes and inter-ethnic relations, an unambiguous outcome of the occupation was the drastic reduction in the size of the Jewish population and in the numerical importance it had in Ukraine. The 1939 census had reported 1,533,000 Jews in Ukraine (old boundaries) and in 1959 this figure had dropped to 840,000. Not a single one of the Jewish institutions — collective farms, schools, theaters, newspapers, and the like — which had managed to survive the purges — survived the war.

Jewish life in Ukraine now became quantitatively and qualitatively different. Though the nationality continued to exist, albeit in reduced numbers, its organized national existence had disappeared. This meant that more than ever Jews in Ukraine were a highly acculturated ethnic group whose ethnicity was less and less linked to the usual appurtenances of an ethnic culture — language, institutions, specific customs — but had become defined both by the **perception** of the "ingroup" as being an ingroup, as well as by the **perception** of the "outgroups" — Russians and Ukrainians in the main — that the Jews were a group apart. This definition of Jews as a group does not depend, however, on subjective perceptions alone. For, as we shall see, Jews in Ukraine do possess certain distinctive characteristics which set them apart from other groups, especially when those characteristics are perceived — and perhaps exaggerated — both by Jews and by others. While losing some of the distinctive cultural traits we normally associate with ethnic groups, Jews have acquired or maintained other characteristics which have become associated with them to such a degree that they become perceived as a distinct **social** group. Since the Soviet system persists in classifying Jews as an ethnic group, or nationality, Soviet Jews have a **legal** status which sets them apart and reinforces the separateness and distinctness of the group which might even be defined solely in terms of its socioeconomic, rather than political-legal, status. In other words, the combination of mass perceptions, self-perception, and legal status conferred by the political system insures that despite the fact that Jews are the most acculturated major nationality in the USSR, they continue to be regarded — and to regard themselves, in most cases — as a distinct group.

Demographic Characteristics of the Jewish Population in Ukraine

In 1970 there were 2,150,707 Jews in the USSR according to the Soviet census.[16] Jews are the twelfth largest nationality among 104 nationalities in the USSR. They are one of the most geographically dispersed ethnic groups in the USSR, with only Russians, Ukrainians, Belorussians, and Tatars more widely dispersed.[17] About 770,000 Jews, or 36.1 percent of the total Soviet Jewish population, live in Ukraine. (In 1959 there were 840,000 Jews in the Ukrainian SSR, constituting 37 percent of the total Jewish population.) Only the RSFSR has a larger Jewish concentration. But whereas in 1959 the Jews made up two percent of the population of Ukraine, in 1970 their percentage had diminished to 1.6. Nevertheless, within republic boundaries there are particular concentrations of Jews. For example, Jews are the second most numerous nationality in Leningrad oblast (including the city of Leningrad). They are the third most numerous nationality in eight oblasts of the Ukrainian republic. The third largest concentration of Jews in the USSR is found in Kyiv oblast (164,600), the fourth in Odesa oblast (117,200), the sixth in Kharkiv oblast (76,500) and the seventh in Dnipropetrovs'k (69,300). As is well known, the Jews are the most highly urbanized Soviet nationality, about 98 percent of them categorized as urban dwellers. This makes them the seventh largest urban nationality in the Soviet Union. In Kyiv, where 152,000 Jews reside, they constitute 9.3 percent of the city's population (only Kishinev, in the neighboring Moldavia, with 14 percent of its residents of Jewish nationality, has

172

a higher proportion of Jews).[18] In other cities of Ukraine Jews make up between 4 and 13 percent of the population. Thus, despite their overall dispersal in the country, their concentration in the cities, and in the larger administrative centers at that — 26 percent of the entire Jewish population lives in Moscow, Leningrad, and Kyiv — make the Jews very highly visible in certain locations, nowhere more so than in the larger urban centers of Ukraine. Since it is in these centers that the political and cultural life of the Soviet state is concentrated, Jews should be favorably located with regard to educational and cultural opportunities and to political and social participation.

Nevertheless, in Ukraine, as in most other parts of the Soviet Union, Jews are a declining proportion of the urban population, as the urban-rural migration of other nationalities increased the size of the cities and of the proportion of the Soviet population that is urban. For example, in 1959, 13.89 percent of Kyiv's population was Jewish, while by 1970 it had fallen to 9.3 percent.[19] In 1926 the 81,000 Jews of Kharkiv made up nearly one fifth of the city's population; by 1939 this had declined to 15.6 percent, despite the fact that the Jewish population was now 130,200; and by 1959, when the population had fallen to 81,500, largely as a result of the holocaust, Jews made up only 8.7 percent of Kharkiv's inhabitants.[20] Overall, whereas in 1926 Jews made up 24.8 percent of the urban population of the Ukrainian SSR, by 1959, they had dropped to 4.3 percent of that population.[21] There is every likelihood that the Jewish proportion in the urban population will continue to decline, since there are no reservoirs of rural Jews upon which to draw. Moreover, the Jews have one of the lowest birth rates in the Soviet Union (the average Jewish family in 1959 consisted of only 3.2 persons[22]), and the Jewish population is skewed in favor of the older age groups. A study in Kharkiv showed that while generally there were 236 births for every 100 deaths, among the Jews in 1960 there were only 800 births as against 977 deaths.[23] The urban population of Ukraine grew by nine percent between 1959 and 1970,[24] while the Jewish population declined absolutely. Curiously, one Soviet study found that in 1967 among those migrating to Kyiv from Ukraine and other republics Jews constituted 2.2 percent, but they made up 3.3 percent of those leaving the city (the destination of the migrants was not indicated).[25] However, this would hardly indicate an out-migration of Jews from the Ukrainian cities.

A second defining characteristic of the Jewish population, and closely linked to its urbanity, is its high level of education. Education has traditionally been highly regarded by Jews, and given their relatively high levels of literacy before the revolution (in 1926 over seventy percent of Ukrainian Jews was literate, while only 41 percent of the Ukrainians and 45 percent of the Russians in Ukraine were literate), and the fact that their urbanity allows them access to the most highly developed Soviet educational institutions, they have emerged as the most educated nationality, by far, in the USSR. According to the third volume of the 1970 census results, 39.9 percent of the Jews in the RSFSR (no data were published for Jews in other republics) who were above ten years of age had some sort of higher education. The second ranking nationality, the Georgians, had only 10.5 percent, while Russians had 5.9 percent and Ukrainians 4.5 percent. If one examines the educational level of the working force population only, one finds that over half the Jews (again, in the RSFSR) have higher education and only 15.4 percent of the Georgians, again in second place, have such education. Fully 82.4 percent of the Jews have more than primary education, which is nearly twice as much as the national average (43.5 percent). Though the Jews are the twelfth largest nationality, in 1973 they ranked third — behind Russians and Ukrainians — in the absolute number of "scientific workers" in the economy.[26] Among those holding the degree of doctor of science they rank second, and among those with the degree of "candidate" they rank third. However, while they still rank third in the number of doctoral candidates (aspiranty), the absolute number of Jews in this category declined by nearly 500 between 1970 and 1973. (Interestingly, the absolute number of Ukrainians increased by only two, while the number of Russians increased by 1,130.)[27] Thus, in 1973, when Jews constituted less than one percent of the Soviet population they made up 6.11 percent of the "scientific workers." Here, too, their proportion has been declining: in 1950 Jews were 15.46 percent of "scientific workers," in 1960, 9.47 percent, and 1970, 6.94 percent.[28] It has been calculated that about forty percent of Jewsih "scientific workers" reside in Moscow, and that perhaps two-thirds of all Jewish "scientific workers" reside in the RSFSR. Nevertheless, it can be assumed that in Ukraine as well — the republic with the second highest number of scientific institutions in the country as well as the second highest number of Jews — the Jews are "overrepresented" among "scientific workers." William Korey asserts that in Ukraine, 283 out of 1,000 Jews over the age of ten have completed higher education.[29] A slightly different picture emerges from the following table, based on 1970 census data.[30]

Educational Level of Soviet Jews
For every 1000 persons over the age of ten, the number of those with education is:

	Higher	Incomplete higher	Specialized secondary	General secondary	Incomplete secondary	Elementary
RSFSR	344	55	135	172	118	116
Latvia	209	72	119	214	159	163
Ukraine	195	37	150	214	151	160
Belorussia	164	37	142	179	188	190
Moldavia	126	34	112	198	190	227

Thus, while the most educated Jews reside in the RSFSR, and the educational level of Latvian Jews is also high, the Ukrainian Jewish population is rather well educated, even in comparison with other Soviet Jews. Nearly 60 percent of Ukrainian Jews have completed some type of secondary education. In 1960 / 61 Jews made up 4.5 percent of all students in higher education in Ukraine, and 24.2 percent of Jewish students in the USSR were studying in Ukraine.[31]

On the basis of an examination of a 1968 directory of doctors (holders of the doctoral degree) and teachers in higher education in Ukraine, Mordechai Altshuler has calculated that about thirteen percent were Jewish. About eighty percent of these Jewish scientists and scholars were concentrated in medicine, technical sciences, and physics-mathematics, and only 8.77 percent of the Jews holding the doctoral degree were in the humanities and social sciences. Furthermore, Jews were much better represented among older age groups, especially in social sciences and humanities, despite the fact that, in general, Jews received their doctorates at a lower age than the average.[32] According to data cited by Yaroslav Bilinsky, at the end of 1960 Jews constituted 12.2 percent of professionals with higher education working in the Ukrainian republic.[33] Thus, Jews are prominent in the professional and scientific-scholarly life of Ukraine beyond what their proportion in the population would indicate. This is true in other republics as well. For example, in Belorussia, where Jews constitute the same proportion of the republic population as they do in the Ukraine (1.6 percent) in 1970 they were the third ranked nationality in terms of specialists with higher education. But while the number of Belorussians, Ukrainians, and Russians with such education more than doubled between 1960 and 1970, for the Jews the number increased by only 67 percent.[34]

Clearly, a high level of education has emerged as an "attribute" or "trait" of the Ukrainian Jew. Since education is closely linked to position in the social-occupational structure, this also means that Jews are unevenly dispersed in the social hierarchy and are concentrated in the professional categories, adding yet another component of the definition of being a Jew in Ukraine and in the USSR as a whole. There is little doubt that Jews themselves as well as other nationalities associate these characteristics with Jews, for better or for worse, and that these have become as much a defining characteristic of ethnic affiliation as language, or religion, or other, more conventional components of ethnicity.

The Political Role of Ukrainian Jews

There is a great deal of evidence that the Communist Party has increasingly recruited from the more educated, and hence the urban, sectors of the population. It is also clear that even in the 1920's those who were literate and urban stood a much higher chance, statistically, of being Party members and government officials than the peasantry and the less skilled and less educated segments of the working class. While Jews in Ukraine, as elsewhere in the Russian Empire, showed no particular inclination toward Bolshevism, despite the fact that some rather atypical Jews were prominent in the Bolshevik leadership,[35] the wave of pogroms in 1918-21 and the sudden opening of educational and employment opportunities hitherto denied the Jews attracted increasing numbers of them to the Soviet regime and Party. As Lenin noted, the Jews replaced the tsarist administrators and part of the intelligentsia for they provided literate and reasonably educated cadres after the disappearance of large numbers of tsarist officials and administrators.

Scrutiny of the Belorussian and Ukrainian republics in the 1920's reveals the importance of education and urbanity for political activity and position. Jews played a larger and more powerful role in the Belorussian than in the Ukrainian Party for they constituted a larger share of the literate and working class population in Belorussia than in Ukraine. In 1926 Jews made up 8.2 percent of the Belorussian Republic's population, and 5.4 percent in Ukraine. Whereas they were 40.2 percent of the urban population in Belorussia they were only 22.7 percent of this population in Ukraine.[36] In Belorussia they also constituted 20.7 percent of all workers, whereas in Ukraine they were 8.7 percent of the proletariat.[37] The difference between the two republics is reflected in Party membership figures: while Jews constituted 26.6 percent of the Belorussian Party, they were 13.1 percent of the Ukrainian Party.[38] The Jewish Sections of the Communist Party in Belorussia enjoyed far more influence and a better relationship with the rest of the Party than in Ukraine, where from the very start the Sections had to struggle against strong pressures in the Party to liquidate or emasculate the Evsektsii. There were several Belorussian Evsektsii activists who were members of the Central Bureau (Committee) of the Belrussian Party, but there were no Evsektsii leaders in the Ukrainian Central Committee. Nevertheless, in both republics Jews by nationality served as first secretaries in the 1920's — Jan Gamarnik in Belorussia and Lazar Kaganovich in Ukraine. By 1927, 4.3 percent of the Ukrainian Central Executive (VUTsIK) members were Jews, as were ten percent of the kraiispolkomy members and 19.3 percent of the city soviets' members.[39] In that year the national composition of the Ukrainian Party was as follows:[40]

Nationality	Number	Percentage	Women	Percentage of Women
Ukrainians	87,185	51.96	8,434	43.78
Russians	46,156	27.51	4,902	25.45
Jews	20,306	12.10	4,645	24.11

Almost half of all the Jewish Communists resided in Ukraine, though their proportion in the Belorussian Party was almost double that in Ukraine (23.8 percent). In the Belorussian Party Jewish women constituted fully 46.5 percent of all female Communists. Finally, in Ukraine Jews were 13.2 percent of the Ukrainian Komsomol and 11.79 percent of all trade union members (24.72 percent in Belorussia).[41]

The Ukrainian Party was divided into two main factions in the late 1920's: one consisted of former members of other Ukrainian parties and some younger nationally

175

conscious Ukrainians, and the other was made up mostly of Russified Ukrainians and Russians.[42] In general, the Jewish Communists tended to side with the Russifying faction. Some Jewish Communists resented what they perceived as antisemitic attitudes among the lower Party apparatus. Others charged that the policy of "nativization" (korenizatsiia) had only partially solved the national problem because in Ukraine it had been used to force national minorities—Russians, Poles, and Jews—to learn Ukrainian. Yuri Larin charged that the Soviet policy of nativization was being transformed into a device for repressing the separate minorities in the republics, just as the majority groups in border areas had been repressed by the Russians before 1917.[43] This question became academic when in the early 1930's a major shift in nationality policy put an end to further progress in "nativization" and a centralizing tendency emerged. The Ukrainian Party leadership was badly hit by the purges, and the Jewish political and cultural leadership was also decimated at this time. Both Ukrainian and Jewish cultural and scholarly institutions were closed and it became clear that "petty bourgeois nationalism" was a far greater sin from the regime's point of view than "great power chauvinism."

Though the proportion of the Jews in the Ukrainian population declined in the 1930's, and though large numbers of Ukrainians (and Russians) were emigrating to the cities and illiteracy was being wiped out, the Jews seem to have managed to maintain their numerical position within the Party up until the outbreak of the war. According to T. H. Rigby, in 1940, 13.4 percent of Party members in Ukraine were Jews.[44] In that year they were but four percent of the delegates to the Ukrainian Party Congress, and it would appear that they had lost their representation in the higher echelons of the Party.[45]

There is no publicly available data for Jewish membership in the Ukrainian Party after the war. We do know that in 1962 Jews constituted 6.4 percent of the Belorussian Party and 6.3 percent of the Moldavian Party. Rigby suggests that since "The prewar position and the recent history of the Jews in Ukraine (is) the same as those in Belorussia" — a suggestion which is open to some question, as we have tried to demonstrate — and since a partial breakdown of the ethnic composition of the Ukrainian Party published in 1958 shows that the 6.3 percent of the republic's population who were neither Ukrainian nor Russian contained 11.5 percent of the Party members, "it seems likely that the Jewish population had a Party membership rate at least twice and possibly three times as great as that for the republic's level as a whole."[46] Armstrong estimates that Jews constitute eight percent of the Ukrainian Party. In light of the educational and urban characteristics of the Jews, Rigby's assumption seems reasonable, though it is likely that Jews are to be found in greater proportions in the lower (Armstrong calculates that in 1956 only 2.6 percent of delegates to the Ukrainian Party Congress were of Jewish nationality) levels of the Party. Probably not a single obkom first secretary or even raikom secretary is Jewish, though the research of Grey Hodnett and others may clarify this point.

It does seem that Jews were underrepresented in the state organs of Ukraine. In 1959 in the Ukrainian Supreme Soviet there was only one Jew of the 457 elected deputies (0.22 percent) and only 0.52 percent of the local Soviet deputies in the republic were of Jewish nationality.[47] This was the lowest representation of Jews in any republic Supreme Soviet. In 1971 there were a total of 6,058 Jews in all Soviet organs in the USSR, only 19 in the republic Supreme Soviet.[48]

There is little doubt that the political position of the Jews has greatly deteriorated, in the country as a whole as well as in Ukraine. With the emergence of the movement for emigration to Israel, the image of the Jew as a person of divided loyalty and of doubtful fealty to the Soviet state and the ideals of Communism is reinforced, and further restrictions on the political activities of Jews, applied more stringently in some republics than in others, can be expected. While once some people included Party membership or sympathy among the components of Jewish identity, that may be decreasingly the case.

Acculturation, Assimiliation, and National Consciousness

There is not a single Jewish school of any kind in the USSR and there are no Jewish cultural institutions, with the exception of a Yiddish monthly published in Moscow and a dwindling number of synagogues tolerated by the authorities. This means that since the late 1930's the education of Jews had been in cultures other than their native one. It is not surprising to find that Jews are the most linguistically assimilated of Soviet nationalities. Whereas in 1970, 93.9 of the Soviet population gave the language of their nationality as their mother tongue, only 17.7 percent of the Jews listed a Jewish language (mainly Yiddish) as their mother tongue (in 1926, 71.9 percent, and in 1959, 21.5 percent of the Jews listed a Jewish language as their mother tongue). However, 25 percent in 1970 indicated substantital familiarity with Yiddish. [49] Seventy-eight percent of the Jews consider Russian their mother tongue; 95 percent have a command of Russian; and 33 percent command other languages of the USSR. [50] In Ukraine only 13.1 percent listed Yiddish as a mother tongue (down from 16.9 percent in 1959), and this was the lowest percentage of Yiddish speakers listed in any republic but the RSFSR. It was also in Ukraine that the steepest decline in percentage of Yiddish speakers occurred between 1959 and 1970. In those cities which were originally part of the Pale of Settlement, and in those which until 1939-40 had been part of Poland or Romania, the percentage of Yiddish speakers is higher than in the Ukrainian cities with a more recent Jewish population and / or one which has been under Soviet rule since the revolutionary period. In 1970 in Kyiv 13 percent of the Jews listed Yiddish as their mother tongue, but in Kharkiv, outside the former Pale, while 73 percent of all Kharkivites gave their national language as their mother tongue, only 7.7 percent of the Jews did so. [52] It is clear that even in the non-Russian republics Jews favor Russian over other languages, especially in the cities. In Kharkiv 92 percent of the Jews listed Russian, and only 0.3 percent listed Ukrainian as their mother tongue.

This tendency to adopt Russian culture probably derives from the conviction that Russian is a more useful language, since it is the lingua franca of the country, and that it embodies a "higher culture" than the other cultures of the USSR. In republics such as Ukraine and the Baltic, where national feelings run high and there is resentment of the Russification of local cultures, the Russian acculturation of the Jews evokes the displeasure of the local nationalities who see the Jews as agents of Russification. On the other hand, the nationalism of the non-Russians is disquieting to the Jews since it is associatedin their minds with antisemitism.

While some have pointed to the linguistic assimilation of Soviet Jews as an indication of their general assimilation, it would be more correct to see this as an index of their acculturation, rather than assimilation. Acculturation involves the adoption of the culture of another group, which most Ukrainian Jews have done, but assimilation means the adoption of another culture to such an extent that one no longer has any characteristics identifying one with his former culture and no longer has any loyalties to his former culture. [53] It is doubtful that very many Ukrainian Jews have assimilated in this sense, since they are officially identified in their passports as Jews, they retain distinctive values and life-styles, and they are regarded by other nationalities as Jews. It would be quite difficult for them to lose consciousness of themselves as Jews, however they may feel about this identification. Soviet scholars themselves have warned against identifying linguistic with psychological assimilation. I. S. Gurvich points to Russianized Germans, Jews, and Tatarified Bashkirs when he notes that "Even while losing the mother tongue and even cultural characteristics, national consciousness is often preserved."[54] Another scholar argues that ethnic change lags behind socioeconomic change and that "Linguistic switchover does not in itself mark a transition to a new ethnic state." [55] Thus, Ukrainian Jews who know no Yiddish and whose culture is Russian may nevertheless be legally, psychologically, and socially Jewish.

Perhaps a better indicator of assimilation, if not of the present generation then of future ones, might be marriage with members of other nationalities. Children of mixed marriages may choose the nationality of either parent and fragmentary evidence on Jews from the Baltic republics, and evidence on other nationalities elsewhere in the USSR, indicates that children, one of whose parents is a member of a national minority, overwhelmingly opt for the majority nationality when they can. Thus, children with one Jewish parent are likely to have their legal identification become other than Jewish and this would undoubtedly go some way to think of themselves as non-Jews.

In the USSR as a whole, for every 1,000 families, 102 are of mixed nationality. The highest proportion of mixed families is in Latvia (158) and the second highest is in Ukraine (150). [56] In the cities of Ukraine 26 percent of marriages are mixed. In 1969 Ukrainian males married Ukrainian females in 83 out of 100 cases; Jewish males married Jewish females in 63 of 100; and Polish males married Polish females in only 22 of 100 instances. [57] In 1958-61 in Ukraine, 20.6 percent of Jewish children had a father of non-Jewish nationality, but 89.7 percent of Jewish urban families were considered ethnically homogeneous. [58] While these data do not provide a comprehensive picture of intermarriage among Ukrainian Jews, it is clear that such marriages are considerably more frequent today than they were in the 1920's.

PERCENTAGE OF MIXED MARRIAGES AMONG UKRAINIAN JEWS [59]

Males			Females		
1925	1926	1927	1925	1926	1927
4.23	4.62	4.97	4.74	5.52	5.53

In a survey of 56 towns in the 1920's, it was found that 96 percent of the Jewish males married endogenously, but in Kyiv, Odesa, Ekaterynoslav, and Kharkiv, 5.7 percent married exogenously (more to Russians than to Ukrainians in these cities, but overall almost equally to Ukrainians and Russians). In Ukraine as a whole it was calculated that 3.7 percent of the Jews married exogenously, but in the 54 largest towns and cities the percentage rose to 4.5. [60] In Kharkiv three times as many Jewish males were married to non-Jews in 1960 as were in 1923, and four times as many Jewish females. [61]

Nevertheless, in comparison with other national minorities the Jewish intermarriage rate is not very high. It might be added that in comparison with such rates among West European and Amerian Jews it is also relatively low. In Kharkiv, in 1960, 720 Jewish women married, 235 of them (32.6 percent) to non-Jews. (Of the 235, 117 married Russians and 108 married Ukrainians.) This was a lower percentage of exogenous marriages than among Russians, Ukrainians, Belorussians, and Tatars. Among 662 Jewish grooms, 177 (26.8 percent) married non-Jews (86 Russians and 72 Ukrainians). [62] A 1970 sample survey taken in the Kyiv marriage registry showed that Jews have the highest "index of attraction" for their own nationality. [63] Though Jewish intermarriage in Ukraine is more frequent than in Moldavia and perhaps the Asian and Transcaucasian republics, it is comparable to intermarriage in Latvia, [64] and is less frequent than one might expect, given the acculturation of the Ukrainian Jews. Perhaps this is an indication of high ethnic consciousness, even among urban and educated peoples, and the existence of ethnic barriers among the nationalities in Ukraine, though these barriers are much lower than they have been in the past.

The situation of Ukrainian Jews, even more so than of Soviet Jews generally, may be described as one of acculturation without assimilation. Jews no longer speak a distinctive language, by and large, and have no cultural institutions of their own. Yet they have a distinctive identity maintained, in part, by Soviet law, and defined by their urbanity, education, life-styles and mores, and by their group consciousness. Social and ethnic strata coincide and sometimes become coterminous. Jewish national consciousness is probably higher than statistics can reveal. [65] As one Jew from Kharkiv puts it, "when they bring a new elephant to the zoo, the first question we ask is, 'is it one of ours or one of theirs?'" Since national consciousness generally is high in Ukraine, Jews also become nationally aware. The influx of Jews from Western

Ukraine undoubtedly strengthened the dwindling Jewish identification of Soviet Jews, and the events of 1941-46 emphasized that Jews were regarded as such no matter how they might regard themselves. Finally, antisemitism also forces the Jew to confront his own national identity.

One indirect measure of national consciousness may be emigration from Ukraine to Israel. It is generally believed that since March, 1971, when Jewish emigration began on a large scale, it has been easier for Jews from the Baltic Republics and Georgia than for those from the interior of the USSR to gain permission to leave. Nevertheless, in 1971 about 2,300 Jews emigrated from Ukraine. In that year they constituted 18 percent of the total Soviet emigration. In 1972 there were 8,500 Ukrainian Jewish emigrants and they made up more than one quarter of all emigrants. At the same time Ukraine had become the republic from which the second largest number of Jews had emigrated. One of the first Soviet Jews to publicly demand that he be allowed to emigrate was the Kyivan, Boris Kochubievsky. Though the center of the emigration movement seems to have been (1971-73) in the Baltic republics and in Georgia, several prominent figures in the movement have emerged in Ukraine, and immigrants have come to Israel from all parts of Ukraine. It is not possible to determine at present what the proportion is of those coming from Western Ukraine, but it is clear that cities such as Kyiv, Kharkiv, and Odesa have contributed significant numbers of immigrants. There have been several cases of Soviet repression of would-be emigrants from Ukraine, though, as elsewhere in the country, there does not seem to be any consistent policy in this regard.

Ethnic Relations in Ukraine

In the absence of survey data, and in the presence of much sensitivity and perhaps prejudice, it is difficult to speak with any certainty about the state of relations among the ethnic groups, or nationalities, in Ukraine. Lacking longitudinal data, it is impossible to ascertain what changes have taken place over time. Here it is only possible to cite some fragmentary evidence, which itself must be treated with great caution, and to warn that, by no means, can it be seen as definitive.

Shortly after World War Two, as part of the Harvard Refugee Project, Ukrainian emigres were questioned on their attitudes towards Jews. It was found that 47 percent of the least educated Ukrainian refugees, 51 percent of the moderately educated, and 36 percent of well educated respondents favored excluding Jews from social contacts. "The middle-educated Ukrainian, the interviewer concluded, was particularly anti-Semitic both in his perceptions of relations between his own national group and Jews, and in expressions of social exclusion he desired." [66] In my survey of 150 Soviet immigrants in Israel (1972), in which 77 percent of the respondents said they had encountered anti-Semitism in the USSR "often" or "sometimes," 86 percent of those coming from Ukraine responded in this way. Some have argued that since in 1961-63 ninety percent of those sentenced to death for economic crimes in Ukraine were Jews, and since this represented a much higher percentage of Jews executed than in other republics and in the USSR as a whole (59 percent), this could be an indication that local anti-Semitic officials were using the campaign against economic crimes in order to punish the Jews, who, after all, at that time constituted only two percent of the republic's population.

A recent Jewish emigre from Ukraine, Izrail Kleiner, has published anecdotal memoirs in which he discusses the problem of Ukrainian-Jewish relations. He argues that:

it is necessary to admit that the relations between Jews and Ukrainians in the USSR, and especially in Ukraine, are extremely strained. From the Ukrainian side we see, and not only among the uneducated strata of the population, hatred for the Jews and repugnance for everything Jewish, openly expressed at every step. Such expressions, for example, as 'we can still arrange another Babyn Yar for you,' or 'it's too bad the Germans didn't succeed in slaughtering all of you, but it's not too late!' — every Jew in Ukraine has heard a dozen times . . . It is not

179

surprising that Jewsih children, having grown up, have become alienated from the Ukrainians and have developed enmity toward them. The disproportionately high cultural level of the Jewish masses compared with the Ukrainians gives the Jews a basis for feeling a certain scorn for Ukrainians. The situation is becoming still worse as a result of the official anti-Semitism which has been Party-state policy for several decades in the USSR. Now it is impossible to encounter a Jew among Party workers, even at the **raikom** level . . . Things have gone so far that they don't even take a Jewish woman as a cleaning lady in a building where there is some kind of Party or KGB institution.

Kleiner claims that the Russian authorities incite anti-Semitism and that "unfortunately, such a policy finds fertile ground in Ukraine. In this way the impression is created among Jews that their most terrible enemy are the Ukrainians and not Russian great power chauvinism. In the event of ... political disorder, pogroms will begin again — in part spontaneously, in part as a result of incitement by the Russian great power forçes. Under such circumstances, Jews will find themselves on the side of Russian imperialism." [67]

In another article, Kleiner describes the Jewish activists in Kyiv and says that they were sympathetic to the "democratic" political oppositionists. "Sympathy for the 'nationalists' was significantly smaller, because of the long-standing hostility between Ukrainians and Jews. Perhaps it would be more diplomatic to say 'between a segment of the Ukrainians and the Jews.' Unfortunately, my experience tells me that these segments in Ukraine approach, if not one hundred, then ninety-nine percent of both peoples." "Many Jews," he says, "sympathized with the Ukrainian nationalist movement, understanding the similarity of our interests. Yet there was widespread skepticism about the perspectives of this movement. From their experience Jews know that any kind of outburst of Ukrainian national feelings takes the form of a great Jewish pogrom." [68]

There have been attempts by some leading Ukrainian dissidents to raise the question of relations with the Jews. In April, 1966 the writer Svyatoslav Karavansky, then in jail, addressed a petition to the Chairman of the Soviet of Nationalities in which he demanded to know why Jewish culture had been suppressed and why there was an unofficial quota against admissions of Jews to educational institutions in Odesa (a fact frequently mentioned by Soviet Jews). He wrote that "the attitude of a society toward its Jewish population is the litmus paper indicating that society's level of international consciousness." [69] The well known Ukrainian dissenter, Ivan Dzyuba, made a now famous address at Babyn Yar on the twenty-fifth anniversary of the massacre (1966) in which he charged that there had been no attempt to combat anti-Semitism after the war and "periodically it was artificially nurtured."

As a Ukrainian, I am ashamed that in my nation, as among other nations, there is this shameful phenomenon, unworthy of humanity, called anti-Semitism. We, the Ukrainians, should combat in our midst every manifestation of anti-Semitism or disrespect to a Jew, and the incomprehension of the Jewish problem. You, the Jews, should struggle against those in your midst who do not respect Ukrainians, the Ukrainian culture and the Ukrainian language, those who unjustly perceive in every Ukrainian a disguised anti-Semite.

He called for both nationalities to become familiar with each other's history and culture and to learn to respect them. [70]

It is impossible to say how much of an impact these statements made on Ukrainian Jewry, or indeed, how widely they are known. But they are testimony to the fact that some Ukrainian intellectuals are willing to confront the question of Ukrainian-Jewish relations, that these relations are still problematic, and that at least a "segment" of Ukrainian opinion is for a decisive improvement in those relations.

Still, it seems premature and overly optimistic to conclude, as Yaroslav Bilinsky does, that "...As the socio-economic difference between the Ukrainian majority and the Jewish minority will diminish by action of the regime, the Ukrainians will increasingly look upon the Jews as their comrades in suffering, that this is likely to happen despite some ugly doing, seems to be assured by the fact that there is no fundamental hostility between the two peoples." [71] This seems to underrate the effect of the religious, socio-economic and even political differences between the two peoples. While some Jews seek to leave Ukraine for Israel, some Ukrainians seek to develop Ukraine and increase its limited autonomy from Moscow. While some Jews see Russians as their protectors against Ukrainians, **Faute de mieux**, some Ukrainians see Jews as the agents of Russification. Moreover, stereotypes and prejudices persist even after objective conditions have changed decisively — and socio-economic change in Ukraine has not been that rapid as to equalize the statuses of Ukrainians and Jews. As Paul Lendvai has pointed out with regard to Eastern Europe, especially Poland, it is even possible to have "antisemitism without Jews."

Conclusion

A recent Soviet monograph on nationalities concludes that "the development of nations and national relations is one of the most complex areas of social life about which to make predictions. First, because such predictions depend on a correct understanding of the development of social processes, which are very hard to understand, both because of ever more rapid social development and because these processes are speeded by the scientific-technological revolution; secondly, because of the special complexities of the study of national psychology and national feelings . . . " [72] This caution is well taken. Few would have predicted the development of the movement for emigration to Israel; it is difficult to gauge accurately the true state of ethnic relations in Ukraine; it is difficult to know what the impact of further economic development will be on inter-ethnic relations; and the eventual effect of emigration on the Ukrainian Jewish community is also not altogether clear.Perhaps, if the emigration continues, the most nationally conscious Jews, on the one hand, and those most sensitive to anti-Semitism, on the other, will, along with those seeking better economic opportunities, leave the country and significantly diminish the size of the Ukrainian Jewish population, while also changing the character of the Jewish community that remains. One can envision developments along the lines of those which occurred in Poland after the war. Large numbers of Jews left for other parts of the world, and only the very old, the committed Communists, and the highly assimilated remained. Of course, Ukrainian Jews are better off materially and better integrated into Soviet life spiritually than were the Polish survivors of the holocaust. It is unlikely that as great a proportion of Ukrainian Jews will emigrate, even if they could do so freely, and there is less objective reason for them to do so. Nevertheless, emigration must now be taken into account as an important determinant of the future of the Ukrainian Jewish community.

Even if there is no substantial emigration, the failure of the Jewish population to reproduce itself — as a result of low birth rates and inter-marriage — means that the absolute number of those officially classified as Jews in Ukraine might well continue to decline, especially since there is not reason to suppose that there will be an in-migration of Jews to the republic. The proportion of Jews in the urban population, in the intelligentsia and educated strata, and in the political elite will continue to decline. In the next decades, with declining birth rates in the European parts of the USSR and rising ones in Central Asia, one possibility is that Central Asians might migrate into Ukraine, where there are industries which will be increasingly hungry for manpower (unless there is a tremendous relocation of industry to Central Asia).. This would further diminish the numerical importance of the Jews, and would also threaten the position of Ukrainians and of Europeans.

From the perspective of the Jewish community itself, unless there are profound changes both in mass attitudes as well as in Soviet nationality policy — both of which are unlikely — the situation will continue to be one of acculturation without assimilation. This will preserve a Jewish nationality in Ukraine, however barren of any cultural-religious substance that community might be. Relative to other groups within Soviet Jewry, Ukraine is likely to continue losing number to the RSFSR, though it is so far ahead of the other areas that it will undoubtedly be "the second Soviet republic" for Jews as well. Though, as we have seen, the Ukrainian Jewish community has certain specific characteristics, its long range future will be determined by that of Soviet Jewry as a whole, as well as by the fate of Ukraine. In turn, this will depend on the future character of the multi-national Soviet state.

FOOTNOTES

1. M.I. Kulichenko, **Natsional'nye otnoscheniia v SSR i tendentsii ikh razvitiia** (Moscow: Mysl, 1972), p. 384.

2. Robert A. LeVine and Donald T. Cambell, **Ethnocentrism** (New York: John Wiley, 1972), p. 161

3. See **ibid.**, pp. 115-135.

4. John Armstrong, "The Ethnic Scene in the Soviet Union: The View of the Dictatorship," in Erich Goldhagen, ed., **Ethnic Minorities in the Soviet Union** (New York: Praeger, 1968), p. 8.

5. For details of Jewish political activity in Ukraine, 1917-1921, see my **Jewish Nationality and Soviet Politics** (Princeton: Princeton University Press, 1972), pp. 155-176.

6. N. Gergel, "Di pogromen in Ukraine in di yorn 1918-1921," in Yacov Lestschinsky, ed., **Shriftn far ekonomik un statistik**, p. 110.

7. See Salo Baron, **The Russian Jew under Tsars and Soviets** (New York: Macmillan, 1964), pp. 220-221, and Yakov Lestschinsky, **Dos sovetishe identum** (New York: Yidisher Kemfer, 1941, p. 70. See also John Reshetar, **The Ukrainian Revolution 1917-1920** (Princeton: Princeton University Press, 1952), pp. 253-256.

8. For documentation, see my **Jewish Nationality and Soviet Politics, op. cit.**, pp. 164-166.

9. S. D. Niepomniashchi to Daniel Charney, private letter dated August 7, 1924, YIVO Archives (New York).

10. Semen Sumny, "Tsvishn a natsmindisher natsmerheit," **Shtern,** May 26, 1927.

11. **Natsional'naia politika VKP (b) v tsifrakh** (Moscow, 1939), p. 49.

12. Based on titles listed in Mordechai Altshuler, ed., **Russian Publications on Jews and Judaism in the Soviet Union 1917-1967,** (Jerusalem, 1970), pp. 51-66.

13. For details, see Solomon Schwarz, **The Jews in the Soviet Union** (Syracuse: Syracuse University Press, 1951), pp. 135-137, 139-145.

14. Quoted in Solomon Schwarz, **Evrei v Sovetskom Soiuze s nachala Vtoroi Mirovoi Voiny** (New York: American Jewish Labor Committee, 1966), p. 97.

15. See Philip Friedmann, "Ukrainian-Jewish Relations During the Nazi Occupation," **YIVO Annual of Jewish Social Science XII** (1958 / 59). See also Schwarz, **ibid.**, pp. 95-114. A prominent figure who helped save many Jewish lives was Metropolitan Sheptytsky, but there were simple peasants and other "ordinary citizens" who risked their own lives to save those of Jews. See Curt Lewin, "Metropolitan Andreas Sheptytsky and the Jewish Community in Galicia," **Annals of the Ukrainian Academy of Arts and Sciences in the U.S.,** VII (1959), 1-2, pp. 1656-1668. For the view that "organized and systematic antisemitism never existed in Ukraine" unless it was aroused by an occupying or foreign power, see Lew Shankowsky, "Russia, the Jews and the Ukrainian Liberation Movement," **The Ukrainian Quarterly,** XVI, 1 and 2 (Spring and Summer, 1960).

16. Data on the 1970 census is derived mainly from the seven published volumes reporting the results.

17. Yakov Kapeliush, "Yidn in Sovetnfarband," **Sovetish Haimland** No. 9, 1974, p. 174.

18. Data from **ibid.**, pp. 175-176.

19. Data for 1959 is taken from **Itogi vsesoiuznoi perepisi naselenia 1959 goda** (Moscow: Gosstatizdat, 1962-1963) and from Mordechai Altshuler, ed., **The Jews in the Soviet Union Census 1959** (Jerusalem, 1963).

20. M. V. Kurman and I. V. Lebedinskii, **Naselenie bol'shogo sotsialisticheskogo-goroda** (Moscow: Statistika, 1968), p. 122.

21. V. I. Naul'ko, **Etnichnyi sklad naselennia Ukrains'koi RSR** (Kyiv: Naukova Dumka, 1965), p. 89.

22. B. Ts. Urlanis, **Rozhdaemost' i prodolzhitel'nost' zhizni v SSSR** (Moscow: Gosstatizdat, 1963), p. 72.

23. Kurman and Lebedinski, p. 128. The same situation, roughly, was found to obtain among other national minorities — Poles, Armenians, Moldavians, and Bulgars. The authors explain this solely in terms of the high rate of assimilation among the minorities in recent times, resulting in the birth of national minority children who are registered as being of another nationality, since one of their parents is likely to be a Russian or Ukrainian. On the other hand, those members of the minorities in the advanced age groups are almost always registered as members of that minority, and so the minority is "overrepresented" in deaths and "underrepresented" in births. In light of evidence on inter-marriage among Jews, to be cited later, and on the smallness of Jewish family size, it would seem that low birth rate must be taken into account as well, at least in regard to the Jews.

24. M. Kulichenko, **op. cit.**, p. 446. This was the national average for the USSR as well.

25. V. V. Onikienko and V. A. Popovkin, **Kompleksnoe issledovanie imigratsionnykh protsessov** (Moscow: statistika, 1973), p. 39. In Transcarpathian oblast, where Jews are only one percent of the population, they provided two percent of the urban migrants. (p. 41.

26. **Vestnik statistiki** No. 4, 1974, p. 92.

27. **Ibid.**, p. 95.

28. See "The Declining Share of Scientists who are Jews and Jewish Emigration in Relation to Brain Drain," **ACES Bulletin, XVI,** / (Spring, 1974), **p. 69. See also** L.G. Churchward, **The Soviet Intelligentsia** (London: Routledge and Kegan Paul, 1973), pp. 29-46.

29. William Korey, "Quotas and Soviet Jewry," **Commentary,** v. 57, no. 5 (May, 1974), p. 57.

30. Y. Kapeliush, **op. cit.**, p. 177.

31. **Vysshee obrazovanie v SSSR** (Moscow: Gosstatizdat, 1961), cited in Michael

Checinski, "Soviet Jews and Higher Education," **Soviet Jewish Affairs**, III, 2 (1973), pp. 9, 14.

32   Mordechai Altshuler, "The Jews in the Scientific Elite of the Soviet Union," **The Jewish Journal of Sociology**, XV, 1 (June, 1973).

33.   Yaroslav Bilinsky, **The Second Soviet Republic** (New Brunswick, N.J.: Rutgers University Press, 1964), p. 397.

34.   Based on data in **Statisticheskii ezhegodnik Belorusskoi SSR** (Minsk: Belarus, 1973), p. 158.

35.   For a discussion of this point, see my **Jewish Nationality and Soviet Politics, op. cit.** pp. 105-118.

36.   S. Schwarz, **Jews in the Soviet Union, op. cit.** pp. 15 and 261.

37.   Y. Kantor, "Si idishe bafelkerung in ukraine loit der folkstsailung fun 1926-tn yor," **Si koite velt**, No. 4, 1928, p. 133; and **Prakticheskoe razreshenie natsional'nogo voprosa v Belorusskoi Sotsialistichekoi Sovetskoi Respublike** (part two) (Minsk, 1928), p. 22-24.

38.   S. Schwarz, **Jews in the Soviet Union, op. cit.**, p. 261.

39.   **Shtern**, November 29, 1927.

40.   Data in **Natsional'naia politika VKP (b), op. cit.**, p. 138.

41.   **Ibid.**, pp. 161, 177.

42.   See Hryhory Kostiuk, **Stalinist Rule in the Ukraine** (New York: Praeger, 1960), p. 142.

43.   See Robert Sullivant, **Soviet Politics and the Ukraine, 1917-1957** (New York: Columbia University Press, 1962), p. 125.

44.   T. H. Rigby, **Communist Party Membership in the USSR 1917-1967** (Princeton: Princeton University Press, 1968), p. 373.

45.   See John Armstrong, **The Soviet Bureaucratic Elite** (New York: Praeger, 1959).

46.   T. H. Rigby, **op. cit.**, p. 386.

47.   See M. Kulichenko, **op. cit.**, p. 433 and **Jews in Eastern Europe**, II, 1 (December, 1962), p. 8.

48.   Y. Kapeliush, **op. cit.**, p. 177.

49.   **Ibid.**

50.   **Ibid.**

51.   For details, based on 1959 data, see J. Armstrong in E. Goldhagen, ed., **op. cit.**, p. 33.

52.   M. Kurman and I. Lebedinski, **op. cit.**, 123.

53. See Arnold Rose, **Sociology: The Study of Human Relations** (New York, 1960, pp. 557-558.

54. "Nekotorye problemy etnicheskogo razvitiia narodov SSSR," **Sovetskaia etnografiia**, No. 5, 1967, p. 63.

55. Yu. V. Bromley, "Toward Typology of Ethnic Processes," paper delivered at the Eighth World Congress of Sociology, Toronto, 1974, p. 10.

56. A. A. Isupov, **Natsional'ny sostav naseleniia SSSR** (Moscow, 1964), p. 38.

57. M. Kulichenko, **op. cit.**, pp. 499-550. See also, A. Boiarskii, "Stranitsy bol'shoi biografii," **Izvestiia**, May 9, 1971.

58. V. Naul'ko, **op. cit.**, p. 110.

59. **Natsional'naia politika VKP (b), op. cit.**, p.4.

60. **Statistika Ukrainy No. 8, tom IV, Seriia 1, Vyp. 2; Pryrodnyi rukh naselennia naivazhlyvishykh mist Ukrainy v 1924 r.** (Kharkiv, 1926), pp. 18 and 36.

61. M. Kurman and I. Lebedinskii, **op. cit.**, pp. 126-127.

62. **Ibid.**

63. V.S. Zhuchenko and V.S. Steshenko, eds., **Vliianie Sotsial-no-ekonomichesikh faktorov na demograficheskie protsessy** (Kyiv: Naukova Dumka, 1972), p. 118.

64. See A. I. Kholmogorov, **Internatsional'nye cherty Sovetskikh natsii** (Moscow: Mysl, 1970), p. 84.

65. For a discussion of the concept of national consciousness, see V. I. Kozlov, "Problema etnicheskogo samosoznaniia i ee mesto v teorii etnosa," **Sovetskaia etnografiia**, No. 2, 1974.

66. B'nai Brith International Council, "The Status of Jews in the Soviet Union," August, 1964, pp. 12-13. Based on an unpublished manuscript by Sylvia Gilliam.

67. Izrail Kleiner, "Ukrainsko-Evreiski vzaemyny i Ukrains'ka emigratsia," **Ukrains'kyi samostiinyk**, XXIV, 6 (June, 1973). Kleiner's articles have been translated for me by Ms. Maryann Szporluk, whom I wish to thank.

68. "Anekdotychna tragediia," **Suchasnist'** No. 9 (153), September, 1973.

69. "To the Council of Nationalities of the USSR," **The New Leader**, January 15, 1968, pp. 12-13. Also **The Chornovil Papers** (New York: McGraw-Hill, 1968), pp. 198-201.

70. Reprinted in **The Chornovil Papers**, pp. 223-226.

71. Y. Bilinsky, **op. cit.**, p. 409.

72. M. Kulichenko, **op. cit.**, p. 535.

Comments on Professor Zvi Gitelman The Social and Political Role of the Jews in Ukraine

by
Ivan L. Rudnytsky
The University of Alberta

At the beginning, I want to make it clear that I am a student of history, and not a specialist in Soviet affairs. This will account for my historically oriented treatment of the subject.

It is my conviction that the present time is particularly propitious to an improvement and normalization of Ukrainian-Jewish relations. This is, in the first place, facilitated by social changes undergone by both peoples in recent decades. There occured a massive urbanization of the Ukrainians, and this trend still continues. As for the Jews, their share within the population of the Ukrainian S.S.R. dropped from 6.5 percent in 1926 to 1.6 percent in 1970, and professionally they became probably more diversified than in the past. During the same time, the Jewish minority became "acculturated." I agree with Professor Gitelman that acculturation is not the same as assimilation, and that it does not involve the loss of a sense of national identity. Still, the Jews of Ukraine have shed the traits (in language, dress, customs, etc.) which in the past visibly differentiated them from the rest of the population. I do not wish to suggest that these social changes have automatically obliterated all actual or potential frictions between Ukrainians and Jews. But at least Ukrainian and Jew will no longer meet each other in the traditional, stereotyped roles of the peasant and the small-town trader. Sociologically, Ukrainian-Jewish relations will increasingly become more similar to those which obtain in other European countries between the host nations and the respective Jewish minorities.

The contemporary political constellation urgently calls for a new Ukrainian-Jewish **entente cordiale**. It is obvious that in the U.S.S.R. both Ukrainian and Jewish national survival is jeopardized by the totalitarian Russian Communist regime. This fact is clearly perceived by Ukrainian and Jewish dissidents under Soviet rule. On the international scene, Soviet policies present a threat to the existence of the State of

Israel. Russian encouragement and aid to the Arab governments prevents their coming to terms with Israel. It is difficult to doubt that the creation of an independent Ukraine, or even the achievement of a limited Ukrainian autonomy through genuine federalization of the Soviet Union, would remove much of the pressure under which Israel is laboring at the present. Thus we have the right to assume that Ukrainian struggle for national liberation corresponds with Jewish interests. On the other hand, Jewish support, or even only benevolent neutrality, would be extremely useful to the Ukrainian liberation movement, both in the country itself (where the Jewish minority, despite its reduced numbers, will continue to play a socially and culturally significant role) and internationally.

Therefore, an improvement in Ukrainian-Jewish relations is not only desirable on general humanitarian grounds, but also would be politically beneficial to both peoples. It is not an accident that the current Soviet press carries frequent attacks against the "unholy alliance" between Ukrainian bourgeois nationalists and Jewish Zionists. The alleged alliance, of course, does not exist in fact. But Soviet propagandists are sensitive to what they perceive as a potential danger.

Professor Gitelman stresses correctly that the road toward a normalization of Ukrainian-Jewish relations is barred by certain painful historical memories. I regret that the limited scope of my paper does not allow for a substantive discussion of the controversial questions in the past mutual dealings between Jews and Ukrainians. I would like, however, to comment on one point which emotionally seems particularly sensitive.

Professor Gitelman refers to the Ukrainian Cossack revolution under the leadership of Hetman Bohdan Khmelnytskyi. The Ukrainians look upon the 1648 uprising against Poland as a glorious event in their country's history, while for the Jews this very same event represents a tragic page in their annals. Thus the unforgotten and unforgettable memories of the Khmelnytskyi era exacerbate Ukrainian-Jewish animosities.

At this point I would like to interject a personal reminiscence. One of my favorite characters in world history is Oliver Cromwell. I do not stand alone in my admiration of Cromwell; I understand that Sigmund Freud named one of his sons after him. Some years ago I happened to teach history in a Catholic college in the eastern United States. I discovered that any positive reference to Cromwell was likely to provoke resentment among my students, many of whom were of Irish descent. While respecting my students' feelings, as a teacher of history I felt obliged to point out to them that the Drogheda massacre, appalling as it was, is not the standard by which Cromwell's personality and historical achievement ought to be ultimately judged. Today most thoughful Englishmen deplore Cromwell's and the Puritan's Irish policy. As a matter of fact, England is still paying a price for it. This, however, does not preclude a positive overall evaluation of Cromwell and the Puritan Revolution. I believe that what has been just said of the English Lord Protector may be applied also to his Ukrainian contemporary, the Cossack Hetman. Ukrainians revere Khmelnytskyi as their country's liberator from foreign rule and the founder of the Ukrainian Cossack State. The respect paid to the memory of this great man does not imply in any way an endorsement of the misfortunes which befell the Ukraine's Jewish population in the course of the revolution headed by Khmelnytskyi.

Generally speaking, how are we to deal with the errors and tragedies of the past? Obviously, whatever happened cannot be undone. It can, however, be overcome and sublimated. A great educational responsibility devolves here on historical science. Objective historical research and frank discussion of controversial and painful issues may exercise a cathartic effect on the minds of the respective communities. What, however, needs to be avoided in such historical explorations is the spirit of narrow partisanship. A historian is not a lawyer, and his task does not consist of painting his own side lily-white, while heaping all the blame on the other side. Much remains to be done for historians in the field of Ukrainian-Jewish relations. It is to be expected that such studies would dispel many ingrained prejudices and lead to a better mutual understanding. In this connection one should mention the recent interesting discussion in **Jewish Social Studies** between Professors Taras Hunczak and Zosa Szajkowski concerning the reappraisal of Symon Petliura.[1]

The normalization of Ukrainian-Jewish relations is obstructed not only by the memories of past conflicts, but also by certain unresolved contemporary issues which divide the two peoples. I would like to point out specifically two grievances, one of the Jews against the Ukrainians, and one of the Ukrainians against the Jews. In my opinion, both grievances are legitimate, and they must be honestly faced, before a genuine mutual trust and friendship between Jews and Ukrainians will become possible.

Let me tackle the first problem. The Ukrainian national movement in the nineteenth and early twentieth centuries was democratic-populist in its character, and the same can be said about the independent Ukrainian People's Republic of 1917-21. Since the 1930's, however, the leadership of the Ukrainian movement outside the U.S.S.R. has been assumed by "integral nationalists," who clearly displayed a totalitarian outlook, similar to Western fascism. I am referring to the Organization of Ukrainian Nationalists (O.U.N.), founded in 1929, and its offshoots. The older democratic Ukrainian parties in Halychyna-Volyn' and in the emigration did not disappear, but they were put on the defensive, and during the war years they became largely inactive. The rise of Ukrainian integral nationalism and its causes cannot be discussed at this place.[2] May it be said that I do not believe that everything was bad about Ukrainian integral nationalism. Most O.U.N. members and supporters were youthful enthusiasts, motivated by a consuming desire to serve the liberation of their enslaved country. This enthusiasm and spirit of self-sacrifice were demonstrated during World War II by the courageous struggle of Ukrainian nationalist guerrillas against both Soviet Russia and Nazi Germany. Nevertheless, the acceptance of a totalitarian ideology by the O.U.N. meant a deviation from the noblest traditions of the pre-Revolutionary Ukrainian movement. It implied a lowering of the level of political culture, an intellectual stultification, and a blunting of the moral sense of the Ukrainian community. In particular, it precluded the establishment of friendly, cooperative relations with other nationalities either outside the country, or those living on Ukrainian soil as minorities.

What is the relevance of the preceding remarks for the Ukrainian-Jewish relationship? During the years of the German occupation, which lasted from 1941 to 1944, Ukraine (like other countries under Hitler's control) became an arena of an unprecedented tragedy: the wholesale extermination of the Jewish population. The primary responsibility lay undoubtedly with Nazi Germany. But what was the Ukrainian's reaction to those terrible events? We know that some Ukrainians, particularly those enrolled in police formations, participated in the perpetration of Nazi crimes. We also know of other Ukrainians who endangered their lives by helping and hiding their Jewish neighbors. In either case, however, these were instances of individual action which did not add up to a collective, political stance. Who could take such a stance? Ukraine, in contrast to other countries under German occupation, did not possess a government-in-exile in the Allied camp, entitled to speak in the name of the nation. Obviously, German atrocities could not be protested by "legal" Ukrainian institutions, precariously tolerated by the occupation authorities and engaged in relief and cultural work under most difficult conditions. But there existed at that time a Ukrainian nationalist underground, endowed with a well-developed organizational network, a clandestine press, and military detachments. Even a rudimentary underground government was formed in 1944, named Ukrainian Supreme Liberation Council (**Ukrainska Holovna Vyzvol'na Rada**, U.H.V.R.). All these revolutionary activities were controlled by the O.U.N. factions. The underground frequently issued various appeals and proclamations to the population. The nationalist underground was, therefore, quite in a position to condemn Nazi atrocities against the Jews and to enjoin the Ukrainian people against any participation in those crimes. It is impossible to tell how many Jewish lives would have been actually saved, but the moral and political significance which such an act would have had is self-evident. It is a fact, however, that the Ukrainian nationalist underground never raised its voice against the slaughter of the Jews. There are situations when silence is morally indefensible, when it amounts to a complicity. The silence of the O.U.N. and the U.H.V.R. about the horrors perpetrated by the Nazis against the Jewish citizens of Ukraine was not fortuitous. It reflected a moral callousness and essential inhumanity which Ukrainian integral nationalism shares with all other totalitarian movements and systems.

I conclude that the Jews are quite justified in mistrusting the Ukrainians as long as the latter have not succeeded in purging their own ranks of totalitarian elements. Improvement is to be expected from the circumstance that national dissent in the Ukrainian S.S.R., which has become vocal in the course of the last decade, displays a distinct libertarian and humanist outlook. The political life of the Ukrainian dispersion, on the other hand, is still largely dominated by epigones of the integral nationalist movement of the 1930s and the 1940s. Recent symptoms of change in Ukrainian emigre politics are due to the stimulating impact of the ideas of the home-country dissidents and to the rise of a new generation, fully trained in Western schools. Should this encouraging trend assert itself more strongly, the time will at last become ripe for a serious Ukrainian-Jewish dialogue.

Now let us move on to a consideration of the principal grievance held by Ukrainians against the Jews. The grievance consists in the fact that Ukrainian Jews., in becoming acculturated, have in overwhelming majority adopted Russian language and culture, thus contributing to the Russification of Ukrainian cities. Professor Gitelman touches upon this problem, but it calls for some additional comments.

In the first place, it is to be noticed that the problem is not a new one. It originated in pre-Revolutionary times, when the Jews of Ukraine began to emerge from their traditional isolation, determined by a strict adherence to religious orthodoxy and ritualistic observances. Here is an excerpt from the diary of Yevhen Chykalenko, a prominent civic leader and the publisher of **Rada**, the first Ukrainian-language daily in Kiev. The entry was made in 1909, during a trip to the countryside:

> Simple, uneducated Jews talk with me, as with everybody else, in good Ukrainian vernacular, and they call themselves "jews" (**zhydy**). The more or less "enlightened" ones obstinately speak Russian, and call themselves "Hebrews" (**yevrei**). They realize that I am a Ukrainian nationalist, but they consider this a fancy, an odd quirk, on my part. I tell them frequently: "I wonder why the (tsarist) government oppresses you and discriminates against you, as you are its agents in Russification. The government alone, without the Jews, would not be capable of Russifying Ukrainian cities and towns as thoroughly as you are doing it." They listen to this complacently, as to a tribute paid to their role as carriers of a superior culture (**kulturtregerstvo**).[3]

It would not be difficult to provide a sociological explanation of this phenomenon. After all, urban ethnic Ukrainians also have been susceptible to Russification, and it would be unreasonable to expect a greater degree of resistance from the Jews. Illuminating parallels can be adduced from other geographical areas. Under Habsburg rule, the Jews of Bohemia and Moravia sided linguistically and culturally with the Germans rather than with the Czechs. A native of Prague, Franz Kafka, was a German, and not a Czech, writer. This did not prevent the Bohemian Jews from later becoming loyal citizens of the democratic Czechoslovak Republic.

The situation obviously calls for patience and forbearance on the Ukrainian's part. This does not mean that Ukrainians will acquiesce in the present situation and accept it as "normal" in the long run. It is morally indefensible, and perhaps politically unwise, for a minority to disregard the vital interests and legitimate claims of the host nation, and to turn themselves into accomplices of the oppressive imperial overlord. For the present, it would suffice if Jewish public opinion were to become cognizant of this Ukrainian grievance and accept its validity. This might serve as a first step toward a future solution of the problem.

The problem is not limited to the territory of Ukraine, and it possesses an international dimension. I refer to the fact that in Western lands, particularly in North

America, Jews have been conspicuously instrumental in spreading pro-Russian sympathies. One can state with assurance that in the United States Jewish scholars, writers, and journalists, in their capacity of voluntary propagandists, have rendered greater services to the Russian cause than have genuine Russians.

The preceding assertion requires some qualifications and explanations. Russia is, and will remain, one of the great nations of the world, in possession of a rich literature, music, etc. Thus a sympathetic interest in Russian culture is understandable and legitimate. It is something else that I have in mind. We encounter a prevalent infatuation with all things Russian, combined with a systematic neglect of the contributions of other Slavic nations, including the Ukrainians. There exists in the Western world a deeply-ingrained "Russocentric" bias in the treatment of the controversial East European historical and political issues. Jewish intellectuals have played a prominent role in the perpetuation of this bias. Some people will perhaps question the accuracy of this charge. It is impossible to provide a detailed documentation within the narrow limits of these remarks. I propose, however, the following simple test. I am not aware of the existence of any single scholar of Jewish background in the United States and Canada (with the exception of one doctoral student at Harvard) who would specialize in the study of Ukrainian history, literature, linguistics, etc., while at least hundreds (many of whom derive from Ukraine) are working on Russian topics. This state of affairs cannot be considered normal, and it is profoundly aggravating to Ukrainians.

A silver lining has appeared on the North American academic horizon in recent times. Many a Ukrainian professor and graduate student could testify from personal experience that anti-Ukrainian prejudice, which was much in evidence in the past, has noticeably decreased in the last few years. This is in part a result of the exertions of Ukrainian scholars, but even to a greater degree of a change of climate in the American academic environment, certainly not unconnected with the Kremlin's anti-Jewish policies. The present Soviet leaders have already succeeded in curing the traditionally most Russophile European nation, namely the Czechs, from its blind infatuation with the Slavic "big brother." It is to be hoped that if Mr. Brezhnev and his colleagues persevere in their good works, the Jewish intellectual community in North America will gradually become more sensitive of and more sympathetic toward Ukrainian concerns and aspirations.

I have already given distinct expression to my conviction that in a discussion of the Ukrainian-Jewish relationship we must not skirt painful and controversial points. But it would also be an error if we were to overlook the positive and encouraging aspects of the record. My chief criticism of Professor Gitelman's paper is that he pays insufficient attention to extant constructive achievements in the relations between Ukrainians and Jews. We may regret that these achievements have not been weightier, but this does not excuse their neglect.

Several decades before the Revolution Ukrainian democratic political thought had already found an approach toward the solution of the problem of Ukrainian-Jewish relations. I am referring to the writings of Mykhailo Drahomanov (1841-1895) who gave much attention to this subject.[4] Drahomanov's originality consisted in his insistence that the Jews of Ukraine should receive not only equal civil rights (denied to them by tsarist Russia) but also an autonomous corporate national organization in educational and cultural matters. This organization should be guaranteed by the country's constitution and enjoy public financial support. Drahomanov's program ran counter to the thinking of nineteenth-century European liberals whose common assumption was that the granting of civic equality would lead to an assimilation of the Jewish minorities by the respective host nations. In contrast, Drahomanov definitely rejected the idea of any forced "Ukrainization" of the Jews and other ethnic minorities. Thus he may be considered a precursor of the concept which in our times is known in Canada under the name of "multiculturalism."

The Drahomanovian idea did not remain a paper plan. During the short era of Ukrainian independence, the government of the Ukrainian People's Republic honestly strove to implement the concept of cultural self-government for ethnic minorities. This is evidenced by the Law on National-Personal Autonomy of January 22, 1918, and the formation of a Ministry on Jewish Affairs.5 Professor Gitelman mentions the anti-Jewish pogroms in Ukraine in 1919. The pogroms were the result of a breakdown of law-and-order, under conditions of civil war, foreign invasion and prevailing general anarchy. In those sections of the country where the Ukrainian administration was more successful in upholding public order — I am thinking of the Western Region of the Ukrainian People's Republic, the former Eastern Halychyna — not a single pogrom occurred. One can state with assurance that no Ukrainian government of the 1917-21 revolutionary era pursued an anti-Jewish policy or was guilty of inciting pogroms. This applies not only to the leftist Ukrainian People's Republic, headed at different times by Mykhailo Hrushevskyi, Volodymyr Vynnychenko, and Symon Petliura, but also to the conservative regime of Hetman Pavlo Skoropadsky. The essential Ukrainian policy toward the Jewish minority was reflected in the Law on National-Personal Autonomy. Ukrainians can take pride in this achievement. The principles underlying the 1918 Law on National-Personal Autonomy have not lost their validity. With proper adjustments, necessitated by changed circumstances, they can serve as a guidepost for the future. Let me finally express the following criticism of Professor Gitelman. He cites approvingly the well-known Babyn Yar speech of the contemporary Soviet Ukrainian dissident, Ivan Dzyuba. However, he fails to notice how much Dzyuba's ideas on Ukrainian-Jewish relations are in line with the tradition of Ukrainian democratic political thought, going back to Drahomanov and the post-1917 Ukrainian state.

The question arises whether the Jews on their part can display some positive achievements in their dealings with Ukrainians. The answer is affirmative. During the Revolution there appeared a few leaders who, combining Jewish national consciousness with patriotism for their native country, gave active support to the Ukrainian struggle for independence. They did not let themselves be deterred by difficulties and disappointments. Their choice was not easy and comfortable, but it indicated vision and moral courage. The representative figures of Arnold Margolin and Solomon Goldelman come to mind in this connection.6 I do not know whether their names mean much to the Jewish community today. But they are kept in grateful remembrance by Ukrainians, and it is to be hoped that their lifework will still bear fruit in the future.

In conclusion, I would like to quote from a recently-published memoir. The passage deals with a crucial debate in the Central Rada, the Ukraine's revolutionary parliament, concerning the response to the Instruction of August 17 (N.S.), 1917, issued by the Russian Provisional Government; the purpose of the Instruction was to curtail the scope of Ukrainian autonomy.

The orators for the (national) minorities advocated an unconditional acceptance of the Instruction. Their chief spokesman was the editor of the largest (local) newspaper, **Kievskaia Mysl**, (the Menshevik M.) Balabanov, a noted journalist and revolutionary. He made a well-documented speech, and sat down contemptuously glaring at the Ukrainians. But now stood up Solomon Goldelman, a member of the Socialist-Zionist Party, and said to everybody's surprise: "Comrade Balabanov's speech does not concern us, because here we are on Ukrainian soil, and we are members of the Ukrainian parliament. Therefore, Petrograd's ways are not our own." This statement created the impression of a bomb, and the Instruction was amended.7

The normalization of Ukrainian-Jewish relations will depend, among other things, also on whether the Ukrainian Jewry will produce in the future fewer Balabanovs and more Goldelmans.

FOOTNOTES

1. Taras Hunczak, "A Reappraisal of Symon Petliura and Ukrainian-Jewish Relations, 1917-1921, "**Jewish Social Studies**, Vol. XXXI, No. 3 (July 1969), pp. 163-183; Zosa Szajkowski, "'A Reappraisal of Symon Petliura and Ukrainian-Jewish Relations, 1917-1921': A Rebuttal," **Ibid.**, pp. 184-213.

2. See my article, "Nationalism," **Entsyklopediia Ukrainoznavstva: Slovnykova chastyna**, ed. by V. Kubijovyc, V (Paris and New York, 1955), pp. 1723-1728; reprinted in Ivan Lysiak-Rudnytsky, **Mizh istorieiu i politykoiu** (Munich, 1973), pp. 233-249.

3. Yevhen Chykalenko, **Shchodennyk** (1907-1917), (Lviv, 1931) pp. 59-60.

4. Ivan L. Rudnytsky, "Mykhailo Drahomanov and the Problem of Ukrainian-Jewish Relations," **Canadian Slavonic Papers**, Vol. XI, No. 2 (Summer 1969), pp. 182-198.

5. See Solomon I Goldelman, **Jewish National Autonomy in Ukraine**, 1917-1920 (Chicago, 1968).

6. The motives and ideas of these men are documented in their writings. See Arnold Margolin, **Ukraina i politika Antanty: Zapiski yevreia i grazhdanina** (Berlin, 1921); also his, **From a Political Diary: Russia, the Ukraine, and America**, 1905-1945 (New York, 1946); Solomon Goldelman, **Lysty zhydivskoho sotsial-demokrata pro Ukrainu: Materialy do istorii ukrainsko-zhydivskykh vidnosyn za revoliutsii** (Vienna, 1921).

7. Mykailo Yeremiiv, "Polkovnyk Yevhen Konovalets na tli ukrainskoi vyzvolnoi borotby," **Yevhen Konovalets ta yoho doba**, ed., Yu. Boiko (Munich, 1974), p. 151.

Russians in Ukraine and Problems of Ukrainian Identity in the USSR

by
Roman Szporluk
University of Michigan

It is only in the most literal, arithmetical sense that Russians in Ukraine are a national minority. Over three million strong in 1926, over seven in 1959, more than nine million in 1970, they are not an ordinary minority. Perhaps they could be considered so if Ukraine were independent, but it is not, and the main areas of the Russian's concentration — the Donbas, Kharkiv — are contiguous to the boundaries of the RSFSR.

It is hardly useful to present here the usual statistics, which would inform about the status and role of the real minority nationalities. Although full data are lacking, we know that Russians have more than their share of the republic's total population in the Party, in the party elite, among the academic, managerial, and other leading groups. (We may presume that they are vastly "overrepresented" in the police). They are concentrated in the cities, where they constitute over 30 percent of population, unlike the Ukrainians whose share in urban population — over 60 percent — is far below their share in the total population (ca. 75 percent).

It is even less necessary to dwell upon the obvious facts of Soviet political life: it is no longer worth arguing that the Russian nation is the leading Soviet nationality, and that the Russians, helped by Russified "nationals", run the Soviet Union. Little pieces of information, such as that all secretaries of the Central Committee of the CPSU are ethnic Russians, are well-known and need not be recalled here.

While these considerations are applicable to other Soviet peoples, there is an issue specific to the Russo-Ukrainian relationship, which is not present in the relations of Russians with Georgians, or Latvians, or Uzbeks: Russians and Ukrainians have a long history of shared experiences, from the period of Kyivan Rus', and throughout the past three centuries. This sharing of experience was so close at times that it gave rise to a view that Russians and Ukrainians either had been, or continue to be to the present day, members of a common, single nation. Only Belorussians, perhaps more so than the Ukrainians, have had this problem about their national identity.

It is fair to argue that it is only in the twentieth century that the differentiation of the two nations, realized and accepted by the wide masses of people and not only by the intelligentsia, has been accomplished.

Rather than being a minority, an external, as it were, body or element within the distinct social and cultural organism of the Ukrainian nation, the Russians of Ukraine, or a significant part of them, have been there for centuries and most of them have felt they had not left their own homeland by living there.

For these reasons — there may be others, no less valid than these — we propose to discuss the Russians in Ukraine under a broad, comprehensive angle, and use their situation and position in Ukraine for answering certain questions concerning the national identity of the Ukrainians, in the Ukrainian SSR and the Soviet Union at large. There should be no objection to doing the latter: it hardly seems possible to consider Russians in Ukraine while forgetting that these Russians in Ukraine, who are a minority in the land primarily inhabited by Ukrainians, are a part of the larger polity which is called the USSR, but to many has been and remains best described as Russia. It might be sensible to bear in mind that our topic could be more broadly titled "Ukrainians in the USSR," or "Ukrainians in Russia." For this reason this paper has a double title: Russians in Ukraine **and** Problems of Ukrainian Identity in the Soviet Union.

It is common knowledge that Ukrainians are seen in the other non-Russian republics as Russians, and even those who know that in principle Ukrainians are a different nationality quite rightly perceive them as those whose function in the national republics is identical to that of the Russians. A recent document of the Estonian **samizdat**, complaining of massive Russian immigration to that country, counts Ukrainians and Belorussians among Russians.[1] It is right to do so insofar as the function of these two East Slavic peoples in the Baltic areas is concerned.

Professor Pokshishevskii, a specialist in nationality problems and urbanizaiton, has usefully classified various ethnic groups from the point of view of their role outside of their proper ethnic area in relation to the Russians and has concluded that in Central Asia and the Caucasus the Ukrainians have traditionally functioned as the Russians' "fellow-travellers" or "Satellites" (**sputniki russkikh**), and were considered Russian by indigenous population.[2]

The concept of **sputniki russkikh** corresponds to the concept which Professor J.A. Armstrong has introduced, that is the view that Ukrainians function as the Russians' "younger brothers." As described by Armstrong, Ukrainians are "younger brothers" of Russians because they are still relatively low in social mobilization, and also close to Russians in major cultural respects. Armstrong expected Ukrainians to become the object of particularly intensive assimilationist efforts by the Soviet regime. The success of the regime, Armstrong thought, would depend on its improving the position of "submerged social strata, particularly the peasantry."[3] Armstrong evidently took the view that the peasantry is the principal group maintaining a separate Ukrainian identity and that improvement of its economic and social position would facilitate its assimilation to Russian nationality.

It is a thesis of this paper that the role of Ukrainians as the Russians' helpers in russifying Estonia, Latvia or Uzbekistan is related to the respective position of Russians and Ukrainians inside Ukraine, to wit, the identification of the city with Russia and the countryside with Ukraine. When Ukrainians move upward, by becoming technicians, scientists, etc., they become **ipso facto** Russified and mobile in the entire USSR. Once they leave Ukraine, regardless of their subjective attitudes, they function as Russians. The party seems to understand that the goal of maintaining Ukrainian culture and the Ukrainian nation in its rural style requires that those Ukrainians who do not fit this description be moved outside Ukraine. How is one to interpret the fact that almost sixty years after the establishment of Soviet power, Ukrainians form just barely more than fifty percent among the scientific cadre in

Ukraine, while more than one third of the scientists of Ukrainian nationality in the USSR work in the other republics? How are these considerations related to the question of Ukrainian identity in the USSR?

It is our thesis that the status of the Russians, and of Russian culture, in Ukraine, has its counterpart in the status of Ukrainians outside Ukraine. While in Ukraine Russian language and Russians are in a superior position, and Russians themselves are expected to, and do, use only the Russian language as the means of communication. Ukrainians outside Ukraine are totally deprived of any nationality rights. Since moreover, the world of modern culture in Ukraine — science, technology, etc. — is the world of the Russian language, the Ukrainian functioning in this world is denationalized; Ukrainian culture is defined only as the culture of literature and the humanities.

A comparison between the Russian and Ukrainian literary newspapers, **Literaturnaia Gazeta** and **Literaturna Ukraina** will drastically point to the difference. The Ukrainian paper writes only about books and problems relating to the belles lettres, poetry, and **publitsystyka**, and does so on an elementary level. Occasionally other topics of professional interest to librarians and elementary, possible high school, teachers are dealt with. The Russian paper writes for the entire intelligentsia, not only the humanistic cadre. Psychology, philosophy, questions of family, urban life, scientific revolution, demography, organization of science, are regularly covered. The paper clearly addresses itself to the intelligent, educated urban reader. International affairs (political perhaps more than literary) receive broad coverage. It is a safe bet that **Literaturnaia Gazeta** has several times more readers in Ukraine than does **Literaturna Ukraina**.

I would like to deal with the Russians in Ukraine both in a broad historical perspective — the emergence of the modern Ukraine as a political, national, and geographic concept and reality — and from a special angle — the role of the Russians as a modernizing force in relation to the Ukrainian population. Accordingly, our discussion will develop the following questions. First, what is Ukraine, what are the origins of what we know today as the Ukrainian Soviet Socialist Republic? Secondly, to what extent is it possible to view the Russians in Ukraine as a modernizing force, broadly conceived, and accordingly, the Ukrainians as the object of those modernizing activities rather than a force in its own right that contains its own modernizing elements. Should one continue to identify the Ukrainians with the countryside and the village way of life and outlook, and the Russians as the representatives of modern, urban culture? Or perhaps there exists evidence suggesting that this simple dichotomy is no longer descriptive of the Russo-Ukrainian relationip in Ukraine?

What is Ukraine, then?

The Soviet Ukrainian republic as we know it today has been in existence for about thirty years. It was only in 1944-45 that its present western **oblasti** were definitely incorporated in the USSR (L'viv, Ternopil', Ivano-Frankivs'k, Volyn', Rivne, Chernivtsi, Transcarpathia). The Crimea was added about ten years later, in 1954. The Ukrainian SSR in its earlier shape, i.e., before 1939, was about twenty years old when its western expansion began. Its pre-1939 boundary was basically established only after the Soviet-Polish war of 1920 (except that in 1923 it lost the Tahanrih and Shakhty regions to the RSFSR).

Ukraine as it existed before the establishment of Soviet power and after the March 1917 revolution did not have firm boundaries for any significant length of time. The area under Hetman Skoropadsky was perhaps the most stable: it survived under German occupation from the Spring of 1918 to December 1918. After the fall of the Hetman, throughout 1919, Ukraine was under a variety of competing forces: Ukrainian, Communist, White Russian, local partisan forces such as Makhno and Hryhoriiv, and the Allied forces in the Black Sea region.

The predecessor of the Hetmanate had been the Ukrainian People's Republic, at first autonomous, but after the fall of the Provisional Government in Petrograd, **de facto** independent, formally proclaiming its independence in January 1918. However, the area under effective control of the Kyiv government was not clear: the authority of the Central Rada did not extend to the south eastern and southern parts of the present Ukrainian SSR, that is to the Donbas, and such cities as Odesa, Kherson, Dnipropetrovs'k, Kryvyi Rih or Zaporizhia. Before that, the autonomous Ukraine, as recognized by the Provisional Government in the summer of 1917, consisted of the following five gubernii: Kyiv, Volyn', Podillia, Poltava and Chernihiv (excluding the last one's northern counties). Such centers as Kharkiv, Odesa, and Dnipropetrovs'k were thus left out.[4] It was not obvious even to the nationally-conscious Ukrainians, let alone others, what exactly should be considered as Ukrainian territory. In principle the answer was simple and easy: the Ukrainian "ethnographic" territory at that time was understood to mean the territory where the peasant population was predominantly Ukrainian. But where should the cities — obviously not Ukrainian "ethnographically" — be assigned? Was Odesa a part of Ukraine, the Odesa where the Ukrainians represented something like one tenth of inhabitants? Small wonder that not only many of its inhabitants but also some Ukrainians felt that "Odesa is not Ukraine."

One of the indications that what we have now come to know and accept as Ukraine was not a single unit, whether administratively, politically, or economically, or ideally, in the perceptions of the population, is the fact that no single city enjoyed a clear position of superiority in the area. Kyiv was, of course, the most famous, historically the "prime city", but neither Odesa (which was a larger city in population until after 1917) nor Kharkiv nor the cities of the Donbas-Kryvyi Rih area were accustomed to consider Kyiv as their capital in any meaningful way. The story of the split in the Bolshevik camp between the Kyivans and Katerynoslavians, the attempt to establish a separate Soviet republic of Donets'-Kryvyi Rih, and an "Odesa Soviet republic", by means of secession for the Soviet Ukrainian republic are well-known. For the purposes of this discussion these cases are directly relevant: when we are speaking about Russians in Ukraine, we have to be sure we know what kind of Ukraine we are thinking of.

What about earlier times, preceding the confused events of 1917-1945? The area of an autonomous Ukraine in the 17th-18th centuries, the Hetmanshchyna and the region of the Zaporizhia Cossacks, roughly corresponded to the present administrative oblasti of Dnipropetrovs'k, Zaporizhia, Poltava, Chernihiv and (partially) Kyiv. To the west of this area, until 1793-1795, was Poland. To the east, were the lands under the direct rule of the tsar, which were being (or had been) colonized by Ukrainians alone or jointly with Russians. These areas included what we know now as the oblasti of Kharkiv and Sumy. Such was then territorial status quo of the 18th century. In the 17th century, before the partition of Ukraine in 1667 (Andrusovo), the independent Ukraine established de facto in 1648 extended to the west of the Dnipro and included also what we call today the oblasti of Cherkasy, Vynnytsia, Zhytomyr, and Kyiv. It did not include the west Ukrainian areas.[5]

It becomes evident that none of these old territorial-political structures (and, we should add, any of their predecessors) extended to the coast of the Black or the Azov seas, and none included what we call now the Donbas. It is worth remembering that Ukrainians began to settle in those areas only in late 18th and in the 19th-20th centuries, when many others, including Russians, Greeks, Serbs, Jews, and Germans were moving in there as well, and when the political or administrative status of those areas was different from that of Ukraine in the stricter sense. Until the end of the tsarist state Ukraine was divided into a number of gubernii belonging to three governorships-general: Kyiv, Odesa, and Kharkiv, directly under St. Petersburg administration.

Although it is true that by and large Ukrainians proved to be the most numerous of all those peoples in the newly settled area, interestingly enough they settled in the country, not in towns, and worked primarily in agriculture. Ukrainians did not show equal readiness or desire to enter the cities of this area or indeed the cities of other area of Ukraine. The Ukrainian peasant appears to have preferred to move to those places where he could get enough land to engage in farming.

In a study of migrations in Ukraine in the light of the 1926 and 1897 censuses, A.

Hirshfeld pointed out that while emigrants from Ukraine to other parts of the Soviet Union (Russian Empire) had been overwhelmingly employed in agriculture, and continued to work in agriculture in their new place (although they included also a white collar element), migrants to Ukraine from the provinces of Russia in a similarly overwhelming proportion were employed in Ukraine as industrial workers. He cited the figures relating to the place of origin of migrants to the Donbas in order to demonstrate that a vast majority of those born outside the region were born outside Ukraine (151,131), while those born in Ukraine other than the Donbas itself numbered much less (49,098).6 Why did migrants from the predominantly agrarian and ethnically Ukrainian areas of the Right Bank Ukraine settle beyond the Urals, in Kazakhstan, etc., rather than move to South-east Ukraine?

It appears we are dealing here with historic inertia of peasant population of the Right Bank and Polissia which has no desire to change its profession and prefers in its move to the East to go beyond the Urals in search of free land.7

These patters of migration, discernible through an analysis of the 1926 census had been in force also before the revolution, as demonstrated by the census of 1897. Hirshfeld hoped that Ukrainian migration from Ukraine would cease in the future (his book was published in 1930), and that Ukrainian agricultural suplus labor would seek employment in industry in Ukraine instead.8 In the meantime, the rapidly growing cities, and urban jobs being created there, to which Ukrainians were not moving, were attracting migrants from the north, ethnic Russians.

Owing to these diverse migratory patterns (in addition to such obvious and self-explanatory circumstances as the fact that Ukraine was a part of Russia and that Ukrainians were considered the "Little-Russian" branch of the Russian nation) the towns, located mainly in the East, and the country in Ukraine differed ethnically and linguistically, up to the time of the revolutionary events of 1917-1921. The prevalence of Russians and corresponding weakness of Ukrainians in the cities in those years was a decisive factor, according to some scholars, in bringing about the failure of Ukrainian struggle for independence.9

It seemed that the Ukrainization policies inaugurated in the 1920's would result in the linguistic integration of the urban East and the rural West of the Ukrainian SSR. These policies were abandoned in the thirties, however, and as Robert S. Sullivant has observed, "the old division of the Ukraine into an urban area which was distinctly Russian and a rural area which was distinctly Ukrainian remained basically unchanged." According to Sullivant, the "striking dichotomy" established in pre-revolutionary years of the urban-Russian East versus rural-Ukrainian West, was not affected by Soviet rule. "Stalin and his successors alike argued that, whatever the language program for the cities, the Ukrainian character of the countryside was to be maintained.10

We do not have to agree with Sullivant that once Ukrainization of the cities was rejected as a policy, Russification proceeded naturally as a product of sociological pressures and a consequence of the advantage enjoyed by the Russian language.11 We might respond by suggesting that the role of force, including terror and deportations, was no less instrumental in producing Russification. Sullivant's statement that the "extent of Russification was more a measure of the Ukraine's urbanization trend and of the growing mobility of the USSR's population than of influence exerted by official Russifying policies" seems to ignore the extraordinary intensity of terror and other administrative measures used under Stalin in order to undo the achievements of the Ukrainian element in Ukraine's cities. However we may distribute the responsibility for what had happened, Sullivant appears to be right in stating that the old dichotomy had survived Stalin and was in evidence during the immediate post-1953 years. The question may be raised whether this generalization is equally valid today.

It is customary to review ethnic conditions in Ukraine by treating that republic as a homogeneous unit, and then to compare the ratio of Russians to the republican nationality in Ukraine to that in Lithuania, Latvia or other Soviet republics. Even on purely statistical grounds this method appears to be questionable. More importantly, we believe, it is faulty for historical reasons, in view of the fact that until 1945, indeed 1954, the present day Ukraine had never in the past formed a single political or administrative unit. But let us begin with some general all-Ukraine comparisons with other European Soviet republics.

Among the European republics of the USSR, Ukraine (19.4 percent) ranks behind Latvia (29.8 percent) and Estonia (24.7) in the percentage of Russians in the total population. In Moldavia (11.6 percent), Belorussia (10.4 percent) and Lithuania (8.6 percent) the percentage of Russians is lower. Russians were increasing in Ukraine, between the censuses of 1959 and 1970, at a rate lower than that in Belorussia, Moldavia, Estonia. The intercensal percentage increase of the Russians in Ukraine and these three republics was 28.7 percent, 42.1 percent, 41.3 percent, and 36.9 percent respectively. In Latvia they gained 26.8 percent and in Lithuania 16.0 percent. The Russians increased at a rate higher than that of their respective titular nations in all republics except Lithuania, where Lithuanians grew by 16.6 percent compered to the Russians' 16.0 percent. In Estonia the Russian rate exceeded the native by a full eleven times, in Latvia by close to eight, in Belorussia by 3.6, in Ukraine by close to three times, and in Moldavia by close to two (Moldavians increasing by 22.1 percent against the Russians' 41.3 percent).[12] As we said, these comparisons suffer from a major limitation in that Ukraine in terms of its population is in a different class: its population more than twice exceeds the combined total of the rest. Even were one to divide Ukraine into the three major economic regions, the South (6.4 million) would be in terms of its population size larger than all the other European republics except Belorussia; the other two regions are over 20 million each, thus exceeding the population of Belorussia more than twice. For this reason, and also considering the historical differences in the pattern of Russian settlement in Ukraine, we have subdivided the entire territory of the Ukrainian SSR into six units (see Table I: Ethnic Composition of Major Regions). They have been ranked in decreasing order of Russian share in the population. The Donbas is clearly the most Russian part of Ukraine, followed by the South, Dnipro, North-East (Kharkiv), Central West (Kyiv) and West (L'viv). In Donbas Russians constitute 41.03 percent, and in West 5.09 percent in the total population. The Donbas and the South surpass Latvia and Estonia in the share of Russian population. The North-East and Dnipro are below these two republics, while the Central West and the West have less Russians than any European republic of the USSR.

The growth rates of the Russian element in the respective regions of Ukraine also display wide diversity, ranging from 40 percent in Dnipropetrovs'k and just under 40 percent in the South to the low of 10.6 percent in the West. While the higher figures resemble the rates of Russian growth in Belorussia, Moldavia, and Estonia, the low figure in the West is lower than the Lithuanian figure of 16 percent.

Considering that most of these regions are large, in size comparable to the Union republics, we propose to analyze some of demographic data in such a regional breakdown, concentrating our attention especially on demographic and ethnic trends in the **urban** sector of the population. The concentration on urban population is warranted by various reasons, not only the fact that the USSR is undergoing a process of urbanization which is likely to continue, but also in view of the peculiar nature of Russo-Ukrainian relationship. We have in mind, of course, the coincidence of the dichotomy urban-rural with that of Russian-Ukrainian, both historically and in the present time.

What is happening in the cities of Donbas, then, from the ethnic point of view?[13]

While the share of Ukrainians in Donets'k oblast's total population declined from 55.56 percent to 53.08 percent during eleven intercensal years, the percentage of the population that considered Ukrainian as its native language dropped from 44.42 to 37.89 percent. In the cities the decline has been even more marked: native speakers of Ukrainian declined from 39.39 percent in 1959 to 30.55 percent in 1970. The speakers of Russian as their native language, including Ukrainians, Greeks, etc., increased from 58.67 percent to 65.38 percent. Not only percentage-wise but also in absolute figures, the number of persons declaring Ukrainian their native language declined in

Donets'k, both in town and in county, while the numbers of Russian-speakers rose in both categories. In the cities Ukrainian speakers declined by 1.86 percent, Russian speakers increased by 30.31 percent. In the Ukrainian ethnic group alone, the total increase was 12.32 percent (compared with Russian of 23.77 percent), of which those speaking Ukrainian declined by 1.89 percent, those Ukrainians declaring Russian rose by 54.81 percent. The importance and significance of these figures is harldy challenged by the data, available for 1970 only, on knowledge of Ukrainian as a second language. According to the census, 488,049, that is 26.11 percent of the Russians (1,869,071) know Ukrainian; also 347,696 Ukrainians or 47.10 percent of the total of 738,182 Ukrainians speaking Russian as their first language know Ukrainian. While in 1959, Russian was the native language to 25.06 percent of urban Ukrainians in Donets'k oblast, by 1970 the figure was 34.54 percent, an increase of almost ten percentage points. (To be precise, there was an annual transfer from Ukrainian to Russian among Donets'k Ukrainians equalling 0.86 percent. At this rate, by the year 2056 all urban Ukrainians in Donets'k oblast will consider Russian their first language.) Those who either consider Ukrainian their first language or declare knowledge of it as a second language constitute 56.74 percent of the total population, and 53.55 percent of urban. Conversely, Russian is a language native to, or known by, 83.64 percent of Donets'k oblast, and 87.77 percent of Donets'k oblast's urban population. There exists, thus, a considerable reciprocally bilingual population, and an absolute majority of Ukrainians who speak Ukrainian also know Russian. Only in the villages a majority of Ukrainians could not speak Russian. (The rural population of the oblast, 613,383, was only 12.60 percent of the total oblast population.) In the cities, besides those 738,182 Ukrainians whose native language was Russian in 1970, an additional 891,879 declared familiarity with it. This leaves only 506,772, that is 23.71 percent of all urban Ukrainians, not speaking Russian. The case of Donets'k (and Donbas at large) seems to indicate that an increasing number of people speak Russian there. The share of those who consider themselves Russian is also on the rise. years? To make any analyses along those lines one would have to compare those data with the data relating the other principal urban centers of Ukraine and also to consider historic, political, and cultural factors which may have influenced the linguistic situation in these various centers.

Before moving on to a review of ethnic composition of other regions, let us briefly pause to note two Soviet sources relating to the Russian element in Eastern Ukraine and its interaction with Ukrainians.

Speaking about the pre-Soviet period, Kurman and Lebedinskii, two recent Soviet authors of a book on Kharkiv, admitted that the immigration of Russians to Ukraine was not only a demographic or social process but also one directly involving the use of force and application of discriminatory practices. As they wrote, Ukrainians were forced to make room for Russians in Kharkiv. The tsarist government pursued a deliberate policy of increasing the ratio of Russians in the population of Kharkiv, according to these writers, and had been sending various administrators to the city ever since pre-Peter times. This process continued after the abolition of serfdom, when railroad construction and industrialization were accompanied by immigration of Russian officials and workers. Another relevant aspect was the Russification policy, including the prohibiion of Ukrainian-language schools. It was this factor, Kurman and Lebedinskii suggest, which must be considered in explaining why, in the 1897 census, only 25 percent of Kharkiv's population declared Ukrainian as their native language — even though over two thirds of the city's inhabitants had been born in Ukraine.[14]

According to Kurman and Lebedinskii, the "flowering of national culture" in the USSR after the revolution, and the rise in national consciousness of Soviet citizens, lies behind the increase of self-declared Ukrainians in Kharkiv: in 1926, over 38 percent, and in 1939, 48.6 percent of the Kharkivite residents were Ukrainian by nationality. By 1959, however, the share of Ukrainians in the city had decreased slightly (to 48.4 percent), while that of Russians rose from 32.9 percent in 1939 to 40.4 percent in 1959. Considering that virtually all Russians declared Russian to be their

TABLE I

ETHNIC COMPOSITION OF MAJOR REGIONS OF UKRAINE

	TOTAL POPULATION			UKRAINIANS					RUSSIANS				
	(1959)	(1970)	Percentage change	(1959)	Percent	(1970)	Percent	Percentage change	(1959)	Percent	(1970)	Percent	Percentage change
Ukraine	41,869,046	47,126,517	12.56	32,159,493	76.81	35,283,857	74.87	9.72	7,090,813	16.94	9,126,331	19.37	28.71
Donbas	6,714,220	7,642,545	13.82	3,784,427	56.36	4,103,479	53.69	8.43	2,551,284	38.00	3,135,551	41.03	22.90
South	5,066,132	6,380,614	25.95	2,883,000	56.91	3,506,931	54.96	21.64	1,566,070	30.91	2,170,150	34.01	38.57
Dnipro	5,386,561	6,377,109	18.39	4,182,207	77.64	4,766,924	74.75	13.98	947,376	17.59	1,327,005	20.81	40.07
North-East	5,665,553	6,037,018	6.56	4,589,545	81.01	4,739,075	78.50	3.26	916,333	16.17	1,129,214	18.70	23.23
Central West	11,237,522	11,944,822	6.29	9,921,534	88.29	10,445,560	87.45	5.28	706,812	6.31	918,761	7.69	29.99
West	7,799,058	8,754,552	12.25	6,797,780	87.16	7,721,898	88.20	13.59	402,938	5.17	445,650	5.09	10.60

Source: Itogi 1959, Ukrainskaia SSR, Table 54, and Itogi 1970, Vol IV, Table 8.

Note: Donbas — Donetsk, Voroshylovhrad
South — Odesa, Crimea, Kherson, Mykolaiv
Dnipro — Dnipropetrovs'k, Zaporizhia, Kirovohrad
North-East — Kharkiv, Poltava, Sumy
Central-West — Kyiv, Chernyhiv, Cherkasy, Zhytomyr, Vinnytsia, Khmel'nyts'ky
West — L'viv, Rivne, Volyn', Ternopil', Ivano-Frankivs'k, Transcarpathia, Chernivtsi

TABLE II

SELECTED OBLASTI OF UKRAINE

	TOTAL URBAN POPULATION			URBAN UKRAINIANS					URBAN RUSSIANS				
	(1959)	(1970)	Percentage change	(1959)	Percent	(1970)	Percent	Percentage change	(1959)	Percent	(1970)	Percent	Percentage change
Donets'k	3,656,240	4,275,596	16.94	1,902,583	52.04	2,137,010	49.92	12.38	1,517,860	41.51	1,878,618	43.94	22.77
Odesa	956,694	1,334,381	39.48	421,126	44.02	633,658	47.49	50.47	341,720	35.72	474,622	35.57	38.89
Kharkiv	1,573,738	1,958,194	24.43	956,369	60.77	1,170,648	59.78	22.40	503,074	31.97	668,708	34.15	32.92
Dnipropetrovs'k	1,898,765	2,548,964	34.24	1,358,025	71.52	1,765,675	69.27	30.02	417,388	21.98	642,951	25.22	54.04
Kyiv (city and Oblast combined)	1,547,907	2,286,725	47.73	1,024,029	66.16	1,595,675	69.78	55.82	312,904	20.21	463,526	20.27	48.14
L'viv	821,338	1,148,649	39.85	575,377	70.05	878,998	76.52	55.77	168,937	20.57	193,042	16.81	14.27
Ukraine	19,147,419	25,688,560	34.17	11,781,750	61.53	16,164,254	62.92	37.20	5,726,476	29.91	7,712,277	30.02	34.68

Source: Itogi 1959, Ukrainskaia SSR, Table 54 and Itogi 1970, Vol. IV, Table 8.

native language, while 35.9 percent declared Russian as their language, the population of Kharkiv in 1959 was divided linguistically in the following way. 15

Russian	628.0 thousand	67.2 percent
Ukrainian	291.6 thousand	31.2 percent
Other	14.5 thousand	1.6 percent
Total	934.1 thousand	

However, although these figures suggest that Russian is clearly a dominant language in Ukraine's second largest city, the authors argue that in fact both languages are widely known in the city. One of the reasons why this is so is that Russian is taught in Ukrainian schools, Ukrainian is a "required" subject in Russian schools. 16 Since the book was published about eight years after the Khrushchevian educational reform abolished the teaching of non-Russian languages in Russian schools as a required subject, one wonders whether the authors are misinformed or the reform proved to be something different from what it was thought to be.

Additional material on ethnic relaitons in Eastern Ukraine may may be found in a study published in 1968 in **Sovetskaia etnografia**. As we noted earlier, Russians had been living in the eastern regions of Ukraine, especially the oblasti of Kharkiv and Sumy, both in town and country, ever since the 17th century. According to the findings of an expedition sent in 1966 by the Institute of Ethnography, Academy of Sciences of the USSR, the bulk of Russians and Ukrainians living there had retained their national consciousness, but there had also been cases of changes of national self-consciousness among those Russians who lived in mixed, Russo-Ukrainian villages. The cases of such a change among Ukrainians had reportedly been rarer. 17 In one village, Aleshnia, which had been settled by Russians in the second half of the 17th century (previously it had been a Ukrainian village), two village soviets were established after the revolution, in view of the mixed ethnic composition of the village. "At the end of the 1950's, considering that a majority of the population of that village came to consider themselves Ukrainian, the two village soviets were combined into one and one secondary school, with Ukrainian as the language of instruction, was formed." This transference in national consciousness occurred apparently in the 1950s-1960s. According to local records, in 1950-1952, Ukrainians and Russians in the village constituted 46.4 percent and 53.6 percent respectively; by 1964-1966 the corresponding figures were 91.2 percent and 8.4 percent. In the 1959 all-Union census all population of the village was recorded as Ukrainian. L.N. Chizhikova, from whose study all these data are cited, gives various examples of how persons with names like Orekhov, Maksakov, Kriukov, Koz'min, Lukianov, Machulin, and Pushkariev, declare themselves now as Ukrainians, even though 12-15 years earlier they gave their nationality as Russian. Sometimes children of Russian parents declare Ukrainian nationality. Russian names at times become Ukrainianized: Krivoguzov becomes Kryvohuz, Maksakov — Maksak, Slin'kov — Slyn'ko. 18

Asked about the reasons of changes in national self-definition, they usually answer that they live in Ukraine and among the Ukrainian people; moreover, many emphasize along with this that it is not of great importance to them what to call oneself — Russian or Ukrainian. Some local residents find it difficult to answer to which nationality they belong, which unquestionably is to be explained by the occurrence in those regions of active processes of ethnic change in the population.

Needless to say the expedition also recorded cases of change of nationality from Ukrainian to Russian, especially in those locations where the population was mixed with a predominance of Russians. The language of the school appears to exert an influence on national self-identification. It is interesting, however, that the terms "Ukrainian" and "Russian" were not the same as those which as late as this century were in common use: even the participants of the 1966 expedition encountered villagers who called themselves "khokhol" or "pereverten" and referred to others as "moskali." These terms were not considered as derogatory but descriptive. 20

Since similar changes from Ukrainian to Russian, and of course much more significant in terms of numbers, have occurred in the predominantly Ukrainian-inhabited districts of the Kuban', and other areas outside the Ukrainian SSR, it may be worth noting that those Ukrainians had often been at a stage of pre-modern national consciousness. Without denying that the policies pursued by the Stalinist regime in the 1930s were very decisive (terror, prohibition of schools and the press in Ukrainian, etc.), one should not fail to add that these objects of Russification made a switch from a "Little Russian," "khokhol" or some such ethnic consciousness to Russian, without having ever consciously accepted the national Ukrainian identity, including its literary language, political symbols, etc. There is no doubt that a similar transfer to Russian nationality did occur in Ukraine, considering that the period of relatively pro-Ukrainian policies in Soviet Ukraine was very brief and even then was more frequently declared in official statements rather than actually implemented in the work of the local administration. 21

How do these statements of Kurmon-Lebedinskii and Chizhikova look in the light of the 1970 census returns?

According to the 1970 census, Russians represented 34.15 percent of the urban population in Kharkiv oblast (in 1959 the ratio was 31.97 percent); of those 30.14 percent declared that they knew Ukrainian fluently, and another 0.97 percent considered Ukrainian their native language. The percentage of Ukrainians in Kharkiv oblast's urban population was 59.78 percent (compared with 60.77 percent in 1959). Of these Ukrainians (considered as 100 percent), 24.27 percent regarded Russian as their native language (in 1959, the figures was 19.21 percent), and 44.62 percent said they knew Russian. However, out of the 284,170 Ukrainians who chose Russian as their first language, 162,795, or 57.29 percent declared a command of Ukrainian as well; this figure represents a 13.91 percent of the total of urban Ukrainians, which means that about 10 percent of all urban Ukrainians in Kharkiv oblast neither consider Ukrainian as their first language nor claim to know it as their second language (284,170 - 162,795= 121,375, or 10.36 percent). 22

It is a matter of guessing to what extent the declarations in census accurately reflect the real language situation, in particular a knowledge of the second language among the Ukrainians and Russians. It may well be that they understate the extent of reciprocal bilingualism. 23 In practice, it seems that the Russians, or rather those who use Russian as their first language in the urban centers of Ukraine, do have a sufficient command of Ukrainian to allow them to read Ukrainian newspapers and journals, to listen to radio broadcasts, etc. In 1970, an evening newspaper was established in the Ukrainian language in Kharkiv, **Vechirnii Kharkiv.** According to a Soviet journalist, some in the publishing circles argued, prior to the appearance of the paper, that it would not sell well if it were published in Ukrainian. However, the paper was proved to be quite successful despite the "handicap" of appearing in Ukrainian. The initial circulation of **Vechirnii Kharkiv** was 100,000 copies daily, and by 1974 it rose to 150,000. 24

Limitations of space do not allow any but the briefest reference to nationality processes in the south of Ukraine, the Crimea and Odesa, or the area of lower Dnieper with the major urban and industrial centers of Dnipropetrovs'k, Zaporizhia and Kryvyi Rih. In Table II we have assembled data on the ethnic composition of the urban population of select oblasti of Ukraine, namely those which contain the metropolitan centres of the republic: Kharkiv, Donets'k, Dnipropetrovs'k, Kyiv and L'viv. As Table II shows, the urban Russian population in Dnipropetrovs'k rose very rapidly between the censuses (54 percent), and was also high in Odesa (39 percent). However, also Ukrainians were increasing relatively fast, especially in Odesa, somewhat more slowly in Dnipropetrovs'k, but still even there faster than in either Donets'k or Kharkiv oblasti. One may speculate that ethnic tensions will accelerate in the south, including the lower Dnipro, since it is an area in which both nationalities remain in a stage of rapid growth. Let us note that Dnipropetrovs'k was the place where students and young intellectuals and artists protested against Russification in 1969 and were put on trial in 1970,[25] and that **samizdat** materials contain information about the prevalence of the Russian element and subordinate position of Ukrainians in Odesa, and the Crimea. Thus **Ukrains'kyi Visnyk** No. 6 refers to the restrictions on Ukrainian language in Crimea's schools and colleges and the virtual absence of that language in common use, while a most recent work, published in the West this year, draws a picture of Odesa which recalls Skrypnyk's statement that during the revolution neither Russians nor Ukrainians felt that Odesa was in Ukraine. Skrypnyk would have been surprised, one imagines, to learn that as late as the 1970s some inhabitants of Odesa remained convinced that their city was not located in Ukraine. Danylo Shumuk, the author of "Za skhidnim obriem," after release from a labour camp, came to Odesa in 1970 and found that unlike Kyiv where that language still could be heard occasionally nobody spoke Ukrainian in Odesa. When he spoke Ukrainian he was met with insults and hostility. One woman commented to him:

Vy, molodoi chelovek, i odety khorosho, i vashe litso kak-budto intelligentoe, a rezgavarivaete kak-to ne pochelovecheski. Neuzheli vy ne znaete russkogo iazyka?

Another added:

A vy znaete, eti khokhly dazhe zdes' v Odesse do togo obnagleli chto predlagali mne biulleten' zapolniat' na ikh khokhlatskom iazyke. A ia im otvetila: "Ia vam ne kolkhoznitsa, ia Odessitka." I ne obrashchaia vnimaniia, zapolnila biuleten' po russki.

When Shumuk replied that in Moscow or Leningrad he would speak in Russian but in Ukraine he always spoke in Ukrainian, a man joined in with this observation (the discussion took place in a street car):

O, vidish, i zdes' kakoi-to bandera poiavilsia, on dazhe Odessu schitaet Ukrainoi.[26]

A little later the author ran into someone he had known in the camps and who had been for the preceding fourteen years employed in construction work in Odesa. The friend was totally resigned about the prospects of Ukraine. He argued that those intellectuals in Kiev — such as Svitlychnyi and Dziuba, whose names he knew — were completely isolated from the masses of the Ukrainian population, and besides, "what can some group of intellectuals do when the entire working class 'hlaholyt' in Russian and does not even want to hear about any such independence . . . We are not a nation, Danylo, not a nation but a Little Russian nationality / 'narodnist' / which is only proud of its varenyky, halushky, borshch, and nothing else."[27]

It is also probably not accidental that this area has been referred to in Russian **samizdat**. A document titled **Slovo Natsii**, "A Word of the Nation" (or more properly "A Nation Speaks") admits that "there exists in Ukraine a strong nationalist movement," but **Slovo Natsii** considers its aims "utterly unreal." "The present-day frontiers of Ukraine . . . do not correspond with its ethnographical/boundaries/." On ethnic grounds, the document says, Ukraine should lose its Eastern and Southern provinces, especially those like the Crimea where Ukrainians do not constitute a majority in population. If the Russian and Russified areas of Ukraine are ceded to Russia, the remaining part would find itself without an outlet to the sea and without the basic industrial areas; the Ukrainians will have no choice — faced as they will be by Polish claims to Ukraine's western regions — but to ask to be accepted back by Russia, "the return of the prodigal son." (The author(s) do not seem to be well aware of the conditions in West Ukraine because they attribute to the population of Ukraine's western provinces a "pro-Polish orientation.")[28]

It is probably also significant that while in his celebrated letter to the leaders of the Soviet Union (1973) Solzhenitsyn expressed readiness to accept the secession, from a state common with the Russians, of various borderland nationalities, in the case of Ukraine he envisioned the possibility that only some "parts of Ukraine" might do so; presumably, he considered some other parts of the Ukrainian Soviet Republic more Russian than Ukrainian.

This view seems to be in accord with the position traditionally taken by Russians of various orientations that Odesa and Donbas are not Ukrainians.

There is evidence that the West and Central West are viewed differently by both Russian and Ukrainians. The area is different in other regards as well. Central West (Table I) is characterized by slow growth of population (the lowest in the republic) and relatively low growth of Ukrainian population. However, to understand the demographic processes at work there, one should consider separately from the rest of the region its center, the city of Kyiv (possibly together with Kyiv oblast, considering the importance of Kyiv's satellite towns providing commuters for the capital). Splitting the Central West region along those lines we get two rather different trends. Our initial impression of rather slow demographic growth becomes reinforced when we subtract from the totals the figures referring to the city of Kyiv. Even when, to avoid distortion, we add to the city data also the data for Kyiv oblast, we observe that the population of Central West minus Kyiv metropolitan area was stagnant in the eleven intercensal years: it rose by less than one percent (0.80 percent). The Ukrainians grew by even less (0.76 percent) but Russians, interestingly enough, rose by as much as 16.98 percent. The developments in Kyiv were notably different. The city and oblast combined rose by 22.60 percent, the Ukrainians by 20.97 percent, and the Russians by 43.92 percent. Since the Russians represented only 11.92 percent of the population in 1959, their rise by such a high percentage, paralleled by a half that rate rise of Ukrainians, resulted in their gain of two percentage points by 1970 (to 13.99 percent). In the capital itself, the increase of the Ukrainian element was higher than that of the Russians, resulting in an increase of the Ukrainian share of the city's population from 60.0 to 64.76 percent. The total population rose by 47 percent, the Russians by 46.5 percent, and the Ukrainians by 58.2 percent. Only in the Crimea was the Ukrainian increase higher (79.5 percent). Kyiv thus proved to be the only one among the five largest cities of Ukraine in which the Ukrainian element has increased ahead of the Russian advance. (L'viv, where the Ukrainians grew faster too, belongs to the somewhat lower class.)

In order to make the Kyiv situation comparable with that in the other major urban centers, we have assembled data on Kyiv city and urban population of the rest of Kyiv oblast together in Table II. As may be seen in Kyiv and L'viv Ukrainians increased faster than Russians; and while in Kyiv the Russian share remained virtually the same, in L'viv the Russians actually declined from 21 to 14 percent of urban population. We shall return to L'viv shortly, but let us note that the comments of the Soviet demographer and geographer, V. V. Pokshishevskii, seem to apply directly to Kyiv. Pokshishevskii argues that the "ethnically oriented state structure" of the USSR, and industrialization of non-Russian areas, gave rise to urban centers in those non-Russian areas which became "the centers of national culture and ethnic consciousness." They became the centers of education, of publishing and broadcasting, and they developed a need for ethnic personnel in administration and in training indigenous workers for industry. For these reasons, these cities "began to attract ethnic contingents from rural areas, in some cases from other union republics and even from cities in those republics. This suggests that in the USSR it is now the city, perhaps more than the countryside, that has become the 'carrier of the ethnos.'" According to Pokshishevskii, the Ukrainian element has been on the rise in Kyiv owing to Kyiv's attraction of Ukrainians from the entire territory of Ukraine, and owing to "further consolidation of the Ukrainian nation and a strengthening of ethnic consciousness. It may be supposed that some Kyivans, after some hesitation whether to consider themselves Ukrainian, later did so with absolute conviction; more children of mixed marriages have also declared themselves Ukrainian."[29]

TABLE III

RUSSIANS IN REPUBLIC CAPITALS

NAME OF CAPITAL CITY	Total Population (1970)	Russians (1970)	Russians in the Republics who know Republic Language (Percent)	Russians in the capital who know Republic Language (Percent)	Russians as Percent of Capital's Population (1959)	Russians as Percent of Capital's Population (1970)	Population of Capital as Percent of Republic Population
Frunze (Kirghizia)	430,618	284,676	1.50	0.72	71.8	66.11	14.68
Alma-Ata (Kazakhstan)	729,633	512,900	0.99	0.73	73.2	70.29	5.61
Ashkhabad (Turkmenia)	253,118	108,144	2.08	1.23	50.3	42.72	11.72
Dushanbe (Tadjikistan)	373,885	157,083	2.36	1.25	47.7	42.01	12.89
Tashkent (Uzbekustan)	1,384,509	564,584	3.77	2.47	43.8	40.78	11.73
Baku (Azerbajdjan)	1,265,515	351,090	7.56	5.14	34.2	27.74	24.73
Kishinev (Moldavia)	356,382	109,313	13.34	11.84	32.1	30.67	9.99
Tallin (Estonia)	362,706	127,103	12.57	12.23	32.0	35.04	26.75
Riga (Latvia)	731,831	312,857	17.08	15.15	39.4	42.75	30.95
Tbilisi (Georgia)	889,020	124,316	10.51	17.86	18.2	13.98	18.97
Minsk (Belorussia)	916,949	214,208	20.60	17.88	22.9	23.36	10.19
Vilnius (Lithuanian)	372,100	91,004	30.76	20.45	29.7	24.46	11.89
Erevan (Armenia)	766,705	21,519	18.95	30.95	4.4	2.81	30.77
Kyiv (Ukraine)	1,631,908	373,569	25.95	41.05	22.7	22.89	3.46

Source: Itogi 1970, Vol. IV, tables 7-29, and Sovetskaia etnografiia, No. 5, 1969, p.8.

In Table III we assembled various information about the capitals of the non-Russian republics in the USSR, ranking them in order of their share of Russians who declared in 1970 that they spoke fluently the language of the respective union republic. In all of the Central Asian republics, in whose capitals the Russians constituted either an absolute majority or exceeded 40 percent, Russians speaking the native language ranged from 0.72 percent to 2.4 percent. In Baku 5.14 percent of Russians knew Azeri; their share in the capital's population was 27.74 percent. The percentage of local-speaking Russians in the Caucasus, besides Baku, reached 14 percent in Tbilisi and as high a figure as 30.95 percent in Erevan. However, in Erevan the Russians constituted only 2.81 percent in 1970, a drop from 4.4 percent in 1959. It is reasonable to imagine that those few Russians were under some pressure to learn Armenian. It is rather strange that only less than a third said that they had actually done so. The more interesting, therefore, seems to be the case of Russians in Kyiv, of whom 41.05 percent declared knowledge of Ukrainian. This, compared with just above 20 percent in Vilnius, 18 percent in Minsk, and 12 percent in Tallin, suggests, in our view, a high degree of reciprocal bilingualism in the Ukrainian capital, indirectly testifying to relatively high status of Ukrainian language and culture. In Minsk — Belorussia seems to be the most suitable for comparison in view of the close resemblance of both Belorussian and Ukrainian to Russian — where the Russians were almost exactly as numerous percentagewise as in Kyiv, they knew Belorussian less than a half as often as their compatriots knew Ukrainian in Kyiv. We may add that the popular daily evening paper **Vechirnii Kyiv**, with a circulation of over 300,000 copies, appears in Ukrainian and must be read by Russians too, while in Minsk a comparable paper has a Russian and a Belorussian edition, the former printing about 150,000 copies, the latter under 2,000.

Capitals, as is well known, influence the country of which they are the center. In the case of Ukraine we may ask: does Kyiv function as the capital of the entire Ukraine (we do not question of course that it functions as the administrative capital of the republic); is it the primate city enjoying a superior position in relation to such giants as Kharkiv, Odesa, or Donets'k? Employing the concepts of urban geography concerning the rank-size order of cities, Professor Chauncy D. Harris has suggested that Kyiv's population in 1959 was about one-third as large as would be expected from the network of 301 cities and towns of more than 10,000 population in Ukraine. "The rank-size analysis suggests that the Ukraine, established on ethnic principles (we have noted that this no longer corresponds to reality, indeed never did exactly), may not be a single urban economic unit but rather that it may be composed of as many as 5 urban network regions."[30] (These were, according to Harris, Kyiv, Kharkiv, Odesa, Donets'k, and Dnipropetrovs'k.) Another American scholar, David Hooson, has taken a somewhat more affirmative view of the relative role of Kyiv among the cities of Ukraine, saying that "Kharkiv may conceivably grow larger, but cannot now challenge Kyiv's pre-eminent position, any more than Milan can supplant Rome as capital of the Italian State."[31]

Without disputing Hooson, I feel that Harris is right in arguing that for Kharkiv, Odesa or Donets'k, Kyiv does not exercise, as yet, the role of the capital city. If it actually establishes its position of the primate city of Ukraine by gaining population far above the population of cities like Odesa or Kharkiv, this will be an indication that the present day Ukraine has gained an economic and social cohesion within its present territorial limits of a Soviet republic. This in turn might promote the growth of a Ukrainian territorial identity as a real factor of (or independently from) any linguistic assimilation. Some scholars have argued in recent years that there exist objective economic conditions for the rise of such a non-linguistic, territorial and economy-concerned community of interest. Thus, for example, Professor David Hooson believes that while the Moscow region has "poor and transitional natural endowments," for which it compensates by its political role of a national metropolis, the Greater Ukraine (this is an area that includes Moldavia, the lower Don and Kuban' lowland) is "physically homogeneous — almost all black earth (**chernozem**) — and rich in a variety of industrial resources and productive activities. It is clearly

208

the region most nearly indispensable to the Soviet Union and conversely the only one comparable in population and potential to the great nation-states of Western Europe."[32] According to Hooson, despite the growth of population, industry and agriculture in the east, north, and south, "most of the economic and other indicators of rationality point to an optimum area for future development and growth in south European Russia. Its core may be broadly encompassed within a radius of six hundred miles from Kharkiv, taking in the whole of the Greater Ukraine region . . ., stretching to Kuibyshev on the Volga, and beyond Moscow and Minsk. This circle contains over half the Soviet population and industrial and agricultural production, rich natural resources, and potential for further development. The area's middle lies at the center of gravity of the population of the whole Soviet bloc, and it contains the densest transport network in the Soviet Union. Labour is plentiful and its productivity is higher than in the south and east. The population is overwhelmingly Slavic in ethnic composition, which is of considerable — though unacknowledged — significance. The potential resurgence of Ukrainian nationalism is a significant unanswered question. **Incidentally, many people in this region, particularly the Ukrainians and Belorussians, are becoming increasingly dissatisfied with the prolonged disproportionate allocation of scarce investment capital to eastern regions, where the return tends to be lower, and with the comparative underestimation of the natural resources of their own regions."[33]**

Whether or not such a development is likely to occur, that is, whether a territorial Ukrainian identity, including those who consider themselves ethnic Russians and those Ukrainians who speak Russian as their first language, will develop, Kyiv has been clearly gaining in importance as the largest city in Ukraine and the third largest in the USSR. Simultaneously it has been becoming more of a Ukrainian city. If one has the impression now that it is a thoroughly Russian city, it is worth remembering that it is also less Russian now than it was ten, twenty, or fifty years ago. Because of this Kyiv, and to a much smaller degree L'viv, are the testing ground for the capacity of the Ukrainian people to establish a Ukrainian presence in the metropolitan framework on the basis of the Ukrainian language. If the attempt succeeds, at least Western and Central Ukraine will be modern while remaining Ukrainian. More broadly, such an achievement will reinforce the Ukrainian ethnic element elsewhere, not only in Eastern Ukraine but also beyond its boundaries and will thus make it possible to redefine the Russo-Ukrainian relationship on a basis different from the present "younger brother" or "country cousin" pattern.

A priori, L'viv could play an even greater modernizing role in Ukraine on the basis of Ukrainian, not Russian, identity. Demographic data cited in Tables I and III show that Western Ukraine as a whole is large in terms of total population (were it a republic of its own it would be among the most populous ones), and urban population of the main oblast, that of L'viv. It is here more than anywhere else in Ukraine that the Russians fit the description of a national minority. They are new, having come only thirty or so years ago; and they are relatively few even though they are in control of "commanding heights" such as party apparatus, the police, and managerial cadres. Here the Russian language and culture have not been traditionally identified with modernity in the popular perception. Historically, it was Polish, German, and Hungarian rather than Russian culture which represented the city, and to a degree not later achieved by Ukrainians under Russia, the Ukrainian society, culture and politics did win for itself a firm position in the city before the coming of the Soviets. If L'viv does not influence Ukraine today as much as it could, however, the reason lies in deliberate efforts to limit its possible impact. It only has one monthly periodical, for example, compared with dozens of weeklies and monthlies which were published there before 1939, in Ukrainian; and it lacks the status symbol of a big city — an evening paper — although many smaller Soviet cities do enjoy this privilege. Its capacity, then, to influence Ukrainian developments is much smaller than that of Kyiv.

It is reasonable to speculate that the presence and role of the Russians in this western area would be perceived by the local population quite differently than in the old, formerly tsarist Russian parts of Ukraine which had been Soviet for two decades preceding 1939. There exist certain documentary **samizdat** materials on Russians in the West, mainly limited to issues involving persecution of dissenters by police and judiciary personnel of Russian nationality. Officially approved accounts, documentary or fictional, dealing with Russo-Ukrainian relations in the West in the conditions of daily life (Ukrainian **pobut**, Russian **byt**) are less frequent. Soviet Ukrainian writers, for example, avoid dealing with inter-ethnic relations in fiction. The more remarkable therefore are those few works which directly address themselves to those themes and thus provide some information about the nationality aspects of daily life in the Soviet Ukrainian cities. The author Iakiv Stetsiuk, born in 1912 in the Zhytomyr region, has been living in Western Ukraine since 1944, first at Ivano-Frankivs'k, and subsequently in L'viv. In 1969 the Kyiv Komsomol literary journal **Dnipro** published a long-story by Stetsiuk entitled "Imenyny materi" (A Mother's Birthday). [34] The story is set in L'viv in the 1960s, although there are flash-backs to the immediate post-war years; the characters include teachers, government officials, and students, both Ukrainian and Russian. Let us briefly note those passages dealing with our subject, the Russians in Ukraine, remembering of course that this is a non-literary approach; we are interested in the work's sociological inferences.

Stetsiuk draws a distinction between the two Russian migrations to Western Ukraine. The first migratory wave, during and immediately after the war, is represented in his story by Oleksii, who decides to stay in the city where he was wounded while fighting the Germans, and where he feels he will be needed more than in his homeland in Russia.

It is commonly known that the towns and cities of Western Ukraine had been mainly Polish and Jewish before 1939, and that they lost most of that population either because of Nazi genocide or as a result of population transfers. Moreover, many of those Ukrainians who lived in the cities before 1939 were arrested and deported by the Soviets, or left with the Germans. For these reasons after the war managerial, economic, technical, engineering and administrative personnel were brought into the area from the outside. Given the political unreliability (from the Soviet point of view) of the local population, it was also necessary to bring into the area numerous administrative, party, police, and ideological cadres from the East. In Stetsiuk's story, then, Oleksii as the Russian immigrant of the 1940s vintage, stands for them all. Oleksii decided to identify his own life and work with people of Ukraine. He learns and uses the Ukrainian language in professional and public work; he also marries a local Ukrainian.

At first, Oleksii is not sure whether his decision to remain was right: he did not know Ukrainian, while schools in the area had been Ukrainian (and of course Polish). He becomes a teacher in a Russian school in which Ukrainian was also taught. A new colleague, the Ukrainian teacher, Mariia Ivanivna, "in order to please him, attempted to speak Russian" to him but did so very poorly. (Let us note that she was supposed to be teaching Ukrainian in a school with Russian language of instruction. It is highly improbable that someone not fluent in Russian would hold such a post.) Oleksii suggests that she should speak her own language, and when she expresses fear he will not understand, he responds:

I will try. Besides, to be frank, it is not you who should be getting used to me, but the reverse. You are the host here.

Mariia teaches Oleksii Ukrainian, he reciprocates by teaching her Russian, and she develops an admiration for the "richness and power" of that language. As one might have guessed, they eventually got married.

Oleksii not only learns Ukrainian but also speaks it at various conferences and meetings. A former army acquaintance chances to attend one such conference and later visits Oleksii and Mariia in their apartment. In a conversation with Oleksii he refers to Mariia as "your baba." This is enough to offend Oleksii, but then the ex-friend remarks:

Zdorov ty cheshesh po yikhniomu. Where did you learn, I wonder? You can do it even with that very ... local accent. Well, well, don't get excited. I know — politics. But why, really? Why play? in any case, everything is moving toward one. One language on the whole planet — that's convenient and simple.

— Chinese? — Oleksii responded at last.

— What you! Ours! — offendedly said the guest.

— And this game is not good for anything. I myself am a descendant of the Zaporozhians. My ancestors used to be Cossacks. But if this has to be done ... so what ...

— And so you will spit into your soul?

Oleksii asks his former friend to leave even though he knows very well that the latter will write about him to "all instantsii."[35]

Later in the story Oleksii dies, and Mariia and their child Yaroslav become the principal "positive" personages of the story. Mariia is now forty-five and Yaroslav a first-year journalism student.

The main negative figure is Ruslan Hlibovych Nosal'skyi, Mariia's second husband and Yaroslav's stepfather. When we meet him, Ruslan Hlibovych is a high figure in the city administration. His previous career merits a brief recounting because it contrasts sharply with the story of Oleksii and symbolizes the second, one is tempted to call it "parasitical," wave of Russian immigration in Western Ukraine. Before coming to Western Ukraine, Orest Hlibovych was a career officer in the Soviet Army. The author presents him as a typical careerist.[36] Internal evidence suggests that he was one of those officers who were released from full-time military career during the celebrated Khrushchevian reduction of the armed forces (1959-60); the author remarks that at the time when Nosal'skyi left the service many other officers did. He was then just over forty, had reached the rank of lieutenant colonel, and his civilian pension was 150 rubles a month. (The author explains that in comparison with what others got this was a relatively low pay for an ex-officer.) Ruslan's first civilian job is "deputy director for economic matters" in the high school in which Mariia is a language teacher. Ruslan has an apartment larger than that of Mariia and her son, and after Ruslan and Mariia marry, they exchange both apartments for a single four-room apartment in a "luxury" house built in "Polish times."[37] Subsequently he is moved to a higher post, and we learn that he is trying to get an even higher promotion. He is a totally despicable character, cheats on his wife, etc., but we will omit all these sides, and look at him only from our special angle. Owing to his official position, he is able to arrange a residence permit in L'viv (even though this is a city of restricted residence) for Maya, the third Russian in the story, a negative type like Ruslan.

Unlike Ruslan who is about fifty and had come a decade or so earlier, Maya is quite young and has just arrived in L'viv. She also lacks any good qualities; the author characterizes her as a morally dissolute person. She comments about L'viv as follows:

In general, the climate here is just good for nothing. Damp, unpleasant. It smells of rottenness. I do not understand why people get so attached to this town. Take Novosibirsk or Omsk ... There's a climate for you ...[38]

Despite L'viv's clear inferiority in comparison with Omsk and Novosibirsk — which Maya seems to know from personal experience — she is determined to get a L'viv residence permit and gets Ruslan to help her. She comes to see Ruslan with Yaroslav's friend, Bohdan, a local Ukrainian, who is a **de facto** professional athlete but officially an employee of some factory. Bohdan sees an open book on Yaroslav's desk and says:

What are you reading, old man? O, you have marked it so much ... Something interesting? — He began to read the passage marked with a red pencil: "The Polish king, Stefan Batory in a letter written in Polish in 1576 invited some Ukrainian lords to come to see him. The lords became angry, and wrote back: 'Your majesty, our liberties and rights are violated because letters are being sent to us from Your Majesty's chancellery which are written in Polish. Therefore, we beg humbly Your Majesty to maintain our privileges in the future, and instruct that letters from Your Royal Chancellery be sent in Rus' language.'" He read this with mock solemn language and then added: there is nothing strange in this.

Maya said— It appears that in those times there were those ... what you call them?

Those present became rather embarrassed, as Maya is obviously groping for the expression "Ukrainian bourgeois nationalists" but she is undeterred: — What's the matter? Am I not right? (**A schcho? Khiba ne tak?**) 39
As far as I know this story has met with no critical response in the Soviet Union and has passed unnoticed in the West despite its unusual content. Its principal significance, it seems to me, is that it shows the second group of Russian immigrants to Ukraine as being socially parasitical and spiritually alien to the people among whom they have decided to settle.

To sum up our discussion, what future do the Ukrainians have in the Soviet Union, and accordingly, and dependent on that, what are the prospects of the Russian population of Ukraine?
For reasons which have been earlier suggested, the prospect that the Ukrainians disappear from their historic area, the South-West region, is very small indeed. Nor is there a likely prospect that this area will acquire a Russian majority or a large minority as appears to be happening in Estonia and Latvia. Rather, somewhat in the pattern of Lithuania and Moldavia, West-Central Ukraine appears to be maintaining an internal cohesion and developing ways to make itself immune to the corroding influence of Russification. On the other hand, it sems to be equally clear — barring unforeseen developments — that the Donbas and the South are either becoming increasingly more Russian and correspondingly less Ukrainian linguistically, or that at least certain parts of that area are on the way to becoming almost exclusively Russian in language (the Donbas); others are possible going to remain bilingual, such as the Dnipropetrovs'k-Zaporizhia area and the Crimea (the latter due to exceptionally large Ukrainian immigration). At any rate, the entire territory beyond the historical Ukrainian lands is unlikely to switch to using mainly Ukrainian as long as Ukraine is part of the USSR. It seems doubtful that even a separation of Ukraine would necessarily be followed by a de-Russification (we are assuming that no major transfers of the population would occur). What bearing, then, do these demographic facts and trends have on the status of the Russians in Ukraine, and on the status of Ukraine in a Russian-dominated USSR?
There seem to be basically two major alternatives for the survival of Ukraine and the Ukrainians within the USSR and for resolving the problem of the Russian element in Ukraine within a Ukrainian context. The first alternative would be to partition the Ukrainian SSR along ethnic-nationality lines: the Donbas and possibly several other oblasti would be separated from Ukraine and the size of the Russian-language element in that smaller Ukraine would be decreased. One imagines that to become acceptable to Ukrainians, this operation would have to reduce the Russian population in that smaller Ukraine to a truly national minority, and not a dominant and privileged element. There would have to be a clear understanding, supported by practical guarantees, that Russification stops at a certain line, and that the status of

the Ukrainian language and culture would be institutionally secure. Some Ukrainians might find this a gain worth paying for with a territorial redefinition of Ukraine. Such a reduced Ukraine would enjoy national rights somewhat comparable to, if not exceeding, those of Armenia or Georgia.

The second alternative would maintain the present territorial integrity of the Ukrainian SSR but would redefine the Ukrainian nationality in a territorial sense: the population of the republic might have the option of considering itself Ukrainian regardless whether its language of communication is Ukrainian or Russian. We have even now many persons who declare themselves to be Ukrainian by nationality, Russian by native language. Both Soviet and non-Soviet commentators consider this phenomenon of Russian-speaking Ukrainians to be an anomaly of sorts, a transitory status to Russian ethnic identity. This may be the case, but the matter should be investigated statistically, among other things, before any firm conclusions can be reached. Do those who declare Russian as their native language actually switch to Russian nationality after some time? Do their children do so? Or is there some retention of this dual identity from generation to generation? Indeed, at least hypothetically, it may be asked whether some of those who start as Russian by both language and nationality do not switch to a Ukrainian identity while retaining their Russian language? We know it is possible to regard oneself Ukrainian while speaking Russian. The question is whether this phenomenon is considered an inherently transitory and unstable one (leading to either complete Russification or return to full Ukrainian identity) or whether a Ukrainian identity can be so redefined as to allow the combination of Ukrainian nationality with Russian language.

We may only suggest here, in passing, that one of the several ways in which this identity option might be tested empirically would be to study the Russian-language press in Ukraine: is it mainly a Russian press by Russians and for Russians who happen to live in Ukraine, or is it in some significant way different from the Russian language press say in the RSFSR, or Kazakhstan, or Latvia? Might one view it as a Russian-medium Ukrainian press?

To admit that Ukrainians may have two languages and still remain "good" Ukrainians would mean to base the Ukrainian identity on territory and community of interests derived from a commonly shared territory rather than a common language. It is impossible to envision this development as a practical prospect. Its acceptance would require not only formal declarations on the part of the regime but also a variety of practical measures, such as the use of Russian language for transmission of Ukrainian national messages. No declaration could by itself transform the millions of declared Russians (by language and nationality) into Ukrainians in the territorial-political sense. A policy shift might facilitate, however, the political assimilation or "naturalization" of some of them, and also slow down or reverse the process of national identity shift from Ukrainian to Russian along with and through linguistic assimilation. I would like to know more in this connection about the nationality processes currently under way in Belorussia, because while the linguistic assimilation of the Belorussians appears to be progressing, it also appears that the Belorussian national identity, based on a political-territorial identity, is not weakening. Will Belorussians remain a separate nation even when they are Russian? Are there any Belorussians who speak Russian but politically have a Belorussian national consciousness? How important are they?

There are no Soviet precedents for this type of national identity, and the only successful case in Eastern Europe seems to be that of Finland where Swedish and Finnish are considered the national languages of the country. (Needless to say, Sweden does not pose anything nearly resembling the threat to the survival of a Finnish-speaking Finland that Russia does in relation to Ukraine.) The cases of Ireland and, more recently, Scotland, where it has been possible to be not only Irish and Scottish but also anti-English via the medium of the English language, on the other hand, suggest that the emergence of Ukrainian nationalism among Russian speakers is not a figment of the imagination.

The adoption of either of these "options" would not resolve the problem of

Ukrainian identity in the USSR. Whether the Ukrainian republic is made smaller (or rather, if it is) or whether the definition of Ukrainian nationality is based on the community of territory, there will remain all over the USSR persons considering themselves Ukrainian. If the Soviet state seriously treats its claims to be a truly multinational structure, it is hard to understand its policy of denying to the Ukrainians a minimum of national-cultural rights beyond the boundaries of the Ukrainian SSR. How is one to justify such a treatment of the close to two hundred thousand Ukrainians who live in the city of Moscow, or over a half of million Ukrainians in Moldavia? Long before 1914 Thomas Masaryk argued in the Austrian Reichsrat that if the Czechs were to accept the Austrian Monarchy as their state, they would have to be given an opportunity to feel equally at home in Vienna as in Prague. To deny them their right to live as Czechs outside their own Czech homeland was tantamount to treating them as less than equal citizens of the state.

The possibility of disentangling the bond between nationality and territory (which makes nationality right dependent on one's place of residence) should be **prima facie** attractive to the leaders of the USSR. To accept it, however, would require on their part a renunciation of their present goal of Russification of non-Russians living outside their national territories. It is impossible to foresee whether a refusal to reform their system along the lines suggested by Masaryk will cause any political difficulties. At any rate, it seems reasonable to suppose that it makes it difficult for Ukrainians to view the USSR as a country in which they are at home everywhere, even though their numbers and relatively wide despersion through the USSR would make it quite practicable to grant them the status of an "all-Union" nationality, which now only Russians possess everywhere — and notable in Ukraine.

FOOTNOTES

1. See "Two Estonian Memoranda to the United Nations," **Baltic News**, 1974, No. 5, p. 2.

2. V.V. Pokshishevskii, "Etnicheskie protsessy v gorodakh SSR i nekotorye problemy ikh izucheniia," **Sovetskaia etnigrafia**, 1969, No. 5, p. 6.

3. John A. Armstrong, "The Ethnic Scene in the Soviet Union: The View of the Dictatorship," **Ethnic Minorities in the Soviet Union**, ed. by Erich Goldhagen (New York: Praeger 1968), pp. 14-21, 32.

4. For the problem of territorial delimitation of Ukraine during 1917-1921, see **Ukraine: A Concise Encyclopaedia**, ed. by V. Kubijovyc, vol. I (Toronto: University of Toronto Press 1963), pp. 797 and 735. See op. cit., p. 811 for the figures indicating the percentage of the Ukrainians in the population of major cities of Ukraine in 1923 and 1933. The ratio of Ukrainians in those cities during the revolution may be presumed to have been lower.

5. The boundaries of Ukraine in the 18th and 17th centuries are presented on the maps on p. 653 and between pp. 642-643 of **Ukraine: A Concise Encyclopaedia**, vol. I.

6. A. Hirshfel'd, **Migratsiini protsesy na Ukraini (v svitli perepysu 1926 r)** (Kharkiv: Derzhvydav "Hospodarstvo Ukrainy," 1930), pp. 81, 86 and 73-74.

7. Hirshfel'd, **op cit.**, p. 82. According to Hirshfel'd's calculations, the number of migrants from the Right-Bank region and Polissia to areas outside Ukraine was 587,849; to other parts of Ukraine — 311,777, but of these only 26,671 had migrated to the Donbas. (**Ibid.**).

8. **Ibid.**, pp. 83 and 87.

9. See, for example, Richard Pipes, **The Formation of the Soviet Union: Nationalism and Communism**, 1917-1923 (New York: Atheneum 1968), p. 149.

10. Robert S. Sullivant, **Soviet Politics and the Ukraine 1917-1957** (New York: Columbia University Press 1963), pp. 296-297.

11. Sullivant, **op. cit.**, p. 300.

12. These calculations are based on table 6 in Roman Szporluk, "The Nations of the USSR in 1970," **Survey**, No. 4 (81), 1971, p.99. The full data are available in **Itogi Vsesoiuznoi perepisi naseleniia 1970 goda**, Vol. IV (Moscow: Statistika, 1973).

13. All calculations relating to the population of Donets'k oblast are based on **Itogi Vsesoiuznoi perepisi naseleniia 1959 goda**, Ukrainian-Skaia SSR (Moscow: Gostatizdat, 1963), table 54, pp. 174 and 180, and **Itogi** 1970, vol. IV, table 8, p. 173.

14. M.V. Kurman, I.V. Lebedinskii, **Naselenie bol'shogo sotsialisticheskogo goroda** (Moscow: Statistika 1968), pp. 121-122.

15. Kurman and Lebedinskii, **op. cit.**, pp. 122-125.

16. **Ibid.**, p. 125.

17. L.N. Chizhikova, "Ob etnicheskikh protsessakh v vostochnykh raionakh Ukrainy (po materialam ekspeditsionnogo obsledovaniia 1966 g.)," **Sovetskaia etnografia**,

1968, No. 1, p. 22.

18. Chizhikova, op. cit., p. 23.

19. Ibid.

20. Ibid., pp. 23-24.

21. It is enough to consult any contemporary document, for example the articles and speeches of Mykola Skrypnyk, in order to learn how common was the opposition to Ukrainianization not only in the predominantly Ukrainian regions of the RSFSR, such as the provinces of Kursk, Voronezh or Stalingrad, or the Kuban' region, but also in the eastern districts of the Ukrainian SSR. See Mykola Skrypnyk, **Statti i promovy z natsional'noho pytannia**, ed. by Iwan Koszaliwec (Munich: Suchasnist' 1974).

22. All these calculations are based on **Itogi 1959 goda, Ukrainskaea SSR**, table 54, p. 180, and **Itogi 1970 goda**, Vol. IV, table 8, p. 187. The following are absolute figures for urban population of Kharkiv oblast in 1959 and 1970 and its Ukrainian and Russian components:

	1959	Native Language		1970	Native Language	
		Ukrainian	Russian		Ukrainian	Russian
Total	1,573,738			1,958,194		
Ukrainian	956,369	772,622	183,699	1,170,648	886,441	284,170
Russian	503,074	5,734	497,317	668,708	6,546	662,122

Of those Russians and Ukrainians whose native language was Russian and Ukrainian respectively in 1970, 522,346 Ukrainians knew Russian, and 201,563 Russians knew Ukrainian.

23. Two Soviet scholars have argued recently that the knowledge of Russian among Moldavians is much wider than indicated by the census. See S.I. Bruk and M.N. Guboglo, "Razvitie i vzaimodeistvie etnodemograficheskikh i etnolingvisticheskikh protsessov v sovetskom obshchestve na sovremennom etape," **Istoriia SSR**, 1974, No. 4, pp. 44.

24. Personal information received by the author. Information contained in issues of **Vechirnyi Kharkiv** in possission of the author.

25. See **Molod' Dnipropetrovs'koho proty rusyfikatsii** (Munich, Suchasnist', 1970); **Ukrayins'kyi visnyk**, No. 6, 1972 (Baltimore: Smoloskyp, 1972); Skrypnyk, **op cit.**

26. Danylo Shumuk, **Za skhidnim obriem** (Baltimore: Smoloskyp, 1974), pp. 440-441.

27. Shumuk, **op cit.**, p. 445.

28. "A Word of the Nation," **Survey**, vol. 17, No. 3 (1971), pp. 196-197. See also Dimitry Pospielovsky, "The Resurgence of Russian Nationalism in Samizdat, "**Survey**, vol. 19, No. 1, 1973, pp. 51-74.

29. V.V. Pokshishevskiy, "Urbanization and Ethnogeographic Processes," **Soviet Geography: Review and Translation**, vol. XIII, No. 2 (February, 1972), pp. 116, 118-119.

30. Chauncy D. Harris, **Cities of the Soviet Union, Studies in Their Functions, Size,**

Density and Growth (Chicago: Rand McNally, 1970), pp. 135 and 134.

31. David Hooson, **The Soviet Union, people and regions** (Belmong, Cal.: Wadsworth 1966), p. 163.

32. David Hooson, "The Outlook for Regional Development in the Soviet Union," **Slavic Review**, vol. 31, No. 3 (September, 1972), p. 540.

33. Hooson, "The Outlook," p. 552. (Emphasis added.) Hooson refers in this connection to Leslie Dienes, "Issues in Soviet Energy Policy and Conflicts Over Fuel Costs in Regional Development," **Soviet Studies**, vol. 23, No. 1 (July, 1971), 26-58.

34. Iakiv Stetsiuk, "Imenyny materi," **Dnipro**, 1969, No. 8, 80-123. For brief biographic data on the writer, see **Literaturna Ukraina**, 15 December, 1972, p. 2, which contains an article by S. Trofymuk in honour of Stetsiuk's fiftieth birthday.

35. Stetsiuk, "Imenyny," pp. 90-93.

36. **Ibid.**, pp. 112-114.

37. **Ibid.**, p. 83.

38. **Ibid.**, p. 95.

39. **Ibid.**

40. One wonders if granting such a status to the Jews, dissociating the availability of national rights from any particular area, would not have made their dissatisfaction less intense and induce some of them at least from seeking to emigrate.

V
Party, State, Society

The Status of the Ukrainian Republic Under the Soviet Federation

by
John N. Hazard
Columbia University

Ukrainian nationalism was a major cause of the formation of the Soviet federation in 1922, and it remains a major reason for expecting that the federation will survive contemporary constitutional reform. If these conclusions prove to be justified, the status of Ukraine in the Soviet federation is prominent indeed: it is the keystone of the arch of fifteen republics forming the federation. It is the bastion resisting pressures for restructuring the Soviet Union as a unitary state.

No one questions either within the Soviet Union or abroad the desire of the founders of the Soviet system of government and of those who perpetuate it today to create a state which will eventually be unitary; in which ethnic hostilities or even loyalties have no place. The Communist Manifesto of 1848 had said very clearly that the workers have no fatherland.[1] Loyalties were to be restructured from those of ethnic origin to those of class affinity. Communists everywhere took the position in 1917 that class had succeeded ethnicity as a basis for cohesion; indeed their attitude had been a primary cause for breaking with the Second International in 1915 to form their own fledgling association in opposition to socialists who put loyalty to the German or French nation above loyalty to the internationalized working class.[2] Out of this beginning was to come the Third International.

When Lenin and his communist colleagues set about creating a new governmental structure for the remnants of the Russian Empire which they controlled, their thought was of a unitary state, but historically oriented ethnic loyalties and animosities forced them to preside over the dismemberment of the former Empire. The Tsarist system had been built upon a policy of "Russification," and the Bolsheviks had played upon the revolutionary sentiments that Russification had created to win friends among the politically unsophisticated masses for their Marxist-oriented cause.

221

Self-determination had become a powerful revolutionary slogan among the minorities of the tottering Russian Empire during World War 1, and the Bolsheviks thought it to their advantage to support the concept not only with words but with deeds. Release of the various ethnic entities on the fringes of the old Russian Empire to go their own way for a time as independent states was Lenin's dramatic manifestation of his party's willingness to follow the route of self-determination.

Tonight's well-informed audience needs no extended development of the historical events between November 7, 1917 and December 30, 1922 when Soviet federation became a legal reality. The facts are well known, but the thinking of the communists who played a part in the process deserves brief resume because it bears directly upon the development of the federation in the fifty-two years since its proclamation and upon the likely structure of the Soviet state as it emerges from the constitutional drafting committee currently at work.

Richard Pipes' classic history of the evolution of the federation of 1922 makes clear the role of Ukrainian communists in the formative years.[3] They hoped to bring about the eventual unification of peoples which the 1848 Manifesto envisaged, but they had increasing doubts about the good will of their Russian colleagues. This led them by 1922 to pass a resolution on October 3, 1922 categorically demanding the preservation of Ukrainian independence and the establishment of relations within the R.S.F.S.R. on the basis of principles formulated by what was called the Frunze commission during the previous May.[4] Pipes tells us that the resistance of the Ukrainian communists to Stalin's draft of a plan of federation grew out of a perception in 1922 of a growing new Russian bureaucracy and the personal ascendancy of Stalin and his coterie.[5] Mykola Skrypnyk, who had become the chief spokesman for Ukrainian grievances, was in Pipes' view convinced that nationalism was a legacy of capitalism, but he was dismayed by its persistence under communism among the Russians and in their extraordinary Georgian spokesman, Joseph Stalin.[6] Skrypnyk had concluded during the discussion of the nationality question at the Eleventh Communist Party Congress in March of 1922 that a powerful faction of the Russian apparatus actually wanted to liquidate his Republic.[7]

Roy Medvedev now tells us that the Skrypnyk-Stalin split dates from a telegram of April 4, 1919 when Stalin wired, "Enough playing at a government and a republic. It's time to drop that game; enough is enough."[8] Skrypnyk had responded in a telegram to the Party in Moscow, saying, "Declarations like that of Commissar Stalin would destroy the Soviet regime in Ukraine . . . They are direct assistance to enemies of the Ukrainian toiling masses."

Lenin had to intervene in 1918 and again in 1922 to prevent an outright break. Pipes indicates that Lenin saw in 1922 that Stalin's draft was undoing the edifice he had built, and on which he relied to mollify and neutralize the nationalist sentiments of the minorities.[9] He summoned Stalin and called for a new federation with a separate government, above the R.S.F.S.R., to be called the "U.S.S.R. of Europe and Asia." This concession was notable because the Ukrainian communists had been prepared at the outset of the Soviet regime to look toward entry into the R.S.F.S.R. itself as soon as the hostility of the masses could be overcome to reunion with the Russians. Pipes reports that the Kharkív Bolsheviks on March 6, 1918 had issued a press editorial saying, "Economically our basin is connected with the Petrograd Republic; politically it is also more convenient for us to join the Russian federation . . . "[10]

Even the General Secretariat of the Ukrainian Central Rada had declared its desire on November 3, 1917 (o.s.) to remain a part of the Federal Russian Republic, denying any striving for independence, despite the Bolshevik coup in Russia.[11] On November 6, 1917 it issued a proclamation that Ukraine was a People's Republic and a component part of the Russian Federation. Within a few weeks the Rada changed its mind because it thought the Bolsheviks trying to Russify Ukraine by establishing the rule of the essentially non-Russian cities over the Ukrainian countryside through convocation of an All-Ukrainian Congress of Soviets which the urbanites could be expected to dominate.[12]

This series of events suggests that the Ukrainians of all socialist persuasions were at the outset of the Russian revolution prepared to join with the Russians in a structure, which although called a "federation," offered few concessions to nationalism, and that they as proletarians anticipated that the leadership would be organized democratically so as to give the Ukrainian communists their fair share of the posts in policy-making and administration. Only when it became evident that the Russians were assuming a dominant and partisan position, did they turn against the plan and begin to assert the right to representation on a basis that would assure local self-government and a definite proportion of places in the apparatus of the central government.

This reversal of an attitude originally favouring denationalization of politics and the advent of working class internationalism worked its way even into the Communist Party structure, where there had been common agreement since the split with the Bund back in 1903 that nationalism had no place at all. Pressure for a federal structure of the Party began to mount in 1919, and was met by a provision in the Program of 1919 denoucing the idea of independence for the Communist Parties functioning within the various republics, although the Party acknowledged that the independence of state units as republics was to be fostered at the time. [13]

It is this Party Program of 1919 which has intrigued Leonard Schapiro in his classic effort to understand communist attitudes toward national minorities. [14] He notes the Program's reaffirmation of respect for the principle of self-determination but with two qualifications: (1) that respect be manifested only in the shape of a federal union of states as a transitional form on the path to complete unity, and (2) that the question be posed as to what element may be regarded, in any particular case, as the bearer of the will of the nation on the issue of expression of a desire to secede from the federation. Schapiro suggests that outsiders must ponder the Program's emphasis upon the need to ascertain persons qualified to determine popular will relating to state structure, and that the authoritative persons will vary with the historical stage in which they speak. This means that those who may speak during the historical stage of development of a nation, they will not be the same as later. During the formative period they will not be the masses as a whole, for that would be what is called "mathematical democracy." The general public is not yet qualified to choose because it is not yet schooled to understand the historical process and the historical forces at work. Only a vanguard of communists is qualified to choose, since they are what a common law lawyer might call the trustees of the national will.

If this be so, then the basic decision made in 1922 to create the U.S.S.R. could be only that of the vanguard of communists. The dispute was not between two wings of the untutored general public, but between wings of communist thought. The split at this level could not be between a nationalist and an internationalist wing, since no communists could believe in traditional nationalism and continue to hold their Party card. The only permissible basis for split on the Ukrainian issue had to be between communist tactitions, all of whom looked forward to a unitary state to emerge with a full flowering of communism but some of whom already distrusted the Russian communists and their Russified comrades from other national groups as wanting consciously or unconsciously to put the non-Russified communists in the position of wards. In short, there would develop a Russified vanguard of the larger communist vanguard, if the Stalin-led wing were allowed to control the center. Skrypnyk and his colleagues looked upon this possibility as fatal to achievement of the non-nationalist society of their dreams because they saw it as a form of Russification. Perhaps it was less evident than the Russification of the Tsarist past, but it was no less likely to arouse animosity based on still lively fears that the Ukrainians were again to be drowned in a Russian šea.

Fortunately for the Ukrainian communists, Lenin saw things their way, and Stalin was leashed, but only for the moment. The tide was to turn, and Stalin could name Lazar Kaganovich General Secretary of the Ukrainian Communist Party. Stephen F. Cohen tells us that only in July 1928 were the Ukrainian communists able to express themselves sufficiently strongly to force the termination of Kaganovich's three-year tyranny in Kharkiv, but again Stalin had the last word, for he controlled the allocation of resources. He saw to it that Ukrainians were denied some of the New capital construction which they wanted. [15]

Stalin's heavy hand was felt most strongly during the Great Purge when the leadership of the Ukrainian Party was decimated along with that of the Belorussian and Polish Parties. Finally, in 1938 all three Parties were dissolved. [16] The abnormal period of the War for the Fatherland with its revelation of conflicting loyalties was followed by Stalin's reassertion of his line on national subordination. He reappointed Kaganovich as First Secretary of the Ukrainian Party for a nine month period in 1947; months which Roy Medvedev calls the "black days" of Ukraine, [17] and he accused writers and Party officials of nationalism, an unjustified charge in Medvedev's view. [18] In retaliation, according to Medvedev, there reemerged a revival of nationalist feelings which had almost vanished in the 1930's. [19]

Adam Ulam concludes that in the period since the end of World War II, the process of Russification of national cultures and indoctrination of the youth in the primacy of, and indissoluble union with, the Russian nation has been especially pronounced. [20] He doubts, however, that such indoctrination can be effective except in the case of small, until recently, primitive tribes or smaller nations. He expects the indoctrinators to be less than efficacious when dealing with national groups like the Ukrainians and Turkic peoples because they number in the millions.

To test the potential of the center's current campaign for unity, we must await Dr. Birch's discussion when he treats the sources of current dissidence. One cannot but wonder in the light of what has gone before whether Ukrainians today resist the Russians because of disillusionment among Ukrainian communists with the internationalist plank of their faith's platform, hoping that they can bring the Russian communists to their senses, or whether they have given up all expectation of reform. Is their opposition built, like Skrypnyk's upon the premise that faith in communism is well founded? Is their complaint only that those who profess to lead from Moscow need to be cautioned lest they attempt to leap prematurely into the promised unitary society.

If we take as evidence the record set forth by Konstantyn Sawczuk in his review of the 1971 "Ukrainian Jurists' Case," the protest is not based on a rejection of communism and a desire to return to capitalism. [21] The seven Ukrainian intellectuals who were the defendants professed to be Marxist-Leninists, driven to despair by what they saw to be discrimination against Ukraine. Their despair led them to think of a campaign to win fellow Ukrainians to the view that only a fresh start would save the situation, and this would require recognition of their right to secession. The U.S.S.R. constitution permits secession, and so they sought to exercise what they thought to be a constitutional right.

These jurists were accused of violating the Ukrainian criminal code's provision on "treason," as a deed intentionally committed to the detriment of territorial inviolability (Art. 64). Sawczuk tells us that in his view Art. 56 of the criminal code is unconstitutional since secession is permitted by the constitution, and it necessarily involes dismemberment of the territory of the Union. This argument was rejected by the court, making the case a juridical puzzle in Sawczuk's view, unless one accepts the view that the constitution is not the law.

From what has been said earlier, it may be seen that the issue is not new. Communists have long argued that not everyone is qualified to express the will of the people, much less to try to create a desire on the part of the people for secession. Only the vanguard may speak, and only the vanguard may prepare the public to take a position. If the constitution be read in this light, the criminal code is compatable with the constitution, for the code is directed against the non-vanguard elements, whether communist-oriented or not.

Reference to the constitution and law reminds me that our organizers have asked for a discussion of the law of the federation. Some of you may be saying that I have avoided my duty up to now by travelling a side road leading into history, personalities and communist philosophy. I have postponed intentionally the moment of legal provisions until something could be said about background, for like Valery Chalidze, writing in his recent book, [22] I do not believe that Soviet law can be examined meaningfully apart from background. Chalidze says that the lawyer must always consider the Communists Party's leadership role in the functioning of the state. Surely, if this be so, and probably all of us here would agree that it is, one cannot consider the right of secession as set forth in the Ukrainian and U.S.S.R.'s constitutions without examing the communist position on the exercise of this right.

If one traces the statements on the subject coming from communist mouths over many years, one finds an unbroken line of explanations, summarized by Merle Fainsod in his noted treatise, [23] and this line indicates that secession is a right which must always be examined in the light of the purpose for which secession is sought. If it is to permit a people to slip back into the epoch from which the have been lifted by a socialist-oriented revolution, the Communist Party is obligated to do what it can to prevent the reversion. Given the paragraph in the Party Rules requiring the convening of a Party caucus in any group in which Party members find themselves, it can be presumed that opponnents of the party line would have a nearly impossible task in winning the group for a vote on secession.

In view of the influence Party members are supposed to have upon the formulation of opinion, the "Ukrainian Jurists' Case" suggests that there has been a breakdown in Ukraine. When the Prosecutor has to step in to prevent proposals for secession, especially among Marxist-Leninists, who must know the history of the Party's position on the subject, faith in Party leadership must have fallen to a low point. The "Jurists" must have concluded that the central Party apparatus and its Ukrainian colleagues had betrayed its trust. Like Tito, the "Jurists" must have thought that there can be quite different roads to socialism, and when the road prescribed by the center is evidently irresponsible, Ukrainian communists should be permitted to strike out on their own.

I am also reluctant to enter upon a discussion of legal formalities concerning federation since Konstantyn Sawczuk has already put a finetooth comb through the law of the subject in his effort to determine whether Ukraine is sovereign and independent, and concluded that it is hard to find it so. [24] Also I have already tried myself here in Canada to consider the relationship of republics to the Soviet federation and to point out how different it is from anything known in Canada or the United States. [25]

To a notable degree the Soviet federation reflects two major features of difference from the two great federations of North America. One is the determination of the Soviet Communist Party leadership to look upon federation as a transitional form on the road to ultimate unity. The other is the monistic economy of socialism which is conceived in terms of centralized planning, centralized administration, and centralized taxation. Decentralization occurs only when the center thinks it desirable for the sake of efficiency, or when there is very strong opposition to centralized direction in a given field, as in primary education.

The will of Soviet communists is, therefore, more important than the legal form of centralism, since the second is but the reflection of the first. If one believes that federation is but a compromise to be overcome as the public learns that compromises are undesirable in the long run, then one centralizes power, both as to decision-making and as to administration as fast as circumstances permit, i.e., as fast as possible without stimulating animosities. Retreat may become necessary, as contemporary Ukrainian communists are sometimes arguing because the centralizing process is pursued too swiftly for a Ukrainian populace still fearful of Russification. The center may have to admit more Ukrainians to the decision-making circle at the center, but such a step is seen as a retreat, and not merely as a revision of a strategic program.

Any apparent decentralization so long as it requires no sharp reversal becomes one of administrative convenience. This is what motivated Nikita Khruschchev's Sovnarkhoz pattern of industrial administration in 1957. This is what seems to have motivated the Moldavian experiment in agricultural administration in 1973. Neither was a grassroots desire to assert a measure of independence, and to conduct an economy as an ethnic minority might wish. Both experiments were subject to centralized inspiration, guidance and control. The ethnic unit was only a laboratory for an experiment, not a people seeking its own way of self-expression.

The legal charter of the republics is Article 14 of the U.S.S.R. constitution. It is here that the reader can find the statement of division of powers between federation and republics. Scholars can and do prepare tables showing how much or how little authority the republics have retained. It is here that socialism plays its part for the division of powers places in the federation the right to determine the course of the economy, and in the absence of pluralism in the ownership of productive wealth, there can be no challenge to the federation's decisions by local producers. It is in this article that one also finds the law making authority of the republics. Currently, each may draft its own codes but they must conform to fundamental principles established by the federal Supreme Soviet.

In a measure, it can be interesting to follow the fluctuations in apparent republic power as evidenced in the right to draft codes of law. One moves from the pre-1923 period when republics were their own bosses, although they often cast an eye to the R.S.F.S.R. for guidance. One moves on the the first federal constitution when the codification process was left with the republics, but subject to a new requirement that these codes conform to such federal principles as might be enacted. Then comes the second federal constitution which placed all code-making authority in the federal Supreme Soviet; an authority which was never exercised because of the advent of the second World War. Then follows amendment to restore the situation of the first constitution, so that codes are again republic in origin, but subject to federal determination of fundamental principles. This federal authority, unlike that of 1923, has been exercised in every field so that Soviet law is today essentially federally directed.

Ziguars L. Zile has examined the republic criminal codes to determine the extent of variation. He finds it only in detail. [26] Increasingly large portions of each code are made to conform to the federal fundamentals. This discovery need not necessarily mean that the republics, including Ukraine, have no input into the formulation of laws. Back in the formative years of Soviet law Ukrainian scholars took pride in innovating and in the fact that Russian codifiers often followed their lead. [27] Some of this seems to follow even today, and Ukrainian law professors argue in conversation that Ukrainian scholars wield considerable influence among their colleagues from other republics when drafts are considered before the formulation of fundamentals. Certainly the procedures established for the preparation of drafts, calling as they do for meetings of republic scholars to discuss desirable changes in the law, give the republics a formal share in the drafting process. Whether Ukrainians avail themselves of the opportunity or sit silently in the meetings we do not know. We can but hope that eventually our Soviet colleagues will satisfy our curiosity by giving us the inside story.

The centralizing role of the federal courts has also been examined elsewhere to determine whether the U.S.S.R.'s Supreme Court is following the same path as the Canadian and United States Supreme Courts in unifying the law through interpretation. [28] The conclusion seems impelling that such centralization has occurred because the U.S.S.R. Supreme Court has been interpreting not only federal statutes and federal fundamental principles but also codes of the republics for which there are no underlying federal fundamentals to which conformity is required. The U.S.S.R. Supreme Court in some cases seems to be exercisng a unifying function as a central court presiding over the practice of republic courts, notably by establishing what might be called a standard of "due process of law" for which there is no specific constitutional authority.

It is time to turn to the constitutional revision of the federal constitution of 1936 which is currently in progress. General Secretary Brezhnev told the XXIV Communist Party Congress in 1971 of the Politburo's plans for reform. He even set a loose timetable, calling for presentation to the XXV Communist Party Congress, which should be held in 1976 if the Party Rules are respected. The key words in his report were that there will be "new steps . . . along the path of the further gradual drawing together of the nations and nationalities of our country." [29]

What do Brezhnev's words mean for the federal structure? Perhaps nothing, but the words were spoken on the occasion of the 59th anniversary of the federation. At that time the Party's anniversary resolution was instructing Party workers to arrange in celebration for emphasis upon the "further growing together of all socialist nations as a benefit to all aspects of life in Soviet society." In Soviet parlance the republics are the formal manifestations of the various nations who live together in the U.S.S.R. Presumably, a growing together of nations would bring the republics into a new relationship. It might eliminate them altogether and usher in the unitary state of communist dreams.

Regrettably we on the outside cannot get enough information on the work of the drafting commission to predict with accuracy what is likely to happen to the federal structure. The drafting of any legislation in the U.S.S.R. is always confidential until the Party has approved a preliminary draft for presentation to public discussion. Such public discussion is promised for the future, but the moment of revelation has not come, nor has the timing of discussion and adoption been established. We know that the drafting process is continuing, for Soviet newspapers and periodicals tell us so. As recently as December 5, 1973, on the anniversary of the promulgation of the 1936 constitution, a **Pravda**, editorial restated that ". . . as is known, a new draft text of the U.S.S.R. Constitution is now being worked out . . ." [30]

The explanations of what is before the draftsmen suggest that there is a division of opinion among the specialists planning for the future constitution. An author in **Voprosy Istorii** has summarized the early reaction to the XXIV Congress's order on convergence of nations and has taken to task most of the interpreters. [31] Apparently, there was misunderstanding among even top Party officials, especially in Ukraine as to what convergence meant for the future of the republics. We read that at the April 1973 plenum of the Central Committee of the Communist Party of Ukraine, its participants severely condemned manifestations of national vanity and ethnocentrism on the part of leading personnel. This can only mean that some high Party personages had taken a position reminiscent of Skrypnyk's decades ago and had expressed fears for the future of the republic.

Perhaps these "manifestations" had been stimulated by alarmist reporting of what convergence was to mean for the Ukrainians, for in a Kyiv publication of 1970 to which the historian refers, one B. A. Martynenko is said to have written, "The progress of convergence contains as much joy as bitterness: in one way or another it violates the holy values of the national spirit, and, clashing with the conservatism of national consciousness, proceeds in a manner that is not painless, not without resistance and zigzags." [32] This statement is hardly clear, but it suggests that convergence had been interpreted by some Ukrainians as bringing an end to their nation.

The Ukrainians seem not to have been alone in expressing fears, for an Erevan author is quoted as having gone so far as to argue dialectically that the process of convergence and merging of nations would lead to the negation of the flourishing of nations. [33] His Moscow critic agrees that flourishing and convergence are indeed in dialectical opposition, but he argues that a nonnational communist culture will occur only "after the triumph of communism all over the world." In other words, the nation will pass away, but not soon. Ukrainian and other nationalists are wooed with the thought that their future is to be a long one, since world-wide communism is still remote.

For the Moscow historian convergence is only a "tendency," which has in his view a leading role to play, but flourishing of cultures will continue, stimulated by economic betterment which is the result of cooperation on the economic front between the nations. This is expected to enrich the entire material and spiritual life of each nation and bring nations closer together. This repeats the familiar argument that it is poverty that causes national rivalries, and that when all are satisfied, there will be no national sentiments, no conflicts, and no need for the compromises which the republic structures were designed to foster.

Translated into terms which are familiar to lawyers, the issues can be raised around the word "sovereignty." How much sovereignty will the republics retain as the sovereignty of the central government is enhanced in the process of the convergence of nations? Years ago a Soviet lawyer argued that the sovereignty of the republics is enhanced by the very existence of the federation. [34] He refused to accept the view that as the sovereignty of the federation was increased by extensions of federal power that there must be a corresponding decrease in the sovereignty of the republics. This was to him a false application of the principle of equivalents, of the principle which calls for the emptying of one bottle as the other is filled.

The same argument has been repeated by the Moscow historian, for he says that as the wealth of a republic is increased through cooperation with other republics in the federation, its sovereignty is increased because it has more choices before it. Impoverished peoples have few choices; wealthy ones have many. It is not too hard to understand the argument because it is made by many in the West in support of a stronger United Nations. When Eastern European statesmen argue that a strong world government will reduce the sovereignty of its members, proponents of such a government have long argued that the existence of a world free of war and with a strong economy will help all nations by increasing the opportunities open to them. In brief, they will have more choices and greater sovereignty than before.

What does convergence mean for Ukraine in view of these arguments? The Moscow historian says that "nations will remain even after communist society has been built," but there will be complete social homogeneity and a high level of communist consciousness, the complete triumph of the ideology of internationalism. He is even prepared to coin a new word to describe these nations. It is "semi-nations." He anticipates that the process of transition from a society of national differences to one in which these differences are absent will not reduce national cultures to "some gray and faceless level identical for all," but that the best of each national culture will be merged in a culture common to all. Perhaps his comparison to colours can be extended to suggest that the end product will not be gray and faceless but multi-coloured and multi-faced like a great Asian multitude gathered to hear their leader, each wearing traditional garb and each with his own physiognamy but all united in one brotherhood and recognizing one source of inspiration.

With convergence there will be the matter of language, for what will the individuals in the multitude speak? Students of nationalist movements know that there is no subject that arouses such conflict as language unification. Stalin suggested in 1930 that eventually one language will emerge from the encouragement given all languages by the state. He believed this to be the result of the dialectical process. Adam Ulam tells us that Stalin changed this view in his notable comment on linguistics, [35] but the original 1930 idea seems still to pervade Soviet thinking, albeit with a variation. Authors now anticipate that a language of general communication must necessarily emerge to provide a basis for general communication of all nations within the U.S.S.R., and this will be Russian. It will become the language of fraternal collaboration and mutual aid. It is not, however, to eliminate the languages of the other nations, but, perhaps, like Swahili in East Africa or Wolof in Senegal, Russian will be only a lingua franca, and the national languages will continue to be used in the home and as a medium of literary expression.

The legal structure to be created by the new constitution has been the subject of an article written by two senior law professors of the Academy of Sciences of the U.S.S.R., namely V. F. Kotok and N. P. Farberov. [36] While dating from mid-1973, it remains the only legal treatment of the impact of current political thinking upon the draft. The startling feature of the article is absence of any comment on the impact of the convergence discussion upon the federal structure. Except for a few words on the tasks facing Soviet society, as including "a constant convergence of classes, social groups, nations and nationalities, the strengthening of the social and political unity of the Soviet people on the basis of the communist ideals of the working calss and the cultivation of a communist social consciousness in all Soviet people," there is no hint as to what will come. One wants to know whether the Council of Nationalities will remain a separate chamber of the Supreme Soviet; whether the republics will lose their current right to enact codes of law; whether the main burden of criminal prosecution and civil litigation will remain in the courts of the republics or pass to new federal inferior courts; whether economic planning and administration will pass to economic regional directorates divorced completely from republic governments.

Albert Boiter in a perceptive analysis for Radio Liberty [37] of the Kotok-Farberov article thought that the present boundaries between union republics and autonomous national regions would become less meaningful and perhaps eliminated altogether in a new redistricting of the country along the lines of economic regions. He went further to suggest that it was unlikely that the right of secession of republics from the federation would be stated at all. If one with Boiter's access to Eastern European thinking could make such predictions, those of us who are more distant must take them into consideration.

In the absence of other articles to suggest what may be done in these areas of federal-republic concern, it is hard to test Boiter's thesis. Perhaps he is supported in some measure by a paper by V. S. Shevtsov, published some months after the Kotok-Farberov study. [38] He was considering the national question, and especially the right of secession. Shevtsov repeats the familiar line that the exercise of self-determination, which if it were to occur in the U.S.S.R. would open the possibility of secession, must be subordinated to the creation of the necessary democratic precondition for the solution of the task. Shevtsov seems to be restating the rule that the untutored population cannot be permitted by communists to demand independence if it would mean reversion to a system which is less socially progressive on the Marxist-continuum of historical epochs. The proponents of secession would have to argue that the communist party had become revisionist, while those seeking to secede wanted to do so in order to be free to return to an orthodox position. Of course, the dissenters from the majority would have a hard time exercising their right of secession in a federation where the other republics were willing to take up arms to prevent it, unless the armed services of the federation were won over because of some currently unthinkable appeal to the position of some ethnic minority.

A signed article in **Pravda** on June 22, 1972 may have been designed to calm the fears of ethnic minorities lest they mount to unmanageable majorities. The author criticized authors "who are in a hurry to throw the national element overboard as something that from their standpoint is archaic." [39] To this author "the nations, as they assimilate general features, will retain their specific features for a long time to come," and, "the Party . . . is striving to make full use of and improve the forms of national statehood of the U.S.S.R.'s people."

In the light of these published explanations it can be surmised that the U.S.S.R. will remain "federal" in form. It is hard to imagine that there will not be continuing recognition in the Supreme Soviet of ethnic differences, although this recognition might be provided in some different way, as, for example, including within a unicameral Supreme Soviet deputies chosen by the various ethnic units to represent them directly. It is unlikely that economic planning will cut increasingly across republic boundaries, and these regional economic boundaries used for planning purposes may no longer amount to no more than groupings of republics according to their economic concerns. It is possible that an economic region's boundary might split Ukraine or Belorussia. This does not mean, however, that there would no longer be a Ukrainian republic on the map for cultural reasons.

Everything suggests that cultural specificities will be respected in the future; that music, art, drama, literature, and even language will be encouraged in all their ethnic variation, although there will be increasing emphasis upon the desirability of learning Russian as a means of inter-communication between peoples. Whether a youth must become "Russified" to the point that his natal language fades away and his native culture a subject for no more than lip service is hard to predict. John Armstrong tells us that the Ukrainians in the central Party and state apparatus have already become "Russified."[40] If this becomes evident to able and ambitious youngsters as necessary to advancement, it can be expected that many will "Russify" themselves. This has happened in many lands where the central government is in the hands of a dominant majority culture group. Education will play the key role here, for the schools play the basic role in acculturation, and there is already an increasing expansion of schools where Russian is the language of instructions.

Communists are having to admit the existence of what is being called outside the communist world "national communism," and this exists in spite of doctrinal strictures against such a concept. While Soviet leaders seem to have reconciled themselves to various roads to socialism in Eastern Europe, there is not likely to be such a novel development in Ukraine. The peoples of all of the republics of the U.S.S.R. are being held to one uniformly defined road to socialism, but this does not mean that the Ukrainian republic is to become in the foreseeable future no more than an administrative region like Krasnoyarsk oblast. I suspect that there are distinctions, and that the time is not yet ripe for the assimilation of the Ukrainian Republic in law as well as in culture with the peoples of the Soviet Union in some new homogenized unitary society and government.[42]

FOOTNOTES

1. Section II.

2. All Soviet histories of the Communist Party indicate that the prupose of the 1915 meeting was to convince socialists that to defend the father-land was to defend the bourgeoisie and the autocracy. See **History of the Communist Party (Bolsheviks). Short Course,** New York, 1939. p. 166.

3. Richard Pipes, **The Formation of the Soviet Union. Communism and Nationalism 1917-1923.** Revised edition. Cambridge, Mass. 1964.

4. **Ibid.** p. 272.

5. **Ibid.** p. 263.

6. **Ibid.** p. 266.

7. **Ibid.** p. 265.

8. Roy Al Medvedev, **Let History Judge. The Origins and Consequences of Stalinism.** New York, 1973. p. 16.

9. **Op. cit., supra,** note 3 at p. 273.

10. **Ibid.,** p. 130.

11. **Ibid.,** p. 115.

12. **Ibid.,** p. 117.

13. **Ibid.,** p. 244.

14. Leonard Schapiro, **The Communist Party of the Soviet Union.** New York, 1964. p. 222.

15. Stephen F. Cohen, **Bukharin and The Bolshevik Revolution. A Political Biography 1888-1938.** New York, 1973. p. 326.

16. **Op. cit., supra,** note 8 at p. 219.

17. **Ibid.,** p. 480.

18. **Ibid.,** p. 484.

19. **Ibid.,** p. 493.

20. Adam B. Ulam, **The Russian Poltical System.** New York, 1974. p. 74.

21. Konstantyn Sawczuk, "Opposition in the Ukraine: Seven versus the Regime," **Survey,** Vol. 20, No. 1 (90) pp. 36-46 (Winter, 1974).

22. Valery Chalidze, **Prava cheloveka i sovetskii soiuz.** New York, 1974, p. 7.

23. Merle Fainsod, **How Russia is Ruled.** Cambridge, Mass. 1963, pp. 55-59.

24. Konstantyn Sawczuk, "Ukraine: A Sovereign and Independent State: A Juridical Approach," **The Ukrainian Quarterly**, Vol. 29, No. 3, pp. 237-257. (Autumn, 1973).

25. John N. Hazard, "Fifty Years of the Soviet Federation," **Canadian Slavonic Papers**, Vol. XIV, ppl. 586-609 (1972).

26. Adolf Sprudz and Armin Rusis, editors. **Res Baltica: A Collection of Essays in Honour of the Memory of Dr. Alfred Bilmanis.** Leiden, 1968. pp. 152-159.

27. For recognition of Ukrainian initiative, see N. I. Avdeenko and M. A. Kabakova, "Grazhdanskoe Protsessual'noe Pravo," pub. in 40 **let sovestkogo prava.** Leningrad, 1957, Vol. I, p. 653, Footnote 36. The Ukrainian decree initiating the NEP preceded that of the RSFSR by over one month. See decree of April 19, 1921 (1921) I. Sob. Uzak. Uk. No. 7, item 193, and decree of May 24, 1921 (1921) I Sobr. Uzak, RSFSR, No. 40, item 212.

28. **Op. cit., supra,** note 25 at pp. 600-02.

29. For English translation of Brezhnev's speech, see **Current Digest of the Soviet Press,** XXIII, No. 14 (1971) p. 3.

30. For English translation of the editorial, see **Ibid,** XXV, No. 49 (1974), p. 7.

31. I. P. Tsamerian, **Voprosy istorii KPSS,** 1973, No. 8, translated as "Certain Theoretical Problems in the Leninist Nationality Policy of the CPSU," **Soviet Law and Government,** XXII, No. 4 (Spring, 1974), p. 3.

32. Cited by Tsamerian as B. A. Martynenko, "Metodologicheskie voprosy dialektiki natsional'nogo i internatsional'nogo," in **Natsional'noe i internatsional'noe v zhizni naroda. Materialy Mezhrepublikanskoi nauchoi konferentsii.** Issue I. Kyiv, 1970. P. 127.

33. Cited by Tsamerian, as G. S. Agadzhanian, **K voprosu o prirode i perspektivakh razvitiia sotsialisticheskikh natsii v SSSR.** Erevan, 1972, p. 156.

34. See B. L. Manelis, "The unity of sovereignty of the USSR and of the union republics," **Sovetskoe Gosudarstvo i Pravo,** No. 7 (Juoy, 1964), pp. 17.

35. See **Op. cit., supra,** note 20 at p. 71, footnote 2.

36. **Sovetskoe Gosudarstvo i Pravo,** No. 6 (June, 1973), pp. 3-12. English translation in **Soviet Law and Government** XII, No. 3 (Winter, 1973-74), pp. 3-20, and **The Soviet Review,** XV, No. 1 (Spring, 1974), pp. 3-20. Also abstracted in **Current Digest of the Soviet Press,** XXV, No. 49 (1974) pp. 7-8.

37. Contrary to general practice this dispatch in the regular series of Radio Liberty dispatches bears no identifying date. It appeared in the autumn of 1973.

38. V. S. Shevtsov, "Natsional'nyi suverenitet: soderzhanie i politiko-pravovoe znachenie," **Sovetskoe Gosudarstvo i Pravo,** No. 12 (December, 1973) pp. 11-18.

39. E. Bagramov, "Drawing Together of Nations Is a Law of Communist Construction, **Pravda,** June 22, 1972. pp. 2-3. English translation in **Current Digest of the Soviet Press,** XXIV, No. 25 (1972) pp. 10-11.

40. John A. Armstrong, **Ideology, Politics and Government in the Soviet Union: An**

Introduction. Third Edition. New York, 1974. p. 177.

41.   Svetlana Alliluyeva, **Twenty Letters to a Friend**, New York, 1967. p. 67.

42.   Cf. "Editorial: Fifty Years of the U.S.S.R.: An Anniversary of Fraud and Deceit," **The Ukrainian Quarterly**, Vol. 29, No. 1 (Spring, 1973) pp. 5-11 and **Ibid.**, No. 2 (Summer, 1973), pp. 158, 163.

Comments on Professor J. N. Hazard The Status of the Ukrainian Republic Under the Soviet Federation

W.S. Tarnopolsky
York University

The problem I as a lawyer have in commenting on a paper outlining "The Status of the Ukrainian Republic Under the Soviet Federation" is that I agree totally with Professor Hazard's thesis, found at the halfway point in his paper, that "the lawyer must always consider the Communist Party's leadership role in the functioning of the state," and that "the will of Soviet communists is ... more important than the legal form of centralism." In the first half of his paper Professor Hazard did not travel "a side road into history, personalities and communist philosophy," it is the only road to an understanding of the constitution of the U.S.S.R.

We must remember that a written Constitution is only a piece of paper unless the sovereign power in the state, be it Parliament, as in the U.K., or the courts and the legislature and the executive as in the U.S., or the military rulers as in Chile, intend it to be binding. It is not the written Constitution of the U.S.S.R. nor, as in Canada or the U.S., the decisions of any Supreme Court that one looks to for guidance, but rather to a body not even mentioned in the Soviet Constitution, i.e., the C.C. of the C.P.S.U. and, more particularly, one looks to the current "Spokesman," whether it be Lenin or Stalin or Khruschchev, or Brezhnev and Kosygin. As Humpty Dumpty said, "When I use a word, it means just what I choose it to mean — neither more nor less".

Thus, an understanding of history and personalities and Communist philosophy is fundamental. Here I must on the whole defer to the far greater expertise of others at this conference for comments on the first half of Professor Hazard's paper. I must, however, make some reference to this part.

Without picking out a particular sentence or paragraph, may I make this general comment that I think Professor Hazard gives too much credit for the formation of the federation in 1922 to Ukrainian Communists and too little to the force of Ukrainian Nationalism. To some extent I believe this is a result of relying almost totally upon

235

Richard Pipes' study. His is "a classic history," but there are other views, and one need only refer to Lawrynenko's bibliography to see that there are other views. But even Pipes makes it clear that the Ukrainian Communist Party (one should say parties, as there was more than one) had to be brought into Ukraine in the saddle bags of the Soviet central forces thrice in two years. Moreover, not even an old Ukrainian Bolshevik like Skrypnyk, was ever First Secretary (the first was in 1953), and at all times non-Ukrainians occupied key positions in the Ukrainian Party and government. Furthermore, by 1922, what few Ukrainians there were in the Party were not all long-time Communists. Some had just defected from the Social Democrats and the Social Revolutionists. And, no doubt, as in any political system anywhere, some were just opportunists. All of them put together may have had some persuasive effect in making Lenin and the Russian Communists recognize that the proclaimed right to "self determination" must at least mean local autonomy.

It was not the Ukrainian Communists themselves as much as the surprising upsurge of Ukrainian-ness that finally convinced both the Ukrainian and the Russian Communist. It is true, of course, that some of this Ukrainian-ness arose in reaction to the not-surprising "Great Russian Chauvinism" which still permeated the Russian Communist party, as it has all Russian political parties.

It is on this point that I find the Pipes' study somewhat silent, and it is perhaps this that makes page four of Professor Hazard's paper somewhat unclear. What is "nationalism?" There is "bourgeois" nationalism and "socialist" nationalism, unacceptable nationalism and acceptable nationalism, Ukrainian nationalism and Great Russian chauvinism. As Chornovil said in his closing statement at his trial on 15 November, 1967:

It seems that I am a nationalist as well. If only it could be established whether I am a bourgeois or, maybe, a socialist one? I did not dwell on the nationalities question in my statements. The conclusion that I am a nationalist has been drawn solely on the basis of the fact that I wrote about violations of legality committed in Ukraine. And if I lived in Tambov and wrote something similar, what kind of nationalist would I be then — a Tambovian one? The procurators in Lviv cannot help dragging nationalism into cases like mine. It seems that in Lviv they see a bourgeois nationalist in every second person.

To return to the point, I think one fails to understand the Central Rada and its socialist leaders, and their motives in 1917 when they spoke of "internationalism" or remaining part of a "federation", just as much as today's authorities in the U.S.S.R. fail to understand the "nationalism" of socialists like Dzyuba or Chornovil, because of a failure to understand that being a "nationalist" does not necessarily mean being a "separatist." (We are only now understanding this in Canada!) In fact, it is rather ironic that Quebec nationalists do not understand the aspirations of Ukrainians better, and Ukrainian-Canadians who look forward to an independent Ukraine are not more sympathetic to Quebec nationalism.

Being a nationalist, to a Ukrainian Socialist in 1917, or to a Soviet Ukrainian today, could mean only the right to use Ukrainian at work, with the government, in the schools, and to have it used by enterprises, by government, by teachers, by the communications media, and in the fine arts, and the right to equality of opportunity while being a Ukrainian. If the only acceptable nationalism is a "Soviet nationalism" which means, as Dzyuba pointed out, "Russification" and the Russians getting all the best or most important positions, then one can see why the Ukrainian socialists of 1917, or the Soviet Ukrainians of recent times, spoke of "internationalism." They did not mean de-nationalization in terms of language and culture loss leading to homogenization and loss of control of one's destiny.

I hope I am not unfair to Pipes and Professor Hazard when I suggest that they do not understand what the Ukrainian socialists of 1917 and the Soviet Ukrainians of today meant by "nationalism" and "internationalism" unless they understand what Dzyuba was talking about:

> For all the great figures of world culture — philosophers, sociologists, historians, writers and artists — this membership of humanity and this work for humanity is inseparable from their memberhsip of their own nation and their work for it. They have all derived their universal humanistic enthusiasm from their highly developed national feeling and national consciousness, without which they did not conceive of genuine internationalism.

This is the important point that the leaders of the Soviet Union have failed, or refused, to grasp from the beginning. Unless they do, "nationalism" and "self-determination" and "federalism" will mean what they say they mean which is that:
1) Ukrainian nationalism is "anti-Soviet agitation and propaganda."
2) "Soviet nationalism" means using Russian in all spheres outside one's home.
3) "Self-determination" is a right to opt into the Socialist (i.e., Communist) sphere, not the right to "opt out," or, as Professor Hazard has described it, a right available only to "the vanguard."
4) "Federalism," to use Professor Hazard's characterization, "is but a compromise to be overcome as the public learns that compromises are undesirable in the long run, then one centralizes power, both as to decision-making and as to administration as far as circumstances permit, i.e., as far as possible without stimulating animosities."

This brings me back again to a consideration of the topic from a legal point of view. First, as to Ukraine's international status. Despite Articles 17 and 18a of the Soviet Constitution, on the right of the Union Republics to secede and to enter into foreign relations, and despite Articles 2, 3, and 4 of the U.N. Charter which speak of the "sovereign equality of all of its members" and of membership being that of "states," Ukraine is not an independent sovereign state. It does not, in fact, conduct its foreign affairs at all, much less independently, and it does not have diplomatic relations with any state, and its membership in the U.N., as Sawczuk points out, is not recognition by other members.

On the other hand, since the Soviet Union wants, and feels it needs, 3 votes rather than 1 in the U.N. and other international organizations, it is not likely to change the Constitution either with respect to Articles 17 or 18a. On this point I do not agree with the reference in the paper to Boiter's comment that this could happen, in the new constitutional revision. These Articles do not mean anything anyway, and the Soviet Union is not likely to risk a challenge in the U.N. to membership of Ukraine and Belorussia by deleting them.

Second, as to Ukraine's status in a federation. The Soviet Constitution for reasons described earlier, is not federal because the position of the C.P.S.U. overrides the Constitution.

Further, even if we take the Constitution at face value, it does not meet the definition of classical federalism, as stated by K.C. Wheare, as we in Canada would understand it, of dividing powers so that the regional and central governments are each, within a sphere, coordinate and independent. It does not matter whether, e.g., the criminal law power is with the regional governments as in the U.S., or with the central government, as in Canada. It does matter, however, whether the central government (or a central authority like the C.P.S.U.), can unilaterally change the coordination at any time. Even apart from the political reality, this is clear from the Constitution itself:
1) Article 146 — amending power in Supreme Soviet of the Union.
2) Article 14 — powers of the Union —
   esp.d) control over observance of the Constitution;
      k) determination of taxes and revenues;
      q) determination of use of mineral wealth, forests and waters;
      r) determination of basic principles in education and public health;

237

u) determination of principles concerning judicial system.
3) Article 20 — supremacy of Union law.
4) Article 49 and Chapter IX — the Praesidium of the U.S.S.R. (49c) gives interpretations of the laws of the U.S.S.R. in operation, whereas the Supreme Court of the U.S.S.R. is nowhere given power to interpret the constitution, but is merely "charged with the supervision of the judicial activities of the judicial organs."

Thus, the U.S.S.R. is no more a "federation" than the Holy Roman Empire was "holy" or "Roman" or an "empire." And Ukraine is not even as independent as Quebec or Hawaii.

Nevertheless, because the U.S.S.R. must keep up on the fiction of independence of the Union Republics if it wants to retain three seats in the U.N., and because, as Adam Ulam points out, as many colonialists have seen, and as Russians of all political persuasions should have realized by now, Russification of a nation of some 40 millions is not going to happen in our millenium except by genocide on a scale that I hope, the present world will not take. In fact, in a world where old-fashioned imperialism is on the retreat, as formerly colonial teritories disappear, I expect that world attention will have to focus on the one area where it is still practised on a large scale in full vigour, i.e., the U.S.S.R.

This brings me to my final point, which is the dilemma faced not only by Russian liberals both within the Soviet Union and without, but by the Soviet authorities themselves. And this is that there will be no civil liberties in the Soviet Union until the Ukrainians disappear as a nation, which is not yet, or until the Soviet Union learns to live with Ukrainian nationalism, even if it is only "socialist" nationalism. There can be no freedom of speech or press or assembly or association in the U.S.S.R. if Ukrainians are not allowed to be Ukrainians. As Valentyn Moroz wrote on May 15, 1968 in a letter to Shelest:

In the centre of the political duel between East and West stands the problem of freedom and the rights of the individual. To persecute a person under these circumstances for the expression of ideas (when the Constitution of the UkrSSR and the Universal Declaration of Human Rights guarantee freedom of speech) means sawing off the branch one is sitting on. In the ideological struggle victory falls not to one who invents more unprintable expressions but to one who opens his sluices to the forces with a future, rather than to those which are dying away.

Will today's Ukrainian communists succeed in finally resurrecting Lenin's policy of Ukrainianization and declare a decisive war against Russian chauvinism in Ukraine? This will determine the success of the ideological struggle with the West. One can proclaim all he likes that the Leninist principles on the national question have been fully revived in Ukraine, but as long as people are prosecuted for their opposition to chauvinism all these professions will be unconvincing. Now there is a new precedent. The communists of Czechoslovakia are demonstrating to the communists of all countries how to jettison what has become ballast and how to open the sluices to those forces which guarantee a future. Will the communists of Ukraine be able to learn this lesson in their own interests?

The National renaissance is today's strongest trend and it is comical to attempt to screen oneself from it with a piece of paper called a verdict. This trend will subside but only when,

Into the open grave will fall
The last chauvinist on the planet.
(Vasyl Symonenko)

The Communist Party of Ukraine After 1966*

by
Yaroslav Bilinsky
University of Delaware

Strange things have been happening to the leaders of the Communist Party of Ukraine (CPU), and the Party as a whole. May 19, 1972 the First Secretary of the CPU Peter Ye. Shelest was abruptly dismissed from his post, so abruptly, in fact, that it surprised the staff of the CPU's Central Committee, the body who had formally elected Shelest First Secretary in July 1963. They heard about the change first in a

* I discussed substantial portions of the paper with Professors Grey Hodnett of York University, Vsevolod Holubnychy, of Hunter College of the City University of New York, and Dr. Myroslav Prokop, of Prolog Research Corporation. Dr. Wasil Hrishko, of Radio Liberty, and Mr. Imre Kardashinetz, of Radio Free Europe, helped me with their rich collection of research memoranda and newsclippings. Professors John A. Armstrong, of the University of Wisconsin, and T. H. Rigby, of the Australian National University, advised me on the intricate question of Party membership. A former Soviet journalist who has recently emigrated from Soviet Ukraine granted me an interview on condition that he remain anonymous. My graduate teaching assistant, Mr. David Sanders, proofread the paper, checked the figures and drew the graphs. At the McMaster University Conference the preliminiary version of the paper was commented upon by Dr. G. Hodnett, the panel chairman, and the two official discussants: Dr. Borys Lewytzkyj, of Munich, Germany, and Professor Jaroslaw Pelenski, of the University of Iowa and the Harvard Ukrainian Research Institute. Mr. Edward Kasinec, Librarian of the Institute, furnished some additional materials, as did Dr. Peter Woroby, of the University of Saskatchewan — Regina. I would like to cordially thank all these persons and to assure them that any possible errors of fact or interpretation are my own.

broadcast of Radio Kyiv. Secretaries of the Ukrainian Provincial (oblast) Party Committees have been purged in turn. Moreover, the total membership of the CPU that had almost doubled under Khrushchev (from over 800,000 full and candidate members in 1956 to almost 1.6 million such members in 1961) and had continued growing at a faster than the All-Union average rate under Brezhnev from 1966 through 1971, in 1972 dropped by 2.2 percent while the All-Union Party on the whole gained 1.3 percent new members (see Table 1, in the Appendix). "Something is rotten in the state of Denmark" (Hamlet, I, iv,90). Or, what is going on in Ukraine?

Too many things have happened which I cannot even mention in this brief study. To answer the question only partially I will trace changes among the top Party cadres of Ukraine from 1966 — the year in which Brezhnev had become firmly established — until the end of 1973, the year in which Shelest's fall was officially confirmed. Changes in the state apparatus of the Ukrainian SSR I will treat much less fully, the Soviet apparatus being of secondary importance only. I will concentrate on the First Provincial Party Secretaries — the systematic information on Party officials below that rank is too difficult to obtain outside the Soviet Union. Occasionally, I will have to go back farther in time and I will also try to be reasonably up-to-date, but in principle the study will begin with the 23rd Congress of the CPU in early 1966 and end with the Party personnel changes in the last months of 1973. But first a brief excusion into theory and then a brief discussion of the membership and composition of the CPU as a whole, for a conceptual and empirical backdrop.

1. A Little Theory

Addressing the second joint colloquium of the Canadian Political Science Association and the Société canadienne de science politique in Quebec City in 1970 on the subject of "Cultural Diversity and Theories of Political Integration" Professor Arend Lijphart said that a "culturally fragmented system" could be integrated through "consociational democracy" or an "overarching co-operation at the elite level."[1] It would seem that Lijphart's proposition could also be applied to non-democratic political systems such as the Soviet Union. To be sure, the Soviet leaders would reject some conditions which make the consociational democratic elite transactions particularly effective such as "a kind of voluntary apartheid policy" in an ethnically divided society or "a multiple balance of power among subcultures" cum individual veto power (is not the Russian subculture already enjoying a clear hegemony in today's USSR? or is, on the contrary, the question not yet finally decided?).[2]

But is not the multi-ethnic Communist Party of the Soviet Union (CPSU) in general and are not its leaders in particular an elite with an overarching interest in holding the country together and in keeping themselves in power, whatever their national origin may be, Russian, Ukrainian, Uzbek, Armenian, or Georgian? The Soviet "new class" with their secret salary supplements, special stores, exclusive doctors, multiple mansions and chauffeured limousines have a vested stake in their comfortable status whether they live in Kyiv or in Moscow.[3] Whatever their nationality, the Shelests, the Mzhavanadzes, and the Rashidovs are widely separated from the common Soviet fellow citizens at whose expense they rule. Power does separate and near absolute power separates almost absolutely.

The fly in the ointment of this "consociational autocracy" — or, possibly, "consociational oligarchy" — is that the individual members of the Soviet Party elite are being kept in circulation by whoever among them reaches the top post. Stalin used to shuffle, reshuffle and them kill; Khrushchev and Brezhnev have not invoked the supreme sanction but have moved their subordinates around too though Brezhnev has so far used this weapon much less often than did Khrushchev, not to speak of Stalin. Within the Soviet Party elite there is an everlasting, almost artificial conflict,[4] whereas in a consociational democratic élite a live and let live accommodation would have been reached. To achieve if only a modicum of political stability, the Soviet Party leaders on the make try to surround themselves with associates and subor-

240

dinates who must be reasonably competent in politics, administration and image making but who above everything else are loyal to the person of the rising leader, not to this or that issue that happens to be the order of the day, but may well be discarded overnight. Thus conflict among individuals is transformed into a conflict among patrons with their retinue of clients among clans or extended feudal families.[5] Some issues such as the predilection for capital goods might admittedly be more persistent and might hamper the maneuvrability of the leaders. But the careers of both Stalin and Khrushchev prove that the dictator reserves unto himself a great degree of tactical flexibility that calls for unlimited personal loyalty from his subordinates rather than devotion to consistent policies.

Given the centralized structure of the CPSU the Republican and Provincial Secretaries are agents of the central leadership rather than representatives of their respective Party organizations and of the people that are controlled by the latter. But in order to fulfill their role as viceroys of the central, highest autocrat, or supreme oligarch, the Republican and Provincial Party leaders must not become completely alienated from the population over which they rule. Separated from them they may well be, but not alienated. Beyond their immediate "family circle" of associates and clients they have to reach out to the popular masses if only to take their pulse. Most likely, they will also discreetly make some small concessions to the non-Party masses and above all to the relatively numerous rank and file Party members in order to obtain their acquiescence or support for measures which both the central and the Republican leaders believe to be necessary. The bolder among the Republican leaders may even attempt to extend their personal following into increasingly wider areas. Even in the Soviet Union with its strong repressive apparatus the political elite are not completely self-contained but try to establish a broader base of support among the aspiring elites and the popular masses. The continuing conflict among the elite makes this reaching out below as necessary to political survival as the formation of self-protective families within.

2. The CPU as a Whole: Membership and Composition

In addressing the 1966 Congress of the CPU the then First Secretary Shelest emphasized with pride the increase in its membership. As of the 1st day of the year the CPU had as many as 1,977,199 full members and 145,697 candidates, or a total of 2,122,816. In the last four years, that is apparently since January 1, 1962, the Party had grown by more than half a million members including candidates, or to be exact, by 513,580 persons, equal to 31.9 percent.[6] If we count back to the CPU membership at the 22nd CPU Congress in 1961 (as of September 1, 1961) we find a total increase of as many as 542,725 full members and candidates, or 34.3 percent.[7] The significance of all this becomes apparent if we consider that from 1961-66 the CPU increased faster than the All-Union Party, the CPSU. Between October 1, 1961 and January 1, 1966 — virtually the same time period — the CPSU grew by only 27.2 percent (see Table 1 in the Appendix and Graph). This disparate trend by the way, goes back to the beginning of the Khrushchev regime. Under Stalin the CPU had relatively few members compared with the CPSU as a whole (weighted by total population). In the first years of Khrushchev's rule the "model" Ukrainian Party, intensely loyal to its one time First Secretary, grew by leaps and bounds. Between the 1956 and 1961 CPU Congresses its membership increased by as many as 88.5 percent compared to a 34.5 percent growth of the All-Union Party.[8] Though conclusive proof may be lacking, it is plausible to assume that a kind of bargain had been struck between the leaders of the CPU and Khrushchev: in return for unquestioning support (was not Kirichenko one of the minority in the Presidium who voted for Khrushchev's economic regionalization plan in June 1957?), Khrushchev would allow Kirichenko and Podgorny to build up their power base by recruiting members for the hitherto disadvantaged CPU.

After 1966, that is after the assumption of power by Podgorny's rival Brezhnev, the membership of the CPU continued to increase more slowly than in 1961-66 and much less dramatically than from 1956-61 but though the rate of growth of the CPU has been slowed down, until 1972 the Ukrainian Party added members faster than did the All-Union Party. In 1972, however, which is also the year in which Shelest was removed, the CPU membership went down by about 55 thousand or 2.2 percent, whereas the All-Union Party continued growing at a diminished rate of 1.3 percent, adding about 190 thousand members (see Table I and Graph). Why? To add to the puzzle, in 1966 and 1971 the membership data given by Shelest do not jibe with the annual series of members' figures printed in the yearbooks of the Great Soviet Encyclopedia. Moreover, those discrepancies are serious. It would appear that either the editing and / or proofreading of the yearbooks has been quite slipshod or — more likely — that the Party apparatus are unsuccessfully trying to hid something. If the latter assumption is correct, what are they hiding? I cannot adequately explain the discrepancy in 1966, except possibly by the implicit exclusion of armed forces and internal security personnel from the yearbook figure. The 1971 yearbook may have repeated the procedure. But the 1972 yearbook went to press when the so-called exchange of party card (read: purge) was being prepared. Giving for the CPU membership on January 1, 1972 the same figure that Shelest had announced for the membership as of January 1, 1971 may be due to an oversight. It may also be a way of deliberately understating the true extent of the purge before January 1, 1973 through the simple expedient of withholding the real January 1, 1972 figure. (See Technical Note "The Mysterious Membership Figures," at end of main text.)

Ever since the Party Congress of 1966 Brezhnev has been hinting at the necessity of restricting entry to the CPSU and of purging undesirable elements.[9] At the 1971 Congress he announced the impending "exchange of Party cards," but significantly in its resolution the Congress did not establish any time limits but delegated the matter to the Central Committee.[10] Shelest apparently belonged to those Party leaders who urged Brezhnev to go slow with the purge. Writing in Moscow's **Kommunist** in August 1971 he pleaded that "much remains to be done to prepare well for this important organizational-political measure."[11] Willy-nilly Brezhnev went along: not until the CPSU Central Committee (CC) Plenum of May 19, 1972 was it decided to carry out that "exchange" over a period of two years, starting with 1973. (The very same plenum also ousted Shelest from the First Secretaryship of the CPU.)[12] No figures have been released on the extent of the purge in Ukraine. We know, however, that practically all (98.8 percent) of the CPU members had received new Party cards by the Spetember 1974 CC CPU Plenum.[13] It has also been disclosed in a revealing recent article by O. Kuznetsov, the Director of the Department of Party Organizational Work of the Odesa Province Party Committee, that initially some district secretaries resisted higher instructions and had to be told again in no uncertain terms that a purge was a purge, and not "essentially a technical operation the aim of which was to verify (the members) records."[14]

An alternative explanation, as suggested by Rein Taagepera,[15] may be that the CPU membership on January 1, 1973 is in line with an extrapolation of membership figures per thousand population from 1966-71 and that it is low only in comparison with the "abnormally high" January 1, 1972 figure. But unless we assume that the 1972 figure is a multiple misprint — a very unlikely event, in my opinion — this alternative hypothesis of normal growth only deepens the mystery of the sudden spurt in the increase of CPU members, which took place either in 1970, according to Shelest's data, or during 1971, if we put our confidence in the editors of the Great Soviet Encyclopedia. (I am strongly inclined to trust Shelest's figures.) This hypothesis also does not solve the mystery of the extent of the "corrective" purge.

For reasons of space I will not analyze the composition of the Ukrainian Party in terms of seniority of membership, age, sex, and education cum social class: in all these respects the CPU does not appear to differ significantly from its parent party, the CPSU.[16] But given the history of strong non-Ukrainian representation in the CPU the question must be asked: to what extent is the CPU an ethnically Ukrainian party and in what measure does it represent — possibly even overrepresent — the national minorities in the Ukraine? In the form of a small table I would like to present the sparse data on the nationality composition of the CPU over time, since 1940:

NATIONAL COMPOSITION OF THE CPU, 1940-1968

| | Percentage of CPU Members | | | | Percentage in total population, Ukr SSR | | |
	1940	1958	1965	1968	1940 estimate	1959 census	1970 census
Ukrainians	63.1	60.3	64.2	65.1	80.0	76.8	74.9
Russians	19.1	28.2	26.9	26.6	n.a.	16.9	19.4
Others	17.8	11.5	8.9	8.3	n.a.	6.3	5.7

SOURCES: 1940 Party data — V. Holubnychy, "Outline History of the Communist Party of the Ukraine," **Ukrainian Review** (Munich), 1958 / 6, 124. 1958: "KPU v tsifrakh," **Partiynaya zhizn'**, 1958 / 12 (June 1958), 59 or Y. Bilinsky, **Second Soviet Republic,** 231; 1965: **Ukrains'ka Radyans'ka Entsyklopediya,** XVII, 201; 1968: Soviet Ukraine, 190. Population figures: 1940 estimate from **Second Soviet Republic,** 55-56; 1959 and 1970 census data from TsSU SSSR, **Itogi vsesoyuznoy perepisi naseleniya 1970 goda,** IV (Moscow, 1973), 12.

The table shows clearly the disproportionately low enrollment of Ukrainians in the CPU compared with their share in the total population and the disproportionately high share of the Russians. Using the 1970 census data on the age structure of the Ukrainians in the Ukrainian SSR and assuming that the unknown age structure of the Russians in Ukraine is proportional to the age structure of the Russians throughout the USSR and combining these data with the nationality of CPU membership data for 1968 we may say that of the adult Russians who live in Ukraine approximately one in every ten (10.1) is a member of the CPU as contrasted with only one in every seventeen (16.6) adult Ukrainians. If we control the figures for sex, we find that one in every six (5.8) Russian men living in Ukraine is a member of the CPU but only one in every nine (9.1) Ukrainian men. The corresponding figure for Russian women is one in every twenty-nine (28.7) compared with one in every forty-nine (49.0) for Ukrainian women. [17] The Russians in Ukraine are definitely a dominant minority.

Why are Ukrainians so underrepresented among the CPU members? Professor T. H. Rigby gives two explanations: the "most important reason" is that the Ukrainians in the Ukrainian SSR still contain a far higher proportion of peasants than do the Russians living in that Republic. Secondly, the Western Ukrainians who had been annexed between 1939-45 still appear to "show relatively low party membership levels — like the indigenous population in other border territories incorporated at this period." [18] I have tried to document the second, minor reason elsewhere. [19] The 1970 census data do bring out that the Ukrainians in Ukraine are much less urbanized, far less highly educated, and thus socio-economically less mobile than are the Russians in that Republic. Thus, 45.8 percent of the Ukrainian majority live in the cities compared with as many as 84.5 percent of the Russian minority. [20] Among the Ukrainians in Ukraine over ten years old only 30 per thousand have completed higher education and only 9 more have incomplete higher education, while among the Russians the corresponding figures are more than double: 66 per thousand are college graduates and 20 per thousand college attenders. Even among the urban residents alone, the Russians tend to be better educated: 75 per thousand Russians have completed higher education compared with only 52 per thousand Ukrainians, while 22 per thousand Russians attended but did not finish college compared with 16 per thousand Ukrainians. [21]

Obviously, the Ukrainians appear to be worse candidates for admission to the political elite — the CPU — than the Russians. In fact, the reasons for the underrepresentation of ethnic Ukrainians in the CPU are far less obvious in the 1970's than they had been in the 1920's. Fifty years ago, the low socio-economic status of the Ukrainians had to be taken for granted as an inheritance from the former Russian Empire. Almost two generations of Soviet rule later, the low social mobility of the Ukrainians appears to be less the result of inevitable socio-economic processes, less of a given than a dependent variable: viz., the consequence of deliberate Soviet nationality policy such as anti-Ukrainian discrimination in schools, the geographical distribution of capital investments now favoring the eastern Republics rather than Ukraine, and last but not least, officially encouraged immigration of highly qualified Russians and the outmigration of highly qualified Ukrainians. [22]

3. Why Did Shelest Fall? (Or, an Essay in Kremlinology)

Party membership is, by itself, only a minimum prerequisite for access to decision-making in the long run. In the short run, participation in policymaking is limited to a more manageable group of Party officials, the republican and provincial elites of our study. Even the more protuberant, more tangible roots of the events of 1972 and 1973, of the dismissal and public humiliation of the leader of the second largest Soviet republic, reach back as far as June 1963. The hidden taproot is the sullenness and barely disguished protest with which the Ukrainian Communist leaders accept the policies emanating from Moscow which they consider injurious to "their" republic and their own positions. It is with the shallower, "Kremlinological" or perhaps "Kyivological" roots that I shall be primarily concerned here but I will have to hint at the deeper root occasionally.

In June 1963 Khrushchev had both Brezhnev and Podgorny elected CC CPSU Secretaries: Brezhnev was the heir-presumptive, while Podgorny was promoted to Moscow as a counter-heir. Shortly thereafter Peter Yefimovych Shelest, an apparent protégé of both Khrushchev and Podgorny, [23] was elected to succeed Podgorny as First Secretary of the CPU over the heads of Podgorny's Secretary Ivan P. Kazanets and Prime Minister Volodymyr V. Shcherbyts'kyi (Had CPU precedents since 1949 been followed the job should have gone to Kazanets', precedents from other Republics, however, pointed to Shcherbyts'kyi.) Moreover, in the Ukrainian reshuffle after Podgorny's promotion Kazanets' was transferred to the Prime Ministership and Shcherbitsky was dmoted to his old 1955-57 position of First Secretary of the Dnipropetrovs'k obkom. At the meeting of the All-Union Party Presidium December 13, 1963 Shelest was inducted as a candidate member, somewhat unceremoniously displacing from that body candidate member and ex-Prime Minister V. V. Shcherbyts'kyi who had been elected to the Presidium at the 1961 CPSU Congress.

The importance of all these moves is that most probably Shcherbyts'kyi's career had been helped by Brezhnev. [24] As Prime Minister of Ukraine in 1961-63 Shcherbitsky may well have incurred Khrushchev's displeasure by opposing All-Union economic policies unfavorable to his Republic, as he would do later at the 23rd CPSU Congress in 1966, though I have not been able to find the concrete issues on which they clashed. Most likely, Shcherbyts'kyi's demotion in 1963 was the byproduct of the power play in Moscow: once Khrushchev had decided to clip Brezhnev's wings it stands to reason that he would do the same to Brezhnev's man in Ukraine. This gave Shelest the chance of his life.

In October 1964 Khrushchev was overthrown and by the end of 1965 Podgorny was removed from the CC CPSU Secretariat. In mid-1965 a campaign was also started against Podgorny's supporters in Ukraine, notable within his old Kharkiv Party organization. The shoe was now on the other foot. In November 1964 Shelest, apparently with Podgorny's help, had been promoted to full member of the CPSU Presidium, but October 15, 1965 Shcherbitsky was back as Ukrainian Prime Minister and in December 1965 he was re-elected as candidate member of the CPSU Presidium. To make room for Shcherbyts'kyi Kazanets was transferred to Moscow to become USSR Minister of Ferrous Metallurgy while the First Secretaryship of the Dnipropetrovs'k Province was filled by another Brezhnev man, Oleksiy F. Vatchenko. 25

The CP of Ukraine was strongly affected by the rout of Podgorny's Kharkiv group. At the 1966 CPU Congress ex-Kharkivite N. A. Sobol was not re-elected Second Secretary of the republican party organization, but effectively demoted to First Deputy Prime Minister responsible for general economic affairs. In that position and in the Politburo of the CPU he was allowed to stay until the last CC plenum under Shelest on March 31, 1972, when he was retired from both, at the age of 62. 26 Into the sensitive post of Second Secretary was now moved Alexander P. Lyashko. Lyashko, an ethnic Ukrainian, since 1952 has been intimately tied with the Donets'k Province Party organization, whose First Secretary he became in March 1960. (His second in command since January 22, 1963 was Vladimir I. Degtyarev, a Russian.) June 28, 1963 Lyashko was appointed to the CC CPU Secretariat and to its Presidium (as a full member) to take the post of shelest as Fourth (Industrial) Secretary and Chairman of the CC CPU Bureau for Industry and Construction. In all likelihood, in 1963 Lyashko enjoyed the confidence of Khrushchev, Podgorny, and Shelest. That in March 1966 Shelest was able to obtain Lyashko's services as Second Secretary might perhaps be attributed to the Donets'k Party organization headed in 1966 by Degtyarev. 27 Or possibly, as Dr. Lewytzkyj has suggested in his comments, the Donets'k faction is eminently acceptable to Moscow since the Donets'k Party leaders coming from a heavily Russified province are relatively isolated from the mainstream of Ukrainian cultural developments and in politics and administration are attuned to think in "All-Union," i.e., centralist terms. In any event, nothing and nobody could really compensate for the indirect blow received by Shelest: the political setback of his old protector Podgorny.

In terms of long-range economic development the Ukrainian Party leaders appeared by 1966 to have lost several battles under Khrushchev and Brezhnev, notably those for obtaining more capital funds to build large electric power stations in Ukraine, as opposed to Siberia, and to further exploit the increasingly more expensive coal mines in the Donets'k Basin. Generally speaking, a few Soviet Ukrainian economists and administrators had turned sour on the entire issue of Russo-Ukrainian economic relations. The extent of their feeling is perhaps best gauged not so much by the cautious scholarly literature 28 as by a remarkably candid even though anonymous contribution in **Samizdat's Political Diary**. The observer was shocked at the vehemence with which the Soviet Ukrainian administrators insisted that Ukraine was being economically exploited by Russia; if they had not had to contribute so much to the Union budget, the Ukrainians would have, e.g., solved the housing problem a long time ago! 29

Knowing that he was dealing with political dynamite, Shelest did not criticize Moscow's economic policies either at the CPU or the CPSU Congress. But it is interesting that in 1966 Shcherbyts'kyi showed less restraint. Speaking from the tribune of the 23rd CPSU Congress in Moscow, the reinstated Ukrainian Prime Minister freely admitted that Ukraine would experience some difficulty in her production of fuel and energy. He laid some of the problems at Khrushchev's door: during the Seven Year Plan (1959-1965) the construction of new coal mines had been slowed down without any justification. Furthermore, if the government wanted Ukraine to overfulfill any industrial plans, the USSR Gosplan should give funds for building more electric power stations and transmission lines, for there were no more energy reserves left in Ukraine. 30

In 1966 on the ideological-political front the situation did not look too bright either. A Ukrainian-Canadian Communist John Kolasky had been enrolled as a student at the Higher Party School of the CC of the CPU from September 1963 until the end of the spring term of 1965. In those two years he had become bitterly disillusioned over the nationality policy in Ukraine and the Russification in particular. The KGB arrested him in late July 1965 and expelled him from the country in mid-August of that year. He was also expelled from the Canadian Communist Party. His well-documented accusations, however, led to a visit in mid-1967 by a Canadian-Communist investigation committee: every Party and government official in Kyiv reportedly trembled at their presence. But already in 1966 Shelest must have found the Kolasky episode a considerable embarrassment. [31]

In order to take wind out of the sails of such foreign Communists as Kolasky and of the indigenous Soviet Ukrainian dissidents, the Ukrainian SSR Minister of Higher and Specialized Secondary Education M. Yu. Dadenkov, himself probably a Russian, in August 1965 called in the rectors of higher educational institutions (vuzy) in the Republic that were under the jurisdiction of his Ministry and instructed them in writing to give the lectures "predominantly in Ukrainian." Such an important change must have been sanctioned by the highest Party officials in Ukraine, probably Shelest himself: it is unrealistic to assume that Dadenkov would have made the step on his own. But thanks to an organized letter-writing campaign of Russian and Russified students' parents who appealed directly to the CC CPSU in Moscow, Dadenkov's letter of instruction was countermanded. [32]

If it be plausible to assume that Shelest had decided in August 1965 to meet the demands of indigenous patriotic Ukrainians with partial concession, it is plausible to argue that he could not but have had considerable misgivings over the first wave of arrests of dissident Ukrainian intellectuals in August-September of that year. Unlike Khrushchev who had come to grief over changing policies in several areas at once (e.g., the relaxation of tensions with the U.S. plus more consumer goods plus greater freedom to intellectuals, from the spring and summer of 1963 through his overthrow in October 1964), Brezhnev has followed a truly Leninist policy of making concessions in one sector (e.g., that of industrial management) but sharply tightening all the screws in other (intellectual freedom, nationality groups). Most likely it was Brezhnev backed by Suslov who ordered the arrests of Ukrainian intellectuals as well as those of Sinyavsky and Daniel in August-September 1965. Unwittingly perhaps, a subordinate of Shelest's, Ideological CC CPU Secretary Andrey D. Skaba whom Shelest had inherited from Podgorny, further embarrassed his present boss when in the fall of 1965 he invited one of the most prominent Ukrainian dissidents Ivan Dzyuba to put his ideas down in writing. The result was the nearly 300 pages long well-argued and relatively well-documented treatise entitled **Internationalism or Russification?** It was addressed to Shelest as First Secretary and Shcherbyts'kyi as Prime Minister of the Ukrainian SSR and was submitted to them in December 1965. The document soon entered the samizdat channels and was published in the West in 1968. [33]

Against this background of growing dissidence and arrests in Ukraine it took considerable courage (or possibly even foolhardiness) on Shelest's part to state at the 1966 CPU Congress that thanks to Leninist nationality policy "lack of friendship and enmity between the nations had been completely liquidated in our country, which (phenomena) had for centuries been imposed and exacerbated by the exploiting classes and their ideologies — the bourgeois nationalists **and the great power** (i.e., Russian — Y.B.) **chauvinists.**" [34] To be sure, Shelest then tried to pour some oil on the waves by promising that Ukraine would forever stay with Russia and the other peoples of the Soviet Union. But then he turned around again and denounced both deviations: Ukrainian **and** Russian nationalisms. Such a formulation would have been perfectly acceptable at the de-Stalinization Congress of 1956 but no longer at the Consolidation Congress of 1966. Either Shelest did not know that the wind from Moscow had changed, or, more likely in the light of his subsequent book on Ukraine, he felt so strongly about the excesses of Russification himself that he did not care.

An analysis of the full and candidate members of the CPU Presidium-Politburo and of the CC CPU Secretaries who were elected at the 1966 CPU Congress shows the advancement of Shcherbyts'kyi's and Brezhnev's Dnipropetrovs'k faction. To that faction belonged, besides the old full member Shcherbyts'kyi himself, possibly the old-timer D. S. Korotchenko, [35] definitely the newly elected full member O. F. Vatchenko, and possibly, if we take Dr. Duevel's word for it, the incumbent First

Secretary of the Kyiv **obkom** and long-time (1948-59) Komsomol leader V.I. Drozdenko. Drozdenko was newly elected full member of the Presidium-Politburo and at the Congress made Third Secretary in charge of the economy. [36] Another newly elected **candidate** member I. S. Hrushets'kyi whom I would put down as essentially a third-ranking CPU leader with experience in West Ukrainian posts has also been identified as a Brezhnev protégé and, by implication, a supporter of Shcherbyts'kyi. [37] Against all these open and secret members of the "Dnipro Mafia" there stood in Shelest's camp the increasingly ineffectual Kharkivites and Podgorny's protégés M. O. Sobol (new full member) and H. I. Vashchenko (new candidate member) and the members of the upcoming Donets'k faction: new full member and new Second Secretary O.P. Lyashko, new full member and new Secretary in charge of industry O. A. Tytarenko, old candidate member V. K. Klymenko (a trade union leader), and new candidate member, the Donets'k Party boss V. I. Degtyarev.

Several processes and events that took place prior to the CPU Congress of March 1971 merit cursory attention. Shelest does not seem to have had much luck with the crucial position of Second Secretary in charge of Party personnel. For reasons unknown, Lyashko was promoted **de iure** but not **de facto** to Korotchenko's old position, the Chairmanship of the Presidium of the Republican Supreme Soviet on April 7, 1969. [38] Into Lyashko's place, on June 19, stepped Ivan K. Lutak. Though Lutak has survived the fall of Shelest (at the time of writing, in September 1974, he is still Second Secretary) it is not easy to determine where his loyalties lay in 1969. Lutak had worked under Shelest in the Kyiv **obkom**. [39]

To reinforce his position in the crucial Party personnel area Shelest had previously, in March 1969, appointed a Ukrainian Party official from the Donets'k province Volodymyr M. Tsybul'ko to head the Organizational Party Work Department of the CC CPU Secretariat (he succeeded in that post veteran Party personnel manager I. I. Vivdychenko, who had held the position since before 1955). But Tsybul'ko did not last in that key post more than a year. April 7, 1970 it went to A. A. Ulanov, whom I have not been able to identify, but whose name sounds Russian. [40] Ulanov, in turn, held the job at least through 1972, but by May 1974 it went to a certain H. K. Kryuchkov, also apparently a Russian. [41]

The personnel changes at the level of First **obkom** Secretaries between the Congresses do not yield a sharp picture, but some of the individual moves point toward difficulties for Shelest. Out of the 25 provinces of Ukraine plus the large Kyiv City organization, 12 experienced a change in their top Party leadership. [42] In three provinces (Odesa, Sumy, and Volyn') the First Secretaries were apparently demoted for punishment, but only in Odesa were the issues made clear. [43] Somewhat bothersome from Shelest's point of view must also have been the fluidity of Secretaries in his old bailiwick, the Kyiv **obkom**. Upon Drozdenko's promotion to the CC CPU Secretariat, his place as First Secretary of the Kyiv **obkom** was taken by F. P. Holovchenko who may have had loose ties with Podgorny and may have been well known by Shelest. For some reason, April 1, 1970 Holovchenko was shifted into the Government as Ukrainian SSR Minister of Automobile Transport, a demotion apparently. [44] His place in the Kyiv **obkom** had to be filled on April 7, 1970 by Tsybul'ko from the key Organizational Party Work Department of the CPU CC. [45] No major scandal adhered to the Kyiv Province Party organization, just an uneasy fluidity in cadres. There was a major scandal in Odesa, however, first the Second, then the First **obkom** Secretaries were removed for protecting freewheeling and arbitrary A. I. Yurzhenko, the President (**rektor**) of Odesa University. The importance of this episode for our theme is that First Odesa **obkom** Secretary M. S. Synytsya may have been close to Shelest: from before 1955 to June 8, 1960 he headed the Kyiv City Party Committee while Shelest was Second and First Kyiv Province Secretary. [46] Synytsya's successor in Odesa is former journalist and First Secretary in Vinnytsya Pavlo P. Kozyr whose ties to Shelest do not appear to be firm. [47]

Concerning the sensitive relations between the secret police and the CPU we must note two things. First and less important, the demoted head of the All-Union KGB

Volodymyr E. Semichastny arrived in Kyiv in May, 1967 and was given the job of First Deputy Chairman of the UkrSSR Council of Ministers. (July 15, 1971 he was degraded to an ordinary Deputy Prime Minister.) His responsibilities seem to lie in transport, communications, and possibly also youth affairs.[48] Much more important is the replacement in July, 1970, of the KGB head in Ukraine Vitaliy F. Nikitchenko, who had been at that post since 1954, by Vitaliy V. Fedorchuk. Nikitchenko was officially given "responsible work" with the KGB in Moscow, but on balance this appears to be a demotion. Nikitchenko has been identified as "Shelest's fired." Fedorchuk has come from outside the Ukrainian KGB apparatus: he reportedly has served in the eastern districts of the Russian SFSR and according to informed sources he has replaced all the regional heads of the KGB in Ukraine, a clear sign that the leadership in Moscow was dissatisfied with Nikitchenko's work. According to rumors circulating in Munich, Fedorchuk disagreed with Shelest's conviction that dissidents should be handled by political not police methods; as soon as Fedorchuk was installed he began to energetically work against Shelest. It is interesting that the decision to replace Nikitchenko was made rather suddenly, for as late as June 14, 1970 Nikitchenko had been elected to the USSR Supreme Soviet from Ukraine. (In 1971 Fedorchuk was elected to the same body in a by-election.)[49]

This leads to the difficult question of Shelest's relationship to the Ukrainian dissidents in general and writers in particular. On balance Shelest's speech to the 5th Congress of Ukrainian Writers on November 16, 1966 was orthodox enough: Soviet workers cannot remain neutral, before the people they must observe "Party honesty." Writers, especially younger ones, must avoid "imprecision and ambiguity and individual poems, stories or critical articles" which could be taken advantage of by bourgeois propaganda and its lackeys, the Ukrainian borgeois nationalists. But in the middle of his speech there was a passage in which Shelest called upon the Ukrainian writers "to treat our native, wonderful Ukrainian language with care and respect." He continued: "This is our treasure, our great heritage, which each one of us and first of all, you writers, must cherish and develop." Moreover, he pledged the continuing support of the Communist Party for the writers' endeavors.[50] Oles' Honchar, the President of the Writers' Union and some others evidently interpreted this passage as an encouragement to defend the use of the Ukrainian language, going as far as to criticize the prevailing Russification policy.[51] Did they misinterpret Shelest? This is unlikely, since Honchar reputedly was quite close to Shelest having written some of his speeches. Probably Shelest sincerely believed that so long as Soviet Ukrainian literature was socialist in content it ought to be allowed to be genuinely national (i.e., Ukrainian) in form. By writing and publishing in 1968 the symbolic and patriotic novel, **Sobor** (The Cathedral) Honchar may have politically embarrassed Shelest and contributed to his later downfall: significantly, the vicious campaign against **Sobor** was led by First Dnipropetrovs'k Party Secretary Vatchenko, the protege of Shcherbyts'kyi (on the pretext that the locale of the novel was in the Dnipropetrovs'kZaporizhia region), while Shelest remained silent.[52] In March, 1968 Shelest finally managed to get rid of his ideological secretary A. D. Skaba who was such an overzealous Russifier that ultimately he proved ineffectual even from Moscow's viewpoint.[53] Shelest chose as his successor the chemist Fedir D. Ovcharenko, who, from 1956-68 had headed the Science and Culture Department of the CC CPU Secretariat.[54] Ovcharenko, however, appears to have been more at home standing behind the chemist's bench than walking the tightrope of ideology. He was replaced soon after Shelest's fall.

1968 was, of course, the year of Czechoslovakia. Shelest's role in the Soviet invasion of that country has been studied in detail by Grey Hodnett and Peter J. Potichnyj. They came to the conclusion that on this issue Shelest was a prominent, possibly even a reactionary hawk, uncompromising in his rejection of Czechoslovak revisionism. Shcherbyts'kyi, on the other hand, was more moderate vis-a-vis the Czechoslovak reformers.[55] If so, Shelest must have feared that extension of the Prague spring to Ukraine would have the Ukrainian dissidents even more rebellious

248

than they were already. Furthermore, according to a recent Soviet refugee, there was a partial Soviet mobilization before the invasion and a Soviet military truck driver who was delivering ammunition to the Czechoslovak border was fired upon while still on Soviet Ukrainian territory. In other words, the situation in Ukraine on the eve of the invasion may have been more serious than is commonly realized, which would explain Shelest's "preventive hawkishness." On the other hand, Vsevolod Holubnychy has drawn my attention to the fact that in a 1967 book which was signed to go to print as late as October 31, 1967, Shelest warmly praised the relations between the Ukrainian Komsomol and the Czechoslovak Youth League.[56] It may be, as Holubnychy asserts, that Shelest knew the attitudes of the Czech and Slovak youth on the eve of Dubcek's coming to power and that he approved of them — at least in the fall of 1967. Whatever his true feelings about the Prague spring may have been, even among the intellectuals in Kyiv he seems to have acquired the reputation of a hawk and possible initiator of the invasion, says a former Kyivan journalist. This added more controversy to Shelest's figure, the more so since his views on Czechoslovakia were not fully shared by Shcherbyts'kyi and — even more importantly — by Suslov.

The proceedings of the 1971 CPU and CPSU Congresses shed some further light on the positions of Shelest and Shcherbytskyi. In his speech in Kyiv Shelest quite openly admitted that generation of electricity in Ukraine had not kept pace with the demands of industry, agriculture, and communal service establishments. He stressed repreated lobbying efforts in Moscow.[57] He also criticized the USSR Gosplan and the USSR Ministry of Coal Industry for not devoting "proper attention" to the Ukrainian demands for coal.[58] Shcherbyts'kyi's speech before the CPU Congress, however, was a dry and singularly non-polemical recital of Ukrainian economic tasks and achievements.[59] In Moscow, before the CPSU Congress Shelest repeated his demands for more coal from the Donets'k basin — he considered it "incorrect" to "lower the attention to the development of coal industry" in favor of the oil and natural gas industries, as had been suggested by "somebody."[60] (A reading of later speeches discloses that that "somebody" was none other than Kosygin speaking for the Soviet government and presumably for Brezhnev as well.)[61] Shelest also demanded from Moscow more and better scientific animal feeds and more farm machinery.[62] Shcherbyts'kyi's speech at the 1971 CPSU Congress, however, was in stark contrast with Shelest's. If Shelest played the insistent, almost truculent defender of the Soviet Ukrainian economy, Shcherbyts'kyi in 1971 — unlike in 1966 — let it be known that he was a loyalist who could be relied upon to accept and further "the most rational location of the productive forces" among the Soviet Republics as decreed by Moscow.[63] Shcherbyts'kyi was also rather fulsome on his praise of Brezhnev though formally he should have addressed himself to Kosygin's report. Brezhnev was explicitly praised three times in a short speech and of those three times he was praised twice as an individual. Such a prominent display of loyalty could not go unrewarded: after the Moscow Congress Shcherbyts'kyi was elected a full member of the CPSU Politburo.[64]

Reviewing the membership of the top CPU organs that were elected at the 1971 CPU Congress we notice three things: the baffling down-ranking of Vatchenko, who was listed third last among the full Politburo members arranged according to political seniority or in fact last, if allowance be made for the two new full members who had just been promoted from alternates and who ranked the lowest (Vashchenko and Degtyarev); the disappearance from the Secretariat of former Kyiv First **obkom** Secretary and presumed Shcherbitsky supporter Drozdenko (shunted off as Ambassador to Romania);[65] and the strong position of the Donets'k group: Lyashko, Tytarenko, and Degtyarev as full members, Pohrebnyak, and Solohub as alternate members of the Politburo, and Pohrebnyak and Tytarenko as Secretaries. Were the Comrades from Donets'k taking over the CPU leadership and threatening Shelest, or, more likely, was Shelest cooperating with the Donets'k faction to keep down the representatives of the Dnipropetrovs'k clan (Shcherbyts'kyi, Vatchenko, and possibly Drozdenko) who apparently had the ear of Brezhnev? If the latter, Shelest's triumph did not last long: at CPSU Congress in Moscow three weeks later Vatchenko and Drozdenko were elected full members of the CC CPSU, and Scherbyts'kyi was also elected full member of the CPSU Politburo.[66] At least until the Party archives are opened to Western scholars we will never know the answer to these questions, for at the may 19, 1972, CC plenum in Moscow Shelest was removed from the First Secretaryship of Ukraine and Shcherbyts'kyi was promptly installed.[67] A more charitable interpretation of Ovcharenko's abilities by Dr. Pelenski is that Ovcharenko was a man for the warm spring season only. Twice he made his appearance when the policy toward the Ukrainian autonomist dissenters was liberal and twice did he disappear with a change in that policy.

The circumstances of Shelest's dismissal are somewhat unusual. He might have attended the CC CPSU plenum but he did not speak: the principal spokesman on the foreign policy issue was Vatchenko.[68] Secondly, as soon as Kyiv Radio — before the announcement in the newspapers on May 21, 1972 — put on the air a TASS teletype message from Moscow that Comrade Shelest had been appointed a Deputy Prime Minister of the USSR and in this connection would leave the post of the First Secretary of the CC CPU, an irate voice from the CPU Central Committee called up the radio's newsdesk: "Are you people joking? Is it all a mistake, or is somebody joking with his head?!"[69] Shelest was not allowed to stay in Kyiv. He and all of his belongings were immediately transferred to Msocow. He took up his new duty already on May 26, 1972, i.e., the very next day after the CC CPU plenum that formally released him from the Secretaryship and just when President Nixon arrived in Kyiv.[70] Third, the official communique from the Ukrainian CP plenum insisted that the CC plenum "unanimously" elected V. V. Shcherbyts'kyi, First Secretary of the CC CPU and that Shcherbyts'kyi was "warmly greeted by the plenum participants" when he made his first speech as Secretary.[71] I agree with Dr. Duevel that these highly unusual formulae indicate that, on the contrary, Moscow's fiat struck the plenum participants as being in bad taste, to say the least.[72]

Shelest was further humiliated in April, 1973. While he was still a full member of the CPSU Politburo, the CPU theoretical journal **Komunist Ukrainy** printed a long editorial in which it denounced his 1970 book **Our Soviet Ukraine** for being on a "low ideological-theoretical and professional level" and for contributing to "sentiments of self-contentment and self-admiration."[73] Such a vicious and explicit attack on a member of the All-Union Politburo is unprecedented in the post-Stalinist period: it reminds me somewhat of the campaign in 1951 against the late Volodymyr Sosyura who was denounced for his patriotic wartime poem, "Love the Ukraine."[74] Not unexpectedly, on April 27, 1973, Shelest was relieved of his seat in the CPSU Politburo "in connection with retirement."[75]

What were the reasons for Shelest's ouster?[76] The timing of his dismissal from Kyiv — on the eve of President Nixon's first visit to the Soviet Union — would seem to indicate some kind of a connection. There have been plausible rumors that Shelest had wanted his colleagues on the Politburo to issue a "negative statement" about the scheduled Nixon visit after the mining of North Vietnamese harbors. Rebuffed by the majority he still insisted that Ukraine was opposed to the visit, a sentiment not shared by Shcherbyts'kyi. In arrogating to himself the making of Soviet foreign policy Shelest had gone too far and had to be removed quickly, especially since Nixon was scheduled to visit Kyiv.[77] At the McMaster Conference one of the . . . discussants and a member of the audience suggested that Shelest's ouster had nothing to do with foreign affairs whatsoever, that such a connection was a piece of deliberate KGB misinformation. Admittedly, I have no positive proof of the link, but neither can my opponents furnish any proof of the absence of such a link. I base my inference on (1) Shelest's well-known hawkishness on Czechoslovakia, China, and Vietnam, and (2) the precipitous way in which Shelest was removed on the eve of Nixon's visit thus overdramatizing possible discord in Moscow. Was this done to facilitate American concessions in Moscow from a position of Soviet "weakness"? I doubt it.

But while opposition to the visit by President Nixon may — or may not — have been the proverbial "last straw" there were at least three other issues involved: economic demands and achievements; Shelest's political infighting with Shchebyts'kyi and Brezhnev; and the question of Ukrainian nationalism.

It has already been pointed out how energetically and persistently Shelest lobbied for more power plants, coal mines, animal feeds, and farm machinery. It is not so well known that Shelest did get his way on one administrative-economic issue: Ukraine was the only Soviet republic to have a republican ministry of Sovkhozes between March, 1969, and late February, 1973. After Shelest's fall the exception was withdrawn and the ministry converted to a union-republican one (i.e., the Ukrainian state farms were no longer exclusively subordinated to Kyiv as in 1969-73 but to Kyiv and Moscow simultaneously).[78] Power-conscious bureaucrats in Moscow could not but look askance at Shelest's successes in maintaining administrative autonomy, Shcherbyts'kyi had to accept **Gleichschaltung**.

Politically, Shelest tried and succeeded in symbolically downgrading Vatchenko in 1971. As we will see in the Muzhitsky affair, Shelest also managed to temporarily protect against charges of corruption the First Secretary of the Poltava **obkom**, despite the fact that the charges were being pressed by USSR Minister of the Interior N. A. Shchelokov, a well-known Brezhnev protege. Finally, there is a very interesting brief paragraph in Shcherbyts'kyi's major speech on cadres at the CC CPU plenum on April 17, 1973. Shcherbyts'kyi said:

It is important to note that (a significant number) of specialists are sent to us from other fraternal republics, while we in our turn appoint many of our higher and technical (secondary) school graduates to work in various regions of the country. This also shows the superiority of the socialist economy, which presents a single national economic complex, as well as the unbreakable friendship and unity of the peoples of the Soviet Union . . .[79]

Since so much of the speech was a transparent polemic against Shelest it may be assumed that this passage, too, was directed against him, that he had been lukewarm against the so-called exchange of cadres.[80]

Was Shelest, above all, a hidden Ukrainian bourgeois nationalist who saw his mission in working for the political independence of Ukraine? I think not. He seems to genuinely believe in an international Communist Commonwealth based on the teachings of Lenin whom he sincerely admires. Would Shelest have then favored a gradual and genuinely voluntary linguistic assimilation of the Ukrainians to Russians, as advocated by Lenin? Possibly yes, but more likely not, for he was also genuinely fond and proud of the Ukrainian language. Under Shelest, I have been told on good authority, applicants for responsible jobs in Ukraine had to pass an examination in understanding Ukrainian, no matter how superb the rest of their qualifications might have been. Shelest appears quite sincere in his hatred for and his denunciation of Ukrainian bourgeois nationalists who have collaborated with the West and also of Czechoslovak revisionists: all of them made his task of governing Ukraine more difficult. Shelest was certainly fond of the comforts and remunerations of political power shared by the top Soviet elite no matter what their nationality. "(His) was nothing but a struggle for power, there was no nationalism involved, I implore you," exclaimed a recent Soviet Ukrainian emigre. He has been described to me as essentially a political boss, a feudal baron fighting for his domain which he regarded with understandable pride; or, to use the terminology of Friedrich and Brzezinski, the archetype of the "feudal lieutenant"[81] who had become excessively attached to his fiefdom. All this is true and yet there are certain national as distinct from nationalistic overtones to this stubborn and arrogant independent-mindedness.

His book on Ukraine which I simply cannot analyze here is not so much nationalistic as it is out of date: his proud references to the Ukrainian past and his strictures against the Russian Tsars would have been perfectly acceptable in 1956-58.

They were not in the pro-Russian forced assimilationist atmosphere of the late 1960's and early 1970's. In the 1970's his stubborn insistence that Lenin had fought against both Ukrainian bourgeois nationalism and Russian great power chauvinism was historically correct, but politically too provocative.[82] One small story will illustrate that occasionally Shelest went beyond words. Visiting Southern Ukraine in the spring of 1972 Shelest, without prior clearance from Moscow, made an inspection tour of a unit of the Soviet Black Sea Fleet anchored off Sevastopil. He told the captain of a cruiser that he wanted to personally award three sailors who had excelled in Marxist political education. Could he recommend three good lads to him? — Comrade First Secretary, there is Ivanov and Doroshenko and Arutunyan. — No, Captain, you have misunderstood me, said Shelest, I want three Ukrainians, please! Even if the story be apocryphal, its circulation in Soviet Ukraine shows that such a statement by Shelest was regarded as plausible.

Generally, however, Shelest would treat Russo-Ukrainian relations with tact and dignity. For instance, October 23, 1965, Brezhnev came to Kyiv to award the city an order of the "Golden Star" for heroism of her citizens during World War II. Brezhnev stressed in his speech the necessity for cooperation between Russians and Ukrainians. Shelest expressed on behalf the participants in the ceremony and on behalf of the workers of Ukraine "the cordial gratitude to all the peoples of the Soviet Union, above all to the Russian people, for their fraternal help in liberating the city of Kyiv and all of the Ukrainian land from the Fascist yoke." In the next paragraph he also managed to thank the Czech and Polish (!) troops that had taken part in the campaign.[83] Throughout Shelest's speeches and writings there are, of course, positive references to the Russian people. But they do not include even an iota of that enthusiastic servility that is so familiar to readers of documents of both the Stalinist period and the period since 1972.

Shelest could also be loyal where loyalty was due: in his book on Ukraine, e.g., he approvingly refers to the 29th and 22nd CPSU Congresses, i.e., Khrushchev's de-Stalinization Congresses of 1956 and 1961, without, however, referring to Khrushchev by name.

To conclude this section, I believe that whatever the specific reasons may have been — opposition to Nixon's visit, economic and political demands and achievements — Shelest fell essentially because he was too independent-minded a person in control of too important a republic. In a nutshell, Shelest defined himself when early in 1965 he told Skaba that "he was not Kaganovich and these were not the times of Stalin."[84] In 1972, when Brezhnev and his associates quietly shifted the big celebration of the 50th anniversary of the establishment of the Soviet Union from the true anniversary date of December 30 to December 21 — which happens to be Stalin's birthday,[85] — Shelest was an anachronism. But it was not Shelest who had changed but Brezhnev.

4. The CPU Under Shcherbyts'kyi, 1972-74:

Shcherbyts'kyi lost no time in removing some of Shelest's appointees and presumed supporters on the republican and provincial levels and appointing new people in their stead. Almost immediately after Shelest's ouster Lyashko was brought back into political circulation by being given Shcherbyts'kyi's old Prime Minister-ship.[86] This left vacant the Chairmanship of the Presidium of the Supreme Soviet of the Ukrainian SSR. After floundering for almost two months, Hrushetskyi was "elevated" to that post and made a full member of the CC CPU Politburo.[87] At the same CC plenum Tsybul'ko, the First Secretary of the Kyiv obkom, was elected candidate member.[88] Had Tsybul'ko who originally had come from Donets'k helped to do Shelest in and was now reaping his reward?

Still on the republican level, at the October 10, 1972, CC CPU plenum Shelest's appointee F. D. Ovcharenko was replaced as both ideological CC Secretary and candidate member of the CC CPU Politburo by Doctor of Historical Sciences Professor Valentyn Yu. Malanchuk. Despite his relative youth (he was born in November, 1928), Dr. Malanchuk, who is an ethnic Ukrainian, is a seasoned ideologist with wide exposure to Western Ukraine, the hotbed of virulent Ukrainian nationalism. If anybody can grasp the nettles of the everchanging ideology, it is Malanchuk.[90]

On the provincial level out of 26 Party organizations (25 **obkoms** and the Kyiv City **gorkom**) 9 changed their First Secretaries after Shelest's ouster and 1, which I will henceforth ignore, changed its head in mid-March, 1972.[91] Of the 9 post-Shelest changes, 2 Secretaries were either transferred or promoted to other First Secretaryships.[92] Four First Secretaries were relieved with a whiff of suspicion and displeasure,[93] and 3 First Secretaries were chased out with explicit criticism.[94] Most interesting are those sessions in which Shcherbyts'kyi himself participated: in Kharkiv, where at first only a whiff of suspicion arose, and in Poltava and Voroshilovhrad, where the shortcomings were made obvious.

In June, 1972, H. I. Vashchenko, First Secretary of the Kharkiv **obkom** and since 1971 full member of the CC CPU Politburo was appointed First Deputy Prime Minister of the Ukrainian SSR, ostensibly following the job of First Deputy Prime Minister M. O. Sobol who went into retirement.[95] This appears like a possible demotion. Shcherbyts'kyi himself attended the meeting of the Kharkiv **obkom** which elected I. Z. Sokolov, the previous Second Secretary, to fill Vashchenko's place.[96] Shcherbyts'kyi handled the demotion with finesse: it was not more than a year later that the hapless Kharkiv **obkom** was again chosen as the target of criticism by the CPSU CC in Moscow, this time for economic inefficiency.[97] It appears that Vashchenko is no favorite of Brezhnev's and Shcherbyts'kyis (the residual of the battle with Podgorny in 1965?). But it is also significant that the new First Secretary Sokolov was promoted from within the Kharkiv Party organization and promptly inducted as alternate member of the Politburo. Possibly from Shcherbyts'kyi's viewpoint, the Party organization as a whole is still trustworthy.

The same cannot be said about M. M. Muzhitsky, former First Secretary of the Poltava Province who at the plenum of January 26, 1973, was retired from political life completely, not just demoted, at the age of 60. The Poltava **obkom** have been accused of consistently not fulfilling their economic plans and of falling short in political, particularly "international" education. Shcherbyts'kyi spoke at the meeting, at which Muzhitsky was not given the floor. A somewhat obscure CC CPU staff member, F. T. Morhun, who had until quite recently been First Deputy Prime Minister of Kirghizia, was given Muzhitsky's place. But there is more than meets the eye in Muzhitsky's dismissal, which also explains Shcherbyts'kyi's presence at the purge in a relatively small Party organization. Several years ago N. A. Shchelokov, USSR Minister of Interior Affairs and Brezhnev protege, wanted to convict Muzhitsky of corruption. (Muzhitsky appears to have been an associate and protege of Podgorny's.) In early 1971 Shchelokov's attempt was foiled when the CC CPU Secretariat under Shelest issued a statement that the charges had not been substantiated. Moreover, November 25, 1972, Muzhitsky published a "fighting" article in **Izvestiya** that is reportedly under the influence of Podgorny in which he attacked full CC CPSU Politburo member Polyansky and in which he may have been sniping at Brezhnev himself. On behalf of Shchelokov, Polyansky and Brezhnev, but probably against Podgorny's wishes, Shcherbyts'kyi fired Muzhitsky with great pleasure in January, 1973.[98]

The situation in Voroshilovhrad was somewhat different in that its long-time First Secretary V. V. Shevchenko who had headed the **obkom** since March, 1961, had been criticized already under Shelest for not effectively supervising Party personnel, i.e., for not running a tight ship. In his place Shcherbyts'kyi in December, 1973, personally installed a Borys F. Honcharenko, who since March 18, 1966 had been in charge of the Machine Building Section of the CC CPU Secretariat. Honcharenko's political loyalties are unknown, but he has been put in charge of the 5th largest' CPU organization and this might incline him to be grateful toward Brezhnev and Shcherbyts'kyi.[99]

Conclusion:

Since the heyday of Khrushchev the CPU has increased much faster than its parent party, the CPSU. This was bound to create problems with the quality of members later on. On top of this, Shelest had increasingly challenged the central Party leaders to give "his" CPU greater autonomy in economic, political and ideological-political matters, including greater freedom to deal with its dissidents. As much as he may have wanted Shelest could not cut himself loose from the Ukrainian milieu, which on the one hand lent him oral strength, but also contributed to his political headaches. In his dealing with Brezhnev Shelest was being slowly undermined on domestic issues. When in addition he challenged Brezhnev on the appropriateness of the Nixon visit, he was promptly ousted from the Secretaryship.

His successor, Shcherbyts'kyi, holds an evident mandate from Brezhnev to use the convenient Union-wide "exchange of Party cards" to cover a wholesale purge of administrative and political deadwood, of any corrupt elements, and of intellectual dissidents from positions of power and the ranks of the CPU in general. It is still too early to guage the full extent of the purge, for it will be completed only at the end of 1974. I hope that the regime will then see fit to release **true** membership for January 1, 1975, which would enable us to estimate how many CPU members have been purged as a whole. But some of the trends have appeared already by the fall of 1974.

First, judging on the basis of the **obkom** meetings which Shcherbyts'kyi attended in person, there is a suspicion in my mind that the reshuffle immediately following Shelest's ouster (in June-July, 1972) and the purge proper (1973-74) have been used to settle old political scores. To be sure, V. V. Shevchenko of Voroshilovhrad appears to have been incompetent beyond repair and his replacement was, therefore, overdue. On the other hand, was Muzhitsky of Poltava really fired because he did not fulfill the province's economic plans and did not "ride herd" on his propagandists or rather because he had crossed swords with Shchelokov but had been retained owing to Podgorny's and Shelest's backing? Significantly he was removed after the harvest of 1972, which was poor throughout the Ukraine, not just in Poltava **oblast**. Finally, to me Vashchenko of Kharkiv is definitely a victim of his ties with Podgorny and Shelest rather than of any economic inefficiency in his old province. He has been made to follow the career of Sobol, downward.

The second trend which has recently appeared is the tendency of putting ethnic Russians into key positions in the CPU. This trend should be viewed in the light of Brezhnev's programmatial speech of December 21, 1972, calling in effect for sharp centralization and accelerated assimilation. Not only is Ukraine's largest Party organization (Donetsk) headed by Degtyarev, a Russian, but so is probably the fourth-largest, Kharkiv under the new Secretary Sokolov. Even more dangerous from the viewpoint of the Ukrainian majority who still have not won a proportionate share of members in the CPU is the fact that since early 1970 the Party Organizational Work Department of the CC CPU (i.e., the Party personnel division) has been headed by two Russians, or at least two Ukrainians with very Russian names, A. A. Ulanov and H. K. Kryuchkov. Will they use the exchange of Party cards to regain for the Russians the positions they had lost under Khrushchev?

Furthermore, to touch on a methodological issue, if my analysis of the Party "family groups" is correct and if it was useful in demonstrating Shelest's difficulties in keeping his "own" Kyiv Provincial Party Organization under control, it could also be applied to the career of Shcherbyts'kyi. It would seem to me that anything that happens to Vatchenko, e.g., is important as an indicator of Shcherbyts'kyi's standing. On the other hand, if Shcherbyts'kyi should later dismiss his formal deputy Lutak this need not be taken as a diminution in Shcherbyts'kyi's authority: as Brezhnev in 1965 got rid of Titov and Podgorny after the reorganization of the CPSU so Shcherbyts'kyi might want to blame the hardships of the purge on Lutak. Lutak has never been a member of Shcherbyts'kyi's "family group."

The final big question is, of course, how long will Shcherbyts'kyi himself last before he unpardonably quarrels with Brezhnev or with Brezhnev's successor in Moscow? I venture to predict that it will not be very long, for the same Shcherbyts'kyi, who in 1971 enthusiastically accepted Brezhnev's leadership and

Brezhnev's Kosygin's "rational" industrial plans for Ukraine, in 1966 had aggressively lobbied in Moscow for more coal and electricty. Furthermore, though the issues between Shcherbyts'kyi and Khrushchev have not been officially spelled out, I would doubt very much that Khrushchev demoted Shcherbyts'kyi over an excess of meekness on Shcherbyts'kyi's attitude toward the Kremlin. The top Soviet elite might prefer to agree among themselves, but the republican, ethnic milieu tends to drive them apart.

TECHNICAL NOTE

The Mysterious Membership Figures

For three dates — January 1, 1966, January 1, 1971, and January 1, 1972 — the figures for CPU membership given in the corresponding volumes of **Ezhegodnik Bol'shoy Sovetskoy Entsyklopedii** significantly diverge from those announced by the top CPU leader. For one date — September 1, 1961 — they are identical. Let's start with the perfect corroboration.

At the 1961 CPU Congress then First Secretary Podgorny gave for the membership the figures of 1,432,806 full and 147,365 candidate members as of September 1, 1961 (RU, Sept. 29, 1971, 5). These figures were confirmed by Mandate Commision spokesman I. I. Vivdychenko (RU, Sept. 28, 1961, 8). Vivdychenko also stated that the armed forces and internal security personnel stationed in the republic had elected delegates to the Congress together with the territorial CPU organization. Adding up of the CPU membership **on the basis of delegates** at the 1961 Congress closely tallies with Podgorny's figure (1,431,000 full and 147,000 candidate members). Ergo, Podgorny's figure includes the Red Army and Navy and MVD personnel stationed in the republic. **Ezhegodnik B.S.E.** 1962, 180, reconfirms Podgorny's figures.

At the 1966 CPU Congress, however, Shelest announced 1,977,119 full members and 145,697 candidates as of January 1, 1966. "In the last four years" — i.e., apparently since 1 / 1 / 62 — the CPU had increased by 513,580 members. (RU, March 16, 1966, 5 or **DSUP**, X / r (April '66), 7). Somewhat less precisely Shelest confirmed the membership figures two weeks later at the CPSU Congress in Moscow: the CPU's total membership was "more than two million," in the last four years it had grown by 513,580 (P, March 31, 1966, 3b). At the 1966 CPU Congress Mandate Commission spokesman I. I. Vivdychenko, however, had confirmed Shelest's precise figures as well as the presence of military, etc., delegates. On the basis of delegates, the CPU had 1,978,600 full and 146,900 candidate members. These figures are very close to Shelest's, ergo, the military are included in the former. (RU, March 16, 1966, 8 or **DSUP**, X / 4,8-9). **Ezhegodnik B.S.E.** 1966, 187b, on the other hand, gives for 1 / 1 / 66 1,833,362 full and 128,046 candidate members, i.e., a total of 1,961,408. This is incompatible with Shelest's figures in Kyiv and in Moscow, the difference between the totals being 161,408 or 7.6 percent! The more contemporary data of Shelest & Vivdychenko should be considered more authoritative, I think. Did the E.B.S.E. 1966 editors slip up? This is rather unlikely. To the best of my knowledge, no major purge of CPU members was taking place in 1966. The only plausible explanation for the deficit is the **implicit** exclusion of the Party members among the military and internal security personnel stationed in Ukraine in the E.B.S.E. data. Border guards fall in the same category.

In 1971 the deficit between the Shelest and Mandate Commission (A. A. Ulanov's) figures on the one hand and the E.B.S.E. 1971 figures on the other hand is 155,772 or 6.1 percent. Though the presence of military delegates is not explicitly admitted in Ulanov's report it can be assumed. Membership figures on the basis of number of delegates (2,424,400 full and 110,200 candidates) is very close to Shelest's figures. See RU, March 18, 1971, 5 & 6; E.B.S.E. 1971, 192a. Apparently E.B.S.E. has again excluded the military members, without alerting its readers to that omission.

But E.B.S.E. action in printing in E.B.S.E. 1972, p. 180a for 1 / 1 / 72 the very same CPU membership figure that in March 1971 Shelest gave for 1 / 1 / 71, viz. 2,424,350 full members and 110,211 candidates, a total of 2,534,561 (see RU, March 18, 1971, 5b), resulting in an increase, if the more authoritative, more contemporary Shelest base figure, is taken, of exactly 0 men and women over 365 days is a little hard to swallow as an editorial or proofreading error. Since the 1972 E.B.S.E. went to press September

11, 1972, i.e., after the "exchange of party cards" had been decided upon at the May 19, 1972 CPSU CC Plenum and after Shelest had been ousted from Kyiv, and since both Brezhnev and Shelest's successor Shcherbyts'kyi might be assumed to be interested in some Party "housecleaning" in Ukraine, it would seem to me that they would stand to gain from, some fudging of the figures. Hence what appears to me a somewhat clumsy suppression of the unknown true CPU membership figure as of 1 / 1 / 72 by substituting Shelest's 1 / 1 / 71 figure, in order to hid the true extent of the purge.

TABLE I

GROWTH OF CP OF UKRAINE AND CP OF SOVIET UNION, 1956 — 1973

(with particular attention to 1966-1973)

| | C.P.U. | | | | | | C.P.S.U. | | |
| Year[a] | Full Members | Candidate Members | Full and Candidate Members | Per thousand increase from preceding year or interval (F & C Ms.) | Total population in Ukraine (thousands) | Party members (Full and Candidate) per thousand population, UkrSSR | Full and Candidate Members, CPSU | Per thousand increase from preceding year or interval | Party members per thousand population, USSR |
(1)	(2)	(3)	(4)	(5)	(6)	(7)	(8)	(9)	(10)
1956	--	--	838,336	N.A.	40,587.0[b]	20.7	7,215,505[c]	N.A.	36.0
1961d	1,432,806P	147,365P	1,580,171P	884.9	43,404.8[d]	36.4	9,716,005[d]	346.5	44.4
1966	1,833,362	128,046	1,961,408	241.3	45,548.4	43.1	12,357,308	271.9	53.2
1966	1,977,119S	145,697S	2,122,816S	343.4S	45,548.4	46.6S	12,357,308	271.9	53.2
1967	1,959,215	84,976	2,044,191	42.2 / -37.0S	45,995.5	44.4	12,684,133	26.5	54.0
1968	2,033,792	105,008	2,138,800	46.3	46,408.2	46.1	13,180,225	39.1	55.6
1969	2,123,283	106,476	2,229,759	42.5	46,778.1	47.7	13,639,891	34.9	57.0
1970	2,212,987	88,670	2,301,657	32.2	47,126.5[e]	48.8	14,001,874	26.5	58.0
1971	2,281,568	97,221	2,378,789	33.5	47,496.1	50.1	14,372,563	26.5	58.9
1971	2,424,350S	110,211S	2,534,561S	101.2S	47,496.1	53.4S	14,372,563	26.5	58.9
1972	2,424,350	110,211	2,534,561	65.5 / 0.0S	47,878.0	52.9	14,631,289	18.0	59.4
1973	2,407,667	71,969	2,479,636	-21.7	48,236.8	51.4	14,821,031	13.0	59.6

NOTES:
(a) Data for January 1 of corresponding year, unless otherwise indicated.
(b) As of April 1956 (official estimate). No estimates available for 1 / 1 / 1956.
(c) "On the eve of the 20th CPSU Congress."
(d) As of September 1, 1961 for the CPU and October 1, 1961 for the CPSU. Population data adjusted accordingly (population of Ukraine on 1 / 1 / 61 plus 8 / 12 of difference between P on 1 / 1 / 62 and P on 1 / 1 / 61; population of USSR on 1 / 1 / 61 plus 9 / 12 of difference).
(e) Population data as of January 15, 1970.
P, S — see immediately below.

258

Table 1 (continued)

SOURCES:

Colums (2) and (3): for 1961, 1966, 1971 CPU Congress data — see M. V. Pidhornyi, **Radyans'ka Ukraina** (henceforth; RU,) Sept. 29, 1961, p. 5; P. Ye. Shelest, March 16, 1966, pp. 2-6 or **Digest of the Soviet Ukrainian Press (DSUP)**, X / 4 (April 1966), 7; and Shelest, R.U., March 18, 1971, 4. These figures and all those derived from them have been marked either P for Pidhorny or S for Shelest. The other figures from **Ezhegodnik Bol'shoy Sovetskoy Entsiklopedii, 1966 (E.B.S.E.)**, p. 187; E.B.S.E., 1967, p. 194; E.B.S.E., 1968, p. 191; E.B.S.E., 1969, p. 178; E.B.S.E., 1970, p. 184; E.B.S.E., 1971, p. 192, E.B.S.E., 1972, p. 180; and E.B.S.E., 1973, p. 183. The meaning of the discrepancy of the 1966 and 1971 figures is discussed in Technical Note, above. There is no discrepancy between the 1961 Pidhorny and the E.B.S.E., 1962 data.

Column (4): 1956 figure from Vsevolod Holubnychy, "Outline History of the Communist Party of the Ukraine," **The Ukrainian Review** (Institute for the Study of the USSR, Munich), 1958, No. 6, p. 124. Other figures from Columns (2) and (3).

Column (5). Calculated by author from data in Column (4).

Column (6). 1956: Statystychne upravlinnya Ukrains'koi RSR, **Narodne hospodarstvo Ukrains'koi RSR: Statystychny zbirnyk (Nar. hosp. URSR)** (Kyiv, 1957), p. 7. 1961: Calculated by author from 1 / 1 / 61 and 1 / 1 / 62 figures in **Nar. hosp. URSR v 1971 r.** (Kyiv, 1972), p. 12. All other figures from same table, **ibid.**, pp. 12-13.

Column (7). Calculated by author from data in Columns (4) and (6).

Column (8). 1956 and 1961: Khrushchev reporting to the 22nd CPSU Congress, **Pravda**, October 18, 1961, p. 10. The other data from "KPSS v tsifrakh (K 70 — letiyu II S"ezda RSDRP)," **Partiynaya Zhizn'**, 1973, No. 14 (July), 10.

Column (9). Derived from Column (8), author's calculations.

Column (10). Data from Column 8, and population data from Tsentral'noe statisticheskoe upravlenie SSR, **Narodnoe khozaystvo SSSR v 1972 g.: Statisticheskiy ezhegodnik** (Moscow, 1973), p. 7. Population figure for 10 / 1 / 61 is an adjusted one (see Notes, d, above).

FOOTNOTES

1. Arend Lijphart, "Cultural Diversity and Theories of Political Integration," **Canadian Journal of Political Science,** IV, 1 (March 1971). 10.

2. **Ibid.,** 11, 12.

3. A knowledgeable recent Soviet refugee, e.g., told me that while he was First Secretary of the CPU Shelest had two residences in Kyiv alone: the palatial mansion that went with the office and a comfortably furnished five room apartment "just in case."

4. See on this Carl A. Linden, **Khrushchev and the Soviet Leadership,** 1957-1964 (Baltimore, Md.: The Johns Hopkins Press, 1966), **passim,** especially Introduction and Chapter 1.

5. For a semi-comical, semi-serious denunciation of such protective "family groups" by Stalin see Merle Fainsod, **How Russia is Ruled** (Cambridge, Mass.: Harvard University Press, 1963; rev. ed.), p. 235.

6. All but the percentage figure taken from Shelest's report, **Radyans'ka Ukraina** (henceforth: **RU**), March 16, 1966, 5 or **Digest of the Soviet Ukrainian Press** (henceforth: **DSUP**), X / 4 (April 1966), 7.

7. See the figures in Podgorny's report, **RU,** September 29, 1961, 5.

8. Borys Lewytzkyj uses the term "model" in **Die Sowjetukraine** 1944-1963 (Cologne-Berline: Kiepenheuer & Witsch, 1964), 154 ff. See also Y. Bilinsky, **The Second Soviet Republic: The Ukraine after World War II** (New Brunswick, N.J.: Rutgers University Press, 1964), 227 ff.

9. See, e.g., **Pravda** (P), March 30, 1966, 8.

10. Cf. Brezhnev's Central Committee report, **Izvestiya,** March 31, 1971, 9 and resolution on this report, **P,** April 10, 1971, 4.

11. As cited by Christian Duevel in "Shelest Ousted from Ukrainian CP Leadership," **Radio Liberty Research Bulletin,** CRD 128 / 72 (May 30, 1972), 8.

12. **Ibid.,** Duevel's assertion that Shelest's plea is unrelated to his ouster is not entirely persuasive. See my discussion of Shelest's removal below.

13. See Scherbyts'kyis's report to the plenum, **RU,** September 21, 1974, 3.

14. O. Kuznetsov, "Stringency and Control," **RU,** June 25, 1974, 2; transl. in **DSUP,** XVIII / 8 (August 1974), 7-8.

15. Privately communicated in his letter of December 10, 1974.

16. See the last complete breakdown in "To the 50th Anniversary of Ukraine's Communist Party. Avant Garde of the Ukrainian Nation. Communist Party of Ukraine in Figures," **RU,** June 30, 1968, 2 or **DSUP,** XII / 8 (August 1968), 6 ff.; and "KPSS v tsifrakh," **Partiynaya zhizn'** (P.zh.), 1967 / 19 (October 1967).

17. The numbers of adult Ukrainians and Russians as of January 15, 1970 have been discounted back to January 1, 1968 — the date of the Party figures — by using the

difference between the general populations of the UkrSSR on those dates. To obtain the numbers of Ukrainian and Russian adult males and females I have assumed that the sex distribution within a nationality would be the same for adults as for the nationality as a whole. In order to obtain more realistic data of female party members I have assumed that the proportion of female party members is the same among the Ukrainians and Russians in the UkrSSR, i.e., 18.8 percent of the contingent. All these are approximations made necessary by imperfect statistics. Breakdowns by age in **Itogi vsesoyuznoy perepisi naseleniya** 1970 **goda,** IV, 360, 377; number of Russians in the Ukraine, **ibid.,** 12; distribution by sex in Ukraine, **ibid,** 154, 156. Party membership from Table in text, p. 10.

18. T. H. Rigby, **Communist Party Membership in the U.S.S.R.** 1917-1967 (Princeton, New Jersey: Princeton University Press, 1968), 389-90.

19. See my article "The Incorporation of Western Ukraine and Its Impact on Politics and Society in Soviet Ukraine," in Roman Szporluk, ed., **The Influence of Eastern Europe and the Western Territories of the U.S.S.R. on Soviet Society** (New York: Praeger, forthcoming).

21. **Ibid.,** Table 40, 475 ff.

22. See V.V. Onikienko & V.A. Popovkin, **Kompleksnoe issledovanie migratsionnykh protsessov: Analiz migratsiy naseleniya USSR** (Moscow: Statistika, 1973), **passim,** esp. 28, 38-44, 72-75, and 155-57 (conclusions).

23. The tie between Shelest and Podgorny is brought out in Grey Hodnett's excellent biographical sketch, "Pyotr Efimovich Shelest," in George W. Simmonds, ed., **Soviet Leaders** (N.Y.: Crowell, 1967), 99, 100, 101.

24. On Shcherbyts'kyi see **Deputaty Verkhovnogo Soveta SSSR: Sed'moy sozyv** (**D.V.S. SSSR,** 1966) (Moscow, 1966), 505; Lewytzkyj, **Die Sowjetukraine,** 356; Grey Hodnett & Val Ogareff, **Leaders of the Soviet Republics** 1955-1972: **A Guide to Posts and Occupants** (Canberra: Department of Political Science, Research School of Social Sciences, The Australian National University, 1973). 168. On Brezhnev's career see the portrait by Hodnett in **Soviet Leaders,** 23 ff.; also John Dornberg, **Brezhnev: The Masks of Power** (N.Y.: Basic Books, 1974), **passim,** esp. 100, 199-200, 276-77.

25. On Shcherbyts'kyi's reappointments see **N.Y. Times,** October 16, 1965, 10:6 and **P,** December 7, 1965, 1. On Vatchenko see **D.V.S. SSSR,** 1966, 83 and **Die Sowjetukraine** ..., 368.

26. For Sobol's biography see Lewytzkyj, **Die Sowjetukraine** ..., 362; **D.V.S. SSSR,** 1966, 413. Identification of Sobol's functions by Hodnett & Ogareff, **Leaders of the Soviet Republics** ..., 357. For his dismissal, RU, April 1, 1972, 1 or DSUP, XVI / 5 (May 1972), 4-5.

27. See Lyashko's official biographies in **D.V.S. SSSR,** 1966, 271 and in RU, June 10, 1972, 1 or DSUP, XVI / 7 (July 1972), 10-11. Also **Die Sowjetukraine** ..., 341. On Degtyarev see **Die Sowjetukraine** ..., 311 and **D.V.S. SSSR,** 1966, 133. See also RU, July 3, 1963, 1 for Lyashko's initial appointment to the CC CPU Secretariat.

28. See, e.g., the technical literature on the location of power plants in Ukraine cited by Vsevolod Holubnychy, "Some Economic Aspects of Relations Among the Soviet Republics," in Erich Goldhagen, ed. **Ethnic Minorities in the Soviet Union** (New York: Praeger, 1968), 87-88, 117-18. The most prominent advocate of building up Ukrainian fuel and power resources is G.B. Yakusha, **Tekhniko-ekonomicheskie osnovy raz-**

vitiya elektroenergetiki ekomonicheskikh rayonov Ukrainskoy SSR (Kyiv, 1965). See also Akademiya Nauk Ukrains'koi RSR, Instytut Ekonomiky (O.O. Nesterenko, ed.), **Natsional'ny dokhod Ukrains'koi RSR v period rozhornutoho budivyntstva komunizmu** (Kyiv, 1963).

29. Politicheskiy Dnevnik, No. 9, June 1965 (**Arkhiv Samizdata** no. 1002).

30. Cf. Shelest in **Pravda Ukrainy**, March 16, 1966 and **P**, March 31, 1966, 2-3 with Shcherbitsky in **P**, April 7, 1966, 2.

31. See John Kolasky, **Education in Soviet Ukraine: A Study in Discrimination and Russification** (Toronto: Peter Martin Associates, 1968) and especially his **Two Years in Soviet Ukraine: A Canadian's personal account of Russian oppression and the growing opposition** (Toronto: Peter Martin Associates, 1970). See also "Report of (the Communist Party of Canada) Delegation to Ukraine: Central Committee Meeting — September 16, 17 and 18, 1967," **Viewpoint** (Discussion Bulletin issued by the Central Executive Committee, Communist Party of Canada, Toronto, Ont.) V. No. 1 (January 1968) 1-13. That the CPU CC's reaction to the Canadian delegation has been one of fearful anticipation has been told by a former Soviet Ukrainian journalist who, unfortunately, used a pungent but non-printable expression. Vyacheslav Chornovil confirms this: "Potemkin's villages" were quickly erected (to be precise, a broken-down fence around a church near Lviv was urgently repaired) and a factory director suddenly started talking in Ukrainian again. See Chornovil, "Yak i shcho obstoyuye Bodhan Stenchuk (66 Zapytan' i zauvah 'internatsionalistovi')," **Ukrains'kyi visnyk**, VI (March 1972) (Paris-Baltimore, Md.: Smolskyp, 1972), 16-17.

32. Dadenkov's letter of instruction "Pro movu vykladannya u vuzakh MVSSO URSR" is summarized by Chornovil, **loc. cit.**, 28-30.

33. Ivan Dzyuba, **Internatsionalism chy rusyfikatsiya?** (Munich: Suchasnist, 1968). An anonymous Soviet emigre asserts that Skaba had requested a study from Dzyuba. Kolasky writes that Dzyuba had protested against Russification at a meeting with Skaba and to get rid of him, Skaba suggested that he write a memo. Both, however, agree that Dzyuba's response had been solicited (see memorandum of REF's Communist Area Analysis Department — USSR, of April 25, 1973), "Ivan Mikhailovich Dzyuba," p. 2 and Kolasky, **Two Years in Soviet Ukraine**, 76. Skaba had been appointed Ideological CC CPU Secretary and candidate member of the CC CPU Presidium October 25, 1959. His biographies in **D.V.S. SSSR**, 1966, 407; Lewytzkyj, **Die Sowjetukraine**, 359, also in Kolasky, **ibid.**, 73-74 (most complete one).

34. **Pravda Ukrainy**, March 16, 1966, 5 (my translation and emphasis added). See also **DSUP**, X / 4 (April 1966), 6.

35. Identified as a former (pre-1938) First Secretary of the Dnipropetrovs **obkom** and "patron of Brezhnev" in Dornberg's **Brezhnev**, 66.

36. See Radio Liberty's "Soviet Affairs Review: First Quarter 1971," CRD 142 / 71 (April 19, 1971), 8. On the other hand, neither Lewytzkyj, nor Brezhev's biographer Dornberg, nor I have found any evidence linking him to the Dnipropetrovs'k group. I would have assumed that in mid-1959 Shelest and his patron Podgorny would not have tolerated a Dnipropetrovs'k Trojan horse in the Kyiv Party organization, in which he held several responsible offices from 1959-1966 becoming Shelest's successor as First **obkom** Secretary. Dr. Duevel has a point, however, when he emphasizes the parallels in the careers of Vatchenko and Drozdenko (both were humiliated either at or just prior to the 1971 CPU Congress, rehabilitated at the CPSU Congress three weeks later). Possibly Drozdenko was not a charter member of the Dnipropetrovs'k faction

262

but a trusted member of Shelest's Kyivan group who joined Shcherbyts'kyi and Co. later.

37. Dornberg, **Brezhnev**, 67.

38. On the date of his appointment, see Hodnett & Ogareff. **Leaders** ..., 377. On the date of his dismissal from the Second Secretaryship RU, June 20, 1969, 1 or **DSUP**, XIII / 8 (August 1969), 2.

39. Biographies in **D.V.S. SSSR**, 1970, 263; RU, June 20, 69, 1 or **DSUP**, XIII / 8 (August 1969), 2-3 also Lewytzkyj, **Die Sowketukraine** ..., 342. See also RU, January 24, 1967 or DSUP, XI / 3 (March 1967), 28, and Hodnett & Ogareff, **Leaders** ..., 347. Also Christian Duevel, "Stalemate in Ukrainian Leadership Reshuffle," Radio Liberty CRD 144 / 72 (June 13, 1972), 3. Dr. Duevel makes the point that Lutak did not speak during the May 19, 1972, CC CPSU plenum unseating Shelest. Presumably this is an indication of his continuing loyalty to Shelest.

40. See **D.V.S. SSSR**, 1970, 474 and Hodnett & Ogareff, **Leaders** ..., 350.

41. See "Informational Announcement," RU, May 18, 1974, 1 and cf. with Hodnett & Ogareff, **Leaders**, 350.

42. Chernyhiv, Crimea, Ivano-Frankivs'k, Khmelnyts'kyi, Kyiv, Kirovohrad, Mykolaiv, Odesa, Sumy, Ternopil. Volyn', and Zhytomyr **oblasts**.

43. On Odesa see below. First Secretary of Sumy **obkom** B. I. Vol'tovsky was appointed Chairman of the State Committee of Nature Conservation on June 8, 1967 — RU June 10, 1967 or DSUP, XI / 7 (July 1967), 29, also Hodnett & Ogareff, **Leaders** . . ., 366. His successor is O. I. Ishchenko. First Volyn' Secretary F. I. Kalyta was dismissed and replaced by S. Ya Zaichenko in August 1969. **Robitnycha Hazeta**, Aug. 9, 1969 or **DSUP**, XIII / 9 (September 1969), 28. Zaichenko served in Dnipropetrovs'k (!) and on the staff of the CC CPU Secretariat — see **D.V.S. SSSR**, 1970, 157.

44. See **D.V.S. SSSR**, 1966, 110; Hodnett & Ogareff, **Leaders** ....., 349, 353, 375.

45. **D.V.S. SSR**, 1970, 474; Hodnett & Ogareff, **Leaders** . . . ., 349, 350.

46. RU, May 8, 1970 or **DSUP**, XIV / 6 (June 1970), 29. In July Synytsya was made the director of the Chief Administration of the River Fleet (RU, July 31, 1970 or **DSUP**, XIX / 9 (Sept. 1970), 28). Cashiered earlier was his Second Secretary Paul P. Voronin — Radio Odesa Nov. 11, 1969 and Kh. K., "Samokritika Odesskogo obkoma partii," Ts. I.O. 277 / 70 (July 27, 1970), 2 in Radio Liberty, **Issledovatel'skii Byulletin' (IB)**, XIV / 30 (July 29, 1970).

47. **D.V.S. SSSR**, 1970, 213

48. See RU, May 20, 1967, 4 and May 30, 1967, 1 or **DSUP**, XI / 7 (July 1967), 29; and Hodnett & Ogareff, **Leaders** ....., 358.

49. RU, July 21, 1970, 1 or DSUP, XIV / 9 (September 1970), 1; **D.V.S. SSSR**, 1970, 313 ("responsible work" in Moscow). Assertion of Nikitchenko's friendship with Fedorchuk's intrigues against Shelest in RFE Research, Communist Area, no. 1900 (8 October 1973); "Ukrainian KGB Boss in Politburo," 3.

50. P. Ye. Shelest, "Boevye zadachi ukrainskoy sovetskoy literatury," **Literaturnaya Gazeta** (Moscow), November 17, 1966, 2. His speech has been reprinted in the

collection P. Yu. Shelest, **Idei Lenina peremahayut'** (Kyiv, 1971), 269-83, the last cited passage on p. 276.

51. A few more details in Y. Bilinsky, "Assimilation and Ethnic Assertiveness Among Ukrainians of the Soviet Union," in Goldhagen, ed., **Ethnic Minorities in the Soviet Union,** 173-75.

52. For a typical critical review see M. Yurchuk, F. Lebedenko, ("In the Face of Reality,") RU, April 26, 1968, 3-4 DSUP, XII / 6 (June 1968), 12-15. Rumors have it that Vatchenko felt he had been caricatured in Honchar's novel and that copies of **Sobor** were rounded up by Komsomol and Party activists in Dnipropetrovs'k and then destroyed.

53. See John Kolasky, **Two Years . . .,** 73-76.

54. See RU, March 30, 1968, 1 for announcement of Ovcharenko's election to candidate member of the CC CPU Politburo and Secretary. **Robitnycha Hazeta,** March 30, 1968, 1 has brief official biography. Both in **DSUP,** XII / 5 (May 1968), 1-2.

55. Hodnett & Potichnyj, **The Ukraine and the Czechoslovak Crisis,** 81-86.

56. See P. Yu. Shelest, **Istorychne poklykannya molodi** (Kyiv, 1967), 134-35.

57. See RU, March 18, 1971, 2c.

58. **Ibid.,** 2d.

59. RU, March 20, 1971, 2-4.

60. P, April 1, 1971, 3f.

61. Cf. Kosygin's speech: Thanks to an emphasis on cheaper strip mining and to large scale mechanization in the 1971-1975 Five Year Plan coal production will increase by 11 percent while the number of coal miners will decrease by 20 percent. P, April 7, 1971, 4a. Strip mining is impossible in the Donets'k Basin!

62. P, April 1, 1971, 3h.

63. P, April 7, 1971, 8 c-d.

64. See P, April 10, 1971, 1.

65. See "Soviet Affairs Review: First Quarter 1971," 8 (as in Note 36, above).

66. Ibid., 9.

67. P, May 21, 1972, and RU, May 26, 1972, 1 or DSUP, XVI / 7 (July 1972), 1.

68. See Christian Duevel, "Shelest Ousted from Ukrainian CP Leadership," (RL CRD 128 / 72: May 30, 1972), 8, citing P, May 20, 1972.

69. I have this detail from a recent emigre who had worked in Kyiv Radio and Television.

70. P, May 27, 1972, I and Duevel, **loc. cit.** (note 68), 2.

71. RU, May 26, 1972, 1 or DSUP, XVI / 7 (July 1972), 1.

72. Duevel, loc. cit. (note 68), 1-2.

73. Editorial, "Pro ser'yozni nedoliky ta pomylky odniyei knyhy," Kommunist Ukrainy, 1973, No. 4 (April 1973), 77-82, quotations on p. 77 and 82. Very convenient facsimile reprint in Za shcho usunuly Shelesta? Dokumenty (Munich: Suchasnist, 1973). Shelest's book is called Ukraino nasha Radyans'ka (Kyiv, 1970); 280 pp.; signed for printing December 31, 1970; edition of 100,000.

74. See Y. Bilinsky, The Second Soviet Republic: The Ukraine After World War II (New Brunswick: Rutgers University Press, 1964), 15-16.

75. P, April 28, 1973, 1. See also Christian Duevel, "An Unprecedented Plenum of the CPSU Central Committee," (RL 145 / 73 — May 3, 1973).

76. Besides the 2 major memoranda by Duevel, cited in notes 68 and 75, above, two useful published articles are Myroslav Prokop, "Padinnya Petra Shelesta," Suchasnist, XIII, 6 (June 1973), 98-110, and Astrid von Borcke, "Das April-Plenum 1973 des Zentralkomitees der KPd-SU und die Umbesetzungen im Politbeuro," Osteuropa, XXIII, 12 (December 1973), 917-29, esp. pp. 919-21.

77. See especially Robert G. Kaiser in The Washington Post, May 26, 1972, A 17 and June 11, 1972 (column on "Creative Art of Kremlinology').

78. See RL 61, 73: March 5, 1973, "Ukrainian State Farms Subordinated to Moscow," 3 pp.

79. V. V. Shcherbyts'kyi, "Pro zavdannya partiynykh orhanizatsiy respubliky po dal'shomu polipshenniu roboty z kadramy u svitli rishen' XXIV Z'izdu KPRS," RU, April 20, 1973, 1 or DSUP, XVII / 6 (June 1973), 15.

80. Von Borcke, loc. cit. (note 76), 920.

81. See Carl J. Friedrich & Zbigniew K. Brzezinski, Totalitarian Dictatorship and Autocracy (Cambridge, Mass.: Harvard University, 1956), 19-20 or same, (N.Y.: Praeger, 1968; 2nd rev. ed.), 35-36. To be precise, the authors speak of the feudal element in the makeup of the totalitarian lieutenant. Shelest personifies this element quite nicely.

82. See, e.g., Shelest, Ukraino nasha Radyans'ka, 9, 58, also his Lenin centennial speech on April 17, 1970 in Idei Lenina peremahayut', 16.

83. Izvestiya, October 24, 1965. Shelest's speech itself is reproduced in the collection of Idei Lenina . . ., 230-23.

84. Kolasky, Two Years . . ., 206.

85. See L. I. Brezhnev's exceedingly important speech "O piatidesyatiletii Soyuza Sovetskikh Sotsialisticheskikh Respublik," P, December 22, 1972, 2-5.

86. RU, June 10, 1972, 1 or DSUP, XVI / 7 (July 1972), 10.

87. RU, July 28, 1972, 1 or DSUP, XVI, 9 (Sept. 1972), 1, 9. See also Christian Duevel, "Stalemate in Ukrainian Leadership Reshuffle," RL CRD 144 / 72 — June 13, 1972, 4 pp.

88. RU, July 28, 1972, 1 or **DSUP**, SVI, 9 (Sept. 1972), 1.

89. See communique plus official biography in **RU**, October 11, 1972, 1 or **DSUP**, XVI / 11 (November 1972), 11-13.

90. RU, September 15, 1973, 1 or **DSUP**, XVII / 10 (October 1973), 3. See also Kh. K., "Popolnenie sostava Politbyuro TsK KP Ukrainy," RL 295 / 73-21 Sept. 1973, in **IB**, SVII / 39 (September 26, 1973). See below for Vashchenko's ouster.

91. In the Khmelnyts'ky **oblast** M. D. Bubnovsky retired, was replaced by T. H. Lisovy — RU, March 15, 1972 or DSUP, XVI / 4 (April 1972), 28-29.

92. On 29 Nov. 1973 Dobryk was promoted from Ivano-Frankivs'k to Lviv (RU, Nov. 29, 1973, 3 or **DSUP**, XVIII, 1 (January 1974), 6; Oct. 5, 1972. I. O Mozhovy moved from Rovno to Kherson. Se **RU**, October 6, 1972 or **DSUP**, SVI, 11 (November 1972), 28. Dobryk has been identified as member of the Dnipropetrovs'k faction by Duevel, **loc. cit.** (note 36), 9.

93. O. S. Hryhorenko thus left the Chernivtsi obkom in early June 1972 — RU, June 13, 1972 or **DSUP**, XVI, 7 (July 1972), 29, ditto H. I. Vashchenko, of the Kharkiv obkom on June 15, 1972 (see **RU**, June 15, 1972 or **DSUP**, XVI, 8 (August 1972), 27-28); Kutsevol left Lviv in late November 1973 — see RU, Nov. 29, 1973 or DSUP, XVIII, 1 (January 1974), 6; and S. Ya. Zaichenko left Volyn' in August of 1973 — RU, Aug. 16, 1973 or **DSUP**, XVII, 10 (October, 1973), 1.

94. Those of the Kherson (A. S. Kochubey), Poltava (O. M. Muzhytsky), and Voroshilovhrad (V. V. Shevchenko) **oblasts**. For Kherson see RU, October 6, 1972 or **DSUP**, XVI, 11 (November 1972) 28; for others below.

95. See (on Vashchenko) RU, June 10, 1972, 1 or **DSUP**, XVI, 7 (July 1972), 11 and on Sobol RU, June 10, 1972, 2, or **DSUP**, XVI, 7 (July 1972), 10.

96. See Note 93, above.

97. TsK KPSS, "Ob organizatorskoy rabote khar'kovskogo obkoma partii po uluchsheniyu izpol'zovaniia rezervov proizvodstva i usileniyu rezhima ekonomii v promyshlennosti i stroitel'stve," **Partiinaia zhizh'**, 1973, No. 20 (October 1973), 5-8.

98. See RU, January 27, 1973, 1 or **DSUP**, XVII / 3 (March 1973), 1-2. Also Christian Duevel, "Protege of Shelest and Podgorny Ousted in the Ukraine," **RL** 27 / 73 (January 29, 1973).

99. RU, December 15, 1973, 1 or **DSUP**, XVIII / 1 (January 1973), 5. For previous, milder criticism under Shelest see RU, April 1, 1972, 1 or DSUP, XVI / 5 (May 1972), 4-5. See also Kh. K., "Smeshchenie Pervogo Sekretarya Voroshilovgradskogo obkoma KP Ukrainy," RL 401 / 73 — December 21. 1973. On Honcharenko see Hodnett & Ogareff. **Leaders** . . ., 353.

The Ruling Party
Organs of Ukraine

by
Borys Lewytzkyj
Munich, Germany

This paper is a survey of the ruling organs of Ukraine as of October 1974. These organs are: the Central Committee of the Communist Party of Ukraine (CPU): the Politburo, Secretariat and Departments of the Central Committee; the first secretaries of the Oblast Committees; and the Council of Ministers of the Ukrainian SSR. The analysis is based on the author's own files and, accordingly, does not include a list of sources.

The first sections of this paper provide a brief analysis of the individual groups. They are followed by sociological deductions in the form of a comprehensive analysis. The appendices consist of a tabulation of the Central Committee members according to their professional and social status, and of a name list with information about the Politburo and the Secretariat.

1. Basic Data
The Party

The present Central Committee was elected at the 24th CPU Congress in March 1971. It consists of 147 full members (of whom 81 were re-elected and 15 were formerly candidate members) and 85 candidate members (of whom 21 were re-elected, while one was formerly a full member). Three full members and one candidate member died between March 1971 and October 1974, and three candidate members acquired full membership. Sixteen full members and 11 candidate members of the CPU Central Committee are also members of the CPSU Central Committee. One candidate member of the CPU Central Committee is a candidate member of the CPSU Central Committee, and two full members of the CPU Central Committee are concurrently members of the CPSU Central Auditing Commission (see appendix with details of the CPU Central Committee members' professional and social status).

The Politburo of the CPU Central Committee had 11 full members and 5 candidate members in October 1974. All CPU Central Committee secretaries are simultaneously members of the Politburo. The length of membership in the Politburo is shown in the following table.

TABLE I
Length of Membership in Politburo

1954	1	1967	1
1957	1	1970	1
1962	1	1971	2
1963	1	1972	2
1966	4	1973	2
			—
			16

Four of the members were in the Politburo before Khrushchev's ouster; four acquired membership after the First Secretary of the CPU Central Committee, Shelest, was transferred to Moscow in 1972.

The following tables show the age and length of Party membership of the Politburo members.

TABLE II
Age and Party Affiliation of Politburo Members

Year of Birth		Party Member since	
1904	1	1928	1
1906	1	1932	1
1914	1	1940	3
1915	2	1941	1
1918	2	1942	1
1919	1	1943	2
1920	2	1944	1
1924	1	1945	1
1926	1	1947	1
1928	2	1950	1
unknown	2	1952	1
		1953	1
Total	16	unknown	1
		Total	16

A comparison of the age structure with that of the CPSU Politburo in Moscow shows that the top politicians in Kyiv are considerably younger. The two oldest members of the Ukrainian Politburo — I.S. Hrushetsky (b. 1904) and N.E. Kal'chenko (b. 1906) — are younger than the oldest members of the CPSU Politburo. Three of the men in the latter body were born before 1904, the oldest being A.Ya.Pelshe (b. 1899), followed by M.A. Suslov (b. 1902) and N.V. Podgorny (b. 1903). Twelve members of the Ukrainian Politburo (80 percent) were born after 1914. The number of CPSU Politburo members in this age group is only 10 (43 percent). A common feature of both Politburos (as well as those of the other Soviet republics) is the absence of representatives of the under-45 age group.

A comparison of the length of Party membership shows that the number of CPU Politburo members who joined the Party before 1939 (2) is very low compared with the number in the CPSU Politburo; it was three times larger during World War II. Only one member of the Ukrainian Politburo joined the Party in 1953, the year of Stalin's death. It is most unlikely that any other member joined the Party after that date.

These figures reflect the practice of keeping communists who joined the Party after Stalin's death — including people who have now been members for as much as 20 years — out of the top Party posts.

The following table shows the educational structure of the Ukrainian Politburo. Fourteen members have a complete college or university education; information on the educational level of the remaining two is not available. Of the fourteen, eleven graduated from technical institutes, two from state universities and one from the Party School. The year of graduation is important for assessing the quality of education: college and university degrees acquired in the 1930s and during World War II do not compare with international standards of the time and are well below the present-day Soviet norms. In the past Soviet "technical colleges" were often merely training schools attached to industrial enterprises. For this reason the table also shows when the members of the Ukrainian Politburo acquired their degrees.

TABLE III
Type of Education and Year of Graduation of Politburo Members

Education			Graduation Year	
College / University	14		1928	1
Unknown	2		1937	1
Type of College / University			1938	1
Technical Institute	11		1941	2
State University	2		1942	2
Party School	1		1947	1
Unknown	2		1950	1
	—		1952	1
	Total	16	1954	1
			1955	1
			1959	1
			1965	1
			Unknown	2
				—
			Total	16

Only seven of the highest Ukrainian Party officials (about 50 percent) acquired what can be called a full college or university education after World War II.

The Secretariat of the CPU Central Committee is headed by the First Secretary, V.V. Shcherbyts'kyi. There are five other Central Committee secretaries, all of whom are in the Politburo. With the exception of A.A. Tytarenko, who joined the Secretariat in 1966 and is responsible for industry (an area in which he is very experienced), and I.A. Lutak, who was transferred to Ukraine in 1969, all the Central Committee secretaries assumed office in 1970. Since almost all the secretaries belong to the relatively "young" generation in the Politburo and have college or university degrees in addition to their experience in Party management, the Party leadership's personnel policy at this level of administration seems to aim at putting the best men in the best positions. Thus, N.M. Borysenko is responsible for agriculture, V.Yu. Malanchuk for ideology, and Ya.P. Pohrebnyak for cadre policy. It would appear that the Party leadership has hit on an optimal solution in this area, since all the secretaries have an excellent reputation among the Party bureaucracy as well-educated, loyal and efficient functionaries. This cannot be said of the Party secretaries in all the republics.

While 12 of the 16 Politburo members are Ukrainian, one is Russian and three are of unascertainable nationality. All of the Secretariat members, however, are Ukrainian.

There are 25 Oblast Party Committees in Ukraine. It proved impossible to obtain information on all the first secretaries of these committees, so the number of unknowns (8 and 9) in the following tables is relatively high. The tables show age structure and length of Party membership.

TABLE IV
Age and Party Affiliation of Obkom First Secretaries

Year of Birth		Party Member Since	
1913	1	1939	2
1914	1	1940	1
1917	3	1943	2
1918	1	1944	4
1920	1	1945	1
1923	1	1947	1
1924	2	1951	1
1925	1	1952	1
1926	1	1953	1
1927	3	1954	1
1930	1	1957	2
Unknown	9	Unknown	8
Total	25	Total	25

Insofar as the age of the first secretaries of the Oblast Party Committees is known, there are virtually no representatives of the under-45 age group. This parallels the phenomenon in the Politburo. The promotion barrier for Party functionaries who joined the CP after Stalin's death also seems to apply to the position of Oblast secretary. Only three people in the above table have overcome this barrier.

Each of the Oblast secretaries whose academic record is known has a college or university education. Eleven of these secretaries graduated from technical institutes, one from a teachers' training institute, one from a state university and three from the Party College. The following table shows how long the Oblast Party Committee secretaries have been in office.

TABLE V
Length of Service as Obkom First Secretary

1962	1	1968	2
1963	1	1970	4
1965	2	1972	5
1966	1	1973	3
1967	3	1974	3
		Total	25

Many Oblast Party Committee secretaries were replaced in the 1960s, and only two have survived Khrushchev's fall. The number of new appointments since Shelest's demotion is also noteworthy: 11 secretaries have been replaced since 1972, three of them in 1974.

Although the number of secretaries whose age is unascertainable is fairly high, we may nevertheless assume that these changes did not rejuvenate the leadership of the Oblast Party Committees. By and large, the secretaryships went to people with many years of experience in Party work. In the CPU, as in the Party as a whole, the recruitment and selection mechanisms for certain positions do not seem to apply to the under-45 age group.

Nineteen of the Oblast secretaries are Ukrainians and three are Russians; the nationality of the other three is unknown.

The following table shows the political weight of this group in the CPU and the CPSU as a whole.

TABLE VI

Positions Held by Oblast Secretaries in Other Organs of the CPU and CPSU

Politburo Members	2
Candidate Members	2
CPU Central Committee Members	19
CPU Central Committee Candidate Members	2
CPSU Central Committee Members	5
CPSU Central Committee Candidate Members	3
Members of the CPSU Central Auditing Commission	1

The Government

The Council of Ministers of the Ukrainian SSR consists of 60 members of government at the present time. These include one chairman, two first deputy chairmen and seven deputy chairmen. Twenty-eight of the 34 ministers are in charge of union-republican and six in charge of republican ministries. Sixteen government members are chairmen of State Committees or directors of Main Administrations. Since the number of unknowns relating to the members of the Council of Ministers is particularly high, the analysis is limited to the period after accession to the present office.

The length of service of members of government can be seen in the following table:

TABLE VIII
Length of Service on the Council of Ministers

1955	1	1967	6
1957	1	1968	4
1959	1	1969	3
1960	1	1970	9
1961	2	1971	5
1962	2	1972	6
1963	2	1973	4
1965	6	1974	1
1966	6		60

None of the members of the present-day Ukrainian Council of Ministers was in office during Stalin's time, and only ten were in office during the Khrushchev period. The fact that as many as 49 were already members of the Council under Shelest indicates the high degree of stability in this organ of power. Since 1972 the Council of Ministers has acquired eleven new members.

2. A Comprehensive Analysis

Before we draw our conclusion about the ruling organs of the CPU it is necessary to discuss several basic questions. The republic's Party organization and its leadership are an operative organ responsible for implementing a uniform Party policy in all areas of life in a specific territory. The performance of this task requires careful consideration of regional social and national features. The levelling function of the CPU within the supraorganization of the CPSU with a view of coordinated action gives a clear picture of the structure of the former's subordination to the latter. The organs of power in Ukraine are not subordinate to the republic itself but to a higher authority into which they are integrated and from which they take their instructions. In the past Soviet interpreters of the history of the CPSU used to make much of the so-called national features of the corporate republican parties. This is no longer the case. The present-day approach to this question was stated explicitly by A.V. Samosudov in an official Party publication:

> In the course of many years the national colouring of these common interests in our multinational land faded to an increasing extent. This was reflected not only in the composition, operational forms and methods of the Party but also in their structure.[1]

The author of this article sums up the allegedly inevitable tendency of the republican parties to grow increasingly similar to the mother-party with the words:

> The internationalization of our entire social life, which is taking place as a natural result of the profound social changes that have occurred during the process of socialist construction in our country, was bound to be reflected in the Party structure, especially in the Party's organizational forms, where a uniform organizational structure is essential.[2]

Samosudov is at pains to find a parallel development of national features:

> As far as national features are concerned, these are reflected in the operational forms of the Party organizations, forms which are becoming increasingly varied.[3]

The organs of power in Ukraine today do not even claim to represent national interests at the local level. The official line, which they are required to implement unconditionally, presupposes that the creation of the material and technical basis of communism will just about automatically solve all national and local problems. The integration of all sections of society into the "Soviet people" will merely accelerate this "now inevitable" development.

The converse is true. This form of "integration" will not be able to preclude conflicts deriving from the national and regional interests of the individual republics. Smaller and larger conflicts of this kind have marked every stage in the development of Soviet society. The reason for this is simply that the Party's aims, organizational structures and fixed functions do not consider, but rather run counter to, the interests of the people whom it tries to press into a common mould. Here it should be remembered that one of the most important organizational aims of the Party leadership is the continual improvement of both the organizational forms and the composition of the republican organs of power. This means that these organs are nothing but an extension of the central authority in Moscow whose function is to implement decisions at the local level. Consequently, it does not really matter whether the key Party posts in Ukraine are occupied by Ukrainians or not. Nor should we overrate the fact that "Ukrainians" are party to high-level political decisions by virtue of their membership in the Politburo of the CPSU Central Committee — a privilege enjoyed by the first secretaries of the central committees of the communist parties of Ukraine, Belorussia, Kazakhstan and Uzbekistan.

On the other hand the Ukrainian Party leadership has a wide variety of possibilities at the operational level, i.e., in the implementation of standardized plans. In this respect there is clear evidence of the Ukrainian leaders' efforts to assert their status as the rulers of the second most important republic, to stress and consolidate their claim of being at least "secundus inter pares". This fact should not, however, deceive us into drawing false conclusions, for the guiding precept of the Ukrainian Party bureaucracy remains: to perfect the Party apparatus and implement in an optimal manner the decisions handed down from above.

The Party leaders in Kyiv have already achieved a remarkable degree of success in this area. This is borne out by the "quality" of the Central Committee Secretariat. It proved impossible to establish whether the same level of achievement applies to the various departments of the Central Committee. The absence of data on the directors of these departments made it impossible to establish their exact number. Accordingly, the list in the appendices is drawn up with the caveat that there may be additional Central Committee departments and that some of those mentioned may have since been abolished. It can, however, be ascertained that the men in charge of those departments, which are responsible for the national aspects of life in the republic, are not only unconditionally loyal and devoted executors of the Moscow line but also highly educated and talented organizers. One example for many is Malanchuk, the Central Committee CPU secretary in charge of ideological work. Another prime example is F.M. Rudych, Director of the Central Committee Department of Science and Educational Establishments. The boldness of a number of ideas expressed in his article "The Integration of State and Public Principles in Industrial Management," in Komunist Ukrainy, aroused great interest, above all in the West.[4] In this article the author defended, inter alia, the idea that the directors of industrial enterprises should be elected officials. Similar qualities can be found in M.G. Ishchenko, the director of the Central Committee's Department of Culture, and, to some extent, in Yu.N. Yelchenko, the director of the Department of Propaganda and Agitation.

A further feature of the present constellation in the ruling organs of Ukraine is the strong position of a group of functionaries who come from the Donets' Basin. They include: V.I. Degtyarev, First Secretary of the Donets'k Oblast Party Committee and Politburo member; A.P. Lyashko, chairman of the Ukrainian Council of Ministers and Politburo member; Ya.P. Pohrebnyak, a Central Committee secretary and alternate member of the Politburo; V.A. Solohub, chairman of the Trade Union Council of the Ukrainian SSR and Politburo member; A.A. Tytarenko, a Central Committee secretary and Politburo member; and V.M. Tsybul'ko, First Secretary of the Kyiv Oblast Party Committee. Another member of this group is Moscow's top representative, the USSR Minister of Ferrous Metallurgy, I.P. Kazanets'.

The careers and influence of these functionaries can only be understood in the context of the great importance which the Donets'k Oblast has for the Soviet Union as a whole. The dominant forces in this major centre of the coal and metallurgical industries are those enterprises and organizations which are directly controlled by all-Union or Ukrainian ministries and make a major contribution to the Soviet economy. This constellation explains why the Donets' Basin has brought forth functionaries with a particular combination of qualities and talents: Their experience and mentality have been moulded by their subordination to all-Union authorities and by the priority of all-Union interests. Because of its particular situation the Donets' Basin was bound to become a cadre school for Party officials who, as individuals and functionaries, personify the "integrative" aspects of CPSU domestic policy. These officials work in an environment where the nationality problem is virtually nonexistent. During the 1970 census 738,000 of the 2.1 million Ukrainians living in the cities of the Donets' Basin gave Russian as their native language. Furthermore, the region's Russian population (1.9 million) is nearly as large as the Ukrainian.

The influence of the officials from the Donets' Basin in the Ukrainian leadership is not a new phenomenon. The USSR Minister of Ferrous Metallurgy, I.P. Kazanets', for example, was second secretary of the CPU Central Committee from 1960 to 1963 and chairman of the Ukrainian Council of Ministers from 1963 to 1965.

Six of the 16 Ukrainian Politburo members began their careers in the Donets' Basin, three in Kharkiv, two in Dnipropetrovs'k, two in Western Ukraine, one in Chernyhiv and one in Cherkasy. It is not known where the remaining Politburo member began his ascent of the ladder of power.

State and economic officials are the closest allies of the higher Party bureaucracy. A form of alliance between the two groups can be observed in Ukraine and the Soviet Union as a whole. The position of the state and economic officials in the republic, however, has its own special characteristics. Over half of the Ukrainian economy is controlled by all-Union authorities. The number of centrally controlled enterprises is not the decisive factor here: what is important is the number of people they employ, their degree of modernization and the quality of their equipment. Although these enterprises are intimately concerned with the territory in which they are situated, neither the Ukrainian government nor the Ukrainian economic organizations have a say in their operations. The republican authorities' first duty in this area is to help the enterprises of all-Union significance. This means that the republic has to provide these enterprises with all kinds of services which, strictly speaking, do not fall within its sphere of competence. Nevertheless, this is one of the central tasks of the CPU Central Committee departments in charge of various branches of industry.

For a proper understanding of the state and economic bureaucracy in the Soviet Union it is necessary to know how its position in Ukraine and the other republics differs from its posibition in the RSFSR. There are, for example, more union-republican ministries in the individual republics than in the RSFSR itself. The RSFSR has "ceded" certain portfolios to the union-republican ministries of the USSR. This is why there are 28 union-republican ministries under the aegis of the Ukrainian Council of Ministers and only 21 under the aegis of the RSFSR Council of Ministers.

At first glance this creates the impression that the rights and privileges of the RSFSR have been curtailed. However, in view of the present Party line and the structure of power in the Soviet Union as a whole, this merely indicates a higher degree of integration in the Russian Federative Republic and, in the final reckoning, a form of preference.

As for ministries which fall entirely within the republican sphere of competence, the fact that their number is steadily decreasing is less significant than their tendency to acquire the status of union-republican ministries as soon as possible. By means of appropriate investment policies and other measures the Soviet Party leadership has succeeded, with the help of the republican parties, in fostering the belief that republican ministries no longer have a future.[5]

The apparatuses in which the higher state and economic bureaucracy operates fall, for the most part, within the union-republican sphere fo competence. Parallel to the state and economic bureaucracy which heads up the republican apparatuses we find influential authorities and institutions and a powerful bureaucracy which, being independent of the republican authorities, lead a separate existence on the territory of the individual republics under the direct control of the Soviet government. This dichotomy weakens the state and economic bureaucracy of the republics and inevitably leads to the conversion of the non-Russian republics into defacto provinces. It is, therefore, quite natural that the greatest tensions are caused by the question of how the spheres of competence of the Union and the republics should be delineated. However this question is approached it means that part of the bureaucracy in an absolutely bureaucratic system is underprivileged. This creates differences of opinion and conflicts which may justifiably be called political.

The republican state and economic bureaucracy is aware of the fact that it is in a state of permanent atrophy. In the model of bureaucratic government which has developed along such truly classic lines in the Soviet Union the bureaucracy is a closed system of power only up to a certain point. It is not entirely homogeneous, for part of this bureaucracy has made its career and achieved positions of power only because of the existence of republican "features". The fact that these features are of declining significance and offer increasingly fewer opportunities for advancement creates an area of serious tension in the Party bureaucracy as a whole.

Appendix I

Occupation of Members and Candidate Members of the Central Committee

Members of the	Members	Candidate Members
Politburo and secretaries of the CPU Central Committee..	6	-
Senior Party officials (directors of the Central Committee departments, Rector of Party School, etc.)............................	11	8
Secretaries of Oblast Party Committees...................	20	3
Secretaries of City Party Committees.....................	4	7
Secretaries of Rayon Party Committees..................	3	4
Members of the Supreme Soviet..........................	2	-
Members of the Council of Ministers.....................	26	17
Administrative officials..................................	7	7
Justice officials...	-	1
Komsomol officials.......................................	-	-
Trade Union officials.....................................	1	-
Army officers...	4	4
Transport officials.......................................	2	-
Cooperative officials.....................................	-	1
Industrial employees.....................................	10	2

of these:

Enterprise directors	3	1
Engineers and technicians	1	1
workers	6	
Agricultural employees...................................	10	

of these:

Kolkhoz chairmen	6
Kolkhoz workers	4

	Members	Candidate Members
Intellectual professions	8	4

of these:

Writers	4		1
Journalists	1		1
Scientists	3		2

	Members	Candidate Members
Others	2	4
Pensioners	5	2
Unknown	26	17
	147	81

THE POLITBURO OF THE CPU CENTRAL COMMITTEE
(as of October 1, 1974)

Name	Date of Birth	Party Member Since	Nationality	Education	Position	In Politburo Since
Full Members						
Borysenko, N.M.	1918	1943	Ukrainian	Kharkiv Zootechnical Institute (1941)	Secretary of the CPU Central Committee since 1970	Candidate Member 1970-1973; Full Member since 1973
Degtyarev, V.I.	1920	1945	Russian	Moscow Mining Institute (1942)	First Secretary of the Donets Oblast Committee since 1963	Candidate Member 1966-1971; Full Member since 1971
Hrushetsky, I.S.	1904	1928	Ukrainian	CPSU Party School (1959)	Presidium Chairman of the Ukrainian Supreme Soviet since 1972	Candidate Member 1962-1972; Full Member since 1972
Kalchenko, N.T.	1906	1932	Ukrainian	Poltava Agricultural Institute (1928)	First Deputy Chairman of the Ukrainian Council of Ministers since 1963	Full Member since 1954
Lutak, I.K.	1919	1940	Ukrainian	Kazakh Agricultural Institute (1942)	Second Secretary of the CPU Central Committee since 1969	Full Member since 1967
Lyashko, A.P.	1915	1942	Ukrainian	Donets'k Industrial Institute (1947)	Chairman of the Ukrainian Council of Ministers since 1972	Full Member since 1963
Shcherbyts'kyi, V.V.	1918	1941	Ukrainian	Dnipropetrovs'k Institute of Chemical Technology (1941)	First Secretary of the CPU Central Committee since 1972	Full Member since 1957

Name	Date of Birth	Party Member Since	Nationality	Education	Postion	In Politburo Since
Solohub, V.A.	1926	1947	N.A.	Union Polytechnic Institute (1952)	Chairman of the Ukrainian Trade Union Council since 1971	Candidate Member 1971-1973; Full Member since 1973
Tytarenko, A.A.	1915	1940	Ukrainian	Zhdanov Metallurgical Institute (1937)	Secretary of the CPU Central Committee since 1966	Full Member since 1966
Vashchenko, G.I.	1920	1943	Ukrainian	Union Polytechnic Institute (1955)	First Deputy Chairman of the Ukrainian Council of Ministers since 1972	Candidate Member 1966-1971; Full Member since 1971
Vatchenko, A.F.	1914	1940	Ukrainian	Dnipropetrovs'k State University	First Secretary of Dnipropetrovs'k Oblast Committee since 1965	Full Member since 1966
Candidate Members						
Fedorchuk, V.V.	N.A	N.A.	N.A.	N.A.	Chairman of the Ukrainian KGB since 1970	Candidate Member since 1973
Malanchuk, V.Yu.	1928	1950	Ukrainian	University (1950)	Secretary of the CPU Central Committee since 1972	Candidate Member since 1972
Pohrebnyak, Ya.P.	1928	1953	Ukrainian	Donets Industrial Institute (1954)	Secretary of the CPU Central Committee since 1971	Candidate Member since 1971
Sokolov, I.Z.	N.A.	1952	N.A.	N.A.	First Secretary of Kharkiv Oblast Committee since 1972	Candidate Member since 1973

Appendix II (continued)

Name	Date of Birth	Party Member Since	Nationality	Education	Position	In Politburo Since
Tsybul'ko V.M.	1944	1924	Ukrainian	Kyiv Institute of Economics (1965)	First Secretary of Kyiv Oblast Committee since 1970	Candidate Member since 1972

Secretaries of the CPU Central Committee

Name	Date of Birth	Party Member Since	Nationality	Education	Secretary Since	Previous Position
Shcherbyts'kyi, V.V.	1941	1918	Ukrainian	Dnipropetrovs'k Institute of Chemical Technology (1941)	1972	Chairman of the Ukrainian Council of Ministers
Lutak, I.K.	1940	1919	Ukrainian	Kazakh Agricultural Institute (1942)	1967-1969; Second Secretary since 1969	First Secretary of Crimean Oblast Committee 1964-1967
Borysenko, N.M.	1943	1918	Ukrainian	Kharkiv Zootechnical Institute (1941)	1970	First Secretary of Chernyhiv Oblast Committee 1964-1970
Malanchuk, V.Yu.	1950	1928	Ukrainian	Lviv University (1950)	1972	Deputy Minister of Advanced and Secondary Special Education of the Ukrainian SSR 1967-1972
Pohrebnyak, Ya.P.	1953	1928	Ukrainian	Donets'k Industrial Institue (1954)	1971	First Secretary of Mykolaiv Oblast Committee 1969-1971
Tytarenko, A.A.	1940	1915	Ukrainian	Zhdanov Metallurgical Institute (1937)	1966	First Secretary of Zaporizh'ia Oblast Committee 1962-1966

Appendix III

KNOWN DEPARTMENTS
OF THE CPU CENTRAL COMMITTEE

Executive Director.. Holoborod'ko, I.I.

Directors of the Departments of:

Administrative Organs..................................... Opanasyuk, D.G.

General Department.. Odnoromanenko, A.M.

Building and Public Works................................. Zlobin, G.K.

Chemical Industry... N.A.

Trade and Public Services................................. N.A.

Culture... Ishchenko, M.G.

Agriculture... Fedan, V.I.

Light and Food Industry................................... Kanivets N.Ya.

Machine Building.. N.A.

Mechanization, Electrification and
Rural Construction.. N.A.

Party Organizational Work................................. Kryuchkov, G.K.

Planning and Fiscal Organs................................ Ivashchenko, A.V.

Propaganda and Agitation.................................. Yelchenko, Yu.N.

Heavy Industry.. Nikolaev, N.F.

Transport, Post and Communications........................ Maevsky, V.V.

Science and Educational Establishments.................... Rudych, F.M.

International Department................................... Peresadenko, I.A.

One of the Central Committee Departments is headed by a certain V.M. Shramenko, who was reported to have attended the **Myasolmolmash 74** Exhibition in Kyiv in his official capacity.

FOOTNOTES

1. A. V. Samosudov, "Proletarian Internationalism in the Organizational Structure of the CPSU", **Voprosy istorii KPSS**, Nr. 5, 1972.

2. **Ibid.**

3. **Ibid.**

4. F. M. Rudych, "The Integration of State and Public Principles in Industrial Management," **Komunist Ukrainy**, July, 1967.

5. I. O. Bisher, "The Ministries of the Union Republics: An Acute Problem," **Sovetskoe gosudarstvo i pravo**, Nr. 5, 1973, p. 30.

Shelest and His Period in Soviet Ukraine (1963-1972): A Revival of Controlled Ukrainian Autonomism

by
Jaroslaw Pelenski
University of Iowa

In order to appropriately assess the Shelest period (1963-1972) in historical perspective, it is necessary first to analyze the circumstances of Shelest's fall, and the official accusations directed by the Soviet leadership against him. Petro Iukhymovych Shelest (1908-   ), the former First Secretary of the Central Committee (CC) of the Communist Party of Ukraine (CPU) and a member of the Politburo of the Communist Party of the Soviet Union (CPSU)[1] was removed from his positions in two successive stages: first, from the post of the First Secretary of the CC of the CPU, in May of 1972, and subsequently, from the Politburo, in April of 1973.

Shelest's removal from the position of the First Secretary of the CC of the CPU occurred under dramatic circumstances and coincided with former President Nixon's visit to the Soviet Union. Before Shelest's ultimate fall, in the spring of 1973, most Western commentators maintained that the decisive reasons for his demise were his conservative and reactionary hawkism and his hardline approach to foreign policy; more specifically, his alleged attitude on the issue of détente and the question of Soviet-American relations, and his active resistance to the policy of coexistence with the United States.

This assessment of Shelest's foreign policy attitudes undoubtedly originated with his position on the issue of handling the Czechoslovak crisis, and the Soviet invasion of Czechoslovakia. In their perceptive study, **The Ukraine and the Czechoslovak Crisis**, G. Hodnett and P. J. Potichnyj have shown quite conclusively that Shelest was a leading hawk who totally rejected the Czechoslovak experiment and who obviously supported the Soviet invasion of that country.[2] Shelest's possible motives for taking this position have not been fully explored, so far. Also, no direct or circumstantial evidence is available to suggest that Shelest actually opposed détente, or the policy of coexistence with the United States. It appears that the allegations of his so-called militancy, anachronistic cold war mentality, and anti-Americanism have been carefully spread and kept alive by those interested in his ouster. Why, after all, would Shelest have been removed from the Politburo on the basis of his oppostion to détente when Marshall A. Grechko and Iu. Andropov (the Chief of the KGB), while entertaining similar attitudes towards détente, have been promoted to full membership in the same body?

The official political criticism directed by the Soviet leadership against Shelest has been formulated in the editorial-review of his book **Ukraino nasha Radians'ka** (O Ukraine, Our Soviet (Country) (1970 / 1971),[3] published in the theoretical journal of the CC of the CPU **Komunist Ukrainy**, in April of 1973. The then-falling Politburo member and former First Secretary of the CC of the CPU was charged with having committed, as an author, and by implication as a political leader, a number of cardinal transgressions, or better, "mortal sins." Specifically, Shelest was accused with the following "shortcomings" and "mistakes": (1) the allotment of disproportionate amount of space to the history of pre-1917 Ukraine, and negligible treatment of epochal events such as the Great October Revolution; (2) idealization of the Ukrainian Cossacks and the Zaporozhian Host, and condoning the glorifcation of **patriarkhal'shchyna** (an official negative term used to attack those who display a positive historicist and patriotic approach to Ukrainian culture); (3) the minimalization of the epochal significance of the "reunification" of Ukraine with Russia in 1654, and its positive consequences for the history of Ukraine; (4) neglect of the fundamental assumption that the history of Ukraine, following the so-called "reunification," cannot be treated outside the framework of that of the Russian state; (5) non-disclosure of the beneficial influence of Russian culture on the formation and development of Ukrainian literature, art and music, and their mutual enrichment; (6) belittling of the role of the Communist Party, its ideology, and practical activities; (7) abstract-humanist and humanitarian interpretation of literary artistic developments; (8) treating of the Ukrainian economy and culture separately from those of the USSR, and advocacy of the conception of economic self-sufficiency for the Ukrainian Republic ("elements of economic autarchism are obvious in the book"[5]); (9) confusing and incorrect assessment of the ideological and socio-political foundations of the Ukrainian bourgeois nationalism. In short, the attack on Shelest embraced the broadest range of ideological, historico-cultural, economic and political accusations.

Shelest's book is, indeed, an exceptional document of Soviet Ukrainian political literature. Its publication exclusively in the Ukrainian language, its title in the vocative form — **Ukraino nasha Radians'ka**, its attempt at mass appeal (edition of 100,000 copies), indicate that this book was intended for wide circulation among the Ukrainian population. It ought to be pointed out that Shelest was the first Soviet Ukrainian politician since the times of Mykola Skrypnyk to have developed authorial ambitions, which in itself represented a novelty. He is the author of three additional books[6] and one of the few Soviet politicians, besides Brezhnev and Suslov, to have had the aspirations and the necessary influence to assure the publication of collections of his speeches and articles in special volumes. It appears from his speeches, as well as his book **Ukraino nasha Radians'ka**, which may have been ghost-written, that Shelest was interested in creating an image not only as a political leader, but also as a political author. His works are devoid of theoretical bent and Marxist scholasticism — characteristics typical of the works of N. Bukharin and M. Skrypnyk, for example. Shelest's writings deal with major topics such as party work and organizations, youth and Komsomol issues, nationality problems and internal political problems of the Soviet Ukrainian Republic, and can best be described as issue-oriented. His statements on, or allusions to, foreign policy are usually formulated in the context of speeches aimed at Ukrainian anniversaries or dealing with internal problems of the Ukrainian Republic.

Shelest's book, **Ukraino nasha Radians'ka**, which became a subject of severe political criticism, is a work of neither great erudition nor exceptional sophistication.

It was apparently written by several people from Shelest's inner circle. There are indications that O. Honchar, former Chairman of the Writers' Union of Ukraine and author of the patriotic and symbolic novel **Sobor (The Cathedral)**, (1968), and S. M. Iampol's'kyi, Shelest's economic advisor and for many years the editor-in-chief of the best Ukrainian professional journal, **Ekonomika Radians'koi Ukrainy (The Economics of the Soviet Ukraine)**, may have been involved in the composition of this collective work. The book is not an integrated work but rather a treatise combining elements of historico-political essay, assessment of the present state of Ukrainian culture and economy, and the superficial generalities of a tourist guide book. Approximately one-third of the book is devoted to a general historico-cultural account and in the remaining two-thirds the author / authors concentrate on an over-all survey of the twenty-five regions of Ukraine. The most striking feature of this work is the extraordinary emphasis on and pride in the achievements of the Ukrainian people, the socio-economic growth and development of the Soviet Ukrainian Republic, and the evolution of Ukraine from an underdeveloped area to a highly developed agricultural and industrial country.

Ukraine is being treated in this book as a constituent part of the Soviet Union but also as a country with her own needs, her own integrated economy, and distinct cultural traditions.[7] A great many of Shelest's claims are mere exaggerations of a propagandistic nature. His enthusiastic account overlooks such serious issues as the neglect of the Ukrainian economy and the repression of the Ukrainian culture by the central political leadership in Moscow. In spite of these obvious shortcomings, however, the book provided the Ukrainian population of the Ukrainian SSR with a highly favorable interpretation of the role of the Ukrainian Republic within the USSR and a positive image of her inhabitants. Such an account, authored by the First Secretary of the CC of the CPU, could serve as a source of inspiration and of growing self-respect for those elements among the Ukrainian population who have been brought up in the belief that Russia and Russian people alone have been capable of achieving and attaining great and respectable goals.

Following the publication of the editorial review of Shelest's book in the **Komunist Ukrainy**, some commentators began to look for internal political causes which could have led to his demise. They concentrated primarily on two sets of problems: namely, on the role Ukrainian nationalism played in the removal of Shelest from his office,[8] and on the interrelated issues of internal operational party politics and the national question.[9] Since the problem of nationalism has been treated rather abstractly by some commentators and, with the exception of Ya. Bilinsky's analysis, in a manner completely isolated from the economic and socio-political factors in the life of the Soviet Ukrainian Republic, it is necessary to review the entire complex of cultural and historical problems in the context of their ideological ramifications, and then to proceed with an evaluation of the economic, as well as general political developments which took place during Shelest's tenure as the First Secretary of the CC of the CPU, in order to arrive at a balanced and comprehensive assessment of a varity of factors which led to his fall, and which justify the characterization of the period from 1963 to 1972 as **shelestivshchyna** and as the age of the revival of controlled Ukrainian autonomism.

When Shelest assumed the position of the First Secretary of the CC of the CPU in July of 1963, he, together with the leadership of the CPU, found himself confronted with two conflicting pressures, i.e., the pressure of the All-Union Party directed at carrying out the policy of merging of nations, on the one hand, and the counter-pressure of the Ukrainian intelligentsia aimed at assuring the Ukrainian language and culture, in the broadest sense of the words, their appropriate place in the Soviet Ukrainian Republic, on the other. These conflicting pressures were already making themselves felt in the 1950's and in the first years of the 1960's at which time the leadership of the CPU tried to cope with them by making tentative compromises and temporary postponements and by avoiding unpleasant decisions. Shelest took over the leadership of the Ukrainian Party when the first major phase of the latest national revival was completed and when the major attempts at implementing cultural policies, which emanated from the theory of merging of nations, were being undertaken. Until 1962 the Ukrainian national revival, which had started in the mid-1950's, was confined to activities of limited groups among the creative and artistic intelligentsia and the Party circles. This national revival concentrated on historico-political issues, such as the rehabilitation of the victims of the purges in Ukrainian cultural life, as well as on Communist party groups and CPU personalities (the Communist Party of Western Ukraine and Mykola Skrypnyk, for example), on activities in defense of the Ukrainian language and culture, and on attempts to rescue the Ukrainian literature from oblivion and to produce modern Ukrainian literary works, particularly in the field of poetry.[10]

Shortly before Shelest rose to the position of First Secretary of the CC of the CPU, the Ukrainian national revival began to assume broader socio-political dimensions and to acquire certain characteristics of a more aggressive nature. This transformation of the Ukrainian national revial from a purely defensive to a more offensive stance manifested itself at the Conference devoted to the question of the status of the Ukrainian language which was held in Kyiv, February 10-15, 1963, and which was attended by over 1,000 Ukrainian writers, teachers and linguists. The Conference was reported by the Soviet Ukrainian press in a terse news-item only. No information as to its proceedings and resolutions was provided. A more detailed account of this Conference appeared, however, in **Nasha Kul'tura** (**Our Culture**), a Ukrainian-language cultural magazine published in Warsaw, Poland.[11] According to **Nasha Kul'tura**, in their resolutions the participants of the Conference appealed to the CC of the CPU requesting among other things that the Ukrainian language be made the official language of instruction in all higher and specialized institutions of learning and that the Ukrainian language become the official language in state and public institutions and all places of work. Furthermore they demanded that a genuine effort be made to assure the publication of a majority of scholarly works, especially those published by the Institutes of the Academy of Sciences of the Ukrainian SSR, in the Ukrainian language. In short, the resolutions of this Conference represented broadly-supported socio-political demands for the "Ukrainization" of cultural and public life in Soviet Ukraine. Although these demands were not met, they nevertheless reflected the transformation which the Ukrainian national revival had undergone: namely, from being a culturally oriented movement to being a socio-political one. The representatives of the Ukrainian cultural sector participating in this Conference assumed at least for a brief time some of the functions of the Supreme Soviet of the Ukrainian SSR, that institution which has been singularly neglecting its obligation to uphold the position of the Ukrainian language as the state language of the Ukrainian SSR.

Shelest tried to diffuse the two opposing pressures by making concessions to both sides and by avoiding taking a clear-cut position until the mid-1960's when postponement could no longer be extended, particularly when it became apparent that demands for the expansion of a limited "Ukrainization" on the one hand, and the official policy of tacit support to Russification on the other, were on a collision course. As a consequence of this confrontation Shelest was forced to take sides on a variety of crucial issues. He thus began openly to defend the Ukrainian language and cultural heritage as exemplified by his speech to the Fifth Congress of Ukrainian Writers, in November of 1966, in which he made his now-famous ideological statement:

The development of the socialist Ukrainian culture and lanaguage in many respects depends on the people who have gathered here today; and it depends, in the first place, not on talks about the necessity for such development, but on your creativity. We must treat our beautiful Ukrainian language with great care and respect. It is our treasure, our great heritage, which all of us, but in the first place you, our writers, must preserve and develop. Novels, short stories and poetry of high ideological content written in our beautiful language on a high artistic level — all are indispensable for further enrichment and development of the national culture and language. Your efforts in this direction always have been and will be supported by the Communist Party [12]

This passage was interpreted by the Ukrainian intelligentsia as official approval by the highest Party dignitary not only of efforts to defend the role of the Ukrainian language, but as approval also of efforts to spread its influence. Some intellectuals drew even more radical conclusions from this statement and dared to question the policy of Russification which was being supported simultaneously by the All-Union Party leadership and by its more obedient followers in Ukraine.

Even before Shelest made his programmatic statement on the role of the Ukrainian language the leadership of the CPU and the Soviet Ukrainian governmental authorities had made an unpublicized attempt to improve the status of the Ukrainian language in higher educational institutions of the Republic. M. Iu. Dadenkov, the Ukrainian SSR Minister of Higher and Specialized Secondary Education, delivered an instructional lecture in August of 1965 at a meeting of the rectors of the higher educational institutions devoted to the problem of the language of instruction used in those institutions. This lecture became the basis for a circular memorandum to the rectors in which the latter were advised to undertake concrete measures aimed at "Ukrainization" of their institutions.[13] Dadenkov's circular memorandum contained the following instructions:

(a)   The language of instruction should be changed to predominantly Ukrainian; socio-political disciplines should be taught in the Ukrainian language; students should be permitted to use the Ukrainian and Russian languages on an equal basis.

(b)   All instructors who have good knowledge of the Ukrainian language should be requested to use this language in their lectures; courses in the Ukrainian language should be organized for all those instructors who are not in full command of this language.

(c)   All academic, as well as nonacademic, institutions involved in publication of textbooks should publish them in the Ukrainian language.

(d)   Scholarly journals and collective works of higher educational instituions should also be published in Ukrainian.

(e)   Priority in admission to degree programmes should be given to those students who are either in full command of the Ukrainian language, are in the process of learning it, or are willing to study it.

(f)   Teaching programmes should reflect special preparation of students for future professional work in Ukraine.

(g)   Administrative work in the institutions of higher education should be conducted in the Ukrainian language.

(h)   Propagandistic-political and cultural-educational work should be conducted predominantly in the Ukrainian language.

There is little doubt that Dadenkov's circular letter must have been approved by the highest Party officials, and by Shelest in particular. The sincerity of the CPU leadership and the government of the Ukrainian SSR "to return to the Leninist norms in educational policies" and to begin "Ukrainization" in all sectors of the public life of the Ukrainian Republic has been attested by the leading Ukrainian dissident Viacheslav Chornovil.[14]

Almost concurrently with the attempts to improve the status of the Ukrainian language, a number of measures aimed at the revival of Ukrainian historical studies were undertaken in Soviet Ukraine. One of these measures was the reactivation of the Institute of Archelogy of the Academy of Sciences of the Ukrainian SSR under its new director F. P. Shevchenko, the leading Soviet Ukrainian historian of the Cossack period. Since the Institute of History of the Academy of Sciences was concentrating its work primarily on the modern and specifically on the Soviet period of the Ukrainian history, an effort was made to conduct serious research on the early periods of Ukrainian history and to publish the results of this research under the auspices of the Institute of Archeology. As the titles of its new publications indicate, **Middle Ages in Ukraine**[15] and **Kyivan Antiquity,**[16] the Institute of Archeology **de facto** also became the Institute of History of the Middle Ages in Ukraine. Interestingly enough, the

Middle Ages were conveniently extended to embrace the period until the end of the seventeenth century, including a major part of the Cossack history. The Institute of Archeology sponsored extremely important archeological field work in Ukraine during the last decade, and was responsible for the training of a number of promising young members of the profession. Following Shelest's fall, however, this Institute was severely criticized for "Serious shortcomings" by Volodymyr V. Shcherbyts'kyi, the succeeding First Secretary of the CC of the CPU, [17] who in the years 1961-63 and 1965-72 held the post of Chairman of the Ukrainian SSR's Council of Ministers. In similar vein F. P. Shevchenko had been dismissed from the directorship of this Institute, following his removal in February of 1972 from the position of chief editor of the **Ukrains'kyi istorychnyi zhurnal (The Ukrainian Historical Journal)** [18] in which capacity he had served for fifteen years. The removal of Shelest from his post, along with the subsequent purge of his group, had, among other effects, far-reaching organizational repercussions for Ukrainian historical scholarship. It particularly affected the participation of Ukrainian historians in international scholarly meetings. Curiously enough, not only F. P. Shevchenko but also his successor to the position of Director of the Institute of Archeology, V. D. Baran, along with P.M. Kalynychenko, who took over as chief editor of the **Ukrains'kyi istorychnyi zhurnal**, were not permitted to attend the Seventh International Congress in Warsaw, in August of 1973, regardless of the fact that their participation in the programme of the Congress had been approved and announced a year and a half before the Congress actually took place. The decision to withdraw the approval was apparently prompted by the great confusion and feeling of insecurity which pervaded the political atmosphere in the CC of the CPU following Shelest's ouster, and the evident desire on the part of the Soviet authorities to prevent contacts between those Soviet Ukrainian scholars who had been personally affected by the recent changes (including the most reliable figures, who replaced the untrustworthy followers of the Shelest policies) and Western scholars. [19]

Another initiative undertaken during Shelest's tenure was an attempt to publish a multivolumed history of Ukraine with clear concentration on the Soviet period. This history, which originally was to bear the title, "The Great History of the Ukrainian SSR," was also anticipated to have even more ambitious scope than its final product, i.e., **Istoriia mist i sil Ukrains'koi RSR v dvadtsiaty shesty tomakh (The History of the Cities and Villages of the Ukrainian SSR in Twenty-Six Volumes)**, [20] published in Ukrainian language. In spite of its evident bias, this work is a mine of information on Soviet Ukrainian affairs, and will need to be thoroughly analyzed be historians, as well as by specialists in other disciplines of the social sciences, before its value can be appropriately appreciated. The work on this voluminous history was undertaken not only as a scholarly project but also as a socio-political one, in which undreds of scholars and cultural workers patrook, in most cases without financial compensation. A great many enthusiastic participants in this enterprise regarded their contributions to this cause as a patriotic gesture on their part. It is not difficult to observe a similarity of conception between **Istoria** and Shelest's book **Ukraino nasha Radian-s'ka**, two-thirds of which represents a journalistic synopsis of **Istoriia**. Indvidual chapters of Shelest's book correspond thematically to the separate volumes of the **Istoriia**, and the two works are permeated by similar emphasis on the achievements of the Ukrainian people and on the socio-economic growth and development of the Soviet Ukrainian Republic. [21] **Istoriia mist i sil Ukrain'koi RSR v dvadtsiaty shesty tomakh** is undoubtedly the most ambitious collective historical work ever produced in Soviet Ukraine, and reflects to a considerable extent Shelest's conception of the historic role of the Ukrainian Republic in the Soviet Union.

An attempt, in 1966, to rehabilitate Mykhailo Hrushevs'ky (1866-1934), the leading protagonist of the Ukrainian national historical school, which must have been approved on the highest political level, and which was brought to an abrupt end after the publication of only two articles, [22] represents another endeavor of the mid-1960's directed at the revival of Ukrainian historical studies. Since the preoccupation with Hrushevs'ky was apparently regarded in Moscow as politically unsafe, it had to be terminated in its initial stage. It should be mentioned at this point that F.P. Shevchenko's participation in the attempted rehabilitation of Hrushevs'ky, along with his antiquarian approach to the study of history, and his alleged excessive willingness to employ Jews in the Institute of Archeology, were later used as arguments to justify his removal from the positions he had previously held.

All these developments connected with the study of Ukrainian history certainly would not have been possible without the support of Shelest, who was very fond of Ukrainian history and who personally encouraged the revival of Ukrainian historical studies. Shelest's positive attitude toward Ukrainian history is best reflected in his book Ukraino nasha Radians'ka, in which he speaks approvingly about the Ukrainian Cossack Period, and especially about the Zaporozhian Host. By placing positive emphasis on the democratic character of the Zaporozhian socio-political system Shelest, by the same token, displayed his adherence to the radical interpretation of the Ukrainian Cossack history derived from Karl Marx, who characterized the Zaporozhian Host as a "Christian Cossack Republic."[23] Paradoxically, Shelest's references to the Zaporozhian Host were more "Marxist" in essence than the position of the reviewer / reviewers of his book on the same subject in Komunist Ukrainy.

It can further be argued that a positive predisposition on the part of Shelest and his group toward Ukrainian historico-cultural problems made possible the publication of literary works such as O. Honchar's novel Sobor (The Cathedral) (1968), R. Ivanychuk's novel Mal'vy (The Mallows) (1969), and many other works which later came under strong criticism. In the mid-1960's two most substantive treatises which later entered the, samvydav were written with tacit encouragement from higher authorities, i.e., Ivan Dziuba's Internatsionalizm chy rusyfikatsia, (Internationalism or Russification),[24] and the equally important, but less publicized Mykhailo Iu. Braichevs'kyi's Pryiednannnia chy voziednannia? (Annexation or Reunification?).[25] In his sophisticated Marxist analysis Braichevs'kyi has undertaken a fundamental revision of the standard Soviet interpretation of the Pereiaslav Treaty (1654), as well as the subsequent Russo-Ukrainian relations resulting therefrom, and of the official "reunification" theory formulated by the CC of the CPSU in connection with the Tercentenary of the Pereiaslav Treaty in 1954.[26] Braichevs'kyi has shown quite convincingly that applying the concept of "reunification" to the relations between Cossack Ukraine and Muscovite Russia as defined by the Pereiaslav Treaty is completely erroneous. He furthermore argues that the tsarist government broke the Pereiaslav agreement, undermined and weakened Ukrainian institutions, and consistently treated Ukrainian territory as a conquered country to be colonized and exploited. He also dispells the Soviet historical myth about the extremely positive consequences of the "reunification" for the Ukrainian culture and economy, and proposes a highly interesting hypothesis, namely that Muscovy's annexation of Ukraine prevented the latter from embarking upon a road of bourgeois or semi-bourgeois socio-political development. Braichevs'kyi's reinterpretations of Russo-Ukrainian relations represented the most far-reaching departure of a Soviet Ukrainian historian from the Party's position on this issue. The views which he expressed were not his alone. They were, rather, reflections of a growing dissatisfaction among Ukrainian historians with the official interpretation of the decisive developments in Ukrainian history, and of the "reunification" theory in particular.

There is no doubt that the cultural policies of the Shelest period are in need of a much more thorough and comprehensive investigation. But this brief and incomplete survey allows some tentative conclusions already. It appears that Shelest, together with his group, following a period of indecision and compromises with regard to the cultural policies in Ukraine, took a conscious step in support of a programme of the "second Ukrainization" in that Republic. Evidence exists that Shelest advocated implementation of some programmes enumerated in the Dadenkov circular memorandum of 1965 regardless of the fact that this memorandum had been disapproved by the All-Union Party authorities. A good example of his supportive position on the issues of "Ukrainization" of the educational process and improvement of the quality of education in Ukraine is his speech of September 3, 1968 to the students of the T. H. Shevchenko University in Kyiv:

We must look more fearlessly into the future, engage more professionals for the all-round development of a "model" future specialist, work on perfecting educational plans, programmes and lecturing methods. It is necessary to take into consideration the requirements which confront the national economy not just today, but five to ten years hence! The time has come to compile new textbooks which measure up to contemporary scientific and technical levels. And, most important of all, these must be published in the Ukrainian language.[27]

Of even greater significance was Shelest's use in his book **Ukraino nasha Radians'ka** of the term "Ukrainization" in a positive context when speaking of the first "Ukrainization" of the 1920's. His discussion of the successful carrying out of the Leninist nationality policy in the field of education includes the crucial statement: "Ukrainization is being conducted in Ukraine in a continuous and consistent manner."[28] Shelest's positive reference to the first "Ukrainization" signified not only a new approach to the historical policies of the 1920's but also represented an endoresement of these policies for his own period in the form of the "second Ukrainization" in Ukraine.

Contrary to the emphasis placed on the aspects of culture and operational politics of Soviet Ukraine during the Shelest period, relatively little attention has been paid to the problem of the economy, although the economy apparently became one of the crucial issues over which confrontation between the CC of the CPU, under Shelest's leadership, and Moscow took place. Since Shelest has been accused of having advocated a conception of economic selfsufficiency for the Ukrainian Republic, the question arises, whether he, together with his economic advisors and administrators of Ukraine, actually aimed at achieving a selfsufficient economic status for Ukraine.

It is a matter of general knowledge that the Ukrainian party leadership, both in the Khrushchev and Brezhnev periods, has attempted to obtain a much greater share of capital funds for investment purposes in Ukraine than it has been actually allocated. In this respect, Ukraine has fared rather poorly as compared to Siberia, for example, which has been receiving extraordinary attention from the Soviet leadership. While the All-Union leadership has been reducing capital investments for Ukraine, it, at the same time, has attempted to extract out of this country as many agricultural and industrial products as possible.[29] Conclusive evidence is available to show that Shelest, as well as Shcherbyts'ky, and to some degree even Podgorny, at different times and not always for the same reasons have opposed this policy, usually with little success.

On the other hand, the economic achievements and economic status of the Ukraine have been receiving much attention in Soviet Ukrainian professional as well as popular literature, and in the statements of both Shelest and Shcherbyts'kyi. It is in this field that some genuine progress has been achieved in Ukraine in the last decade, in spite of unfavourable economic policy decisions made in Moscow. Ukrainian economists began to entertain critical views concerning the subordinate economic status of the Soviet Ukrainian Republic and the exploitative nature of the All-Union economic policy vis-a-vis Ukraine. As a consequence, both economists, and a growing number of individuals from other strata came to the obvious conclusion that if the Ukrainian economy could operate according to its own necessities and possibilities the Ukrainian Republic would be much better off economically. Since the Ukrainian Republic possesses a very favourable combination of natural resources (with the exception of oil, of course), agriculture, industry, and a highly developed and professionally well-structured labour force, the notion of economic selfsufficiency has been the most natural conclusion to arrive at. Obviously enough, in the contemporary world, countries with well-developed economies have a greater chance of survival. These assessments and attitudes of the economists have been augmented by the growing demand in Soviet Ukraine for goods and services, and by an obsessive desire on the part of the Soviet Ukrainians to acquire items of personal use such as gadgets, clothing and other things which are part and parcel of the prevailing conception of contemporary life, i.e., materialist hedonism.

During Shelest's tenure the preoccupation with economic problems on theoretical, scientific and popular levels reached respectable heights. Not only did the **Ekonomika Radians'koi Ukrainy**, the leading theoretical economic journal in the Soviet Ukraine, edited by Shelest's economic advisor S.M. Iampol's'kyi, attain professionally a most reputable standing, but other serious popularizing endeavors in the field of economic leterature such as the publication of the **Entsyklopediia Narodnoho Hospodarstva Ukrains'koi RSR (Encyclopedia of the National Economy of the Ukrainian SSR)**, under the editorship of S.M. Iampol's'kyi,[30] and of the **Ukrains'ka Sil's'ko-hospodars'ka Entsyklopediia (Ukrainian Encyclopedia of Agriculture)**, under the editorship of V.F. Peresypkin,[31] both in Ukrainian language, and both of which, to the dismay of a historian, are professionally superior to the **Radians'ka Entsyklopediia Istorii Ukrainy (Soviet Enclyclopedia of the History of the Ukraine)**, edited by A.D. Skaba,[32] were carried out in the late 1960's and early 1970's. Another major popular work which should be mentioned is **Ukraina v period rozhornutoho budivnytstva komunizma (Ukraine in the Period of the Developing Construction of Communism)**, published in five volumes in connection on the celebration of the Fiftieth Anniversary of the October Revolution, the aim of which has been to present Ukraine's achievements in various fields.[33]

In addition to defending the conception of economic selfsufficiency for Ukraine, Shelest and his group developed a rather unorthodox view concerning Ukraine's special role as a "model republic" within the framework of the Soviet economy. Whereas these notions were not intended as a direct challenge to the All-Union Party leadership, they nevertheless served as evidence of Ukrainian resistance to the centralization policies advocated by Russian suprematists in the Politburo and the CC of the CPSU. Shelest's views concerning the integrated and complementary character of the Ukrainian economy and about Ukraine's role as a "model republic" were based upon the Ukrainian Republic's achievement of definite successes in this area. He saw and understood the necessity for modernizing economy, and especially for developing an automated (computerized) system of planning and management of the national economy. He furthermore suggested that these programmes should be initiated and experimented with in Ukraine because Ukraine, in his view, had the scientific personnel and had attained concrete achievements in this field. His views on problems of the economy were presented in his speech at the XXIVth Congress of the CPSU, in 1971:

> Ukraine accounts for a large percentage of All-Union production. There is no branch of industry that could not make a substantial contribution to a further increase in All-Union production and to the satisfaction of the country's needs. Realizing their responsibility to the Party and the country, the CC of the CPU and the Republic's Party, Soviet and economic organs have concentrated their attention on the mobilization of all possibilities for the fulfillment and over-fulfillment of state plans and on the more efficient utilization of production capacities and capital investments. Extensive work is under way on the integrated mechanization and automation of production and the introduction of scientific achievements, progressive technology and the scientific organization of labour. More than four thousand models of new machines, mechanisms, instruments, equipment and materials have been put into serious production.

> Automated management is a matter of extremely great importance. The CC of the CPSU and the Council of Ministers of the USSR have posed the task of creating an all-state automated system for the management of the country's national economy. Obviously, it would be expedient to begin work, by way of experiment, on the creation of an automated system of management in one of the Union republics that has scientific cadres and has achieved definite successes in this area.[34]

Shelest's economic proposals were not without justification since, beginning with the 1950's, all the major projects of economic reform aimed at decentralization of the Soviet economy and designed at improvement of the Soviet standard of living have originated in the Ukrainian Republic. Study and research on methods of automating the planning and management of a national economy have been inaugurated by the Institute of Cybernetics of the Academy of Sciences of the Ukrainian SSR under academician Hlushkov. This Institute enjoys the reputation of one of the most outstanding scientific institutions in the USSR, a fact reluctantly admitted by Soviet Russian specialists. The Institute of Cybernetics of the Academy of Sciences of the Ukrainian SSR was established in Kyiv in 1962 as an outgrowth of the Computer Center of the Academy of Sciences of the Ukrainian SSR which was founded in 1957 with the aim of developing research in the field of cybernetics and computer techniques. The research work in this area was begun in Ukraine at the end of the 1940's when cybernetics was still officially classified in the Soviet Union as a "bourgeois science." [35] In fact, Ukrainian scholarship has achieved great success in this field. The journals of the Institute in question, **Kibernetika** and **Avtomatika**, both published in Russian, are among the few Soviet scientific journals which have been translated in the USA and which are taken seriously in the West. Soviet Ukrainian scholarship has recently produced an impressive contribution in the field of cybernetics, namely, the **Entsyklopediia Kibernetyky (Encyclopedia of Cybernetics)**, under the editorship of V.M. Hlushkov. [36] The publication of this work in the Ukrainian language appears to be one of the great events in Ukrainian cultural and scientific life of the twentieth century. According to available information this is the first publication of its kind in the Soviet Union, and obviously will have to become the model for an analogous Russian work. It is common knowledge that in the Russo-Ukrainian **Kulturkampf** the problem of the relative development of the respective languages has always played a role of great significance. Those opting for the Russian side have tended to regard Russian as the only well-developed Slavic language, and Ukrainian as a literary language at best, and a dialect at worst. After the publication of the **Entsyklopediia Kibernetyky** such views will be difficult to maintain.

To sum up, during the eventful years when Shelest was the First Secretary of the CC of the CPU Ukraine not only completed her development into a "model republic" within the framework of Soviet economy, a fact of which he, as well as many other Ukrainians were proudly aware of, but she also successfully entered the technotronic age.

In considering the political developments in Ukraine during Shelest's tenure, three problems deserve special attention:
(1) internal party politics;
(2) Russo-Ukrainian relations;
(3) Shelest as a political figure.

One of Shelest's major concerns during his career as First Secretary of the CC of the CPU was the expansion and strengthening of the Ukrainian party organization. As has already been demonstrated by Ya. Bilinsky in his revealing analysis of the membership figures of the CPU, the membership of the CPU continued to increase in the post-Khrushchevian period, and precisely until the fall of Shelest, albeit less dramatically than in the previous years, as compared to the growth of the All-Union Party. In spite of this growth, however, the disproportionally low enrolment of ethnic Ukrainians in the CPU as compared to their share in the total population, and the disproportionally high enrolment of Russians continued. [37] Whereas these facts point to the obvious conclusion that the Russians represent a diminant minority in Ukraine, which would explain for their disproportionally high enrolment in the CPU, the intriguing phenomenon of the uneven growth of the CPU's membership as compared to that of her parent party the CPSU indicates that Shelest and his associates were not following the accepted trend of party politics with regard to membership recruitment.

Even more interesting was Shelest's approach in selecting members for his inner circle in the process of the formation of his group. Even before becoming First Secretary Shelest had long been associated (1954-1962) with the Kyiv party organization, both the city and the **oblast'**. It is only natural that this organization later provided members for his inner group.

One of Shelest's closest political associates and his protege was Drozdenko (an ethnic Ukrainian), the former First Secretary of the Komsomol organization in Ukraine, Shelest's successor to the leadership of the Kyiv party organization and his staunchest supporter in the Presidium and the Secretariat of the CC of the CPU, until his ouster in 1971 from these bodies.[38] and his subsequent transfer to the politically lower-rank position of ambassador to Romania. Another of his potential protégés, also with Kyivan background, was Lutak (an ethnic Ukrainian), who in June of 1969 was appointed to the strategic position of Second Secretary of the CC of the CPU in charge of Party personnel, after being elected in January of 1967 to full membership in the Politburo and to a position as a Secretary of the CC of the CPU .[39] Lutak seems to be the only prominent party politican relatively closely associated with Shelest, to have survived his fall. Shelest promoted the careers of some ethnic Ukrainians from other party organizations also. The more prominent names were: Liashko, the present Chairman of the Ukrainian SSR's Council of Ministers,[40] and Tsybul'ko, another professional party bureaucrat, both from the Donets'k party organization, and Vashchenko, from the Kharkiv party organization.[41] He especially supported Kutsevol, the First Secretary of the Poltava **oblast'** party organization, both of Muzhyts'kyi, the First Secretary of the Poltava **oblast'** party organization, both of whom were his confirmed followers and members of his inner group.[42]

Shelest's 1968 appointment of Ovcharenko, a chemist by profession, to the crucial position of CC Secretary responsible for ideological affairs, a position which usually is connected with the responsibilities of a Candidate Member of the Politburo, represented another addition to his inner circle. From 1959 to March 1968, a period which included the first five years of Shelest's tenure, this position had been held by Skaba, who distinguished himself in that capacity as a narrow-minded ideological **aparatchik** and a faithful executor of the Russification policy in Ukraine.[43] Since his demotion Skaba, on the basis of some marginal claims to the historical profession, has become the Director of the Institute of History of the Academy of Sciences (Ukrainian SSR). Since Ovcharenko may be regarded as Shelest's ideal appointee, it is worthwhile to cite the official biography published in connection with his election:

He is a Ukrainian who was born in 1913 into an impoverished peasant family in the Sums'ka **oblast'**. A member of the CPSU since 1939, he completed his higher education at the Hlukhiv Pedagogical Institute.

The year 1936 found him serving in the Soviet Army. In 1937 he began lecturing at the Kyiv Veterinary Institute. He spent the years 1941 through 1945 in the front lines of the Great Patriotic War. After demobilization he went back to lecturing. Between 1949 and 1956 he was engaged in scientific work at the Institute of Inorganic Chemistry, Academy of Sciences, Ukrainian SSR. At the same time he has served as Party Committee Secretary at the Aacademy of Sciences, Ukrainian SSR. From 1956 to 1958 he headed the Science and Culture Department in the CC of the CPU. In 1958 he returned once again to scientific work at the Academy of Sciences, Ukrainian SSR. In recent years he has been serving as Director of the Institute of Colloidal Chemistry and the Chemistry of Water, Academy of Sciences, Ukrainian SSR, doctor of chemistry, and a professor. Since 1964 he has headed the Executive Board of the "Znannia" (Knowledge) Society of the Ukrainian SSR. In addition to being a member of the CC of the CPU, he is a Deputy of the Supreme Council of the USSR.

Various medals and orders of the Soviet Union have been awarded to him.[44]

Ovcharenko enjoyed a good reputation among the Ukrainian intellectual and scientific community as a man of sound scholarly judgement and political responsibility, and as a level-headed person in his approach to bureaucratic matters. He appeared twice on the political scene, in 1956-1958 and in 1968-1972. i.e., at times of relative moderation and relaxation. While adhering to the official ideological line, Ovcharenko was not associated with the ideological excesses typical of the periods preceding and following him.

Since Shelest's fall Ovcharenko has been succeeded by Malanchuk, a hardline ideological aparatchik with a doctorate in historical sciences and a professor's title, who has the distinction of being one of the Party's chief experts on the nationalities question. Malanchuk is justly regarded as being notorious advocate of the Russification policy, not so much because of his personal convictions but rather on account of his career considerations. His official biography[45] and the publications which he has written or edited[46] speak for his personality and his sentiments. At the same time they point to the differences between him and his predecessor, Ovcharenko, and provide an explanation for the change of ideological climate in Ukraine in the years since he replaced Ovcharenko.

Besides relying upon party bureaucrats Shelest was ready to listen to professional and political advice from persons such as Iampol's'kyi and Honchar, both of whom had a good reputation for sound and moderate judgement, and both of whom apparently also belonged to his inner circle. While it is not quite clear whether Nikitchenko, the KGB chief in Ukraine (1954-1970),[47] was also a part of Shelest's group, the relationship between the two seems to have been quite amicable. Until... Nikitchenko's sudden removal from his post in 1970 and his replacement by Fedorchuk KGB operations in Ukraine, and the handling of the problem of Ukrainian dissenters in particular, seem to have been subordinated to Shelest's political control.

Reviewing the personalities of Shelest's group, it can be observed that this group was basically Kyiv centered, although Shelest had made attempts at drawing into his circle party bureaucrats from other oblast' party organizations, such as the Donets'k and the Kharkiv organizations, with the exception, obviously enough, of the Dnipropetrovs'k party organization. Besides party bureaucrats, his group included distinguished professionals and intellectuals of a middle-of-the-road political orientation. Another important point which should be stressed is that Shelest tried to make his group all-Ukrainian in composition. All the prominent members of the Shelest group were of Ukrainian ethnic background and, what is more significant, their fundamental political concerns became progressively more Ukrainian in nature.

The next question which arises is what was the relationship between Shelest's group and the other influential party orgnaizations in Ukraine? Tentatively speeking, Shelest made attempts at establishing working relations with the Donets'k party organization, the largest among the Ukrainian party organizations, and the Kharkiv party orgnaization, the fourth largest in Ukraine. Of greater interest was Shelest's relationship with the rapidly rising Donets'k party organization for the very reason that its leadership cadres consisted mainly of ethnic Russians and Russified Ukrainians. As B. Lewytzkyj has correctly argued, the Donets'k oblast' is regarded by the All-Union Party leadership as the model oblast' for solving the nationality problem in Ukraine, and the Donets'k aparatchik as the ideal type of the "Ukrainian" aparatchik with an All-Union orientation.[48] Shelest apparently tried to strengthen the Ukrainian ethnic elements within this group by supporting their appointments to higher positions. With regard to the Kharkiv party organization, it appears that Shelest succeeded in drawing this organization into his sphere of influence basically on account of his good relations with N.V. Podgornyi, who at one time was in charge of it. Shelest's failure to gain influence in the Dnipropetrovs'k party organization can basically be attributed to his being in constant competition with Shcherbyts'kyi, who, at different times, was its First Secretary.

Since Shcherbyts'kyi and the Dnipropetrovs'k party group, including some new followers such as Malanchuk and Morhun, (the latter, the First Secretary of the

Poltava oblast' organization), have succeeded Shelest and his group to the key positions in Ukraine, a brief account of Shcherbyts'kyi's attitudes on selected Ukrainian problems would help to better understanding of Shelest's occasionally strange and unpredictable behavior in matters of Ukrainian politics and international Communist affairs.

In the early 1960's, i.e., before Shelest's assumption of the First Secretaryship of the CC of the CPU, Shcherbyts'kyi was already enjoying the reputation of being a nationally conscious Ukrainian svidomyi ukrainets') and of a political leader in whom the Ukrainian intellectual community thought to have had a protector.[49] A number of concrete pieces of evidence substantiate this assessment:

1. The announcement concerning Shcherbyts'kyi's election in 1961 to the position of a Candidate Member of the Presidium of the CC of the CPU included a clear and unmistakable reference to his national background, i.e., Ukrainian. It should be remembered that until that time the national background of prominent Soviet political figures from Ukraine had not been advertised. This is exemplified in the early treatment of Podgorny's natioanl origin, wich was obscured by references such as "from a worker's family in Ukraine." Only relatively late in his career has Podgorny been referred to directly as Ukrainian.

2. Soon after Shcherbyts'kyi's appointment to the post of Ukrainian Prime Minister (February of 1961), the literary monthly Vitchyzna, which at that time printed articles and literary materials of considerable relevance to the quest for national selfassertion, published a highly publicized interview with Shcherbyts'kyi.[50] This interview stressed the extraordinary achievements of the Soviet Ukrainian Republic and extended support to the development of Ukrainian culture.

3. Shcherbyts'kyi was the leading author of a collection of articles, entitled Sotsialistychna diisnist' i natsionalistychni vyhadky (Socialist Reality and Nationalist Inventions),[51] which aimed at disproving the findings of a number of historians and political scientists working on Ukrainian topics and living in Western countries. Among other things this collection includes an article by M. Lypovchenko (also an editor of this collection), entitled "Against Great Power Arrogance and National Narrow-Mindedness" which criticizes both Russian and Ukrainian nationalism as equal vices.[52]

4. Finally, Shcherbyts'kyi's article in honor of the Fiftieth Anniversary of the Communist Party of Ukraine published in Izvestiia on July 5, 1968, was more Ukrainian in content than Shelest's analogous statement.[53]

Comparing the two figures, one can observe than until 1968 Shcherbyts'kyi's record on Ukrainian national affairs was as good or even better than that of Shelest. In 1968, when the invasion of Czechoslovakia was being decided, and the Dubcek experiment was being suppressed, Shcherbyts'kyi, contrary to Shelest's hard-line and extreme position, displayed relatively moderate and flexible attitudes towards those issues. Shcherbyts'kyi's stance made him a sympathetic politician in the eyes of nationally conscious Ukrainians of progressive and liberal orientation. There is a good chance that Shelest's position on the Czechoslovak problem was motivated by his desire to prove his absolute loyalty to the All-Union Party Leadership. Exposing himself on the Ukrainian national issue, he could not afford a risk of being tainted with revisionism. A victory of revisionist forces would have endangered his position for a competing politician, with the reputation of being a better Ukrainian, in the person of Shcherbyts'kyi, was waiting in the wings.

Brezhnev's protégé Shcherbyts'kyi has won the competition and has replaced Shelest. The All-Union leadership on its part has exploited the competition between the two Ukrainian political leaders and their respective groups for its own purposes. For one thing, it has weakened the Ukrainian elements in the CPU. Secondly, it has advanced the cause of the ambitious and aggressive Donets'k faction with its Sll-Union and basically Russian orientation. And, finally, and ironically enough, it has arranged for Shcherbyts'kyi together with the help of the Donets'k group, to carry out the repression of the "second Ukrainization" in Ukraine, which was initiated under Shelest's auspices. All this once again proves the old historical wisdom that leaders of the Russian political elite are the best experts on the Ukrainian question.

Shelest's approach to the problem of Russo-Ukrainian relations was a very realistic one under the given circumstances. He recognized the historically dominant position of the Russian state and the Russian nation, and acknowledged the absolute necessity for the closest Russo-Ukrainian cooperation. But he was against the merging of nations, the forced assimilation of the Ukrainians, and the degradation of the Ukrainian language and culture. Throughout his career he consistently regarded Russian great power chauvinism and Ukrainian bourgeois nationalism as equal evils. Shelest, however, was apparently sincerely committed to the idea of the perpetuation of the USSR on the foundation of mutual respect and theoretical equality of all the nations and peoples of the Soviet multinational state (recognizing Russians, of course, as the first among the equals). He always paid due homage to the official shibolets such as the "friendship of nations," "brotherly cooperation," and "mutual help and mutual enrichment." Contrary to most Soviet Ukrainian politicians, including those in office before and after his tenure, Shelest always preserved a certain dignity and never demonstrated a degrading servility when he spoke positively and respectfully of Russia and the Russian people. When referring to Russians Shelest tended to avoid the use of the phrase "older brother," an ominous term coined in the Stalinist period. Similarly, when he discussed issues or arrangements indicative of the subordinate status or role of Ukraine or other non-Russian republics he attempted to treat them in a realistic and detached manner.

In the later part of his career Shelest went beyond his cautious and balanced approach to the problem of Russo-Ukrainian relations. The new approach became particularly evident in his book **Ukraino nasha Radians'ka** in which he revealed himself as a spokesman for the revival of Ukrainian autonomism. This can be deduced from his assessment of the Pereiaslav Treaty (1654) and the subsequent Russo-Ukrainian relations, an assessment which represents a subtle modification of the Party's interpretation of the "reunification" theory.[54] A comparison of the relevant passages from the CPSU interpretative document "Theses Concerning the Tercentenary of the Reunification of Ukraine with Russia" and the Shelest book will reveal the crucial difference between the two:

Theses	Shelest
The most ferocious enemy of the Russian, Ukrainian and other peoples of Russia was the tsarist autocracy. Relying on the reactionary upper class of landlords and bourgeoisie, tsarism conducted a policy of cruel national-colonial subjugation of non-Russian peoples. In Ukraine tsarism liquidated local self-administration, brutally oppressed the national liberation movement by suppressing aspirations for Ukrainian statehood, conducted a repressive policy of Russification, and obstructed the development of the Ukrainian language and culture.[55]	In order to strengthen its rule in Ukraine, the tsarist government conducted a ruthless policy of great-power repression, and even **liquidated the remnants of the Ukraine's autonomy** which had been **provided by the Pereiaslav Treaty. Tsarism was especially concerned with the Zaporozhian Host and its autonomous status.**[56]

Although not questioning the "historic necessity" of the Pereiaslav Treaty, Shelest, nevertheless, pointed to the Russian's failure to adhere to its provisions and pointed out the imperial government's abolition of the Ukrainian autonomy it provided. This evaluation of the consequences of the Pereiaslav Treaty, together with the substitution of the broader political concept of autonomy for the more limited notion of local self-administration, and the application of the term "autonomy" to entire Ukraine, as well as to the Zaporozhian Host, signified a criticism by Shelest of the Pereiaslav "reunification" theory and, at the same time, implied his tacit approval of the endeavors already undertaken by the historian Braichevs'kyi to revise this theory.

Almost concurrently with these attempts, and more specifically during the period from 1967 to 1972, a number of legal articles were published in Ukraine. These articles discussed problems such as the concept of the "sovereignty" of the Ukrainian SSR and the characteristics of the Soviet Ukrainian state. They were written with an intent to prove Ukraine's active participation in international relations by virtue of her exercising the prerogatives of membership in the United Nations, signing treaties, and hosting consulates of other countries.[57] They were also aimed at disproving the "claims" and "falsifications" put forward by "bourgeois" Western experts and Ukrainian scholars living abroad, who question assertions concerning the "sovereign" character of the Ukrainian SSR on the grounds of her not entertaining diplomatic relations with other countries. The problems touched upon in these articles in reality reflected the Soviet Ukrainian scholars' genuine concern with the elements of Ukrainian autonomy, a much more appropriate concept than the freely used term "sovereignty," and represented a careful defense of the meager republican prerogatives against the growing encroachments upon the rights of the republics by the All-Union state organs, and in particular, against the pressures generated in Moscow that were aimed first at reducing the importance of and finally at obliterating the boundaries of the republics in the USSR. A successful obliteration of the boundaries of the Union republics would signify the beginning of a process which could eventually lead to complete abolition of these republics.

Shelest opposed these menacing tendencies, and apparently wished to preserve the territorial, administrative and political integrity of the Ukrainian Union Republic. A good example of his concern for the further development of Ukrainian theoretical thought in the realm of state and international law and for the continuous growth of scholarly legal institutions was the belated establishment in 1969 of the Institute of State and Law of the Ukrainian Academy of Sciences, Ukrainian SSR.[58] This Institute, incidentally, is the successor of the Sector of State and Law, which was founded within the framework of the Ukrainian Academy in 1949.

The Shelest period (1963-1972), which in terms of Russo-Ukrainian relations was characterized in Ukraine by resistance to the policies of centralization, by efforts to defend the Ukrainian Republic's rights and prerogatives, and by policies directed at internal cultural, economic, and institutional developments, may appropriately be defined as the age of the revival of controlled Ukrainian autonomism.

In conclusion, a few remarks about Shelest as a political figure. Shelest was neither a hidden Ukrainian nationalist, who dreamed of political independence for Ukraine, nor simply a political boss, or a "feudal lieutenant,"[59] and certainly not an "avowed Stalinist."[60] He rather represented a new type of a Ukrainian party leader which emerged in the post-Stalinist period, the period which signified a revival of relative political respectability in Ukrainian party politics. In some respects Shelest can be compared to O. I. Kirychenko (born in 1908, the year of Shelest's birth), the first ethnic Ukrainian to have held the position of First Secretary of the CC of the CPU, from 1953 to 1957, and who from 1955 to 1960 was also a member of the CC CPSU Presidium and one of the All-Union CC Secretaries, and who fell in 1960 under mysterious circumstances.[61] On the basis of circumstantial evidence the fall of Kirychenko has been partially explained by his favoritism for the native cadres in the non-Russian republics — in Ukraine in particular.[62] Shelest seems to have enjoyed the political support of Kirychenko, and may have been indebted to him and perhaps also to Podgorny for his re-elevation into the ranks of the Ukrainian party elite.[63] This policy of promoting native ethnics to party leadership positions, which was implemented during the period from 1953 to the beginning of the 1960's, certainly benefitted Shelest in his career.

Throughout his career Shelest proved himself to be a competent party bureaucrat, who understood industrial and agricultural management and who sensed the important role of the sciences. He also supported legal and historical scholarship in Ukraine, and even displayed some interest in Ukrainian studies abroad. During his tenure some flirtation with the Ukrainian intellectual community in the diaspora was tolerated. Shelest succeeded in forming his own group and in inspiring the loyalty of a considerable following in the Ukrainian party machinery. Some highly revealing information about his fall and the strength of his group has been provided by the **Ukrains'kyi visnyk (Ukrainian Herald)** (No. 7-8), which appeared in the Ukrainian **samyvdav** in Spring of 1974, following a two-year interruption, and which has since been published in Paris in February of 1975.[64] According to the **Ukrains'kyi visnyk**, Shelest's removal was decided in Moscow. He was prevented from attending and speaking at the May 25, 1972 CC CPU Plenum because of a concern by the Moscow leadership that he might convene the CC CPU Plenum and be reconfirmed by that body. The **Visnyk** further informs that Shelest enjoyed the support of the majority of the **oblast'** party organizations first secretaries, among whom he had only three open enemies:[65] Degtiarev, the First Secretary of the Donets'k **oblast** party organization,[66] Vatchenko, the First Secretary of the Dnipropetrovs'k **oblast'** party organization,[67] and Dobryk, the First Secretary of the Ivano-Frankivs'k **oblast'** party organization. The purge (arrests, dismissals and demotions) of Shelest's followers has been quite extensive. In 1973, thirty-four instructors of the Higher Party School of the CC CPU were dismissed, to give one example.[68] The final count of the purge of Shelest's group is still incomplete. It may very well reach the number of approximately one thousand people. Shelest was also quite popular among broader segments of the nationally conscious Ukrainian population. In some circles he was even referred to as "**bat'ko** Shelest." All these factors have prompted the author of this study to apply the term **shelestivshchyna** to define the period from 1963 to 1972.

There are some indications that Shelst conceived of himself as an architect in the development of the Ukrainian republic, its builder and **hospodar**. In spite of his awareness of the necessities of contemporary times, Shelest was basically a traditionalist and a conservative. He hardly expected the sad outcome of his otherwise remarkable career. After he was caught in the web of the currents and crosscurrents of his times he tilted toward the Ukrainian side, trying in vain to defend his own, as well as his Republic's, reputation and respectability, and in the final analysis he became the reviver of Ukrainian autonomism. In the already-quoted issue of the **Ukrains'kyi visnyk**, Shelest is referred to as having been in charge of "liberally inclined leading party cadres in Ukraine," as an author whose works have been placed on the KGB "black" list, and as a politically repressed Ukrainian national figure.[69] This highly favourable assessment of Shelest's political personality by the Ukrainian dissident journal sheds light on Shelest's attitudes toward the Ukrainian dissident movement. Shelest has been credited with having been opposed to the excesses of repressive policies against Ukrainian dissidents by being consistently in favor of a political, rather than a police-type approach to this problem.

This relationship between Shelest and his group and the Ukrainian dissidents leads to the question of the relative significance of these two groups in the internal developments in Ukraine and, in fact, in the entire USSR. Since the Ukrainian dissident movement has received much greater international attention than the Shelest problem, it seems necessary to put the impact of this movement and the role of Shelest and his group into a more appropriate political and historical perspective. With all due respect for the heroic efforts of the Ukrainian dissident movement and in particular for individuals such as Valentyn Moroz, it should be kept in mind that this movement is of lesser importance for the Soviet Ukrainian, and even more so for the All-Union politics, than the Shelest problem. While it is correct to assume that the Ukrainian dissident movement has much deeper and stronger roots in Soviet Ukrainian society than does its Russian counterpart in Russia, from a general point of view it still remains a secondary, and in the opinion of some analysts a marginal political problem in the Soviet Union. Shelest and his group, on the other hand, constituted an integral part of the Soviet political establishment, and their conflict with its Russian leadership is indicative both of the Russian leadership's continuing inability to permanently solve the historic Ukrainian problem and of the difficult transformation which the Soviet political system is still undergoing, namely from totalitarianism to authoritarian partocracy. The very fact that a group of political leaders, which later had to be treated as having a national-deviationist orientation could emerge within the CPU and was able to dominate the Ukrainian party apparatus for at least five years, represents an unprecedented event both in the Ukrainian, as well as the Soviet history of the third quarter of the twentieth century.

The next crucial question which arises is why would a man like Shelest, who had achieved the highest political position in the establishment, probably the fourth-ranking standing in the Politburo, risk his power, status, privileges and rewards for the defense and support of rather abstract and vague concepts such as a national idea, or Ukrainian republican rights? After all, he was neither a naive student nor a radical intellectual, but a hard-nosed realist and a ruthless careerist. According to standard behavioralist assumptions, Shelest should have adjusted to the changing general line (he knew how to do it well), should have kept his nose clean, and should have acted primarily from the point of view of his own self-interest. He, however, behaved in a manner which brought about his fall. Somewhere along the road he apparently put abstract values above self-interest and fell victim to the historical patterns and traditions of Russo-Ukrainian relations, which, qualitatively speaking, have changed little over the past two-and-a-half centuries.

Shelest can best be compared with Ukrainian Hetmans of the first third of the eighteenth century, such as Ivan Skoropads'kyi (1708-1722),[70] Pavlo Polubotok (1722-1724)[71] and Danylo Apostol (1727-1734),[72] political leaders who attempted to maintain correct relations with the imperial center, on the one hand, and who tried to defend the autonomy of the Ukrainian Hetmanate, its institutions and its special interests, on the other. It is not a coincidence that Shelest was referred to in the Ukrainian intelligentsia circles of Kyiv as **malorosiis'kyi polityk** (Little Russian politician). In fact, an especially close parallel can be drawn between Hetman Pavlo Polubotok and Shelest. Following his removal from the Hetmanate, Polubotok had been brought to St. Petersburg and incarcerated in the SS. Peter and Paul Fortress by Peter the Great. In a similar manner, immediately after his demotion from the position of First Secretary, Shelest was brought to Moscow and since then has been confined under house arrest at a **dacha** in the vicinity of Moscow.

FOOTNOTES

1. For the history of Shelest's career until his promotion in November of 1964 to full membership in the CC CPSU Presidium, see the informative biographical article by G. Hodnett, "Pyotr Efimovich Shelest," G. W. Simmonds (ed.), **Soviet Leaders** (New York: T. Y. Crowell Company, 1967), pp. 95-103. A valuable biographical research guide on careers of party leaders of the Soviet Republics is the work by G. Hodnett and V. Ogareff, **Leaders of the Soviet Republics: A Guide to Posts and Occupants** (Department of Political Science, Research School of Social Sciences, The Australian National University, Canberra, 1973).

2. G. Hodnett and P.J. Potichnyj, **The Ukraine and the Czechoslovak Crisis** (Occasional Paper No. 6, Department of Political Science, Research School of Social Sciences, Australian National University, Canberra, 1970), pp. 81-86.

3. P.Iu. Shelest, **Ukraino nasha Radians'ka** (Kyiv: Vydavnytstvo politychnoi literatury Ukrainy, 1970 / 1971), pp. 278.

4. "Pro seriozni nedoliky ta pomylky odniiei knyhy," **Komunist Ukrainy,** April, 1973, pp. 77-82.

5. **Ibid.,** p. 80.

6. **Istoricheskoe prizvanie molodezhi** (Moscow: Molodaia gvardiia, 1968); **Kommunist — aktivnyi boets partii** (Kyiv: Izdatel'stvo politicheskoi literatury Ukrainy, 1969); **Idei Lenina peremahaiut'** (Kyiv: Vydavnytstvo politychnoi literatury Ukrainy, 1971) (in Ukrainian); **Idei Lenina pobezhdaiut** (Kyiv: Izdatel'stvo politicheskoi literatury Ukrainy, 1971) (in Russian).

7. "We, the legal inheritors of the Ukrainian culture, cherish it greatly and develop it creatively" (**Ukraino nasha Radians'ka,** p. 82).

8. For two examples of traditional and purely "nationalist" evaluation of Shelest's removal from his office, see M. Prokop, "Padinnia Petra Shelesta," **Suchasnist',** XIII, 6 (1973), pp. 98-110 and T. Kharchuk, "Ukrainian Nationalism and the Fall of Petro Shelest," **International Socialist Review,** November, 1973, pp. 14-17; 34-37.

9. A.v. Borcke, "Das April-Plenum 1973 des Zentralkomitees der KPd-SU und die Umbesetzungen im Politburo," **Osteuropa,** XXIII, 12 (1973), pp. 917-929, and especially pp. 919-921, as well as the highly informative and well-researched contribution to this volume by Ya. Bilinsky, "The Communist Party of Ukraine after 1966."

10. For the best accounts of the cultural, as well as political, developments of this period, see the excellent works by Ya. Bilinsky, **The Second Soviet Republic: The Ukraine After World War II** (New Brunswick, N.J.: Rutgers University Press, 1964) and B. Lewytzkyj, **Die Sowjetukraine, 1944-1963** (Koln & Berlin: Kiepenheuer & Witsch, 1964). Information on and analysis of the literary revival in Ukraine in the late 1950's and early 1960's has been provided by J. Pelenski, "Recent Ukrainian Writing," **Survey,** No. 59 (April, 1966), pp. 102-112; Ya. Bilinsky, "Assimilation and Ethnic Assertiveness among Ukrainians of the Soviet Union," in E. Goldhagen (ed.), **Ethnic Minorities in the Soviet Union** (New York: Praeger, 1968), pp. 166-175 and G. Luckyj, "Turmoil in the Ukraine," **Problems of Communism,** XVII, 4 (1968).

11. **Nasha Kul'tura,** No. 3, 1963.

12. P.Iu. Shelest, "Militant Goals of Soviet Ukrainian Literature," **Literaturna**

Ukraina, November 17, 1966, p. 2; for a reprint of this speech, see **Idei Lenina pobezh-daiut,** pp. 283-291; for the relevant quotation cf. p. 291.

13. For a summary of Dadenkov's circular memorandum, entitled "Pro movu vykladannia u vuzakh MVSSO URSR," see V. Chornovil, "Iak i shcho obstoiuie Bohdan Stenchuk (66 Zapytan' i zauvah 'internatsionalistovi'), **Ukrains'kyi visnyk,** VI (March, 1972) (Paris & Baltimore, Md.: Smoloskyp), pp. 25-30.

14. **Ibid.,** p. 30.

15. F.P. Shevchenko (ed.), **Seredni viky na Ukraini,** Vyp. I (Kyiv: Naukova Dumka, 1971); the second issue of this projected series has been published, but is unavailable to me.

16. **Kyivs'ka starovyna,** Vyp. I (Kyiv, 1972).

17. Cf. V.V. Shcherbyts'kyi's address in "Educating Dedicated Fighters for Communism: Meeting of the Aktiv of the Kyiv **Oblast'** and Kiev City Party Organizations," **Radians'ka Ukraina,** March 17, 1973, pp. 1-2

18. F.P. Shevchenko's name as the chief editor of the **Ukrains'kyi istorychnyi zhurnal** last appeared in the first (January) issue of 1972. Beginning with the second (February) issue of 1972 P.M. Kalynychenko became the chief editor of this journal. This substitution of the editors of the **Ukrainian Historical Journal** which was indicative of a major change in Ukrainian historico-cultural field, went completely unnoticed in the West.

19. For the information on the Ukrainian aspects of the Seventh International Congress of Slavists, see P. "Ukraintsi i ukrains'ka tematyka na os'momu Mizhnarodnomu Kongresi Slavistiv u Varshavi," **Svoboda,** October 24, 1973.

20. **Istoriia mist i sil Ukrains'koi RSR v dvadtsiaty shesty tomakh** (Vols. I - XXVI, Kyiv, 1967-1974; Holovna Redaktssia Ukrains'koi Radians'koi Entsyklopedii, P.T. Tron'ko — editor-in-chief).

21. In the editorial-review of his book Shelest was charged with having taken "dry encyclopedic pieces of information" from the **Ukrainian Soviet Encyclopedia** and from the **History of the Cities and Villages of the Ukrainian SSR** (**Komunist Ukrainy,** April, 1973, p. 82). The only difference between Shelest's outline and the individual volumes of the History is a special chapter in Shelest's book on the Dnipro River (**Ukraino nasha Radians'ka,** pp. 271-275) which appears to be a substitute for the volume in the History dealing with the city of Kyiv.

22. The first of the two articles devoted to Hrushevs'ky contributions was authored by I. Boiko and Ie. Kyryliuk, "Mykhailo Hrushevs'kyi. On the 100th Anniversary of His Birth," **Literaturna Ukraina,** September 30, 1966, pp. 3-4. For an incomplete translation of this article, see **Digest of Soviet Ukrainian Press** (cited hereafter as DSUP), X, 11 (1966), pp. 21-25. The second article was written by F.P. Shevchenko, "Chomu Mykhailo Hrushevs'kyi povernuvsia na Radians'ku Ukrainu?" **Ukrains' kyi istorychnyi zhurnal,** 1968, No. 11, pp. 13-30.

23. Shelest, **Ukraino nasha Radians'ka,** pp. 19-20.

24. The original Ukrainian version of his work was published in Germany (I. Dziuba, **Internatsionalizm chy rusyfikatsiia?** (Munich: Suchasnist', 1968)). An English translation of Dziuba's work appeared in Great Britain (I. Dzyuba, **Internationalism or Russification?** (London: Weidenfeld and Nicolson, 1968)).

25. M.Iu. Braichevs'kyi, **Pryiednannia chy vozz'iednannia** (Krytychni zavvahy z pryvodu odniiei kontseptsii) (Toronto: Novi Dni, 1972), reprinted in **Shyroke more Ukrainy** (Dokumenty samvydavu z Ukrainy, Dokumenty VII) (Paris — Baltimore: Smoloskyp, 1972), pp. 241-312) including a brief account of this historian's career (pp. 235-237).

26. For a discussion of the Party's concept of "reunification" and the literature on this problem, see J. Pelenski, "Soviet Ukrainian Historiography after World War II," **Jahrbucher fur Geschichte Osteuropas**, XII, 3 (1964), pp. 375-418, and especially pp. 381-389.

27. "A Meeting with the Students," **Radians'ka Ukraina**, September 4, 1968, p.1.

28. Shelest, **Ukraino nasha Radians'ka**, p. 87.

29. For a discussion of the All-Union Party leadership's attitudes toward the Ukrainian economy and the economic relations between Soviet republics during the early part of Shelest's tenure, see the perceptive study by V. Holubnychy, "Some Economic Aspects of the Relations Among the Soviet Republics," in E. Goldhagen (ed.), **Ethnic Minorities in the Soviet Union**, pp. 50-120, and especially pp. 86-93; cf. also Ya. Bilinsky, "The Communist Party of Ukraine after 1966."

30. **Entsyklopediia Narodnoho Hospodarstva Ukrains'koi RSR** (4 vols.; Kyiv, 1969-1972; Holovna Redaktsiia Ukrains'koi Radians'koi Entsyklopedii, S.M. Iampol's'kyi — editor-in-chief).

31. **Ukrains'ka Sil's'ko-hospodars'ka Entsyklopediia** (3 vols.: Kyiv, 1970-1972; Holovna Redaktsiia Ukrains'koi Radians'koi Entsyklopedii, V.F. Peresypkin — editor-in-chief).

32. **Radians'ka Entsyklopediia Istorii Ukrainy** (4 vols.: Kiev, 1969-1972; Holovna Redaktsiia Ukrains'koi Radians'koi Entsyklopedii, A.D. Skaba — editor-in-chief).

33. **Ukraina v period rozhornutoho budivnytstva komunizmu** (5 vols.; Akademiia Nauk Ukrains'koi RSR, Kiev: Naukova Dumka, 1967); Vol. I: **Velyki zvershennia** (Instytut istorii, K.K. Dubyna (ed.)); Vol. II: **Stvorennia material'no-tehnichnoi bazy komunismu** (Instytut filosofii, P.D. Koval' (ed.)); Vol. V: **Rozkvit orhanizatsiia suspil'stva** (Sektor derzhavy i prava, V.M. Korets'kyi (ed)); Vol. IV: **Korinni sotsial'ni zminy** (Instytut filosofii, P.D. Koval' (ed.)); Vol. V: **Rozkvit kul'tury** (Instytut mystetstvoznavstva, fol'kloru i etnografii, K.H. Huslystyi (ed.)).

34. "Rech' tovarishcha P.E. Shelesta," **XXIV S'ezd Kommunisticheskoi Partii Sovetskogo Soiuza, 30 marta — 9 aprelia 1971 goda, Stenograficheskii otchet** (2 vols.; Moscow, 1971), vol. I, pp. 149-150.

35. For a discussion of the history and the contributions of the Ukrainian Institute of Cybernetics, see the informative study by V. Holubnychy, "The Present State of Cybernetics and the Republic-Level Economic Planning," in this volume.

36. **Entsyklopediia Kibernetyky** (2 vols.: Kyiv, 1973, pp. 572, 582; Akademiia Nauk Ukrains'koi Radians'koi Sotsialistychnoi Respubliky, Holovna Redaktsiia Ukrains'koi Radians'koi Entsyklopedii, V.M. Hlushkov — editor-in-chief).

37. Ya. Bilinsky, "The Communist Party of Ukraine after 1966."

38. For Drozdenko's biography, see **Deputaty Verkhovnogo Soveta SSSR** (Sed'moi sozyv) (Moscow, 1966) (cited hereafter as DVS SSSR 7), p. 146 and Lewytzkyj, **Die**

Sowjetukraine, 1944-1963, pp. 313-314.

39. For Lutak's earlier career, confer **Deputaty Verkhovnogo Soveta SSSR** (Vos'moi sozyv) (Moscow, 1970) (cited hereafter as **DVS SSSR** 8), p. 263 and Lewytzkyj, **Die Sowjetukraine**, 1944-1963, p. 342.

40. For Liashko's biography, consult **DVS SSSR** 8, **p. 264 and Lewytzkyj, Die Sowjetukraine**, 1944-1963, p. 341.

41. For Vashchenko's biography, see **DVS SSSR** 8, p. 78.

42. For Kutsevol's and Muzhyts'kyi's biographies, confer **DVS SSSR** 8, pp. 244, 299.

43. For Skaba's biography, see **DVS SSSR** 7, p. 407 and Lewytzkyj, **Die Sowjetukraine**, 1944-1963, p. 359.

44. **Robitnycha Hazeta**, March 30, 1968, p. 1 (for an English translation, see **DSUP** XII, 5 (1968), pp. 1-2). Consult also **DVS SSSR** 7, p. 329.

45. "V.Iu. Malanchuk was born on November 13, 1928 in the city of Khmel'nyts'kyi in the family of a white-collar worker. He is a Ukrainian, a member of the CPSU since 1950, and has a higher education — he is a graduate of the Ivan Franko State University in L'viv. V.Iu. Malanchuk began his career as a state farm employee, who later worked in a sugar refinery in Khmel'nyts'kyi **oblast'**. From 1945 to 1950, he studies at L'viv's Ivan Franko State University. While a student at this institution, V.Iu. Malanchuk worked as a university Komsomol organizer for the Ukrainian Komsomol Central Committee. In 1950 V.Iu. Malanchuk was elected Secretary of the L'viv **oblast'** Komsomol Committee. After this he worked for 12 years as a party instructor in the L'viv **oblast'** Party Committee, as lecturer, and as head of the Department of Science and Culture. In 1963 Malanchuk was elected Secretary of L'viv **oblast'** Party Committee and placed in charge of ideological work. V.Iu. Malanchuk is a doctor of historical sciences and a professor. He has been awarded two orders and medals" (**Radians'ka Ukraina**, October 11, 1972, p. 1; for an English translation, see DSUP, XVI, 11 (1972), pp. 12-13).

46. V.Iu. Malanchuk is the editor of the following publications: **KPZU — Orhanizator revoliutsiinoi borot'by; Spohady kolyshnikh chleniv Komunistychnoi Partii Zakhidnoi Ukrainy** (L'viv, 1958); **Na choli vyzvol'noi borot'by; Spohady kolyshnikh aktyvnykh diiachiv Komunistychnoi Partii Zakhidnoi Ukrainy** (Kyiv, 1965); **Pamflety, statti, narysy, opovidannia, poezii**, Vstup. stattia: V.Iu. Malanchuk (L'viv: Vyd. Kameniar, 1967-), V(1)3; **Pravda pro Uniiu; Dokumenty i materialy** (L'viv: Kameniar, 1968); **L'vivs'ka oblast'; Istoriia mist i sil Ukrains' koi RSR** (Kyiv, 1968); **Sotsialistychna revoliutsiia i natsional'ni vidnosyny** (Kyiv: Vydavnytstvo Kyivs'koho Universytetu, 1968). He is also the co-author of the following works: With I. Petriv, **Nas iednaie velyka meta** (L'viv: Kameniar, 1965); with M. Kulichenko, **V.I. Lenin i rozv'iazannia natsional'noho pytannia na Ukraini** (Kyiv: Politvydav Ukrainy, 1971).

47. For Nikitchenko's biography, consult **DVS SSSR** 7, p. 319 and **DVS SSSR** 8, p. 313.

48. For B. Lewytzkyj's perceptive comments on the Donets'k group, see, "The Ruling Party Elite of Ukraine" in this volume.

49. The text of Shcherbyts'kyi's official biography reads as follows:
"Volodymyr Vasyl'ovych Shcherbyts'kyi was born on February 17, 1918 into a worker's family. He is Ukrainian, has been a CPSU member since 1941, and has a higher education. In 1941 he graduated from the Dnipropetrovs'k Chemical-Technological Institute.

From 1934 he was engaged in Komsomol work, then studied at the Institute, and upon graduation worked as a mechanical engineer. At the beginning of the Great Patriotic War, V.V. Shcherbyts'kyi was sent to study at a military academy. From 1942 he served in the active units of the Soviet Army.

After demobilization in 1945 he held engineering posts in Dniprodzerzhyns'k in Dnipropetrovs'k oblast', and from 1948 worked in party organs — as secretary of the party bureau at the Ordzhonikidze Coke-Chemical Plant in Dniprodzerzhyns'k and as a party organizaer at the Dzerzhyns'kyi metallurgical plant in Dniprovs'k.

In 1952 he was elected First Secretary of the Dniprodzerzhyns'k City Party Committee. From 1954 he served as Second Secretary, and from 1955 as First Secretary of the Dnipropetrovs'k oblast' Party Committee.

In 1957 com. V.V. Shcherbyts'kyi was elected member of the Presidium and Secretary of the CC of the CPU, and in 1961 appointed chairman of the Council of Ministers of the Ukrainian SSR. Between 1963 and 1965 he worked as First Secretary of the Dnipropetrovs'k oblast' Party Committee. From 1965 — as Chairman of the Council of Ministers of the Ukrainian SSR. Between 1956 and 1961, com. V.V. Shcherbyts'kyi was an elected member of the Central Auditing Commission of the CPSU, and from 1961 he was a member of the CC of the CPSU. From 1961 to 1963 and from 1965 to 1966 he was a candidate member of the Presidium of the CC of the CPSU, and from 1966 to 1971 a candidate member of the CC CPSU Politburo. Since April 1971 he has been a full member of the CC CPSU Politburo. He is also a member of the CC CPU Politburo. Com. V.V. Shcherbyts'kyi was a Deputy of the USSR Supreme Soviet of the Fifth, Sixth, Seventh and Eighth Convocations, and a Deputy to the Ukrainian SSR Supreme Soviet of the Fourth, Fifth, Sixth, Seventh and Eighth Convocations.

He has been awarded three Orders of Lenin and medals.''
(**Radians'ka Ukraina**, May 26, 1972, p. 1; for an English translation, see **DSUP**, XVI, 7 (1972) pp. 1-2).

50. ''Radians'ka Ukraina 1961 roku'' (Rozmova Holovy Rady Ministriv Ukrains'koi RSR tov. Shcherbyts'koho V.V. z chlenom redkolehii zhurnalu ''Vitchyzna''), **Vitchyzna**, 9 (1961), pp. 3-10.

51. M. Lypovchenko (ed.) **Sotsialistychna diisnist' i natsionalistychni vyhadky** (Kyiv: Vydavnytstvo politychnoi literatury Ukrainy, 1968). Shcherbyts'kyi's article ''50 rokiv Ukrains'koi Radians'koi Sotsialistychnoi Respubliky'' appears on pp. 16-38.

52. **Ibid.**, pp. 96-119.

53. For an analysis of this speech, see Hodnett and Potichnyj, **The Ukraine and the Czechoslovak Crisis**, pp. 84-85.

54. Cf. n. 26.

55. **Tezy pro 300-richchia vozz'iednannia Ukrainy z Rosiieiu** (1654-1954 rr.) (Skhvaleni Tsentral'nym Komitetom Komunistychnoi Partii Radians'koho Soiuzu) (Kyiv, 1954), pp. 48-49.

56. Shelest, **Ukraino nasha Radians'ka**, p. 29.

57. V. Korets'kyi and B. Babii, ''Radians'ka behatonatsional'na derzhava — uosoblennia iednosti i druzhby bratnikh respublik,'' **Radians'ke pravo**, 10 (1967), pp. 10-15; V. Terlets'kyi, Leninist Teachings on the Socialist State and Contemporaneity,'' **Ekonomika Radians'koi Ukrainy**, 4 (1970), pp. 3-12; I. Lukashuk, ''Ukrains'ka RSR — chlen Orhanizatsii Ob'iednanykh Natsii,'' **Radians'ke pravo**, 9 (1970), pp. 34-39; M. Malyshko, ''Zdiisnennia federatyvnykh nachal u vidnosynakh derzhavnoho aparatu URSR z orhanamy Soiuzu RSR (Do 50-richchia utvorennia Soiuzu RSR),'' **Radians'ke pravo**, 2 (1972), pp. 37-46; S. Makohon, ''Rozvytok nat-

sional'noi derzhavnosti Ukrains'koi RSR u skladi SRSR," **Radians'ke pravo,,** 10 (1972) pp. 37-42; R. Pavlovs'kyi, "Vkhodzhennia do skladu Soiuzu RSR — osnovna umova vsebichnoho rozvytku Ukrains'koi RSR," **Radians'ke pravo,** 11 (1972), pp. 14-18.

58. B. Babii and V. Mryha, "Instytut derzhavy i prava Akademii Nak Ukrains'koi RSR — novyi naukovyi zaklad respubliky," **Radians'ke pravo,** 10 (1969), pp. 24-26.

59. Ya. Bilinsky, "The Communist Party of Ukraine after 1966."

60. T. Kharchuk, Internationalist Socialist Review, November 1973, p. 14.

61. For Kirichenko's biography, see Lewytzkyj, **Die Sowjetukraine,** 1944-1963, p. 327.

62. Ya. Bilinsky, **The Second Soviet Republic,** pp. 245, 247-248.

63. G. Hodnett, "Pyotr Efimovich Shelest," p. 99.

64. **Ukrains'kyi visnyk,** VII — VIII (Spring 1974) (Paris & Baltimore, Md.: Smolskyp).

65. For Degtiarev's biography, see **DVS SSSR** 8, p. 122.

66. For Vatchenko's biography, consult **DVS SSSR** 8, **p. 77.**

67. For Dobryk's biography, confer **DVS SSSR** 8, p. 133.

68. **Ukrains'kyi visnyk,** VII — VIII.

69. **Ibid.,**

70. For the biography of Ivan Skoropads'kyi, confer the studies of K. Khranevych, "Skoropads'kyi, Ivan Il'ich, hetman Malorossii (1708-1722 gg.)," in **Russkii biograficheskii slovar'** (vol. Sabanev-Smyslov) (St. Pesburg104), pp. 611-614. T. Kostruba, **Het'man Ivan Skoropads'kyi** (1709-1722) (L'viv, 1932); O. Pritsak, "Rid Skoropads'kykh (Istorychnogeneal'ogichna studiia)," in **Za velych natsii** (L'viv, 1938, **2nd ed. New York, 1955), pp. 64-90, especially pp. 65-69.**

71. For the biography of Pavlo Polubotok and his activities, consult V. Modzalevskii, **Pavel Polubotok** (1903); and M. Vasylenko, "Pavlo Polubotok," **Ukraina,** 6 (1925).

72. For the best study on Danylo Apostol, see B. Krupnyts'kyi, **Het'man Danylo Apostol i ioho doba** (1727-1734) (Augsburg: UVAN, 1948).

The Nature and Sources of Dissidence in Ukraine

by
Julian Birch
University of Sheffield

Introduction

Studies of dissidence in Ukraine have long tended to concentrate exclusively upon the nationalist element — itself a rather varied phenomenon. More recently, **samizdat**/**samvydav** literature has thrown light on a much broader range of manifestations. It now has to be recognized that even in one single republic dissidence is an extremely complex issue wherein a variety of types may be distinguished, each receiving support from differing quarters of what is one of the largest and most populous territories in Europe.

Clearly the full range of dissidence evident in Moscow is not to be found in Ukraine. Kyiv, whatever its historic significance, remains a large but provincial city, while the centres of decision-making power lie in its northern rival. The absence of a variety of nationalities alone would preclude Kyiv from attaining a similar status in the field of dissent.

Nevertheless, a substantial cross-section of the all-union level dissent is present in Ukraine and the individual patterns and actions often mirror in microcosm many of those present in the Soviet capital.

In fact, its very complexity necessitates some clarification by dealing separately with its different forms — primarily nationalist, religious, civil rights, and that based on economic grievances. Subdivisions will also be drawn within these categories. On the strength of an empirical examination of these various types of dissent, whose names indicate much of their raison d'etre as well as giving an initial clue to the

307

sources of support, it is the intention here to draw some conclusions on the social basis of dissidence in general in the republic.

National Dissent

In addition to the Ukrainian nationalists and the Hutsuls, Jews, Crimean Tatars, and Magyars must also be considered in this category in order to obtain a fully rounded picture.

Ukrainian Nationalists

The background and activities of dissidents involved in openly proclaiming or defending Ukrainian national aspirations in the 1960s have already been the subject of extensive study in recent years [1] and are now amply documented with primary source materials. [2] The present writer's own work on the subject attempted to analyze and categorize the various strands of this activity into some form of comprehensive framework, partly on the basis of its social context. [3] This revealed that the nationalist element of Ukrainian dissidence took a wide variety of forms with a commensurately broad range of aims and demands. The support afforded these differing shades of nationalism, extensive as it was, similarly demonstrated a marked degree of variation in its background in terms of location, social origin, and occupational status. The latter, though markedly urban in character, was particularly varied, including both intelligentsia and workers — this in itself something of an achievement. Participants were, moreover, drawn from both worker and peasant families, with the latter predominating, as far as can be ascertained, and very few the offspring of the intelligentsia. The movement was thus rooted heavily in traditional, rural, Ukrainian values. Complementing this, the geographical distribution of the various activities revealed an almost predictable pattern. The most virulent, active nationalism, in the form of underground secessionists, was still largely a product of the Western Ukraine, and primarily of those Volyn' and Halychyna oblasti, centering on Lviv, incorporated as late as 1944. This positive, even extreme, brand of nationalist fervour was underpinned by a more passive support for autonomy, seldom pressed in any positive way, which, though naturally centred on certain elements of the Kyivan intelligentsia, was to be found, often in isolated instances, in places as widely dispersed as Odesa, Kharkiv and Dnipropetrovs'k.

Ideally it would be useful if the various social background syndromes of the nationalists could be set against the spectrum of aims and aspirations in order to accurately assess the degree of correlation, but inadequate data on the views of many of those involved prevents this. However, insofar as a typical nationalist could be identified on the basis of the reasonably full data then available, he could be characterized as someone born in the 1930s, as the offspring of a generation of pre-war Polish or Czechoslovak citizens. A high proportion of these parents were, moreover, peasants, though the children frequently attained higher education and took up urban professions.

More recently, the pattern of nationalist activity has continued much as before. The precedents established then have tended to be repeated, in what is an even larger range of fully documented incidents.

Many dozens of additional cases of persecution and arrest are now known to have occurred in the late 1960s, [4] in addition to that of the Dnipropetrovs'k intellectuals, [5] but whether this host of individual, mainly unconnected cases which have come to light was really the result of any upsurge of activism at that time or merely of the better coverage afforded by the advent of the **Ukrainskyi Visnyk** is not entirely clear. The Visnyk can probably be given a good deal of the credit, indeed samvydav has, in the past, belatedly revealed cases previously totally unknown. [6]

Overall analysis of these various nationalist manifestations since the mid-1960s reveals them to be the product of **five principal sources**, undoubtedly with a degree of overlap in some instances.

Firstly, there remains the traditional nationalism of West Ukraine. Although concentrated in the more recently acquired territories, this also embraces some members of the Kyivan intelligentsia of West Ukrainian origin. While it is very varied in its hopes and aspirations, it does include virtually all of the more virulent strands of nationalist thought and action — that is the outright secessionist element.

The majority of instances of individual involvement cited in the various editions of the **Khronika** since 1968 have fallen into this western category, though comparatively little is known of their socio-economic background and status. Certainly there were a considerable number of teachers, as well as a melange of folk musicians, poets, artists and authors. Doctors,[7] manual workers[8] and even secondary school children[9] complemented this picture of artistic / cultural intelligentsia participation. Often quite young in age, these individuals revealed a relatively high level of educational attainment.

The most significant manifestations of this continuing pattern of west Ukrainian activism (though by no means necessarily secessionist) came, however, with the arrests of 1972, and particularly the first wave on 12th of January.[10] Of the twenty persons known to have been detained immediately on or about that day for their involvement in the production of **samvydav**[11] (and these are fully representative of those which followed in April / May and August 1972), little is again known of their social origins, beyond the peasant background of two of them.[12] As with the original 1965 / 66 detainees, the group (for their cases were clearly linked) was primarily composed of a generation from the 1930s, with at least nine definitely born between 1930 and 1940, and possibly others as well. Beyond this core of the group at the extremes of the distribution, were to be found, on the one hand, two members of an older generation born before World War I, and, on the other, a nineteen year old girl — one of only four in the group. Just over half of these arrested were residents of Kyiv, while the remainder were almost all from Lviv. However, at least three of the 'Kyivans' originated from Western Ukraine,[13] and possibly even more. Many were certainly well acquainted with one another, sometimes over a number of years, and even related in one case.[14]

In almost all cases they had undergone complete higher education, and their occupations further served to place them in the intelligentsia. The artistic and literary worlds were again well represented, with 10 of them variously engaged in journalism, writing, criticism and the creative arts. The academic world was represented by a lecturer, a teacher and a student, while the scientific community provided an engineer, a chemist and a doctor. Thus, representatives were drawn from quite a wide range of professions, with the humanities perhaps inevitably predominating as a consequence of their propensity for publishing their thoughts. Only two former party members were known to be among their ranks,[15] and in fact at least four of the group had previously suffered imprisonment on similar grounds.[16] These west Ukrainians were thus not to be counted among the regime's most loyal supporters.

Closely related to this first source of Ukrainian nationalism, has been the second — that of the Hutsuls, an 'ethnic group of Ukrainians'[17] numbering some 300,000,[18] living in the highland areas of Ivano-Frankivs'k and Chernivtsi oblasti and in Rakovskyi district of the Zakarpats'ka oblast. A number of these mountain farmers, foresters and itinerant miners have entered the ranks of the dissidents as a result of attempts to preserve their cultural heritage and religious traditions.

Villagers in Kosmach, Kosiv district — many of them Stalin era deportees — have campaigned since 1964 for the restoration of local historical treasures taken from their church-museum for use in a film and never returned.[19] Although details of the support are scarce, it has included not only the villagers (presumably including the famous local handicraft workers), but also the museum curator Vasyl Babyuk (a prewar, pre-Soviet member of the peoples' militia),[20] and a number of members of the Lviv and Kyiv intelligentsia.[21] The support for the Hutsul's cause offered by Valentyn Moroz (better known for his involvement in more general Ukrainian causes), and his arrest in 1970 partly as a direct consequence, added further momentum to the activity. Several Kosmach villagers actively came to Moroz's defence, and hence more indirectly their own,[22] along with the local Orthodox priest, Vasyl Romaniuk (a Moscow trained 48 year old, originally from Chernivtsi, but active in Kosmach from the mid-1960s),[23] albeit to little avail. Indeed local officialdom responded firmly to any manifestation even hinting at nationalism such as the painting of the church merely in one of the national colours.[24]

The closing of the church in another Hutsul village, Bystritsi, in 1969 similarly produced open oppostion from the kolkhoz peasants.[25]

Another of the sources of nationalism, the third, was to be found in student circles and members of the younger intelligentsia, especially in Kyiv and Lviv. This activity may possibly be attributable to a youthful dabbling in the unconventional, or a fashionable, sometimes idealised, resurrection of a rural, pre-industrial ethnic / cultural heritage in an urban environment. Certainly much of this activity is to be found among those studying or teaching philology, Ukrainian language, literature and history. The principal centres of this type of activity, and the objects of official response have been Lviv University,[26] Kyiv Polytechnic Institute,[27] the "Homin" ethnographic ensemble in Kyiv,[28] Kyiv university,[29] ethnographically oriented institutes of the Academy of Sciences of Ukraine[30] and the Ukrainian literary fraternity.[31]

A fourth source of support for nationalist tendencies among the Ukrainians is rather more unusual. This category is composed of former or disillusioned Marxists who have seen their hopes of flowering of national cultures within an international spirit thwarted by official policies. Drawn from a member of areas of the republic and from a variety of socioeconomic backgrounds, their diversity extends to both the period of their Marxist commitment and to the date and precise cause of disillusionment.[32] Thus while they obviously overlap into the other categories outlined here, there remains some variation in their views. They have, however, made up with their eloquence for their relatively small numbers.

The fifth, and final, major source of nationalist manifestations definitely revealed by available data is to be found among those industrial cities of Eastern Ukraine possessing particularly large Russian communities. Although not confined to any single section of the population in the manner of the first three sources for instance, this source finds its unity in being a predominantly non-secessionist, or autonomist, nationalism. It is essentially a defensive, protective activism, protesting against the excessive Russification brought about by the influx of newcomers, as opposed to the more promotional, positive activism of the secessionists. A product of the different historical contacts of Eastern Ukraine, this source has given rise to both the protest of the Dnipropetrovs'k intellectuals,[33] and the mass disturbances which reportedly took place in June 1972 in Dniprodzerzhins'k, and in Dnipropetrovs'k in September of that year.[34]

Such then are the principal sources of the primary form of nationalism encountered in the republic — a form of dissidence which even the massive official counter-action in recent years has failed to eliminate.

Jewish Dissent

Jewish dissent in the USSR as a whole takes two principal forms. On the one hand it constitutes part and parcel of the general reformist or democratic movement in support of civil rights, whether this be specially related to the national and religious rights of those Jews wishing to remain in the Soviet Union, or to the more general application of legal / constitutional guarantees.

In respect of this type of Jewish dissent, it is noticeable that comparatively little effort is concentrated in Ukraine. It remains a predominantly Muscovite Jewish preserve.

It is possible however, that some of those Jews permitted to emigrate would have achieved prominence in this area had their demands been frustrated for a longer

TABLE I

Imprisoned Jews from Ukraine 1968-1974

Name	Date of Birth	Place of Residence	Marital Status	Education	Occupation	Date of Arrest	Date of Trial	Sentence
Boris L. Kochubievskyi	1936	Kyiv	Married	Higher	Engineer	30 / 11 / 68	13 / 5 / 69	3 years
Raiza Palatnik	1936	Odesa	Single		Librarian	12 / 1970	6 / 1971	2 years
Khaim Renert	1923	Chernivtsi		Higher	Physician	1971		5 years
Yuly Brind	1929	Kharkiv	Bachelor		Mechanic	24 / 3 / 72	1 / 6 / 72	2½ years
Yury Pokh	1950	Odesa	Bachelor			5 / 1972	20 / 6 / 72	3½ years
Grigory Berman	1946	Odesa	Bachelor	Higher	Linguist	26 / 5 / 72	10 / 8 / 72	2½ years
Izaak Shkolnik	1936	Vinnytsia	Married		Worker	5 / 7 / 72	11 / 4 / 73	10 years
Aleksandr Feldman	1948	Kyiv		Higher	Engineer	18 / 10 / 73	1973	3½ years
Gennady Avramenko		Kyiv	Married				17 / 4 / 74	1 year
Zinaida Avramenko		Kyiv	Married				17 / 4 / 74	8 months

Sources: Khronika; Focus on Soviet Jewry; The Jewish Chronicle, and Jews in the U.S.S.R.

period; and official action served, or may even have been designed, to forestall just such an eventuality.

The other aspect of Jewish dissent in Ukraine has involved a parallel, and usually separate, campaign concerned with the question of emigration. Official policies towards Israel and the Middle East served to supplement the entrenched and widespread anti-Jewish feeling which has persisted in the face of a large concentration of Jews in the republic, and which manifested itself openly in three days of riots in Dnipropetrovs'k in May 1972. [35]

The emigration movement in Ukraine is, on the whole, unexceptional and forms but a part of the broader all-Union pattern, as far as can be ascertained from the limited data available. Distorted patterns would in any event probably be revealed in the figures for the first one or two years from 1968, when the emigration appears to have been confined to limited localities within the Soviet Union. Since then, Ukrainian Jews have clearly constituted a not inconsiderable proportion of the 100,000 and more who have been allowed to join this form of voting with one's feet. One of the few actual estimates to appear, albeit unofficial and far from precise, on the Ukrainian contribution came in a statement released at a news conference for foreign journalists in Moscow staged by ten dissident Jews on October 18th, 1972. This claimed that, "among 2,000 Jews who leave the Soviet Union a month, 10 percent are from Georgia, 20 percent are from Central Asia and about 40 percent are from the Baltic republics, Ukraine and Moldavia''. [36]

Some indications of the nature of this Ukrainian contribution can nevertheless be gleaned from available data. It is clear at the outset that the emigration is by no means confined to activist dissidents and long-standing civil rights campaigners. Mere application for an exit visa has proved sufficient to bring Jews into conflict with the authorities. As so often has been the case in other areas of dissent, the official response has proved to be the catalyst which has created an active dissident from a simple 'drop-out'. Comparatively few of the Ukrainian-Jewish, would-be emigrants have however, figured among the cause celebre — with the notable exception of Kochubievsky, [37] Palatniuk, [38] and Shkolnik[39] — and then usually in isolated individual cases, often with little prior record of activism (this being particularly true of Palatnik). Few have in fact actually been imprisoned for anything other than the almost routine 15-day detentions which have followed police dragnets against Jewish demonstraters. Data indicating the social composition of this group of imprisoned Jews is summarized in Table 1.

Though small, even this collection of individual cases serves to reveal both the disparate nature of the alienated Jews (especially in terms of age and occupation), and the firm response to widespread Jewish dissent on the part of the police authorities in Odesa — a response to be encountered again in the case of the Baptist dissidents.

In addition to those dealt with in this way, numerous other instances of individual suffering and persecution in Ukraine, as elsewhere, have become known. Cases have been reported so frequently (for instance, in almost all editions of the samvydav Khronika) [40] as to make what in isolation would be viewed as extraordinarily, little more than commonplace and unexceptional. The concentration of many of the incidents in the western part of the republic, the area of most active Ukrainian nationalism and self-assertion, seems unlikely to be entirely coincidental.

Soviet restrictions on the level of emigration of young people of conscript age and of skilled professionals would serve to distort any image of this communal dissent based on age and occupational analysis purely of the successful emigrants. However, the reported cases of direct conflict with the authorities by those still in Ukraine do provide some clearer indications of the social background to this type of dissent.

While the Jewish population as a whole is found disproportionately among the urban intelligentsia, the would-be emigrants are by no means exclusively drawn from a stratum of well-read Zionist intellectuals. The cases of Yuli Brind[41] and Izaak Shkolnik, cited already, are but two of numerous examples of the involvement of ordinary workers in a movement provided with momentum by the discriminatory circumstances in which many Jews have found themselves in recent years.

Age similarly appears to have little bearing on the potentiality for support of emigration drive, and cases have been reported involving teenagers[42] as well as aged pensioners (whose limited value to the Soviet Union has been indicated by the comparative ease with which many have gained exit visas).

Nor is the movement confined in any way to fervently religious Jews, for insofar as party membership can be equated with some measure of active support for the sytem ceteris paribus, a considerable number of regime supporters have joined the alienated thousands in opposing Soviet Middle East policy and in seeking a promised land elsewhere.[43]

The Crimean Tatars

In some respects the position and dissident role of the Crimean Tatars is a non-Ukrainian issue in that when settled in their pre-war territories they did not constitute part of Ukraine, and now, in the course of their campaign, when their territory forms part of the republic,[44] they themselves are largely outside. Nonetheless, the issue does affect Ukraine, and rather more than indirectly at that.

Shortly after rehabilitation, hundreds of families returned to the Crimea where jobs and homes were available, only to be met by the local police and expelled again. Subsequent statements giving them conditional rights of registration and settlement were frustrated in practice by a range of officially inspired impediments.

Thus, it has been reported in the Tatar documentation, by December 1967, only three single men and two families of Tatars succeeded in getting themselves registered in the Crimea. The remainder of the 6,000 who had moved to the peninsula were either re-deported, or had to leave as a result of the financially onerous obstructions placed in the way of their settlement there.

The following year, in the face of a planned mass departure for the Crimea, some improvement was made to the situation when Crimean provincial officials visited Uzbekistan and allowed a certain number of non-activist Tatars to conclude labour contracts for work in their old homeland.[45] The first of these official settlers arrived in April 1968, at a sovkhoz in the village of Nekrasovo, near Simferopol.[46] This new programme was not carried through very rigorously as far as can be ascertained, and only a very limited number of Tatars were permitted to resettle their former territory — some 148 families in all in 1968.[47] The fortunate few appear to have been given reasonably generous aid in moving, some 35 percent of the cost of new housing (the remainder financed in the form of loans), loans for livestock, etc., and a temporary tax exemption.[48]

Simultaneously, unofficial self-repatriation continued to form the main agency of return, in spite of the fact that both jobs and registration permits remained elusive. The response to these would-be settlers, who refused to be daunted by an official attitude designed to discourage them, was nothing if not firm — several instances of police seizure and redeportation from the Crimea back to Uzbekistan have become known. They include:

1. Sixty Tatars camped at Simferopol reservoir in May, 1968.[49]

2. Ninety-eight camping near the village of Marino on 27 May, 1968.[50]

3. Eleven families occupying empty sovkhoz buildings in Chervonohvardiis'k district (having received permission from the oblispolkom to settle in the Crimea), together with four families from another farm in Dzhankois'k district, on 15 July, 1968.[51]

4. Four families who had bought houses and settled under the recruitment scheme, in Bilohors'k district in June, 1969. This group returned but found their houses boarded up.[52]

In at least one case, in June 1969, those so dealt with were in the process of registering a complaint at their treatment with the chairman of the local oblispolkom [53] — an action which resulted in the full imprisonment of one of the protesters held initially for a short period before deportation.

In this way, the first year or so of the Tatars' actions resulted in the successful return of 18 families and 13 single people, while another 12,000 had been expelled by the Crimean authorities — with seventeen being imprisoned. [54] Some others did, however, manage to settle temporarily nearby in neighbouring Krasnodar Krai.

No comparison was offered to those dispossessed in this way, in spite of a series of protest appeals to the local and central governmental authorities. Most of the appeals and lobbying activity has in fact been concentrated in Moscow, where it is likely to have the maximum effect. Nonetheless, some appeals have also been more locally directed, as in the case of the petition from 456 Tatars against the treatment of families in Ukraine, which was sent, among other recipients, to the First Secretary of the Crimean Obkom of the Ukrainian Party in 1970. [55]

The dissident campaign thus continued unabated for the redress of an increasingly wide range of grievances, and some of the Tatars resident in Ukraine were delegated to join the lobby in Moscow in 1970; [56] while an appeal to the Party Congress of the following year provides grim details of the actions of and methods practised by the police in Ukraine — including, it is said, murder and incitement to suicide, as well as more mundane illegal arrests and theft of property. Certainly a number of trials of Tatar dissident activists have taken place in Ukraine itself. [57]

Those Tatars who have succeeded in settling in the Crimea as a result of the labour recruitment programme have apparently been employed largely as farm labour, being tied to the farm and unable to move, without the threat of deportation — not that kolkhoz workers as a whole have a great deal of latitude in this respect. The Tatar children have reportedly been excluded from higher educational facilities in Ukraine. The sparse reference to the settlers in Soviet sources tend, however, to convey a far more favourable picture of the situation.

The dissident movement among the Tatars as a whole seems to cut across socio-economic boundaries in the basis of its support, including both the young as well as the older pre-deportation Tatars, workers and farmers as well as intellectuals. [58] Some 45,000 of the Tatars in Uzbekistan are said to be industrial workers and another 30,000 farmers on sovkhozy and kolkhozy, and while many of the official settlers in the Crimea have been from the latter category, there is no reason to presume that the support is any less strong among the urban worker element. Indeed the Tatars provide a good example of social cohesion achieved through a strongly developed national consciousness. The absence of any apparent divorce between the worker and intelligentsia elements is particularly notable, [59] and inevitably adds great internal strength to the movement and a more formidable united front to the outside world.

It is clear, moreover, that a considerable, indeed surprising number of the Tatar dissidents have been party members. By April 1969, some 40 of the Tatars had been expelled from the party or the Komsomol for their participation in the movement, [60] and an appeal from 350 Crimean Tatar communists was sent to the Party leadership at the time of the Lenin centenary in April, 1970. [61]

The movement thus appears to have wide support among the Tatars themselves, and has even given rise to a form of supportive dissidence among some of their potential hosts — the Ukrainians.

Magyars

Visible Magyar self-assertion is not only confined to the western Trancarpathian oblast' of Ukraine (of historical and demographic necessity), it has thus far been confined to a very small number of members of the younger, artistic and cultural intelligentsia directly engaged in the propagation of Magyar language and literature in Uzhhorod. A strong identification with their native language has produced among the relatively small Soviet Magyar population [62] a measure of resistance to assimilationist and Russificatory tendencies and what is officially viewed as an unhealthy interest in Hungarian culture. This has found its support or expression variously in the Magyar department for teaching training at Uzhhorod university,[63] the Magyar section of the 'Carpathians' publishing house,[64] and in the Hungarian literary group (mainly composed of Uzhhorod university students) in the regional division of the Writers' Union.[65] As such Magyar nationalism remains but a minor albeit noteworthy phenomenon.

Religious Dissidence — the Initsiativniki Baptists

Since their break with the officially recognized Baptist Church in 1961, and their coming to international prominence in the mid-1960s,[66] the Council of Churches of the Evangelical Christians and Baptists (the CCECB, better known perhaps as the "Initsiativniki") have provided one of the outstanding examples of dissent, and survival under pressure, in distinctly adverse conditions.

Analysis of 611 Initsiativniki imprisoned between 1961 and 1973[67] reveals some 139, or slightly less than 23 percent to be from Ukraine, while the Ukrainian population constitutes approximately 19 percent of the total Soviet population. This group includes some of the principal breakaway Baptist leaders such as Presbyter Alexei F. Prokof'ev (one of the two founding figures);[68] Iosif D. Bondarenko (from Odesa);[69] and Georgi Vins or Viens (who, in spite of German nationality and a mobile career, has been based in Kyiv in recent years along with his wife, when not actually in prison).[70]

Although their names indicate that by no means of all the 139 are definitely Ukrainian by nationality, the Ukrainian element constitutes an overwhelming majority of the 139. Moreover, a number of known and probable Ukrainians living outside the Ukrainian S.S.R. were also imprisoned (eight definite, and 43 possibles) — notably from the neighbouring and formerly Ukrainian territories around Rostov and Krasnodar.

The distirbution of the 139 within Ukraine reveals one or two interesting points. Some 79, or 57 percent, were residents of cities with populations in excess of 100,000. A further 21, or 15 percent, came from towns of over 30,000 inhabitants. Of the remaining 39, or rather less than one third of the total, 14 lived in towns of 10,000 or more citiznes. Thus only 25 inhabited very small towns or villages. It is clear from this that the Baptist activism is primarily an urban — indeed large urban — as opposed to a rural phenomenon.

As far as the actual scatter is concerned, the list of domiciles provides the following distribution in cases where more than one person has been arrested from a particular locality:

Odesa	16	Chernihiv		
Kyiv	12	Luhansk		
Krivyy Rih	10	Protopivka		
Sumy	7	Rivne		
Kharkiv	6	Seredyna-Buda	}	2
Kergachi		Shostka		
Khmel'nyts'kyi	} 4	Simferopol		
Kirovohrad		Smila		
Cherkasy		Vovkivchyki		
Chernivtsi		Zhovti Vody		
Chervonoarmiis'k		Zhytomyr		
Krasnodon				
Lviv	3			
Marganets'				
Saki				
Shevchenkovo	}			

The activism is revealed to be fairly evenly distributed across Ukraine, with only a few major cities such as Donets'k and Dnipropetrovs'k notable for their absence. It is the figures for Odesa and Krivyy Rih which really attract the attention. This relatively high level of activism may merely reflect larger Baptist communities in those cities (though, in the absence of any statistics, this is difficult to ascertain), or may indicate a variation in police alacrity in dealing with such cases. Details of charges, other than the relevant article of the criminal code, are only available in a few instances and throw little light on the matter.[71] The rather international nature of Odesa's population coupled with the likelihood of correspondingly heightened police vigilance, is not a factor obviously involved here; for while a considerable number of the Baptist prisoners elsewhere in the Soviet Union are clearly Germany by nationality, all the Odesa cases involve Ukrainians or Russians. It may not be entirely coincidental, however, that Odesa, with approximately 110,000 Jews in a population of 667,000,[72] has also been faced with a large measure of Jewish activism.

Occupational background is not indicated in the lists of Baptist prisoners and only infrequent reference is made to this factor in other documents or Soviet press attacks on the dissenters. It would, therefore, be unwise to make any generalizations on this nonetheless important matter. The extent of the urban basis of the support does tend to complement the manual working-class characteristic indicated in the few known cases. Certainly the intelligentsia does not appear to be widely represented in their ranks — an impression reinforced by the sparse attention devoted to the Baptists in the dissident intelligentsia's house journal, the **Khronika Tekushchikh Sobytiy.**

The low proportion of women among the prisoners (12 of the 139) runs contrary to the stereotype image of present-day Soviet believers as aging, female war-widows, though it may indicate a more lenient official line in dealing with them, especially where families are involved.

The age distribution is similarly revealing, as well as being rather convenient for analysis in percentages. Of the 99 whose birthdates are known, only two were born before 1900 and 20 before 1920. The majority (62) were born between 1926 and 1940. This is perhaps rather younger than might be anticipated from the usual Soviet official image. Indeed, at least one Soviet publication has commented upon this situation in relation to the "Initsiativniki" as a whole, remarking that, "Among Baptists who have come under the influence of the Action Group (the CCECB), young people are represented more widely than in regular ECB congregations; sometimes supporters of the Action Group have been called Young Baptists. Some of these groups are comprised of more than fifty percent young people."[73] And yet this group clearly represents a first post-revolutionary generation — many doubtless from the families of pre-revolutionary believers. Five of the prisoners were nonetheless born after World War II.

In addition to outright imprisonment, short-term arrests, fines and other forms of harassment have been applied to the Ukrainian Baptists in an attempt to achieve conformity with the regime's terms of acceptable religious activity. As early as 1967, it was reported that, "In Kyiv alone there have been eighty-five cases of ten to fifteen day arrests" of participants of worship.[74] Violence has clearly been employed on occasions, and Ukrainians have been among those who have died while under police detention.[75]

Below this level of indictable activism, the Ukrainian Initsiativniki communities have also been involved in other types of dissidence, particularly in supporting petitions and appeals to the Soviet authorities. A number of these documents have a hundred or more signatures appended to them,[76] and yet, coming, as they do, largely from the CPR (that is from the immediate families of prisoners) they reveal patterns of distribution of activity very similar to the prisoner lists. Thus one such appeal of November 1969, with 62 clearly legible signatures, contains four from Odesa, four from Kyiv, three each from Lviv and Krasnodon, and one each from Sumy, Kirovohrad and Luhans'k.[77]

Some of the Initsiativniki communities in these cities, whether or not met with

TABLE II

Social Background of the Kharkiv Civil Rights Activists — 1969

Name	Nationality	Date of Birth	Education	Occupation	Party Membership
Genrikh O. Altunyan	Armenian	1933	Higher	Radio-technician / engineer	?
Sofia Karasik	Ukrainian	?	Higher	Senior engineer	?
Lev Kornilov	?	?	Higher	Senior engineer	?
Aleksandr Kalinovskyi	?	?	Higher	Senior engineer	?
Arkady Z. Levin	Jewish	1933	Higher	Chief design engineer	?
D.A. Lifshits	Jewish	?	Higher	Engineer	?
Vladislav Nedobora	?	1933	Higher	Senior engineer	?
S.K. Podolskyi	?	?	Higher	Engineer	?
Vladimir V. Ponomarev	Russian ?	1933	Higher	Engineer	?

Source: Khronika, Nos. 9 and 11.

commensurate repressions, are clearly very large indeed. One 1967 appeal to the Soviet government (concerning alleged militia brutality) was sent on behalf of the Kyiv community of 400.[78] A service held outside Kharkiv on 2 May 1973, was reportedly attended by a congregation of as many as 1,500.[79]

The Ukrainian Baptists represent an extremely active, even bold, dissident element, with few signs that its vigour has been daunted by the regime's reaction to it — all the more the case as some of its members have attached themselves to the civil rights cause as a whole.

The Uniates

Closely inter-woven as it is with the nationalism of Western Ukraine and the Hutsuls, members of this church, which reputedly had some three and one half to four million adherents at its liquidation in 1946,[80] became visibly active again in the 1960s, following the release of a number of their former leaders in the late 1950s.[81]

As with the cases of a number of sects, whose activities have lately been revealed by official and samvydav sources,[82] it is difficult to assess the current extent and nature of the support for this Eastern Rite Catholicism. Certainly non-clergy elements have been the subject of police action:[83] however, most of the reported incidents of renewed activism and official counter-action have involved members of the Uniate clergy. Its widespread character is moreover indicated by the claim that in the spring of 1969 "all over Western Ukraine dozens of searches were carried out among Greek-Catholic priests and in flats inhabited by former nuns".[84] Those arrested have mainly been aging survivors of the pre-1946 movement,[85] and most of the cases reported in the sparse documentation thus far have been concentrated in Lviv and Ivano-Frankivs'k oblasti.

Civil Rights Dissidence

While it could be argued that most or all of the dissidents under discussion here are, in one way or another, concerned with issues of civil rights, it nonetheless seems possible to distinguish a form of civil rights dissent distinct from the others. It is distinct, because it involves people who, for the most part, have not openly allied or identified themselves with any of the other specific group interests but have concentrated on the civil rights issue as an entity in itself, above and beyond the question of the narrower application of those rights to certain social groups. Ukraine took on an added importance in this field with the appearance in Kyiv, in January 1970, of the **Ukrainskyi Visnyk**, a counterpart to the Moscow **Khronika Tekushchikh Sobytiy**.

This is not to say that links do not exist between civil rights campaigners and other dissenting groups. The overlap which has been forged at various levels between the different types of dissenters may well in fact strengthen their potential effectiveness, if not their present actual bargaining position with the authorities.

This aspect of dissent has taken on a number of varied forms and drawn its support from a wide range of social sources. As such, characterization and classification is made somewhat difficult. Nevertheless, an initial framework of analysis to draw together the diverse strands.

At one level, individual Ukrainian members of the intelligentsia such as ex-Maj. Gen. Grigorenko[86] and, more recently, Yuri Shikhanovich[87] have participated in all-Union level civil rights activities; while others like Genrikh Altunyan and Leonid Plyushch have been involved with the Action Group for the Defence of Civil Rights in the USSR.[88] Vyacheslav Chornovil, as a supporting signatory of the Group's petitions, provided a link between the general civil rights and the specifically Ukrainian interest.

Plyushch, and especially Altunyan, were not, however, alone in their involvement with the Action Group. Among the other signatories in support of the group's petition to the United Nations, in May 1969, were eight associates of Altunyan's from Kharkiv,[89] whose socio-economic background is indicated in Table 2. Although of different nationalities, their common age, education and occupation indicates the basis of their association.

Altunyan's imprisonment generated its own additional Ukrainian civil rights dissidents.[90] Similarly, Plyushch's arrest in January 1973 produced an appeal by nine supporters, of whom five, however, were members of the Action Group.[91]

Plyushch himself represents a link with another level of this dissidence — that based on the Kyivan intelligentsia, paralleling, as it does in microcosm, the activities of Moscow's dissident intellectuals. Centred in part, since 1970, around the Ukrainskyi Visnyk and its editorials, this collection of civil rights activists has manifested itself in a variety of ways through petitions, appeals and individual acts of protest.

Probably the most outstanding example of openly declared concern over civil rights at this level was the April 1968 petition of 139 Ukrainians to the General Secretary of the CPSU and others.[92] Although concerned with distortions in the nationality policy of the Soviet government in Ukraine and prompted in part by the Ukrainian trials of 1965-66, this petition came hard on the heals of the 1968 Moscow dissident trials and was directed both at them and at more general "forms of suppression of civil activity and social criticism absolutely necessary for the health of any society". It constituted in effect a critique of any restoration of Stalinist methods. The petition was remarkable not merely for the size of its support, but for the breadth of the social basis of this support, as indicated in Table 3. It included six professors, five corresponding members of the Ukrainian Academy of Sciences and a Lenin prize winner, alongside a large group of manual workers — nearly 19 percent of the total. Moreover, the signatories encompassed those like Dzyuba, Svitlichnyi and Sverstiuk, associated primarily with the national claims of Ukraine, as well as others, like Viktor Nakrasov, with records of consistently broad involvement with civil rights issues.[93]

TABLE III

The 139 Civil Rights Petitioners of April 1968

Occupation	Numbers
Artists and Writers	50
Scientists	34
Engineers	11
Doctors	3
Lawyers	1
Teachers	3
Students	6
Manual Workers	26
Others	4

Source: Appeal of the 139.

Besides this somewhat amorphous activity, and supplementing similar developments in the nationalist movement, Ukrainian civil rights activists have been directly involved in, or responsible for, the formation of a number of specific organizations or groups, however pretentious their claims to such status may have been in reality.

An attempt to form the "Organization for the Struggle for Social Justice" in 1968 resulted in a three year prison sentence for Nikolai P. Bogach, a twenty-four year old Kuban' cossack, then studying at the Agricultural Technical College in Mykolaiv.[94]

A marginally more successful and less solo effort was achieved by Nikolai F. Dragosh, with his "Democratic Union of Socialists", also in South West Ukraine. Dragosh, a thirty-two year old mathematics graduate of Odesa University and

Headmaster of a young workers' school in Tarutino district of Odesa oblast', and Nikolai A. Tarnovskyi, a twenty-four year old teacher at the same school were convicted in nearby Moldavia in September 1964, of forming the organization; of recruiting others into it, including Cherdyntsev, another teacher at their school, along with three students at the Kishinev Institute of Arts; and or printing a broadsheet, in newspaper form, entitled **Pravda narodu**. Details of the background of the supporters of this group are summarized in Table 4. Little or nothing is known of the goals of the Union, and its activities were curtailed when the members were all imprisoned for between five and seven years.[95]

TABLE IV

Social Composition of the Democratic Union of Socialists — 1964

Name	Nationality	Date of Birth	Education	Occupation
Mykola F. Dragosh	Ukrainian	1932	Higher	Headmaster
Mykola A. Tarnavskyi	Ukrainian	1940	Specialist	Teacher
Sergei Chemertan	?	1938	Higher	Student
Ivan A. Cherdyntsev	Russian ?	1938	Higher	Teacher
Nikolai S. Kucerianu	Moldavian	1941	Higher	Student
Vasili V. Postalaki	?	1936	Higher	Student

Source: **Khronika**, No. 20.

Beyond this group type of participation in civil rights protests, only a very small number of isolated individuals are known to have involved themselves sufficiently actively in this area of dissent, within Ukraine itself, to merit the attention of the state organs. The **Khronika**, concerned as it is with civil rights, gives some indications of this pattern of involvement in its annual lists of political prisoners in 1969 and 1970. Excluding the extremely small selection of religious activists in the lists, the remaining 164 arrested and / or convicted in those two years included 18 from Ukraine,[96] and only one of these is known to have been engaged in individual protests against state infringements of human rights.[97]

In many of the other cases, as has been seen, the regime response to activism over civil rights has been one of the straight-forward imprisonment of those concerned. However, incarceration in labour camps or psychiatric hospitals has not stopped the activism. Indeed it has continued within that milieu.[98]

Such then is the range of Ukrainian dissent in the general field of civil rights. With the exception of the important appeal of the 139, activism of this type, and interest in more abstract and nebulous freedoms, are revealed as principally the concern of a section of the well educated intelligentsia, though by no means limited to any narrow span of occupational groups within that stratum. Scientists and engineers have played a significant part, alongside employees of the arts and humanities. The interests of the workers and peasants, if directed at all at such issues, clearly are to be found elsewhere, in areas of more tangible, immediate concern. While such a situation prevails, as in Poland in 1968 and 1970, it has the effect of strengthening the hand of the regime in resisting change, by permitting it to apply the approach of divide-and-rule — a lesson presumably not entirely lost on Soviet dissidents as they assess their position in what has become a period of retreat.

Economically Based Dissent

It is rather unusual to refer to economic grievances as a form of dissent, but, given the tradition of almost total regime support and the public passivity over the last half century on the part of Soviet workers (disturbed only infrequently by events such as the demonstrations against the serious bread shortages of the early 1960s) it seems an appropriate usage. This is particularly the case when the grievances are articulated and acted upon in a manner unacceptable to the regime, with its desire for at least an appearance of unanimity, if not fervent support. Indeed, some of these cases have been taken up by the **Khronika** as manifestations of dissent.

Vocal discontent from what is said to be the very basis of the regime's support, that is the proletariat, must inevitably be viewed as a very serious matter indeed, and the authorities can be expected to react in such a way as to isolate any one instance from another. Nonetheless, such discontent has been increasingly voiced — and quite openly — in recent years.

Examples of this type of dissent have naturally varied considerably in content and form, differing according to location and the nature of the grievance. They have ranged from specific, narrow, localized grievances, particularly concerned with wages and housing conditions, voiced through protest letters[99] and strikes, [100] to more generalized expressions of alienation and discontent manifested in responses to questionnaires[101] and in mass demonstrations.[102]

Rarely is any precise detail of the background of those involved available: and yet it is notable that the incidents reported so far have not merely been confined to those proletarian elements offering chauvinistic support to nationalist aspirations in Western Ukraine, but rather have embraced workers in the industrial heartland of the eastern part of the republic — notably Voroshylovhrad and Dnipropetrovs'k. The grievances, many of which are common to industrial workers throughout much of the world, do, moreover, appear to be shared by young and old alike, and thus probably present rather more of a challenge to the regime than all manner of uncoordinated nationalisms.

Conclusion

It is clear from the foregoing analysis that dissent in Ukraine comes in a wide variety of forms — lacking only in any significant generalized political opposition groupings offering total alternative programmes of a not merely nationalist character. The dissent furthermore derives its support from a range of quite different, albeit very occasionally overlapping, sources, involving hundreds, indeed thousands, of persons whose motives and aspirations extend from the general to the particular, but whose persistence is both remarkable and rarely open to doubt. It thereby defies any simple generalizations as to its overall social basis — each case has to be viewed in its own right.

Nonetheless, much of the activity undoubtedly does derive from the western part of the republic, with its residue of anti-Russian, anti-Communist, strongly religious feeling, among a first generation of Soviet citizens — a pattern common also to the Baltic States.

Indeed, Ukrainian dissidence is far from unique or special, even in the context of the Soviet Union. It is remarkable primarily for making its presence both apparent and felt on such a scale. Though the manifestations are numerous, they are perhaps no more than one might realistically anticipate from a population of that size even in other less authoritarian circumstances — in fact possibly somewhat less. And yet, given the nature of the system and the fact that in the KGB the dissident activists have a very much more effective opponent than their nineteenth century counterparts had in the Okhrana, it remains an impressive display of spontaneous participation and activity. One would however be well advised not to elevate the dissent out of all perspective from its position of being somewhat peripheral to the mainstream and more regular processes of Soviet political life. Equally, however, the examples of Portugal and Greece in 1974 indicate the fallacy of accepting the surface quiescence of the bulk of a population as an indicator of popular feeling.

With the pressures enforced by the Soviet regime since 1971, it will be interesting to see whether any further growth in open dissent will take place, and whether the patterns of its social sources revealed thus far will undergo fundamental as opposed to chronologically generated change.

FOOTNOTES

1.   E.g., T. Szamuely, "The Resurgence of Ukrainian Nationalism," **Interstate,** Aberystwyth, No. 5, 1968 / 69; J. Kolasky, **Two Years in Soviet Ukraine** (Toronto: Martin, 1970); G. Hodnett and P. Potichnyj, **The Ukraine and the Czechoslovak Crisis,** Occasional Paper No. 6 (Canberra: Australian National University, Department of Political Science, 1970); V. Moroz, **Among the Snows — Protest from the Ukraine** (London: Ukrainian Information Service, 1971); V. Swoboda, "Cat and Mouse in the Ukraine," **Index,** London, No. 1 (1973).

2.   I. Majstrenko (foreward), **Ukrains'ki Yurysty pid Sudom KGB** (Munich: Suchasnist', 1968); V. Chornovil, **The Chornovil Papers** (Toronto: McGraw Hill, 1968); S.D.O., **Voices of Human Courage** (New York: Association for Free Ukraine, 1968); S. Stetsko (ed.), **Revolutionary Voices — Ukrainian Political Prisoners Condemn Russian Colonialism** (Munich: ABN); **Ukrains'ka Intelligentsiya pid Sudom KGB** (Munich: Suchas 1970); V. Moroz, **A Chronicle of Resistance in Ukraine** (Baltimore: Smoloskyp, 1970); I. Dzyuba, **Internationalism or Russification** (London: Weidenfeld, 1970); M. Browne (ed.), **Ferment in the Ukraine** (London: Macmillan, 1971); Radio Liberty, **Arkhiv Samizdata** (Munich), vols. 18 & 19.

3.   J. Birch, **The Ukrainian Nationalist Movement in the USSR Since 1956** (London: Ukrainian Publishers, 1971).

4.   See the list compiled in **The Ukrainian Review,** London, Vol. XVIII, No. 1 (1971), pp. 36-41; No. 3 (1971), pp. 91-93; various editions of the **Ukrains'kyi Visnyk;** also **Khronika Tekushchikh Sobytiy** (Moscow), Nos. 17, 18, 19 and 24.

5.   Documentation on this case has been considerably improved as a result of the trials which resulted.

6.   This was particularly evident in the cases of the O.P.V.U., U.R.S.S., and U.N.K.

7.   E.g., the Korolchuk case in Lviv, **Ukrainskyi Visnyk,** No. 5, and **Khronika,** No. 22.

8.   E.g., the Medvid case in Lviv, **Ukrainskyi Visnyk,** No. 5, and **Khronika,** No. 22.

9.   See the case of three schoolboys from Snyatyn, Ivano-Frankivs'k oblast', **Ukrainskyi Visnyk,** No. 6.

10. For full details of these arrests see, Reuter reports in **The Times, Daily Telegraph,** London, and **The Scotsman,** 15 January 1972; **New York Times,** 15 January 1972; **Le Figaro,** Paris, 15-16 January 1972; **RFE Research Paper,** USSR / 1267, 17 January 1972; **Agence France Presse** reports of 17 and 20 January 1972; **Nene Zurcher Zeitung,** 19 January 1972; **The Guardian,** London, 20 January 1972; **The Times,** 16 February 1972; **The Economist,** London, 26 February 1972; **Die Welt,** Hamburg, 2 March 1972; **The Guardian,** 13 March 1972; **Radyanska Ukraina and Pravda Ukrainy,** 11 February 1972; **Ukrainskyi Visnyk,** No. 6; **Khronika,** Nos. 24, 25, 26 and 27; **The January 1972 Arrests in the Ukraine,** Committee for the Defence of Soviet Political Prisoners, Woodhaven, New York; **Index,** London, No. 1, 1973; index p. X; and **Posev** Frankfurt, No. 2, 1973.

11. Data drawn from lists in **The Ukrainian Review,** London, Vol. XIX, No. 2, 1972, pp. 92-96; No. 3, 1972, pp. 82-86, Vol. XX, No. 2, 1973, pp. 88-91, 93-94; Vol. XXI, No. 1, 1974, pp. 56-59; **ABN Correspondence** Munich, Vol. XXIII, No. 4, 1972, pp. 27-37; and details in **Ukrains'kyi Visnyk,** No. 6, and **Khronika,** Nos. 24 and 25.

12. M.H. Osadchyy, and H.P. Kochur.

13. E. Sverstiuk, V. Stus and D. Shumuk.

14. Shumuk being married to the sister of Ivan Svitlichnyy.

15. M.H. Osadchyy and D. Shumuk.

16. Chornovil, Osadchyy, Shumuk, and Svitlichnyy (the latter not a west Ukrainian but from Luhans'k oblast').

17. **Bolshaya Sovetskaya Entsiklopediya**, Moscow, 1972, Vol. 7, p. 1399.

18. See **Bolshaya Sovetskaya Entsiklopediya**, Moscow, 1953, Vol. 13.

19. See V. Moroz, "A Chronicle of Resistance", samvydav document of January 1970, summarized in **Khronika**, No. 14, and published in full in V. Moroz, **Report from the Beria Reserve** (Chicago: Cataract Press, 1974), pp. 55-84. See also the commentary by R. Boiter, "The Hutsuls — Tribulations of a National Culture in the USSR," **Radio Liberty Research Paper**, Munich, CRD 370 / 70, 22 October 1970.

20. Moroz, **op. cit.**, p. 61.

21. E.g., O. Honchar, the writer; Hrabovets'kyi the historian; and S. Hebus-Baranets'ka, the artist — Moroz, **op. cit.**, pp. 61-62; and **Khronika**, No. 17.

22. See **Ukrainskyi Visnyk**, No. 3. The letter to the authorities from seven villagers is also cited in **Khronika**, No. 18.

23. See **Ukrainskyi Visnyk**, Nos. 2, 3 and 4. Following a search of his house on 4 / 5 / 1970, Romaniuk was transferred from Kosmach to the Kokyttya; wrote a protest letter on 27 / 11 / 1970, against Moroz's trial (**Ukrainskyi Visnyk**, No. 4 and V. Moroz, **op. cit.**, pp. 136-37); was held by the police for three days in September / October 1972 (**Ukrainskyi Visnyk**, No. 6); was arrested again in Kosmach in January 1972, and finally sentenced in Ivano-Frankivs in July 1972, to seven years imprisonment and three years exile (**Khronika**, No. 25),

24. **Ukrainskyi Visnyk**, No. 6.

25. **Ukrainskyi Visnyk**, No. 5, and **Khronika**, No. 22.

26. Though the involvement was not confined to them, numerous students have been expelled in recent years for association with one or other of the strands of nationalism (see particularly **Ukrainskyi Visnyk**, Nos. 4 and 5; and **The Ukrainian Review**, Vol. XVIII, No. 3, 1971, pp. 93-93, and Vol. XXI, No. 2, 1974, pp. 88 and 94-95). Among those actually arrested was the student son of a lecturer in the German department, who, along with a number of those expelled was apparently involved in the production of a samvydav journal entitled "Postup", (see **Index**, No. 1, 1974, index p. xi, and **ABN Correspondence**, Vol. XXV, No. 2, 1974, p. 38). The dismissals went on to include a number of very senior faculty staff and others in the Institute of Social Studies in Lviv of whom little is known (**The Ukrainian Review**, Vol. XXI, No. 2, 1974, p. 88).

27. Students there have been involved in a number of activities such as the organization of a Ukrainian poetry evening (**Ukrainskyi Visnyk**, No. 4), traditional New Year carolling (**ibid.**), circulating a prohibited journal (**ibid.**, No. 5), and participation in the "Homin" choir (**ibid.**, No. 6). Modest though these may have been,

even in terms of 'national' content, this enthusiasm for Ukrainian culture produced a disproportionate official reaction including room searches and interrogation by the KGB (**ibid.**, No. 6).

28. Operative from the late 1960s until September 1971, some 42 members of this group were subjected to various repressive measures (**Ukranskyi Visnyk**, Nos. 4 and 6). Nearly a third of these were from the generation of the thirties, while over half were born after the beginning of World War II (1941). Teachers, students and young workers in the arts constituted half of those persecuted — although the group also contained 11 engineers, three manual workers, and 12 Komsomol members.

29. Six students from the university were tried in January 1972, reportedly for voicing nationalistic sentiments, circulating leaflets demanding greater sovereignty for the republic, and calling for the removal of Shelest (**ABN Correspondence**, Vol. XXIII, No. 3, 1972, p. 11) while others apparently staged protests against Russification in August 1973 (**Index**, No. 1, 1974, index, p. xi).

30. The arrest of two protesters from the Institute of Philosophy in July 1972 (see **Khronika**, No. 27, and **Index**, No. 2, 1974, index p. xii — they were tried and sentenced in December 1973 to five and three years imprisonment) was followed in September by an all around staff cut of 4 percent, aimed at any suspected of nationalist sympathies, which struck at many in those centres and institutes safeguarding the past and future of Ukrainian culture (**Khronika**, No. 27). Many others found themselves demoted (see **The Ukrainian Review, Vol. XXI, No. 1, 1974, pp. 62-63, and No. 2, 1974, p. 88**). Significantly, these moves were followed by the foundation of a department for theoretical probelms of the relations between nationalities in the cleansed Institute of Philosophy (**Visnyk Akademii Nauk Ukrainskoi RSR**, Kyiv, No. 5, 1973, p. 103).

31. Several writers have been expelled from the writers union though details of the precise charges remain sparse (see e.g., the cases cited in **Literaturna Ukraina**, Kyiv, 20 October 1972, and **Index**, No. 2, 1972, index p. xii).

32. E.g., D. Shumuk, born 1914 in West Ukraine; member of pre-war Communist Party of West Ukraine; professional prisoner. M. Osadchyy, born 1936 in a peasant family in Sumy province; member of CPSU 1962-65; university lecturer. I. Dzyuba, born 1931 in a peasant family in Donets'k district; Marxist but not formal party member; graduate and literary critic. V. Chornovil, born 1937 in village teacher's family in Cherkasy province; Komsomol member (and later official) 1952-1965; graduate and journalist. Other former Marxists or Party members in the nationalist oriented ranks include Lev Lukyanenko, Stepan Virun, Vasyl Luts'kiv and Yosyp Borovnyts'kyi of the Ukrainian Workers' and Peasants' Union, 1959-60; and M.T. Skoryk, R. Stepanenko, H. Prokopenko and V. Kapysh of the Dnipropetrovs'k case.

33. See their open letter to the Chairman of the Council of Ministers et al, in **Suchasnist'**, Munich, February 1969, and **The Ukrainian Review**, Vol. XVI, No. 3, 1969, pp. 46-52, and commentary in Radio Free Europe: "Russification and Socialist Legality in the Dnipropetrovs'k Area," **RFE Research Paper** USSR / 39, Munich, 10 March 1969. The subsequent fate of many of those involved was reported in **Khronika**, Nos. 7, 8, 10, 11 and **Ukrains'kyi Visnyk**, Nos. 1, 2, 3 and 4. The letter itself referred to 'the crazily Russified Dnipropetrovs'k, and indeed in 1970 there were 643,000 Russians in a total population of 863,000 — see **Itogi Vsesoyuznoi perepisi naseleniia 1970 goda**, Moscow, 1973, p. 171.

34. See **The Ukrainian Review**, Vol. XIX, No. 3, 1972, p. 91 and Vol. XXI, No. 1, 1974, pp. 26-27.

35. Reported in **Khronika**, No. 27, these started with a purely domestic quarrel between a Jew and a Ukrainian and the accidental defenestration of the latter, but resulted in rioting, and damage to Jewish graves in the old cemetery.

36. **The Israel Digest**, Jerusalem, Vol. XV, No. 22, 27 October 1972, p. 1.

37. Boris Kochubievskyi, arrested in 1968 after openly opposing Soviet Middle-East policy and anti-semitism in Ukraine. His desire to emigrate was not assisted by the fact that the father of his Russian wife was an official in the KGB. Following his trial and imprisonment, he was eventually allowed to leave the USSR in December 1971. On his case see **Khronika**, Nos. 6, 8, 9, 12 and 23; **Focus on Soviet Jewry**. London May 1969; June / July, 1969; and September / October 1969; and M. Decter (ed.), **A Hero of Our Times: The Trial and Fate of Boris Kochubievsky**, Academic Committee on Soviet Jewry. New York, 1970.

38. Raisa Palatnik, arrested in 1970 on rather dubious charges of circulating libellous fabrications about the Soviet system — based on her possession of a few samvydav documents. She too served part of a prison sentence, and became the subject of much campaigning in the west, before being permitted to leave in 1973. See particularly **Khronika**, Nos. 17, 18, 20 and 21; and **Focus on Soviet Jewry**, May / June 1971.

39. Isaak Shkolnik, arrested in July 1972, he was eventually charged with espionage and sentenced accordingly. See **Khronika**, No. 27; **The Times**, London, 12 and 13 February 1973; and **Soviet News**, London, 17 April 1973.

40. Different Ukrainian cases may be found for instance in **Khronika**, Nos. 6, 8, 12, 13, 17, 24, 25, 26, and 27. The Zionist samvydav journal **Iskhod**, published in Moscow, also reported a number of cases, e.g., No. 3, November 1970.

41. On the Brind case see also **Khronika**, No. 25.

42. E.g., Leonid Kolchinskyi — see below.

43. For example the mother of Mariya Kahsburg from Kharkiv, whose case was reported in the **Jewish Chronicle**, London, 27 August 1971.

44. It was transferred from the RSFSR to Ukrainian jurisdiction on 19 February 1954.

45. **Khronika**, No. 7.

46. **Soviet Weekly**, 23 August 1969.

47. **Khronika**, No. 7.

48. **Soviet Weekly**, 23 August 1969.

49. A. Sheehy, **The Crimean Tatars and the Volga Germans**, Minority Rights Group report, London, 1971, p. 18.

50. Appeal to Soviet government and public opinion, c. February 1969, in **Novyi Zhurnal**, New York, No. 197, 1969, and details in **Khronika**, No. 7.

51. **Khronika**, Nos. 5 and 7.

52. **Khronika**, Nos. 8 and 18; and the six appeals to the U.N. and other agencies relating to this case, in **Posev-Shestoy Spetsial'nyi Vypusk**, 1971, pp. 45-56.

53. Appeal of c. February 1969, **op. cit.**, and **Khronika**, No. 7.

54. **Khronika**, No. 5.

55. Reported in **Khronika**, No. 14.

56. **Khronika**, No. 13 reports on Tatar representatives from Melitopol, not actually in the Crimea, but in Ukraine.

57. See e.g., **Khronika**, No. 7.

58. The trial of the so-called Tashkent ten in 1969 included a fitter, a bulldozer drive, two nurses, a welder, a foreman, an engineer, a physicist, a pensioner, and a teacher-trained bricklayer — see **Khronika**, No. 9.

59. At least 12 of the dissidents are reported to have been expelled from higher educational establishments for their activities — see Sheehy, **op. cit.**, p. 22.

60. **Ibid.**

61. **Ibid.**, p. 20. Indeed one of the defendants in the Tashkent trial, Izzet Khairov, was a party member, **Khronika**, No. 9.

62. 96.6 percent of the 166,000 Soviet Magyars named Hungarian as their native tongue in 1970 (Census returns in **Pravda**, 17 April 1971).

63. One of the lecturers there, Sandor Fodo, was dismissed in March 1971, after displaying what seems to have been viewed as an excess of interest in encouraging Hungarian folk-dancing, see **Khronika**, No. 19.

64. Two writers employed there were dismissed in 1971 following the appearance of an article by them on Transcarpathian Hungarian literature in a journal in Hungary (**Khronika**, No. 22).

65. Those purged from this group in August 1971 — associated as they apparently were with one of the writers dismissed from the publishing house — were attacked for their apolitical attitudes and the spirit of alienation in their writings, and a commission of investigation was set up by the Regional Party Committee to look into the attitudes of students of Hungarian in the Philology faculty at Uzhhorod (**Khronika**, No. 22).

66. See e.g., W.C. Fletcher, "Protestant Influences on the Outlook of the Soviet Citizen Today," in W.C. Fletcher and A.J. Strover (eds), **Religion and the Search for New Ideals in the USSR**, New York and London 1967; M. Bourdeaux and P. Reddaway, "Soviet Baptists Today," **Survey**, No. 66, January 1969, pp. 48-66; M. Bourdeaux, **Religious Ferment in Russia** (London: Macmillan, 1969); M. Bourdeaux & P. Reddaway, "Church and State and Schism — the Recent History of Soviet Baptists," in M. Hayward & W.C. Fletcher, **Religion and the Soviet State** (London: Pall Mall, 1969) pp. 105-141; R. Harris and X. Howard-Johnston, **Christian Appeals from Russia** (London: Hodder and Stoughton, 1969); M. Bourdeaux, **Faith on Trial in Russia** (Hodder and Stoughton, 1971); P. Reddaway, **Uncensored Russia** (London: Cape, 1972); pp. 330-31; K. Murray, "The Council of Baptist Prisoners' Relatives 1964-1972," **Religion in Communist Lands**, Vol. 1, No. 1, Jan.-Feb. 1973, pp. 12-15 and later editions of this journal; M. Bourdeaux et al., **Religious Minorities in the Soviet Union 1960-1970** (London: Minority Rights Group, 1970), Report No. 1, pp. 21-24.

67. Listed in Bourdeaux, **Religious Ferment in Russia**, pp. 211-229; Harris and Howard-Johnston, **op. cit.**, pp. 92-143; a samvydav document produced by the Council of Prisoners' Relatives, 1 November 1969; and in lists published in **Dein Reich Komme**, Stuttgart, No. 2, 1972 and Nos. 2, 4 and 5, 1973.

68. On Prokof'ev's activities, see Bourdeaux, **Religious Ferment in Russia**, particularly pp. 22-26.

69. On whose second trial, see **Pravda Ukrainy**, Kyiv, 4 October 1966.

70. For biographical data on Vins see Bourdeaux, **Faith on Trial in Russia**, particularly pp. 60-100.

71. One such case from Odesa in 1962 is cited in detail in a letter from two of the Baptist leaders, Kryuchkov and Shalashov, to Party First Secretary, Khrushchev, 13 August 1963 (published in Bourdeaux, **Religious Ferment in Russia**, p. 63). Another Odesa trial, in 1967, is the subject of M. Bourdeaux, **Russian Christians on Trial** (London: European Christian Mission, 1970).

72. See J.D. Newth, "Jews in the Ukraine — A Statistical Analysis," **Bulletin on Soviet and East European Jewish Affairs**, No. 3, January 1969, p. 19; and I.I. Millman, "Major Centres of Jewish Population in the USSR," **Soviet Jewish Affairs**, No. 1, June 1970, p. 15.

73. Article by A.I. Klibanov and L.N. Mitrokhin in **Voprosy Nauchnogo Ateizma**, No. 3, 1967.

74. Appeal to the UN Secretary General of 15 August 1967, cited in Harris and Howard-Johnston, **op. cit.**, p. 43.

75. For example K.S. Kucherenko in Mykolaiv on 22 January 1962, see Bourdeaux, **Religious Ferment in Russia**, p. 92.

76. One such document of March 1969, had 1,453 signatures from all over the Soviet Union. From the Kyiv congregation alone, an appeal dated 24 May 1966, had 116 signatures while another from the same community on 25 February 1968 had 176. A 1968 letter from the Odesa community had 180 signatures.

77. Samvydav appeal to all Christian Churches and Christians of the World, 20 November 1969.

78. Dated 5 April 1967, this was appended to a more general CPR appeal to the UN General Secretary of 5 June 1967.

79. Samvydav document, quoted in **Sunday Telegraph**, London, 2 December 1973. As with similar meetings in other parts of the country, this one was broken up by the state security forces. Similar instances have been reported for example from Kyiv in May and June, 1966 (Appeal from Kyiv of 24 May 1966 cited in Bourdeaux, **Religious Ferment in Russia**, pp. 120-21; and appeal to the UN Secretary General of 15 August 1967, in Harris and Howard-Johnston, **op. cit.**, pp. 42-43), and from Krivyi Rih in early 1970 (document cited in Bourdeaux, **Faith on Trial in Russia**, p. 163).

80. See M. Bourdeaux, **Faith on Trial**, p. 20, and M. Bourdeaux, **Religious Minorities in the Soviet Union**, p. 19.

81. This casual relationship has been suggested by W.D. Fletcher in his article

"Religious Dissent in the USSR in the 1960s," **Slavic Review**, Vol, 30, No. 2, 1971, p. 305.

82. A number of members of the related sect of Pokutnyki have, for instance, been arrested in recent years, see **Khronika**, No. 18.

83. See e.g., the case of the Ivasyuk family of Liskiv reported in **The Ukrainian Review**, Vol. XIX, No. 2, 1972, p. 97.

84. **Khronika**, No. 8.

85. Archbishop Vasyl Velichkovs'kyi of Kolomyia, aged 65 on his arrest in 1969 (see biographical details in **Ukrainska Dumka**, London, No. 19 (1152), 1 May 1969, p. 3 — arrest reported in the **Daily Telegraph**, 27 February 1969 and **Le Monde**, Paris, 28 February 1969); Father Danylo Bakhtalovs'kyi of Kolomyia, aged around 70; Father Petro Horodets'kyi of Lviv; and Father Antin Potochniak of Stryi, aged 56 (see on their cases **Khronika**, Nos. 7, 8 and 24; **Ukrains'kyi Visnyk**, No. 1, and W. Mykula, "The Gun and the Faith — Religion and Church in the Ukraine," **The Ukrainian Review**, Vol. XVI, No. 3, 1969, p. 2).

86. Born in Borisovka village, Zaporizhia oblast', but long a resident of Moscow, where his involvement in protests began at the age of 54 in 1969 — see particularly **Khronika**, No. 8.

87. On Shikhanovich's arrest see **Khronika**, No. 27. Details concerning him may be found in an article by a friend V. Belotserkovskii, "V ozhidanii suda nepravogo-o Yurii Shikhanoviche," **Posev**, No. 2, 1973, pp. 15-17.

88. The cases and subsequent arrests of both men were taken up widely in the western press largely on the basis of material from the **Khronika**. In the case of Altunyan (an Armenian, former army major and military academy lecturer, latterly a radio technician and engineer in Kharkiv, as well as party member 1957-68) this may be found in **Khronika**, Nos. 8, 9, 10, 11, 12, 21, and 22; **Ukrains'kyi Visnyk**, No. 2, and documents concerning his arrest in **Posev-Piatyi Spetsial'nyi Vypusk**, 1970, pp. 45-50. In the case of Plyushch (born 1939, Odesa graduate and cyberneticist from Kyiv) see **Khronika**, Nos. 1, 5, 8, 9, 10, 11, 24 and 26; **Posev-Tret'ii Spetsial'nyi Vypusk**, 1969, pp. 59-60; and **RFE Research Report**, Munich, USSR / 1962, 31 January 1973.

89. See **Khronika**, No. 8.

90. Cases reported in **Khronika**, No. 13. The text of the petition is published in **Posev-Piatyi Spetsial'nyi Vypusk**, 1970, pp. 49-50. The additional signatories were those of Levin's sister (herself subsequently persecuted, see **Khronika**, No. 13), and Kalinovskyi's wife.

91. **UPI** dispatch from Moscow, 25 January 1973.

92. Text published firstly in **Svoboda**, New Jersey, 11 October 1968 — translation in **The Ukrainian Review**, London, Vol. XV, No. 4, 1968, pp. 37-39. The document was earlier reported in **The New York Times**, 3 May 1968.

93. Stalin prize winning novelist Nekrasov has variously protested against anti-semitism, the trial of the Red Square demonstrators of 1968 (see **Khronika**, No. 5), press attacks on the 139 for their defence of imprisoned Ukrainians (see the 1968 petition in M. Browne, **Ferment in the Ukraine**, London, 1971, document 30), as well as the controls placed on writers, including Solzhenitsyn, and the methods of the KGB

(for this latter, he was deported from Moscow back to his home in Kyiv in March 1974 — see **The Guardian**, 23 March 1974.

94. **Khronika**, No. 18.

95. **Khronika**, Nos. 15, 18 and 20.

96. Supplement of **Khronika**, No. 17.

97. Leonid Kolchinskyy (born 1952) from Kharkiv — a would be Jewish emigrant and schoolboy civil rights activist — see **Khronika**, Nos. 17 and 18.

98. See e.g., cases cited in **Khronika**, Nos. 23 and 24.

99. Such an appeal concerning poor housing, signed by 600 workers at the Kyiv hydro-electric power station in the village of Berizka, was sent to the CPSU Central Committee in May 1969. One of the delegation sent to deliver it was arrested, and this resulted in a further letter — see report in **Khronika**, No. 8 (republished in G. Saunders, **Samizdat**, Monad Press, New York, 1974, pp. 419-20) and text of the second letter in **Posev-Vosmoi Spetsial'nyi Vypusk**, Frankfurt, 1971, pp. 61-63.

100. A short-lived march was held in the case cited in footnote 99 above, while another apparently successful strike in support of higher wages was reported to have occurred at a machine construction plant on the Brest highway in Kyiv in May 1973 (see **The Ukrainian Review**, Vol. XXI, No. 2, 1974, p. 85). A further brief strike is said to have occurred at the Petrov metal work plant in Dnipropetrovsk in June 1973, following a protest suicide against allegedly pro-Russian discrimination in housing allocation (see **ABN Correspondence**, Vol. XXV, No. 2, March-April, 1974, pp. 42-3; and **The Ukrainian Review**, Vol. XXI, No. 2, 1974, p. 89).

101. Two-thirds of 496 young workers, aged under 25, at the October Revolution Diesel Locomotive Plant in Voroshylovhrad declared themselves dissatisfied with their wages in 1973. Over 70 percent thought the plant poorly equipped and the hygiene conditions bad, and 28 percent were generally dissatisfied with their jobs (see survey published in **Izvestiia**, 23, 24 and 25 October 1973 — also reported in **The Financial Times**, London, 15 November 1973 and **The Guardian**, 11 February 1974). It is perhaps no coincidence that the oblast' party first secretary was dismissed a few weeks later for shortcomings in his leadership (see **Radyanska Ukraina**, 15 December 1973).

102. A demonstration or possibly strike by Dnipropetrovs'k workers in support of a claim for a higher standard of living was reportedly fired upon by troops on 19 September 1972 (see **The Daily Telegraph**, 10 October 1972, **The Ukrainian Review**, Vol. XIX, No. 3, 1972, p. 91; and **US News and World Report**, 18 December 1972).

Brezhnev's two day visit to industrial plants in Kharkiv in April 1970, and particularly one of his speeches there (text in **Pravda Ukrainy**, 14 April 1970) gave rise to speculation that openly voiced discontent with living standards on the part of the workers was the real motive for the exercise — speculation prompted by his reference to labour indiscipline and the need to overcome meat, consumer goods and housing shortages. No corroboration of anything resembling strike or protest action has in fact come to light and Brezhnev's speech was consonant with the general campaign of tightening discipline he had launched at the Central Committee plenum the previous December. Reported protest actions by workers in Kyiv and Kharkiv in January 1971 (see e.g., **The Ukrainian Review**, Vol. XIX, No. 3, 1972, p. 90) have also been inadequately substantiated.

Comments on Professor Julian Birch
The Nature and Sources of Dissidence
in Ukraine

by
Bohdan R. Bociurkiw
Carleton University

Unlike other studies of dissent in Soviet Ukraine, which have focused mainly on the opposition to the Soviet nationalities policy, Dr. Birch's paper attempts to examine all forms of dissidence that may be discerned within the borders of the Republic, not merely what he classifies as "Ukrainian nationalist" dissent. Accordingly, Dr. Birch extends his inquiry to the local manifestations of "all-Union" protest movements, such as those of the Jews and Crimean Tatars; the civil rights ("democratic movement"); and the Baptist **initsiativniki**. At the same time, he brings into focus the Uniate catacomb church, traces of ferment among the Hungarian minority in the Trans-Carpathian **oblast'**, the Hutsul unrest (which, somewhat surprisingly, is treated as a separate variety of national dissent); as well as the largely anomic articulations of economic grievances. Missing from the picture are, however, the stirrings of protest within the Russian Orthodox Church in Ukraine (protests against the closing of individual churches; prolonged struggle of the monks and believers to save the Pochaiv Lavra from the fate of most other Ukrainian monasteries; etc.); the Pentecostal "illegals"; and the well structured underground of the Jehovah's Witnesses.

Save for these omissions, Dr. Birch has amassed an impressive body of evidence on the different manifestations of dissidence in Ukraine and has, undoubtedly, enriched our understanding of the Ukrainian scene since Stalin's death. His categorization and evaluation of this information and his generalizations would have benefitted, I think, from further examination of the interrelationships among the different protest currents in Ukraine, and, in particular, from an analysis of the linkages between the Ukrainian national dissent and the factional politics within the republican Party-State elite.

The inclusion, alongside the Ukrainian national dissent, of the local manifestations of the Union-wide opposition currents makes good sense but only if more emphasis is placed on a multi-dimensional comparison of these including their structural differences as well as diverse movements, their linkages and overlaps among them. Several questions come to mind in this connection: Why has there been so little success attained in forging a "common front" of the Jewish, civil rights and the Ukrainian national rights movements in the Republic? Indeed, it seems that the Ukrainian dissenters have had more success in finding some common ground with the Moscow-based civil rights' spokesmen than with their counterparts back home. Why has there been a distinct lack of sympathy and co-operation between the Ukrainian oppositionists and the "sectarian" dissenters? Are the differences between the Kyiv and Kharkiv dissidents primarily those of "civil rights" vs. "nationalism"? Or are both of them civil rights movements separated by their respective attitudes to the nationality problem in Ukraine?

Some of the paper's generalizations about the social bases of the individual dissent currents may not be well founded. For example, the association of the Uniate Church strength with "rural Carpathia" is clearly too narrow, geographically and sociologically (in fact the staunchest opposition to the ecclesiastical annexation of Halychyna by Orthodox Church came from the ranks of the local intelligentsia); there is also some evidence to show that the reawakening of the interest in religion among the young intellectuals in Western Ukraine has been benefitting the Uniate much more than the official Orthodox Church. It would have been fruitful to pursue further the overlaps between the Uniate and the national dissent movements and to explore the inter-relationship between the "recalcitrant" Uniates in the ecclesiastical underground and the "secret Uniate" among the forcibly "converted" clergy of the Orthodox Church. Recently, new evidence has come to light about the linkages between the Uniates and the massive dissent movement within the Lithuanian Catholic Church. Separate questions which could have also been explored are the importance of contacts with the Ukrainian minorities in Czechoslovakia and Poland in sustaining the national and Uniate dissent currents and providing them with their "windows to the West"; the role of the foreign Ukrainian communists and fellow-travellers (in particular in Canada) in articulating certain dissident grievances and demands; and, of course, the differing relationship of various dissent currents to the large and vocal Ukrainian emigration in the West.

The exploration of some important dimensions of the problem has been complicated, I feel, by the pooling together under the general category of "Ukrainian nationalism" of a rather wide spectrum of Ukrainian dissidence, which tends to blur considerable ideological and tactical differences separating individual dissenters and groups including important contrasts between the two "generations" of Ukrainian dissent — the men of the "sixties" and those of the "seventies", if we are to judge by the orientation and style of the revived **Ukrains'kyi Visnyk (Ukrainian Herald)** (issues 7-8, 1974).

Of special importance, I suggest, for the understanding of the dissident-regime confrontation from the early 1960's to 1972 appears to be the linkage between the "left," "internationalist" wing of the Ukrainian dissent — for which Dzyuba was the most articulate spokesman — and Shelest's so-called "Ukrainian faction", an interrelationship which confronted the Soviet regime with a challenge that potentially, at least, was probably more serious than that coming from any other source of dissidence in the USSR.

In conclusion, I should like to suggest a few generalizations to amplify and supplement Dr. Birch's findings. Apart from a sense of "relative deprivation", the immediate sources of all forms of dissidence in Ukraine, as elsewhere in the USSR, seem to lie in the following features of the Soviet system:

1. The continuing tension between the ideological and legal norms of the regime, on the one hand, and its behavioural patterns, on the other hand;
2. The failure of the official structures — not only the Party-State institutions but also creative unions and leaders of the recognized religious organizations — to articulate the real political, ethnocultural or religious interests of the social groups they claim to represent; and
3. The suppression or distortion of information about both the actual official behaviour and the genuine grievances and demands of the politically "disfranchised" sections of Soviet society.

It is the elements of creative and scientific intelligentsia that — taking advantage of some relaxation of thought controls and the weakening of the system's coercive mechanisms after 1953 — have resumed the traditional role of the intelligentsia as the articulator of the "people's" interests to and against the "state". Deprived of adequate access to the public communication media, the dissident intelligentsia had to develop its own autonomous communication network — **samvydav** or **samizdat** in its various forms — which was indispensable not only for the collection, evaluation and dissemination of reliable information about the grievances and demands and the official response to them, but also for developing solidarity and cohesion in their own ranks. In this way, as well as under the pressure of the Regime's reprisals, what was originally a loose conglomeration of overlapping "friendship circles" evolved into a semi-structured "movement" — or, more precisely — into a number of dissident "currents", united above all in their demands for the strict observance by the regime of its own constitutional "guarantees" of civil rights.

With particular reference to the Ukrainian national dissent, one may discern the following three major areas of emphasis in the movement's orientation and activities:

a. Resocialization of Ukrainian society, especially the youth, in a participatory political culture radically different in its operational values from the dominant political culture;
b. Appealing to the ethno-cultural values and self-interest of the Ukrainian members of the Republic's political elite to have them assume, more decisively and consistently than before, the defence and promotion of the neglected interests of the Ukrainian nation; and
c. Influencing the Republican and the all-Union decision-makers through embarrassing publicity and the mobilization of support for the dissident cause both within the USSR and abroad, in order to reverse the Soviet nationalities policy or at least to minimize its detrimental effects upon Ukraine and the Ukrainians.

VI
Ukrainian Studies in the West:
Problems and Prospects

Ukrainian Studies in the West: Problems and Prospects

by
John S. Reshetar, Jr.
University of Washington, Seattle

As one looks back on the past quarter century and compares the status of Ukrainian studies in the 1970's with the 1940's and early 1950's many changes are evident. Certainly a conference such as this one would have been unthinkable at that time. In the interim many obstacles have been overcome to a considerable degree. The circumstances that prevailed in the early post-World War II period made research on Ukrainian subjects in the social sciences and in history an undertaking that involved a degree of professional risk. Ukraine was both **terra incognita** and, in certain influential academic circles, it was taboo as well. It was either given the silent treatment in courses that dealt with "Russia" or the Soviet Union or was regarded as something of interest only to "nationalists." Persons who entered academic life and Soviet studies at that time can testify to the impediments encountered and to the unsympathetic response frequently experienced at the hands of various academic gate-keepers, censors and impresarios. The response varied from hostility and suspicion to skepticism and indifference.

Although one could dwell on these obstacles at some length — since certain of their remnants can be said to persist in Soviet studies to this day — mention must be made of the numerous achievements that have occurred in Ukrainian studies in the intervening quarter century. A number of substantial monographs have been published by university presses (Columbia, Princeton, Rutgers, Yale). A significant number of scholars have been trained in the social sciences and humanities and are contributing to Ukrainian studies. The various publications of the Ukrainian Free

Academy of Sciences in Canada and of the Ukrainian Academy of Arts and Sciences in the U.S. and the appearance of **Ukraine, a Concise Encyclopaedia** in English translation (Shevchenko Scientific Society and University of Toronto Press), and greater attention accorded Ukraine in the **Canadian Slavonic Papers** and in the **Slavic Review** have provided an impetus and a means of introducing Ukrainian studies to a hitherto closed academic audience. The development of several archival collections and of university library collections of Ukrainiana have served to promote further interest and to provide needed bibliographical resources. The establishment of the Ukrainian Research Institute and the three endowed chairs at Harvard University can be said to have provided a capstone for the past quarter century of achievement. As one looks back one must make mention of the inestimable contribution of the late Philip E. Mosely who at that time — in what was a most unsympathetic academic milieu — offered wise counsel, a professional interest in Ukraine as a historian of Eastern Europe and as a diplomatist, and much active support the extent of which is not fully appreciated. The achievements of Ukrainian studies during the past 25 years would, at the very least, have been delayed had it not been for the late Philip E. Mosely's aid and encouragement.

Scholarship can never rest on its laurels and must move on to new issues and questions. If Ukrainian studies are not to be consigned to the taxidermist an agenda must be prepared, long-range plans pursued, and obstacles identified and overcome. I should like first to identify some of the neglected areas of interest and investigation that should be given consideration and then turn to some of the persistent obstacles that require attention.

As a part of a research strategy in the social sciences and history I would urge that consideration be given to the following issues and problems. There is need for a complete history of the Ukrainian national movement especially prior to the 1917-1920 Revolution. Nation-building got underway during the century prior to 1917 in the face of adverse circumstances, and the interplay of development and reaction, of resistance and accommodation has not been adequately studied. Such a work would integrate the linguistic, literary, intellectual, religious, historiographic and ethnographic aspects of the phenomenon of nation-building in its early stages. There is now reason to hope that the study of the Kievan Period and the Mongol and post-Mongol periods and the uses of the Chronicles in the capable hands of the Harvard Ukrainian Studies Program will produce a series of basic monographs and annotated documentary collections that will resolve the fundamental questions that have made those historical periods so controversial.

We need a scholarly but not scholastic history of the Cossack Period and of the entire Cossack phenomenon and movement. In the cultural sphere there is need for a thorough history of Ukrainian music. Regional histories should be undertaken in order to facilitate understanding of regional differences and how they have affected the development of the national movement. In particular, attention needs to be given the regions of Kyiv, Poltava, Slobids'ka Ukraina, Podill'ia, Halychyna, Volyn', and Carpatho-Ukraine. There is still a need for a history of the Ukrainian SSR and for a fuller treatment of the historical development of the Communist Party of Ukraine. Biography has been sorely neglected; we have yet to produce adequate full-length biographies of Hrushevsky and Petliura and of other prominent figures in Ukrainian political and literary history.

Among the problems meriting investigation in the social sciences is the question of the Soviet regime's language policies. If language retention (or linguistic distinctiveness) is an absolute condition of national existence and identity — and some would dispute this on the basis of the cases of Ireland, the Latin American peoples and other countries — then the political implications of Soviet language policy cannot be ignored nor can they be the exclusive province of specialists in sociolinguistics. For this is an important area of cross-cultural research involving study of the inter-action of the **lingua franca** and the native language. If widespread bilingualism is the professed intermediate-range goal of the Kremlin's nationalities policy-makers, then

338

the systematic study of the conditions and possible consequences of bilingualism must be given attention. The costs and the effectiveness of a bilingualism policy must be studied in terms of who pays what costs (and how) and who obtains what benefits. For here is one index — though by no means the sole index — by which to measure the efficacy of Soviet nationality policy.

In this context it is also appropriate to make a beginning — however modest — in the study of the Ukrainian character or the Ukrainian ethos as it has been affected by conditions of pre-Soviet and Soviet rule. If the Ukrainians enjoyed national independence I would be proposing the study of their political culture, but since this is not the case such research must have a different focus. The study of national character and investigation of the interaction of culture and personality have always elicited controversy not only regarding the findings — which usually can be stated only as hypotheses — but also regarding the kinds of data to be used. Of course, a people and its culture can be studied at a distance, and in the absence of survey research findings obtained in the Ukrainian S.S.R. a modest beginning could be made in several ways. A typology of Ukrainian portraits might be obtained from a study of basic personality types encountered in Ukrainian literary sources (here the literary scholar and critic and the student of political culture might join forces). Another approach would be to collect a sufficient number of biographies — both of prominent and of lesser known Ukrainians — which could provide an empirical basis for a study of the Ukrainian character. The regional dimension could also be incorporated into such an investigation insofar as Galician, Volynian, Poltavan and other types or subtypes may be said to exist within a generic type(s).

The purpose of such a study of the Ukrainian character would be to facilitate a better understanding of the situation "Amidst the Snows" — if we may use Valentyn Moroz's figure of speech to refer to the impact on Ukrainians of the harsh and inclement political climate that emanates from the North. In particular the delineation of a Ukrainian character typology would throw light on the genesis of the various levels of response to the Kremlin's policies regarding language, cultural content, personnel selection, foreign contacts, and the like. It would appear that the Kremlin applies its policies in Ukraine on the basis of a certain model or partial model of the Ukrainian character. If we are to perceive fully the various dimensions of Ukrainian-Russian relations and evaluate the effectiveness of the Ukrainian struggle for ethnic identity and nation-maintenance then the problem of the Ukrainian character must be probed and not ignored.

Despite past achievements in Ukrainian studies and our ability to prepare research agendas and plan specific projects, it must be recognized that there are a number of serious obstacles and unfulfilled needs that require attention:

1. There remains a need to overcome academic vested interests and to challenge the inertia of the academic establishment. One still encounters too many academic persons who equate the history of the U.S.S.R. with the history of Russia and who ignore the fact that the Russia that preceded the U.S.S.R. was an empire in name as well as in fact. Obviously there are various reasons that can be cited to explain the inertia of academia: cultural Russophilism, fear of offending the "Elder Brother," the tendency to disparage all nationalism except the Russian variety, fear of "Balkanization" of Eastern Europe, confusion regarding what is or is not "progressive" and the like. The motives and rationalizations are not really of great import, but their consequences are important because they have led to a skewed development of Slavic and Russian studies.

2. The study of the Ukrainian language has not been accorded its proper place in the curricula of most departments of Slavic languages. Effective Ukrainian language instruction is a prerequisite for the full development of research interests and capabilities. The allocation of a certain number of language study fellowships by the SSRC / ACLS for Ukrainian would contribute to this end; it would also demonstrate a willingness on the part of fellowship selection committees to sup-

port Ukrainian studies.

3. There is a need to break the "fellowship barrier" and to find greater financial aid not only for the promising doctoral candidate who is writing a dissertation on a Ukrainian topic but also to find means to enable established scholars to pursue research. Ukrainian studies have advanced as far as they have largely as a result of the dedication and personal sacrifice of individual scholars, but this cannot be a long-range method of operation.

4. There is need for **direct** scholarly exchanges with the principal centers of the Ukrainian S.S.R. Ukraine has for the most part been ignored in academic and scholarly exchanges with the Soviet Union. The barriers that have prevented or impeded exchanges of personnel and of bibliographic materials and all forms of data must be lowered.

5. A scholarly journal devoted to Ukrainian studies is needed. Whether an annual journal — really a yearbook — like the projected **Harvard Ukrainian Studies will fulfill this need remains to be seen, but it will be an important step contributing to this end.**

6. There is a need for a series of fundamental monographs comparable to the series published by the Ukrainian Scientific Institute (U.N.I.) in Warsaw in the period between the two World Wars.

7. Adequate annotated bibliographical aids are required, although the **Harvard Ukrainian Studies** journal promises to accomplish much in fulfillment of this need.

These and other obstacles persist because of work that has not been done, and they serve as reminders of what must be overcome.

Ukrainian Studies in the West: Problems and Prospects

by
John A. Armstrong
University of Wisconsin

Ukrainian studies in Western Europe and North America have heavily emphasized literary and cultural subjects. This is a laudable and valuable line of inquiry, and one which must, as other panelists have noted, continue. Several Ukrainian scholars (notably Volodymyr Kubiyovych, Yaroslav Bilinsky, and Borys Lewytzkyj) have also made striking contributions not only to the study of Ukrainian social structure, but to the general analysis of Soviet problems. Nevertheless, on the whole Ukrainian studies in the West have neglected social science analysis. Since, as Professor Simirenko reported, Soviet Ukrainian studies have also emphasized literary and cultural subjects at the expense of social science analysis, we are confronted with two problems:

1. Ukrainian studies in the West should act as a surrogate for Soviet Ukrainian scholarship, especially in areas like social science analysis where the regime imposes severe restrictions.[1] On the whole Ukrainian studies in the West have failed to provide this surrogate activity; hence large areas and extensive bodies of data remain unanalyzed, and our projections of developments in Ukraine are consequently shaky.
2. The simultaneous neglect of social science analysis by Ukrainians outside as well as inside the USSR (even in comparison to the neighboring Poles and the Polish emigration, or the Russians in Moscow or abroad) leads one to ask whether there is not some fundamental reason, approachable through the sociology of

knowledge, for this neglect.

Some light can be shed on the sociological reasons for the neglect by comparison with two somewhat similar situations in vastly different cultural contexts. In British public life the dominant emphasis for a century has been the English (not Scots) tradition of the gentleman amateur educated humanistically. During the heyday of imperial expansion this emphasis, with its appeal to qualities required for diplomacy, military command, and colonial governance, may have served British social purposes well. As Lord Charles Snow has pointed out, however, excessive emphasis on the humanist amateur has produced the phenomenon of "two cultures" in contemporary England, a stultifying breakdown in communication between the humanist generalist and the scientist. As I have argued in **The European Administrative Elite** (1973), the anachronistic emphasis on the gentleman amateur represents, today, a defensive ideology of the English elite. But the price the country pays, as nearly everyone now recognizes, is very high in terms of national economic growth and political influence. In North America and France, and increasingly throughout the Continent, the gap between the "two cultures" has been bridged to a considerable extent by the analytic social sciences. They constitute, in a sense, a general language of discourse as well as a unifying point of view and common fund of knowledge. Consequently, British prestige may well be suffering further losses as British intellectuals lose touch with the most dynamic Western worlds of discourse.

As a Roman Catholic, I have been impressed by the parallel way in which inability to communicate with the main intellectual centers may hamper a religious subculture in Western societies. Prior to the 1960s excessive emphasis on scholastic terminology and categories tended to isolate Catholic intellectuals. Writers like my former classmate at the University of Chicago, Father Joseph Fichter, S.J., who tried to integrate Catholic ethics and sociological categories, were frowned upon. Dominant Catholic circles feared that social science analysis would contaminate or jeopardize cherished philosophical positions — many of which we now recognize were not integral parts of our faith. More recently, Catholic intellectuals have embraced — too hastily and rather naively, in many instances — contemporary social science fashions. Nevertheless entry into the world of social science discourse was indispensable if we — like the English elite — are not to be restricted to talking to ourselves.

Both these situations have, I think, lessons for Ukrainian communities in the West — which run a grave risk of talking only to themselves. During the nineteenth century and the first part of the twentieth, the prime need of the ethnic group was to cultivate and elaborate the national "myth" (I use the term in the sociological sense, which carries no implication of truth or falsity) composed of linguistic uniqueness, superlative literary achievement, and heroic history. In response to German romantic nationalism and Russian cultural imperialism, writers from Shevchenko to Hrushevsky provided a Great Tradition for their fellow countrymen. In the second half of the twentieth century, however, the needs of the Ukrainian community throughout the world have shifted (as suggested above) to fundamental analysis of social, economic, demographic, and political problems within Soviet Ukraine. Equally vital is the problem of "putting Ukraine on the map" by entering into broad and intense discourse with the main centers of intellectual activity in the West. This can come about only by adoption (as a partial but major emphasis) of the modes of analysis and the categories of discourse which increasingly predominate there.

I can make only a few concrete suggestions at this point. One is the extreme importance of reexamining Ukrainian history from a developmental point of view. Currently the use of history for social science analysis is becoming a dominant theme in Western scholarly circles — for example, the triennial International Political Science Congress (Edinburgh, 1975) will make the relationship between history and political science the central theme. Surely Ukrainian historical experience, embodying the rapid development of one of the largest European nations from an agricultural society (including new settlement areas as well as centuries-old

342

"traditional" agricultural communities) to the position of an urbanized, industrialized society contains significant lessons. They would intensely interest Western scholars if properly analyzed. As yet, however, Ukrainian scholars have hardly touched upon the developmental aspects of Ukrainian history.

Where feasible, both historical and contemporary analysis ought to be quantitative. As Murray C. Murphey shows,[2] even chronologically remote topics can be subjected profitably to statistical analysis by refined techniques; the raw Soviet data for such analysis is increasingly available. Where possible, such analyses should be machine-readable, for Western scholars are increasingly attracted to topics which readily lend themselves to computer-programmed comparison. Not all topics are suitable for quantification. On the other hand, almost any topic can be related to the world of contemporary social science discourse by utilization of proper conceptual frameworks. A severe defect of Soviet studies in general, and Ukrainian studies in particular, has been invention of ad hoc frameworks for each subject treated, instead of adapting social science concepts already elaborated for other scholarly areas. Instead of isolating Ukrainian subjects in their own little world, which has no apparent relevance for general intellectual discourse, utilization of basic social science conceptual approaches, with their implicit comparative dimension, would bring Ukrainian studies into the mainstream of analytic social science scholarship. Skill and discretion in borrowing conceptual frameworks are, of course, indispensable. Generally speaking, the value of Freudian approaches for examining elite or other group behavior appears dubious. For individual biographies, on the other hand, these and other psychological approaches appear promising. How fascinating it would be if someone examined Shevchenko's remarkable life in categories similar to those used by Erik Erickson for Luther's biography! And what an impression such a biography of Shevchenko would make on the Western intellectual world! To conclude, therefore, I want to re-emphasize that, much as I rejoice in the remarkable development of Ukrainian studies in North America during the past twenty years, I hope most sincerely that this development constitutes only the prelude to a rapid broadening of the field.

FOOTNOTES

1. See my "New Prospects for Analyzing the Evolution of Ukrainian Society," Ukrainian Quarterly, XXIX, 1973, 349-57.

2. Murray C. Murphey, Our Knowledge of the Historical Past, 1973.

Ukrainian Studies in the West: Problems and Prospects

by
Omeljan Pritsak
Harvard University

During the XIV-XVI centuries in the "Latin" West a firm basis was established for national identity (the introduction of vernacular literary languages, creation of native universities, interest in the collection of native documents and chronicles). In the East, however, with the victory at Poltava and subsequent official proclamation of the Russian Empire (1721), a new variant of Eurasian imperialism appeared; this empire profited, though only superficially, by the achievements of the Latinized West. The tragedy of Ukraine was that historical circumstances proved most unfavorable during both these periods. It missed the western development due to the disappearance of the Halych-Volynian State in 1340, and later the new Russian imperialism gradually eased the Cossack Hetman State out of existence (in the years 1709-1764-1783).

Because of these developments, the Ukrainian identity has been pitted in an uneven match against all other nations. Here it will suffice to recall an axiom of Boris Antonenko-Davydovych (who is again being repressed by the Soviets) contained in his marvelous travelogue "Through Ukrainian Lands," written during the so-called period of Ukrainization. According to Antonenko-Davydovych, it is axiomatic (just as two times two equals four) that French is spoken in Paris and German in Berlin. In Kyiv, Kharkiv or Odesa, however, this axiom does not function — it is only a theory, which still has to be proven.

Ukrainian identity, which is the basis of cultural and political activity, as well as the drawing force for the new generation, cannot normally exist without the determined aid of the three Ukrainian disciplines: language, literature, and history (in that order).

Language (along with ethnography) is the common "code" of Ukrainian communities, both in the native land and in emigration, without which Ukrainianhood loses its reason for existence. Literature (with folklore and the arts) is the artistic shaping of the language, spiritual nourishment for the higher levels of culture. History (with archaeology) is the common memory of the Ukrainian community, which without history would be like a robot without a will of its own. The three critical Ukrainian disciplines can develop and function properly only when they are pursued simultaneously on two parallel levels:
(a) instructional — the Chairs of Ukrainian Linguistics, Ukrainian Literature, and Ukrainian History;
(b) research — a Ukrainian Academy of Sciences (a maximal requirement), or a Ukrainian Research Institute (a minimal requirement).

Both the Chairs and the Research Institute must have a solid financial basis and they must be able to function freely, without influence by any political power, and in a gentlemanly fashion (with dignity and without the inferiority complex and paranoia typical of a ghetto mentality).

Unfortunately, there is no Ukrainian state which would take an interest in the problem of Ukrainian identity, and consequently there exist no national universities nor a national Academy of Sciences which would cultivate the three above named disciplines on the highest level. In the theoretically sovereign Ukrainian Soviet Socialist Republic (URSR), the "elder brother" (whom one must love more than oneself) vigilantly prevents the rise of a higher Ukrainian culture — particularly in the areas of linguistics, literature, and history. According to imperial practice only one higher imperial culture is permitted, which is to provide the drawing force for strengthening imperial identity. Ukraine, the "younger brother," must be content with a lower form of culture which emphasizes "folksiness".

In such a situation the Ukrainian emigration in North America, which outnumbers many an independent nation (Iceland, for instance, has a population of 200,000) must assume the burden of creating a basis for Ukrainian identity on the highest level. The Ukrainian emigrants can emulate the formation of the Israeli State and the Poles in the 19th century. They must unite and work together, disregarding national boundaries, since the problem of establishing a basis for Ukrainian identity is equally relevant to the Ukrainians in the United States and to those in Canada.

There are two possible ways that a national group can maintain three Chairs (Language, Literature and History) and a Research Institute:
1) by establishing a separate university, with major emphasis placed on the three Chairs and a Research Institute, or;
2) by creating three Chairs and a Research Institute at an American university, with the stipulation that it must be the best American university.

The Jews chose the first alternative in 1948 and established their own university — Brandeis, in Waltham, Massachusetts. Brandeis is not a large university. There are approximately 2,000 students and some 400 lecturers and professors. In order to operate on such a high level it naturally had to have a solid financial base. Its annual operating cost is around 30 million dollars. This does not include physical plants, libraries, museums, etc. which were donated by private Jewish families and are valued at several hundred million dollars. Brandeis does have an endowment of 45 million, which, however, only covers a small portion of daily expenses.

It would be unrealistic to expect the Ukrainians in North America to be able to spend 100 million dollars for real estate, buildings, furnishment, libraries, museum, and so on, plus 20-30 million annually to maintain a top level university. The other alternative is to enter into a partnership with an established American university. Considering the exceptional importance of the matter, only the best American university can be considered for an agreement of this kind. And this is precisely what has been done in our case. The Ukrainian Studies Chair Fund decided to establish three Chairs and a Research Institute at Harvard University, which is recognized in all competent circles as the oldest, the best, the wealthiest, and the most prestigious American university. After its agreement with the Ukrainian Studies Chair Fund, Harvard University, in the persons of its presidents, deans, and department heads, proudly assumed responsibility for the development of Ukrainian Studies. For this purpose, A Committee on Ukrainian Studies was established.

What were the tasks of the Committee? There were at least three: (1) to develop the resources of the various Harvard libraries in order to serve the needs of the growing Ukrainian disciplines; (2) to prepare and to introduce courses in Ukrainian disciplines into the university curriculum; (3) to create a basis for scholarly research in Ukrainian studies.

The Committee, however, was faced with special difficulties. As I have pointed out elsewhere, never (except for the years 1920-1930) have all three Ukrainian Chairs existed simultaneously in a normally functioning university (such as Harvard). The University of Lviv had only one Chair, that of Ukrainian (Ruthenian) Philology, during the years 1849-1939. As a result, there was no reservoir which could provide accomplished scholars, of suitable age, who could immediately occupy the Chairs. There was also a lack of textbooks in English, or even in Ukrainian for that matter, suitable for university instruction.

Taking all this into consideration the Committee, ever-conscious of its responsibility to the Ukrainian people, decided to take the approach which could be described as grafting and cultivation. It means that the Ukrainian disciplines at Harvard will not be haphazardly planted with people selected at random. Rather the professors will be chosen according to a clear, purposeful and well-thought out plan. This plan foresees the first fifteen years as a preparatory period during which emphasis will not be placed on instruction in the general university program, but on an "incubatory" process in order to prepare new cadres and textbooks.

During this period, which consists of three five-year stages: (1) the most-talented, dedicated and specially-selected young candidates will receive the very best training in their discipline both at Harvard (where, in addition to already existing instructors, outside specialists in Ukrainian Studies are often invited and, if necessary, also from European Universities); (2) having defended their dissertations these young people will have the opportunity, under expert guidance, to express their capabilities either as instructors or as researchers; (3) foundations will be laid for the realization of a professional international journal of Ukrainian Studies, a current bibliography, and other indispensable publications; (4) international symposia and conferences on important scholarly topics will be held. This plan is the only possible route which will lead the Ukrainian disciplines to the most advanced levels as equal and independent national disciplines.

When this becomes an established fact, the Ukrainian emigration in the U.S. and Canada can be proud that they have accomplished their common Ukrainian goal. Then, even in Ukraine, the matter of Ukrainian identity will come out of the sphere of theory, which always has to be proven, and its existence will become as axiomatic as Borys Antonenko-Davydovych could have wished.

Ukrainian Studies in the West: Problems and Prospects

by
George S.N. Luckyj
University of Toronto

I want to approach today's topic "Problems and Prospects" from a rather narrow angle. I am sure my colleagues will have dealt with it in its wider aspect. Yet I feel that we are too much inclined to look for the "big" problems — the need for pure research, creative and original contributions and the performance of our scholarship vis-a-vis the Soviet Ukraine. All these are important issues and I do not wish to minimize them. I will, however, say as a point of departure for my own argument, that I consider the achievement of Professor Kubiyovych in publishing the Ukrainian encyclopaedia in Ukrainian and in English as a far greater achievement than all the rest put together. Why I think so will become clear from my approach to this whole subject.

I shall limit myself, both in scope and in time, to one practical problem, which in my view is at the root of all the other problems. I have in mind the equipment with which we are conducting our courses (especially undergraduate courses) in Ukrainian studies. In my opinion we are very poorly equipped. I am not thinking of libraries, which are getting better from year to year, or the number or quality of students who are also increasing every year. I have in mind the lack of adequate textbooks, necessary for proper instruction in undergraduate courses in Ukrainian language, literature history and political science. I am not going to offer a critical analysis of the texts we use. This would take too long and would be an exercise in futility. We all know that even in a field which relies totally on textbooks — the field of Ukrainian language — there is no adequate book for first, second or third year instruction. The situation is much worse in literature and history not to mention political science.

Let me make one point clear. By a textbook I mean what all Canadian and American undergraduates know as a textbook: a short or long and inexpensive paperback which offers basic knowledge in a given field, subject or period. They are not borrowed from the library, but bought by students. They are the backbone of any course in any subject, no matter what additional reading list the instructor may recommend. Where are the Ukrainian textbooks? To be sure, there are some, but I submit to you that most of them are inadequate. If we are to see a solid development of Ukrainian studies (and at the present moment I estimate that over 500 undergraduates are studying Ukrainian in Canada alone), we need many more modern, well prepared and attractive textbooks in all fields. They will have to be in Ukrainian and in English and some of them even bilingual.

It is with this idea in mind that we in Toronto have created a Ukrainian Research Project. We are not aiming at what Harvard and other places are trying to achieve. Our objective is much more modest, but it is nevertheless important. In the next five years we plan to publish 20 such textbooks in Ukrainian language, literature, history and political science. Let me give you an example of what we are trying to do. First four volumes, two in Ukrainian and two in English are in advanced stage of preparation. The first, History of Ukrainian Literature by D. Chyzhevsky in English translation is coming out in February 1975. It is a volume of 650 pages, a fundamental reference work for the students of Ukrainian literature. We hope to put out a cheap paperback edition as well. The second volume in English is an anthology of Ukrainian political dissent, edited by Professor Bociurkiw. It will contain what is best from the works of Chornovil, Moroz, Dziuba, Sverstiuk, Lisovy, Braichevsky and others. Two Ukrainian volumes, both in literature, are also ready to be published, one of them a history of modern Ukrainian literature by a leading Ukrainian scholar. This is only a beginning. We plan to continue our project and in 1976-77 publish a textbook of Ukrainian grammar, a Ukrainian reference grammar for advanced students, two volumes of Readings in Ukrainian history and in political science in English translation and a bibliographical guide to Ukrainian studies. We also want to continue the series Ukrainian Classics in translation started by me two years ago. A translation of Kulish's Sonata Pathetique will come out in March 1975. It will be followed by translations of Kotsiubynsky and Yanovsky. More parallel-text editions are needed. Following Modern Ukrainian Short Stories which will be reprinted in paperback we plan a volume on Short Ukrainian Prose (Dovzhenko, Gzhytsky, Honchar and others). A series of monographs on Ukrainian writers in English will be continued. The first volume was D. Struk's book on Vasyl Stefanyk. A shorter version of Ukraine — A Concise Encyclopaedia, published by the University of Toronto Press in two volumes and costing over 100 dollars will come out in paperback edition (one volume with updated chapters on language, literature and history) costing less than 10 dollars, a price which the students can afford.

For all this we need funds, but we are confident that we shall get them. I do not wish to bore you with further details of our plans. But I think we have made a start towards filling an important gap and I invite you all to collaborate with us and to help us bring our research and publication project to a successful completion.

In starting our project we have no intention of monopolizing it. Its success will depend on the degree of collaboration by all scholars in Canada, England and the United States. But it will also depend on planning. While it is impossible to plan creative research (for, after all, we are free to do what we want to do in writing our books and articles) it is not only possible but desirable to plan a project like ours — which is to produce a series of texts. I think the prime consideration in such planning is the observance of high standards. The texts which we plan to publish will undergo rigorous scrutiny by specialists in the field. They must also answer the real needs of the undergraduate programme and therefore we plan to commission certain texts to be written. We shall, of course, be in constant touch with other centers, wherever they may be, which may plan similar projects. There is no need for unnecessary duplication, although a certain amount of duplication may be unavoidable and is not be regretted.

Finally, in our plans we shall move cautiously and, I hope, realistically. We want to avoid the impression that this is yet another gradiose Ukrainian plan to cure all our ills. It is not. It is a modest proposal of limited, but nevertheless vital scope.

Ukrainian Studies in the West: Problems and Prospects

by
C. Bida
University of Ottawa

The question of Ukrainian studies at the university level has recently become very topical. They are widely discussed on the pages of the Ukrainian press in Canada, in the United States and in Western Europe, in social cultural and student organizations. In comparison with the situation in the early 1950's, when Ukrainian studies in Canada were the subject of concern and interest to only a few professors pioneering in this field, by the end of the 1960's and the early 1970's the idea of these studies assumed much greater popularity in this country and in the United States. It seems that the Ukrainian community in the West began to consider their university studies as an indispensable factor in the preservation of their cultural heritage, in the development of their humanistic science and in compensation for those losses in their culture and science which are occurring in their native land due to the injurious policy and great restrictions practiced in this area by the Soviet regime. And — no doubt — this is a very sound reaction by this community in the Western world. Deprived of many possibilities in their homeland, this community makes efforts to continue and develop its cultural and scholarly work under the more favourable conditions in the West. There is no need to explain how vital this type of work is in the framework of Ukrainian life. We should not, however, lose sight of the difficulties and problems connected with the topic under discussion. We know that some cultural phenomena may flare up and then slowly die out if they are built on overly optimistic premises.

One must take into consideration all the needs and difficulties encountered in order to confront reality and in order to find a proper solution. I will point out here some of those needs connected with the development of Ukrainian university studies.

I should like to stress that there is an urgent need for textbooks, and reference books in the foreign languages, particularly English, as well as for translations of the Ukrainian literary and scholarly works into English. Working in the field of the literature I am stressing the needs in this area although, I believe, my remarks have reference also to other disciplines. All that which has been done up to now, through the initiative and efforts of the individual authors, does not satisfy the requirements of the programmes planned or already approved in the university curriculum. There is a vital need for monographs on Ukrainian writers and on various aspects of the culture, which would supply information to readers not familiar with the Ukrainian language. Without a sufficient number of translations and scholarly works in the foreign language, particularly in English (here we stress English because we are working mostly in the English-speaking world) Ukrainian studies will always be limited to those who know the language. These studies will, therefore, be destined to a marginal role in the university curriculum. Needless to say, because of this situation the Ukrainian scholarly or literary themes are given even less than marginal attention in the Western encyclopedias and anthologies, or are simply passed over in silence.

Some very outstanding figures in Ukrainian literature are completely unknown in the West and remain beyond the Western literary world's sphere of interest — not because their literary production is insignificant but because it is inaccessible owing to the language barrier. Only a constantly increased number of scholarly and literary Ukrainian works published in foreign languages (particularly in English) would remove the obstructive barrier.

Closely connected with the Ukrainian language problem is the question of the quality of scholarly publications and other sources related to Ukrainian studies. In most cases the students and teachers have at their disposal sources published in the Soviet Union. Many of them must be considered as serious contributions to science. To this cathegory belong rare text editions, linguistic and lexicographical works and reference books and, for example, monographs on the Ukrainian arts (not to mention other disciplines). We know, however, how tendentiously literary works are interpreted by Soviet authors. Forced by the officials dogma to write in the spirit of social realism, they ignore the essence of literary work by evaluating it from the sociological point of view, by neglecting to see in it the real ideological and esthetic values.

A long rich period of baroque literature is virtually ignored by them because it has religious overtone; the writers who have been classified as "bourgeois — nationalistic" have been removed from the pages of the literary history. In the West, where social realism and other dogmas do not hang over writers' heads like a sword of Damocles, much can be done in this direction. Well interpreted source materials and monographs can be produced which should be written in the spirit of objective scholarly research methods. This task, so closely related to the question of Ukrainian studies, is not insurmountable — provided there are experts in the individual academic fields. We must touch here, however, on another problem which evolves from the former.

There is a certain disproportion between the needs and the means — between the theoretical planning and the realistic possibilities. In order to supply the pedagogical and scholarly market with a sufficient number of valuable publications a pool of experts (specialists in the individual humanistic sciences) is indispensable. The situation, as we see it now, is not particularly encouraging. A comparatively substantial number of graduates receive advanced academic degrees in Ukrainian studies, it seems, however, that in an overwhelming number of cases scholarly production does not go beyond the thesis. Teaching careers and other practical occupations draw the graduates — potential scholars — away from the productive scholarly work which is so essential to the future of these studies. When the older generation of scholars — active in the West — passes on, the new one must continue the work. In two recent decades a number of prominent scholars have passed on. It would be too optimistic to say that a new generation has come in its turn to continue and develop the work of their predecessors.

Finally, we should touch upon the problems as it applies to the interest of students in Ukrainian studies. One may observe that among the young generation there is a prevailing tendency to choose very practical professions. As a result of this the number of candidates for the study of medicine, law and practical disciplines exceeds the number of those studying humanities. The pragmatic trend which presently dominates the minds of the young generation may tremendously affect Ukrainian studies as well. Much has to be done here through the school channels, much has to be done by the parents and community to avert the wave of pragmatic orientation and to implant in the minds of the new generation the idea that there is still adequate opportunity in various segments of Ukrainian and non-Ukrainian life for their active and valuable contributions, which they would not be able to make without proper preparation in Ukrainian studies: that, for example, there is a need for professionally-trained teachers of Ukrainian language and literature in the schools of the major Canadian provinces; that the young Ukrainian clergy must be well acquainted with the language and culture of the community in which they are active; that various Universities seek individuals who are competent to teach about Ukraine in Social Science and Humanities disciplines.

These are the problems which deserve the attention of academic circles and the community at large.

Gaps, difficulties and obstacles convince us that the work must be carried on with greater intensity than in the past. Ukrainian studies carried on in the West have good prospect of developing provided that certain conditions are met.

First, the existing Ukrainian studies and research centres must be strengthened; some new institutes should be established to increase the study of important problems and to carry out research in various fields of Ukrainian humanities; the teachers and researchers in this field must come from the ranks of the younger generation; a series of publication projects on Ukrainian problems must be undertaken by the scientific institutions and by the study and research centres.

Ukrainian scholarly production, which has been normally done by individual scholars on their own initiative and, very often, at their own expense, must become a subject of common interest.

Larger and well-chosen topical research and publication projects should be planned and performed if necessary by groups of scholars. This will guarantee closer co-operation between the experts in the field and thus enlarge scholarly output.

Ukrainian problems in all fields of the humanities: in history, political science, literature, etc., should attract attention and become the objects of studies of non-Ukrainian scholars also. There is a great disproportion between the important geopolitical role of Ukraine and Eastern Europe and the very small amount of interest evidenced in Ukraine by Western scholars.

The planning, realization and future development of Ukrainian studies depends greatly upon the Ukrainian community in the West, also on their understanding of the fact that even the most costly investment in national culture and science is, in fact, the best investment.